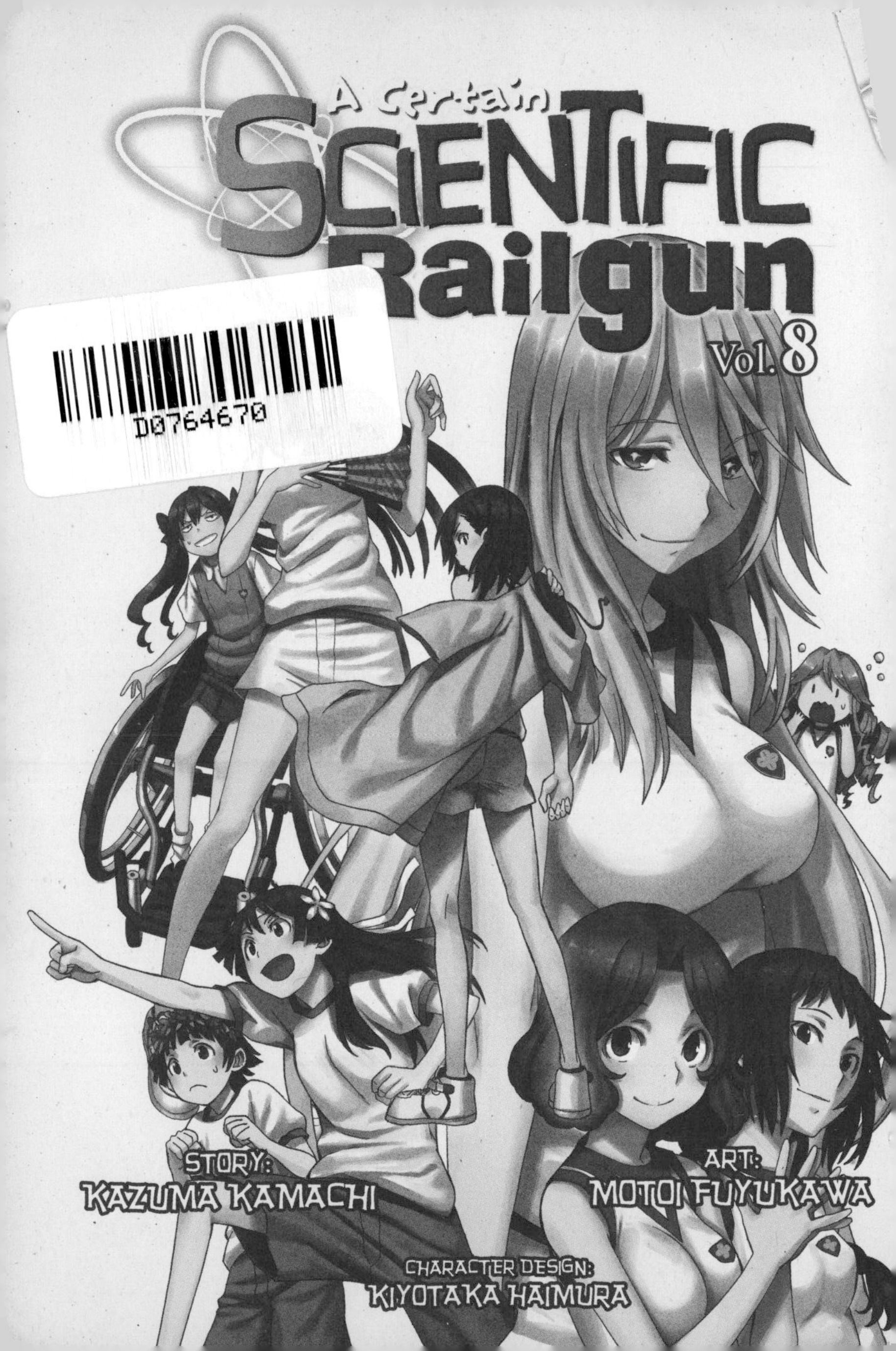
A Certain
SCIENTIFIC
Railgun
Vol. 8
STORY:
KAZUMA KAMACHI
ART:
MOTOI FUYUKAWA
CHARACTER DESIGN:
KIYOTAKA HAIMURA

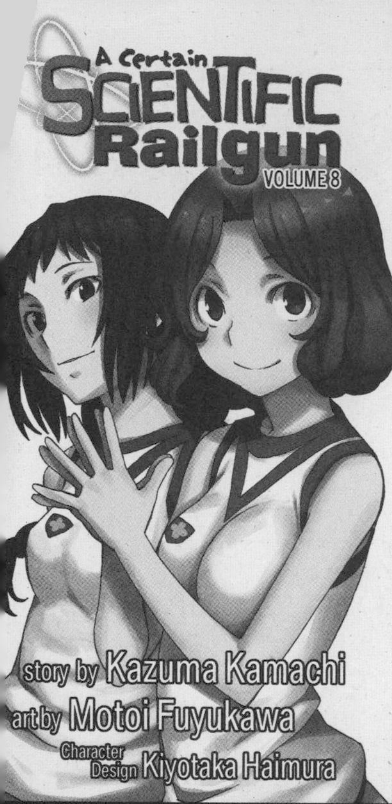
A Certain
SCIENTIFIC
Railgun
VOLUME 8
story by Kazuma Kamachi
art by Motoi Fuyukawa
Character Design Kiyotaka Haimura

STAFF CREDITS

translation Nan Rymer
adaptation Maggie Danger
lettering Roland Amago
layout Bambi Eloriaga-Amago
cover design Nicky Lim
proofreader Shanti Whitesides, Janet Houck
assistant editor Alexis Roberts
editor Jason DeAngelis

publisher Seven Seas Entertainment

A CERTAIN SCIENTIFIC RAILGUN VOL. 8

ISBN: 978-1-937867-39-3

Printed in Canada

First Printing: August 2013

10 9 8 7 6 5 4 3 2 1

READING DIRECTIONS

This book reads from ***right to left***, Japanese style. If this is your first time reading manga, you start reading from the top right panel on each page and take it from there. If you get lost, just follow the numbered diagram here. It may seem backwards at first, but you'll get the hang of it! Have fun!!

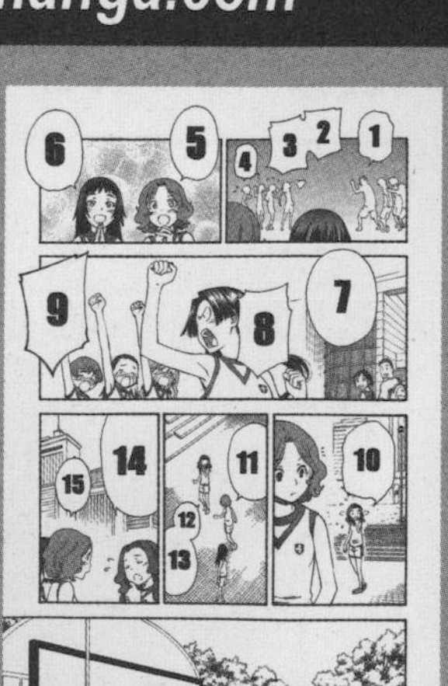
1
2
3
4
5
6
7
8
9
10
11
12
13
14
15

CHAPTER 45: AMBUSH

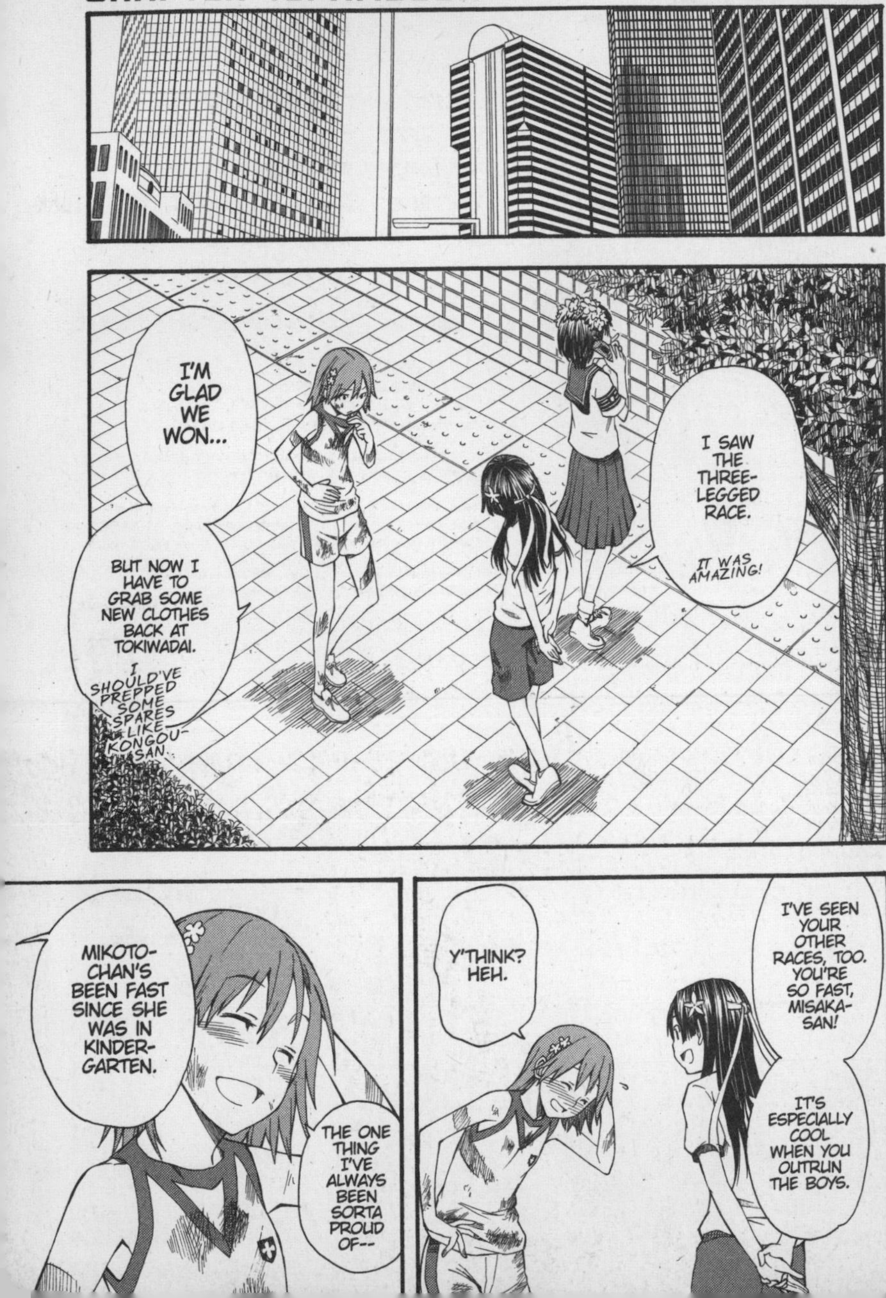
I SAW THE THREE-LEGGED RACE.
IT WAS AMAZING!
I'M GLAD WE WON...
BUT NOW I HAVE TO GRAB SOME NEW CLOTHES BACK AT TOKIWADAI.
I SHOULD'VE PREPPED SOME SPARES LIKE KONGOU-SAN.
I'VE SEEN YOUR OTHER RACES, TOO. YOU'RE SO FAST, MISAKA-SAN!
Y'THINK? HEH.
IT'S ESPECIALLY COOL WHEN YOU OUTRUN THE BOYS.
THE ONE THING I'VE ALWAYS BEEN SORTA PROUD OF--
MIKOTO-CHAN'S BEEN FAST SINCE SHE WAS IN KINDER-GARTEN.

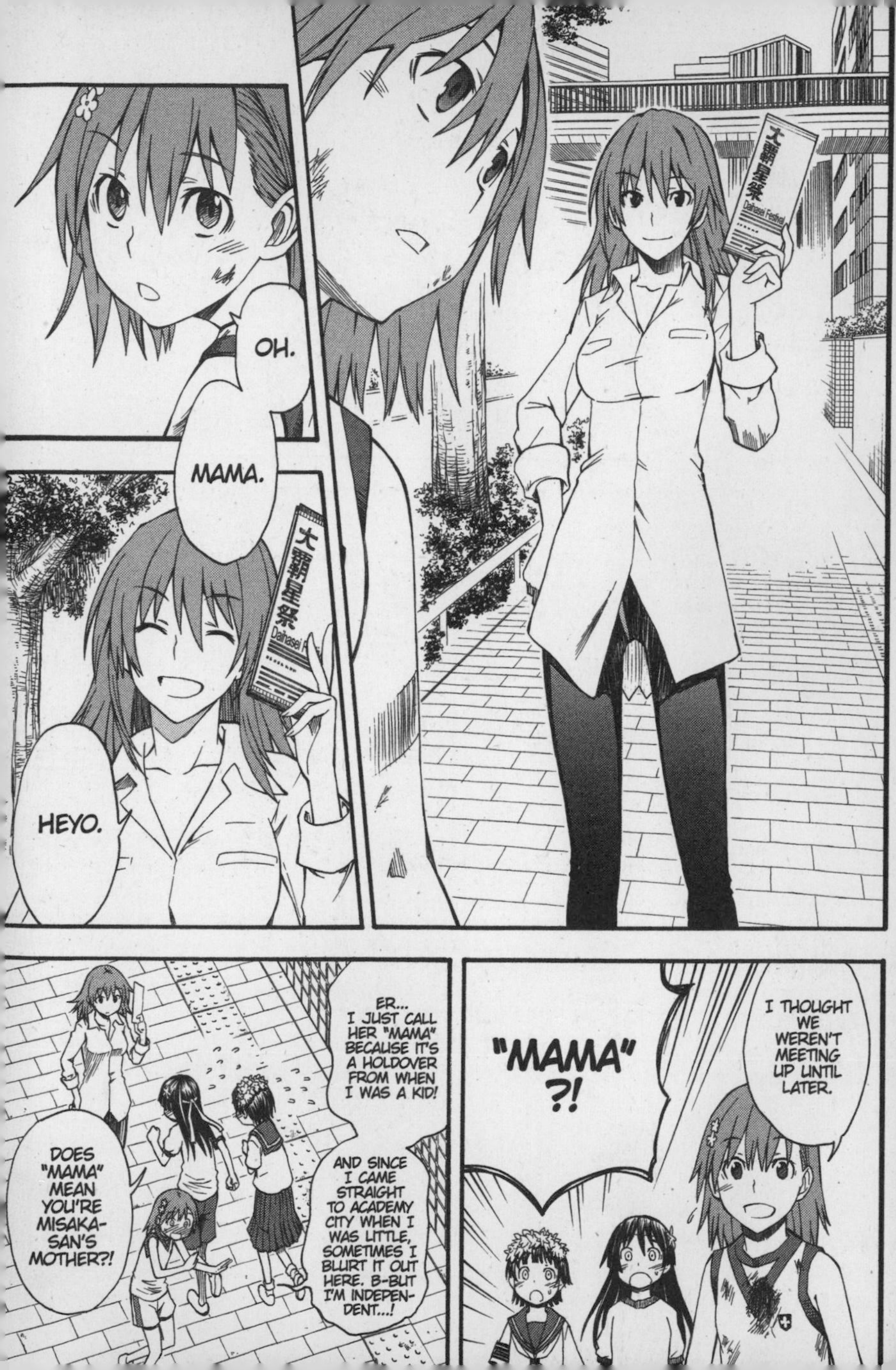
大覇星祭
Daihasei Festival
OH.
MAMA.
HEYO.
I THOUGHT WE WEREN'T MEETING UP UNTIL LATER.
"MAMA" ?!
ER... I JUST CALL HER "MAMA" BECAUSE IT'S A HOLDOVER FROM WHEN I WAS A KID!
AND SINCE I CAME STRAIGHT TO ACADEMY CITY WHEN I WAS LITTLE, SOMETIMES I BLURT IT OUT HERE. B-BUT I'M INDEPENDENT...!
DOES "MAMA" MEAN YOU'RE MISAKA-SAN'S MOTHER?!

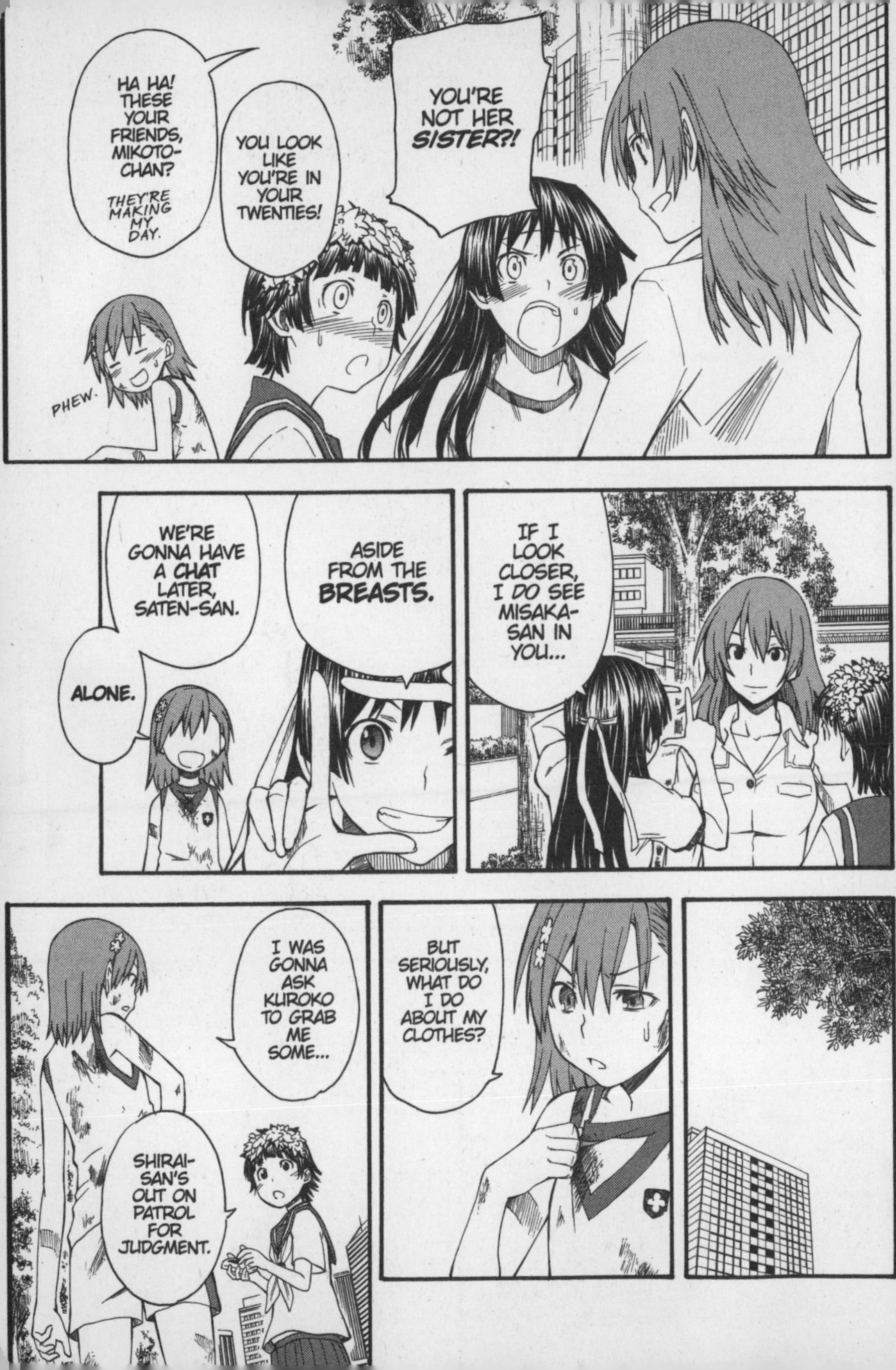
YOU'RE NOT HER SISTER?!
YOU LOOK LIKE YOU'RE IN YOUR TWENTIES!
HA HA! THESE YOUR FRIENDS, MIKOTO-CHAN?
THEY'RE MAKING MY DAY.
PHEW.
IF I LOOK CLOSER, I DO SEE MISAKA-SAN IN YOU...
ASIDE FROM THE BREASTS.
WE'RE GONNA HAVE A CHAT LATER, SATEN-SAN.
ALONE.
BUT SERIOUSLY, WHAT DO I DO ABOUT MY CLOTHES?
I WAS GONNA ASK KUROKO TO GRAB ME SOME...
SHIRAI-SAN'S OUT ON PATROL FOR JUDGMENT.

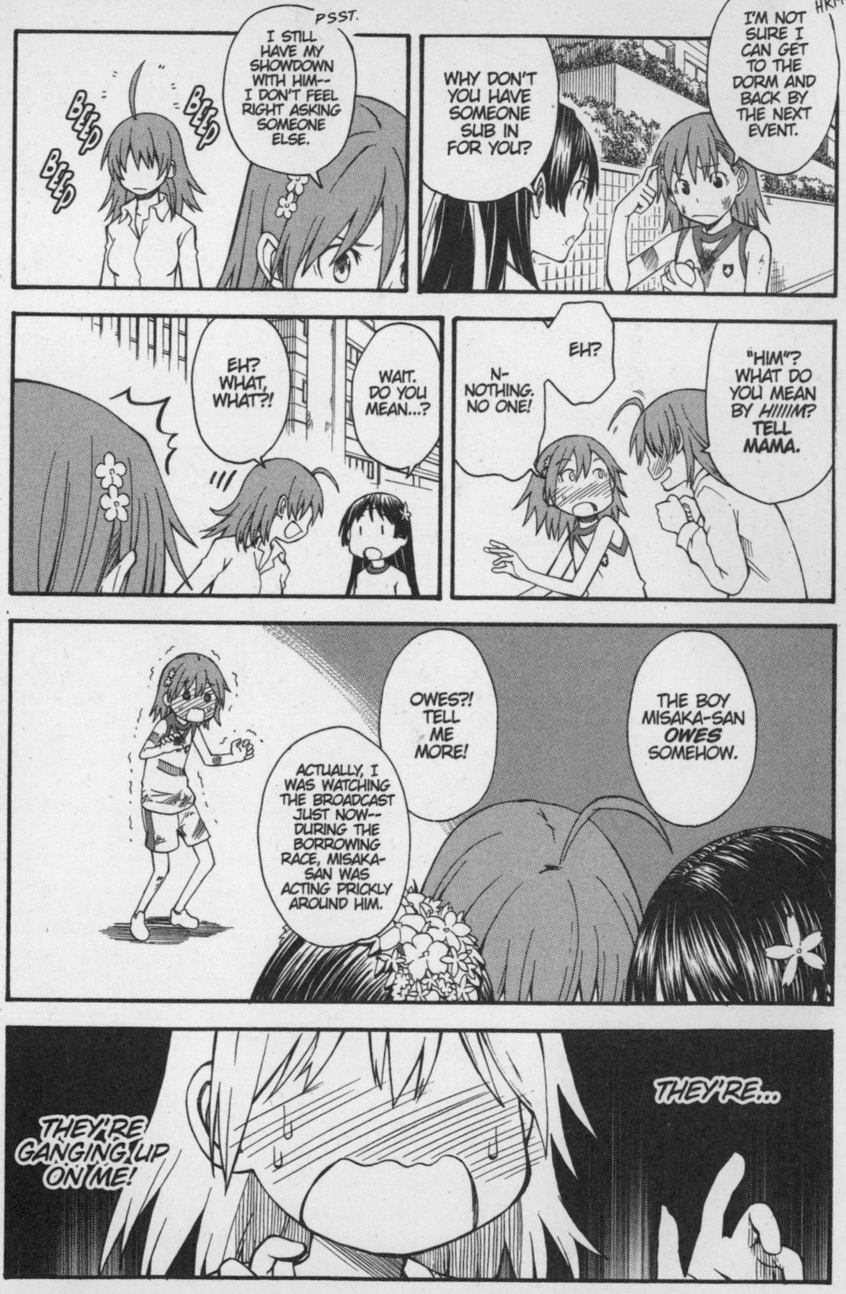
HRM...
I'M NOT SURE I CAN GET TO THE DORM AND BACK BY THE NEXT EVENT.
WHY DON'T YOU HAVE SOMEONE SUB IN FOR YOU?
PSST.
I STILL HAVE MY SHOWDOWN WITH HIM-- I DON'T FEEL RIGHT ASKING SOMEONE ELSE.
BEEP
BEEP
BEEP
"HIM"? WHAT DO YOU MEAN BY HIIIIIM? TELL MAMA.
EH?
N-NOTHING. NO ONE!
WAIT. DO YOU MEAN...?
EH? WHAT, WHAT?!
THE BOY MISAKA-SAN OWES SOMEHOW.
OWES?! TELL ME MORE!
ACTUALLY, I WAS WATCHING THE BROADCAST JUST NOW-- DURING THE BORROWING RACE, MISAKA-SAN WAS ACTING PRICKLY AROUND HIM.
THEY'RE...
THEY'RE GANGING UP ON ME!

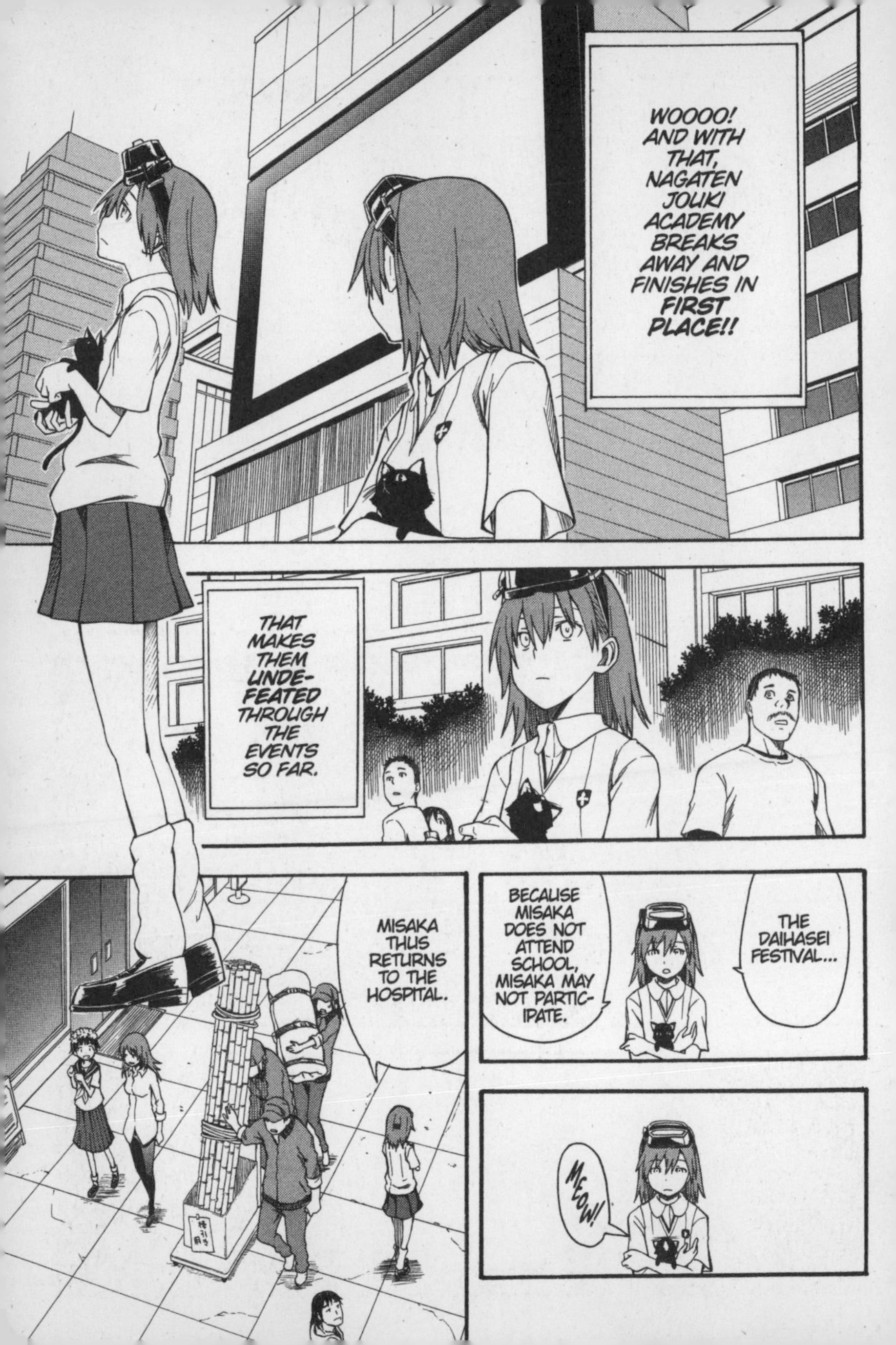
WOOOO! AND WITH THAT, NAGATEN JOUKI ACADEMY BREAKS AWAY AND FINISHES IN FIRST PLACE!!
THAT MAKES THEM UNDEFEATED THROUGH THE EVENTS SO FAR.
THE DAIHASEI FESTIVAL...
BECAUSE MISAKA DOES NOT ATTEND SCHOOL, MISAKA MAY NOT PARTICIPATE.
MEOW!
MISAKA THUS RETURNS TO THE HOSPITAL.

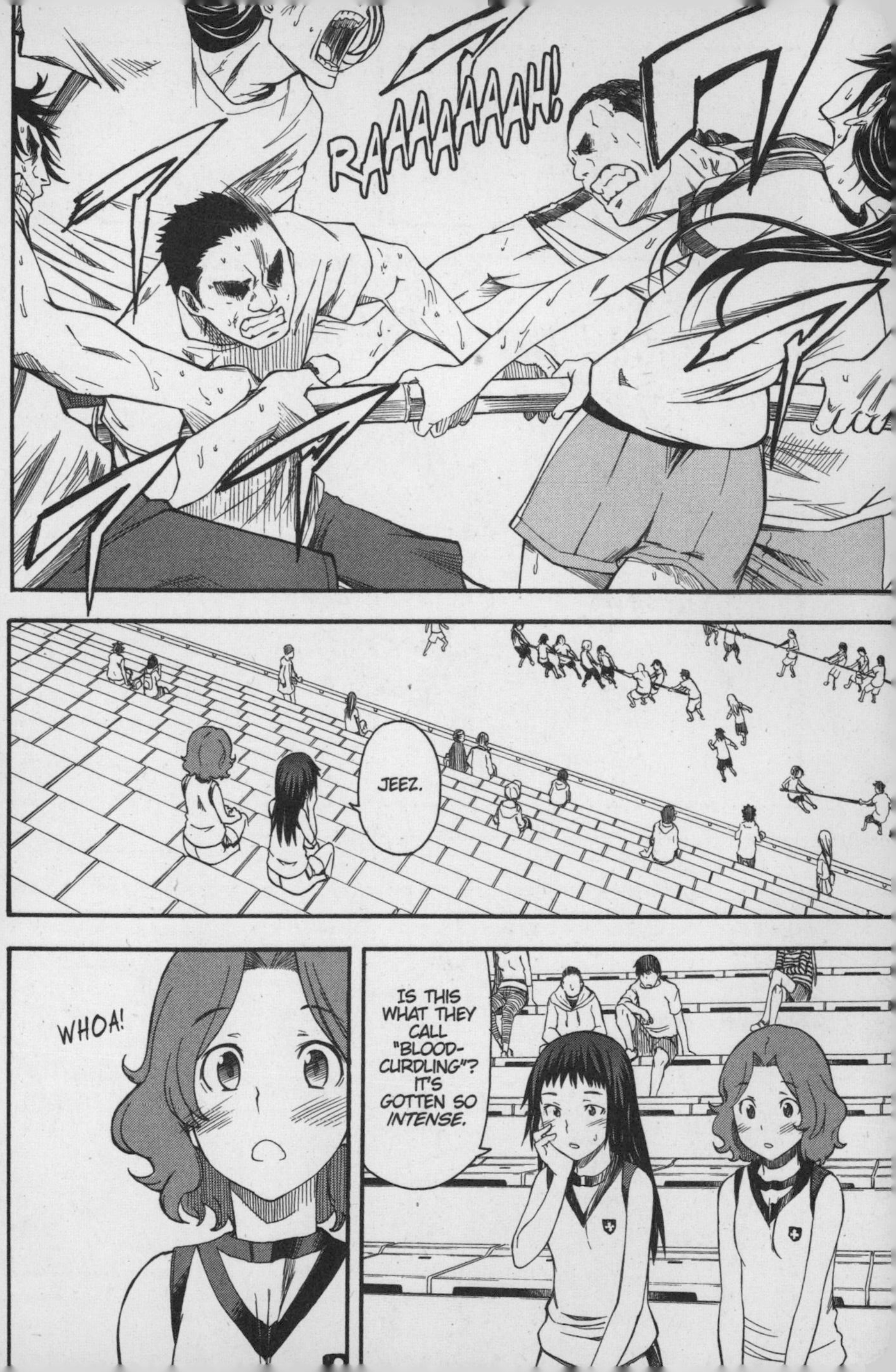
RAAAAAAAH!
JEEZ.
IS THIS WHAT THEY CALL "BLOOD-CURDLING"? IT'S GOTTEN SO *INTENSE.*
WHOA!

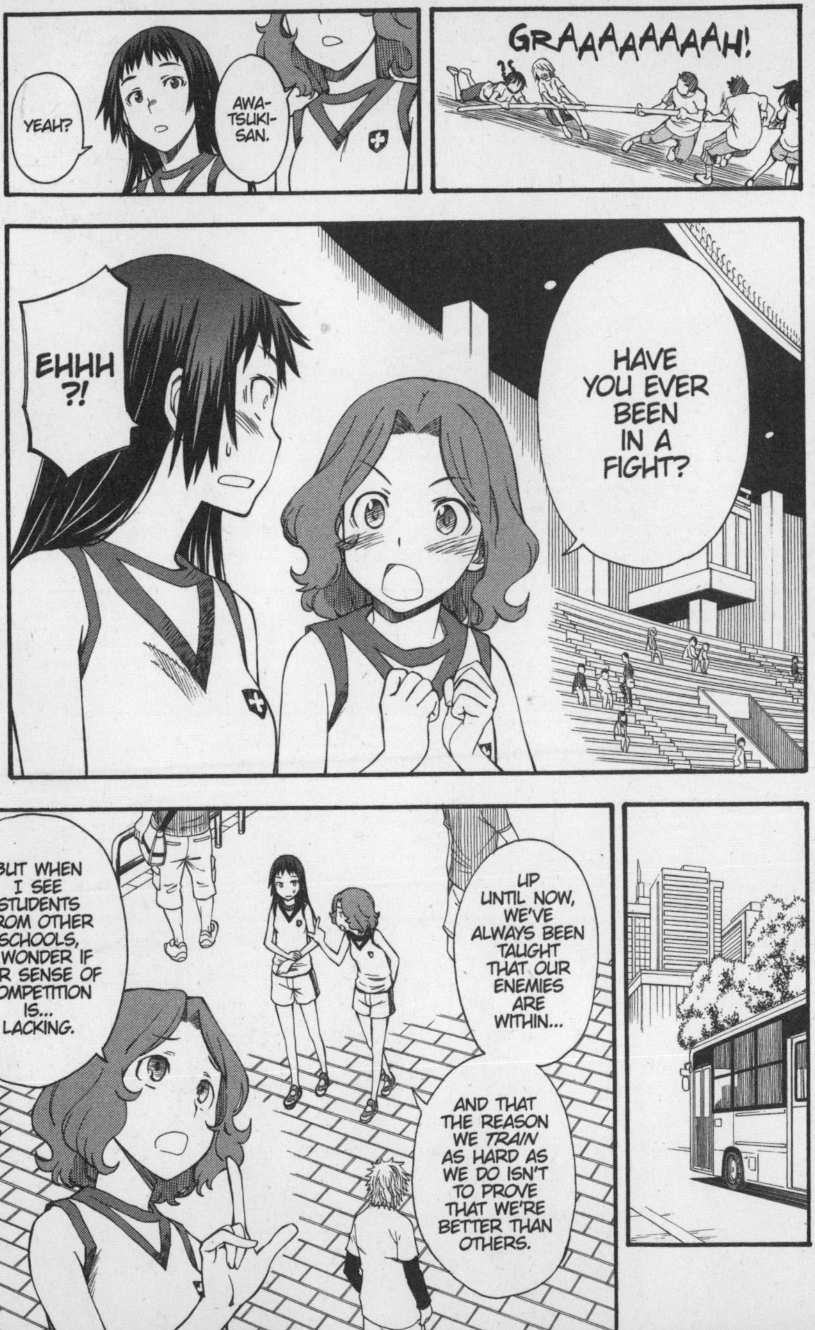
GRAAAAAAAAH!
AWA-TSUKI-SAN.
YEAH?
HAVE YOU EVER BEEN IN A FIGHT?
EHHH ?!
UP UNTIL NOW, WE'VE ALWAYS BEEN TAUGHT THAT OUR ENEMIES ARE WITHIN...
AND THAT THE REASON WE *TRAIN* AS HARD AS WE DO ISN'T TO PROVE THAT WE'RE BETTER THAN OTHERS.
BUT WHEN I SEE STUDENTS FROM OTHER SCHOOLS, I WONDER IF OUR SENSE OF COMPETITION IS... LACKING.

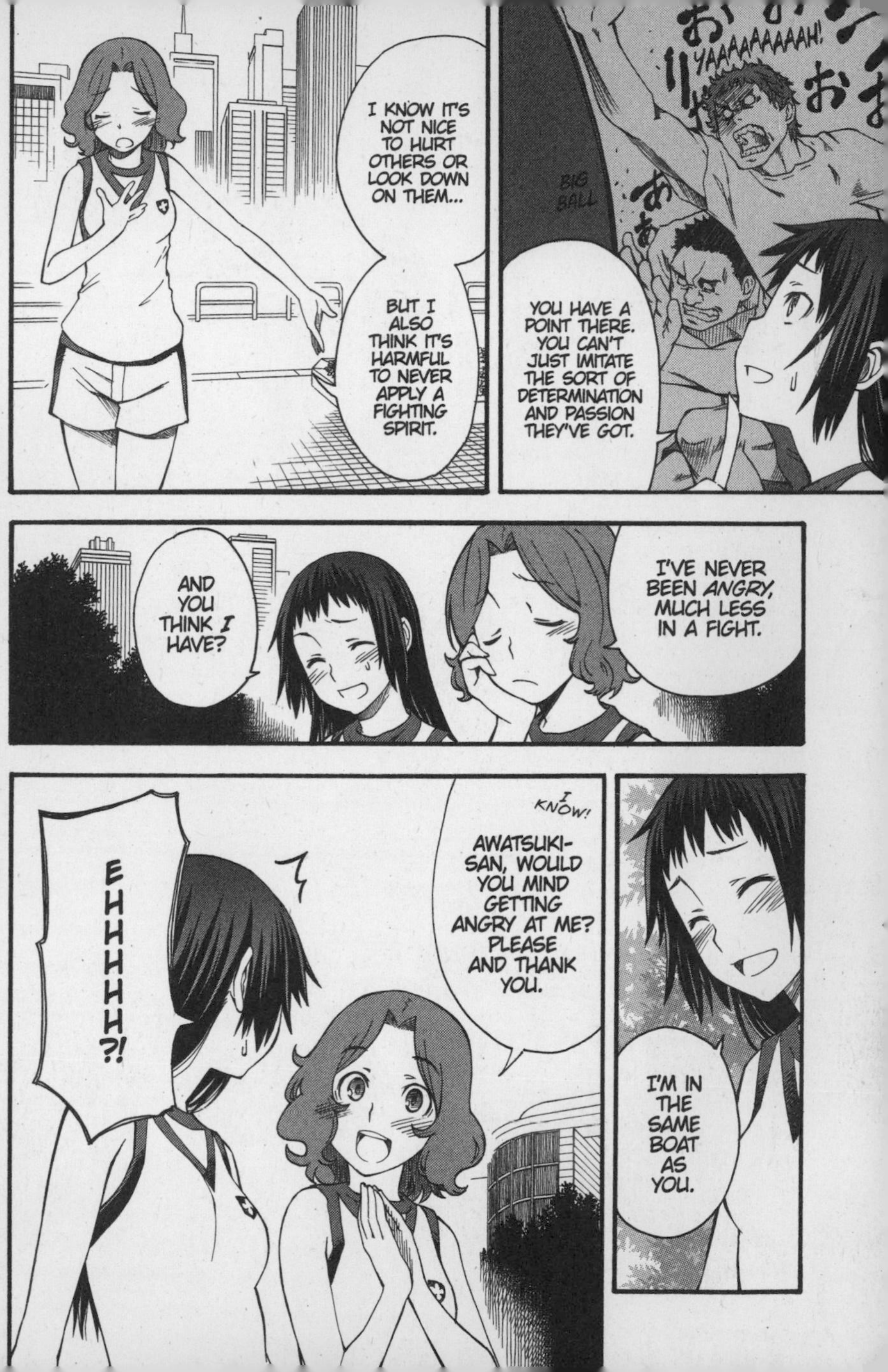
YAAAAAAAAAH!
BIG BALL
YOU HAVE A POINT THERE. YOU CAN'T JUST IMITATE THE SORT OF DETERMINATION AND PASSION THEY'VE GOT.
I KNOW IT'S NOT NICE TO HURT OTHERS OR LOOK DOWN ON THEM...
BUT I ALSO THINK IT'S HARMFUL TO NEVER APPLY A FIGHTING SPIRIT.
I'VE NEVER BEEN *ANGRY*, MUCH LESS IN A FIGHT.
AND YOU THINK *I* HAVE?
I'M IN THE SAME BOAT AS YOU.
I KNOW!
AWATSUKI-SAN, WOULD YOU MIND GETTING ANGRY AT ME? PLEASE AND THANK YOU.
EHHHHHH?!

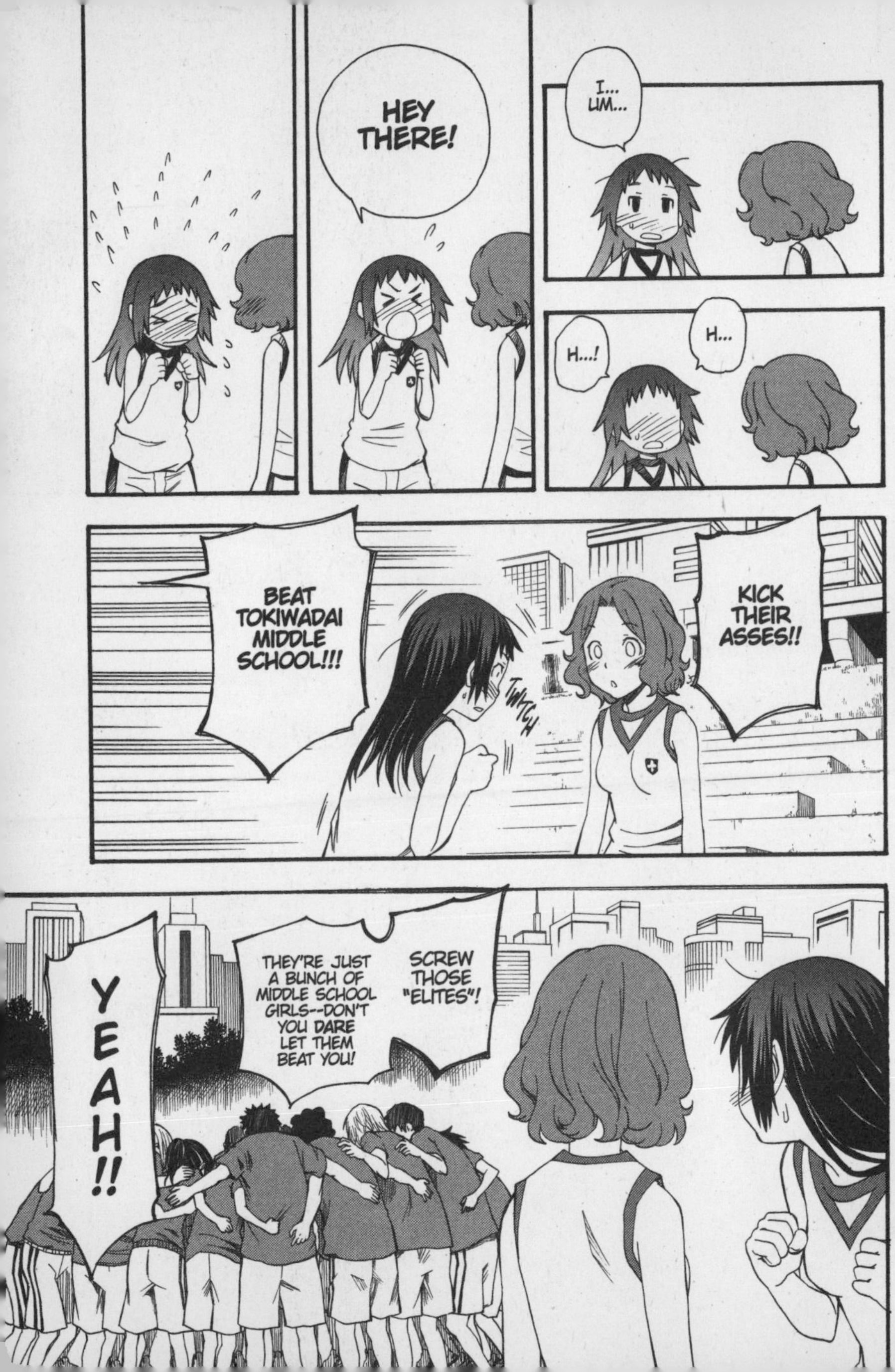
I... UM...
H...
H...!
HEY THERE!
KICK THEIR ASSES!!
BEAT TOKIWADAI MIDDLE SCHOOL!!!
TWITCH
SCREW THOSE "ELITES"!
THEY'RE JUST A BUNCH OF MIDDLE SCHOOL GIRLS--DON'T YOU DARE LET THEM BEAT YOU!
YEAH!!

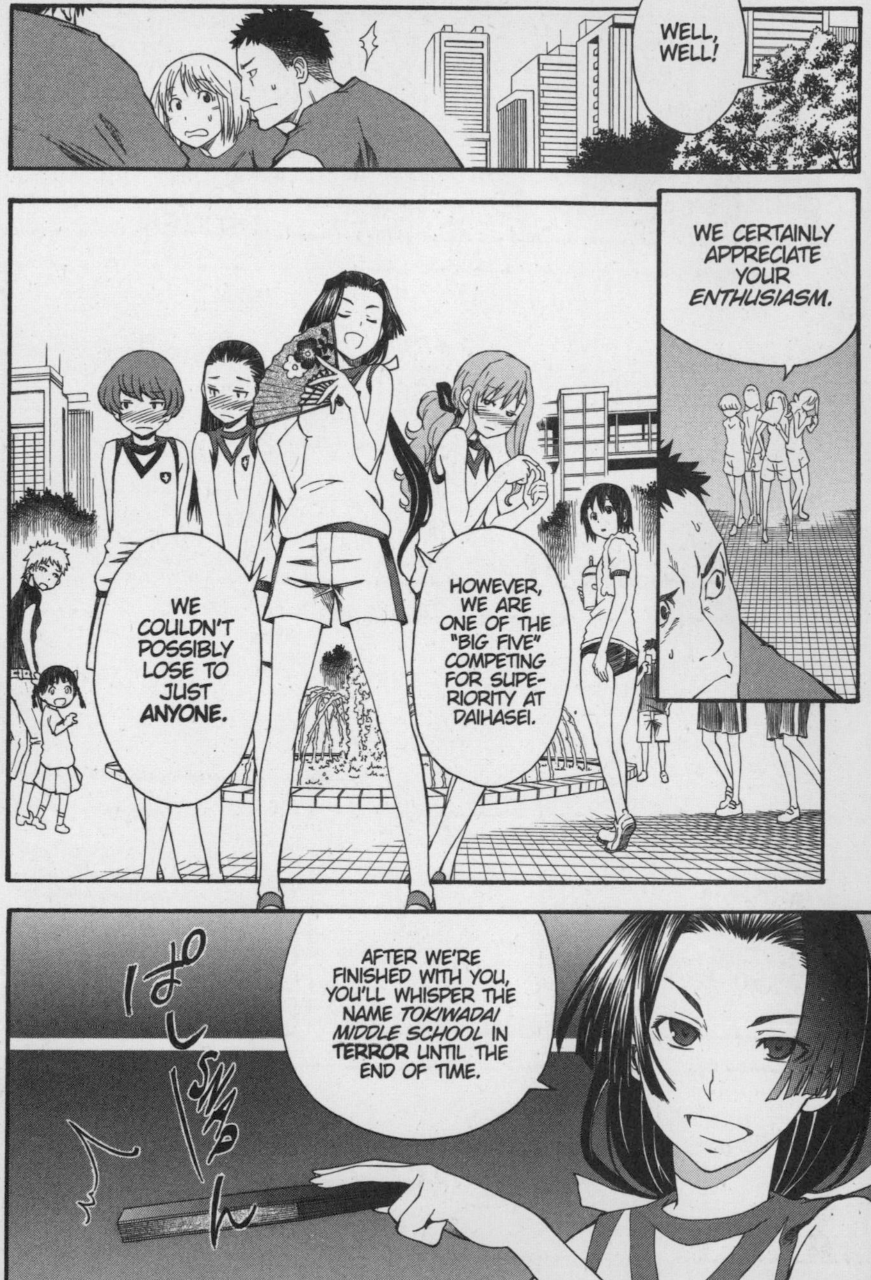
WELL, WELL!
WE CERTAINLY APPRECIATE YOUR *ENTHUSIASM.*
HOWEVER, WE ARE ONE OF THE "BIG FIVE" COMPETING FOR SUPERIORITY AT DAIHASEI.
WE COULDN'T POSSIBLY LOSE TO JUST **ANYONE.**
AFTER WE'RE FINISHED WITH YOU, YOU'LL WHISPER THE NAME *TOKIWADAI MIDDLE SCHOOL* IN **TERROR** UNTIL THE END OF TIME.
ぱしん
SNAP

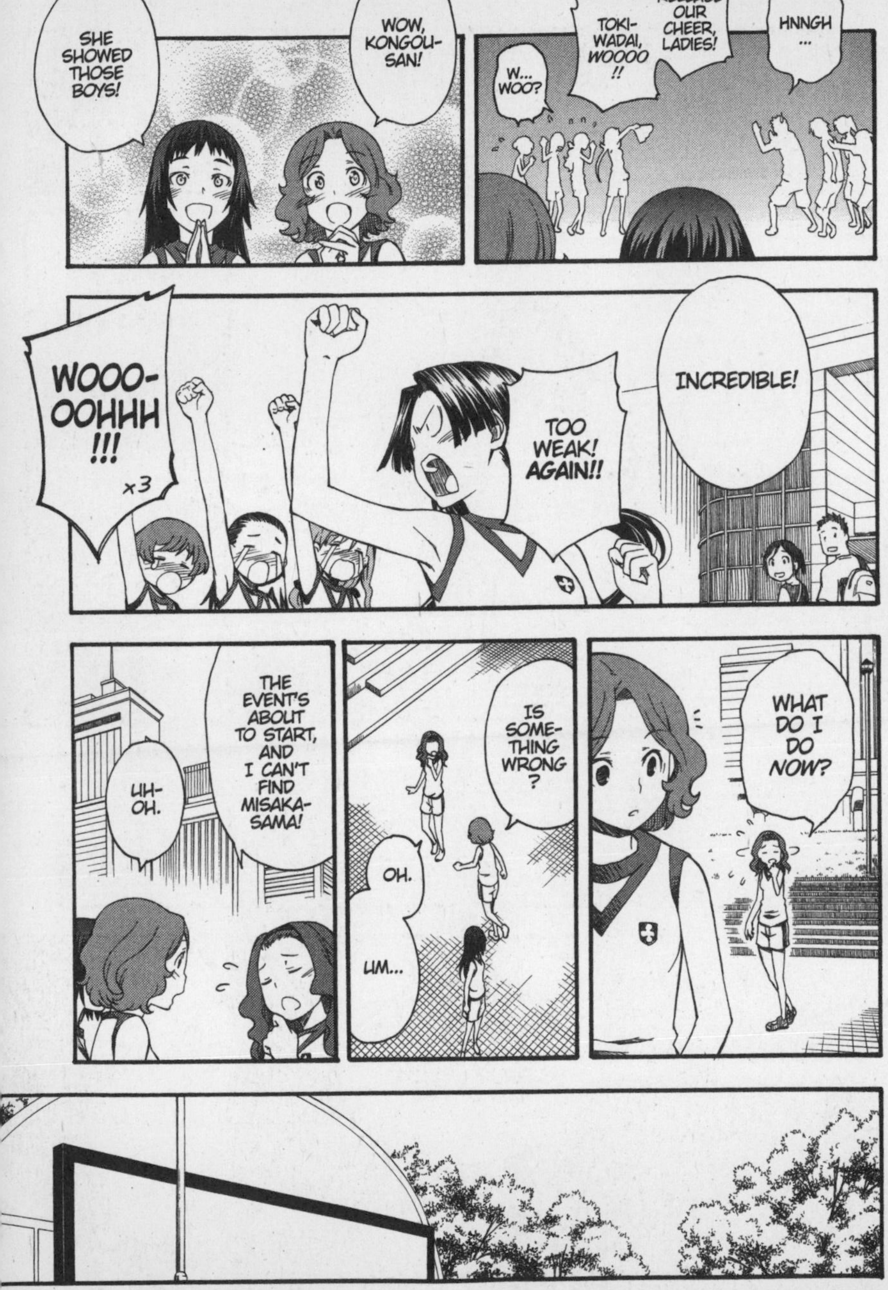
HNNGH ...
RELEASE OUR CHEER, LADIES!
TOKI-WADAI, WOOOO!!
W... WOO?
WOW, KONGOU-SAN!
SHE SHOWED THOSE BOYS!
INCREDIBLE!
TOO WEAK! AGAIN!!
WOOO-OOHHH!!!
x3
WHAT DO I DO NOW?
IS SOMETHING WRONG?
OH.
UM...
THE EVENT'S ABOUT TO START, AND I CAN'T FIND MISAKA-SAMA!
UH-OH.

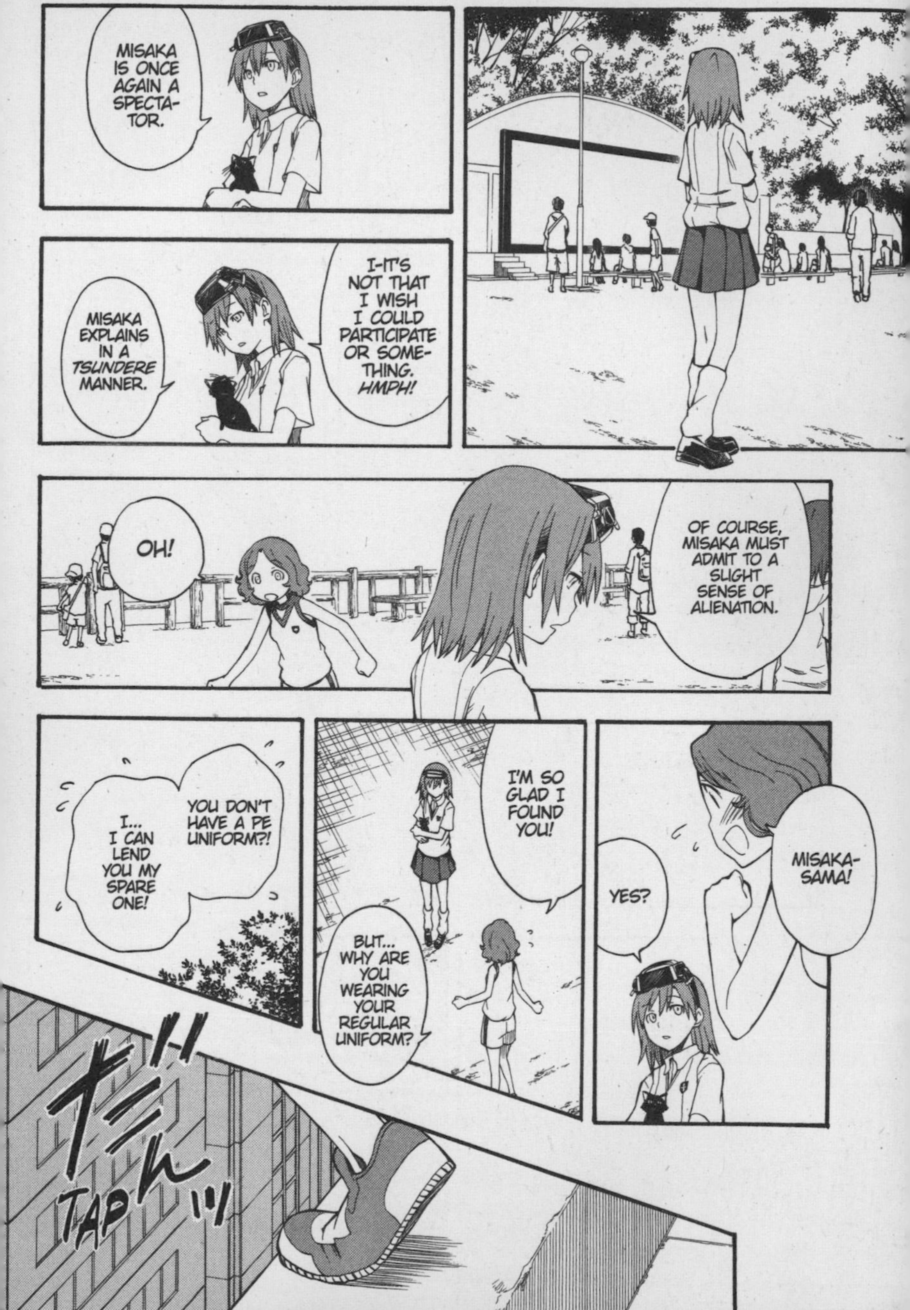
MISAKA IS ONCE AGAIN A SPECTATOR.
I-IT'S NOT THAT I WISH I COULD PARTICIPATE OR SOMETHING. *HMPH!*
MISAKA EXPLAINS IN A *TSUNDERE* MANNER.
OF COURSE, MISAKA MUST ADMIT TO A SLIGHT SENSE OF ALIENATION.
OH!
MISAKA-SAMA!
YES?
I'M SO GLAD I FOUND YOU!
BUT... WHY ARE YOU WEARING YOUR REGULAR UNIFORM?
YOU DON'T HAVE A PE UNIFORM?!
I... I CAN LEND YOU MY SPARE ONE!
TAP

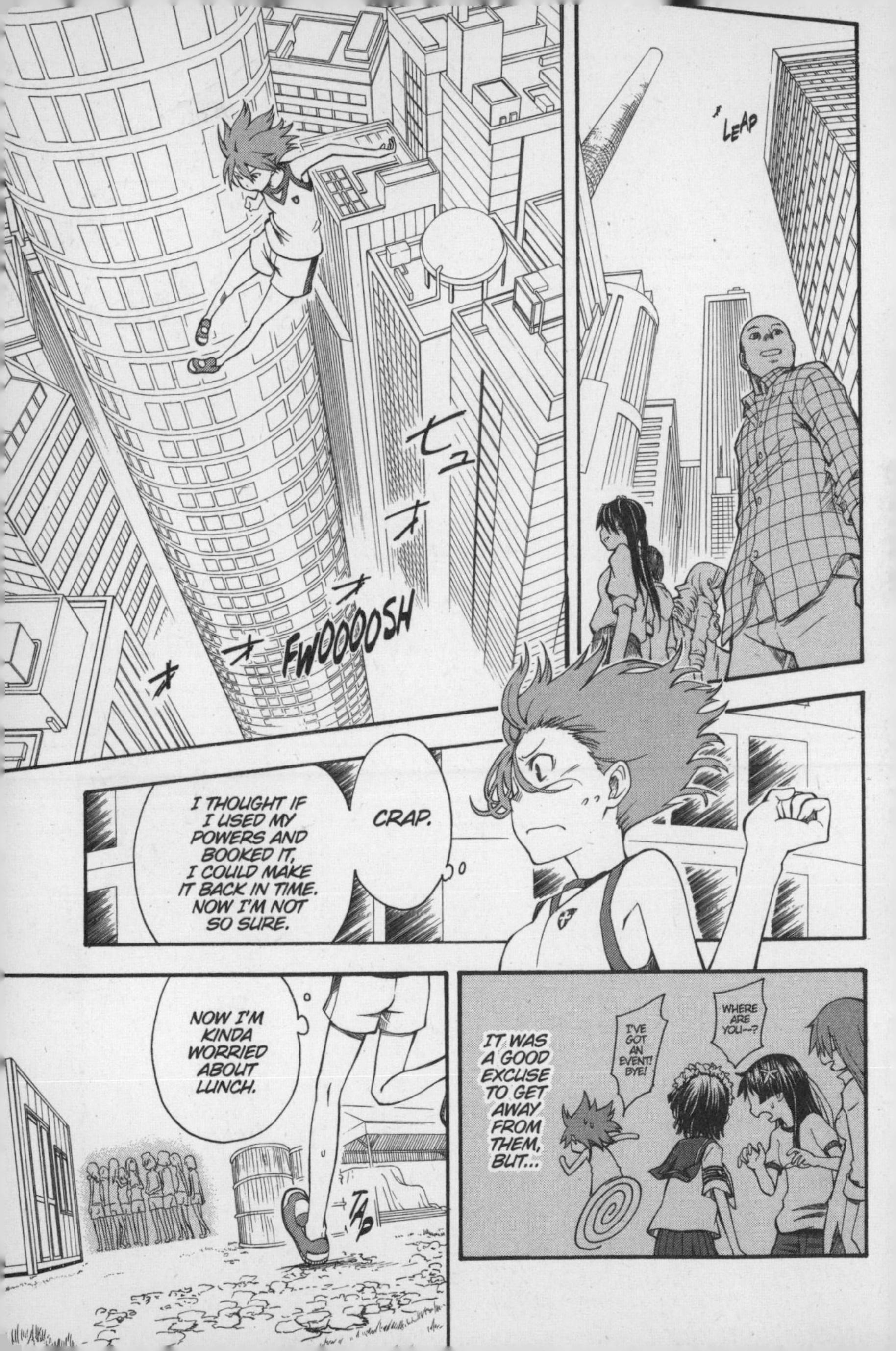
LEAP
ヒュオオオオ
FWOOOOSH
CRAP.
I THOUGHT IF I USED MY POWERS AND BOOKED IT, I COULD MAKE IT BACK IN TIME. NOW I'M NOT SO SURE.
WHERE ARE YOU--?
I'VE GOT AN EVENT! BYE!
IT WAS A GOOD EXCUSE TO GET AWAY FROM THEM, BUT...
NOW I'M KINDA WORRIED ABOUT LUNCH.
TAP

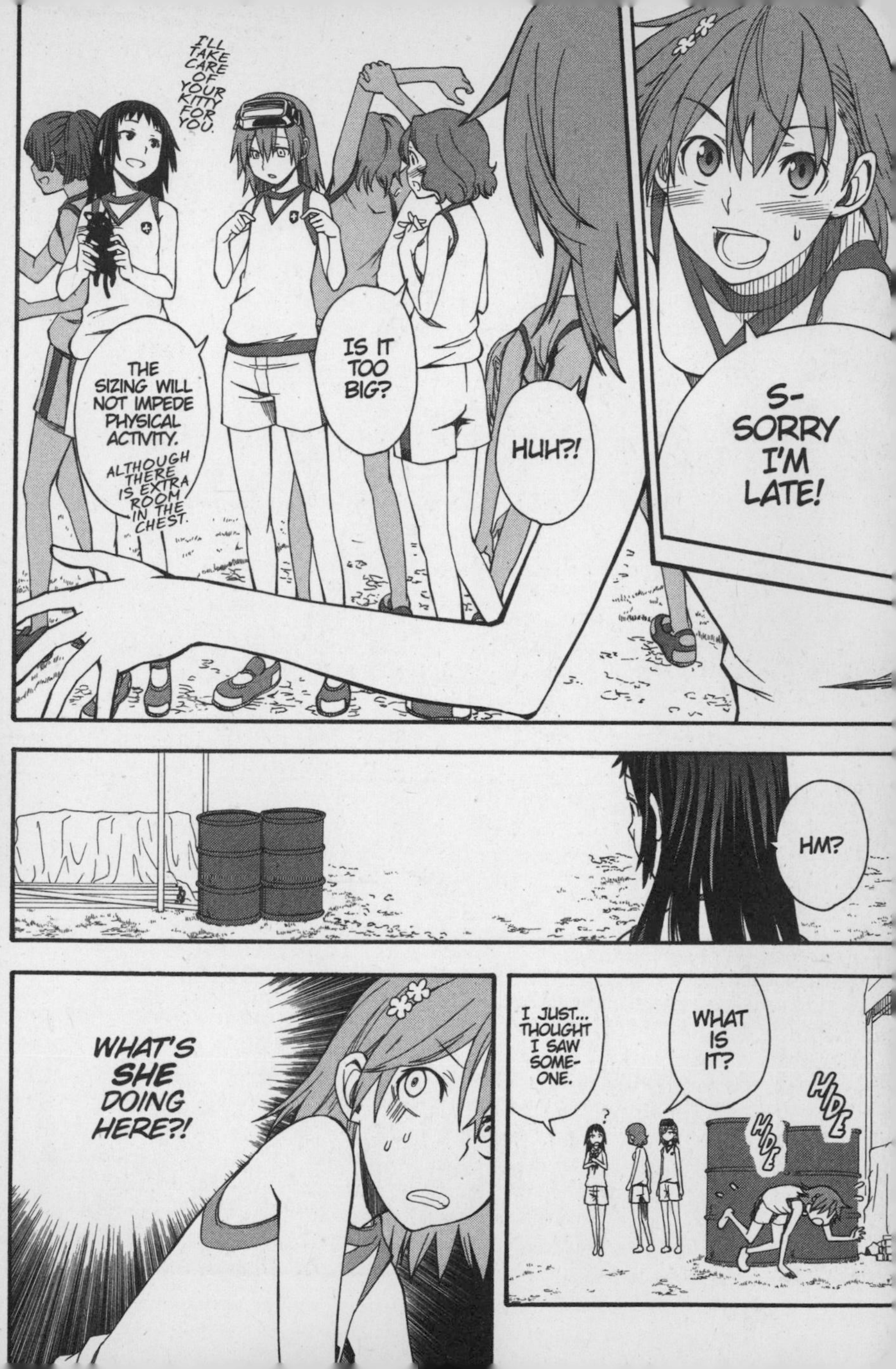
S-SORRY I'M LATE!
HUH?!
IS IT TOO BIG?
I'LL TAKE CARE OF YOUR KITTY FOR YOU.
THE SIZING WILL NOT IMPEDE PHYSICAL ACTIVITY.
ALTHOUGH THERE IS EXTRA ROOM IN THE CHEST.
HM?
WHAT IS IT?
I JUST... THOUGHT I SAW SOME-ONE.
?
HIDE
HIDE
WHAT'S SHE DOING HERE?!

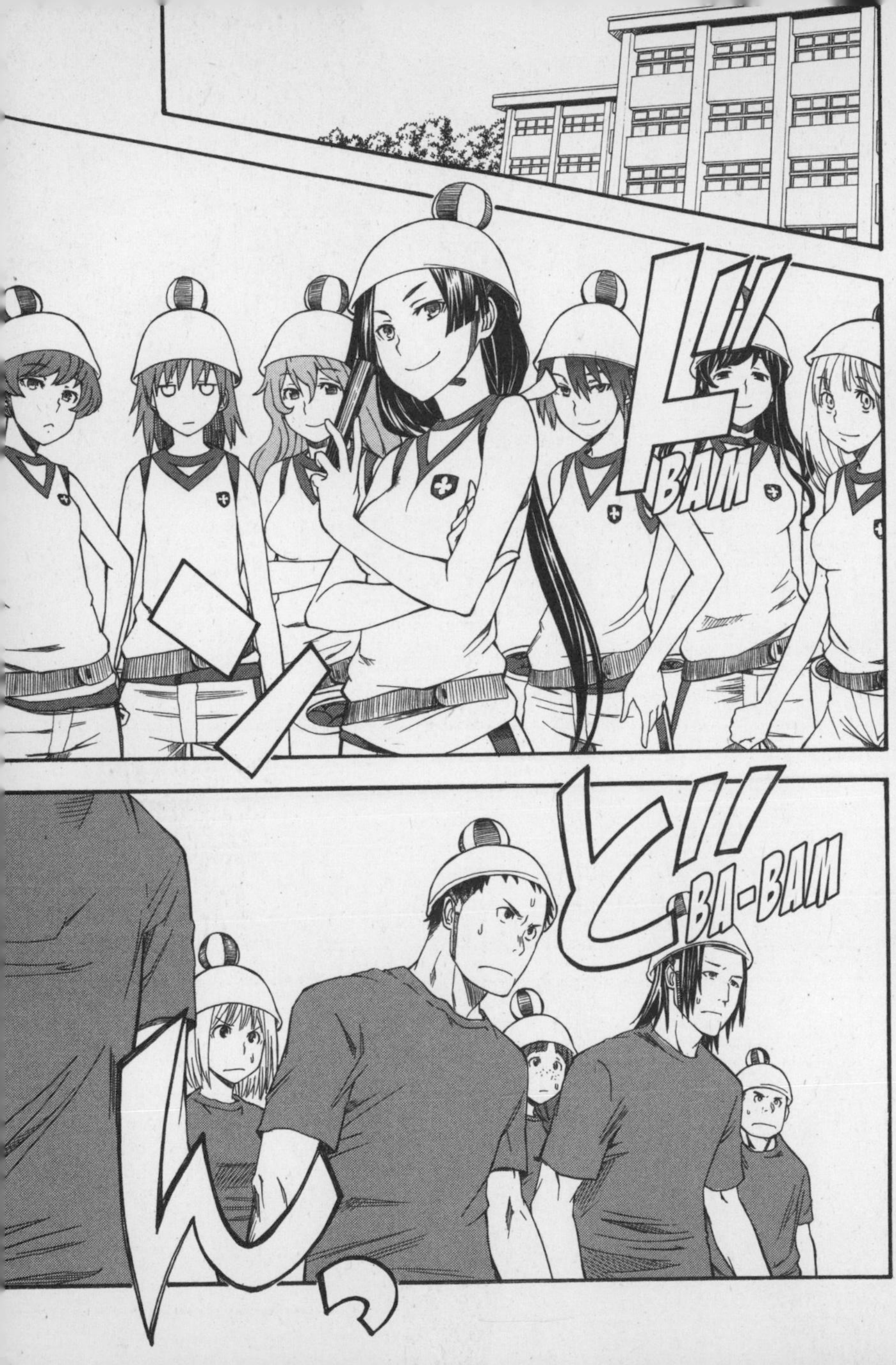
BAM
BA-BAM

BALLOON HUNTER

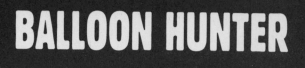

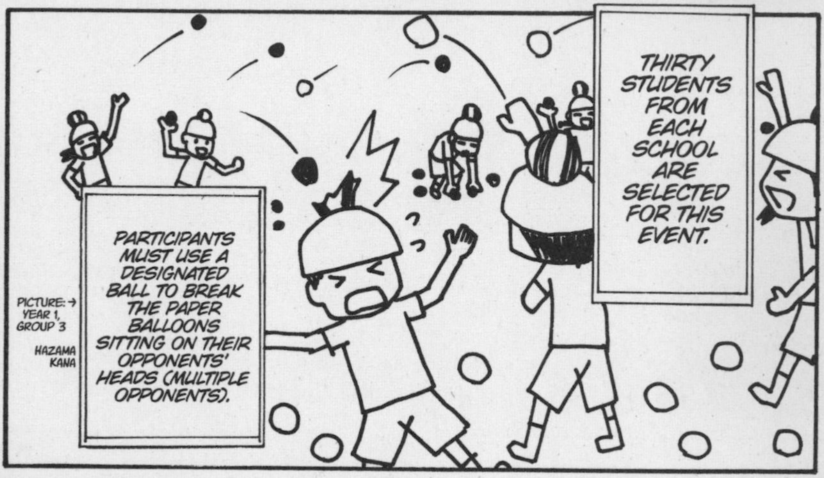
THIRTY STUDENTS FROM EACH SCHOOL ARE SELECTED FOR THIS EVENT.
PARTICIPANTS MUST USE A DESIGNATED BALL TO BREAK THE PAPER BALLOONS SITTING ON THEIR OPPONENTS' HEADS (MULTIPLE OPPONENTS).
PICTURE: → YEAR 1, GROUP 3
HAZAMA KANA

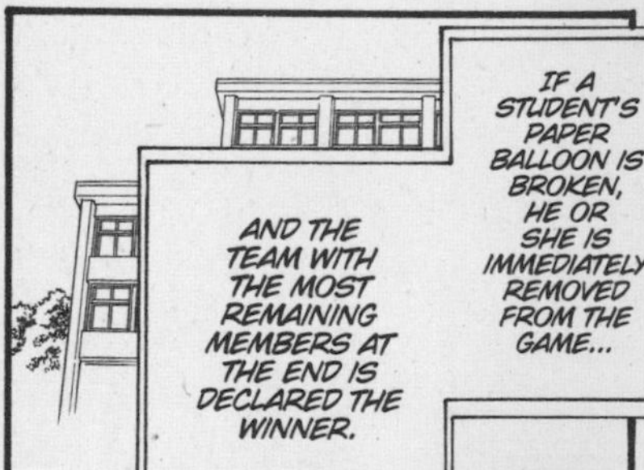
IF A STUDENT'S PAPER BALLOON IS BROKEN, HE OR SHE IS IMMEDIATELY REMOVED FROM THE GAME...
AND THE TEAM WITH THE MOST REMAINING MEMBERS AT THE END IS DECLARED THE WINNER.

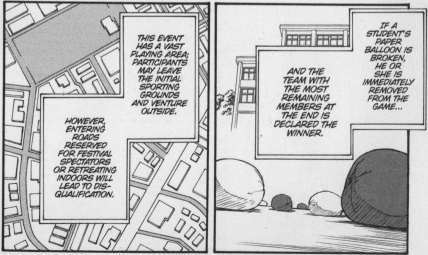

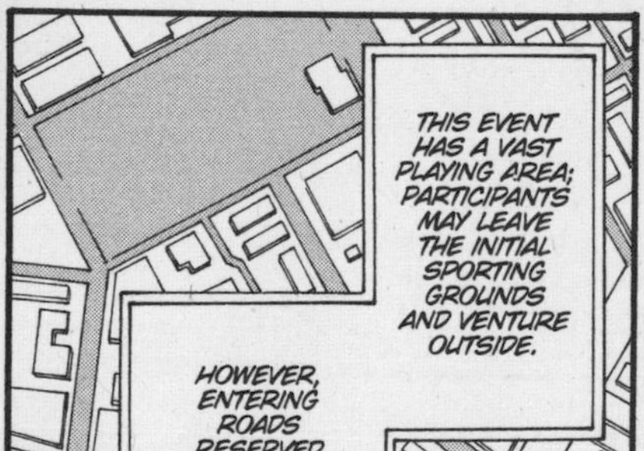
THIS EVENT HAS A VAST PLAYING AREA; PARTICIPANTS MAY LEAVE THE INITIAL SPORTING GROUNDS AND VENTURE OUTSIDE.
HOWEVER, ENTERING ROADS RESERVED FOR FESTIVAL SPECTATORS OR RETREATING INDOORS WILL LEAD TO DIS-QUALIFICATION.

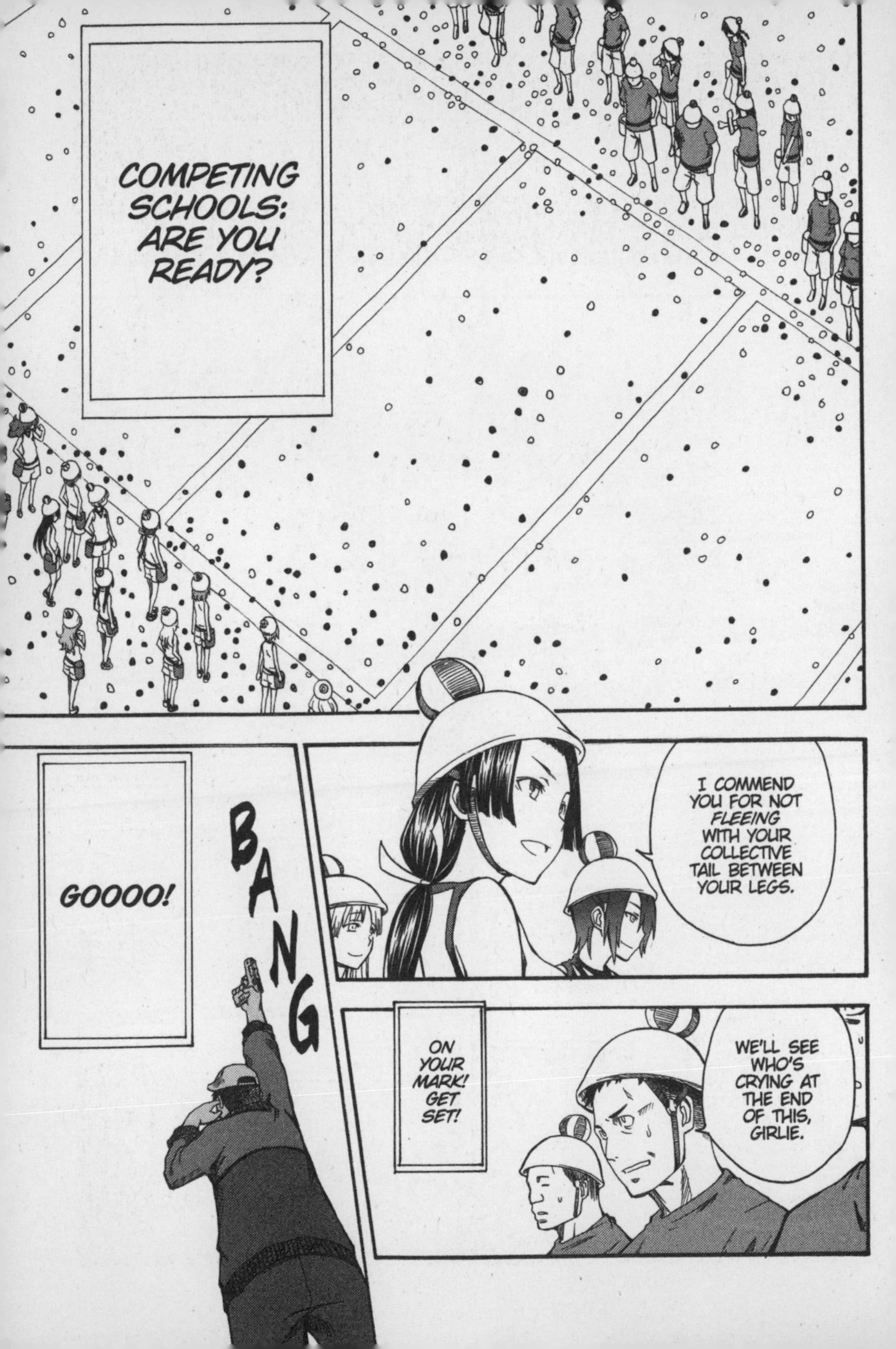
COMPETING SCHOOLS: ARE YOU READY?
I COMMEND YOU FOR NOT *FLEEING* WITH YOUR COLLECTIVE TAIL BETWEEN YOUR LEGS.
WE'LL SEE WHO'S CRYING AT THE END OF THIS, GIRLIE.
ON YOUR MARK! GET SET!
GOOOO!
BANG

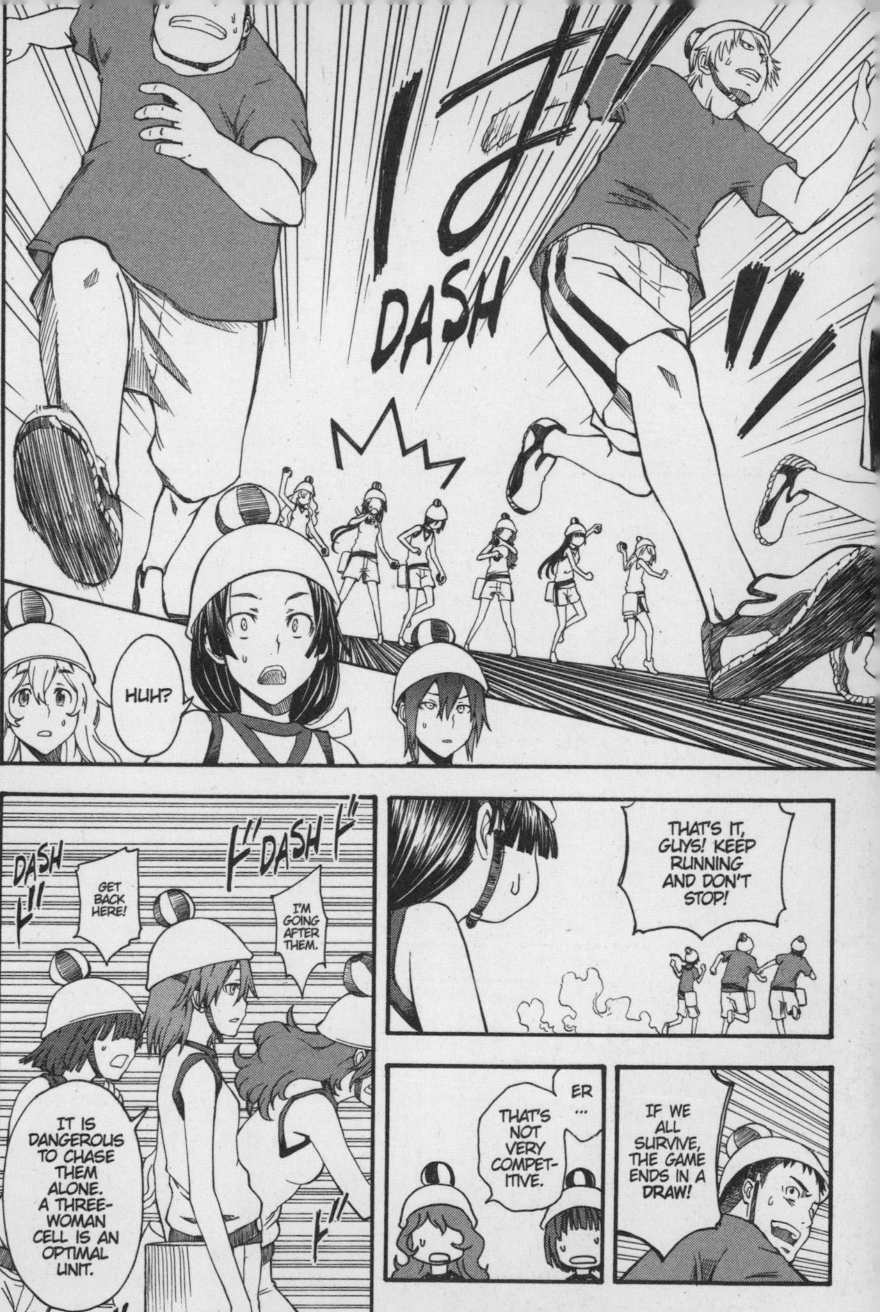
DASH
HUH?
THAT'S IT, GUYS! KEEP RUNNING AND DON'T STOP!
IF WE ALL SURVIVE, THE GAME ENDS IN A DRAW!
ER ...
THAT'S NOT VERY COMPETITIVE.
DASH
I'M GOING AFTER THEM.
GET BACK HERE!
DASH
IT IS DANGEROUS TO CHASE THEM ALONE. A THREE-WOMAN CELL IS AN OPTIMAL UNIT.

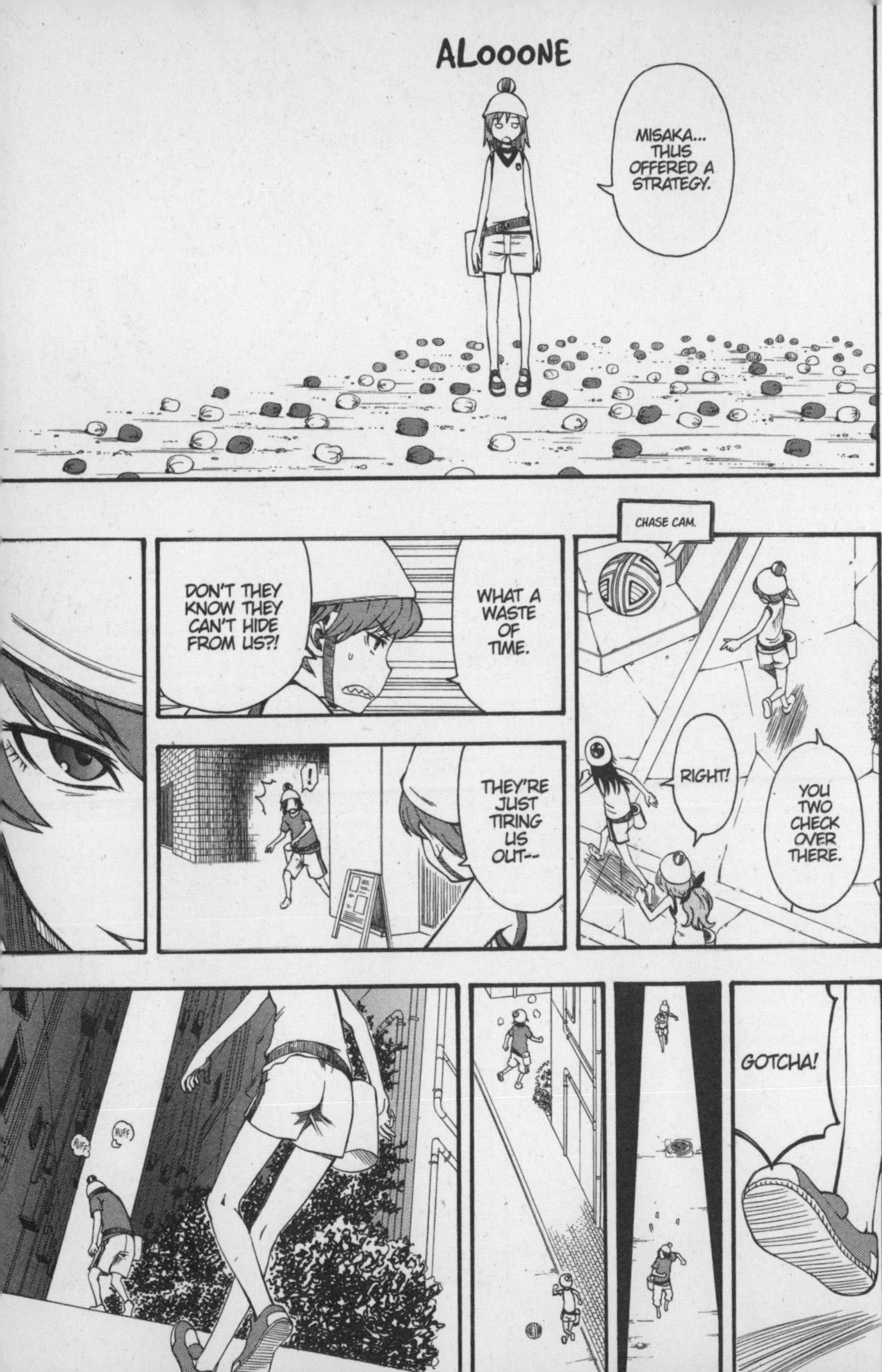
MISAKA... THUS OFFERED A STRATEGY.
ALOOONE
CHASE CAM.
YOU TWO CHECK OVER THERE.
RIGHT!
WHAT A WASTE OF TIME.
DON'T THEY KNOW THEY CAN'T HIDE FROM US?!
THEY'RE JUST TIRING US OUT--
!
GOTCHA!
HUFF
HUFF

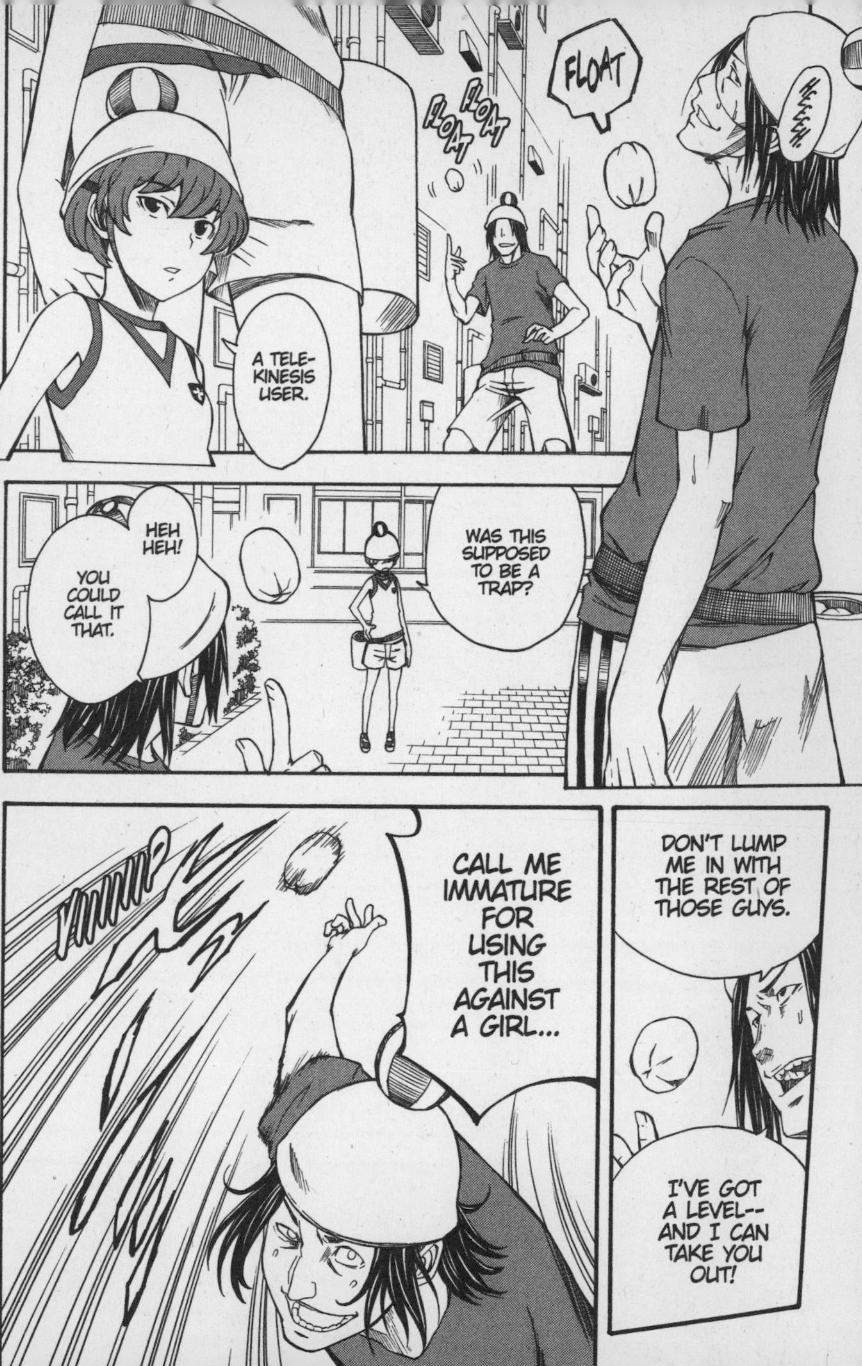
HEEEEH!
FLOAT
FLOAT
FLOAT
A TELE-KINESIS USER.
WAS THIS SUPPOSED TO BE A TRAP?
HEH HEH!
YOU COULD CALL IT THAT.
DON'T LUMP ME IN WITH THE REST OF THOSE GUYS.
I'VE GOT A LEVEL-- AND I CAN TAKE YOU OUT!
CALL ME IMMATURE FOR USING THIS AGAINST A GIRL...

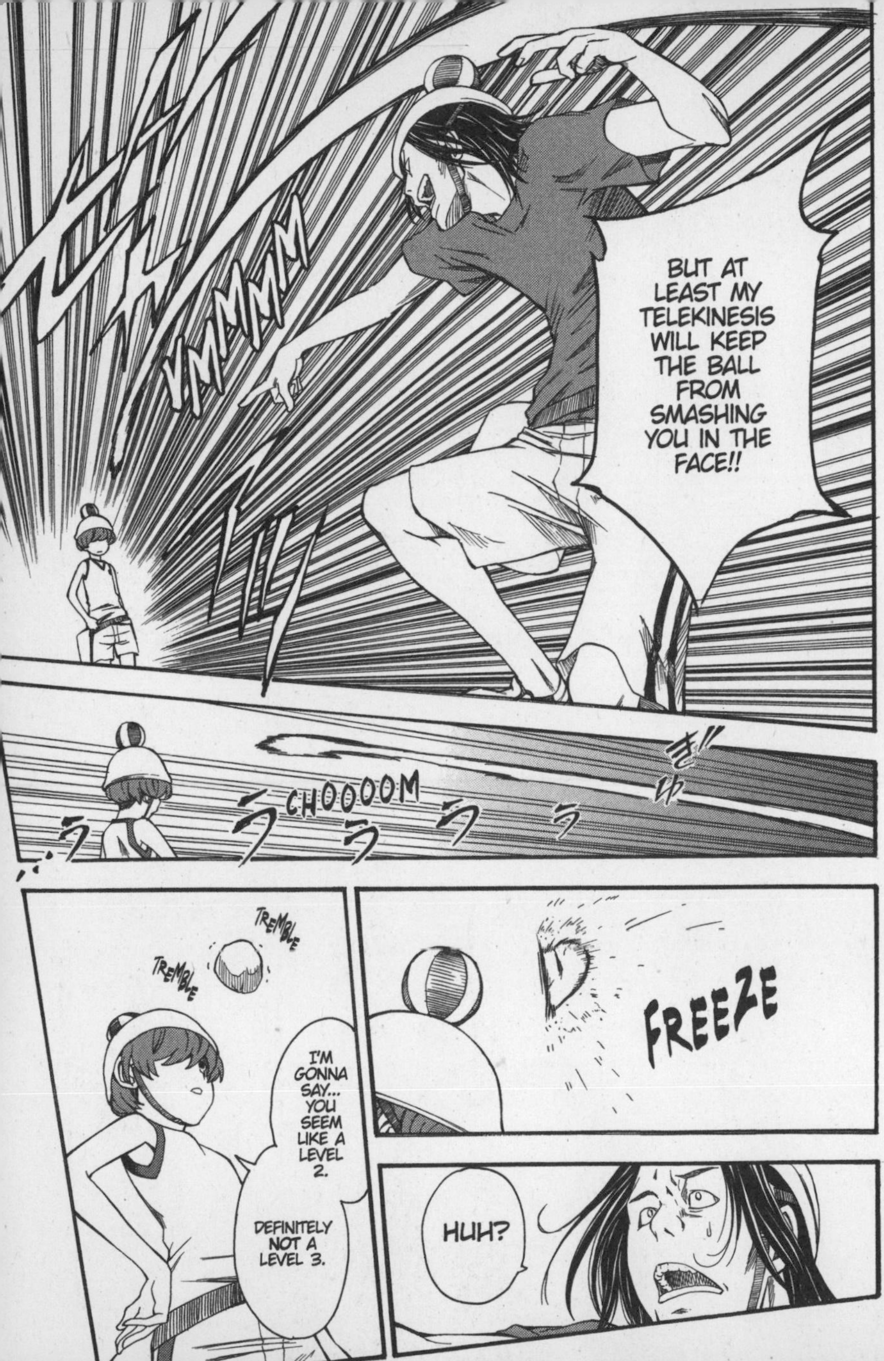
BUT AT LEAST MY TELEKINESIS WILL KEEP THE BALL FROM SMASHING YOU IN THE FACE!!
VMMMM
CHOOOOM
FREEZE
HUH?
TREMBLE
TREMBLE
I'M GONNA SAY... YOU SEEM LIKE A LEVEL 2.
DEFINITELY NOT A LEVEL 3.

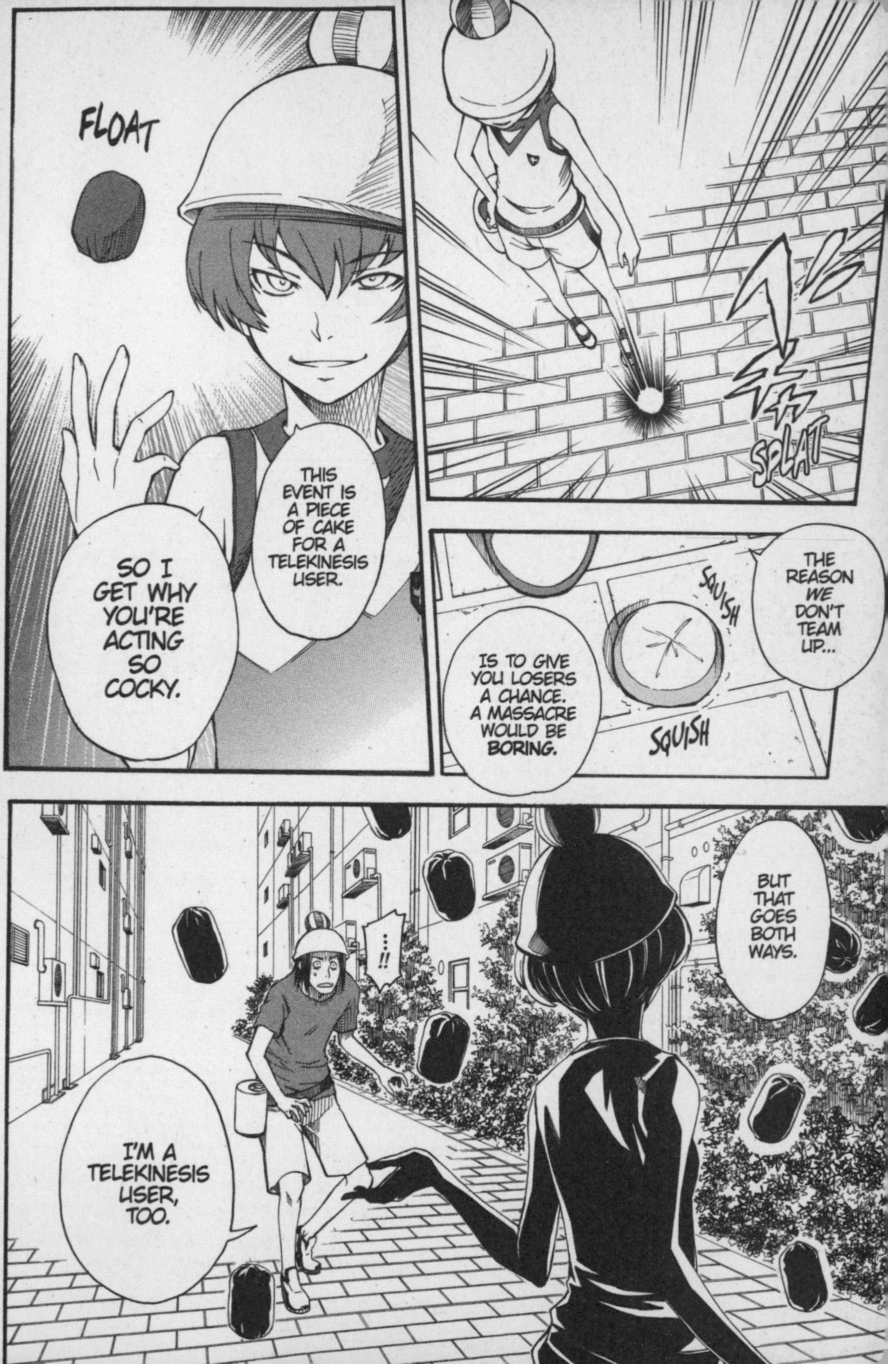
SPLAT
THE REASON WE DON'T TEAM UP...
SQUISH
IS TO GIVE YOU LOSERS A CHANCE. A MASSACRE WOULD BE BORING.
SQUISH
FLOAT
THIS EVENT IS A PIECE OF CAKE FOR A TELEKINESIS USER.
SO I GET WHY YOU'RE ACTING SO COCKY.
BUT THAT GOES BOTH WAYS.
...!!
I'M A TELEKINESIS USER, TOO.

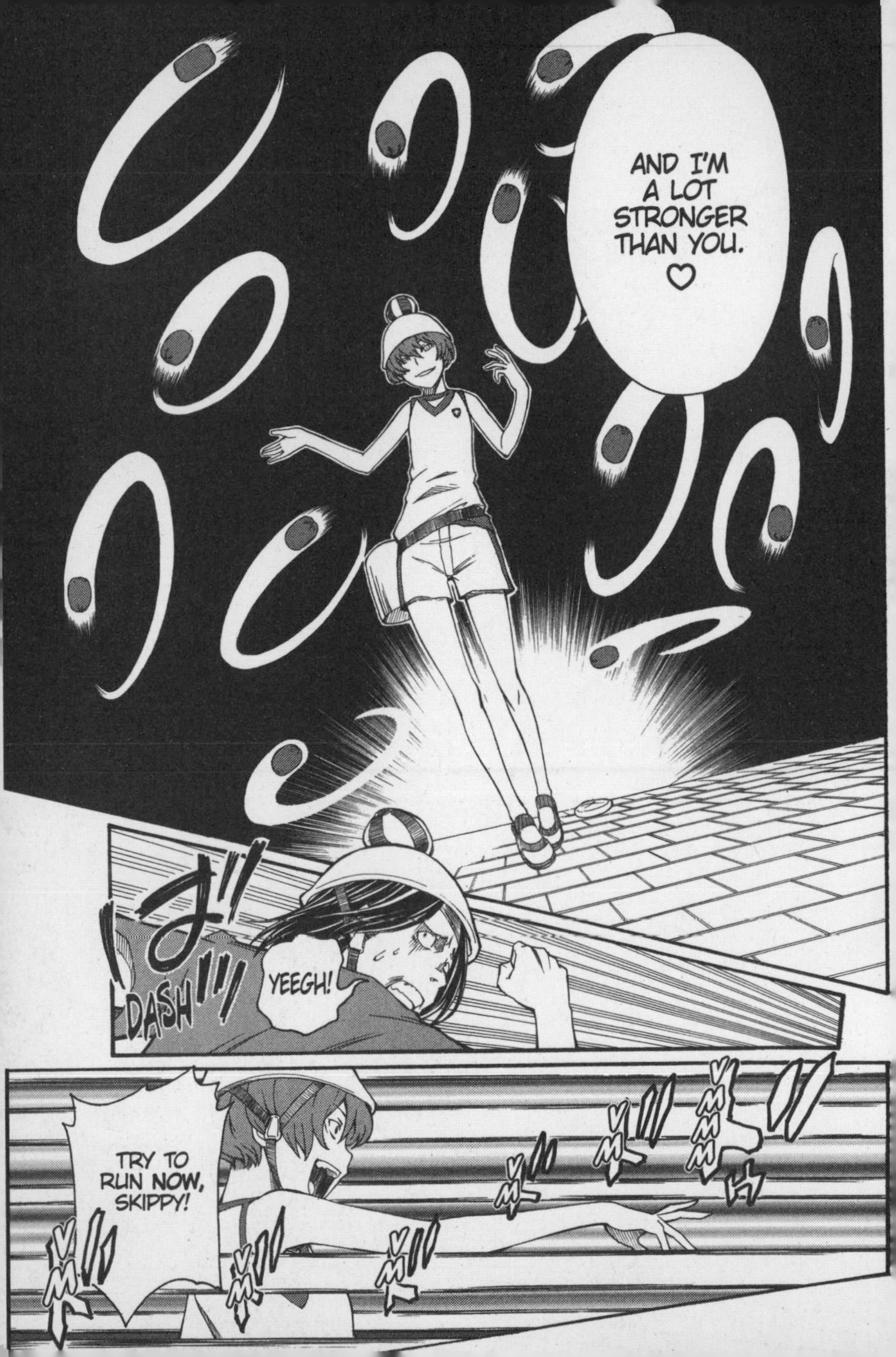
AND I'M A LOT STRONGER THAN YOU. ♡
DASH
YEEGH!
TRY TO RUN NOW, SKIPPY!

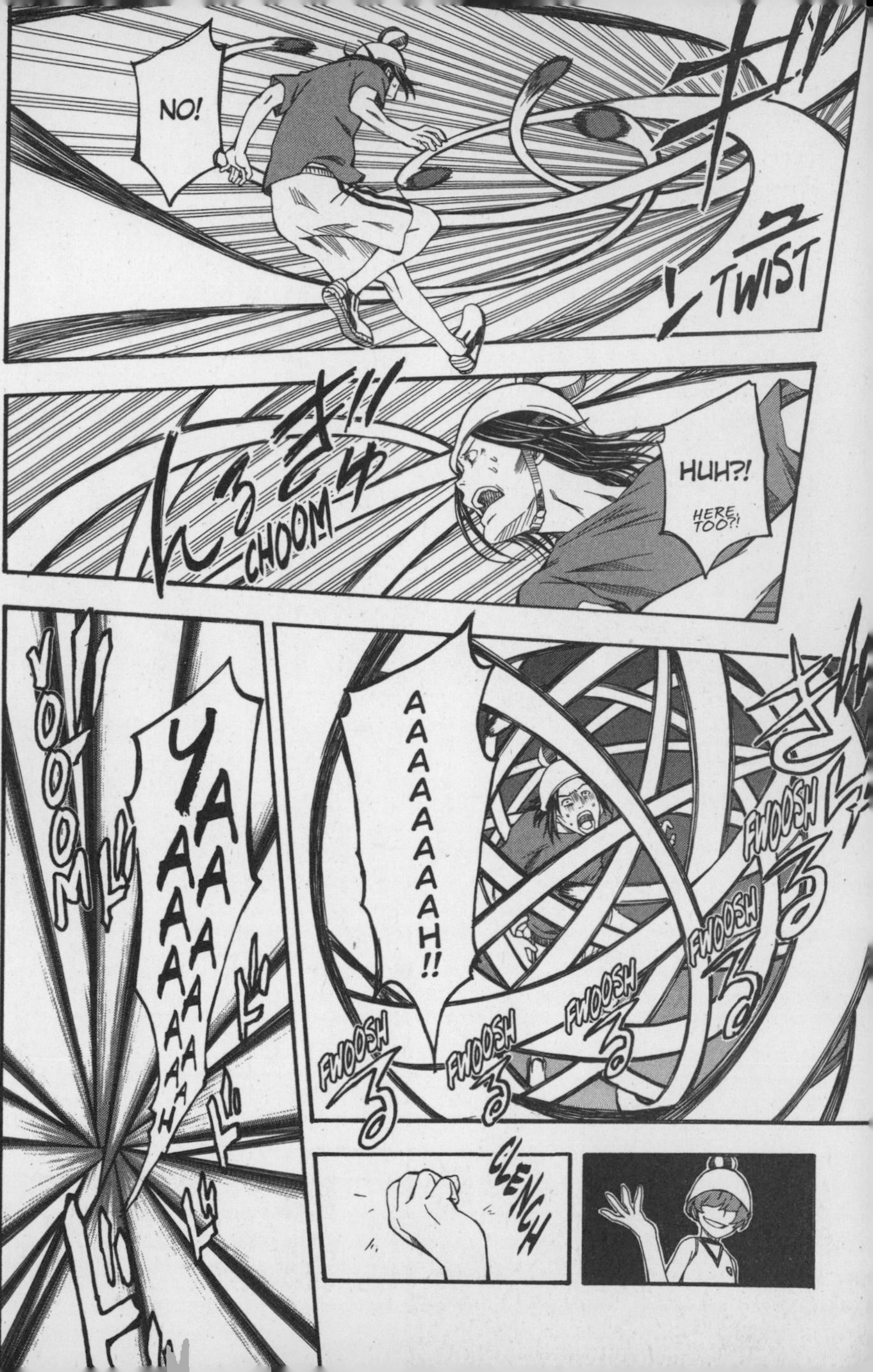
TWIST
NO!
HUH?!
HERE, TOO?!
CHOOM
AAAAAAAAAAAAH!!
FWOOSH
FWOOSH
FWOOSH
FWOOSH
FWOOSH
CLENCH
YAAAAAAAAAAAAAH
VOOOOOM

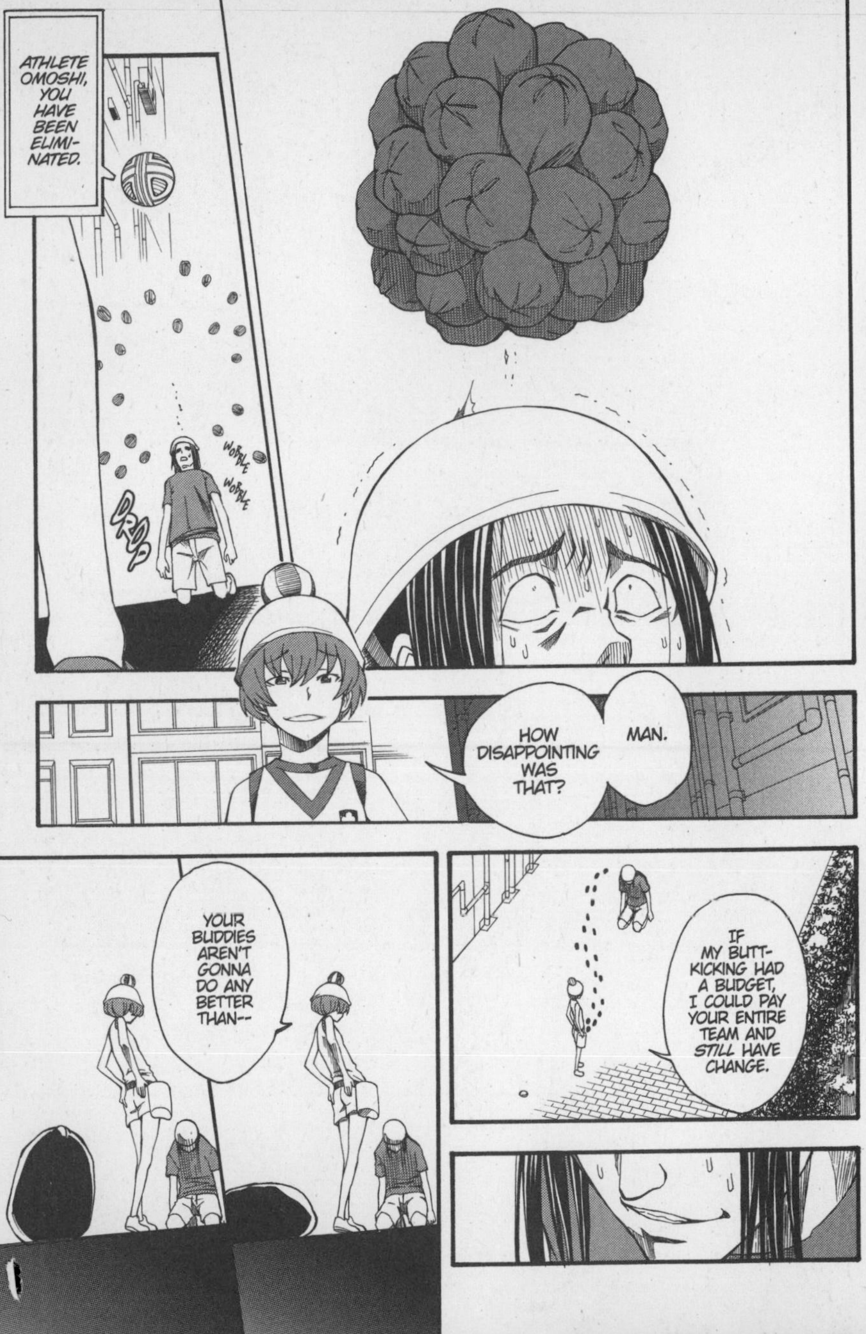
ATHLETE OMOSHI, YOU HAVE BEEN ELIMINATED.
WOBBLE
WOBBLE
DROP
MAN.
HOW DISAPPOINTING WAS THAT?
IF MY BUTT-KICKING HAD A BUDGET, I COULD PAY YOUR ENTIRE TEAM AND STILL HAVE CHANGE.
YOUR BUDDIES AREN'T GONNA DO ANY BETTER THAN--

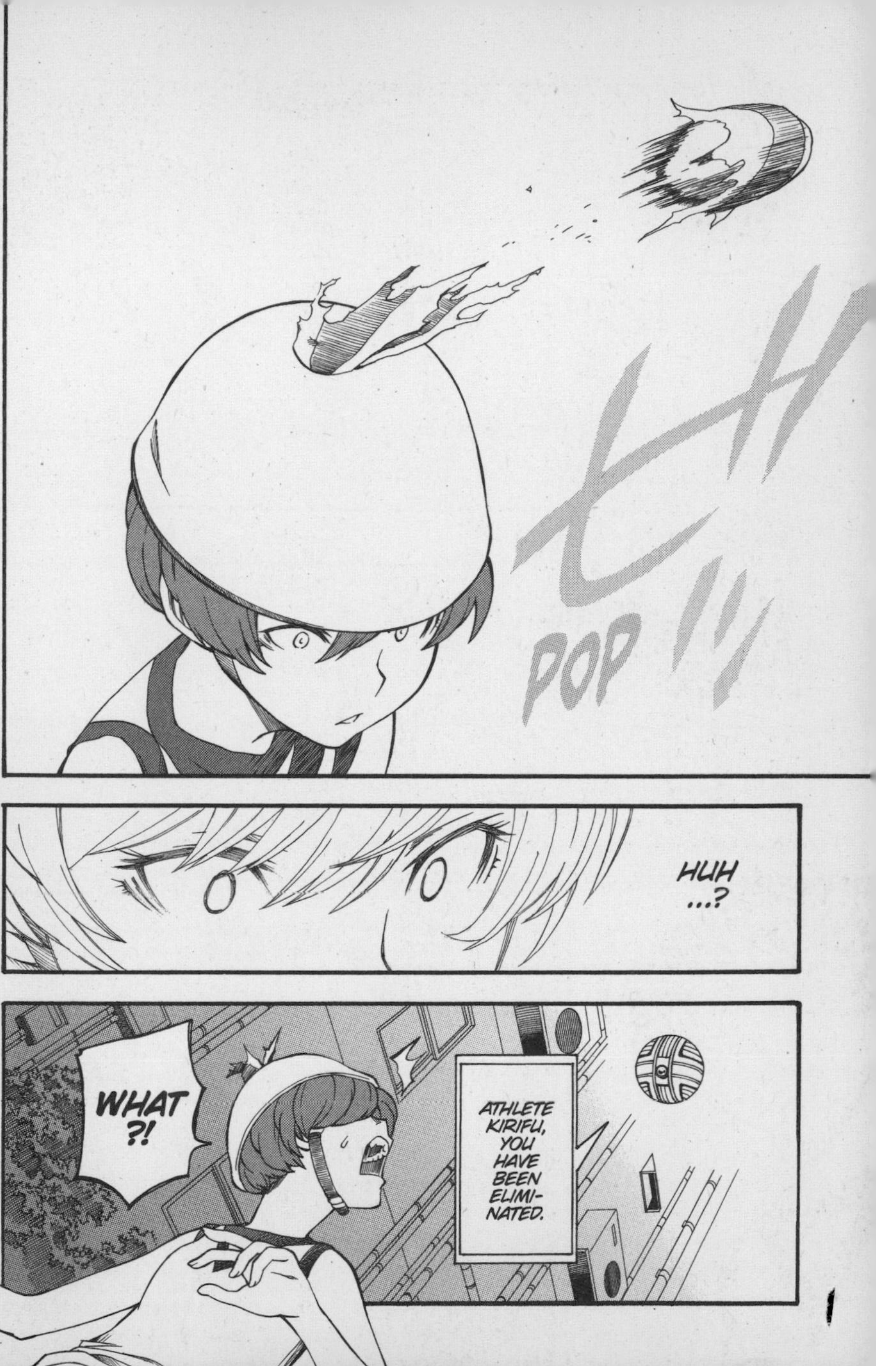
POP!!
HUH ...?
ATHLETE KIRIFU, YOU HAVE BEEN ELIMINATED.
WHAT?!

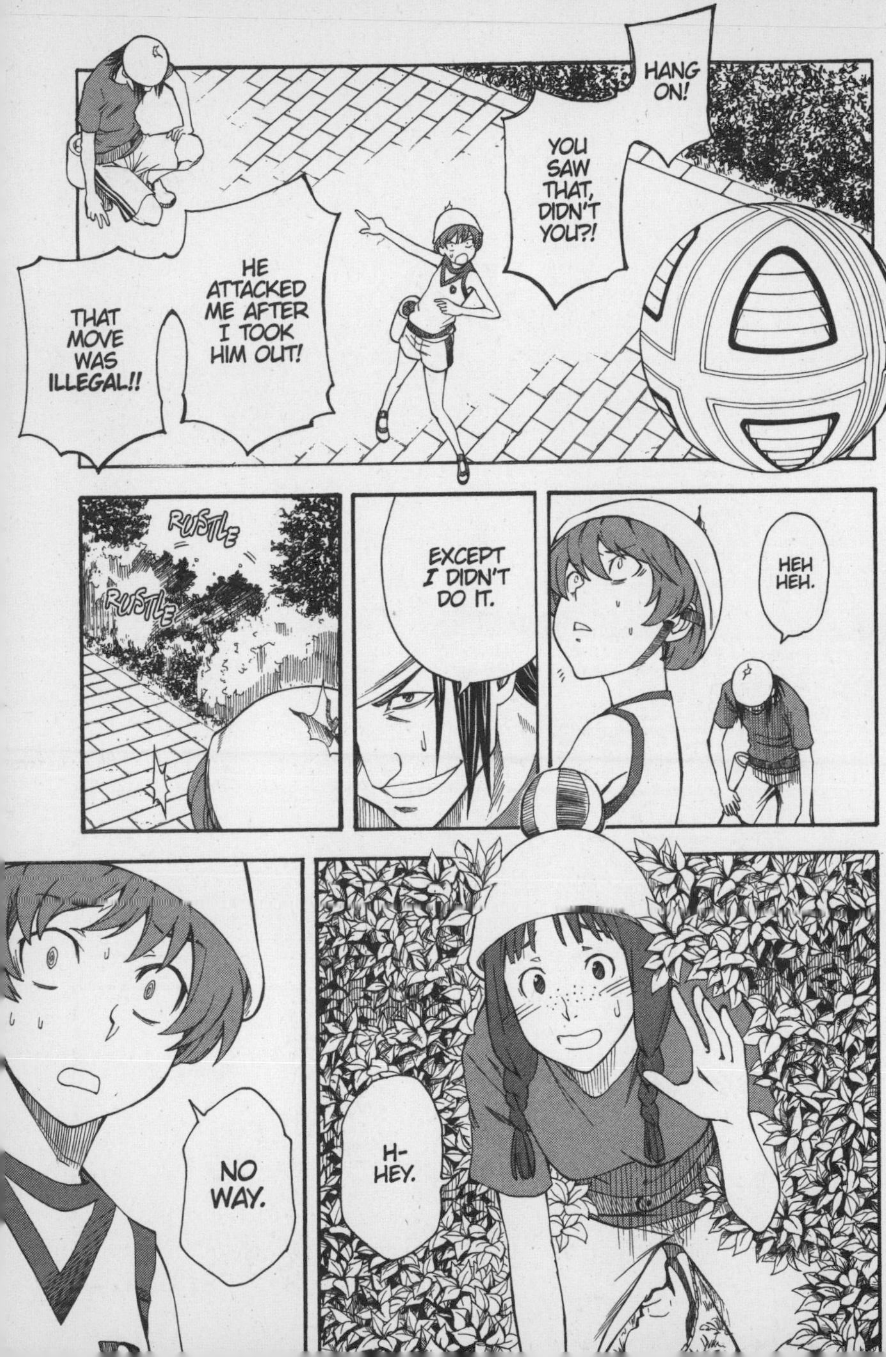
HANG ON!
YOU SAW THAT, DIDN'T YOU?!
HE ATTACKED ME AFTER I TOOK HIM OUT!
THAT MOVE WAS ILLEGAL!!
HEH HEH.
EXCEPT I DIDN'T DO IT.
RUSTLE
RUSTLE
H- HEY.
NO WAY.

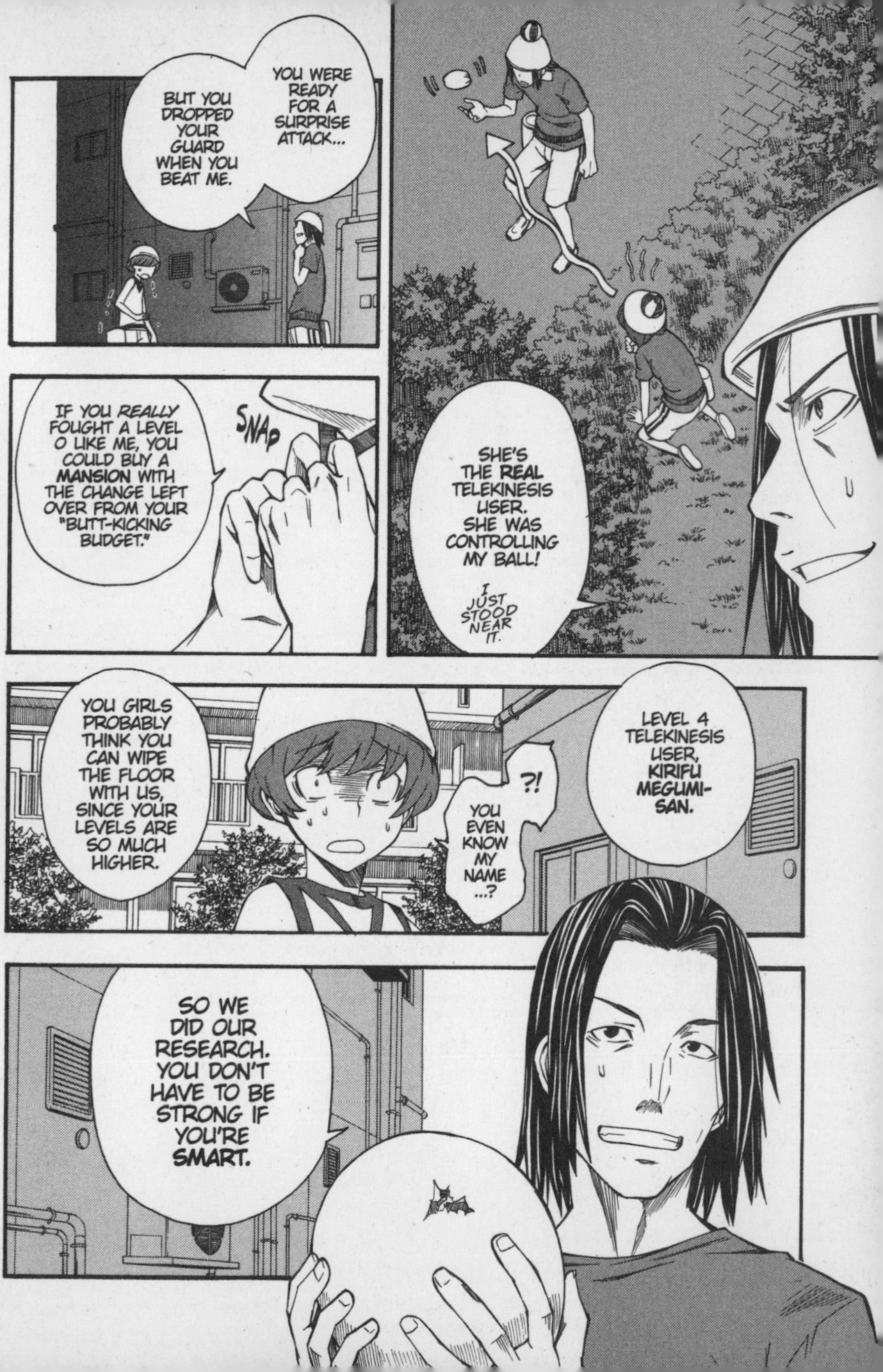
SHE'S THE REAL TELEKINESIS USER. SHE WAS CONTROLLING MY BALL!
I JUST STOOD NEAR IT.
YOU WERE READY FOR A SURPRISE ATTACK...
BUT YOU DROPPED YOUR GUARD WHEN YOU BEAT ME.
SNAP
IF YOU REALLY FOUGHT A LEVEL 0 LIKE ME, YOU COULD BUY A MANSION WITH THE CHANGE LEFT OVER FROM YOUR "BUTT-KICKING BUDGET."
LEVEL 4 TELEKINESIS USER, KIRIFU MEGUMI-SAN.
?!
YOU EVEN KNOW MY NAME...?
YOU GIRLS PROBABLY THINK YOU CAN WIPE THE FLOOR WITH US, SINCE YOUR LEVELS ARE SO MUCH HIGHER.
SO WE DID OUR RESEARCH. YOU DON'T HAVE TO BE STRONG IF YOU'RE SMART.

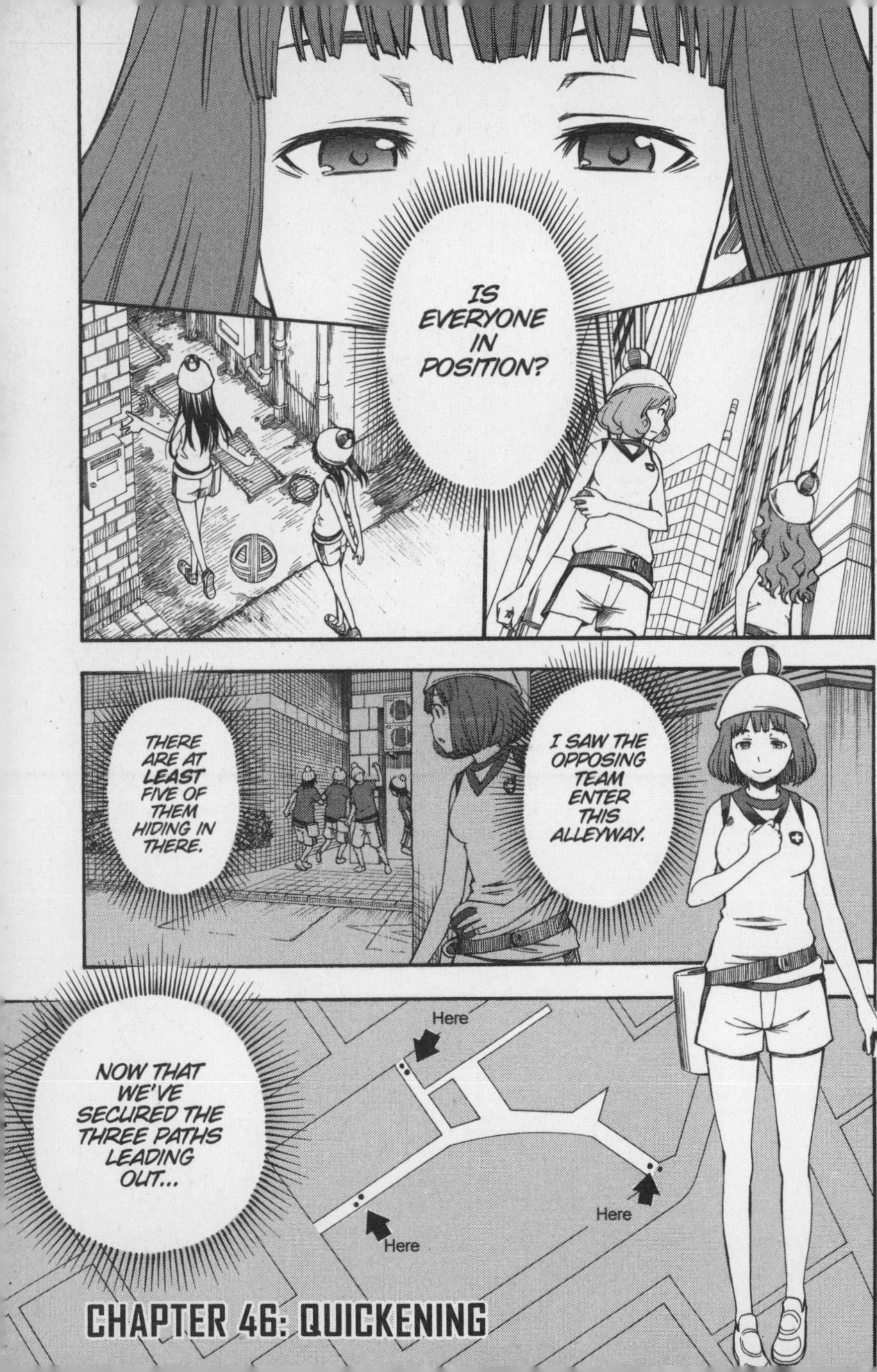
IS EVERYONE IN POSITION?
I SAW THE OPPOSING TEAM ENTER THIS ALLEYWAY.
THERE ARE AT LEAST FIVE OF THEM HIDING IN THERE.
NOW THAT WE'VE SECURED THE THREE PATHS LEADING OUT...
Here
Here
Here

CHAPTER 46: QUICKENING

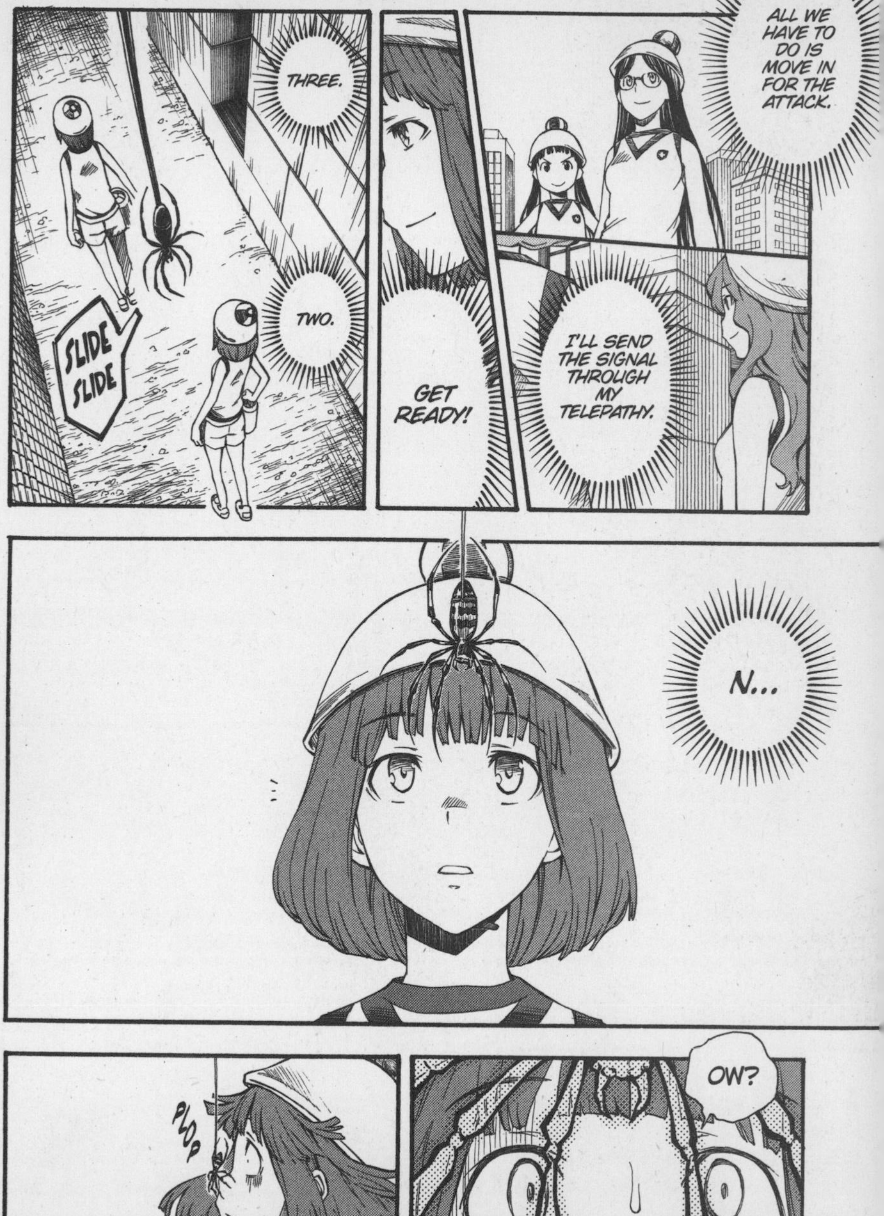
ALL WE HAVE TO DO IS MOVE IN FOR THE ATTACK.
I'LL SEND THE SIGNAL THROUGH MY TELEPATHY.
GET READY!
THREE.
TWO.
SLIDE SLIDE
N...
OW?
PLOP

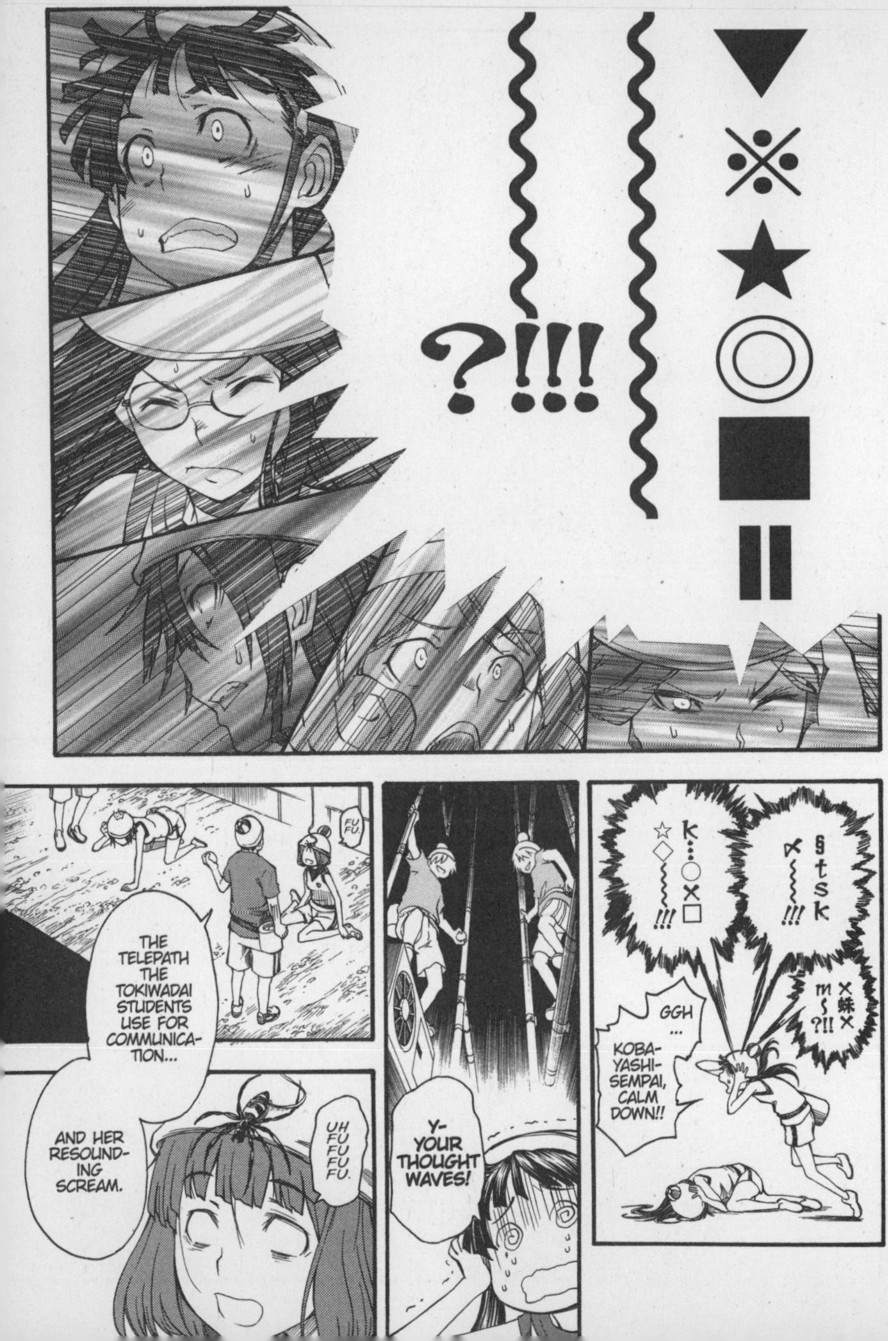
▼※★◎■〓
~~~~~?!!!
§tsk 〆~~!!!
k…○×□ ☆◇~~!!!
×蛛× m~?!!
GGH…
KOBA-YASHI-SEMPAI, CALM DOWN!!
Y- YOUR THOUGHT WAVES!
FU FU.
THE TELEPATH THE TOKIWADAI STUDENTS USE FOR COMMUNICA-TION…
UH FU FU FU FU.
AND HER RESOUND-ING SCREAM.
~~~~~

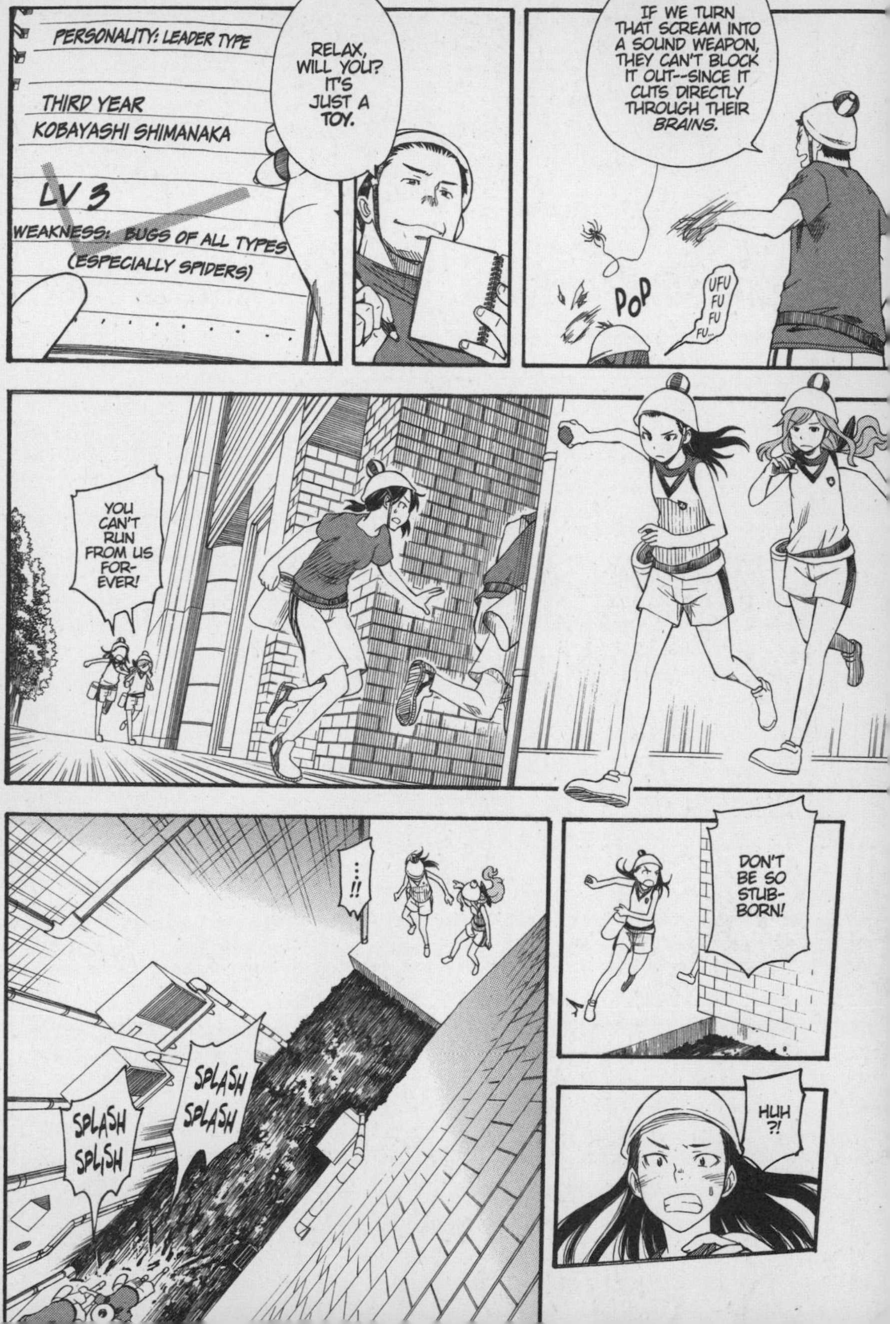
IF WE TURN THAT SCREAM INTO A SOUND WEAPON, THEY CAN'T BLOCK IT OUT--SINCE IT CUTS DIRECTLY THROUGH THEIR *BRAINS.*
UFU FU FU FU...
POP
RELAX, WILL YOU? IT'S JUST A TOY.
PERSONALITY: LEADER TYPE
THIRD YEAR
KOBAYASHI SHIMANAKA
LV 3
WEAKNESS: BUGS OF ALL TYPES (ESPECIALLY SPIDERS)
YOU CAN'T RUN FROM US FOR-EVER!
DON'T BE SO STUB-BORN!
HUH ?!
...!!
SPLASH SPLASH
SPLASH SPLSH

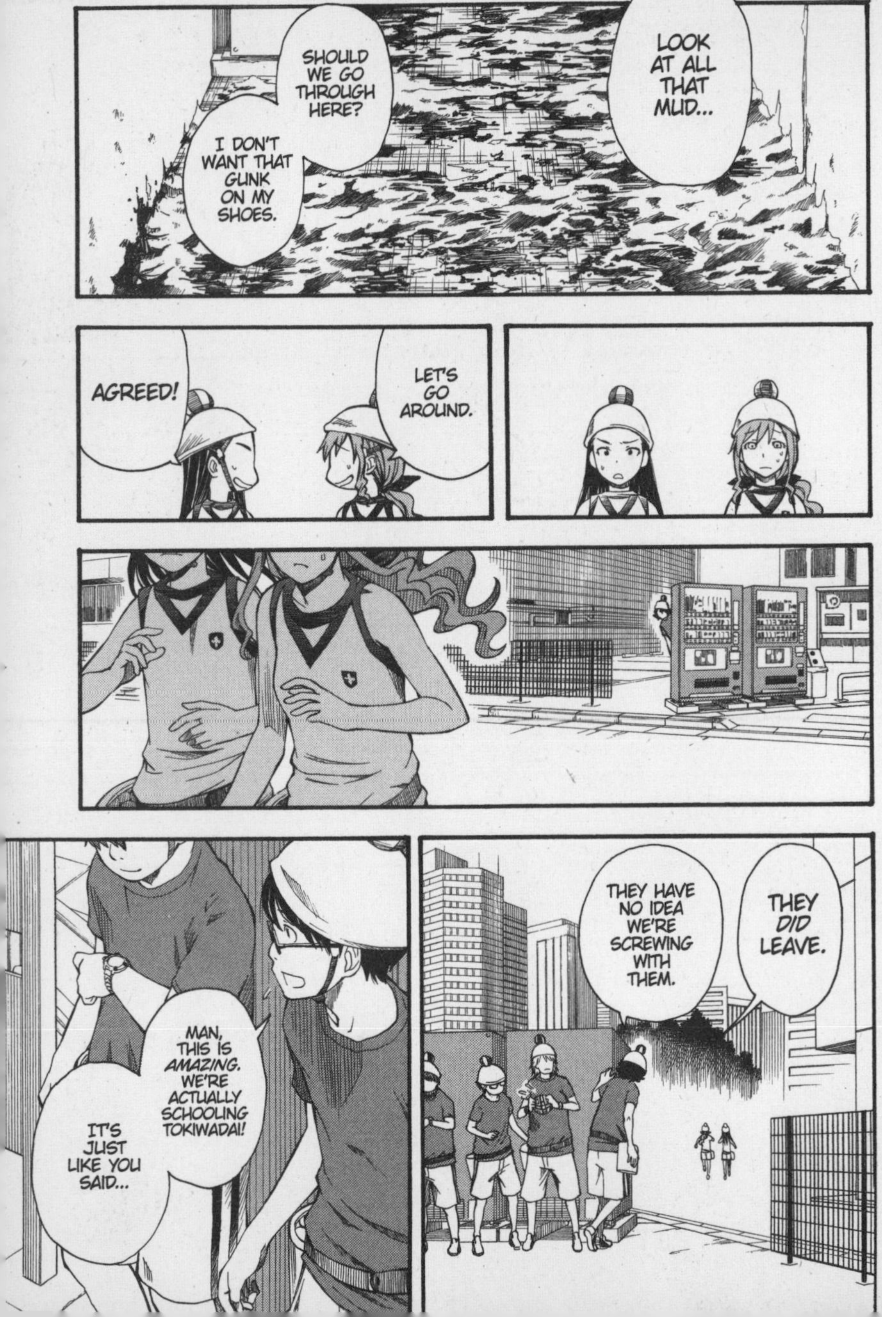
LOOK AT ALL THAT MUD...
SHOULD WE GO THROUGH HERE?
I DON'T WANT THAT GUNK ON MY SHOES.
LET'S GO AROUND.
AGREED!
THEY *DID* LEAVE.
THEY HAVE NO IDEA WE'RE SCREWING WITH THEM.
MAN, THIS IS *AMAZING*. WE'RE ACTUALLY SCHOOLING TOKIWADAI!
IT'S JUST LIKE YOU SAID...

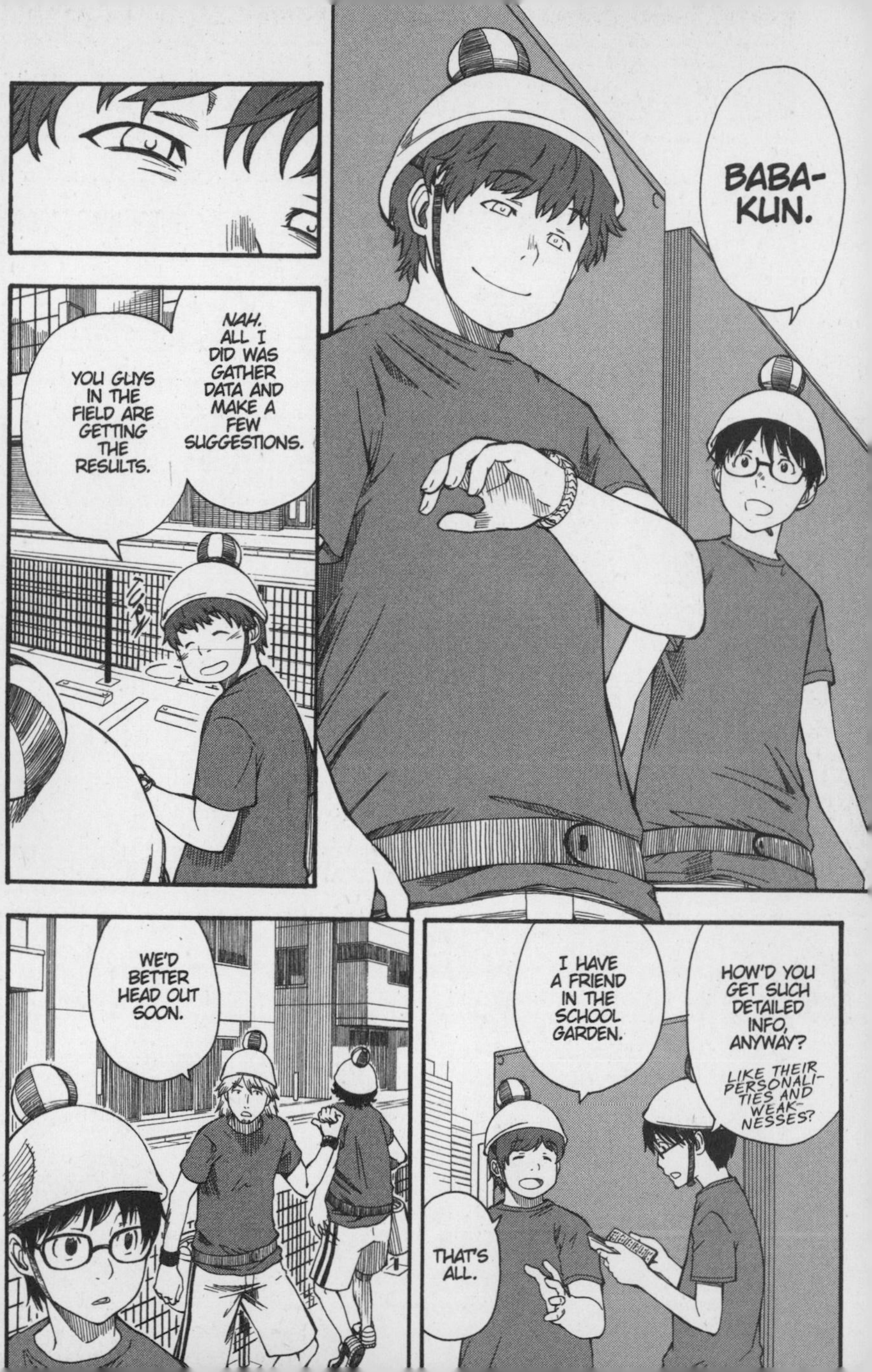
BABA-KUN.
NAH. ALL I DID WAS GATHER DATA AND MAKE A FEW SUGGESTIONS.
YOU GUYS IN THE FIELD ARE GETTING THE RESULTS.
TURN
HOW'D YOU GET SUCH DETAILED INFO, ANYWAY?
LIKE THEIR PERSONALITIES AND WEAKNESSES?
I HAVE A FRIEND IN THE SCHOOL GARDEN.
THAT'S ALL.
WE'D BETTER HEAD OUT SOON.

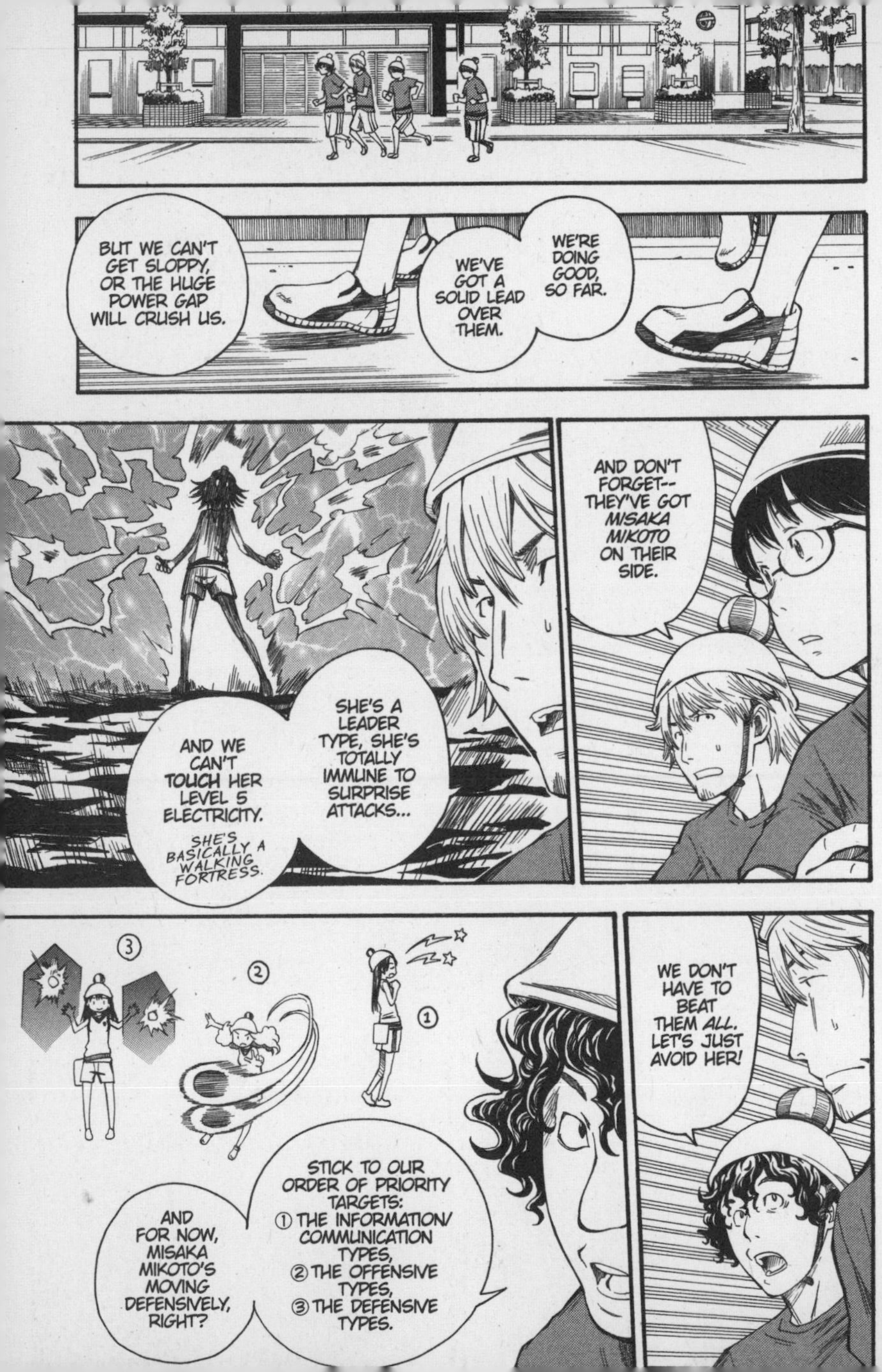

WE'RE DOING GOOD, SO FAR.
WE'VE GOT A SOLID LEAD OVER THEM.
BUT WE CAN'T GET SLOPPY, OR THE HUGE POWER GAP WILL CRUSH US.
AND DON'T FORGET-- THEY'VE GOT *MISAKA MIKOTO* ON THEIR SIDE.
SHE'S A LEADER TYPE, SHE'S TOTALLY IMMUNE TO SURPRISE ATTACKS...
AND WE CAN'T TOUCH HER LEVEL 5 ELECTRICITY.
SHE'S BASICALLY A WALKING FORTRESS.
WE DON'T HAVE TO BEAT THEM *ALL*. LET'S JUST AVOID HER!
①
②
③
STICK TO OUR ORDER OF PRIORITY TARGETS: ① THE INFORMATION/ COMMUNICATION TYPES, ② THE OFFENSIVE TYPES, ③ THE DEFENSIVE TYPES.
AND FOR NOW, MISAKA MIKOTO'S MOVING DEFENSIVELY, RIGHT?

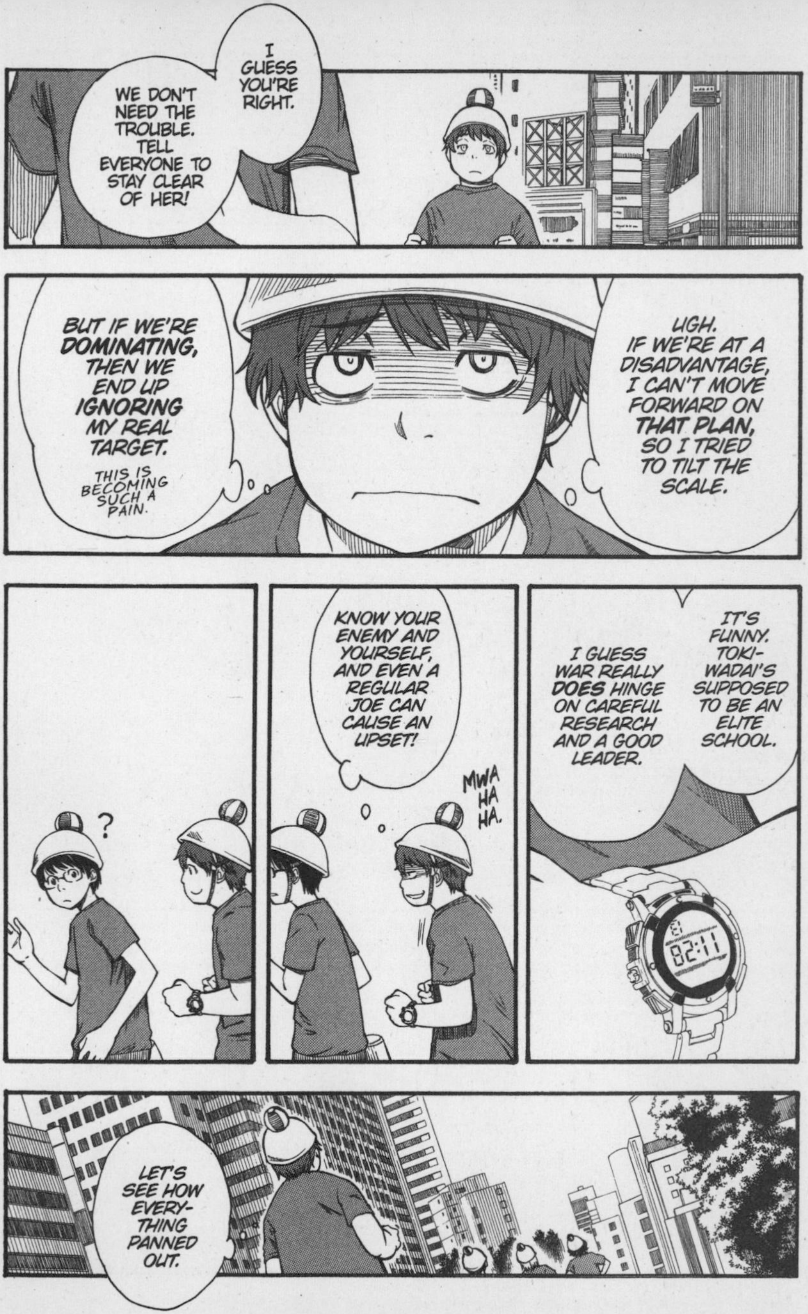
I GUESS YOU'RE RIGHT.
WE DON'T NEED THE TROUBLE. TELL EVERYONE TO STAY CLEAR OF HER!
UGH. IF WE'RE AT A DISADVANTAGE, I CAN'T MOVE FORWARD ON THAT PLAN, SO I TRIED TO TILT THE SCALE.
BUT IF WE'RE DOMINATING, THEN WE END UP IGNORING MY REAL TARGET.
THIS IS BECOMING SUCH A PAIN.
IT'S FUNNY. TOKI-WADAI'S SUPPOSED TO BE AN ELITE SCHOOL.
I GUESS WAR REALLY DOES HINGE ON CAREFUL RESEARCH AND A GOOD LEADER.
02:11
MWA HA HA.
KNOW YOUR ENEMY AND YOURSELF, AND EVEN A REGULAR JOE CAN CAUSE AN UPSET!
?
LET'S SEE HOW EVERY-THING PANNED OUT.

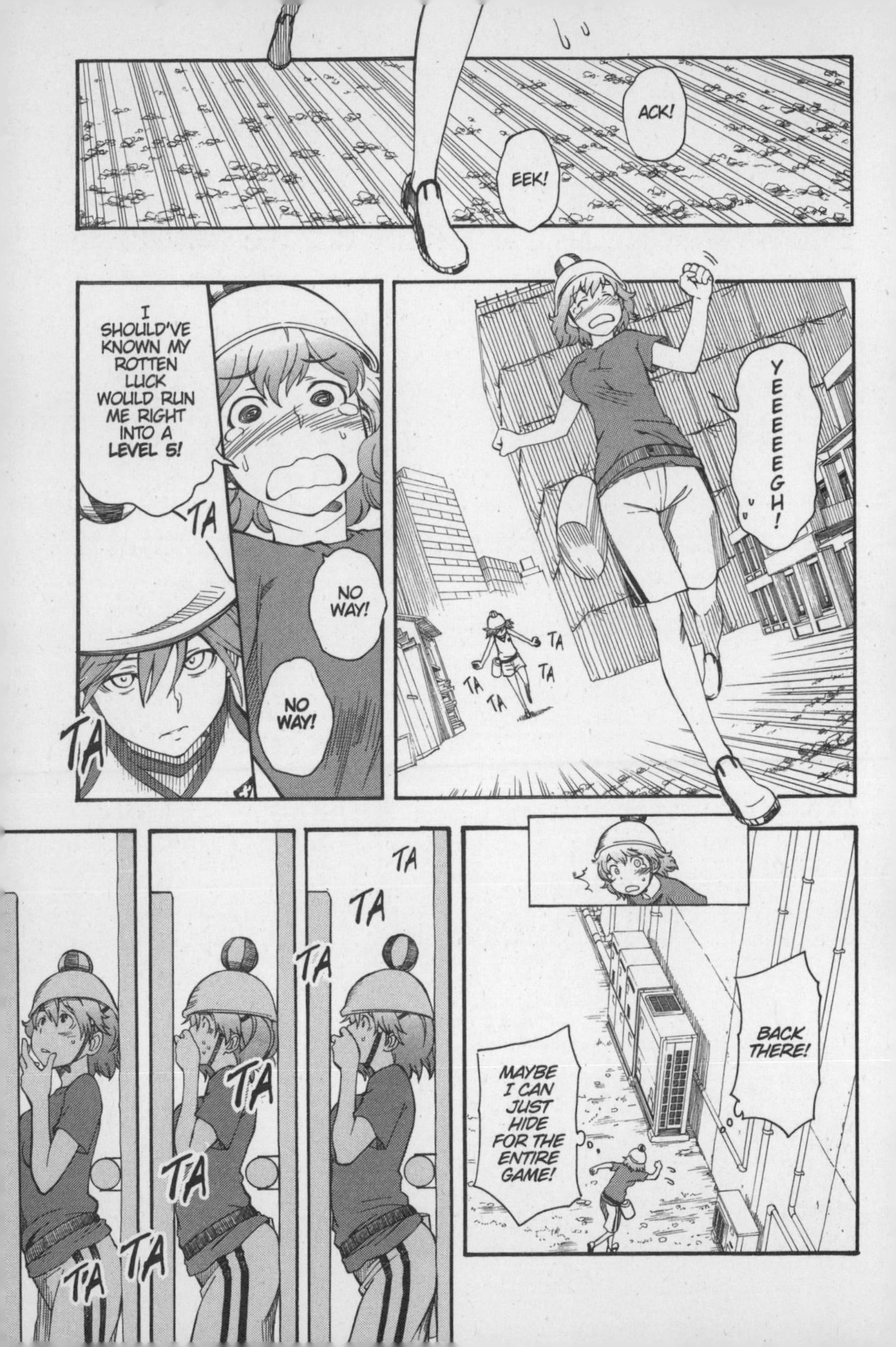
ACK!
EEK!
YEEEEEEGH!
TA
TA
TA
TA
I SHOULD'VE KNOWN MY ROTTEN LUCK WOULD RUN ME RIGHT INTO A LEVEL 5!
TA
NO WAY!
NO WAY!
TA
BACK THERE!
MAYBE I CAN JUST HIDE FOR THE ENTIRE GAME!
TA
TA
TA
TA
TA
TA
TA

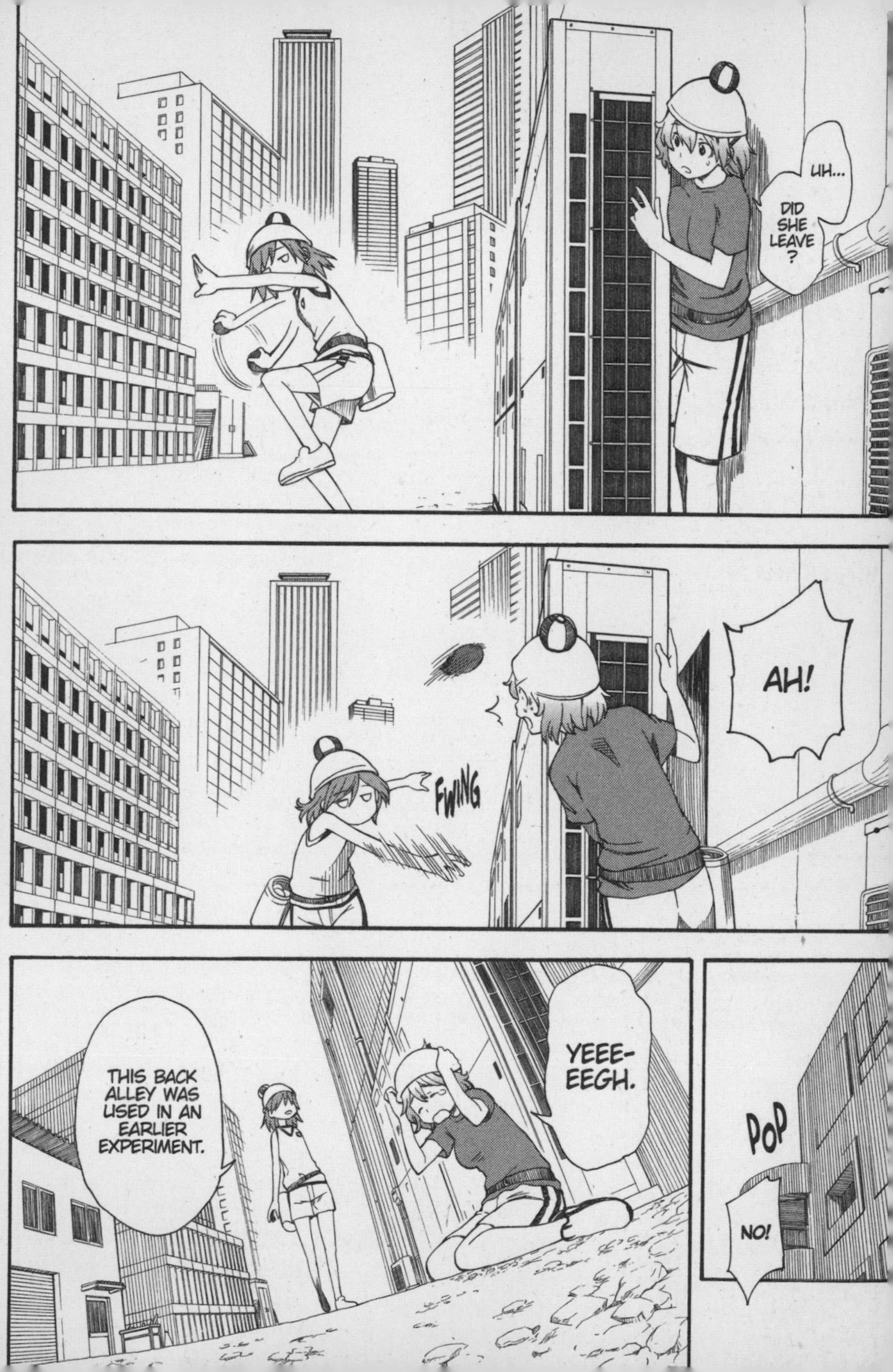
UH... DID SHE LEAVE?
AH!
FWING
NO!
POP
YEEE-EEGH.
THIS BACK ALLEY WAS USED IN AN EARLIER EXPERIMENT.

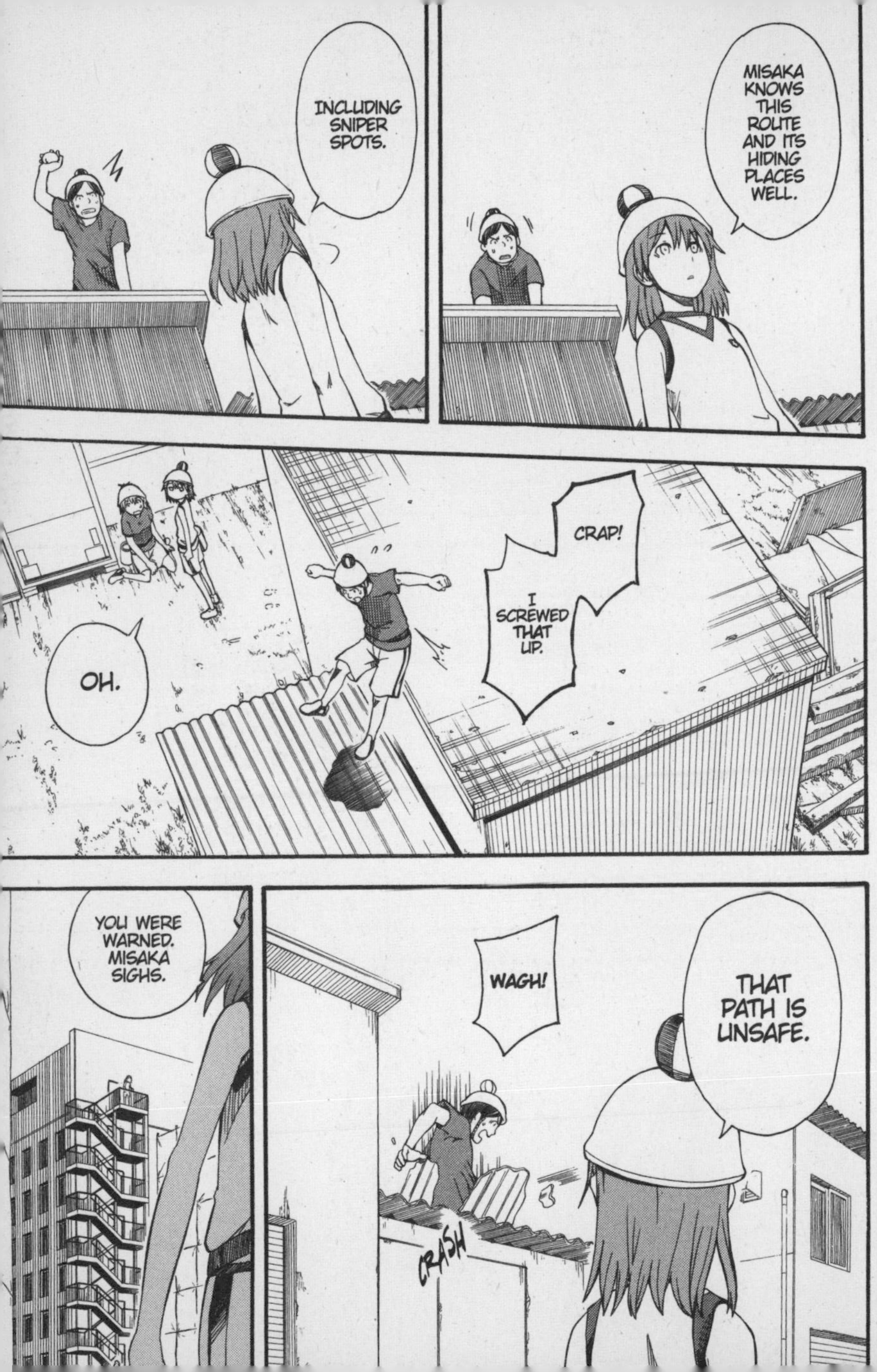
MISAKA KNOWS THIS ROUTE AND ITS HIDING PLACES WELL.
INCLUDING SNIPER SPOTS.
CRAP!
I SCREWED THAT UP.
OH.
THAT PATH IS UNSAFE.
WAGH!
CRASH
YOU WERE WARNED. MISAKA SIGHS.

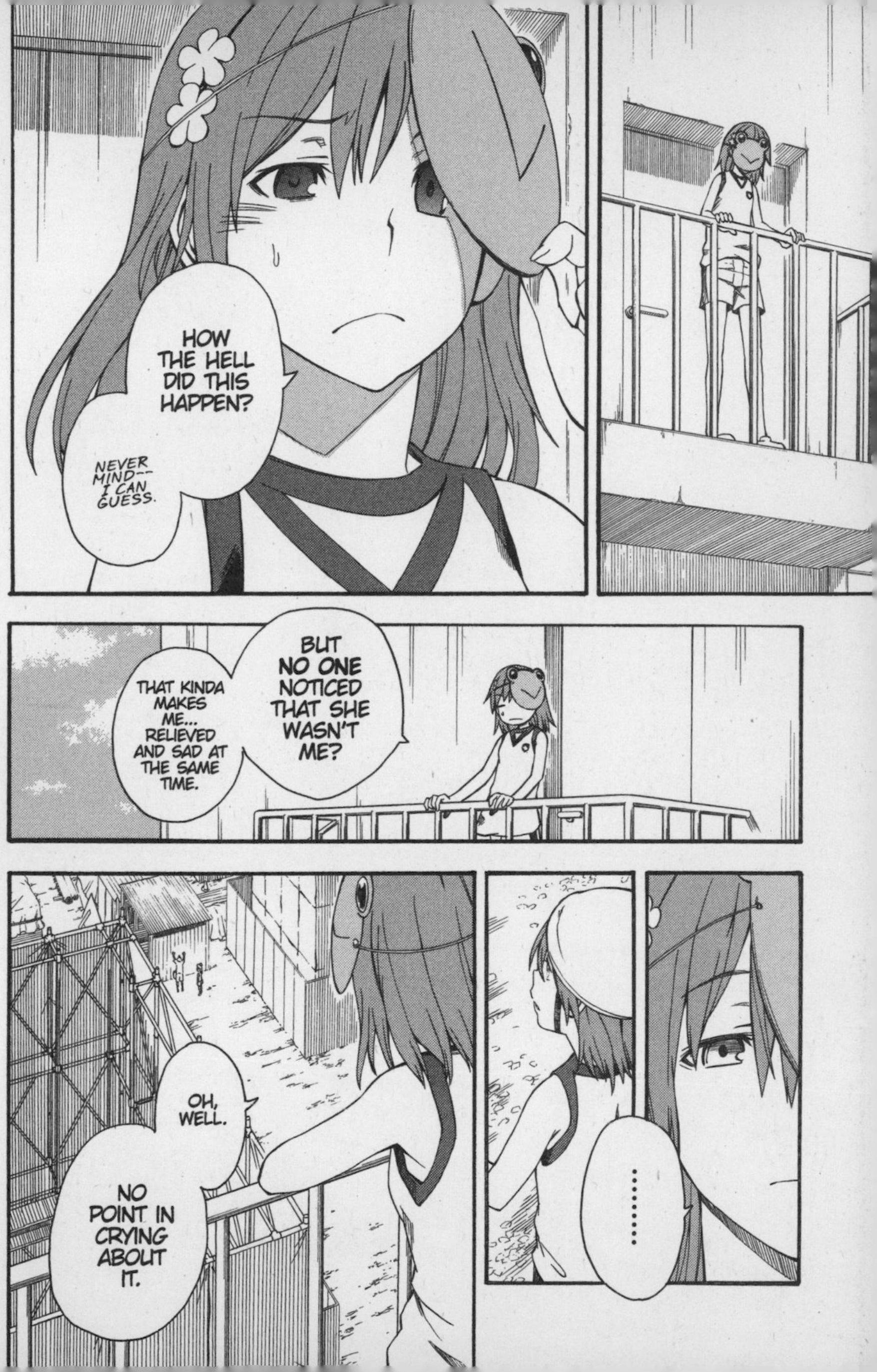
HOW THE HELL DID THIS HAPPEN?
NEVER MIND-- I CAN GUESS.
BUT NO ONE NOTICED THAT SHE WASN'T ME?
THAT KINDA MAKES ME... RELIEVED AND SAD AT THE SAME TIME.
....
OH, WELL.
NO POINT IN CRYING ABOUT IT.

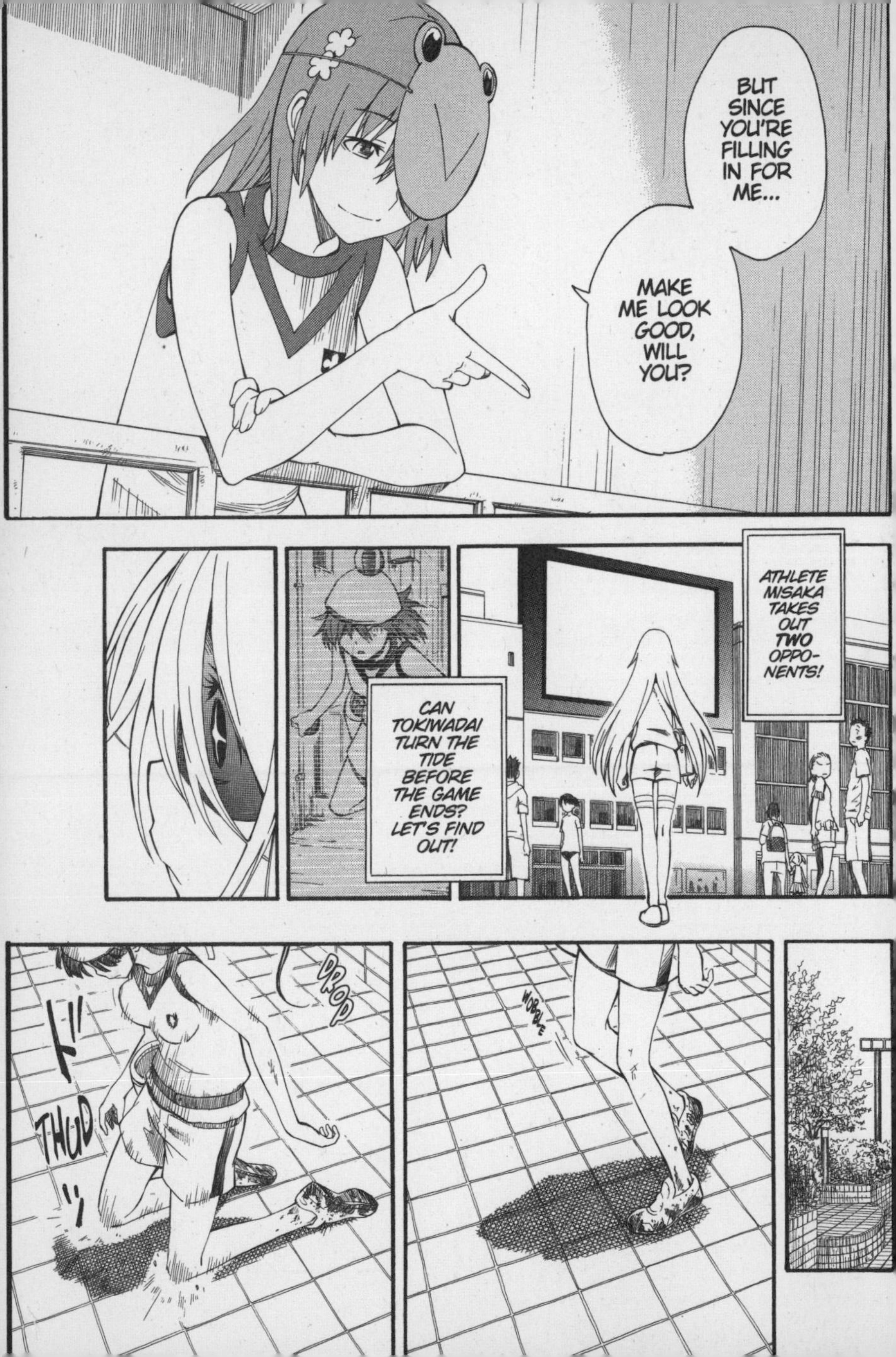
BUT SINCE YOU'RE FILLING IN FOR ME...
MAKE ME LOOK GOOD, WILL YOU?
ATHLETE MISAKA TAKES OUT TWO OPPO-NENTS!
CAN TOKIWADAI TURN THE TIDE BEFORE THE GAME ENDS? LET'S FIND OUT!
WOBBLE
DROP
ド
THUD
ッ

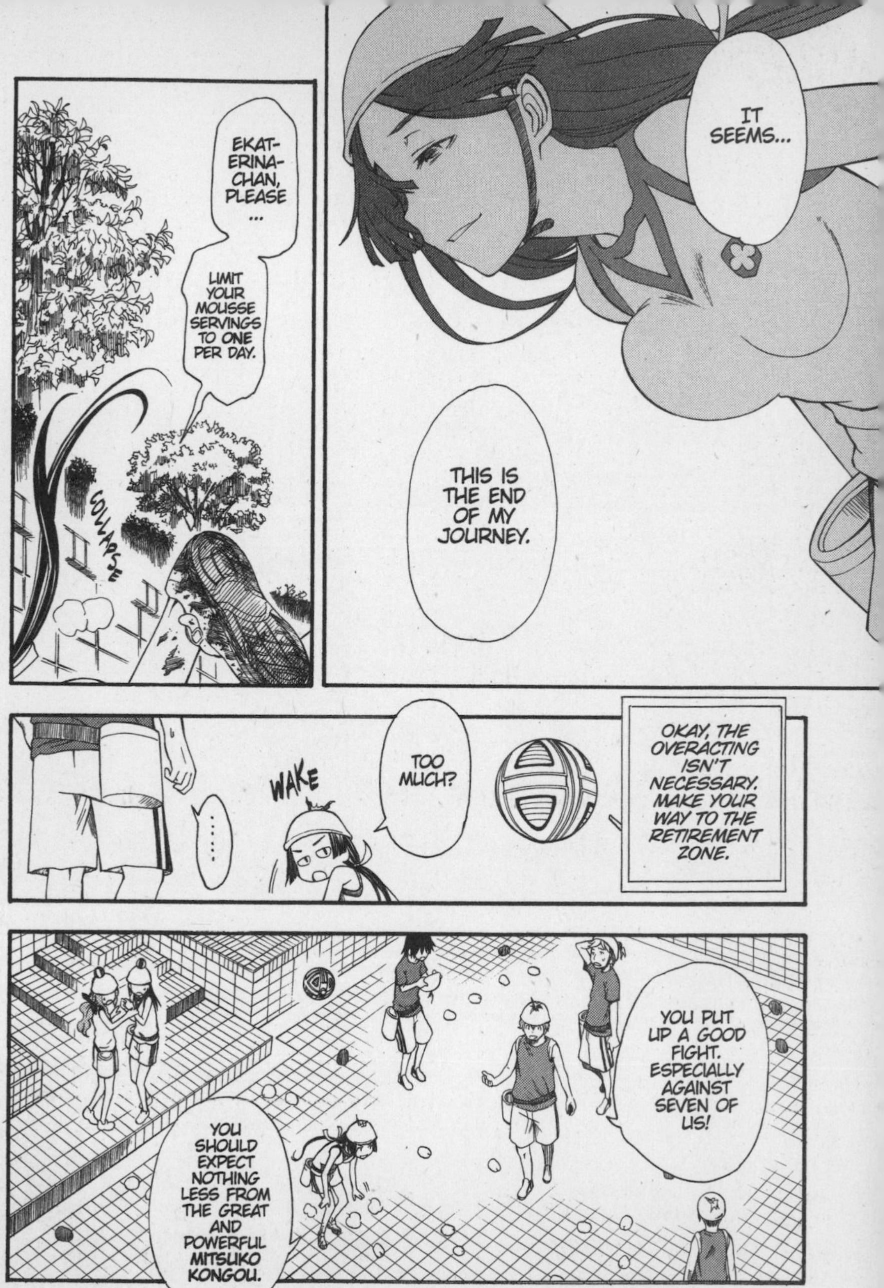
IT SEEMS...
THIS IS THE END OF MY JOURNEY.
EKAT-ERINA-CHAN, PLEASE ...
LIMIT YOUR MOUSSE SERVINGS TO ONE PER DAY.
COLLAPSE
OKAY, THE OVERACTING ISN'T NECESSARY. MAKE YOUR WAY TO THE RETIREMENT ZONE.
TOO MUCH?
WAKE
......
YOU PUT UP A GOOD FIGHT. ESPECIALLY AGAINST SEVEN OF US!
YOU SHOULD EXPECT NOTHING LESS FROM THE GREAT AND POWERFUL MITSUKO KONGOU.

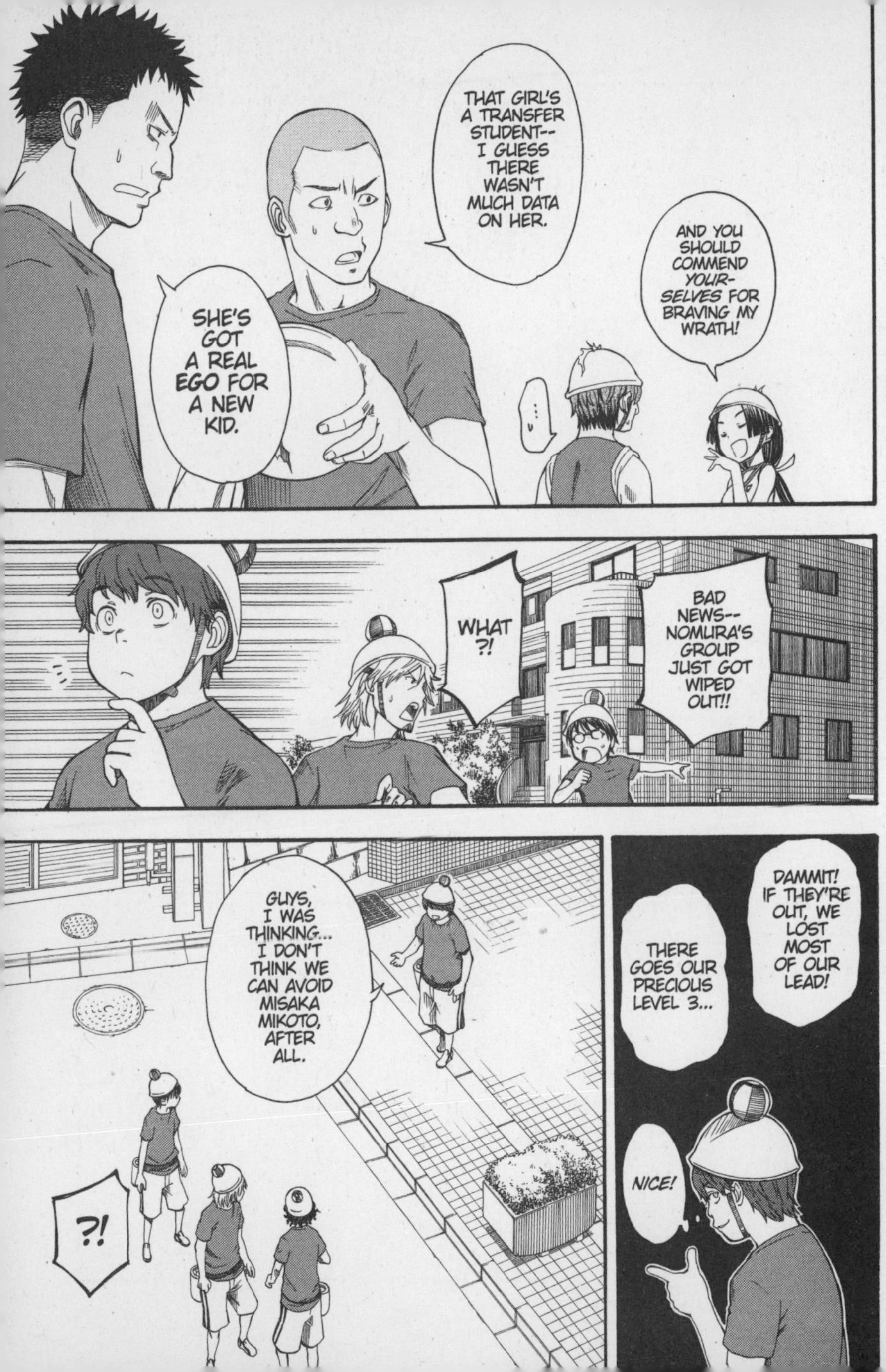
AND YOU SHOULD COMMEND *YOURSELVES* FOR BRAVING MY WRATH!
...!
THAT GIRL'S A TRANSFER STUDENT-- I GUESS THERE WASN'T MUCH DATA ON HER.
SHE'S GOT A REAL EGO FOR A NEW KID.
BAD NEWS-- NOMURA'S GROUP JUST GOT WIPED OUT!!
WHAT ?!
...!
DAMMIT! IF THEY'RE OUT, WE LOST MOST OF OUR LEAD!
THERE GOES OUR PRECIOUS LEVEL 3...
NICE!
GUYS, I WAS THINKING... I DON'T THINK WE CAN AVOID MISAKA MIKOTO, AFTER ALL.
?!

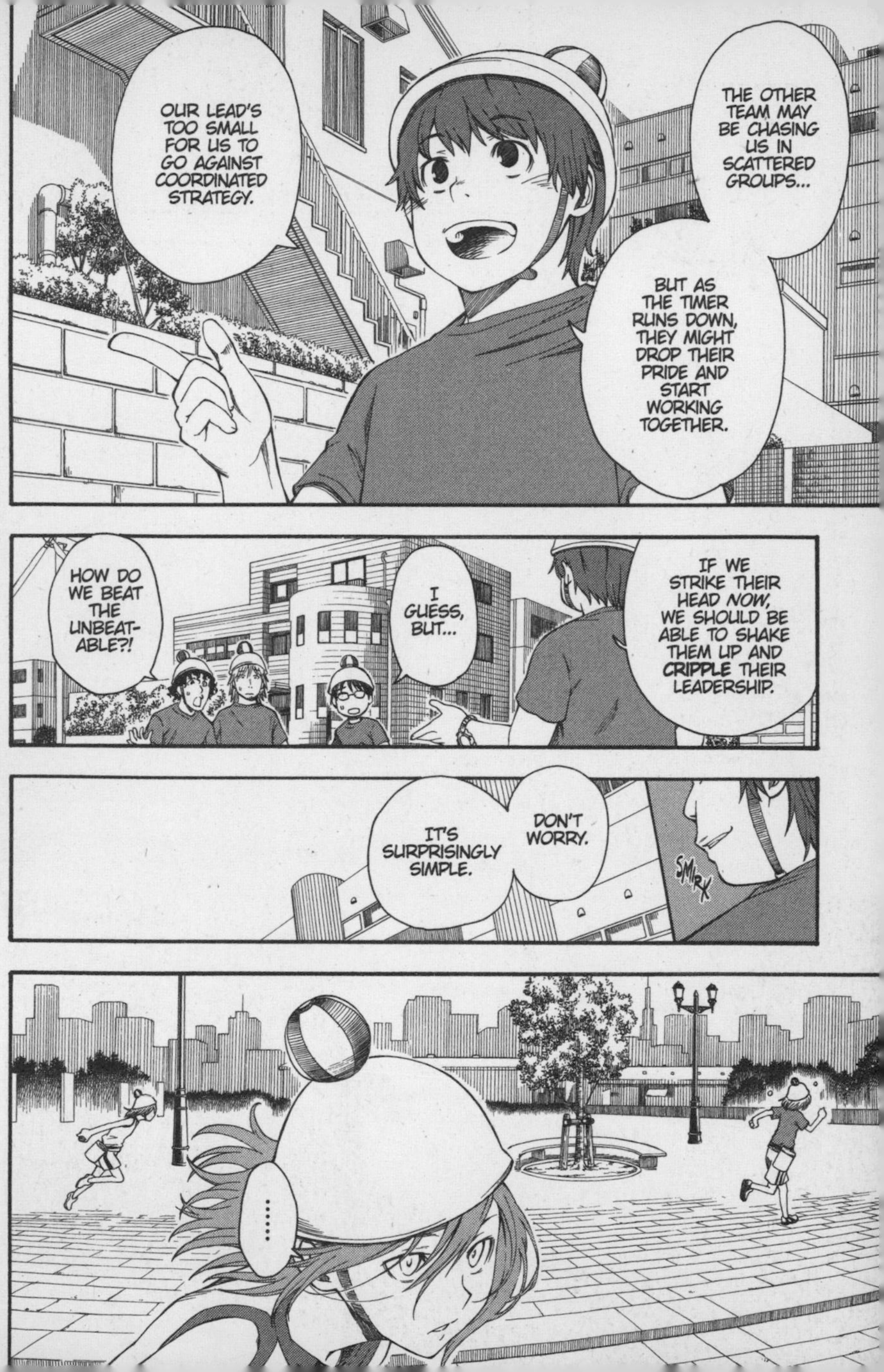
THE OTHER TEAM MAY BE CHASING US IN SCATTERED GROUPS...
BUT AS THE TIMER RUNS DOWN, THEY MIGHT DROP THEIR PRIDE AND START WORKING TOGETHER.
OUR LEAD'S TOO SMALL FOR US TO GO AGAINST COORDINATED STRATEGY.
IF WE STRIKE THEIR HEAD *NOW*, WE SHOULD BE ABLE TO SHAKE THEM UP AND **CRIPPLE** THEIR LEADERSHIP.
I GUESS, BUT...
HOW DO WE BEAT THE UNBEAT-ABLE?!
SMIRK
DON'T WORRY.
IT'S SURPRISINGLY SIMPLE.
......

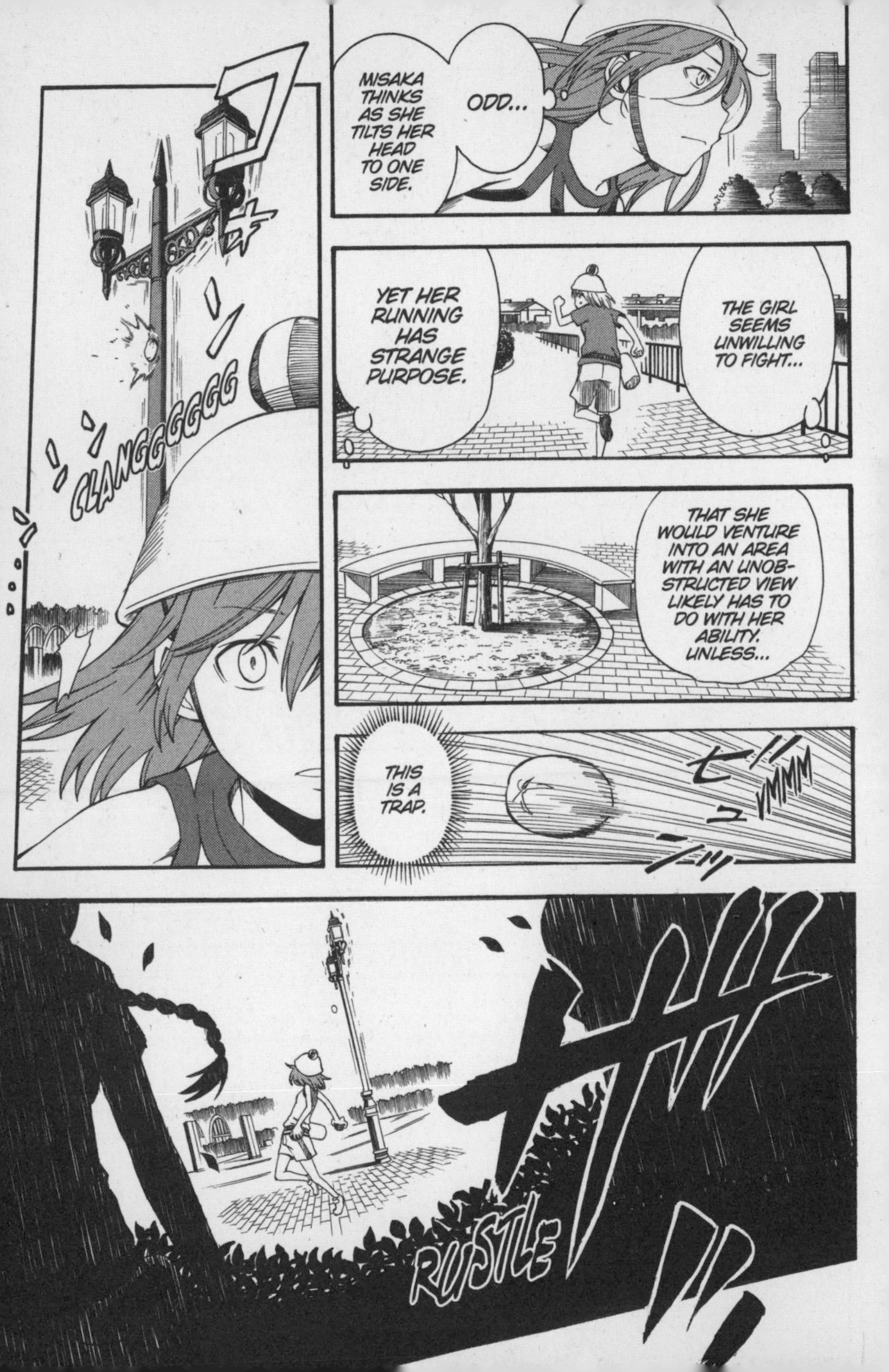
ODD...
MISAKA THINKS AS SHE TILTS HER HEAD TO ONE SIDE.
THE GIRL SEEMS UNWILLING TO FIGHT...
YET HER RUNNING HAS STRANGE PURPOSE.
THAT SHE WOULD VENTURE INTO AN AREA WITH AN UNOBSTRUCTED VIEW LIKELY HAS TO DO WITH HER ABILITY. UNLESS...
VMMM
THIS IS A TRAP.
CLANGGGGGG
RUSTLE

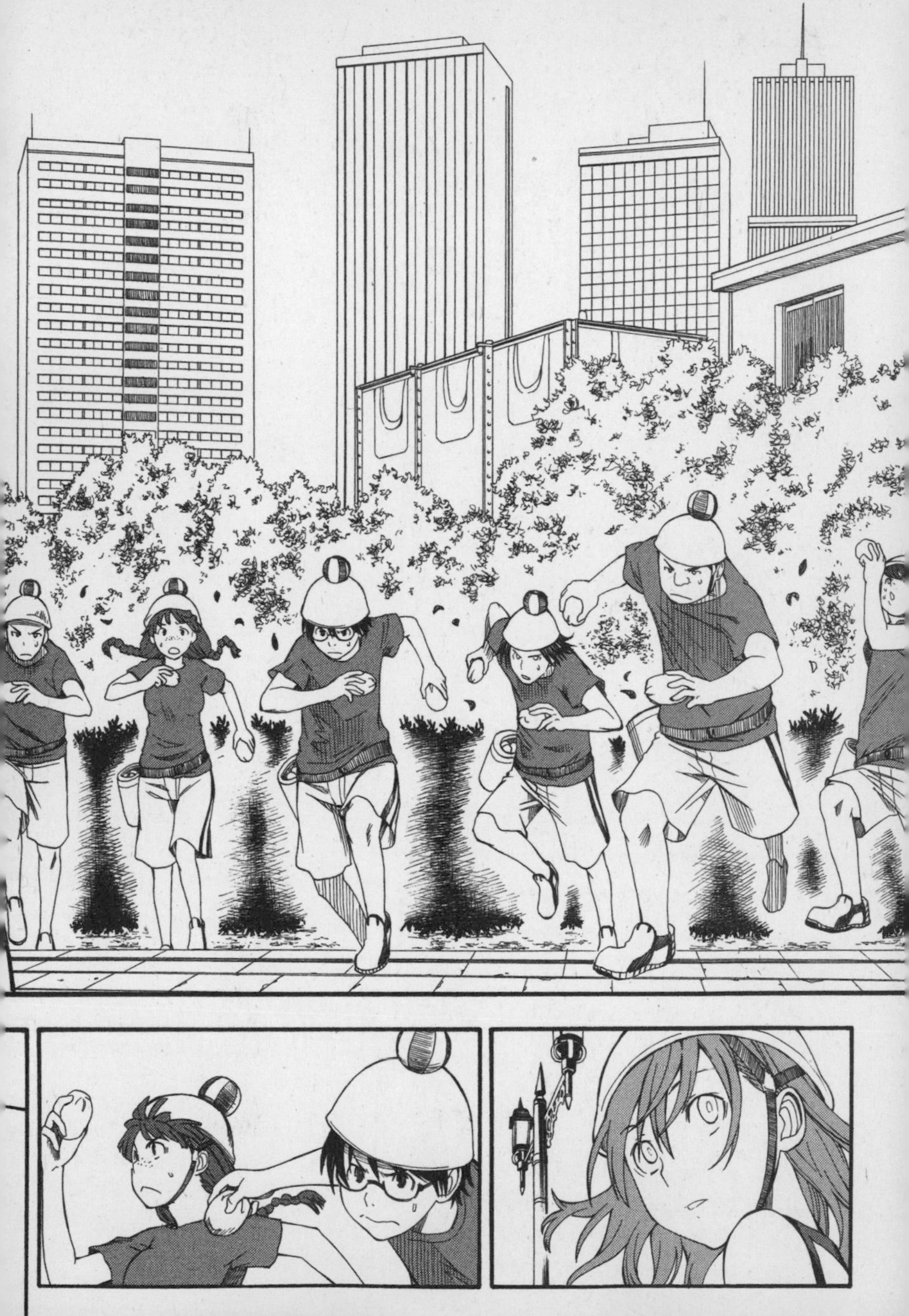

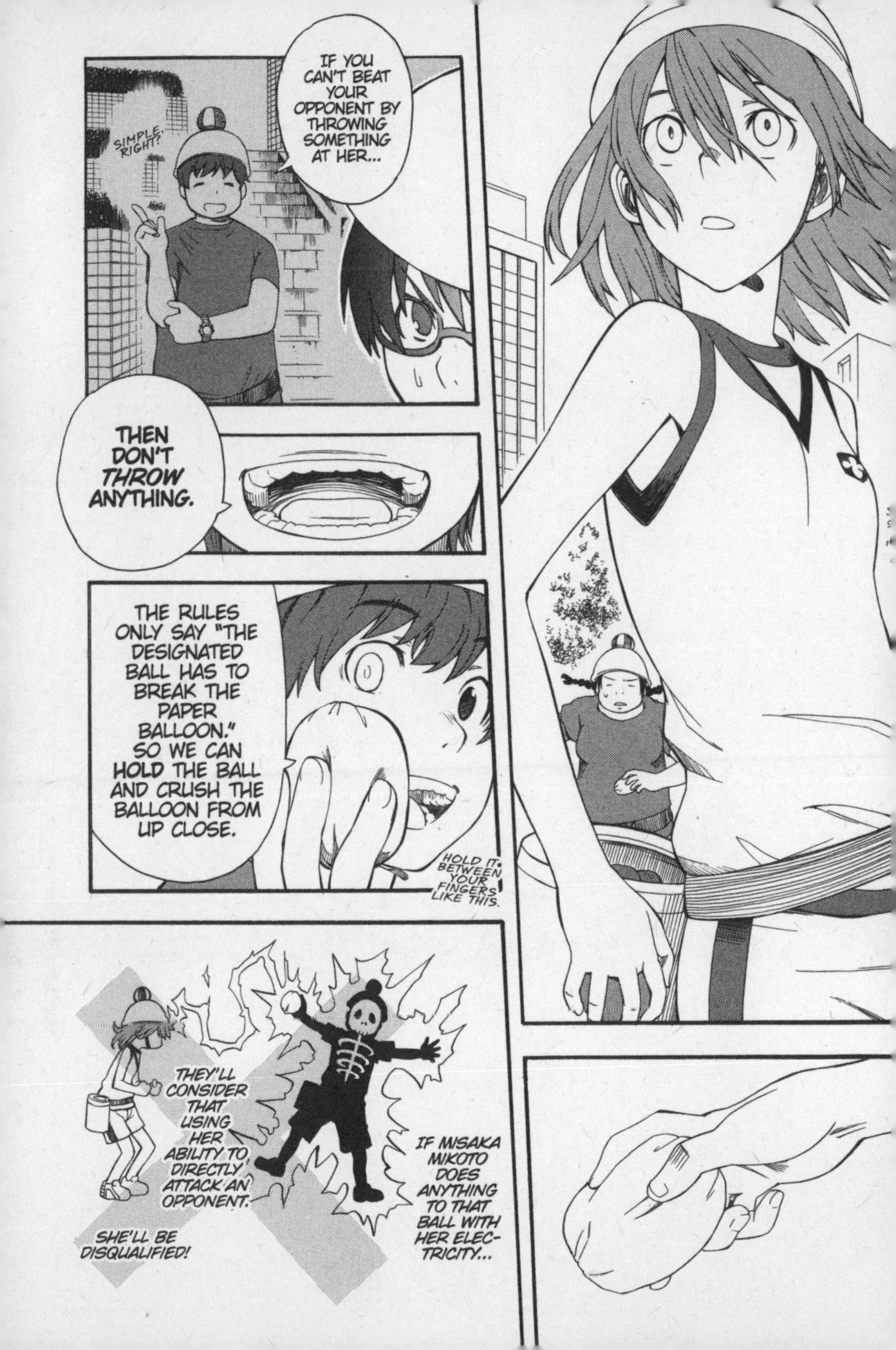
IF YOU CAN'T BEAT YOUR OPPONENT BY THROWING SOMETHING AT HER...
SIMPLE, RIGHT?
THEN DON'T *THROW* ANYTHING.
THE RULES ONLY SAY "THE DESIGNATED BALL HAS TO BREAK THE PAPER BALLOON." SO WE CAN HOLD THE BALL AND CRUSH THE BALLOON FROM UP CLOSE.
HOLD IT BETWEEN YOUR FINGERS LIKE THIS.
IF MISAKA MIKOTO DOES ANYTHING TO THAT BALL WITH HER ELEC-TRICITY...
THEY'LL CONSIDER THAT USING HER ABILITY TO DIRECTLY ATTACK AN OPPONENT.
SHE'LL BE DISQUALIFIED!

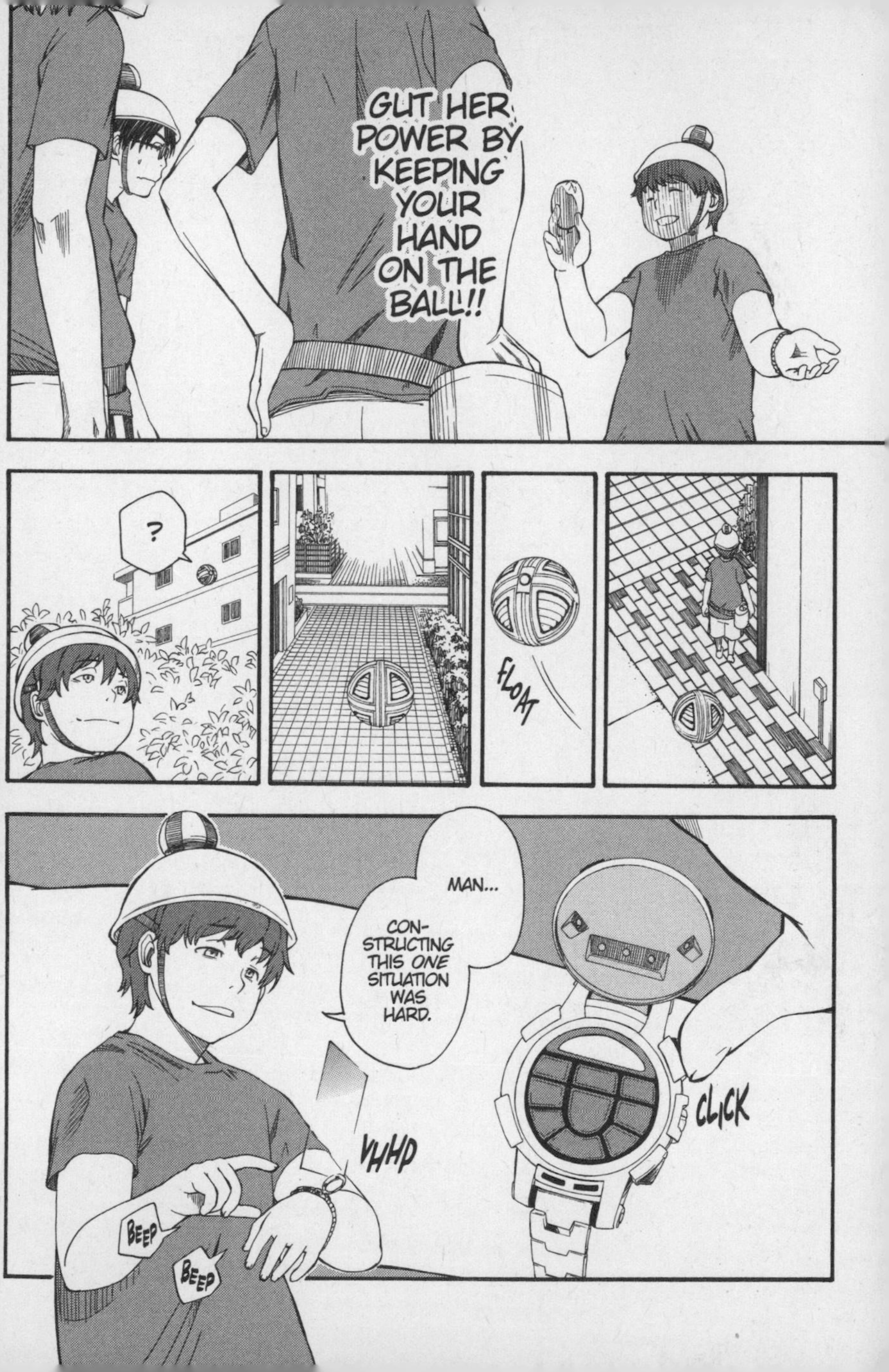
GUT HER POWER BY KEEPING YOUR HAND ON THE BALL!!
FLOAT
?
CLICK
MAN...
CON-STRUCTING THIS *ONE* SITUATION WAS HARD.
VHHP
BEEP
BEEP

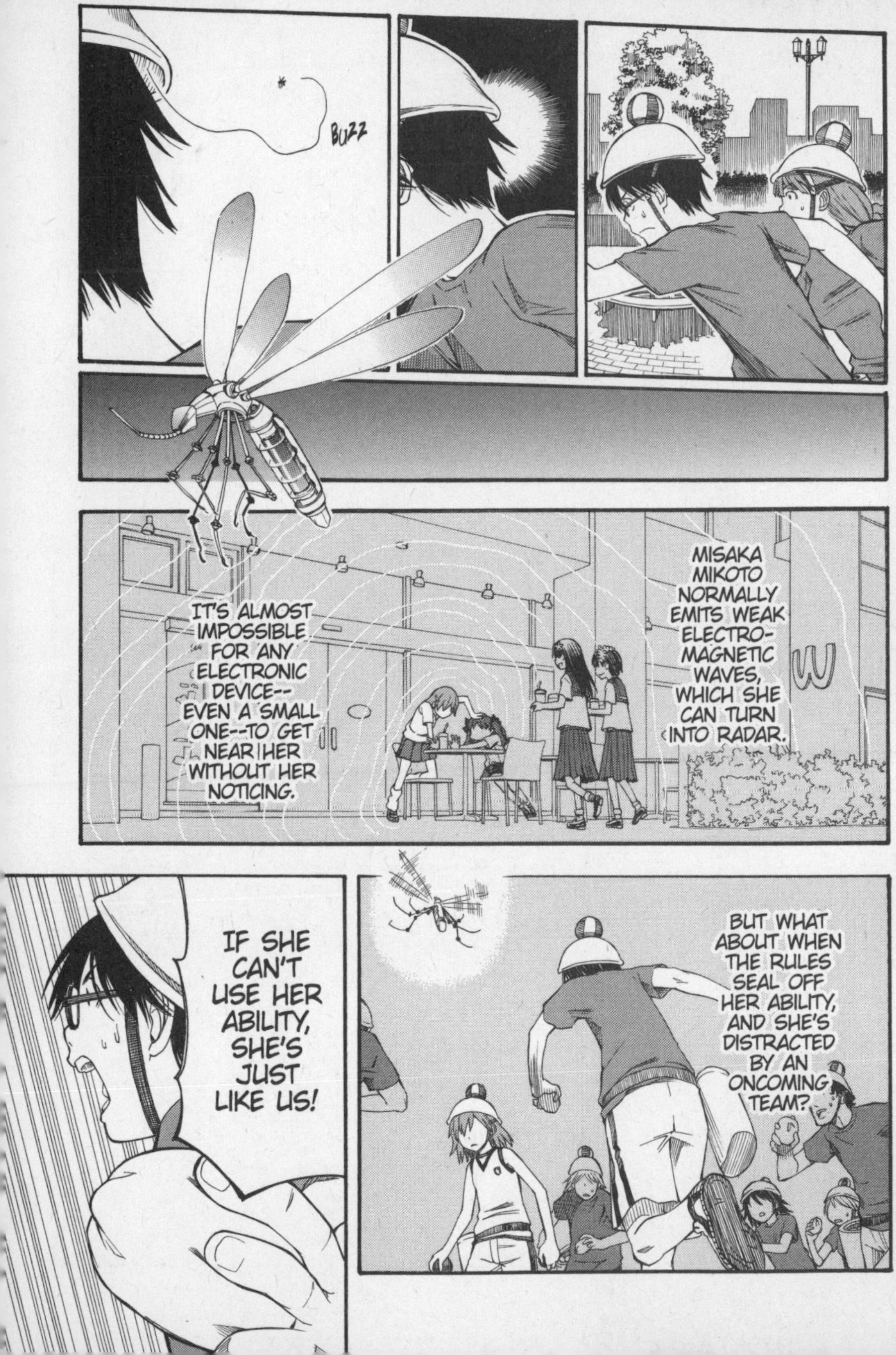
BUZZ
MISAKA MIKOTO NORMALLY EMITS WEAK ELECTRO-MAGNETIC WAVES, WHICH SHE CAN TURN INTO RADAR.
IT'S ALMOST IMPOSSIBLE FOR ANY ELECTRONIC DEVICE-- EVEN A SMALL ONE--TO GET NEAR HER WITHOUT HER NOTICING.
BUT WHAT ABOUT WHEN THE RULES SEAL OFF HER ABILITY, AND SHE'S DISTRACTED BY AN ONCOMING TEAM?
IF SHE CAN'T USE HER ABILITY, SHE'S JUST LIKE US!

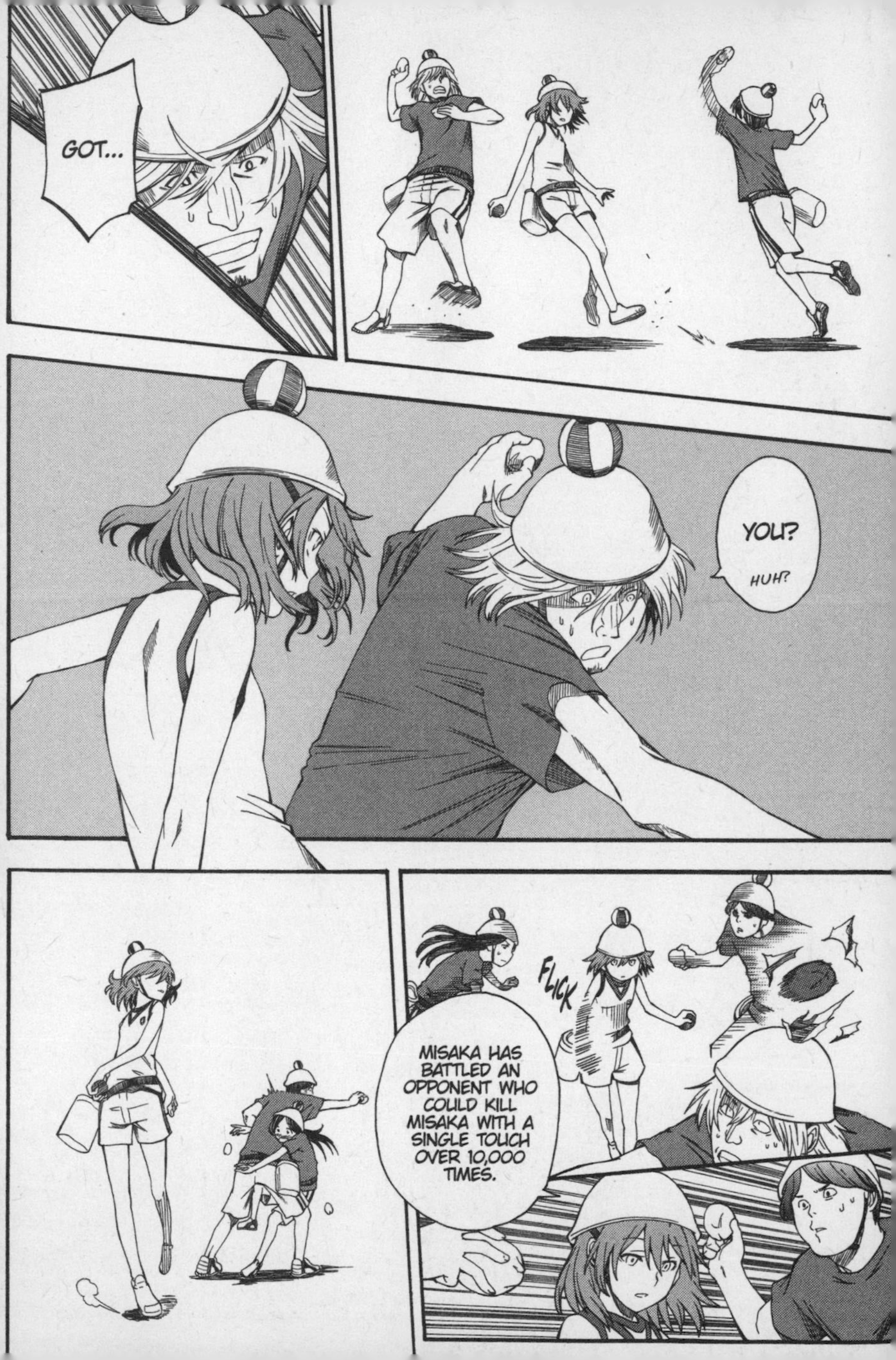
GOT...
YOU?
HUH?
FLICK
MISAKA HAS BATTLED AN OPPONENT WHO COULD KILL MISAKA WITH A SINGLE TOUCH OVER 10,000 TIMES.

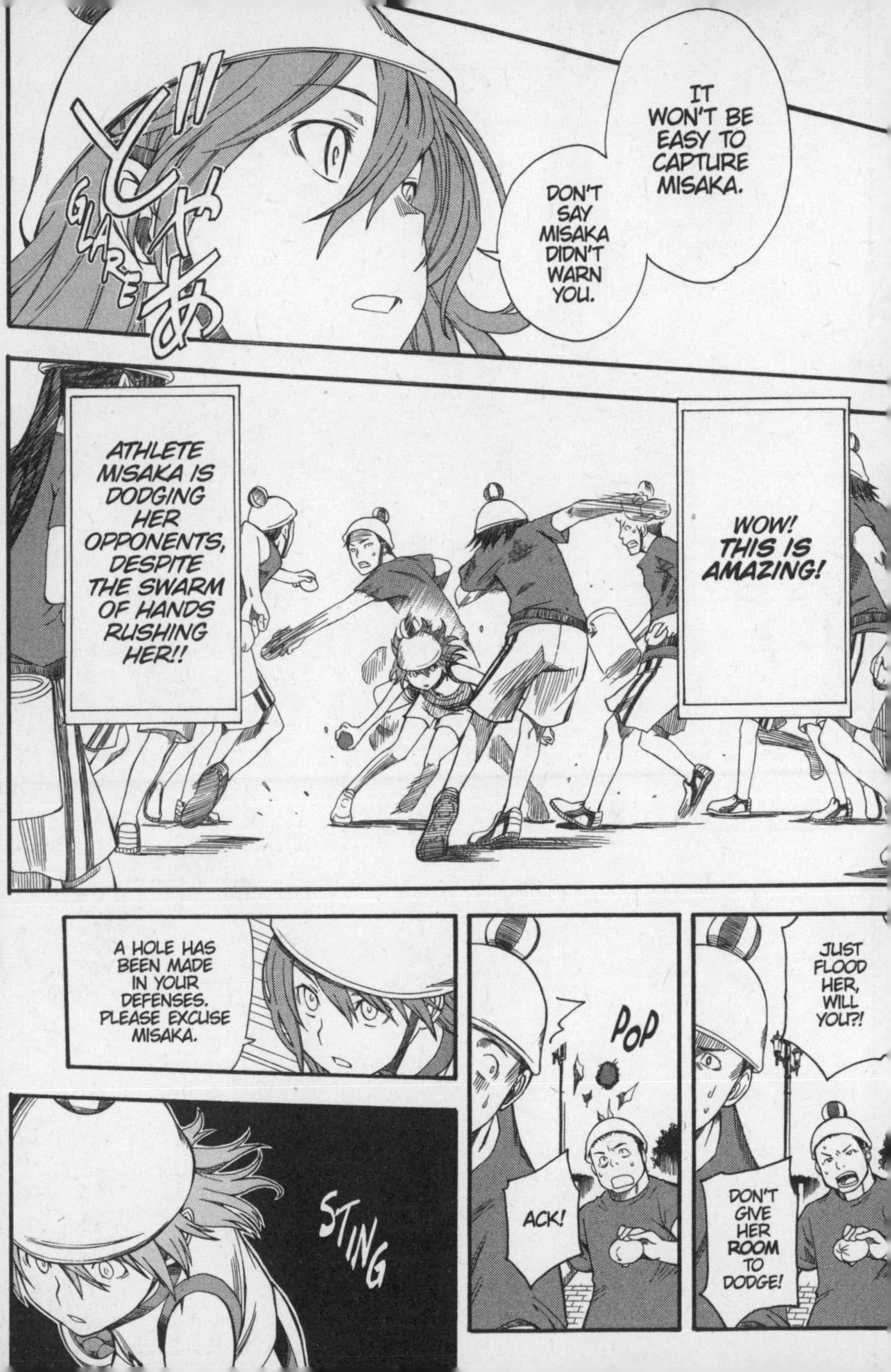
IT WON'T BE EASY TO CAPTURE MISAKA.
DON'T SAY MISAKA DIDN'T WARN YOU.
GLARE
WOW! THIS IS AMAZING!
ATHLETE MISAKA IS DODGING HER OPPONENTS, DESPITE THE SWARM OF HANDS RUSHING HER!!
JUST FLOOD HER, WILL YOU?!
DON'T GIVE HER ROOM TO DODGE!
POP
ACK!
A HOLE HAS BEEN MADE IN YOUR DEFENSES. PLEASE EXCUSE MISAKA.
STING

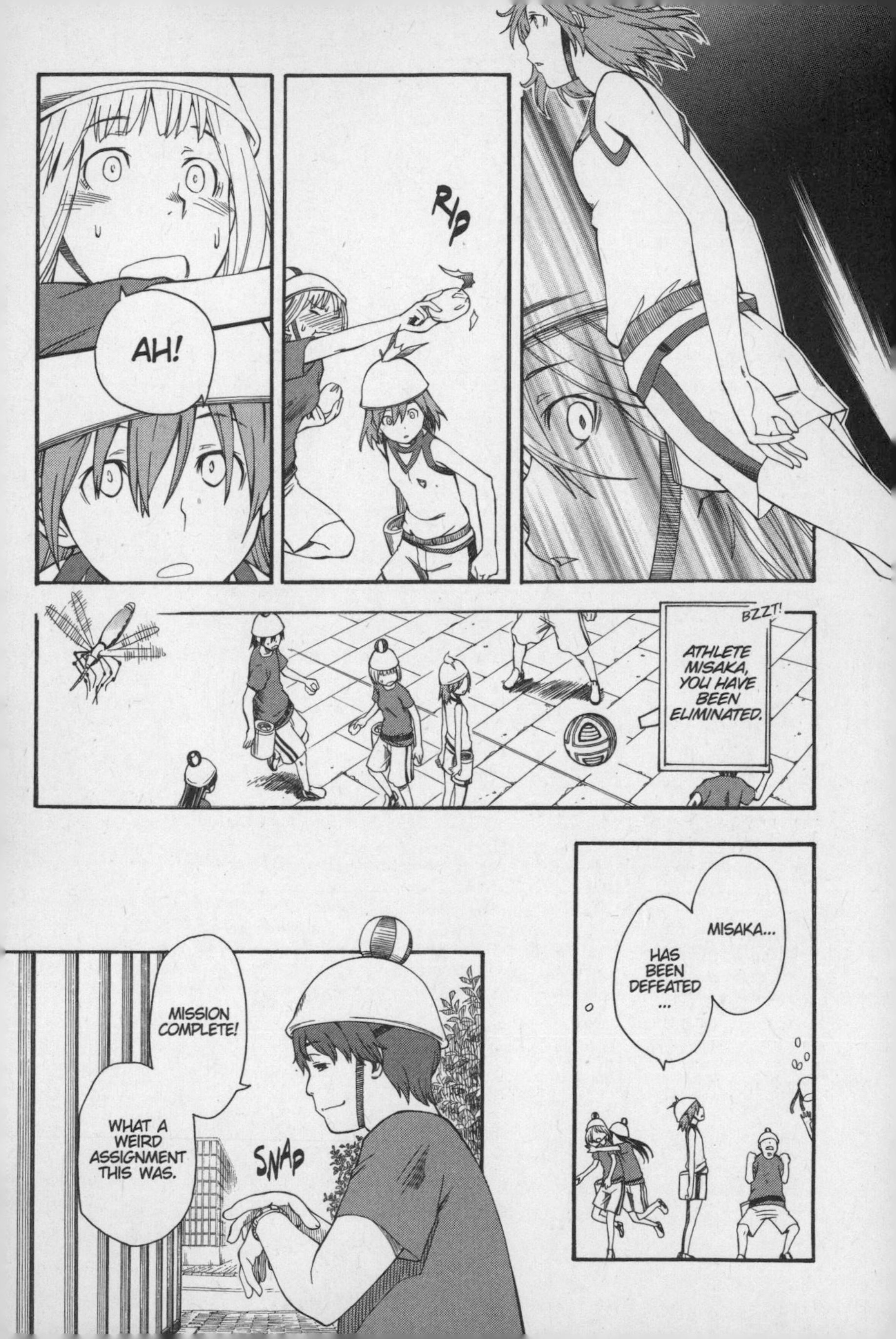
RIP
AH!
BZZT!
ATHLETE MISAKA, YOU HAVE BEEN ELIMINATED.
MISAKA...
HAS BEEN DEFEATED ...
MISSION COMPLETE!
WHAT A WEIRD ASSIGNMENT THIS WAS.
SNAP

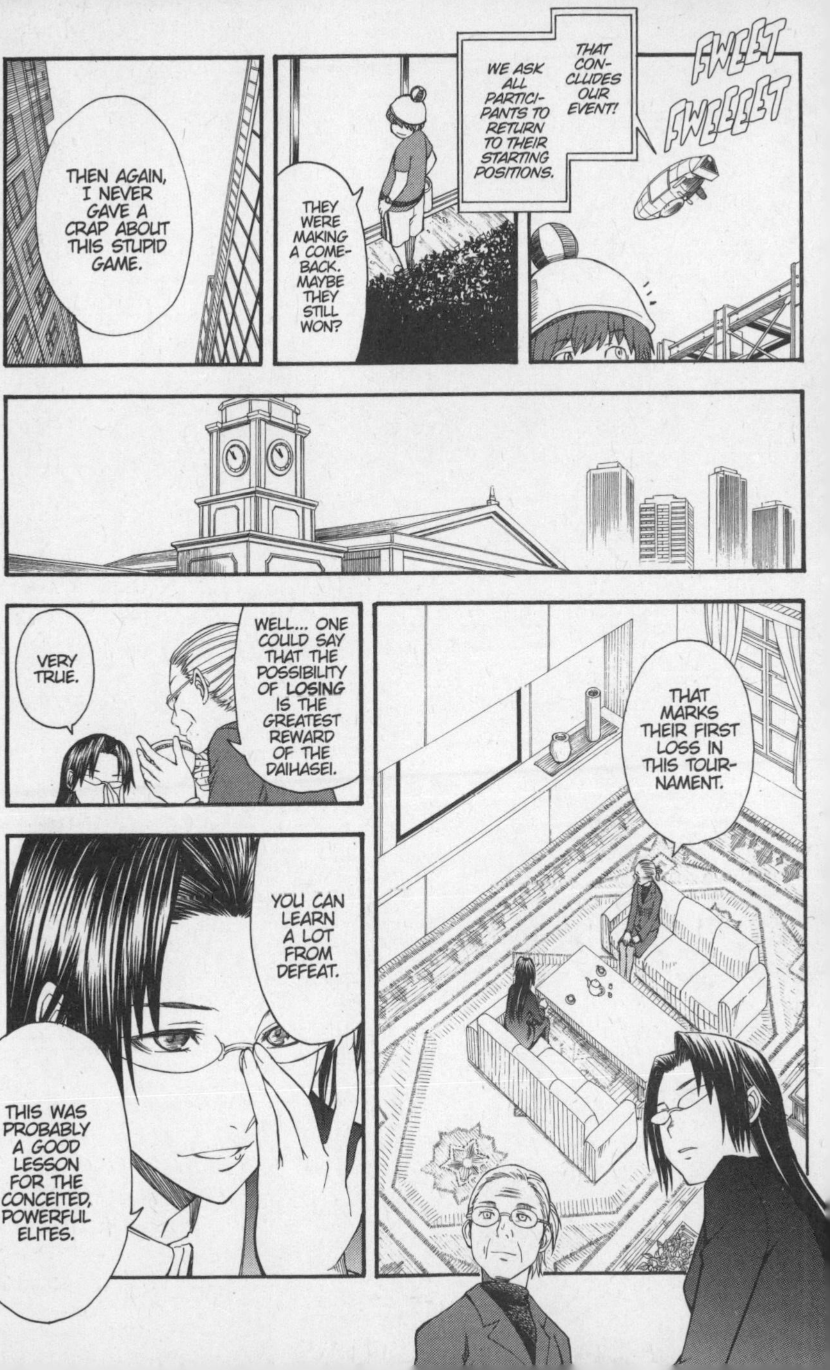
FWEET
FWEEEET
THAT CONCLUDES OUR EVENT!
WE ASK ALL PARTICIPANTS TO RETURN TO THEIR STARTING POSITIONS.
THEY WERE MAKING A COMEBACK. MAYBE THEY STILL WON?
THEN AGAIN, I NEVER GAVE A CRAP ABOUT THIS STUPID GAME.
THAT MARKS THEIR FIRST LOSS IN THIS TOURNAMENT.
WELL... ONE COULD SAY THAT THE POSSIBILITY OF LOSING IS THE GREATEST REWARD OF THE DAIHASEI.
VERY TRUE.
YOU CAN LEARN A LOT FROM DEFEAT.
THIS WAS PROBABLY A GOOD LESSON FOR THE CONCEITED, POWERFUL ELITES.

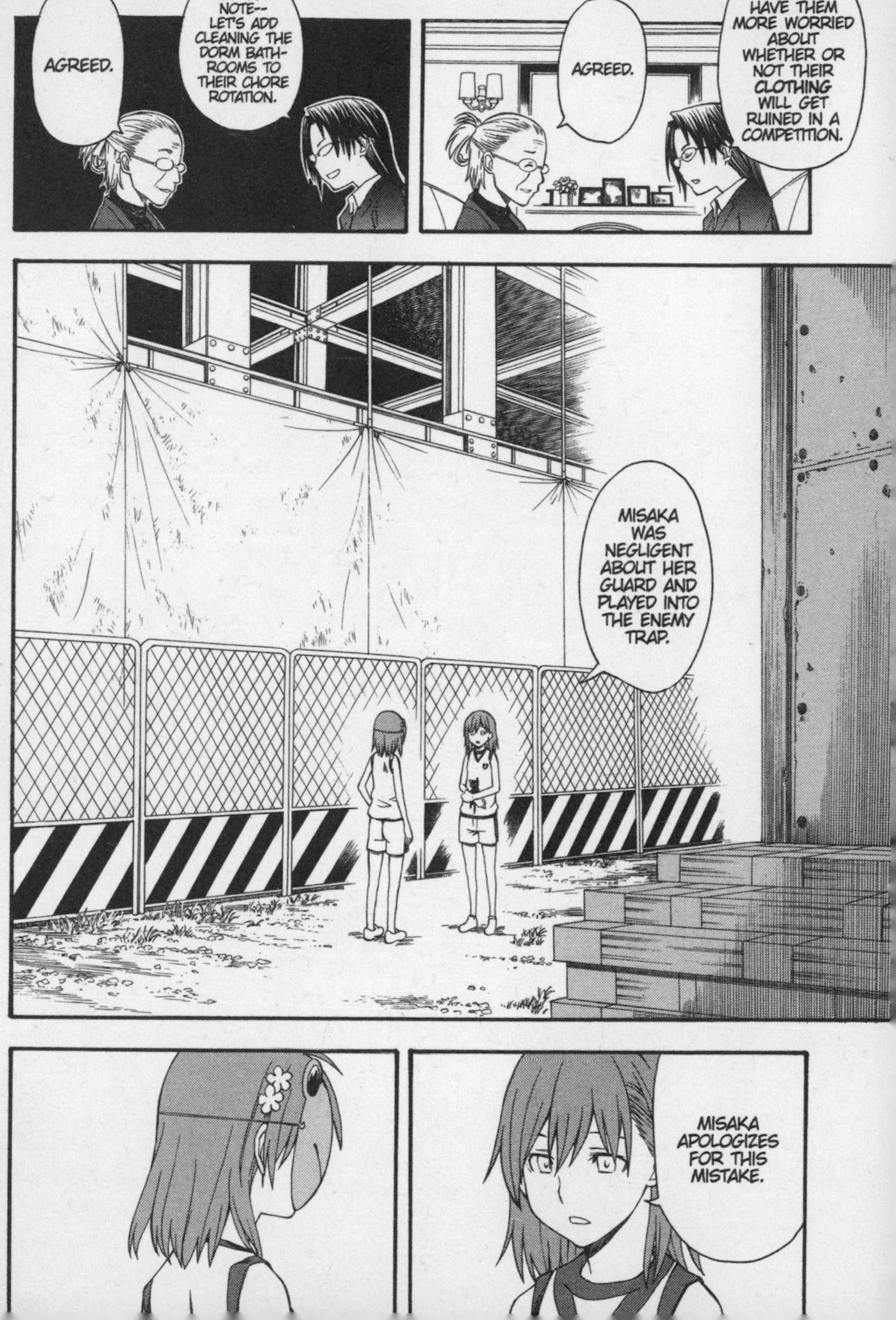
WE CAN'T HAVE THEM MORE WORRIED ABOUT WHETHER OR NOT THEIR CLOTHING WILL GET RUINED IN A COMPETITION.
AGREED.
ON THAT NOTE-- LET'S ADD CLEANING THE DORM BATH-ROOMS TO THEIR CHORE ROTATION.
AGREED.
MISAKA WAS NEGLIGENT ABOUT HER GUARD AND PLAYED INTO THE ENEMY TRAP.
MISAKA APOLOGIZES FOR THIS MISTAKE.

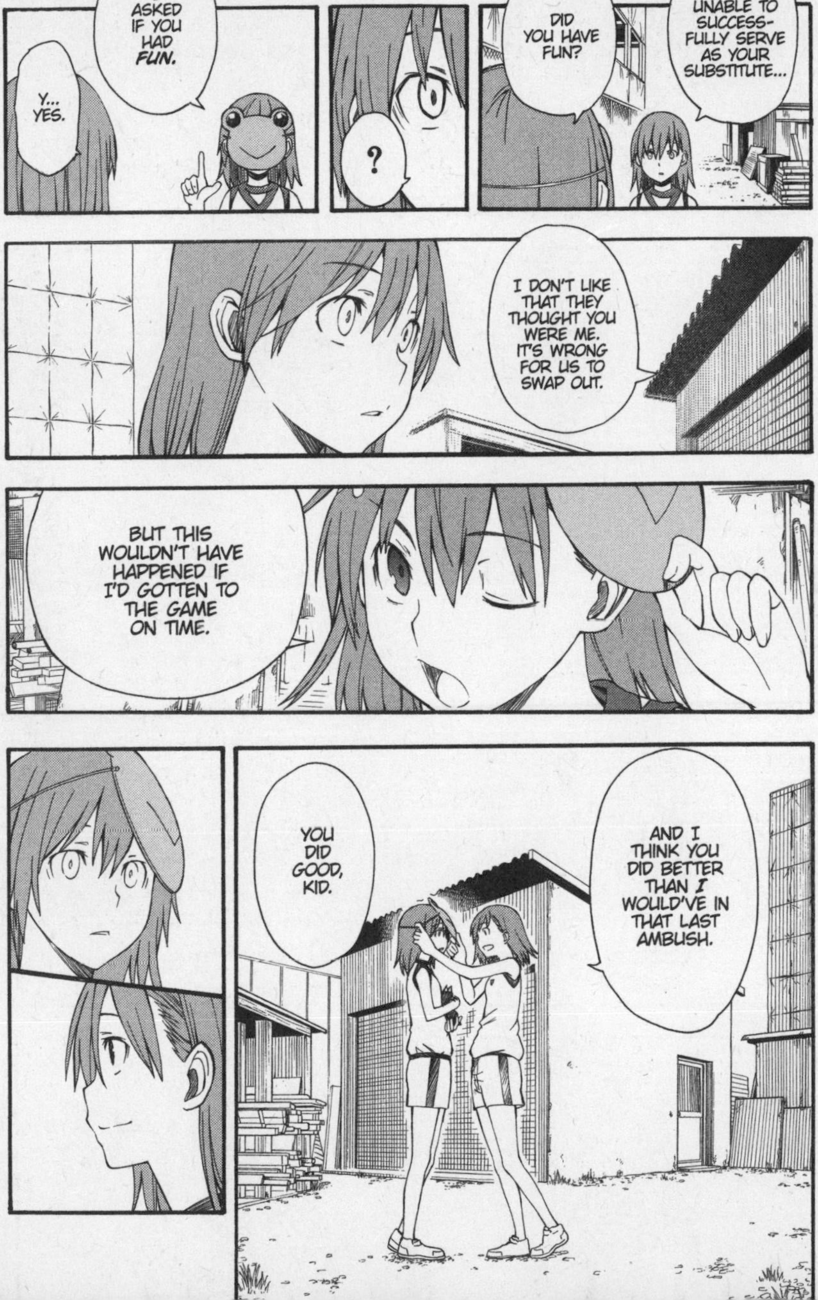
MISAKA WAS UNABLE TO SUCCESS-FULLY SERVE AS YOUR SUBSTITUTE...
DID YOU HAVE FUN?
?
I ASKED IF YOU HAD *FUN.*
Y... YES.
I DON'T LIKE THAT THEY THOUGHT YOU WERE ME. IT'S WRONG FOR US TO SWAP OUT.
BUT THIS WOULDN'T HAVE HAPPENED IF I'D GOTTEN TO THE GAME ON TIME.
AND I THINK YOU DID BETTER THAN *I* WOULD'VE IN THAT LAST AMBUSH.
YOU DID GOOD, KID.

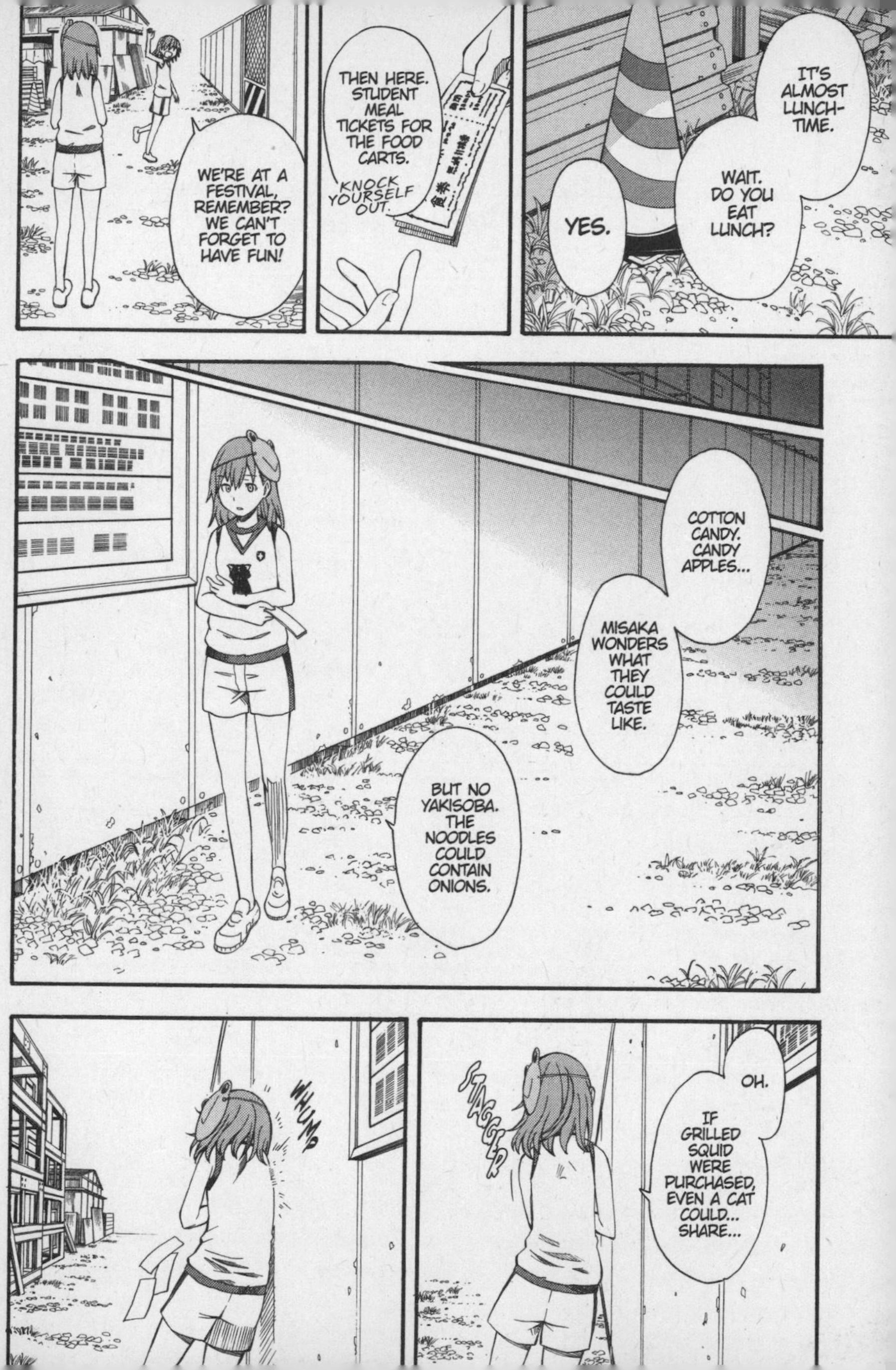
IT'S ALMOST LUNCH-TIME.
WAIT. DO YOU EAT LUNCH?
YES.
THEN HERE. STUDENT MEAL TICKETS FOR THE FOOD CARTS.
KNOCK YOURSELF OUT.
WE'RE AT A FESTIVAL, REMEMBER? WE CAN'T FORGET TO HAVE FUN!
COTTON CANDY. CANDY APPLES...
MISAKA WONDERS WHAT THEY COULD TASTE LIKE.
BUT NO YAKISOBA. THE NOODLES COULD CONTAIN ONIONS.
OH.
IF GRILLED SQUID WERE PURCHASED, EVEN A CAT COULD... SHARE...
STAGGER
WHUMP

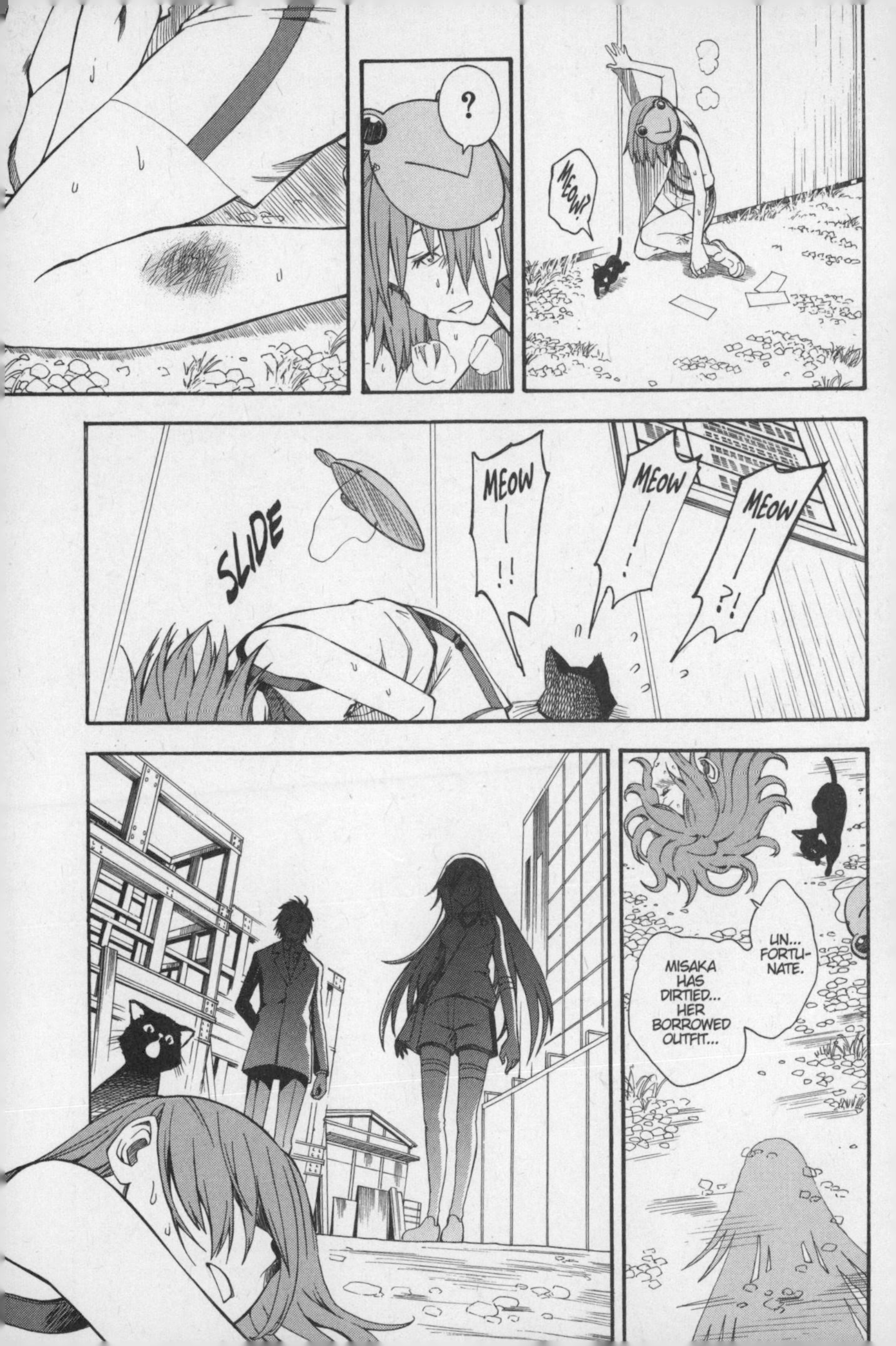
MEOW?
?
MEOW ——?!
MEOW ——!
MEOW ——!!
SLIDE
UN... FORTUNATE.
MISAKA HAS DIRTIED... HER BORROWED OUTFIT...

A Certain Skill Returns

ATHLETE MISAKA IS DODGING HER OPPONENTS...
DESPITE THE SWARM OF HANDS RUSHING HER!!
DODGE
DODGE
DODGE
DODGE
DODGE
DODGE
TH...
DODGE
DODGE
DODGE
TA-DAH!!
THAT SPECIAL SKILL!!

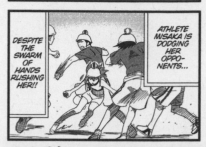

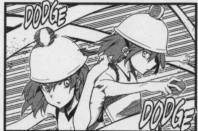

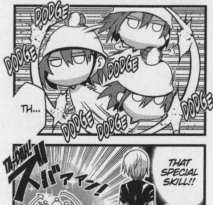

※*Please see the bonus comics in Volume 5!*

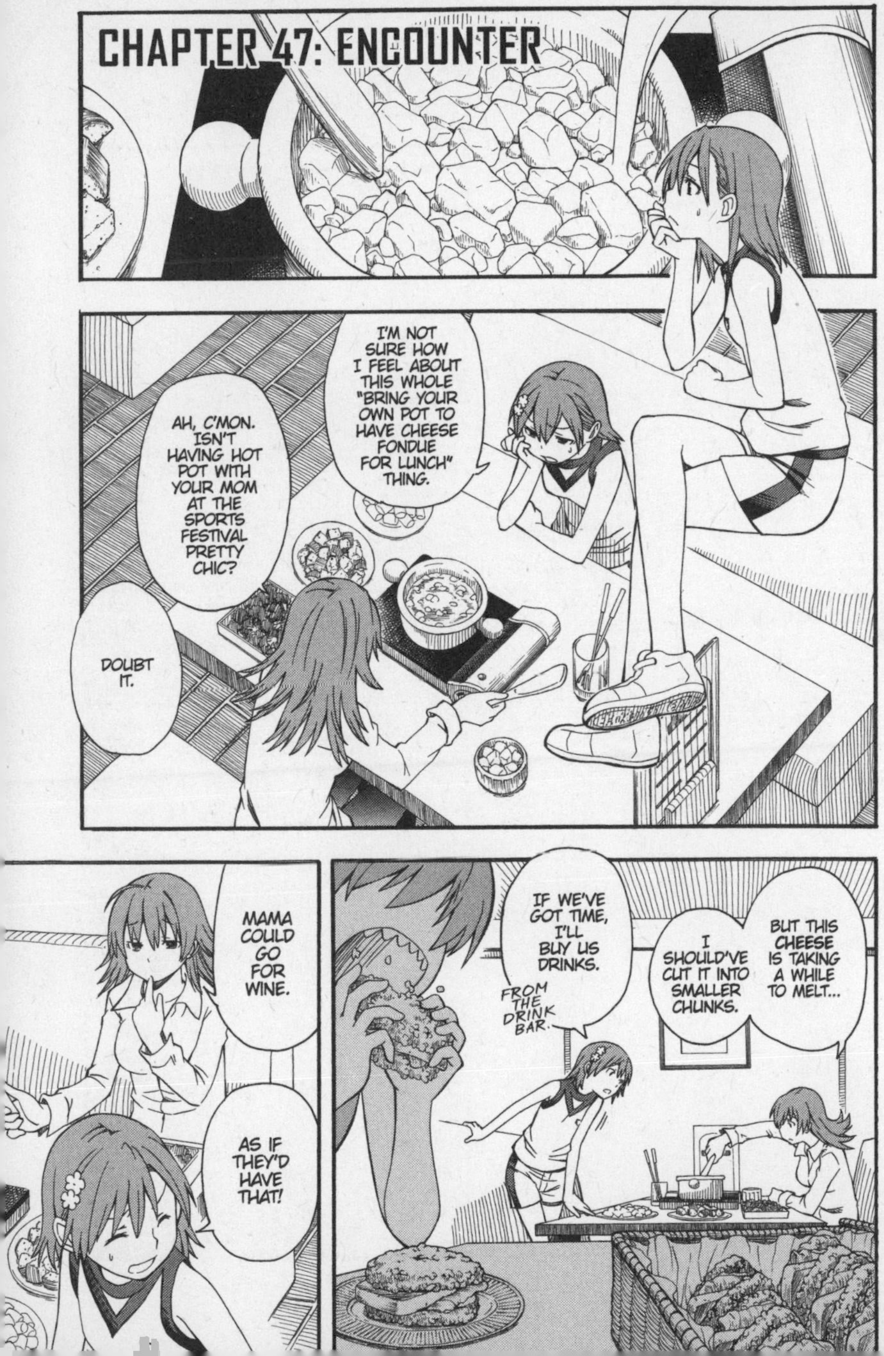
CHAPTER 47: ENCOUNTER
I'M NOT SURE HOW I FEEL ABOUT THIS WHOLE "BRING YOUR OWN POT TO HAVE CHEESE FONDUE FOR LUNCH" THING.
AH, C'MON. ISN'T HAVING HOT POT WITH YOUR MOM AT THE SPORTS FESTIVAL PRETTY CHIC?
DOUBT IT.
BUT THIS CHEESE IS TAKING A WHILE TO MELT...
I SHOULD'VE CUT IT INTO SMALLER CHUNKS.
IF WE'VE GOT TIME, I'LL BUY US DRINKS.
FROM THE DRINK BAR.
MAMA COULD GO FOR WINE.
AS IF THEY'D HAVE THAT!

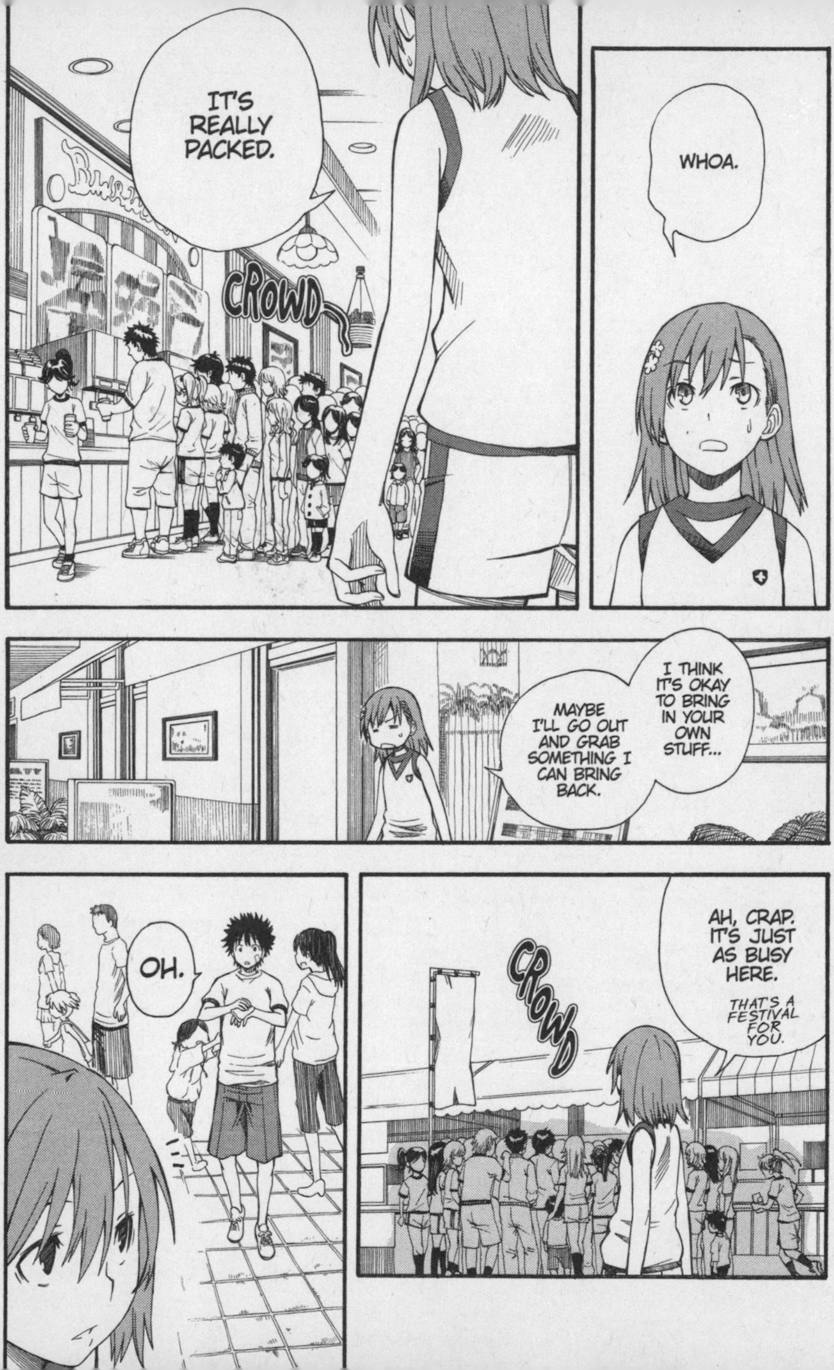
WHOA.
IT'S REALLY PACKED.
CROWD
I THINK IT'S OKAY TO BRING IN YOUR OWN STUFF...
MAYBE I'LL GO OUT AND GRAB SOMETHING I CAN BRING BACK.
AH, CRAP. IT'S JUST AS BUSY HERE.
THAT'S A FESTIVAL FOR YOU.
CROWD
OH.

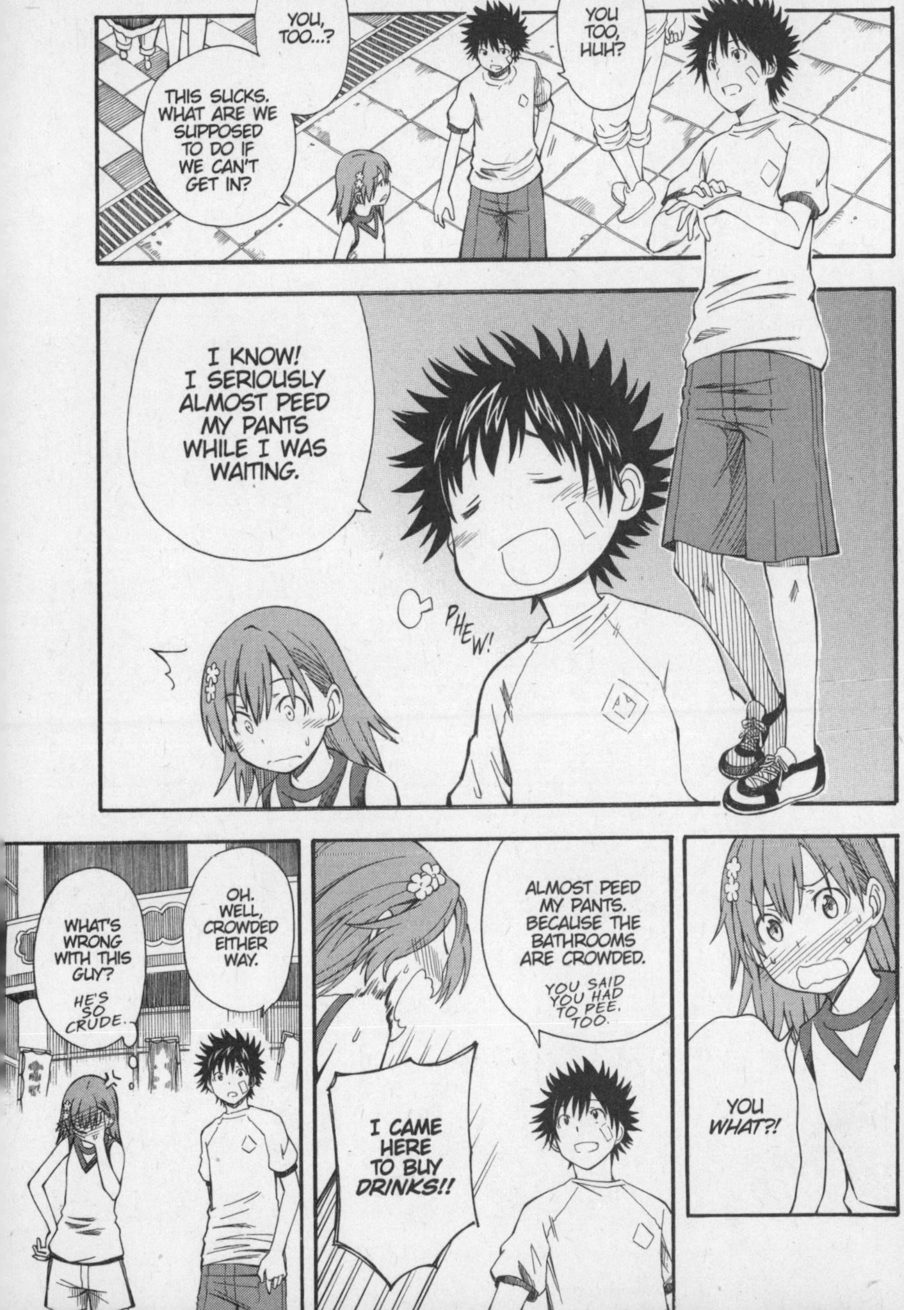
YOU TOO, HUH?
YOU, TOO...?
THIS SUCKS. WHAT ARE WE SUPPOSED TO DO IF WE CAN'T GET IN?
I KNOW! I SERIOUSLY ALMOST PEED MY PANTS WHILE I WAS WAITING.
PHEW!
YOU WHAT?!
ALMOST PEED MY PANTS. BECAUSE THE BATHROOMS ARE CROWDED.
YOU SAID YOU HAD TO PEE, TOO.
I CAME HERE TO BUY DRINKS!!
OH. WELL, CROWDED EITHER WAY.
WHAT'S WRONG WITH THIS GUY?
HE'S SO CRUDE.

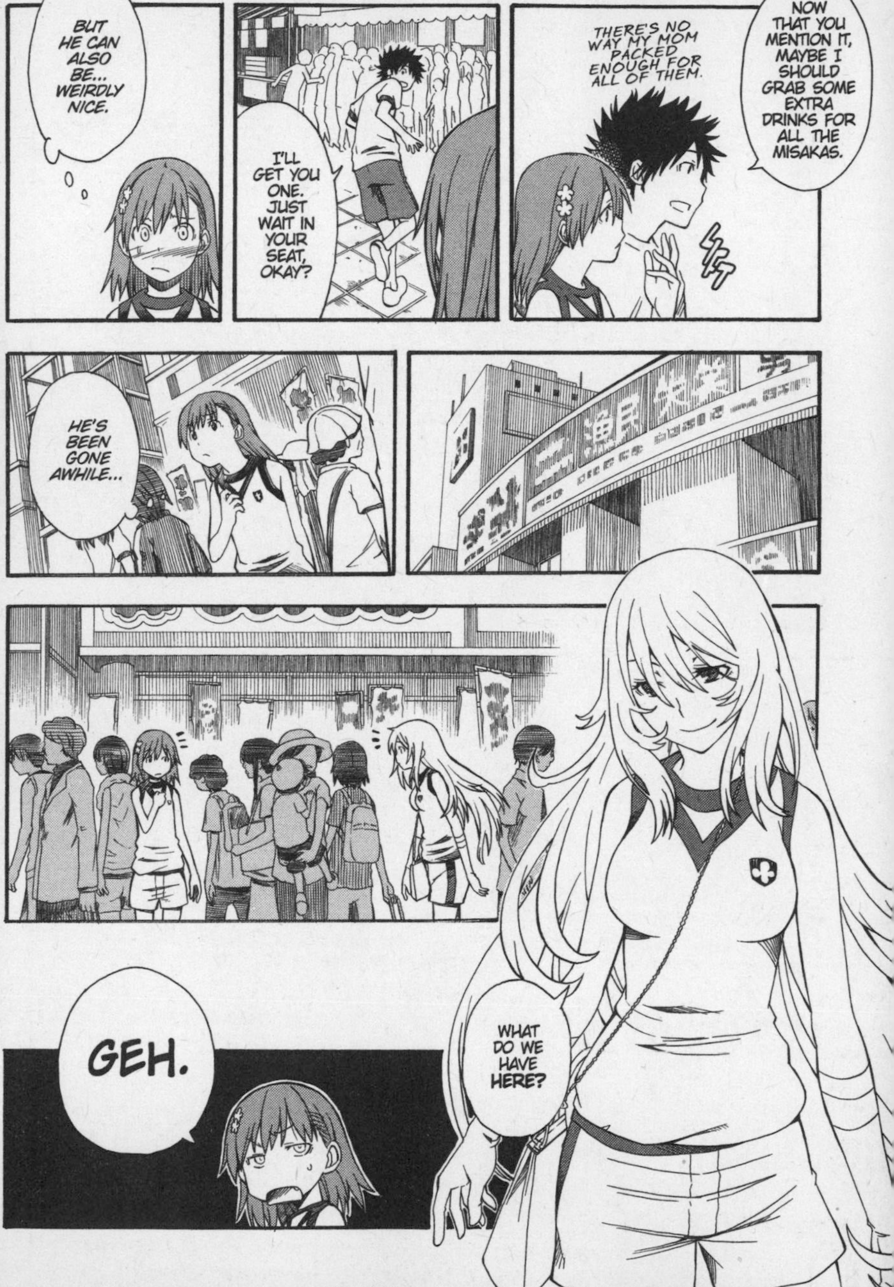
NOW THAT YOU MENTION IT, MAYBE I SHOULD GRAB SOME EXTRA DRINKS FOR ALL THE MISAKAS.
THERE'S NO WAY MY MOM PACKED ENOUGH FOR ALL OF THEM.
I'LL GET YOU ONE. JUST WAIT IN YOUR SEAT, OKAY?
BUT HE CAN ALSO BE... WEIRDLY NICE.
HE'S BEEN GONE AWHILE...
WHAT DO WE HAVE HERE?
GEH.

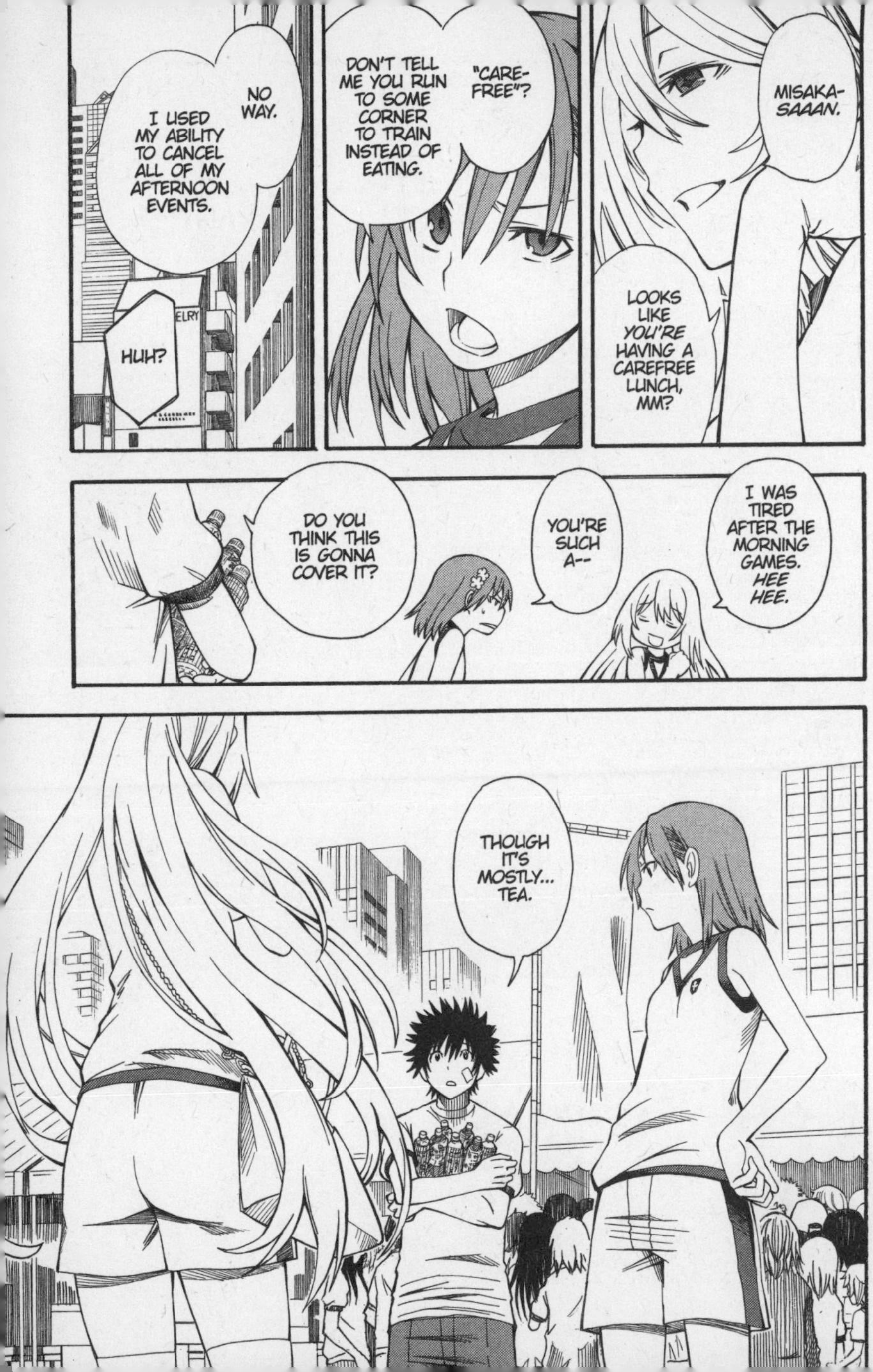
MISAKA-SAAAN.
LOOKS LIKE YOU'RE HAVING A CAREFREE LUNCH, MM?
"CARE-FREE"?
DON'T TELL ME YOU RUN TO SOME CORNER TO TRAIN INSTEAD OF EATING.
NO WAY.
I USED MY ABILITY TO CANCEL ALL OF MY AFTERNOON EVENTS.
HUH?
I WAS TIRED AFTER THE MORNING GAMES. HEE HEE.
YOU'RE SUCH A--
DO YOU THINK THIS IS GONNA COVER IT?
THOUGH IT'S MOSTLY... TEA.

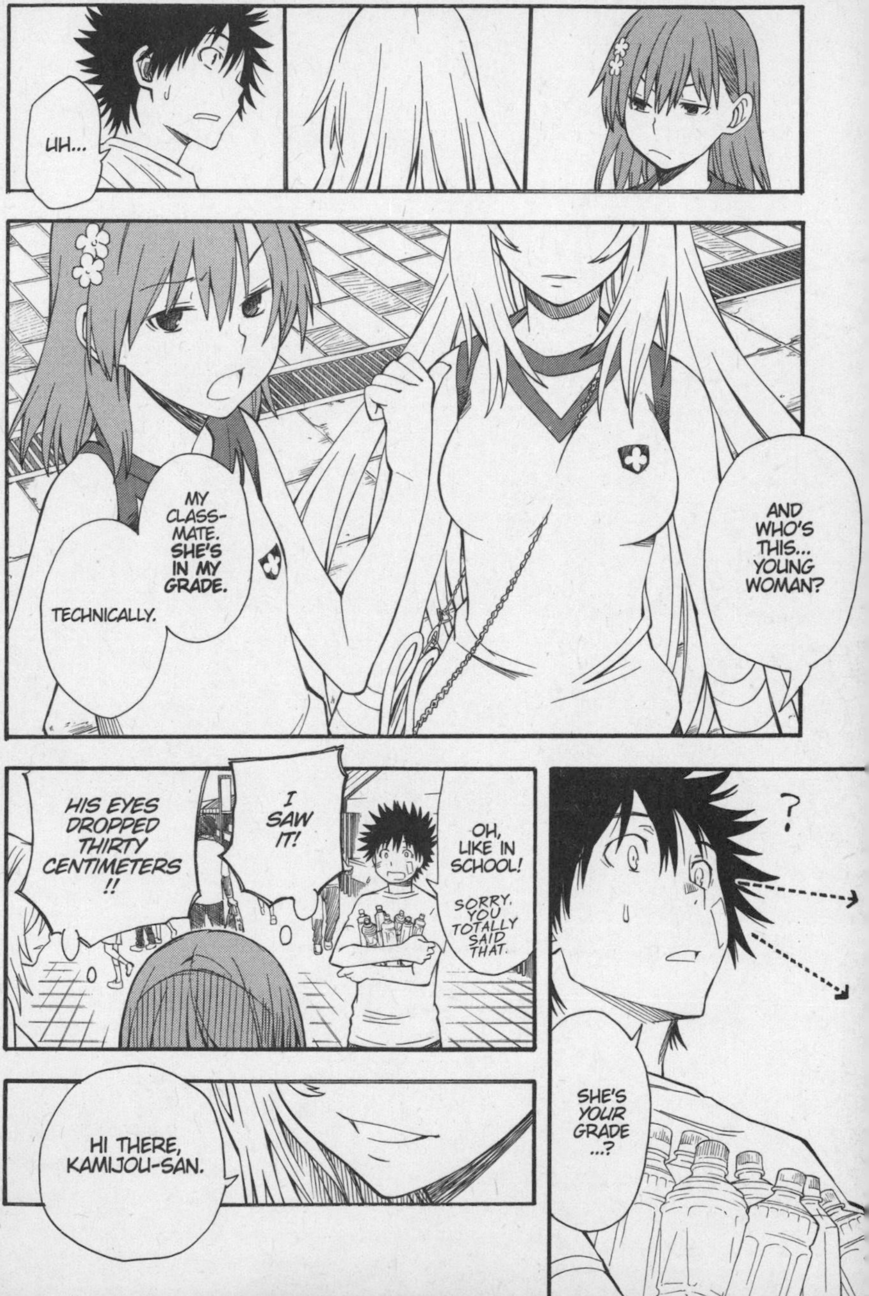
UH...
AND WHO'S THIS... YOUNG WOMAN?
MY CLASSMATE. SHE'S IN MY GRADE.
TECHNICALLY.
?
SHE'S YOUR GRADE ...?
OH, LIKE IN SCHOOL!
SORRY, YOU TOTALLY SAID THAT.
I SAW IT!
HIS EYES DROPPED THIRTY CENTIMETERS !!
HI THERE, KAMIJOU-SAN.

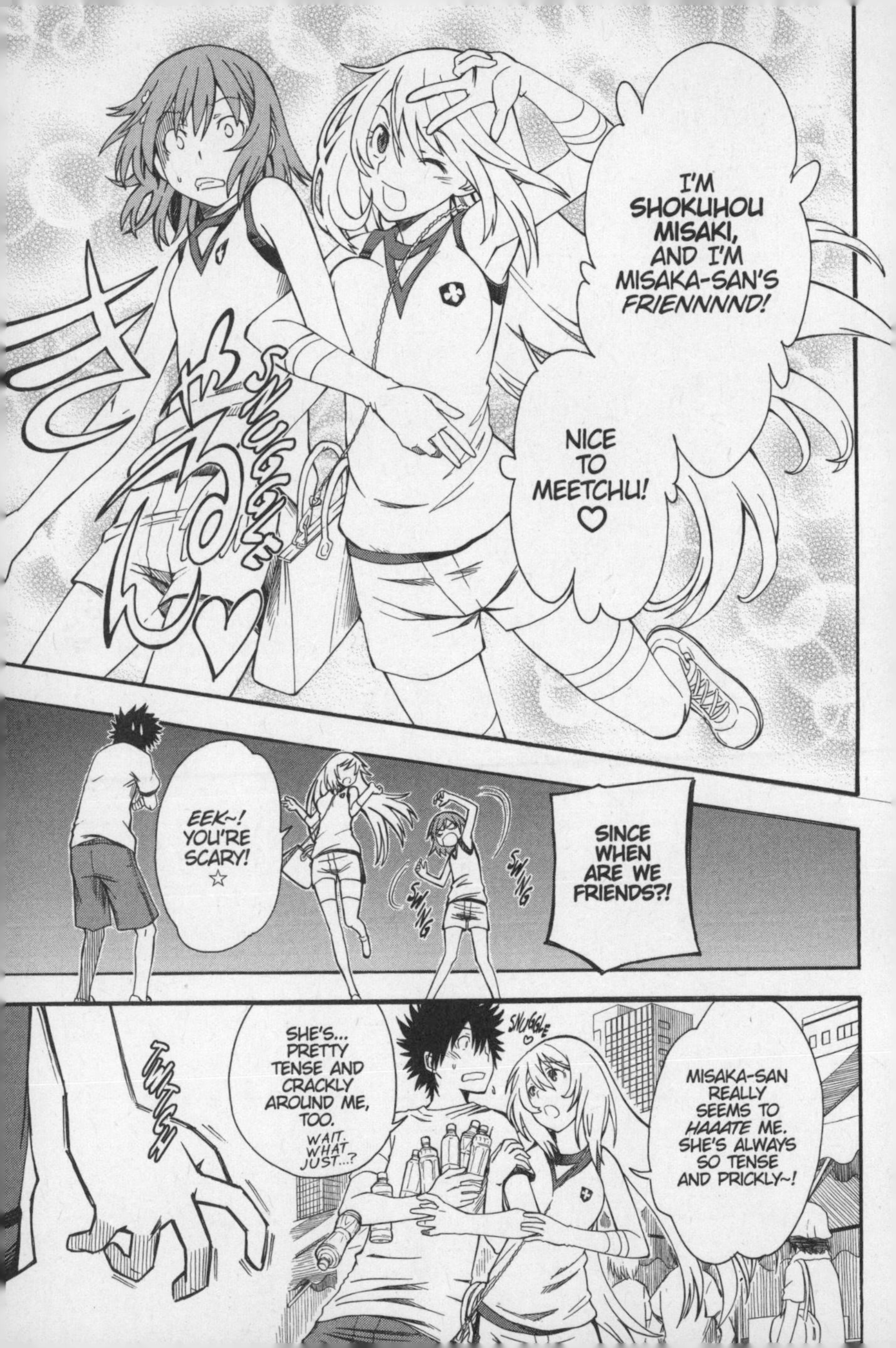
I'M SHOKUHOU MISAKI, AND I'M MISAKA-SAN'S *FRIENNNND!*
NICE TO MEETCHU! ♡
SNUGGLE
SINCE WHEN ARE WE FRIENDS?!
SWING
SWING
SWING
EEK~! YOU'RE SCARY! ☆
MISAKA-SAN REALLY SEEMS TO *HAAATE* ME. SHE'S ALWAYS SO TENSE AND PRICKLY~!
SNUGGLE ♡
SHE'S... PRETTY TENSE AND CRACKLY AROUND ME, TOO.
WAIT. WHAT JUST...?
TWITCH

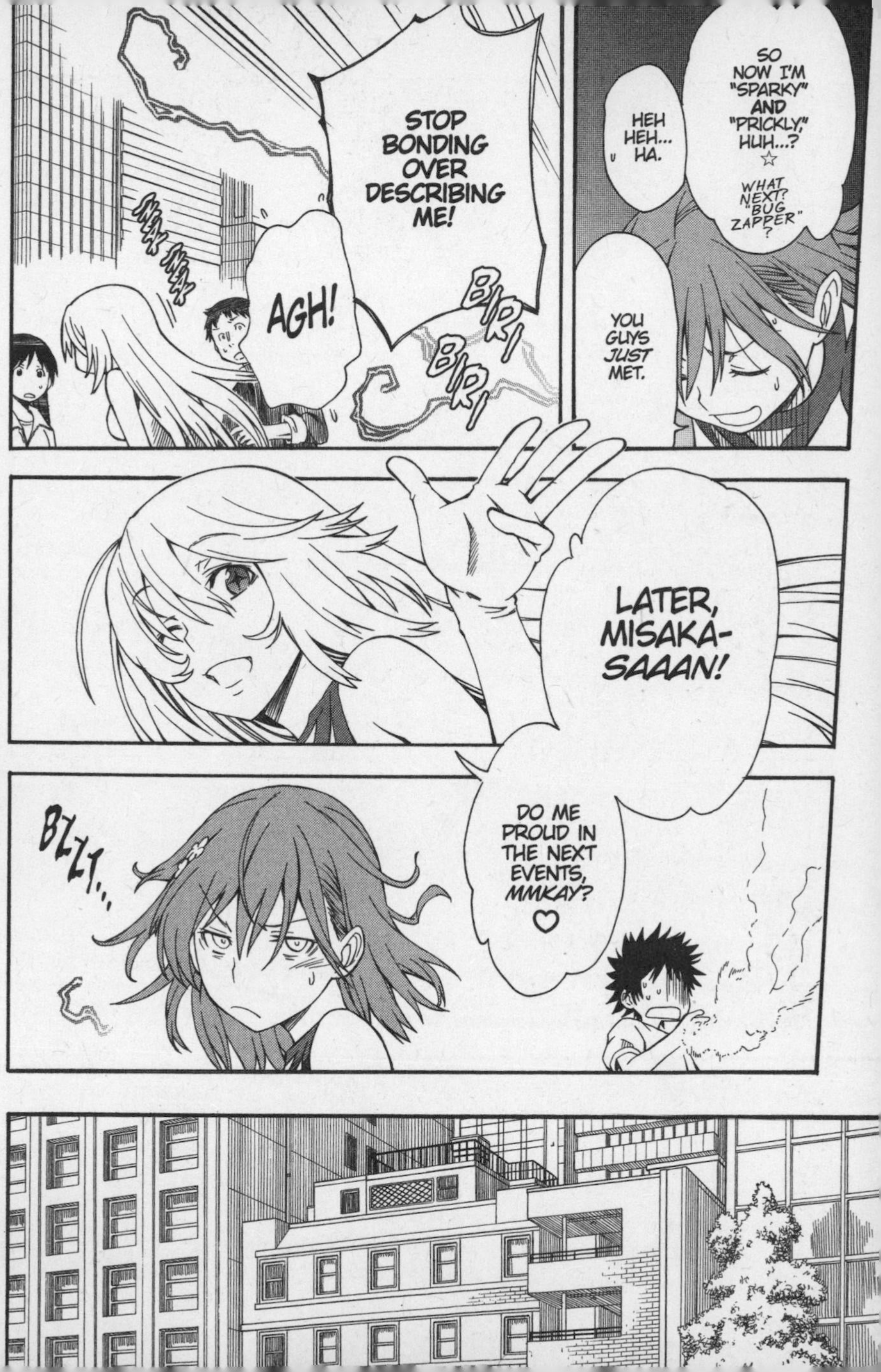
SO NOW I'M "SPARKY" AND "PRICKLY," HUH...? ☆
WHAT NEXT? "BUG ZAPPER"?
HEH HEH... HA.
YOU GUYS JUST MET.
STOP BONDING OVER DESCRIBING ME!
BIRI BIRI
AGH!
LATER, MISAKA-SAAAN!
DO ME PROUD IN THE NEXT EVENTS, MMKAY? ♡
BZZT...

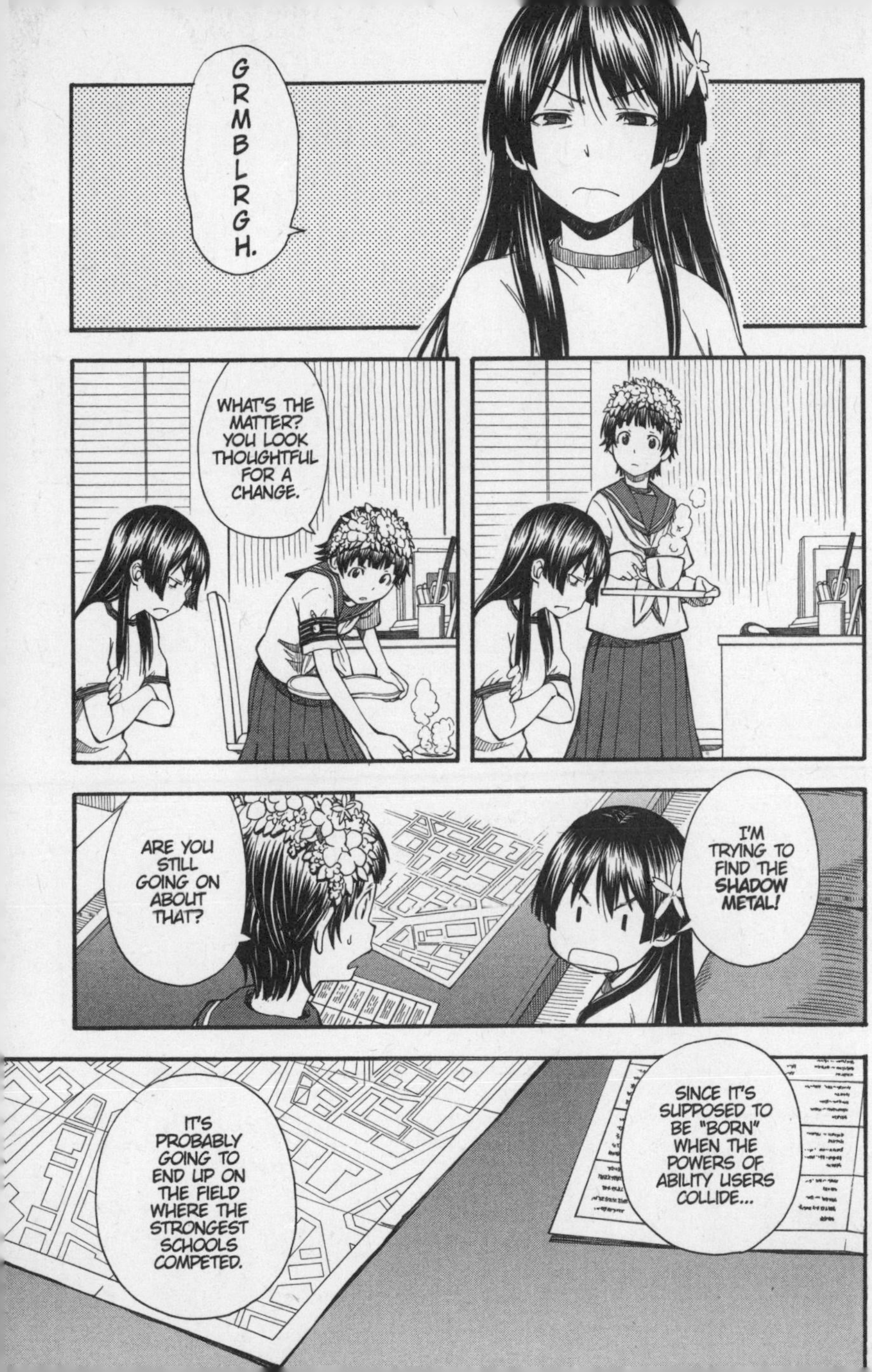
GRMBLRGH.
WHAT'S THE MATTER? YOU LOOK THOUGHTFUL FOR A CHANGE.
I'M TRYING TO FIND THE SHADOW METAL!
ARE YOU STILL GOING ON ABOUT THAT?
SINCE IT'S SUPPOSED TO BE "BORN" WHEN THE POWERS OF ABILITY USERS COLLIDE...
IT'S PROBABLY GOING TO END UP ON THE FIELD WHERE THE STRONGEST SCHOOLS COMPETED.

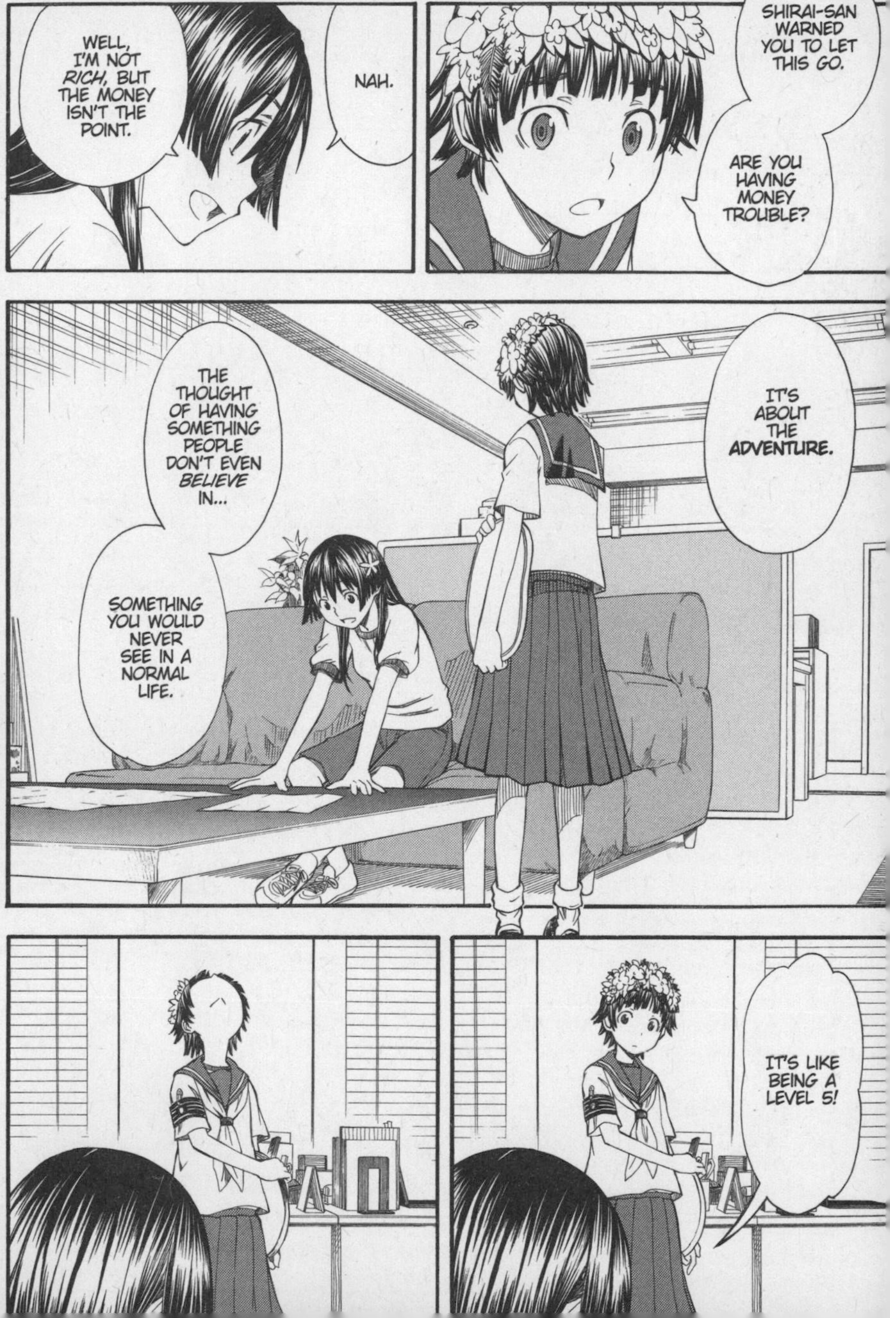
SHIRAI-SAN WARNED YOU TO LET THIS GO.
ARE YOU HAVING MONEY TROUBLE?
NAH.
WELL, I'M NOT *RICH*, BUT THE MONEY ISN'T THE POINT.
IT'S ABOUT THE **ADVENTURE.**
THE THOUGHT OF HAVING SOMETHING PEOPLE DON'T EVEN *BELIEVE* IN...
SOMETHING YOU WOULD NEVER SEE IN A NORMAL LIFE.
IT'S LIKE BEING A LEVEL 5!

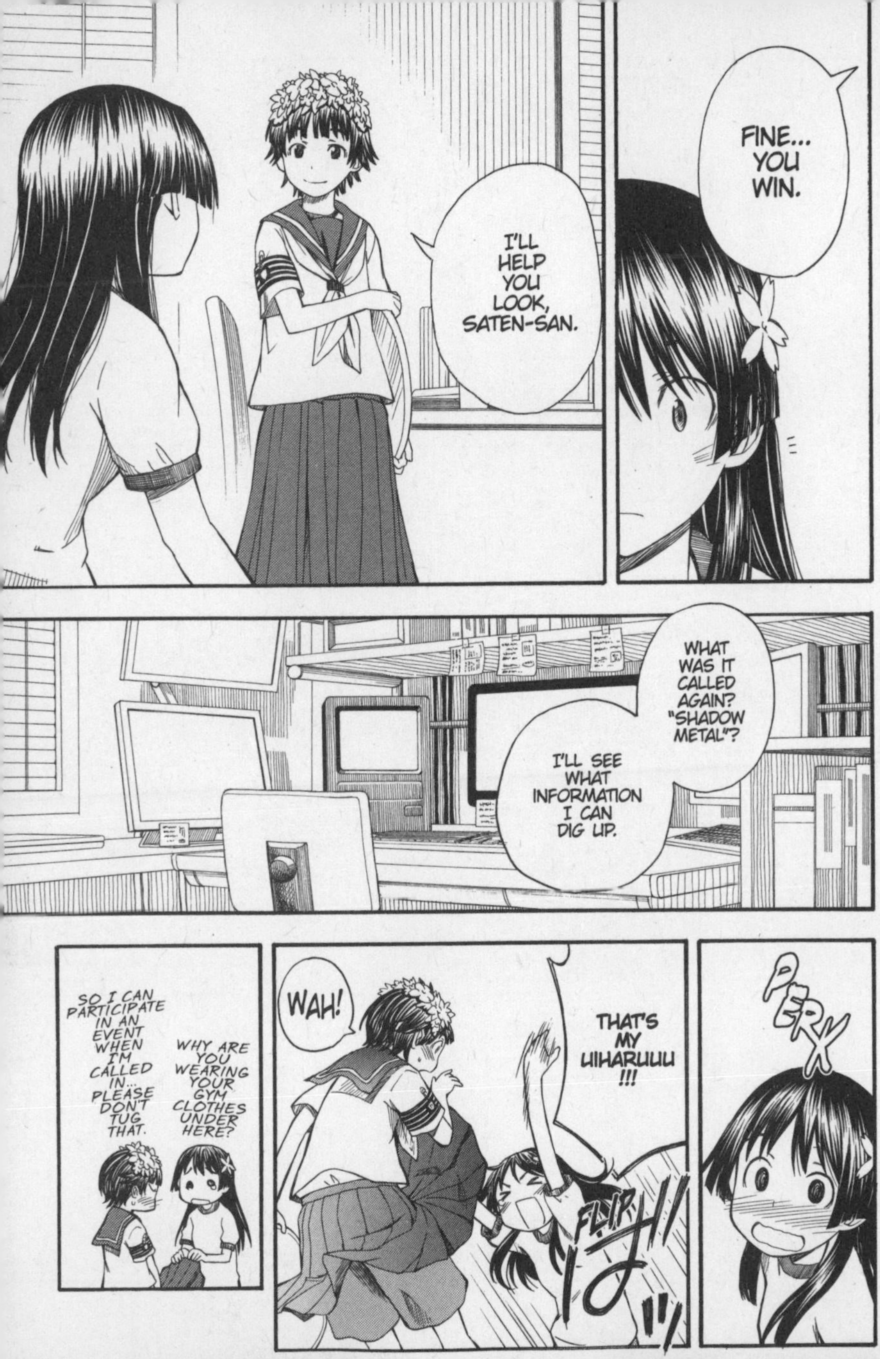
FINE... YOU WIN.
I'LL HELP YOU LOOK, SATEN-SAN.
WHAT WAS IT CALLED AGAIN? "SHADOW METAL"?
I'LL SEE WHAT INFORMATION I CAN DIG UP.
PERK
THAT'S MY UIHARUUU!!!
WAH!
FLIP
WHY ARE YOU WEARING YOUR GYM CLOTHES UNDER HERE?
SO I CAN PARTICIPATE IN AN EVENT WHEN I'M CALLED IN... PLEASE DON'T TUG THAT.

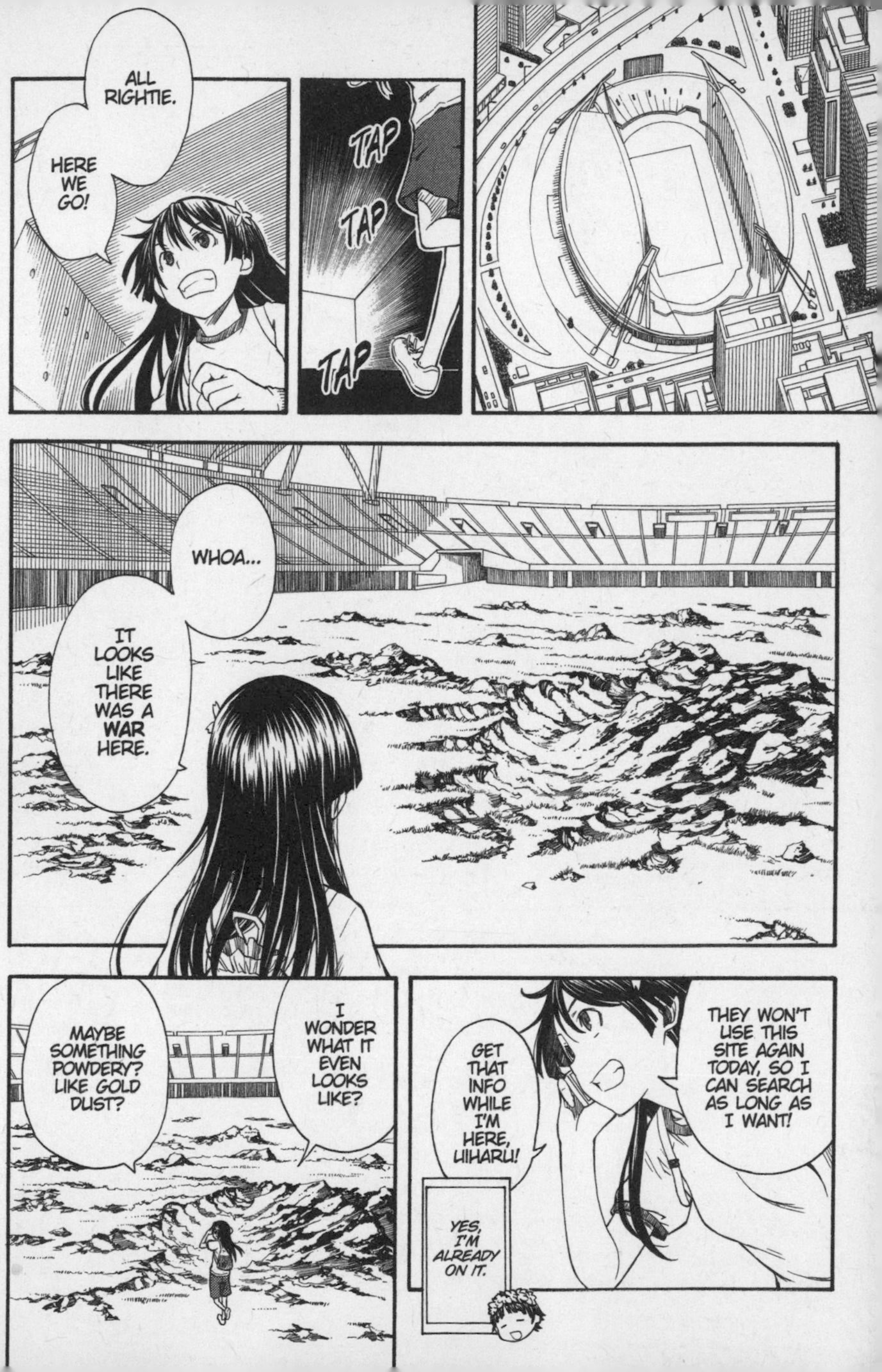
TAP
TAP
TAP
ALL RIGHTIE.
HERE WE GO!
WHOA...
IT LOOKS LIKE THERE WAS A WAR HERE.
THEY WON'T USE THIS SITE AGAIN TODAY, SO I CAN SEARCH AS LONG AS I WANT!
GET THAT INFO WHILE I'M HERE, UIHARU!
YES, I'M ALREADY ON IT.
I WONDER WHAT IT EVEN LOOKS LIKE?
MAYBE SOMETHING POWDERY? LIKE GOLD DUST?

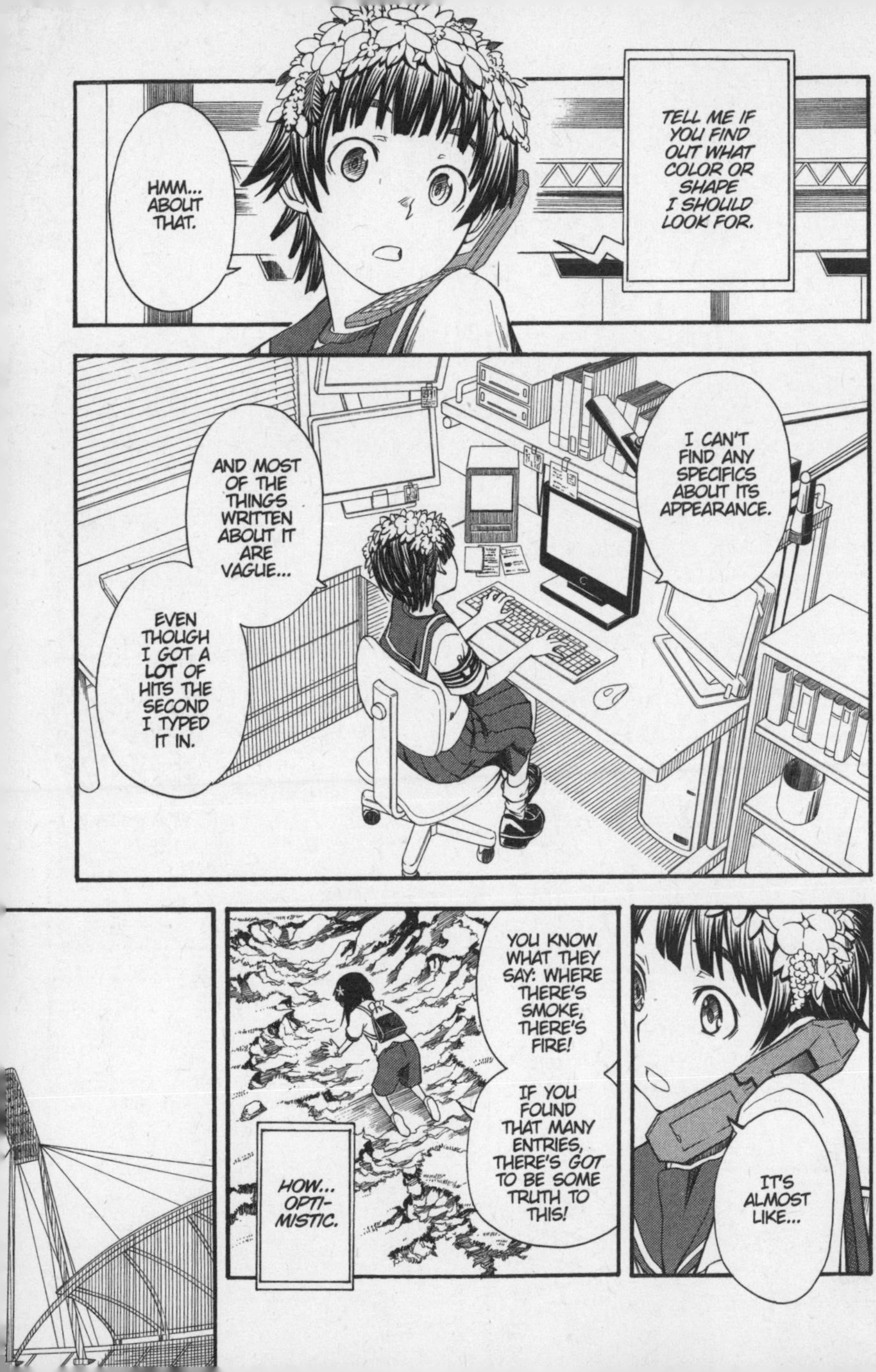
TELL ME IF YOU FIND OUT WHAT COLOR OR SHAPE I SHOULD LOOK FOR.
HMM... ABOUT THAT.
I CAN'T FIND ANY SPECIFICS ABOUT ITS APPEARANCE.
AND MOST OF THE THINGS WRITTEN ABOUT IT ARE VAGUE...
EVEN THOUGH I GOT A LOT OF HITS THE SECOND I TYPED IT IN.
YOU KNOW WHAT THEY SAY: WHERE THERE'S SMOKE, THERE'S FIRE!
IF YOU FOUND THAT MANY ENTRIES, THERE'S GOT TO BE SOME TRUTH TO THIS!
IT'S ALMOST LIKE...
HOW... OPTI-MISTIC.

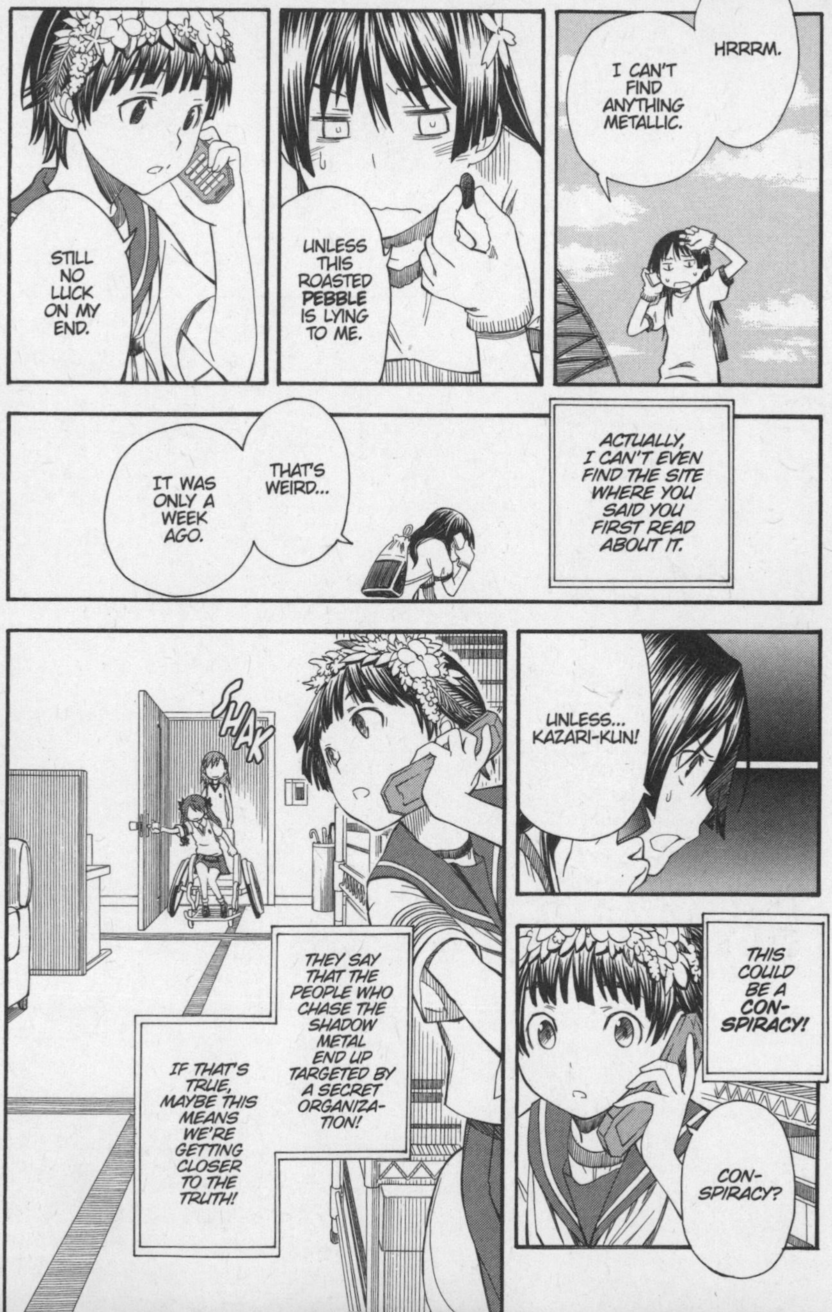
HRRRM.
I CAN'T FIND ANYTHING METALLIC.
UNLESS THIS ROASTED PEBBLE IS LYING TO ME.
STILL NO LUCK ON MY END.
ACTUALLY, I CAN'T EVEN FIND THE SITE WHERE YOU SAID YOU FIRST READ ABOUT IT.
THAT'S WEIRD...
IT WAS ONLY A WEEK AGO.
UNLESS... KAZARI-KUN!
THIS COULD BE A CON-SPIRACY!
CON-SPIRACY?
SHAK
THEY SAY THAT THE PEOPLE WHO CHASE THE SHADOW METAL END UP TARGETED BY A SECRET ORGANIZA-TION!
IF THAT'S TRUE, MAYBE THIS MEANS WE'RE GETTING CLOSER TO THE TRUTH!

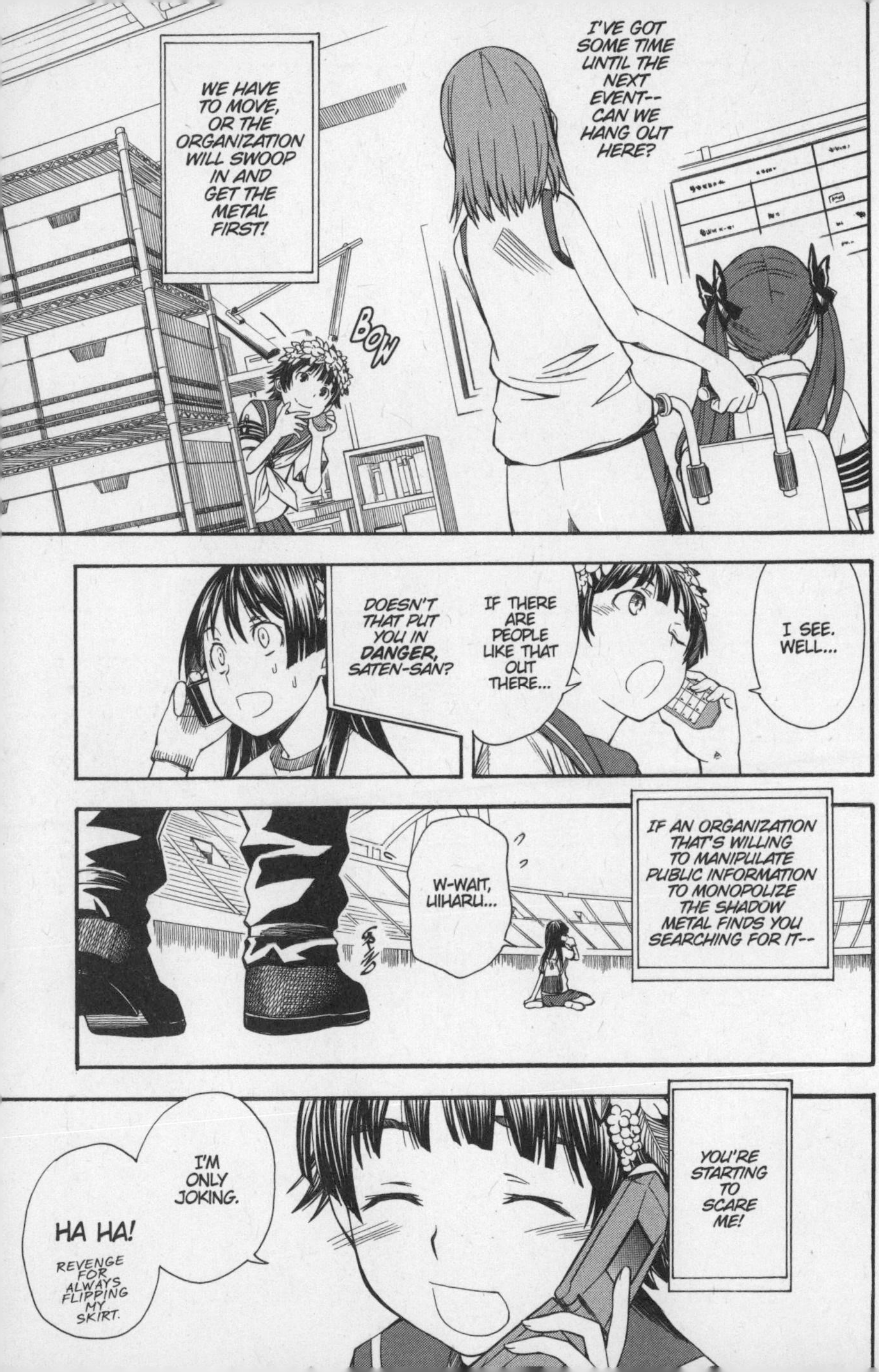
I'VE GOT SOME TIME UNTIL THE NEXT EVENT-- CAN WE HANG OUT HERE?
WE HAVE TO MOVE, OR THE ORGANIZATION WILL SWOOP IN AND GET THE METAL FIRST!
BOW
I SEE. WELL...
IF THERE ARE PEOPLE LIKE THAT OUT THERE...
DOESN'T THAT PUT YOU IN DANGER, SATEN-SAN?
IF AN ORGANIZATION THAT'S WILLING TO MANIPULATE PUBLIC INFORMATION TO MONOPOLIZE THE SHADOW METAL FINDS YOU SEARCHING FOR IT--
W-WAIT, UIHARU...
YOU'RE STARTING TO SCARE ME!
I'M ONLY JOKING.
HA HA!
REVENGE FOR ALWAYS FLIPPING MY SKIRT.

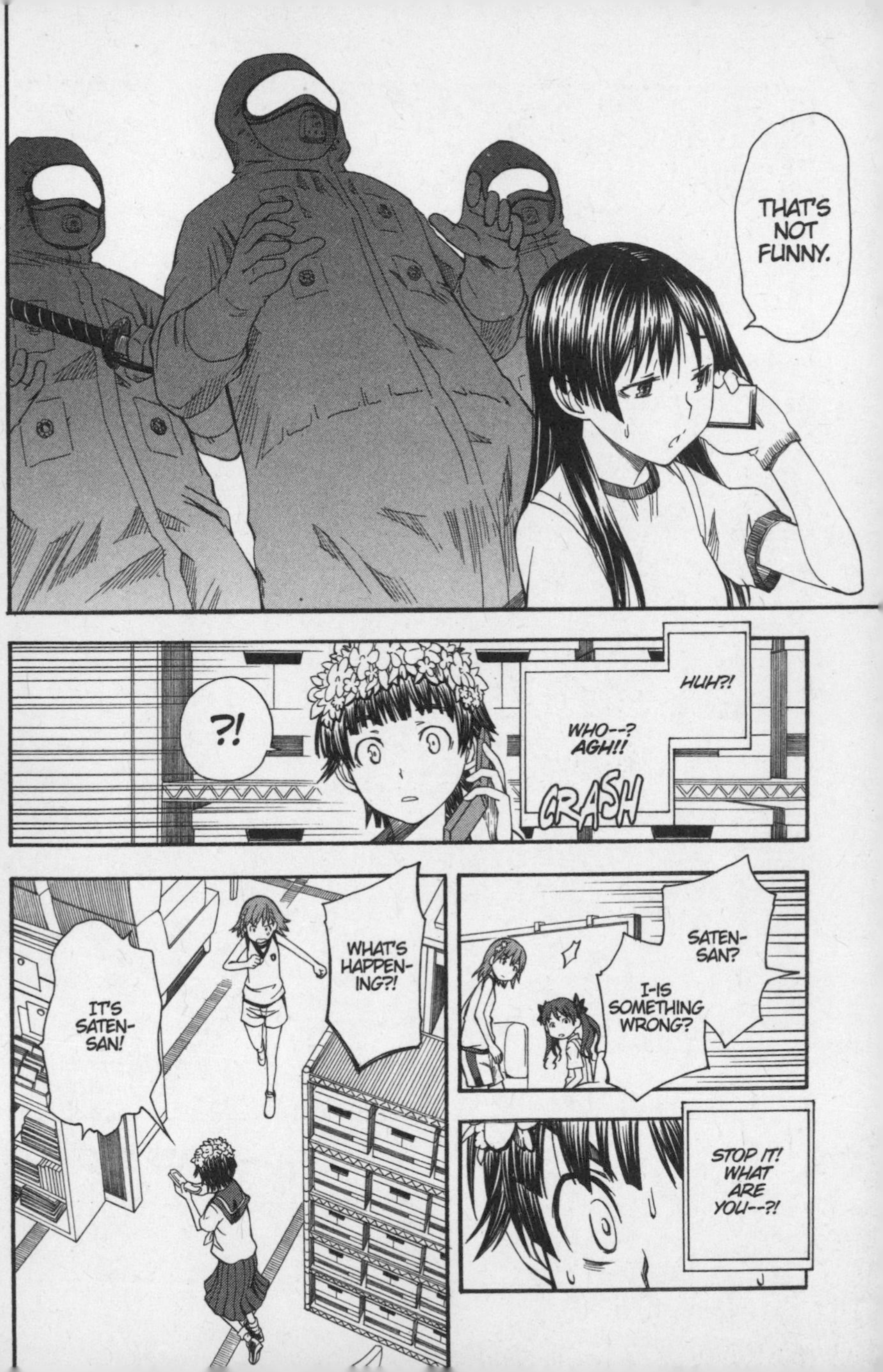
THAT'S NOT FUNNY.
HUH?!
WHO--? AGH!!
CRASH
?!
SATEN-SAN?
I-IS SOMETHING WRONG?
STOP IT! WHAT ARE YOU--?!
WHAT'S HAPPEN-ING?!
IT'S SATEN-SAN!

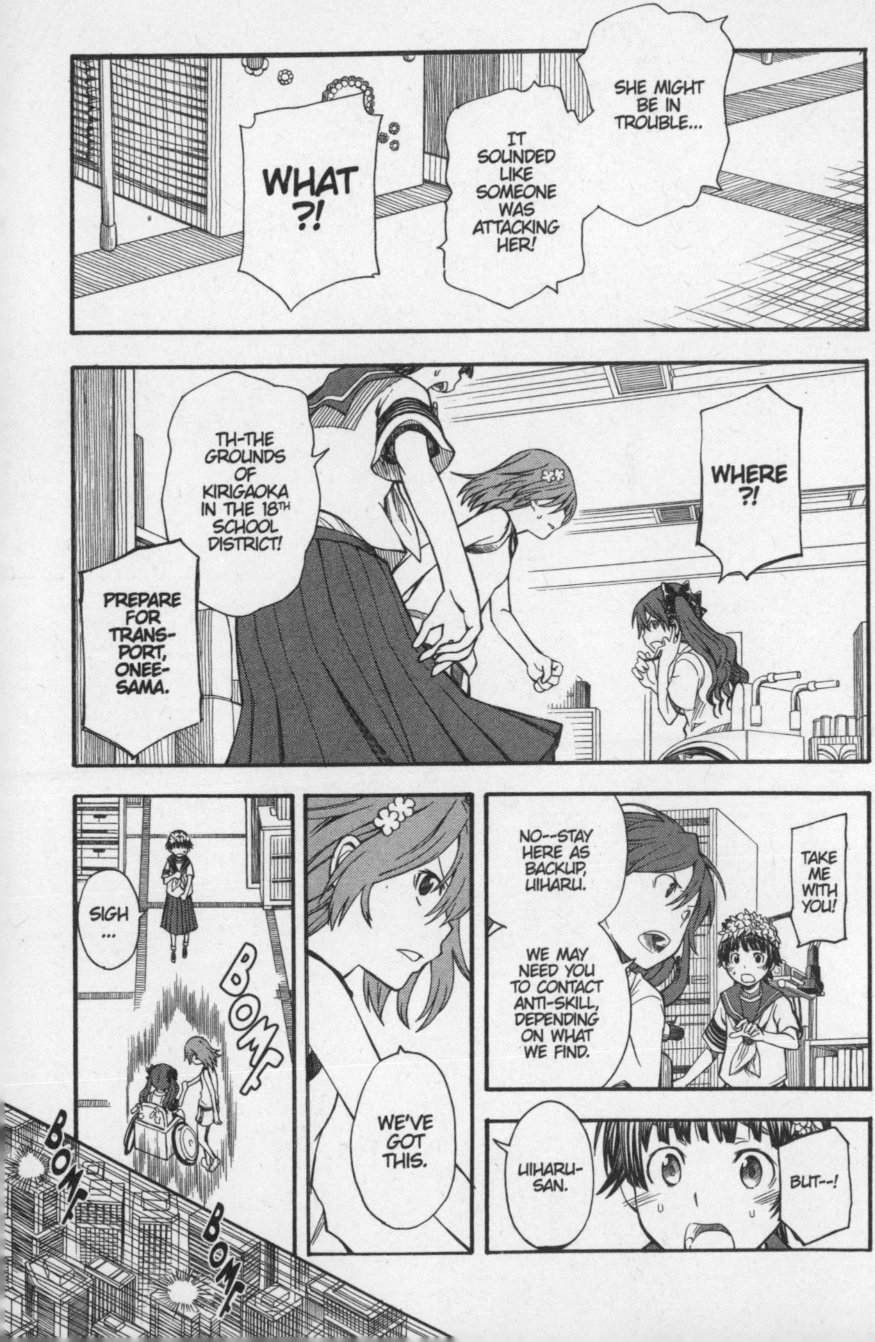
SHE MIGHT BE IN TROUBLE...
IT SOUNDED LIKE SOMEONE WAS ATTACKING HER!
WHAT ?!
WHERE ?!
TH-THE GROUNDS OF KIRIGAOKA IN THE 18TH SCHOOL DISTRICT!
PREPARE FOR TRANSPORT, ONEE-SAMA.
TAKE ME WITH YOU!
NO--STAY HERE AS BACKUP, UIHARU.
WE MAY NEED YOU TO CONTACT ANTI-SKILL, DEPENDING ON WHAT WE FIND.
BUT--!
UIHARU-SAN.
WE'VE GOT THIS.
SIGH ...
BOMF
BOMF
BOMF
BOMF

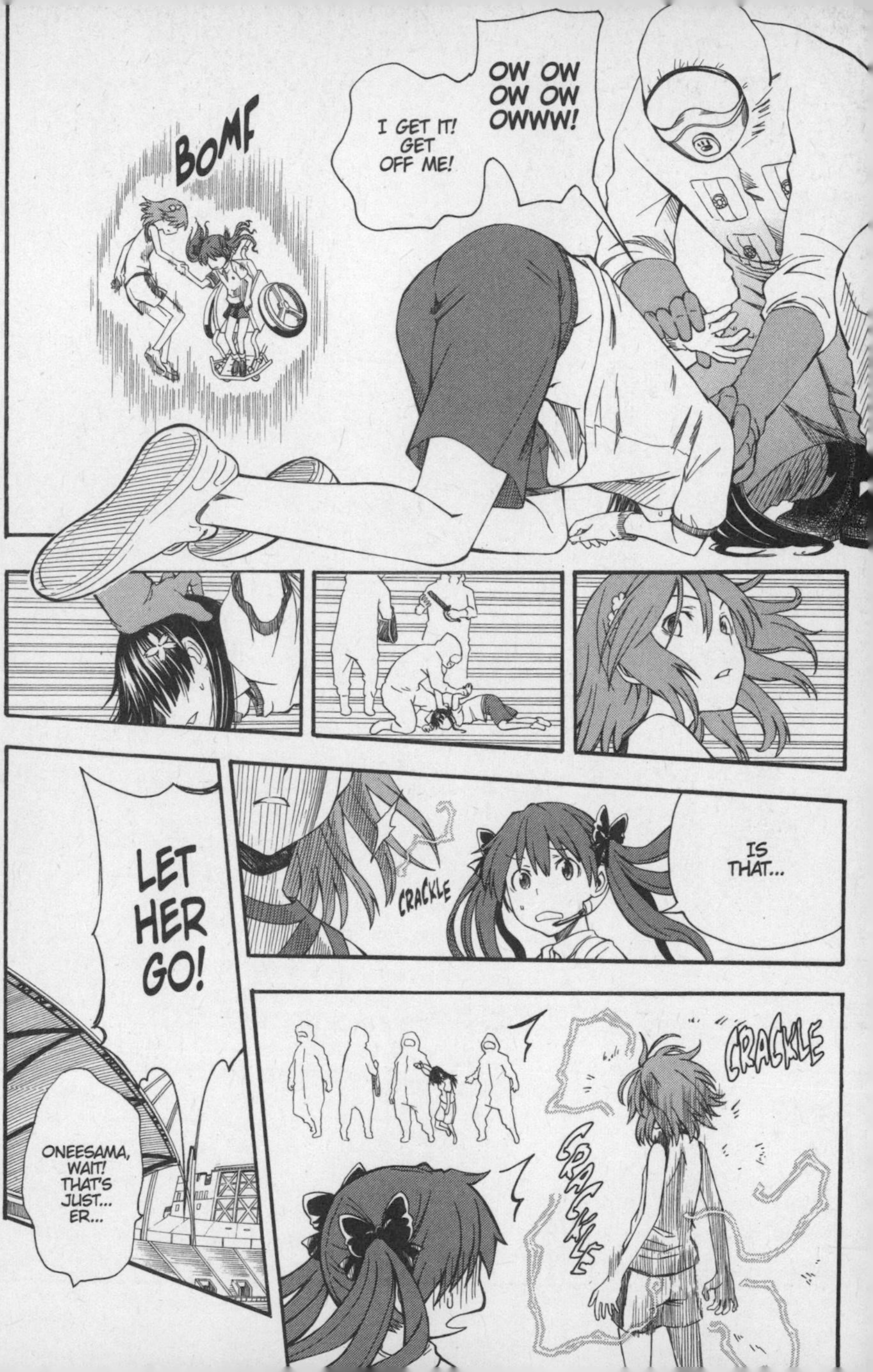
OW OW OW OW OWWW!
I GET IT! GET OFF ME!
BOMF
IS THAT...
CRACKLE
CRACKLE
CRACKLE
LET HER GO!
ONEESAMA, WAIT! THAT'S JUST... ER...

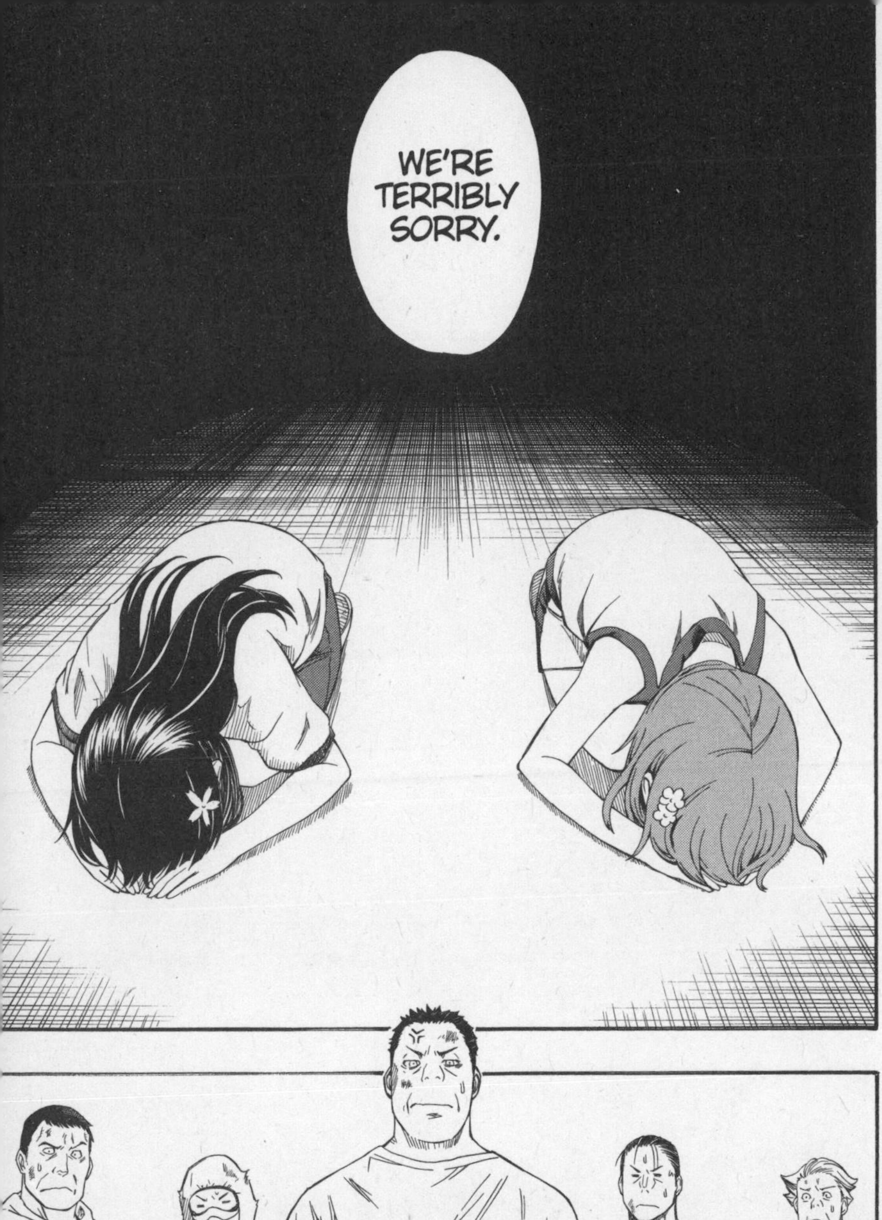
WE'RE TERRIBLY SORRY.

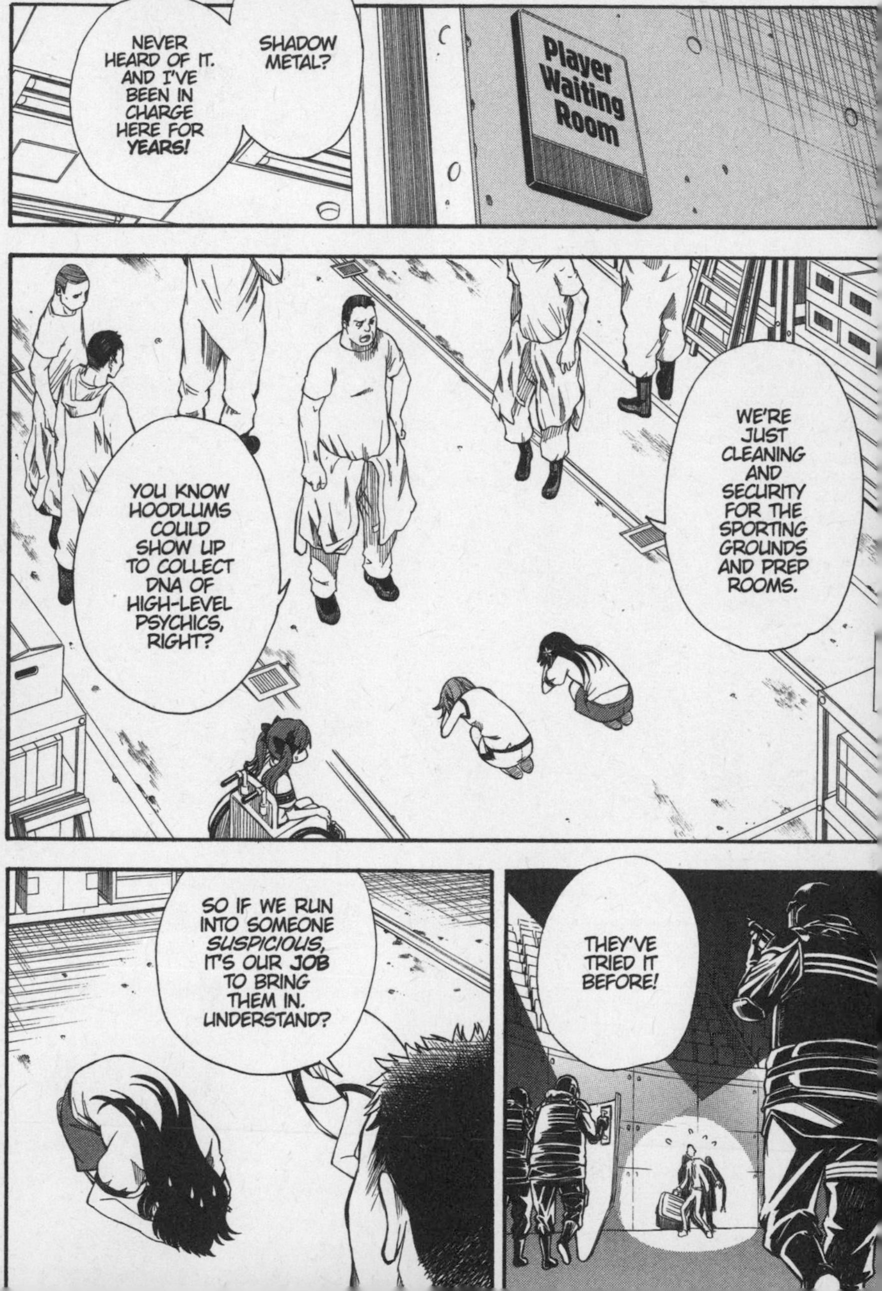
Player Waiting Room
SHADOW METAL?
NEVER HEARD OF IT. AND I'VE BEEN IN CHARGE HERE FOR YEARS!
WE'RE JUST CLEANING AND SECURITY FOR THE SPORTING GROUNDS AND PREP ROOMS.
YOU KNOW HOODLUMS COULD SHOW UP TO COLLECT DNA OF HIGH-LEVEL PSYCHICS, RIGHT?
THEY'VE TRIED IT BEFORE!
SO IF WE RUN INTO SOMEONE SUSPICIOUS, IT'S OUR JOB TO BRING THEM IN. UNDERSTAND?

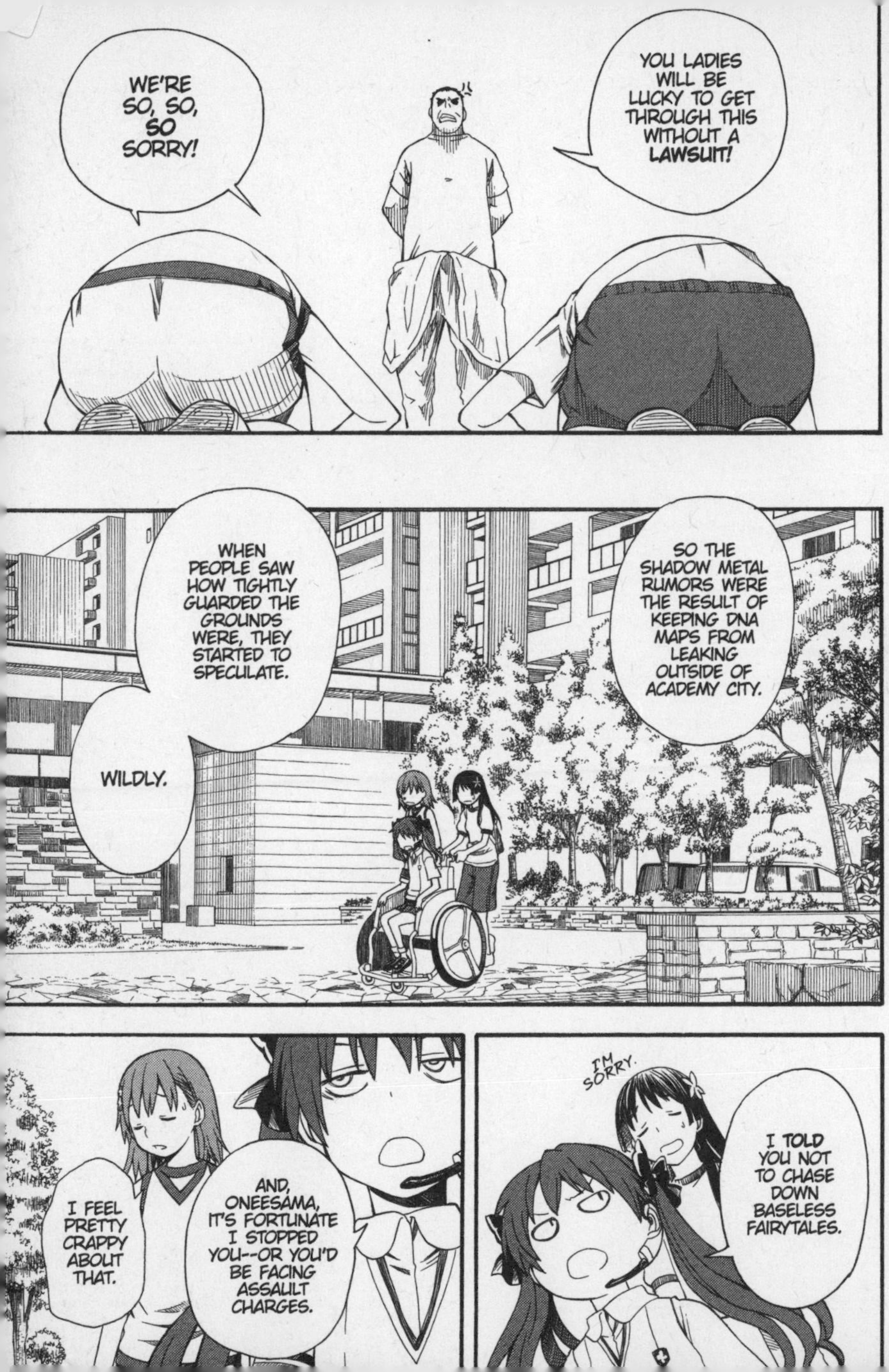
YOU LADIES WILL BE LUCKY TO GET THROUGH THIS WITHOUT A LAWSUIT!
WE'RE SO, SO, SO SORRY!
SO THE SHADOW METAL RUMORS WERE THE RESULT OF KEEPING DNA MAPS FROM LEAKING OUTSIDE OF ACADEMY CITY.
WHEN PEOPLE SAW HOW TIGHTLY GUARDED THE GROUNDS WERE, THEY STARTED TO SPECULATE.
WILDLY.
I TOLD YOU NOT TO CHASE DOWN BASELESS FAIRYTALES.
I'M SORRY.
AND, ONEESAMA, IT'S FORTUNATE I STOPPED YOU--OR YOU'D BE FACING ASSAULT CHARGES.
I FEEL PRETTY CRAPPY ABOUT THAT.

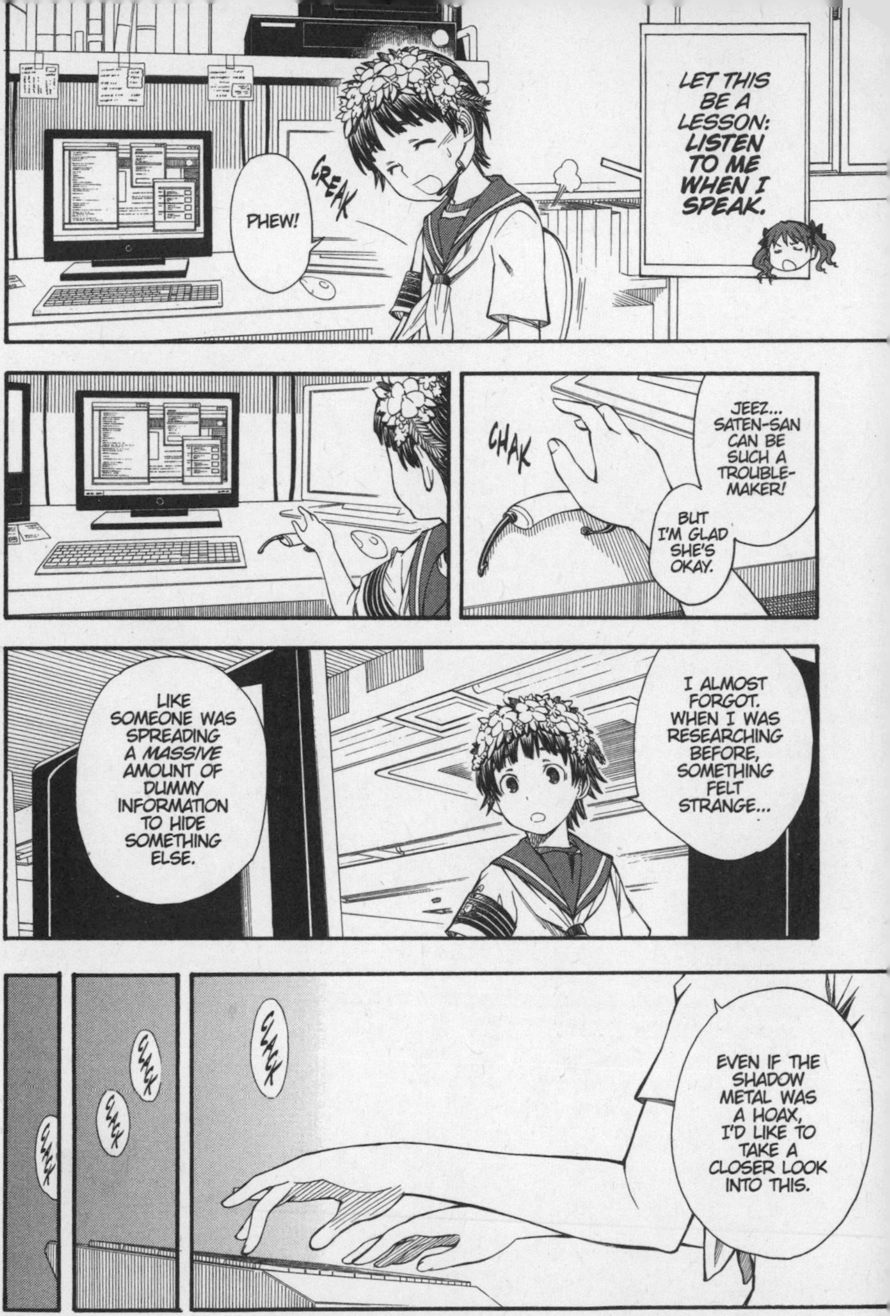
LET THIS BE A LESSON: LISTEN TO ME WHEN I SPEAK.
CREAK
PHEW!
JEEZ... SATEN-SAN CAN BE SUCH A TROUBLE-MAKER!
BUT I'M GLAD SHE'S OKAY.
CHAK
I ALMOST FORGOT. WHEN I WAS RESEARCHING BEFORE, SOMETHING FELT STRANGE...
LIKE SOMEONE WAS SPREADING A *MASSIVE* AMOUNT OF DUMMY INFORMATION TO HIDE SOMETHING ELSE.
EVEN IF THE SHADOW METAL WAS A HOAX, I'D LIKE TO TAKE A CLOSER LOOK INTO THIS.
CLACK
CLACK
CLACK
CLACK

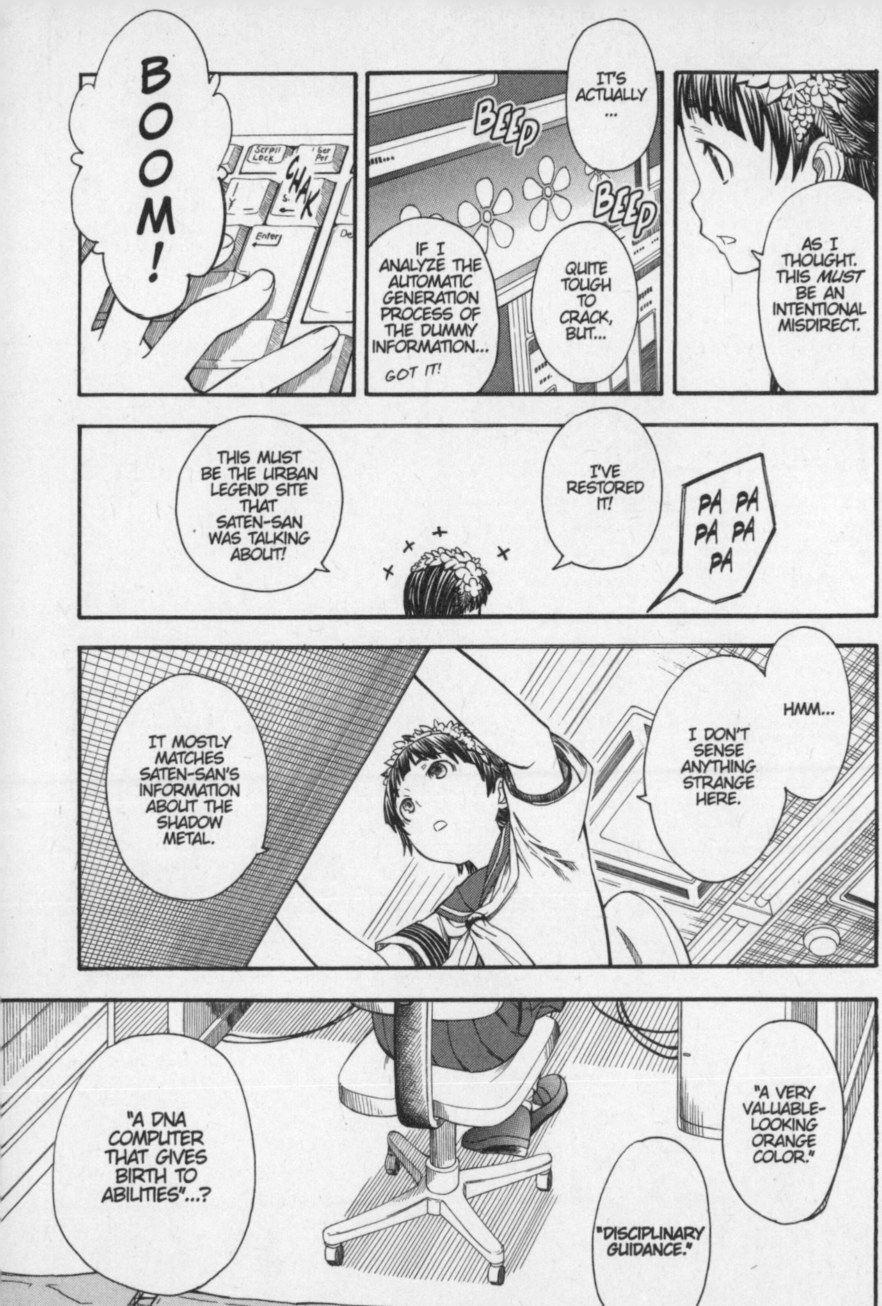
AS I THOUGHT. THIS *MUST* BE AN INTENTIONAL MISDIRECT.
IT'S ACTUALLY ...
BEEP
BEEP
QUITE TOUGH TO CRACK, BUT...
IF I ANALYZE THE AUTOMATIC GENERATION PROCESS OF THE DUMMY INFORMATION...
GOT IT!
CHAK
BOOM!
PA PA PA PA PA
I'VE RESTORED IT!
THIS MUST BE THE URBAN LEGEND SITE THAT SATEN-SAN WAS TALKING ABOUT!
HMM...
I DON'T SENSE ANYTHING STRANGE HERE.
IT MOSTLY MATCHES SATEN-SAN'S INFORMATION ABOUT THE SHADOW METAL.
"A VERY VALUABLE-LOOKING ORANGE COLOR."
"DISCIPLINARY GUIDANCE."
"A DNA COMPUTER THAT GIVES BIRTH TO ABILITIES"...?

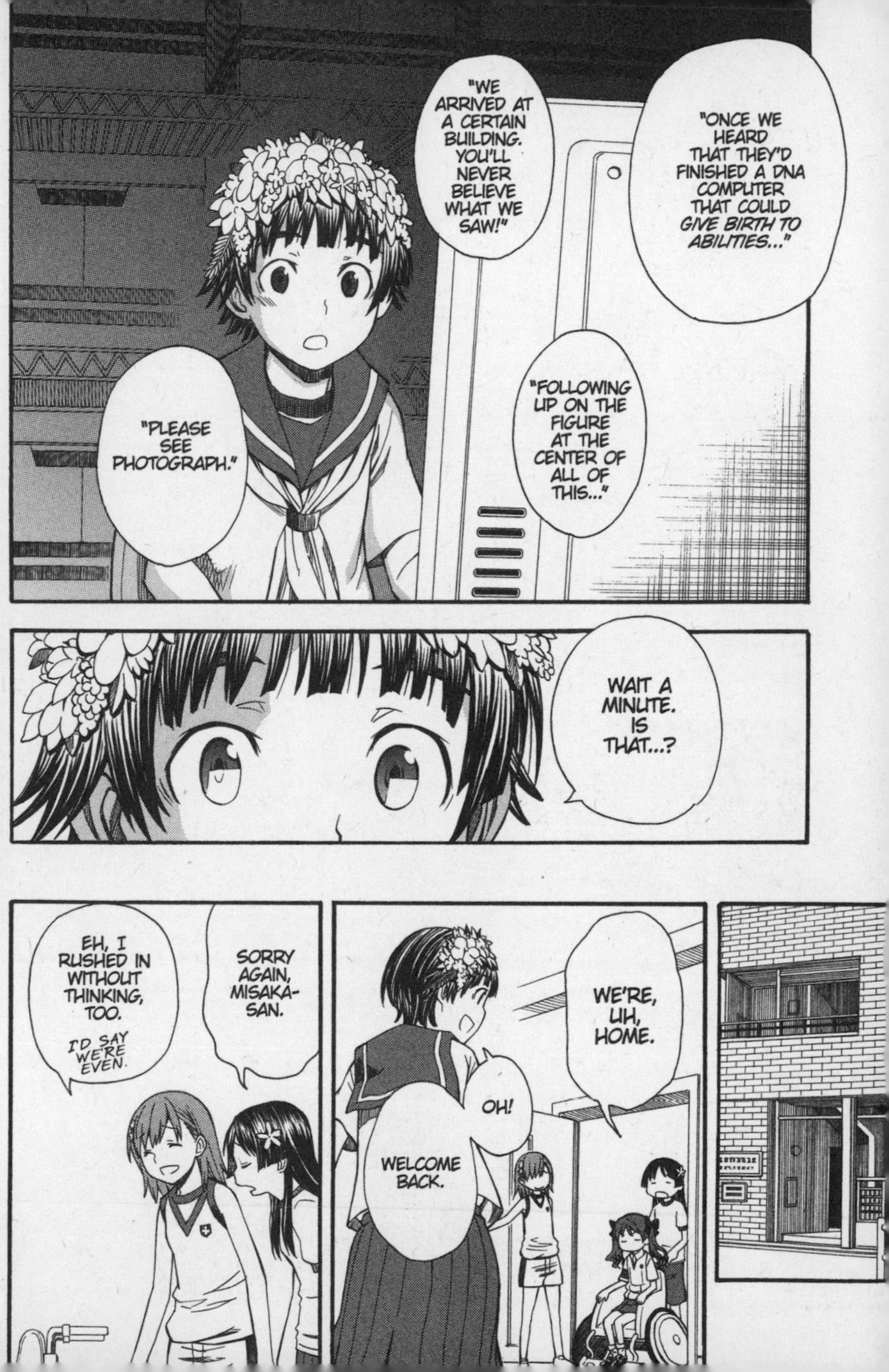
"ONCE WE HEARD THAT THEY'D FINISHED A DNA COMPUTER THAT COULD *GIVE BIRTH TO ABILITIES...*"
"WE ARRIVED AT A CERTAIN BUILDING. YOU'LL NEVER BELIEVE WHAT WE SAW!"
"FOLLOWING UP ON THE FIGURE AT THE CENTER OF ALL OF THIS..."
"PLEASE SEE PHOTOGRAPH."
WAIT A MINUTE. IS THAT...?
WE'RE, UH, HOME.
OH!
WELCOME BACK.
SORRY AGAIN, MISAKA-SAN.
EH, I RUSHED IN WITHOUT THINKING, TOO.
I'D SAY WE'RE EVEN.

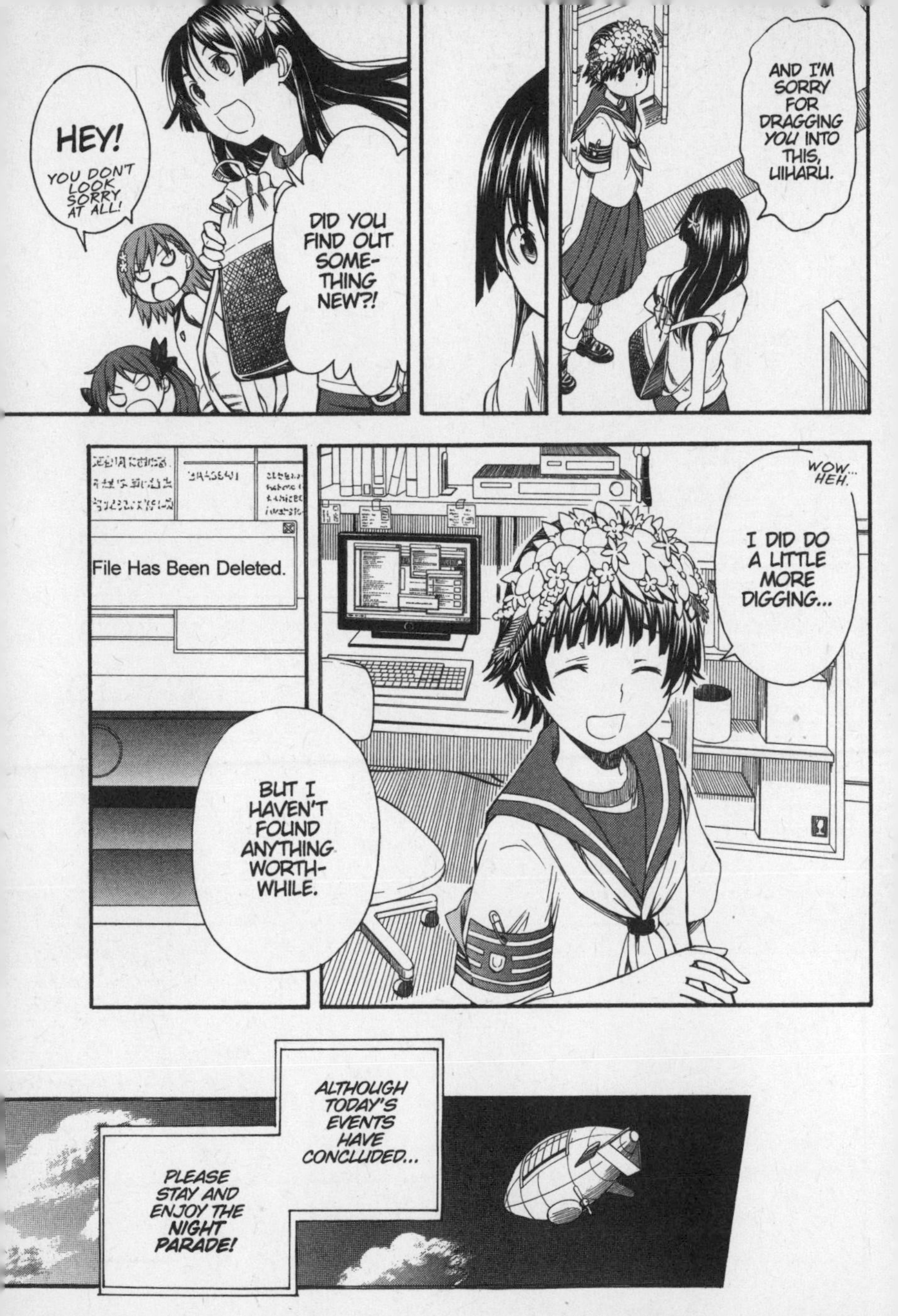

AND I'M SORRY FOR DRAGGING YOU INTO THIS, UIHARU.
DID YOU FIND OUT SOMETHING NEW?!
HEY! YOU DON'T LOOK SORRY AT ALL!
WOW... HEH.
I DID DO A LITTLE MORE DIGGING...
BUT I HAVEN'T FOUND ANYTHING WORTHWHILE.
File Has Been Deleted.
ALTHOUGH TODAY'S EVENTS HAVE CONCLUDED...
PLEASE STAY AND ENJOY THE NIGHT PARADE!

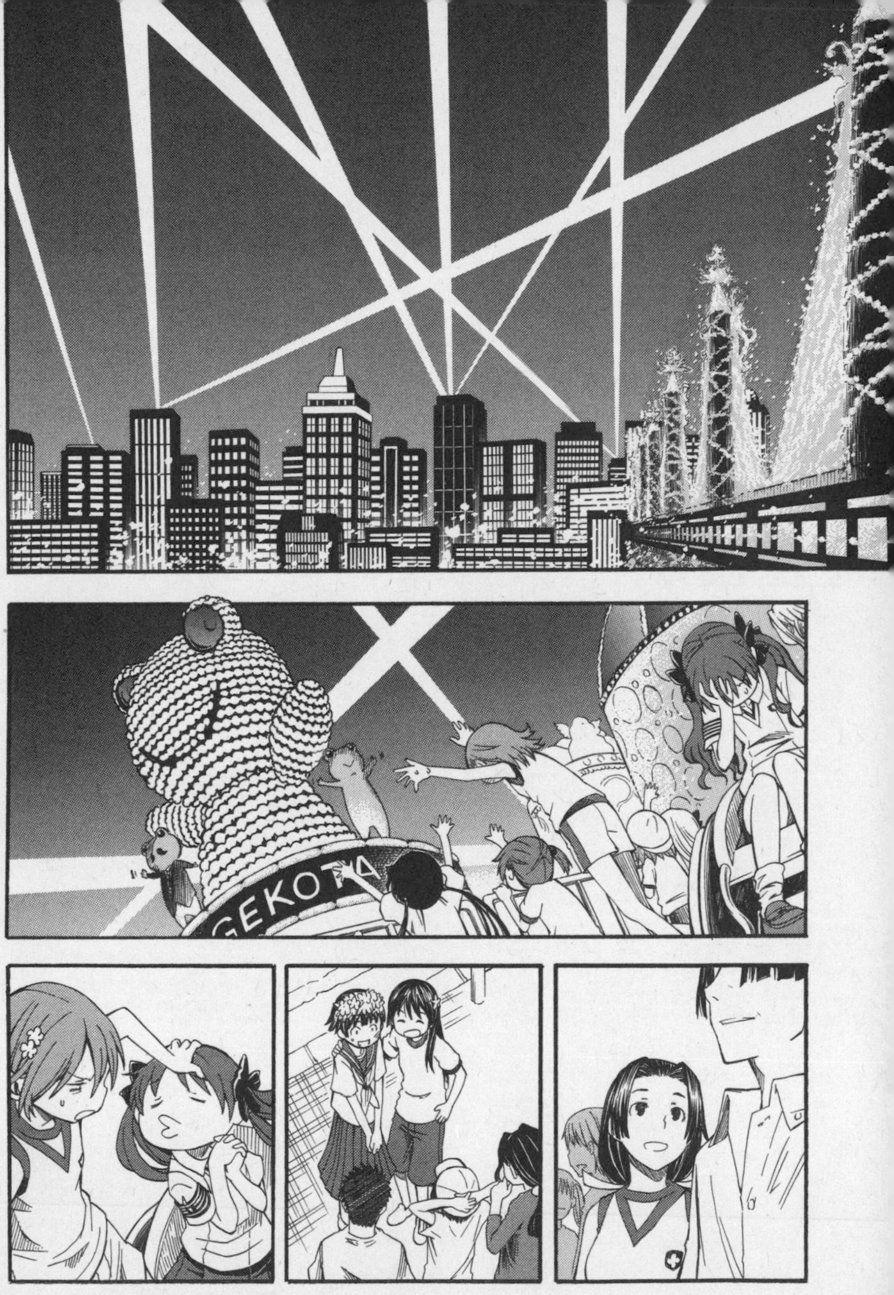
GEKOTA

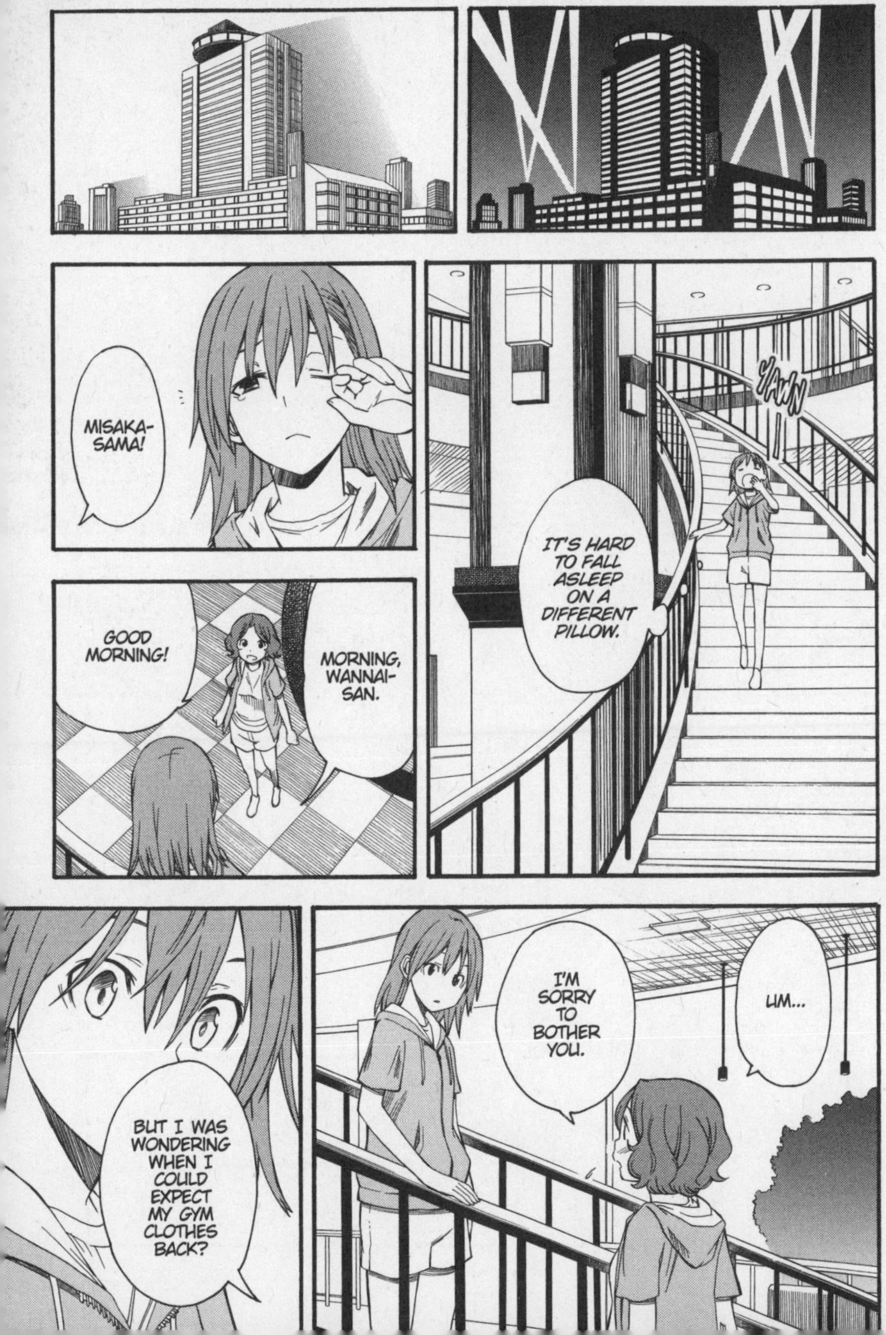
YAWN
IT'S HARD TO FALL ASLEEP ON A DIFFERENT PILLOW.
MISAKA-SAMA!
MORNING, WANNAI-SAN.
GOOD MORNING!
UM...
I'M SORRY TO BOTHER YOU.
BUT I WAS WONDERING WHEN I COULD EXPECT MY GYM CLOTHES BACK?

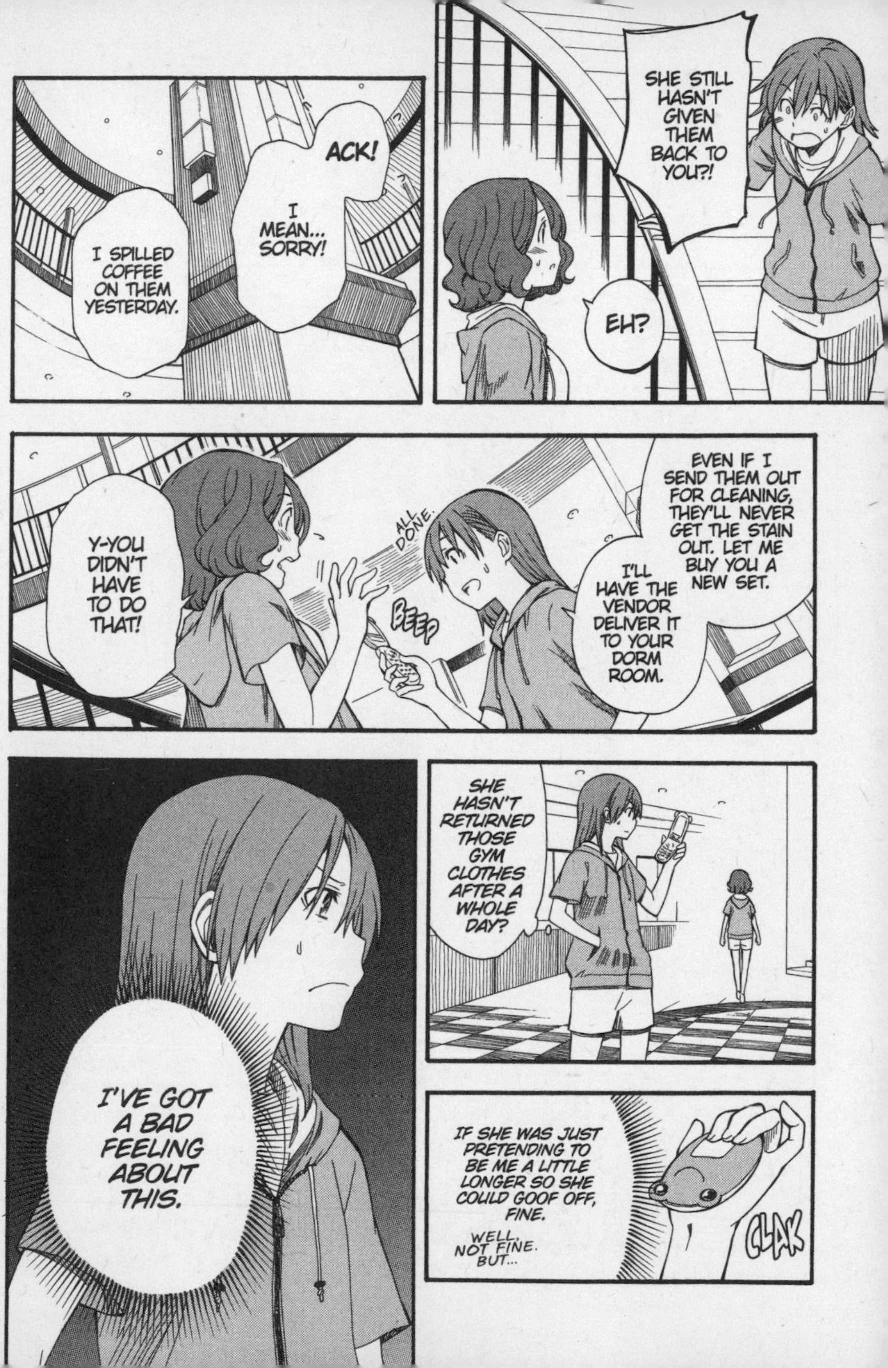
SHE STILL HASN'T GIVEN THEM BACK TO YOU?!
EH?
ACK!
I MEAN... SORRY!
I SPILLED COFFEE ON THEM YESTERDAY.
EVEN IF I SEND THEM OUT FOR CLEANING, THEY'LL NEVER GET THE STAIN OUT. LET ME BUY YOU A NEW SET.
I'LL HAVE THE VENDOR DELIVER IT TO YOUR DORM ROOM.
ALL DONE.
BEEP
Y-YOU DIDN'T HAVE TO DO THAT!
SHE HASN'T RETURNED THOSE GYM CLOTHES AFTER A WHOLE DAY?
CLAK
IF SHE WAS JUST PRETENDING TO BE ME A LITTLE LONGER SO SHE COULD GOOF OFF, FINE.
WELL, NOT FINE. BUT...
I'VE GOT A BAD FEELING ABOUT THIS.

A Certain SCIENTIFIC Railgun

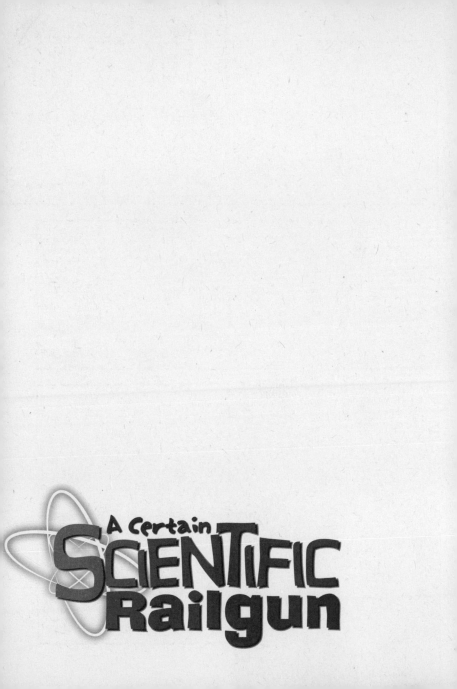

A Certain JC Jealousy

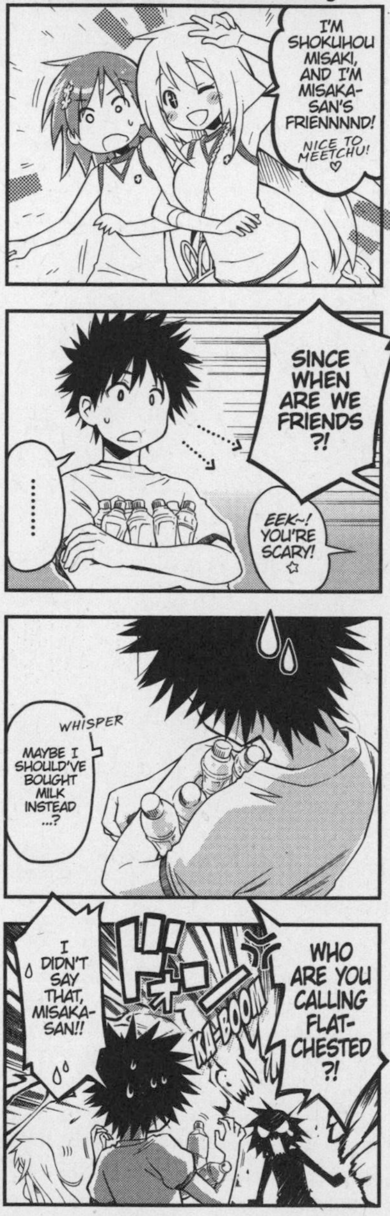
I'M SHOKUHOU MISAKI, AND I'M MISAKA-SAN'S FRIENNNND!
NICE TO MEETCHU! ♡
SINCE WHEN ARE WE FRIENDS?!
EEK~! YOU'RE SCARY! ☆
......
WHISPER
MAYBE I SHOULD'VE BOUGHT MILK INSTEAD...?
WHO ARE YOU CALLING FLAT-CHESTED?!
KA-BOOM
I DIDN'T SAY THAT, MISAKA-SAN!!

CHAPTER 48: EROSION

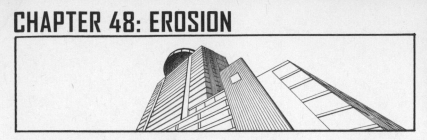

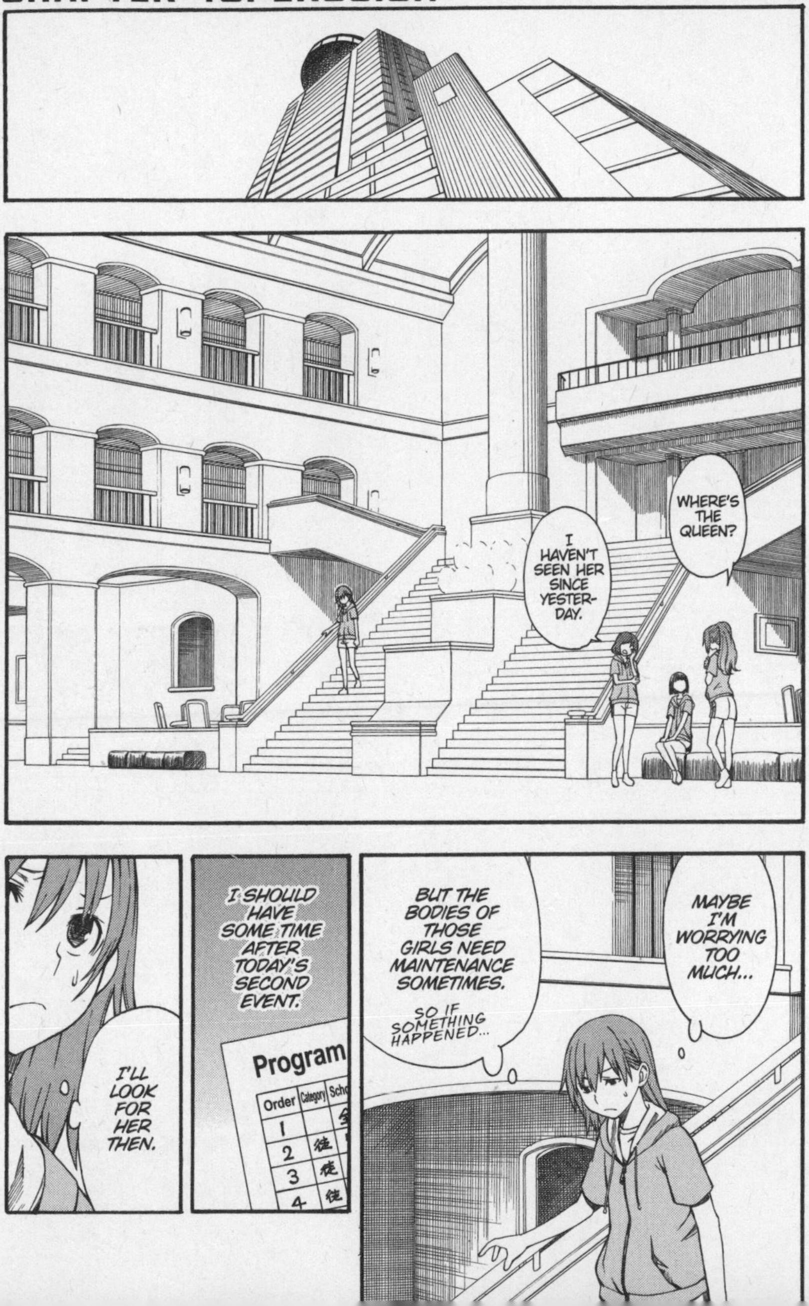
WHERE'S THE QUEEN?
I HAVEN'T SEEN HER SINCE YESTERDAY.
MAYBE I'M WORRYING TOO MUCH...
BUT THE BODIES OF THOSE GIRLS NEED MAINTENANCE SOMETIMES.
SO IF SOMETHING HAPPENED...
I SHOULD HAVE SOME TIME AFTER TODAY'S SECOND EVENT.
Program
Order
Category
I'LL LOOK FOR HER THEN.

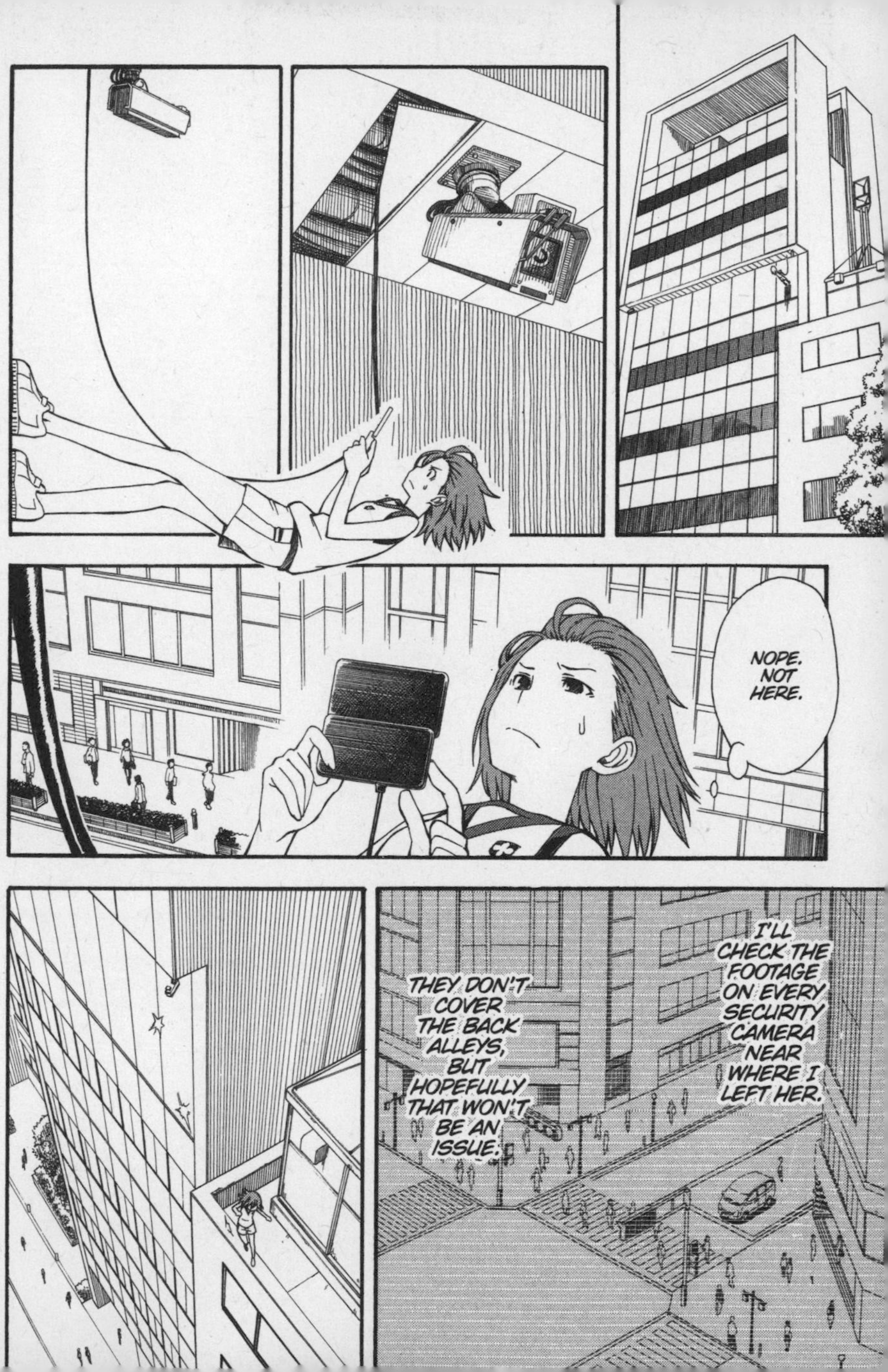
NOPE. NOT HERE.
I'LL CHECK THE FOOTAGE ON EVERY SECURITY CAMERA NEAR WHERE I LEFT HER.
THEY DON'T COVER THE BACK ALLEYS, BUT HOPEFULLY THAT WON'T BE AN ISSUE.

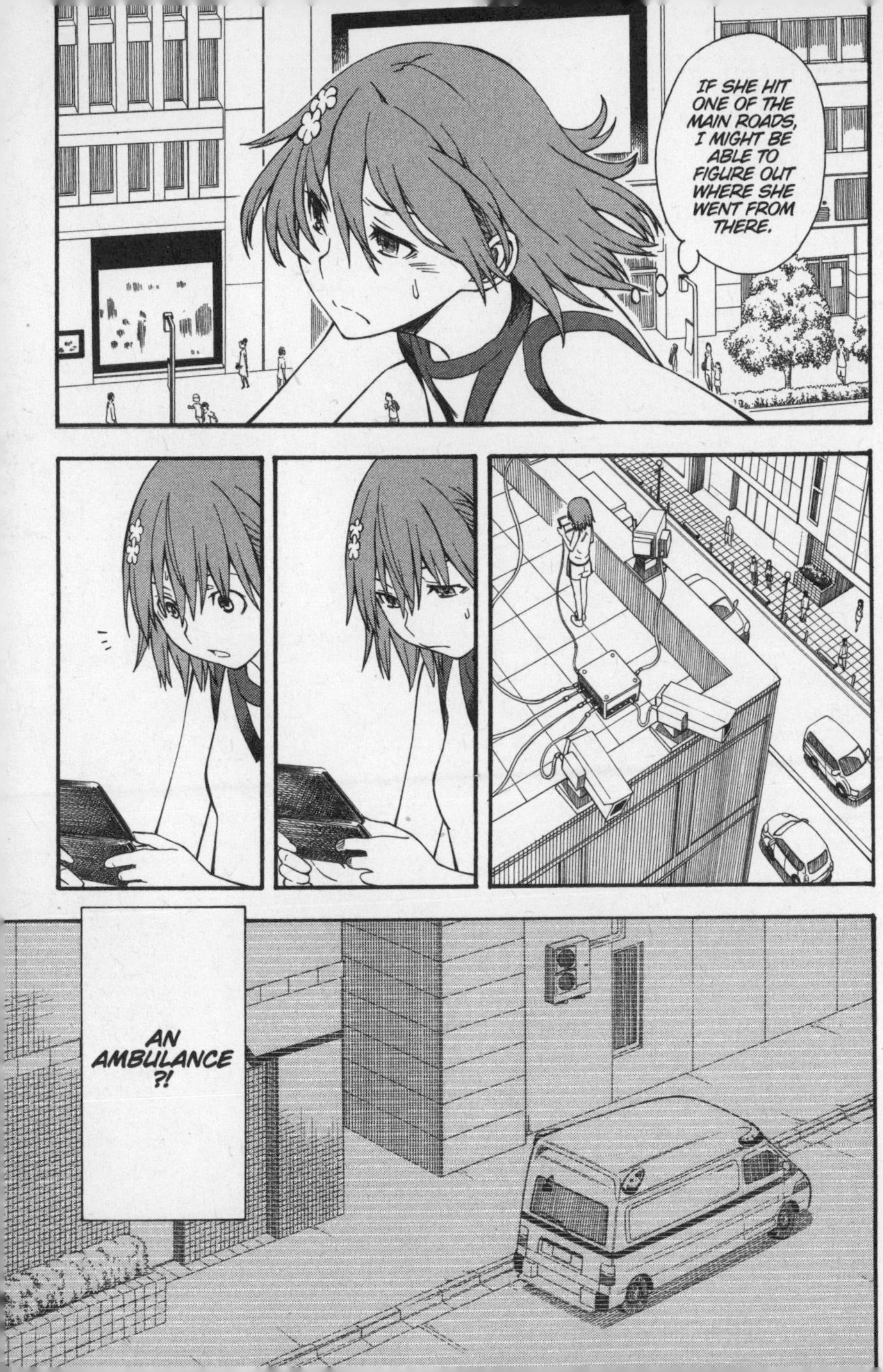
IF SHE HIT ONE OF THE MAIN ROADS, I MIGHT BE ABLE TO FIGURE OUT WHERE SHE WENT FROM THERE.
AN AMBULANCE ?!

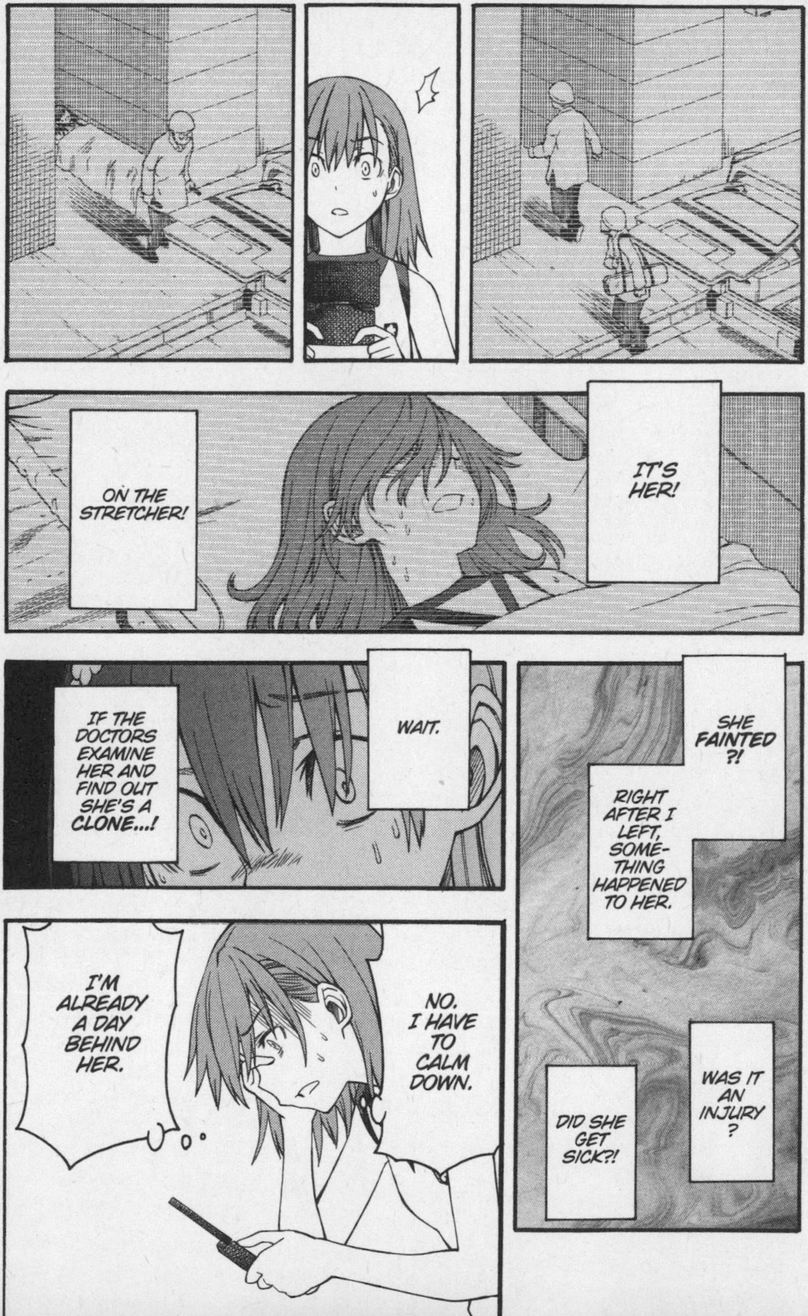
IT'S HER!
ON THE STRETCHER!
SHE FAINTED?!
RIGHT AFTER I LEFT, SOMETHING HAPPENED TO HER.
WAS IT AN INJURY?
DID SHE GET SICK?!
WAIT.
IF THE DOCTORS EXAMINE HER AND FIND OUT SHE'S A CLONE...!
NO. I HAVE TO CALM DOWN.
I'M ALREADY A DAY BEHIND HER.

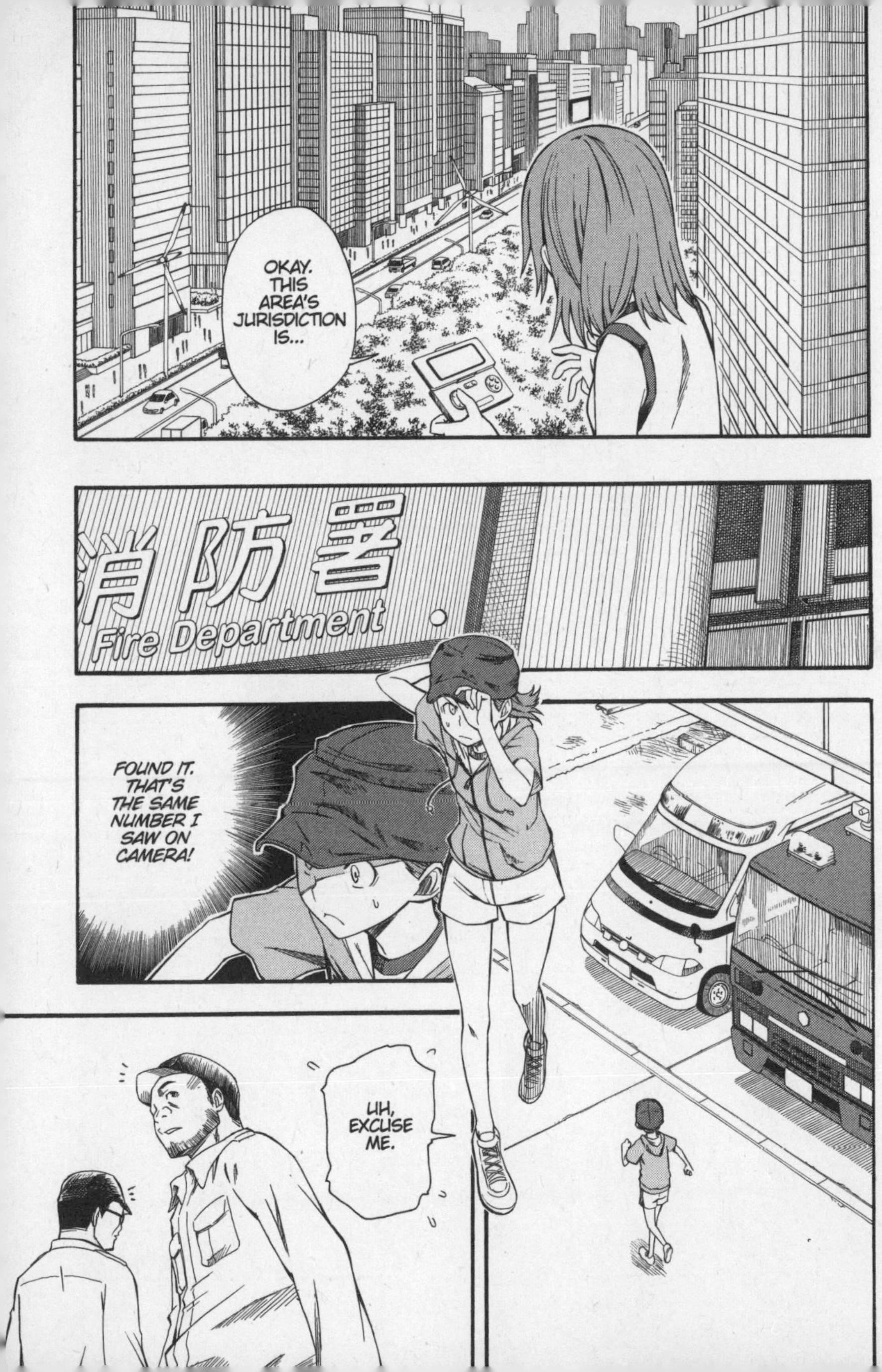
OKAY. THIS AREA'S JURISDICTION IS...
消防署
Fire Department
FOUND IT. THAT'S THE SAME NUMBER I SAW ON CAMERA!
UH, EXCUSE ME.

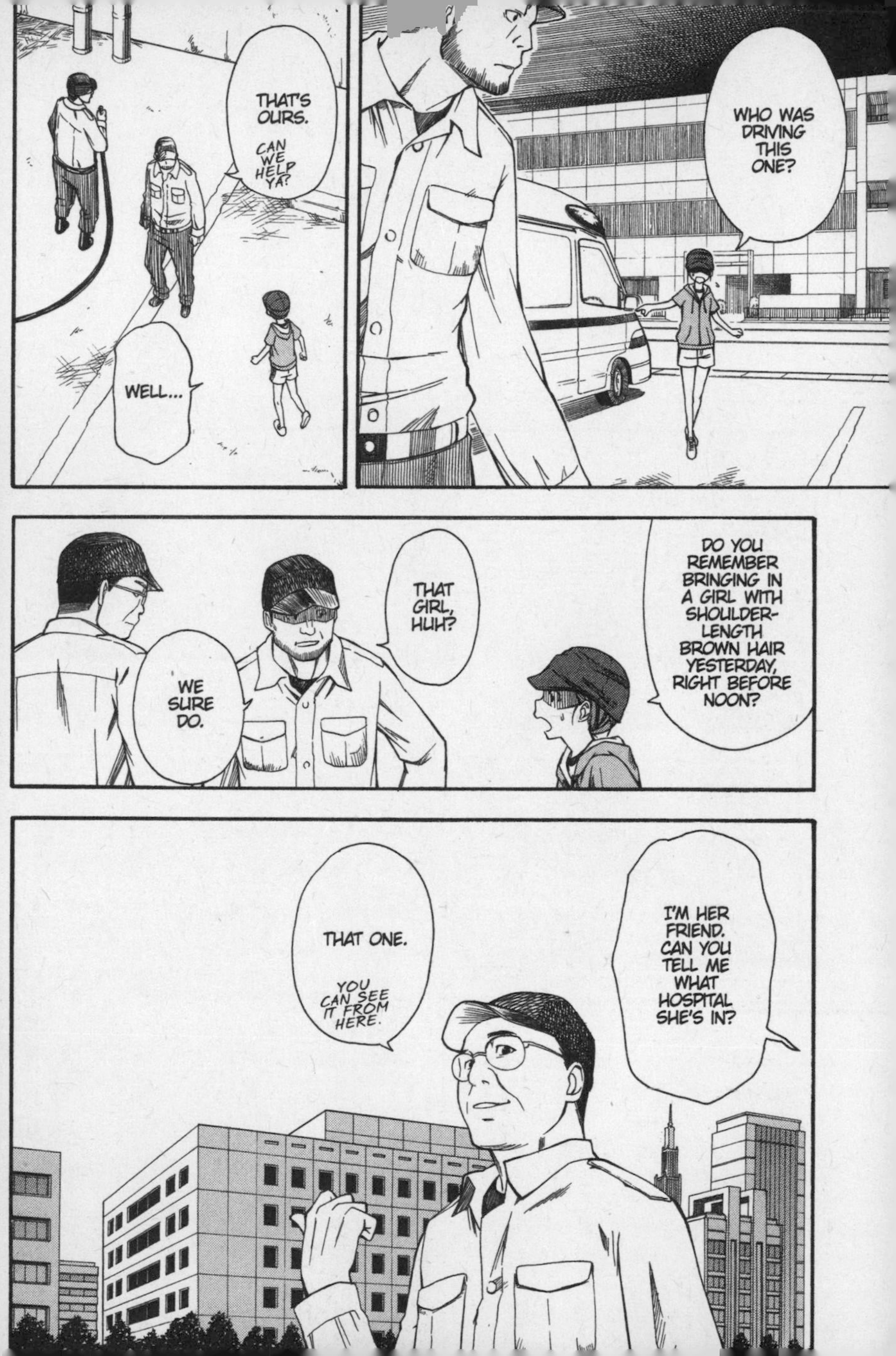
WHO WAS DRIVING THIS ONE?
THAT'S OURS.
CAN WE HELP YA?
WELL...
DO YOU REMEMBER BRINGING IN A GIRL WITH SHOULDER-LENGTH BROWN HAIR YESTERDAY, RIGHT BEFORE NOON?
THAT GIRL, HUH?
WE SURE DO.
I'M HER FRIEND. CAN YOU TELL ME WHAT HOSPITAL SHE'S IN?
THAT ONE.
YOU CAN SEE IT FROM HERE.

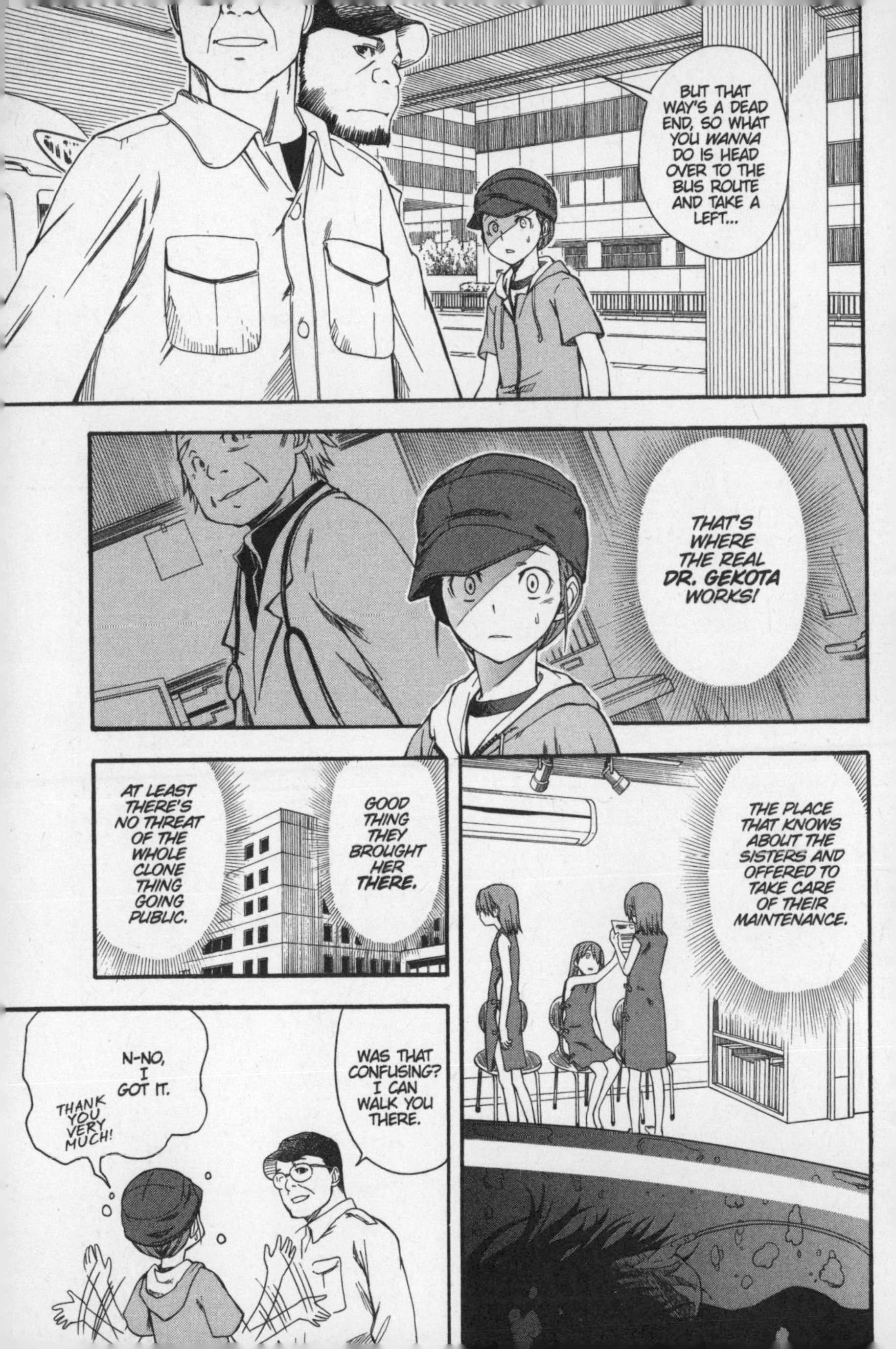
BUT THAT WAY'S A DEAD END, SO WHAT YOU WANNA DO IS HEAD OVER TO THE BUS ROUTE AND TAKE A LEFT...
THAT'S WHERE THE REAL DR. GEKOTA WORKS!
THE PLACE THAT KNOWS ABOUT THE SISTERS AND OFFERED TO TAKE CARE OF THEIR MAINTENANCE.
GOOD THING THEY BROUGHT HER THERE.
AT LEAST THERE'S NO THREAT OF THE WHOLE CLONE THING GOING PUBLIC.
WAS THAT CONFUSING? I CAN WALK YOU THERE.
N-NO, I GOT IT.
THANK YOU VERY MUCH!

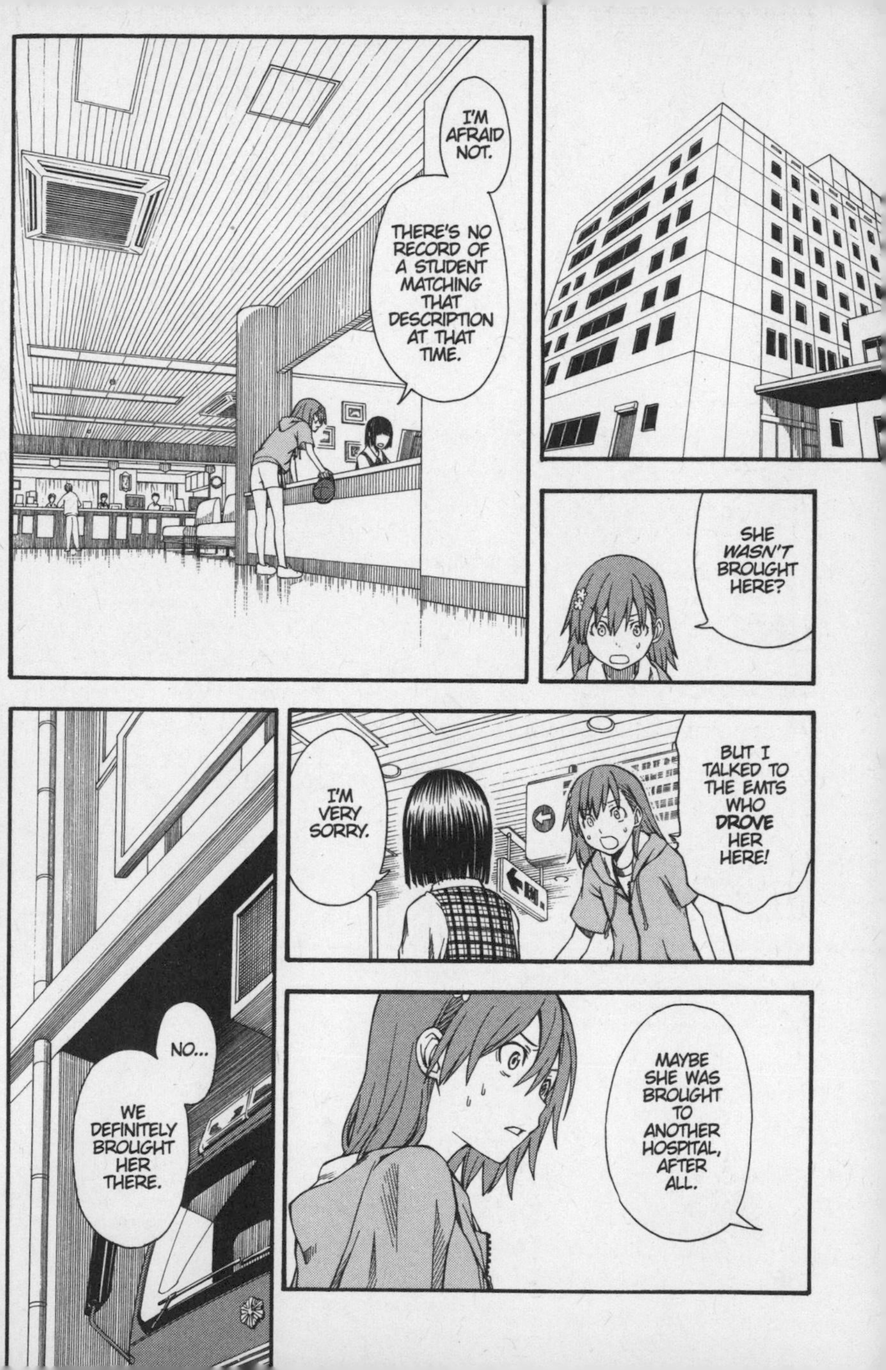
SHE *WASN'T* BROUGHT HERE?
I'M AFRAID NOT.
THERE'S NO RECORD OF A STUDENT MATCHING THAT DESCRIPTION AT THAT TIME.
BUT I TALKED TO THE EMTS WHO **DROVE** HER HERE!
I'M VERY SORRY.
MAYBE SHE WAS BROUGHT TO ANOTHER HOSPITAL, AFTER ALL.
NO...
WE DEFINITELY BROUGHT HER THERE.

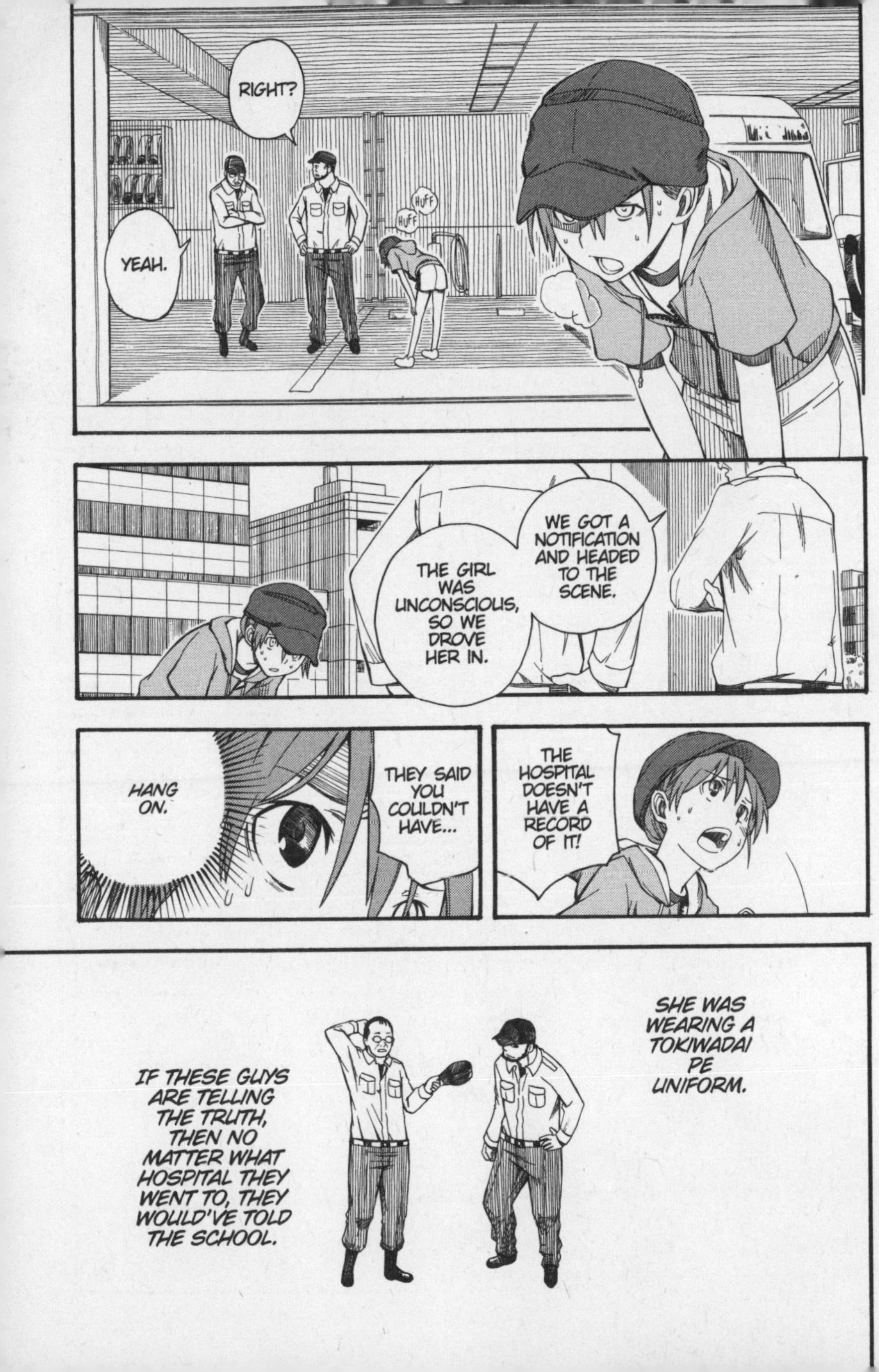
RIGHT?
HUFF
HUFF
YEAH.
WE GOT A NOTIFICATION AND HEADED TO THE SCENE.
THE GIRL WAS UNCONSCIOUS, SO WE DROVE HER IN.
THE HOSPITAL DOESN'T HAVE A RECORD OF IT!
THEY SAID YOU COULDN'T HAVE...
HANG ON.
SHE WAS WEARING A TOKIWADAI PE UNIFORM.
IF THESE GUYS ARE TELLING THE TRUTH, THEN NO MATTER WHAT HOSPITAL THEY WENT TO, THEY WOULD'VE TOLD THE SCHOOL.

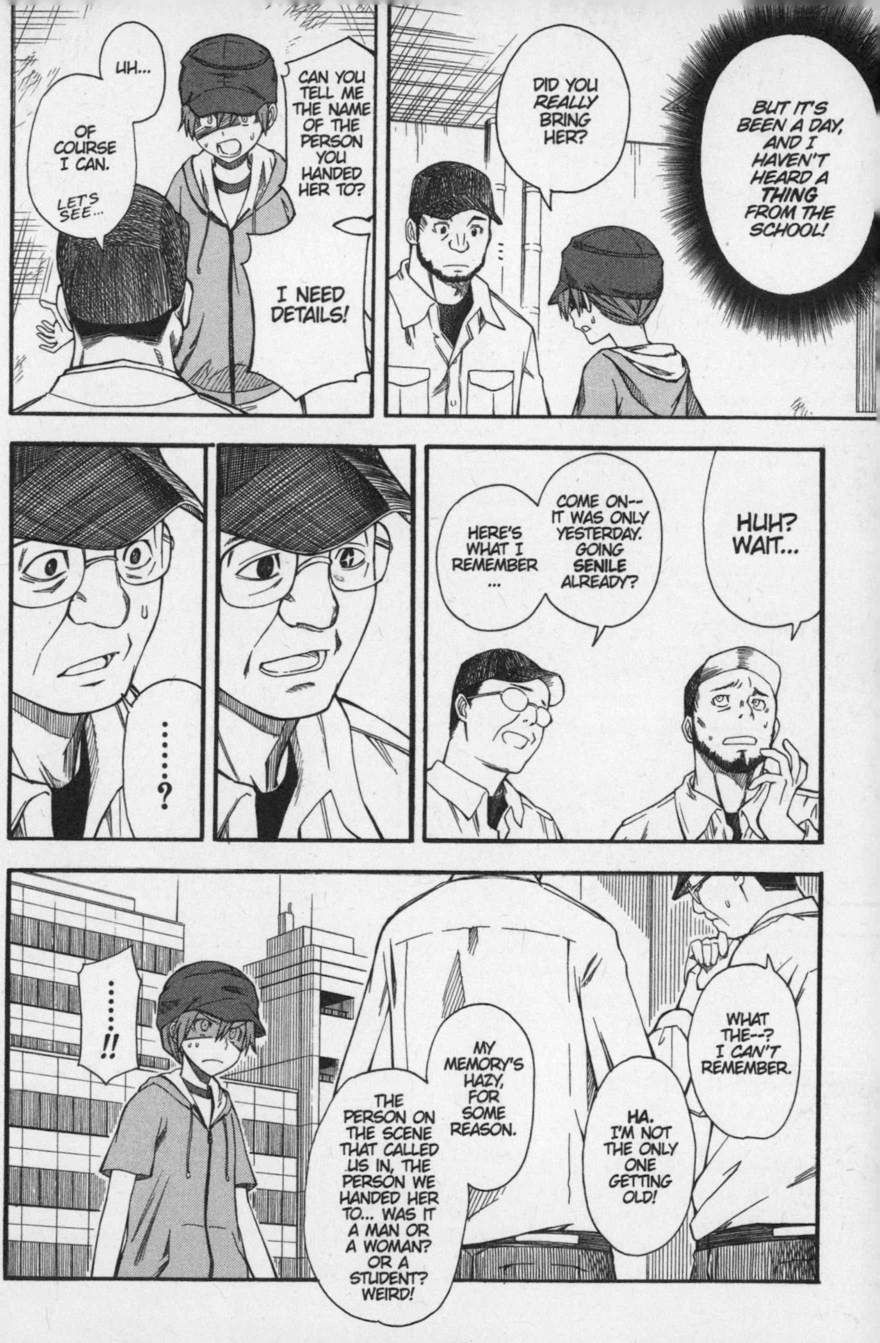
BUT IT'S BEEN A DAY, AND I HAVEN'T HEARD A THING FROM THE SCHOOL!
DID YOU REALLY BRING HER?
...
CAN YOU TELL ME THE NAME OF THE PERSON YOU HANDED HER TO?
I NEED DETAILS!
UH...
OF COURSE I CAN.
LET'S SEE...
HUH? WAIT...
COME ON-- IT WAS ONLY YESTERDAY. GOING SENILE ALREADY?
HERE'S WHAT I REMEMBER ...
......?
WHAT THE--? I CAN'T REMEMBER.
HA. I'M NOT THE ONLY ONE GETTING OLD!
MY MEMORY'S HAZY, FOR SOME REASON.
THE PERSON ON THE SCENE THAT CALLED US IN, THE PERSON WE HANDED HER TO... WAS IT A MAN OR A WOMAN? OR A STUDENT? WEIRD!
......!!

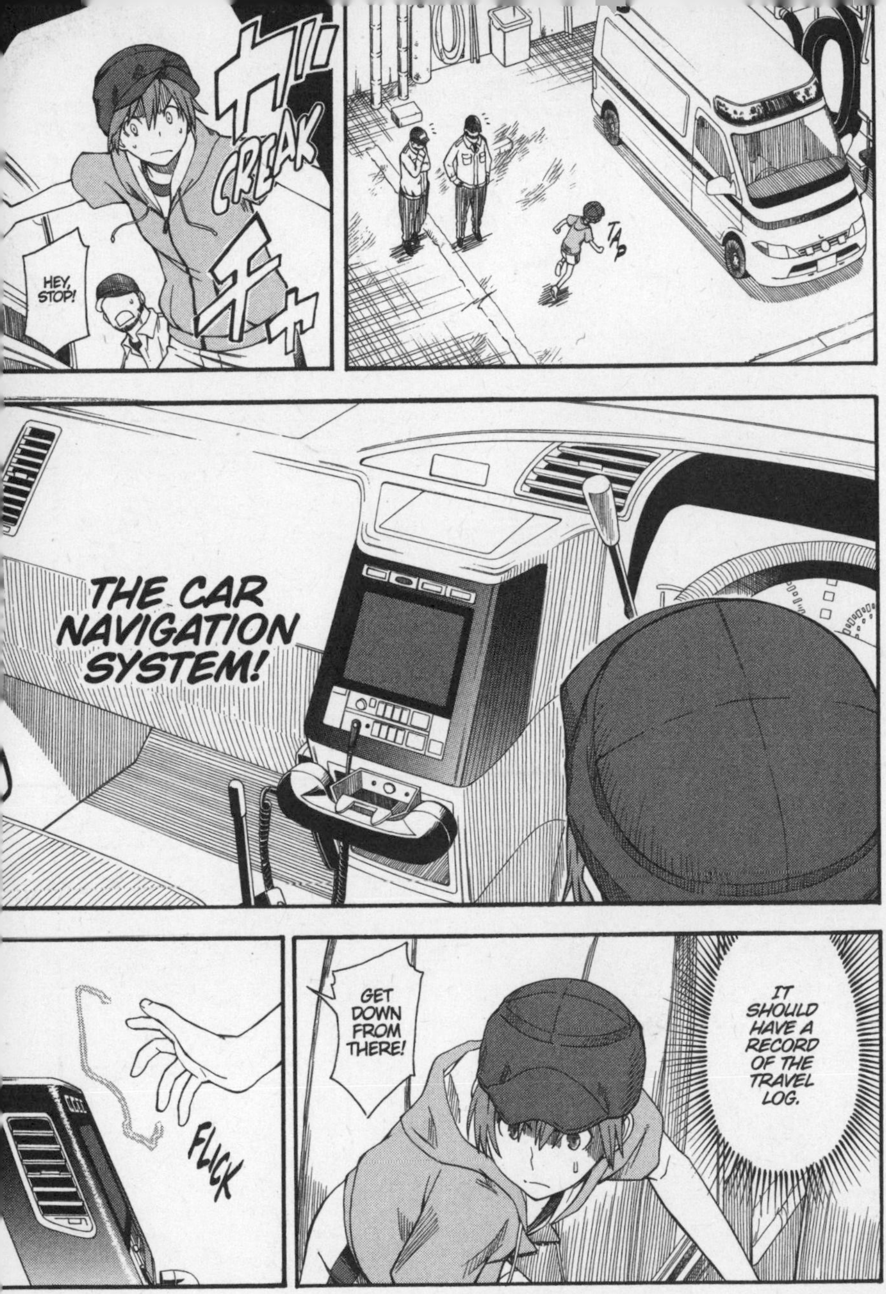
TAP
CREAK
HEY, STOP!
THE CAR NAVIGATION SYSTEM!
IT SHOULD HAVE A RECORD OF THE TRAVEL LOG.
GET DOWN FROM THERE!
FLICK

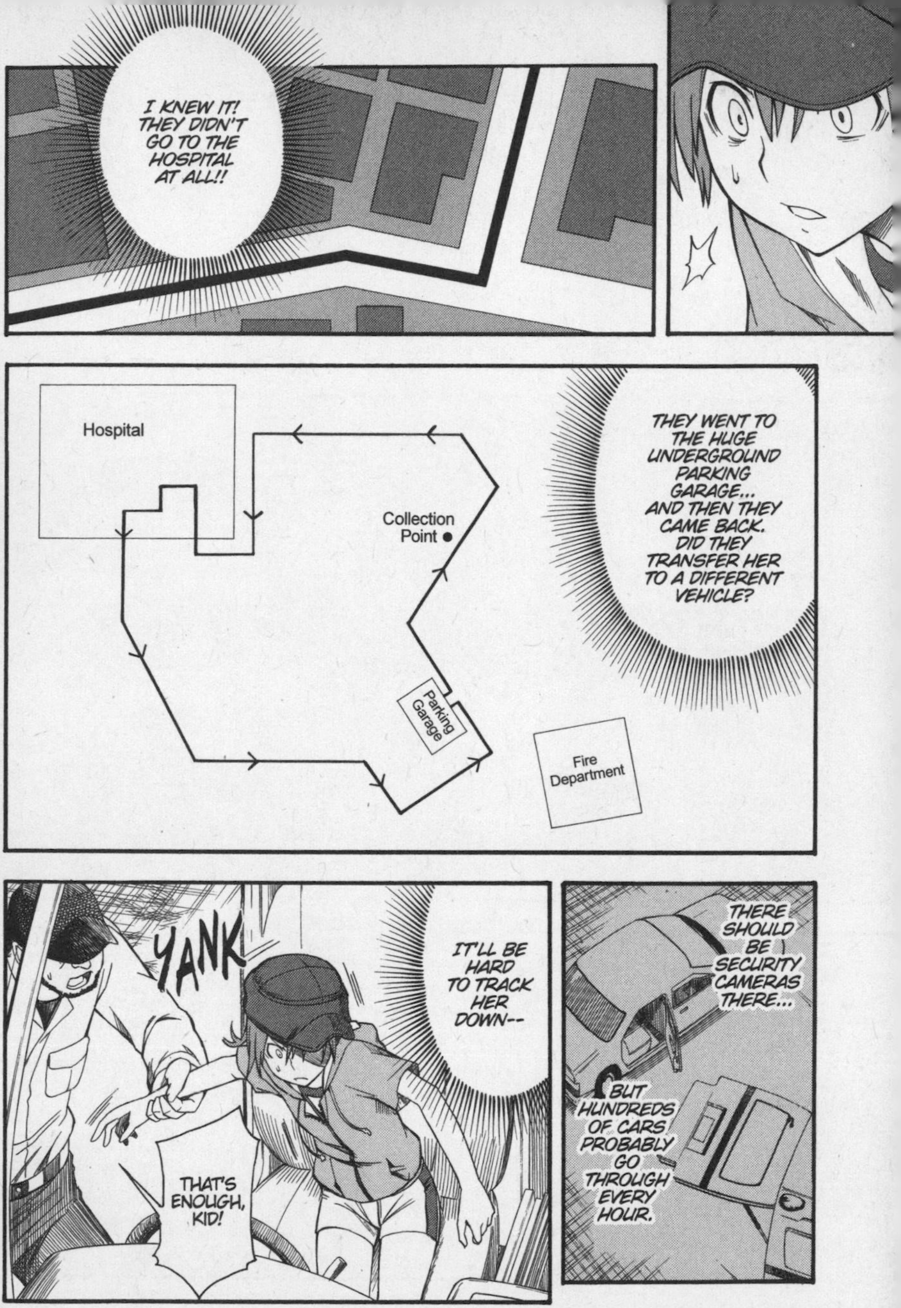
I KNEW IT! THEY DIDN'T GO TO THE HOSPITAL AT ALL!!
THEY WENT TO THE HUGE UNDERGROUND PARKING GARAGE... AND THEN THEY CAME BACK. DID THEY TRANSFER HER TO A DIFFERENT VEHICLE?
Hospital
Collection Point
Parking Garage
Fire Department
THERE SHOULD BE SECURITY CAMERAS THERE...
BUT HUNDREDS OF CARS PROBABLY GO THROUGH EVERY HOUR.
IT'LL BE HARD TO TRACK HER DOWN--
YANK
THAT'S ENOUGH, KID!

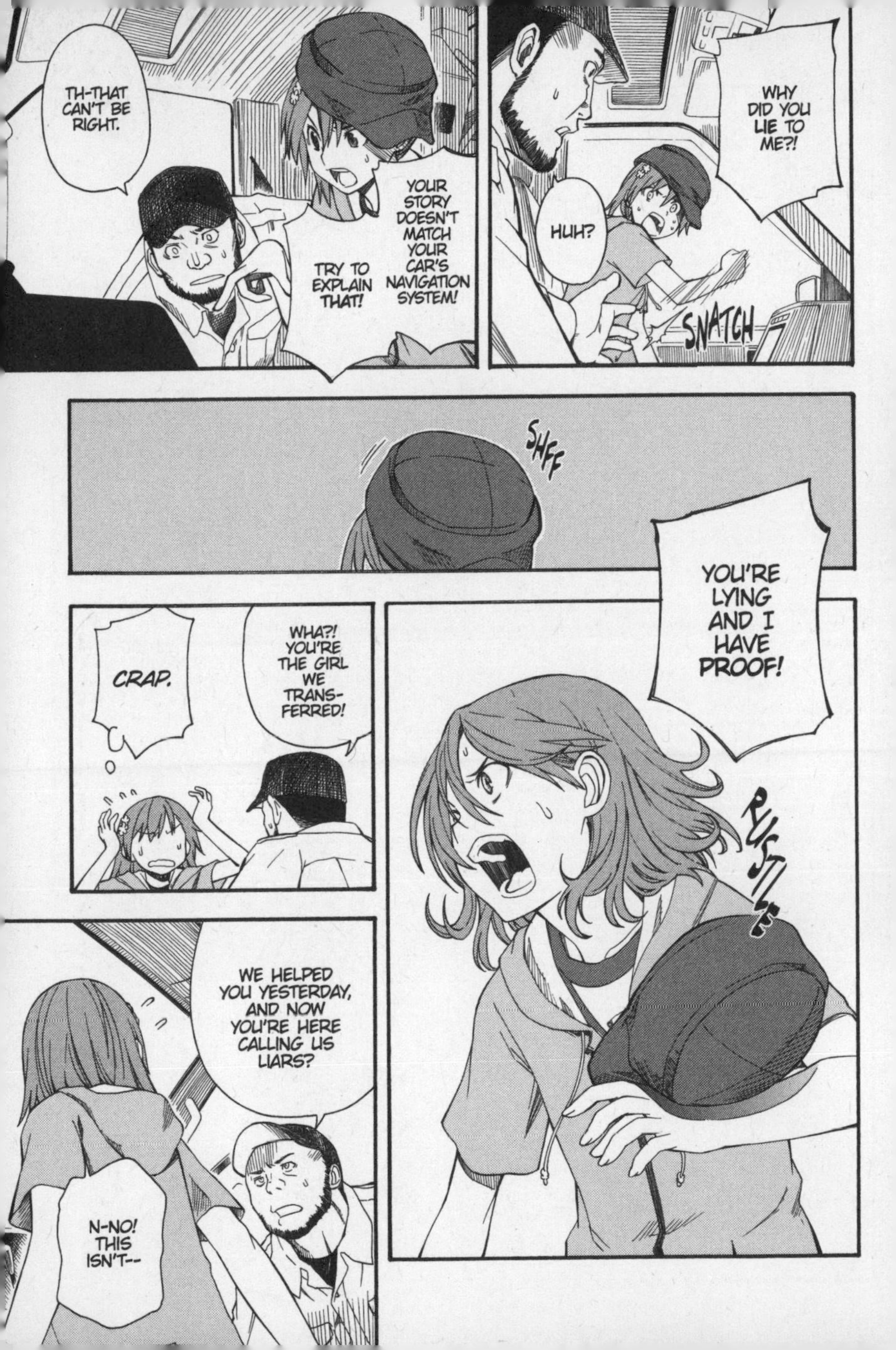
WHY DID YOU LIE TO ME?!
HUH?
SNATCH
YOUR STORY DOESN'T MATCH YOUR CAR'S NAVIGATION SYSTEM!
TRY TO EXPLAIN THAT!
TH-THAT CAN'T BE RIGHT.
SHFF
YOU'RE LYING AND I HAVE PROOF!
RUSTLE
WHA?! YOU'RE THE GIRL WE TRANS-FERRED!
CRAP.
WE HELPED YOU YESTERDAY, AND NOW YOU'RE HERE CALLING US LIARS?
N-NO! THIS ISN'T--

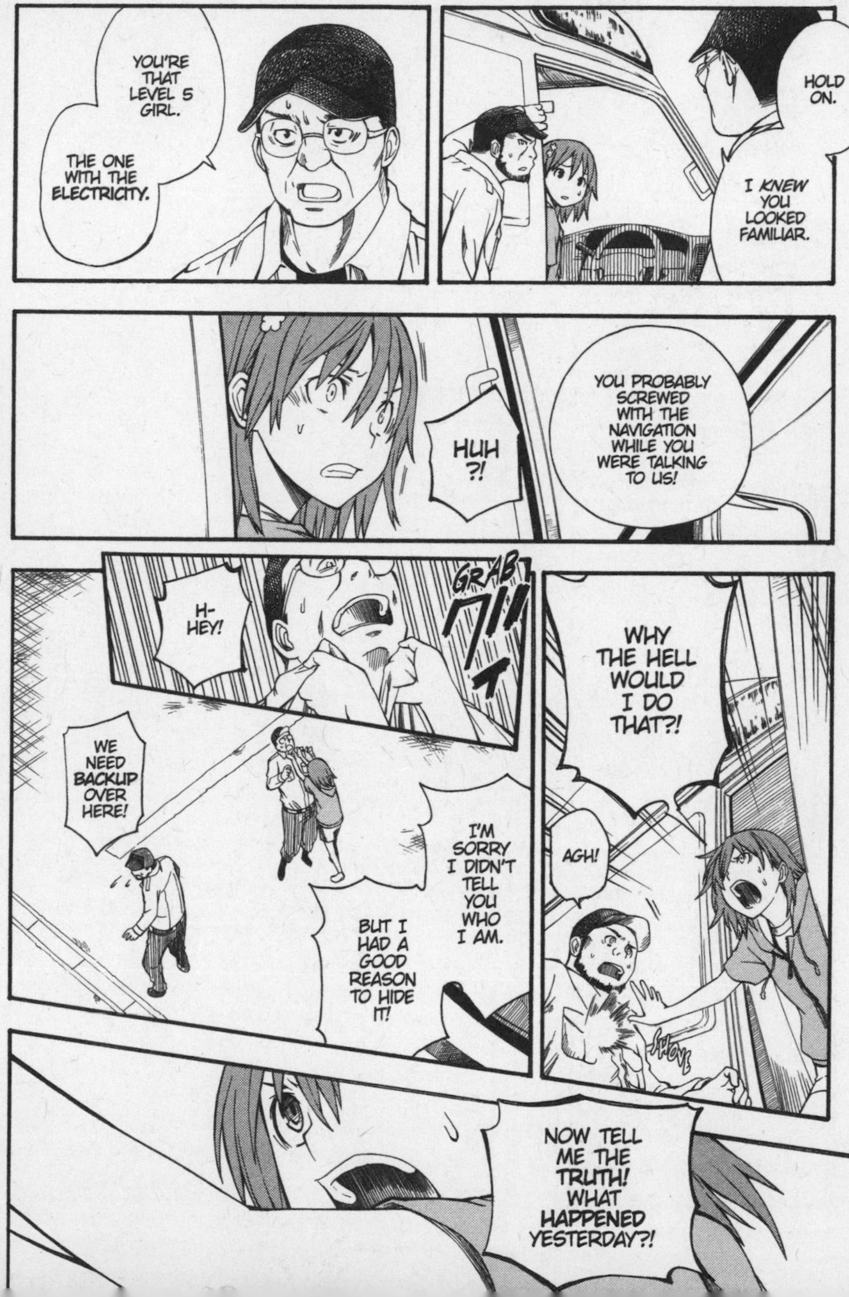
HOLD ON.
I *KNEW* YOU LOOKED FAMILIAR.
YOU'RE THAT LEVEL 5 GIRL.
THE ONE WITH THE ELECTRICITY.
YOU PROBABLY SCREWED WITH THE NAVIGATION WHILE YOU WERE TALKING TO US!
HUH?!
WHY THE HELL WOULD I DO THAT?!
AGH!
SHOVE
GRAB
H-HEY!
I'M SORRY I DIDN'T TELL YOU WHO I AM.
BUT I HAD A GOOD REASON TO HIDE IT!
WE NEED BACKUP OVER HERE!
NOW TELL ME THE TRUTH! WHAT HAPPENED YESTERDAY?!

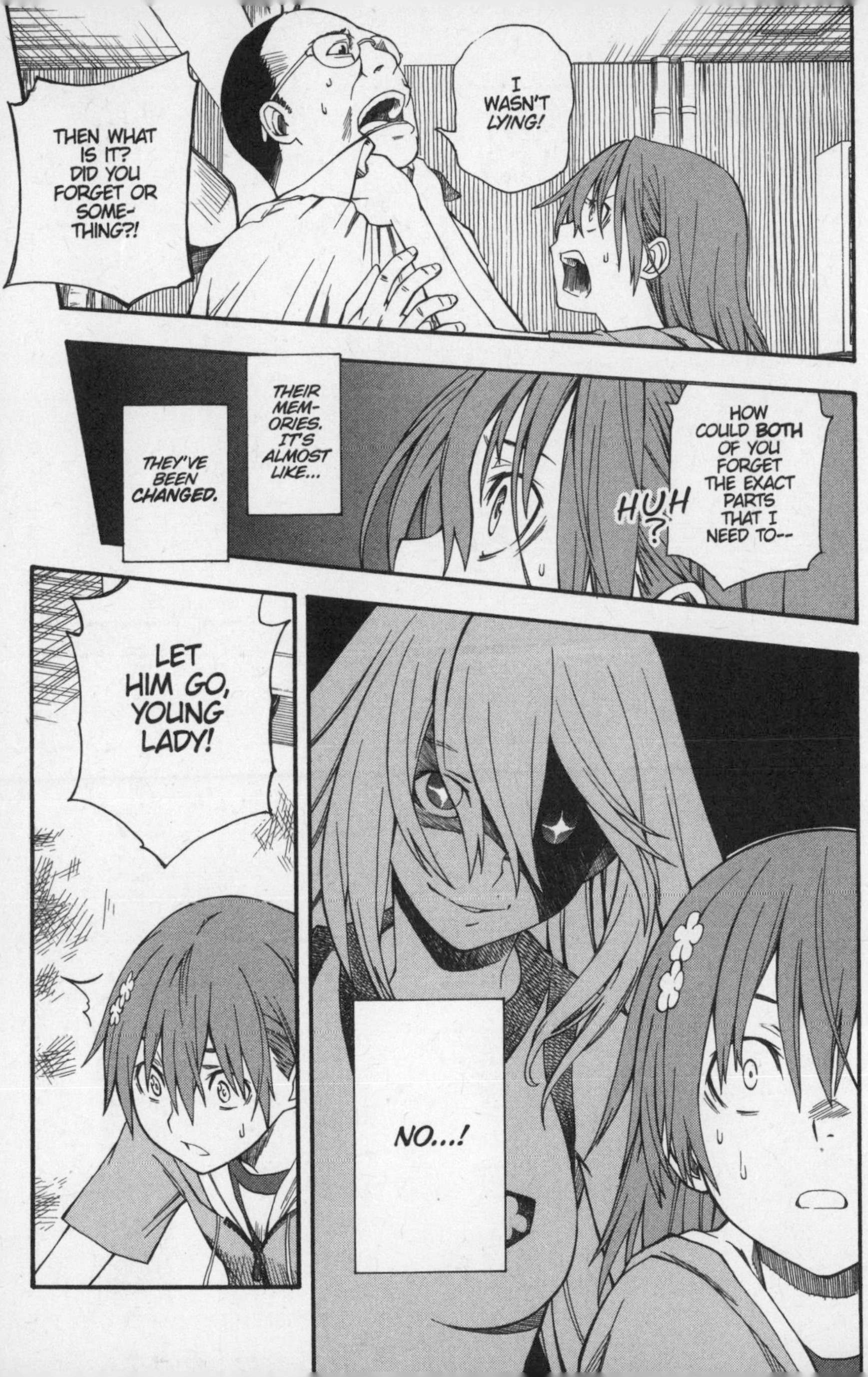

I WASN'T *LYING!*
THEN WHAT IS IT? DID YOU FORGET OR SOME-THING?!
HOW COULD **BOTH** OF YOU FORGET THE EXACT PARTS THAT I NEED TO--
HUH?
THEIR MEM-ORIES. IT'S ALMOST LIKE...
THEY'VE BEEN CHANGED.
NO...!
LET HIM GO, YOUNG LADY!

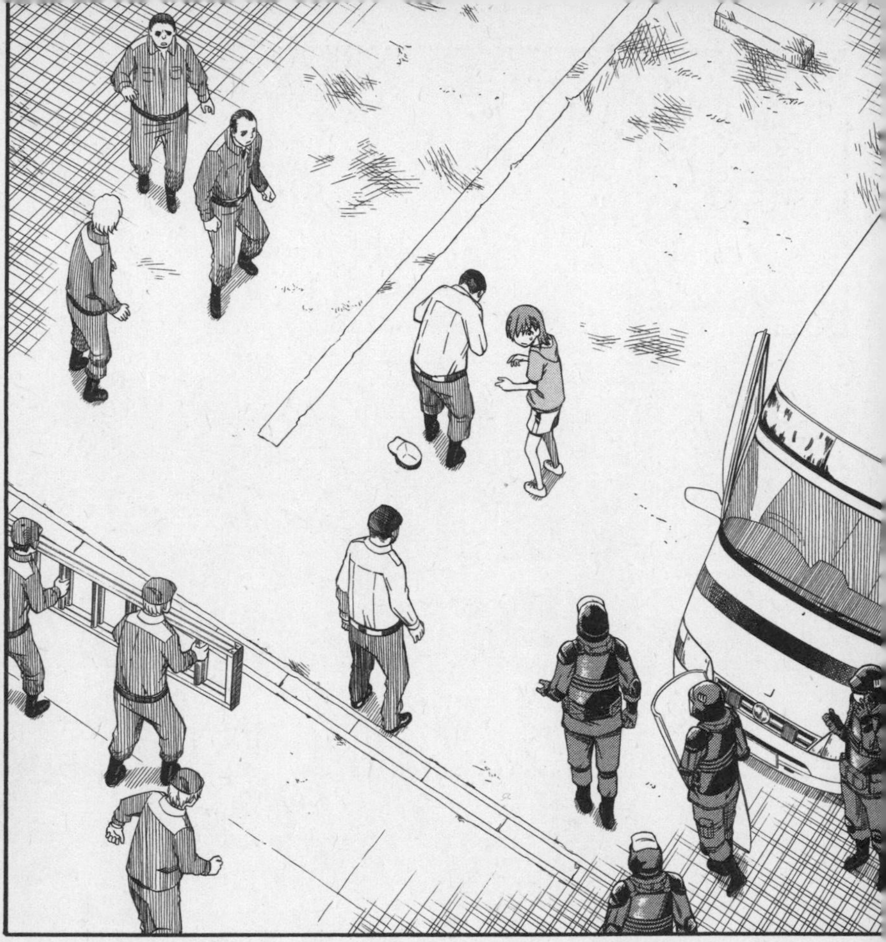
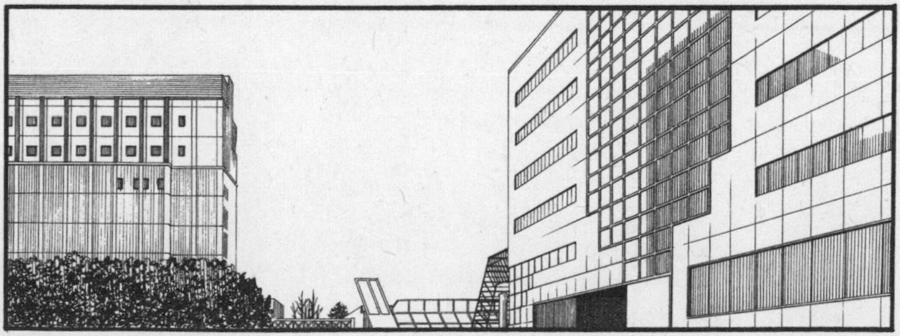

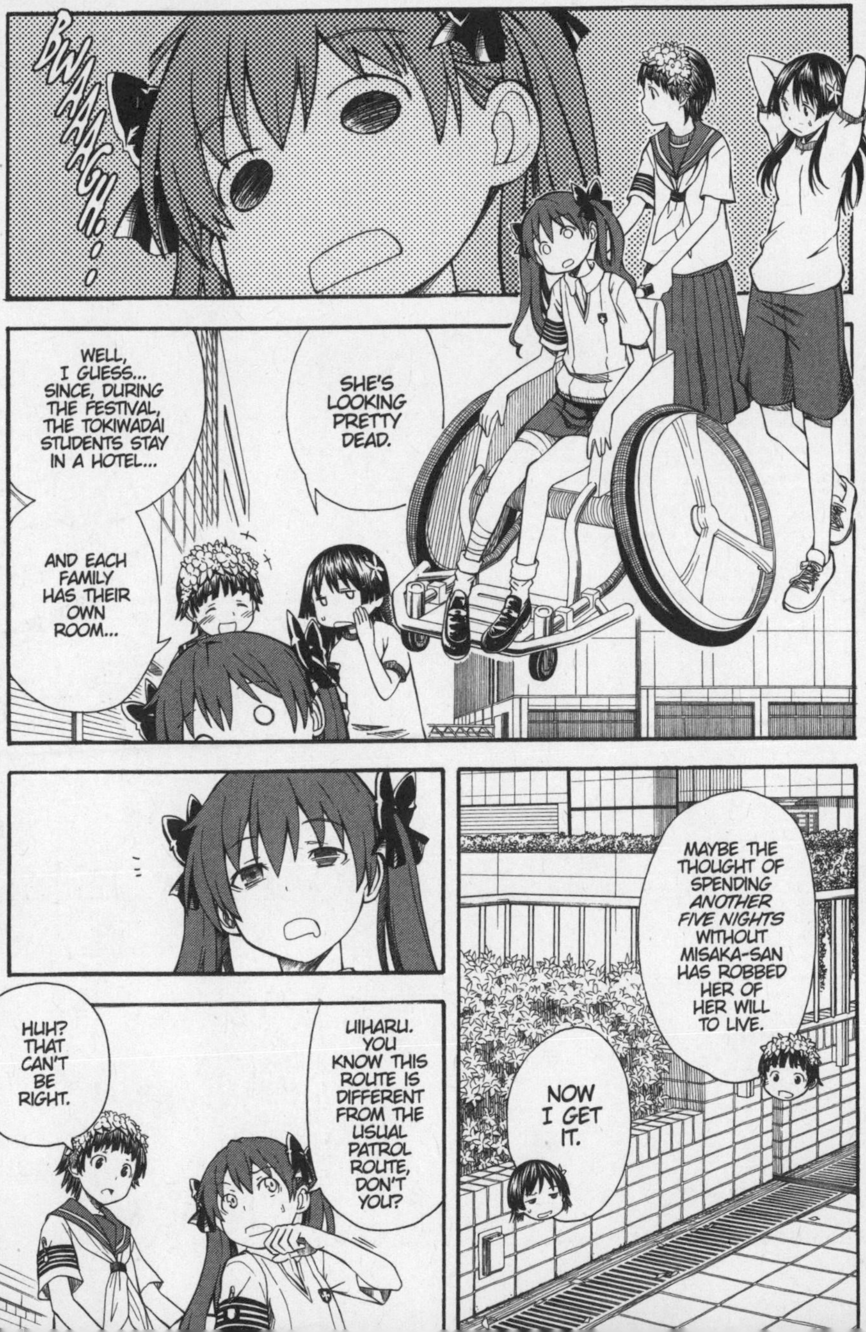
BWAAAGH...
SHE'S LOOKING PRETTY DEAD.
WELL, I GUESS... SINCE, DURING THE FESTIVAL, THE TOKIWADAI STUDENTS STAY IN A HOTEL...
AND EACH FAMILY HAS THEIR OWN ROOM...
MAYBE THE THOUGHT OF SPENDING *ANOTHER FIVE NIGHTS* WITHOUT MISAKA-SAN HAS ROBBED HER OF HER WILL TO LIVE.
NOW I GET IT.
UIHARU. YOU KNOW THIS ROUTE IS DIFFERENT FROM THE USUAL PATROL ROUTE, DON'T YOU?
HUH? THAT CAN'T BE RIGHT.

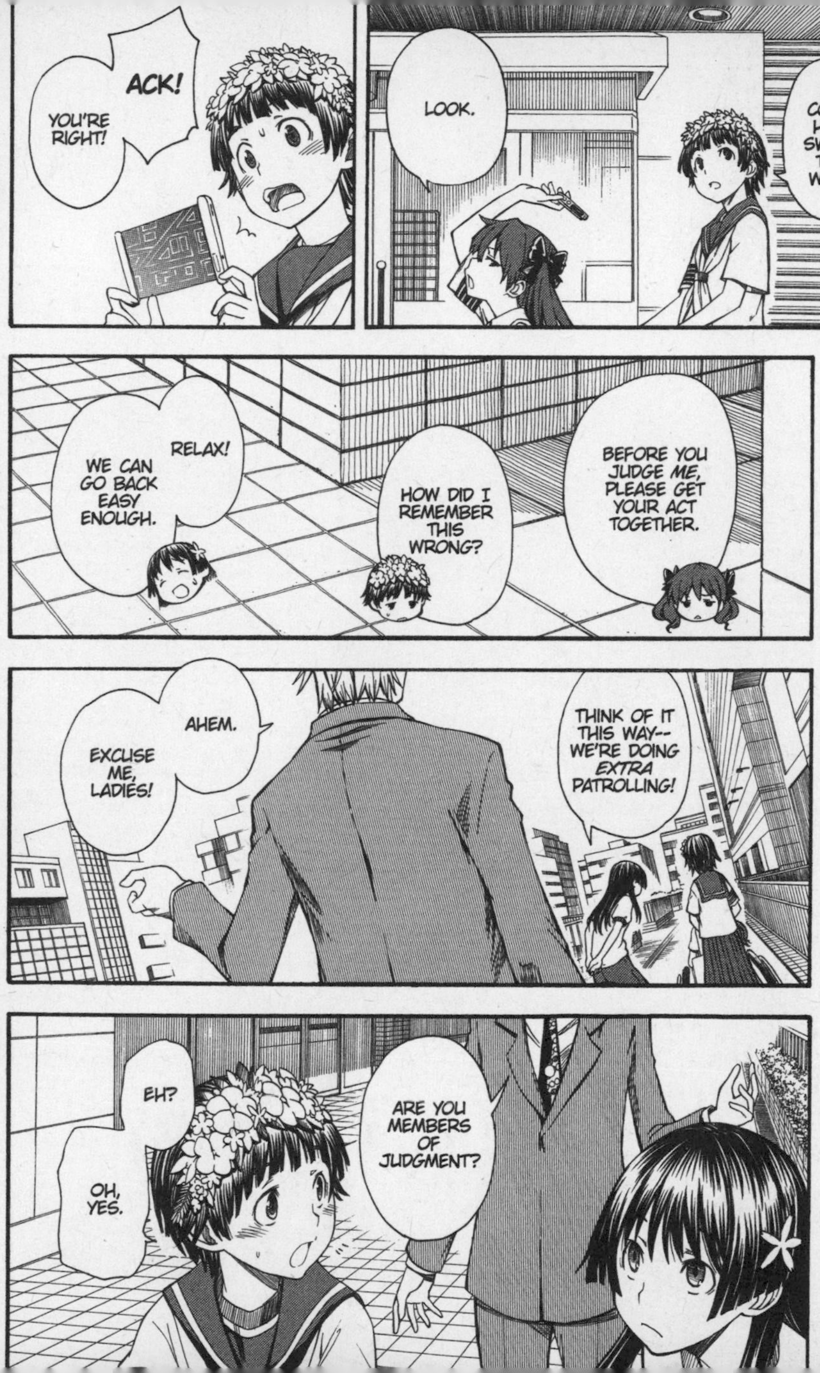
I COULD HAVE SWORN THIS WAS...
LOOK.
ACK!
YOU'RE RIGHT!
BEFORE YOU JUDGE *ME*, PLEASE GET YOUR ACT TOGETHER.
HOW DID I REMEMBER THIS WRONG?
RELAX!
WE CAN GO BACK EASY ENOUGH.
THINK OF IT THIS WAY-- WE'RE DOING *EXTRA* PATROLLING!
AHEM.
EXCUSE ME, LADIES!
ARE YOU MEMBERS OF JUDGMENT?
EH?
OH, YES.

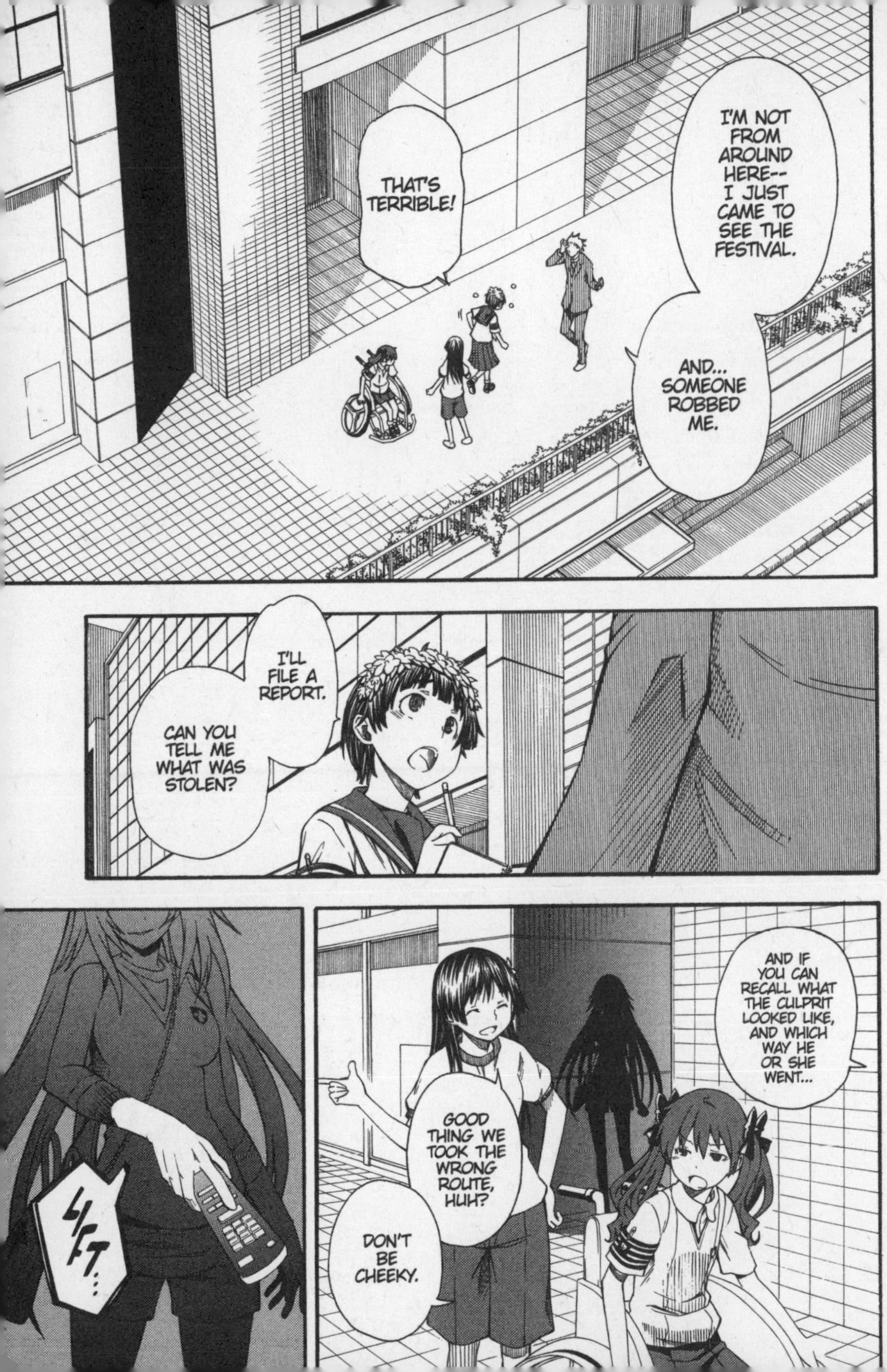
I'M NOT FROM AROUND HERE-- I JUST CAME TO SEE THE FESTIVAL.
AND... SOMEONE ROBBED ME.
THAT'S TERRIBLE!
I'LL FILE A REPORT.
CAN YOU TELL ME WHAT WAS STOLEN?
AND IF YOU CAN RECALL WHAT THE CULPRIT LOOKED LIKE, AND WHICH WAY HE OR SHE WENT...
GOOD THING WE TOOK THE WRONG ROUTE, HUH?
DON'T BE CHEEKY.
LIFT...

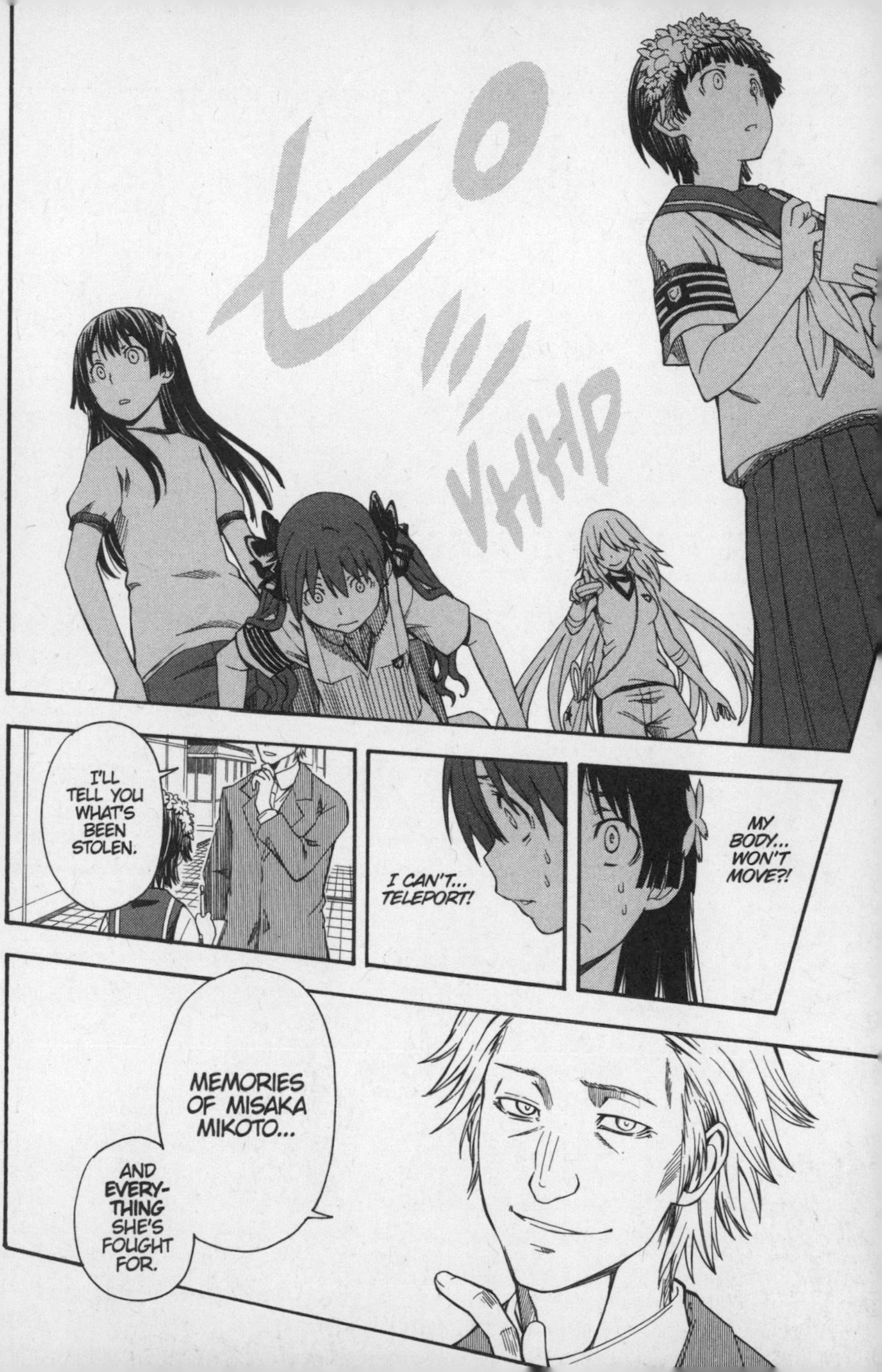
VHHP
MY BODY... WON'T MOVE?!
I CAN'T... TELEPORT!
I'LL TELL YOU WHAT'S BEEN STOLEN.
MEMORIES OF MISAKA MIKOTO...
AND EVERYTHING SHE'S FOUGHT FOR.

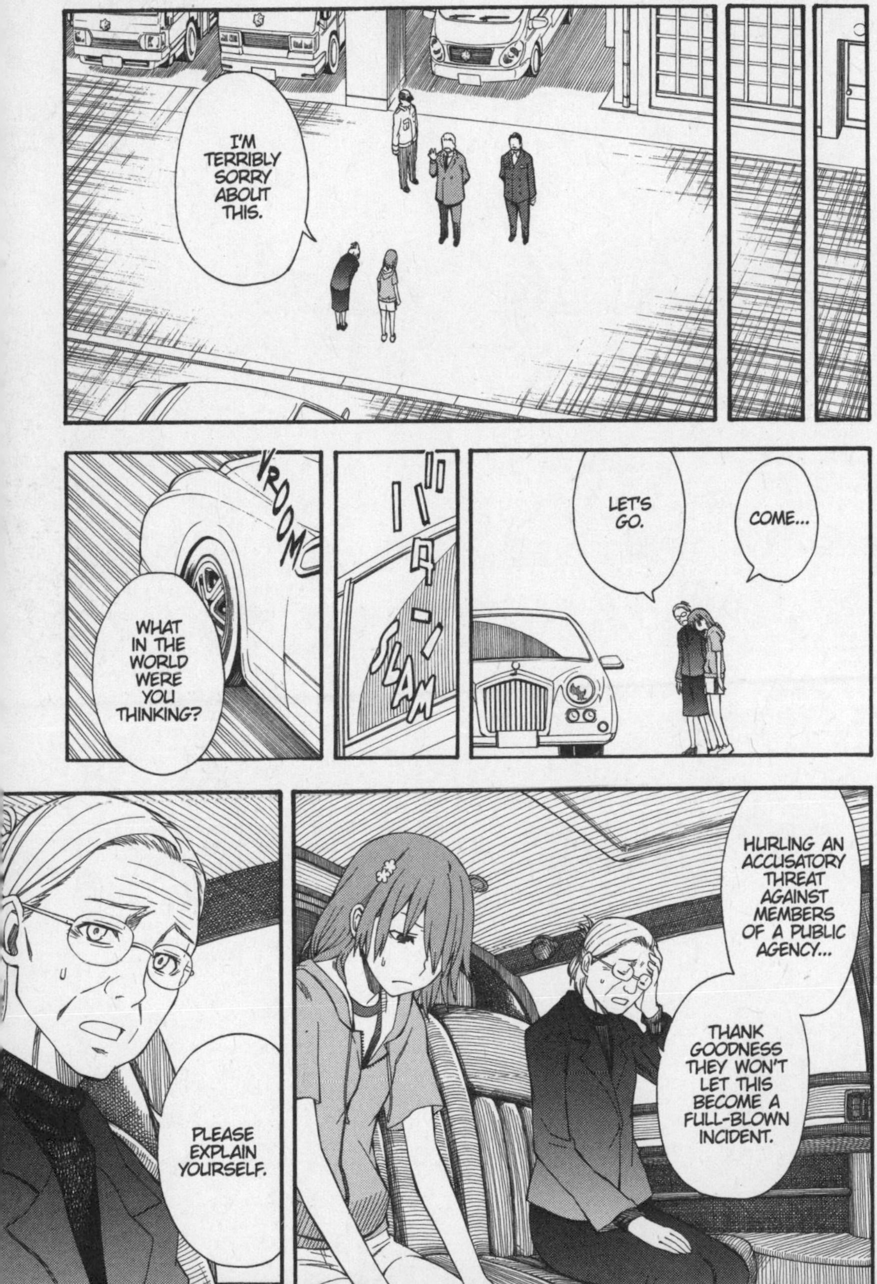
I'M TERRIBLY SORRY ABOUT THIS.
COME...
LET'S GO.
SLAM
VROOM
WHAT IN THE WORLD WERE YOU THINKING?
HURLING AN ACCUSATORY THREAT AGAINST MEMBERS OF A PUBLIC AGENCY...
THANK GOODNESS THEY WON'T LET THIS BECOME A FULL-BLOWN INCIDENT.
PLEASE EXPLAIN YOURSELF.

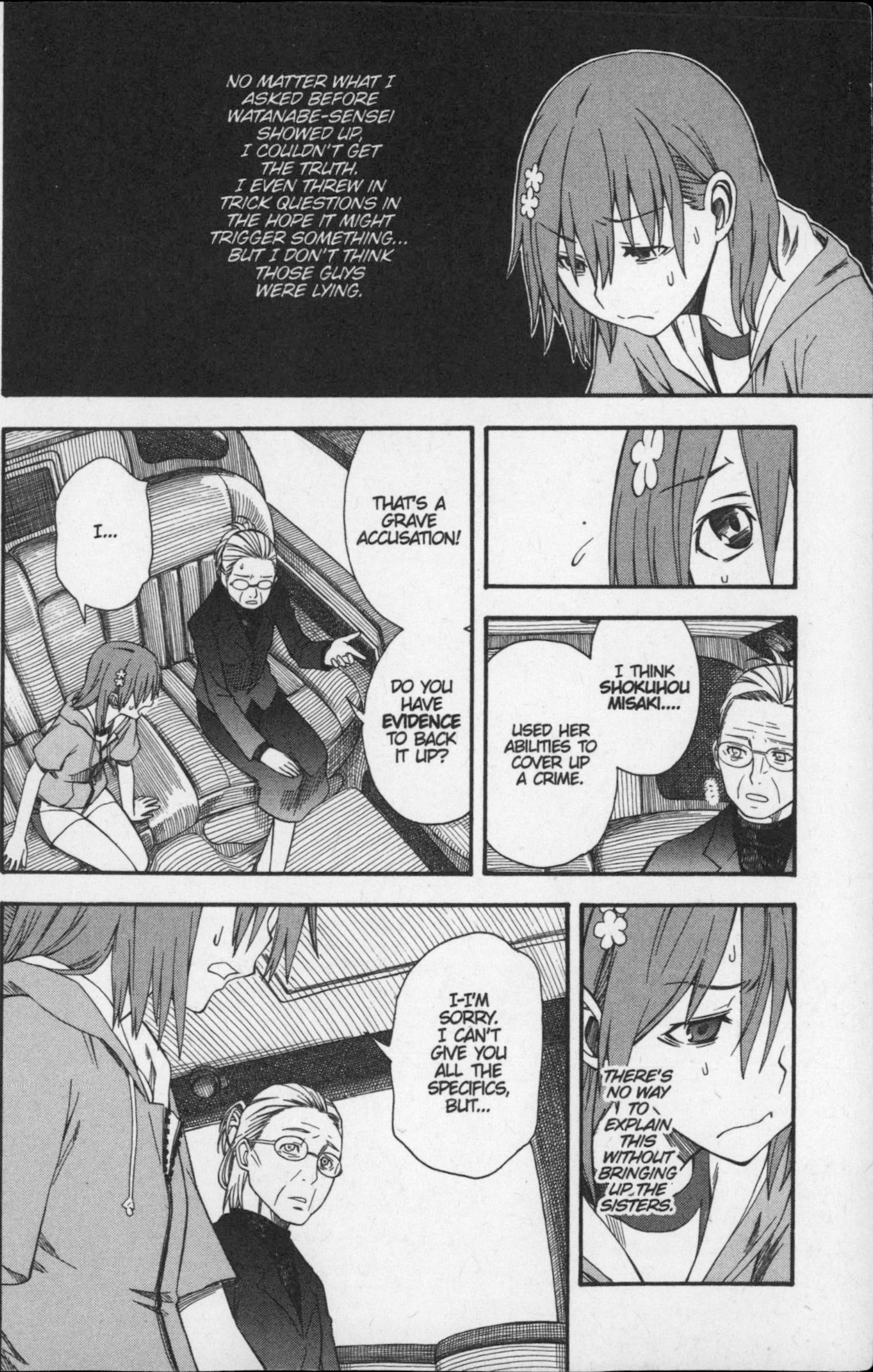
NO MATTER WHAT I ASKED BEFORE WATANABE-SENSEI SHOWED UP, I COULDN'T GET THE TRUTH. I EVEN THREW IN TRICK QUESTIONS IN THE HOPE IT MIGHT TRIGGER SOMETHING... BUT I DON'T THINK THOSE GUYS WERE LYING.
I THINK SHOKUHOU MISAKI....
USED HER ABILITIES TO COVER UP A CRIME.
THAT'S A GRAVE ACCUSATION!
DO YOU HAVE EVIDENCE TO BACK IT UP?
I...
THERE'S NO WAY TO EXPLAIN THIS WITHOUT BRINGING UP THE SISTERS.
I-I'M SORRY. I CAN'T GIVE YOU ALL THE SPECIFICS, BUT...

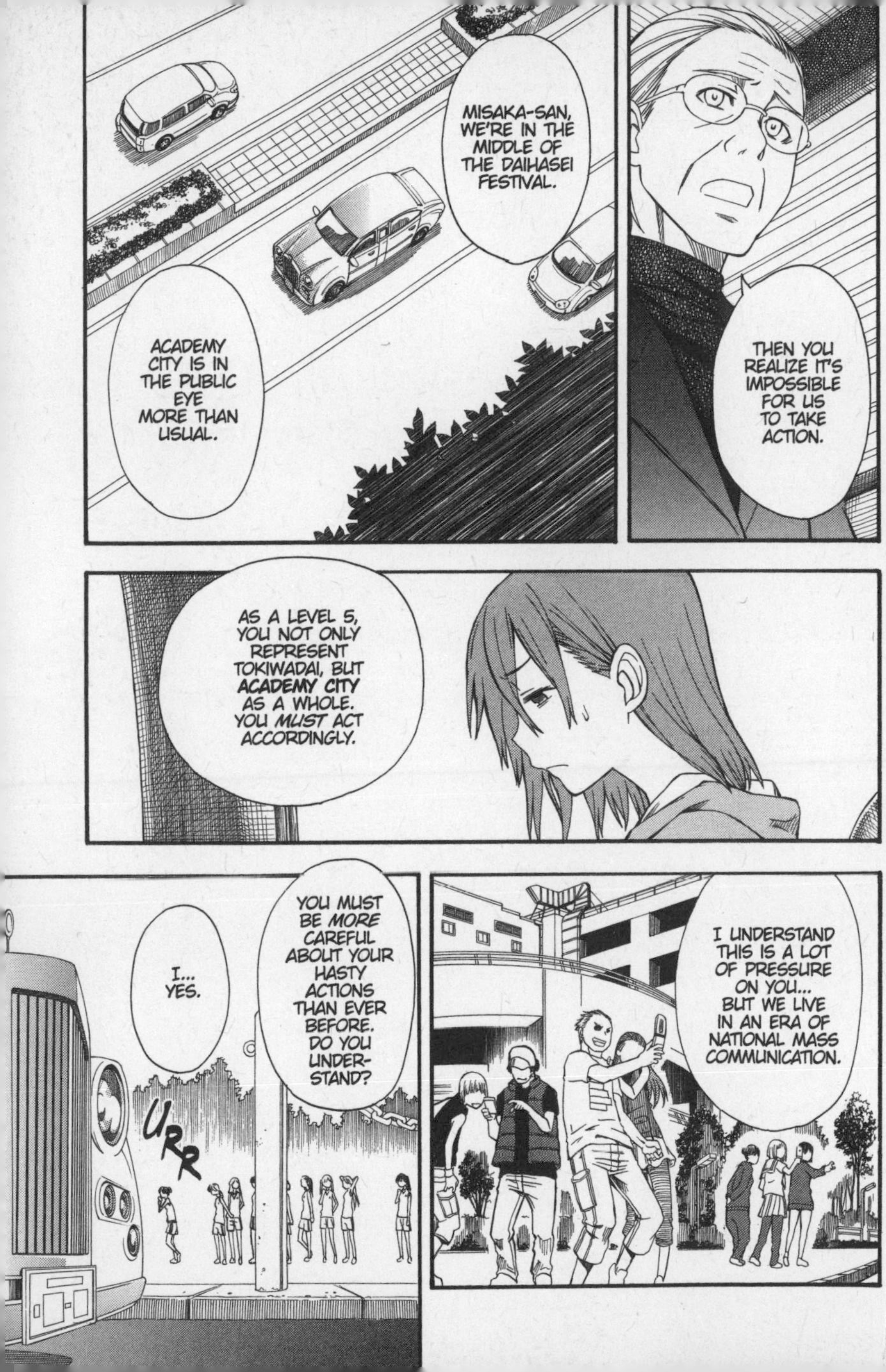
THEN YOU REALIZE IT'S IMPOSSIBLE FOR US TO TAKE ACTION.
MISAKA-SAN, WE'RE IN THE MIDDLE OF THE DAIHASEI FESTIVAL.
ACADEMY CITY IS IN THE PUBLIC EYE MORE THAN USUAL.
AS A LEVEL 5, YOU NOT ONLY REPRESENT TOKIWADAI, BUT **ACADEMY CITY** AS A WHOLE. YOU *MUST* ACT ACCORDINGLY.
I UNDERSTAND THIS IS A LOT OF PRESSURE ON YOU... BUT WE LIVE IN AN ERA OF NATIONAL MASS COMMUNICATION.
YOU MUST BE *MORE* CAREFUL ABOUT YOUR HASTY ACTIONS THAN EVER BEFORE. DO YOU UNDER-STAND?
I... YES.
URR

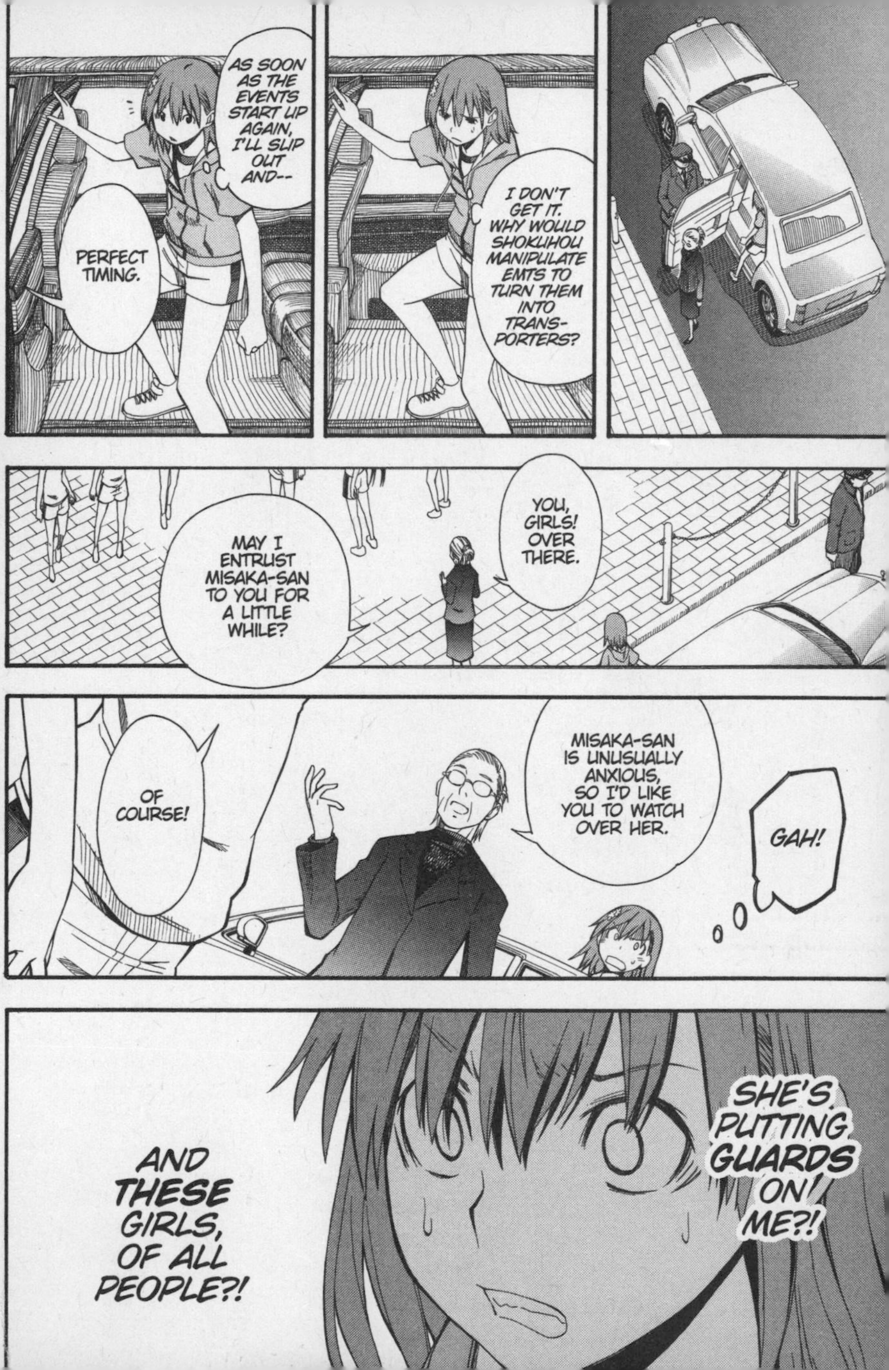
I DON'T GET IT. WHY WOULD SHOKUHOU MANIPULATE EMTS TO TURN THEM INTO TRANS-PORTERS?
AS SOON AS THE EVENTS START UP AGAIN, I'LL SLIP OUT AND--
PERFECT TIMING.
YOU, GIRLS! OVER THERE.
MAY I ENTRUST MISAKA-SAN TO YOU FOR A LITTLE WHILE?
MISAKA-SAN IS UNUSUALLY ANXIOUS, SO I'D LIKE YOU TO WATCH OVER HER.
GAH!
OF COURSE!
SHE'S PUTTING GUARDS ON ME?!
AND THESE GIRLS, OF ALL PEOPLE?!

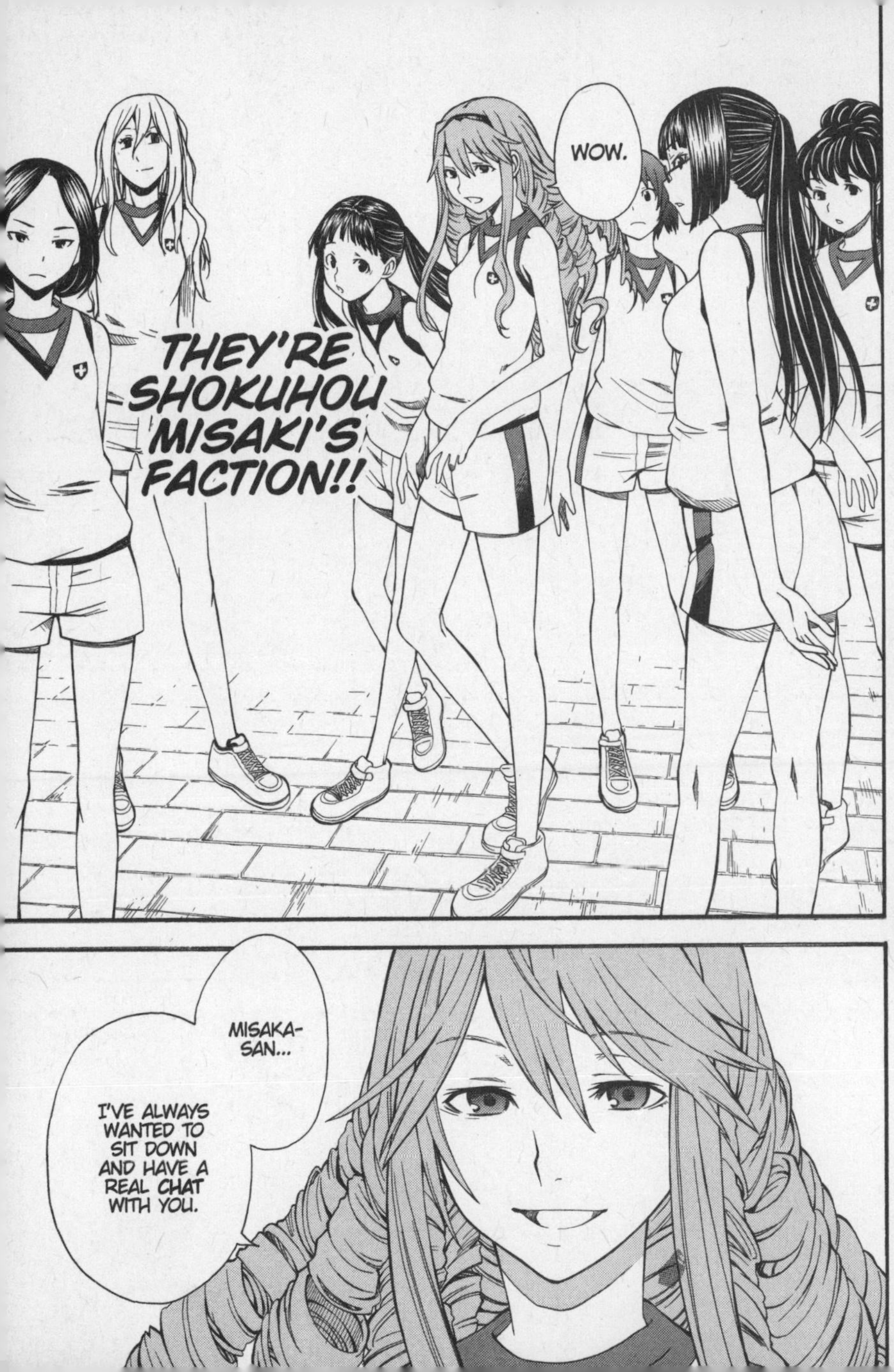
WOW.
THEY'RE SHOKUHOU MISAKI'S FACTION!!
MISAKA-SAN...
I'VE ALWAYS WANTED TO SIT DOWN AND HAVE A REAL CHAT WITH YOU.

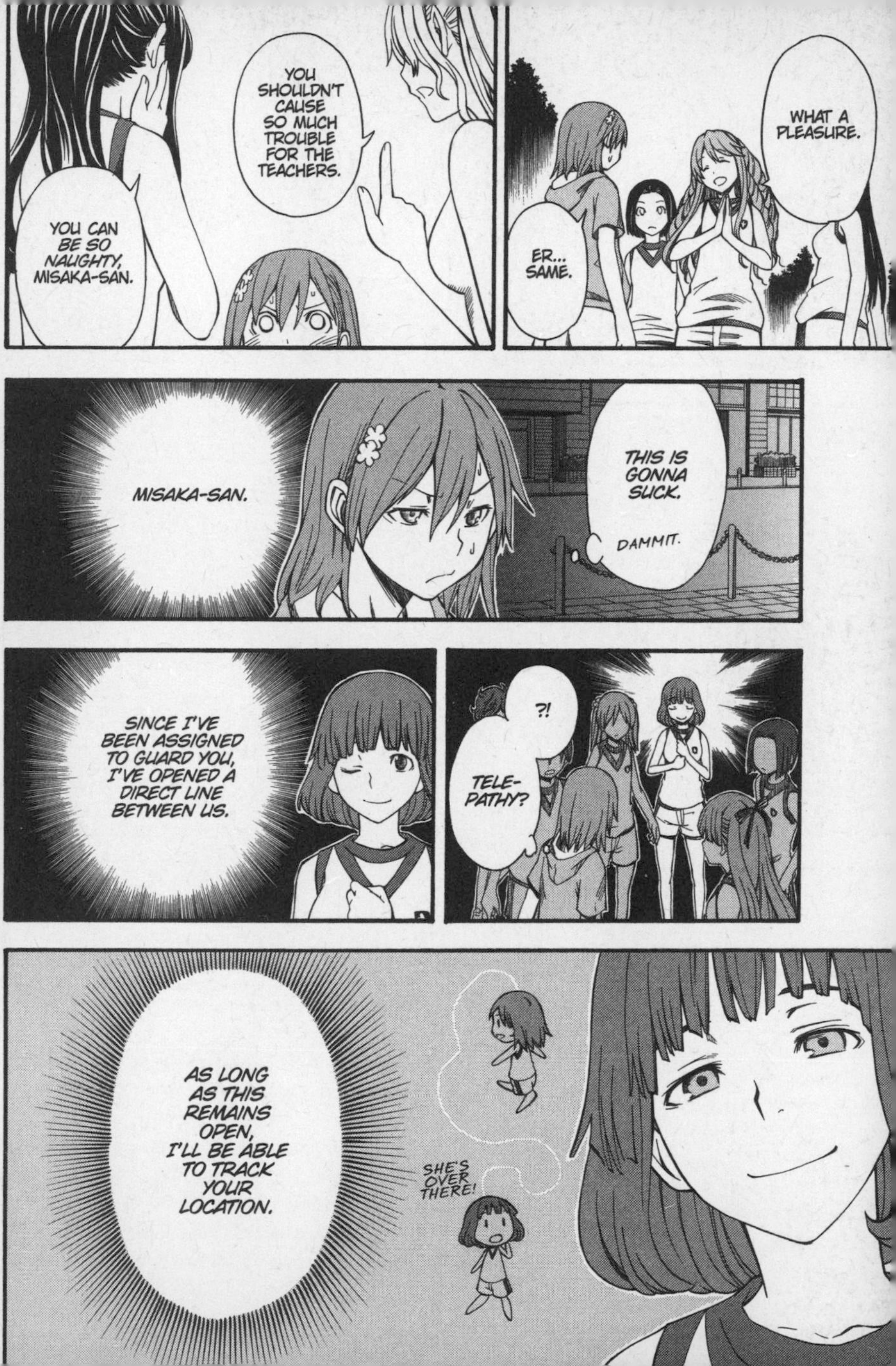
WHAT A PLEASURE.
ER... SAME.
YOU SHOULDN'T CAUSE SO MUCH TROUBLE FOR THE TEACHERS.
YOU CAN BE SO NAUGHTY, MISAKA-SAN.
THIS IS GONNA SUCK.
DAMMIT.
MISAKA-SAN.
?!
TELE-PATHY?
SINCE I'VE BEEN ASSIGNED TO GUARD YOU, I'VE OPENED A DIRECT LINE BETWEEN US.
AS LONG AS THIS REMAINS OPEN, I'LL BE ABLE TO TRACK YOUR LOCATION.
SHE'S OVER THERE!

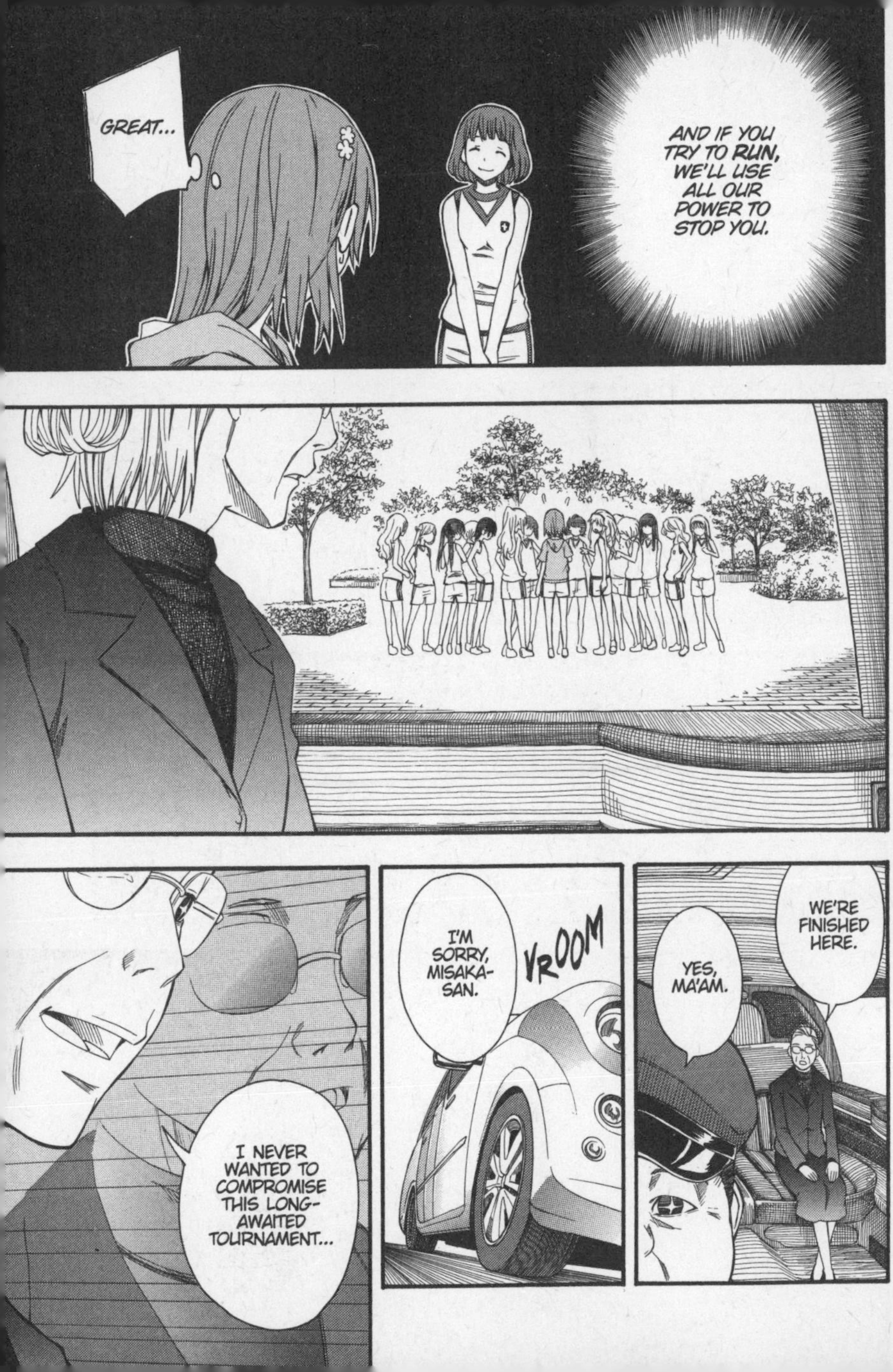
AND IF YOU TRY TO RUN, WE'LL USE ALL OUR POWER TO STOP YOU.
GREAT...
WE'RE FINISHED HERE.
YES, MA'AM.
VROOM
I'M SORRY, MISAKA-SAN.
I NEVER WANTED TO COMPROMISE THIS LONG-AWAITED TOURNAMENT...

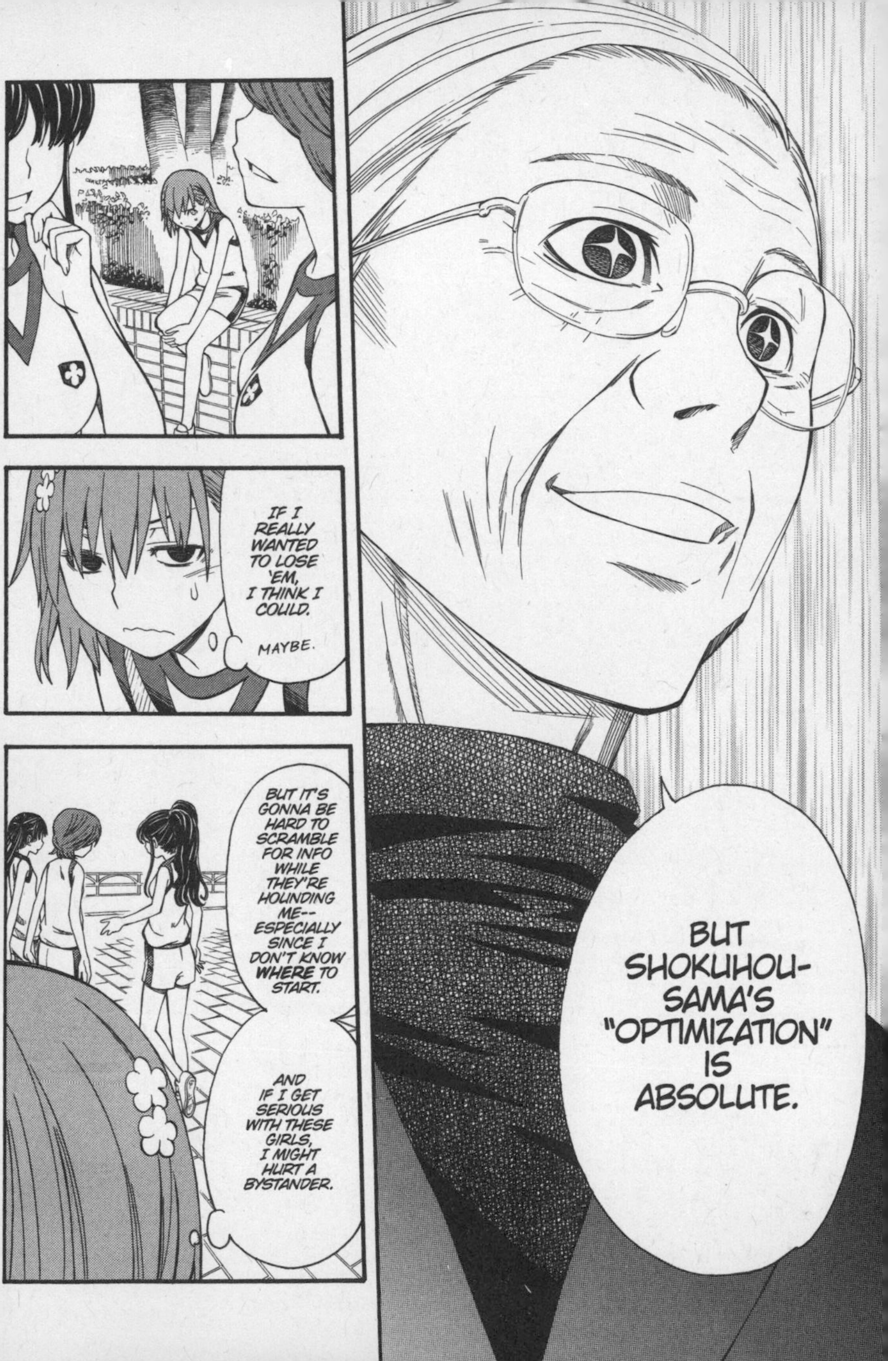
BUT SHOKUHOU-SAMA'S "OPTIMIZATION" IS ABSOLUTE.
IF I REALLY WANTED TO LOSE 'EM, I THINK I COULD.
MAYBE.
BUT IT'S GONNA BE HARD TO SCRAMBLE FOR INFO WHILE THEY'RE HOUNDING ME-- ESPECIALLY SINCE I DON'T KNOW WHERE TO START.
AND IF I GET SERIOUS WITH THESE GIRLS, I MIGHT HURT A BYSTANDER.

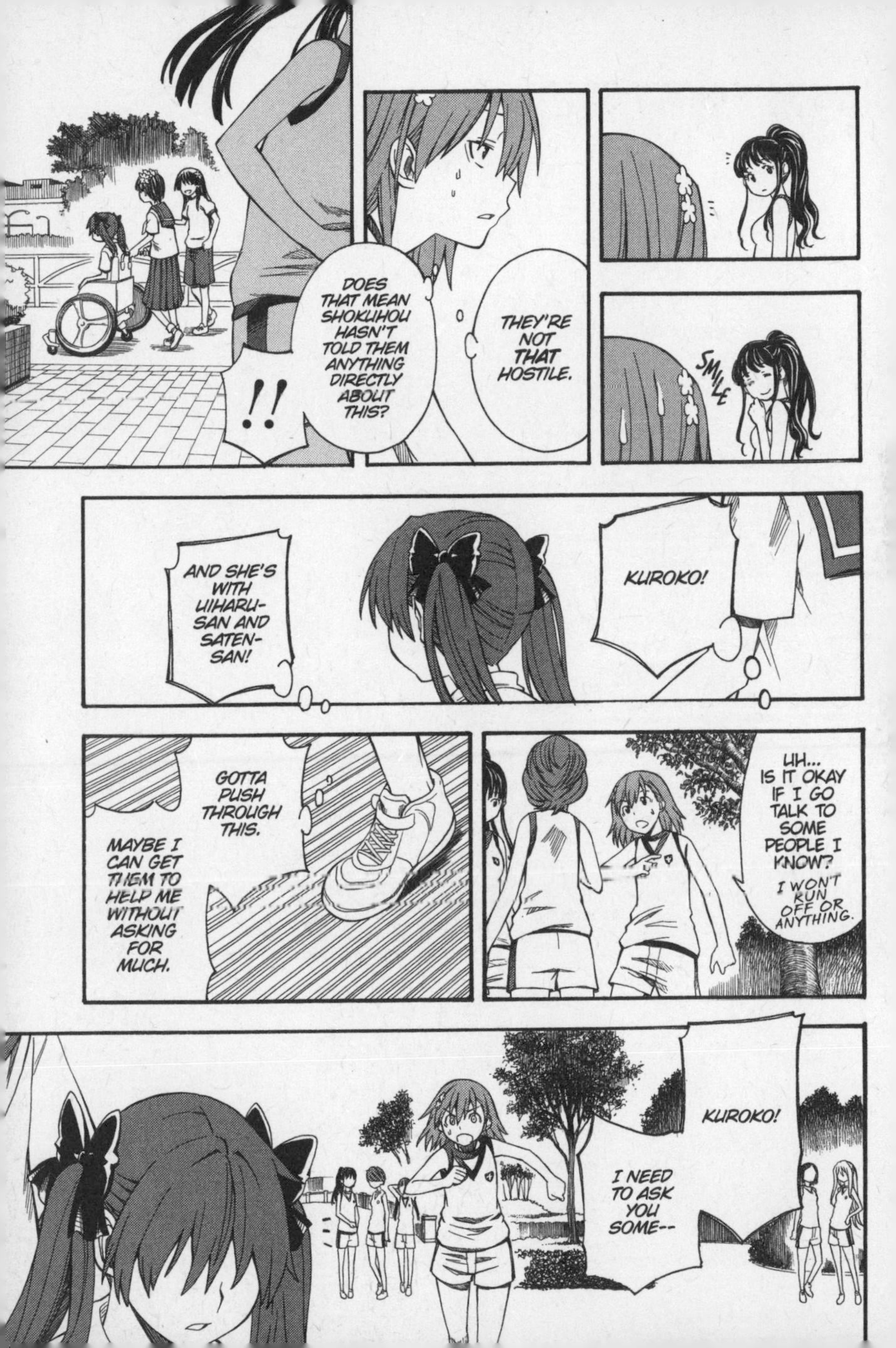
SMILE
THEY'RE NOT THAT HOSTILE.
DOES THAT MEAN SHOKUHOU HASN'T TOLD THEM ANYTHING DIRECTLY ABOUT THIS?
!!
KUROKO!
AND SHE'S WITH UIHARU-SAN AND SATEN-SAN!
UH... IS IT OKAY IF I GO TALK TO SOME PEOPLE I KNOW?
I WON'T RUN OFF OR ANYTHING.
GOTTA PUSH THROUGH THIS.
MAYBE I CAN GET THEM TO HELP ME WITHOUT ASKING FOR MUCH.
KUROKO!
I NEED TO ASK YOU SOME--

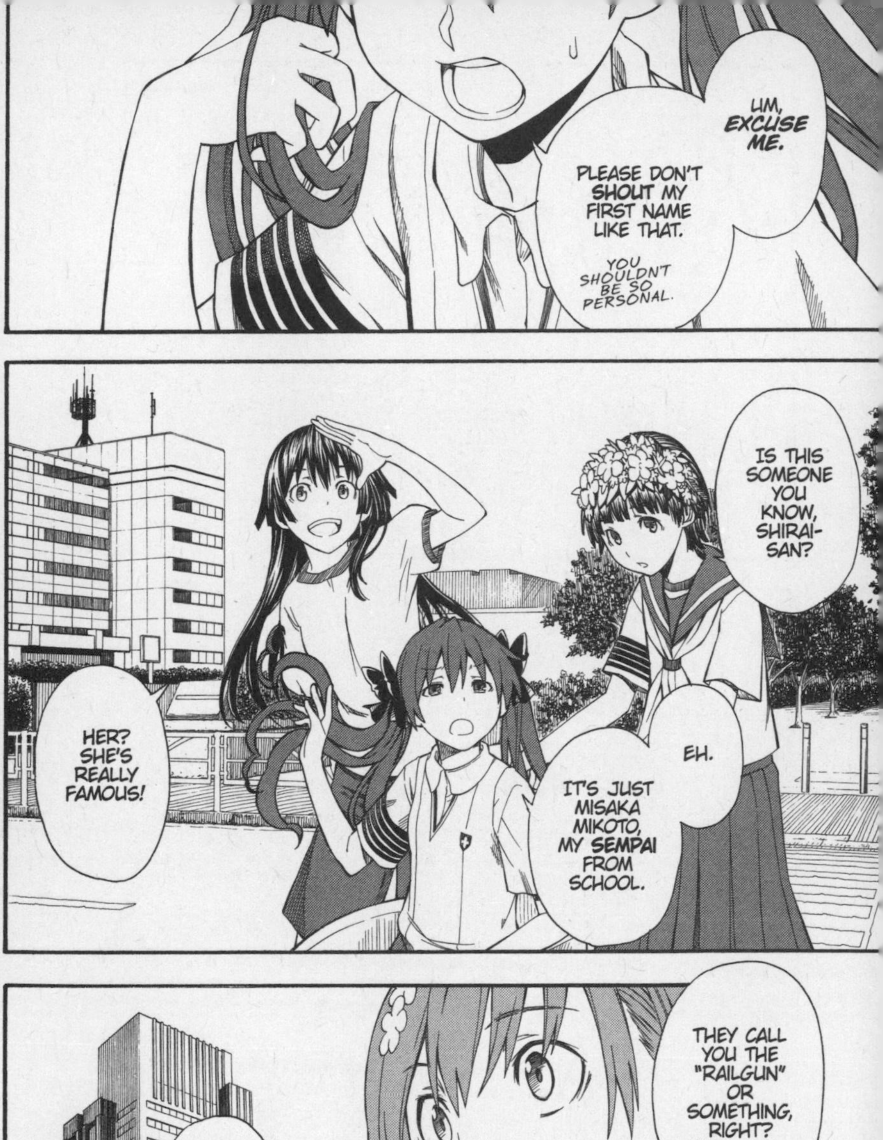
UM, EXCUSE ME.
PLEASE DON'T SHOUT MY FIRST NAME LIKE THAT.
YOU SHOULDN'T BE SO PERSONAL.
IS THIS SOMEONE YOU KNOW, SHIRAI-SAN?
EH.
IT'S JUST MISAKA MIKOTO, MY SEMPAI FROM SCHOOL.
HER? SHE'S REALLY FAMOUS!
THEY CALL YOU THE "RAILGUN" OR SOMETHING, RIGHT?
HUH...?

CHAPTER 49: TRUST

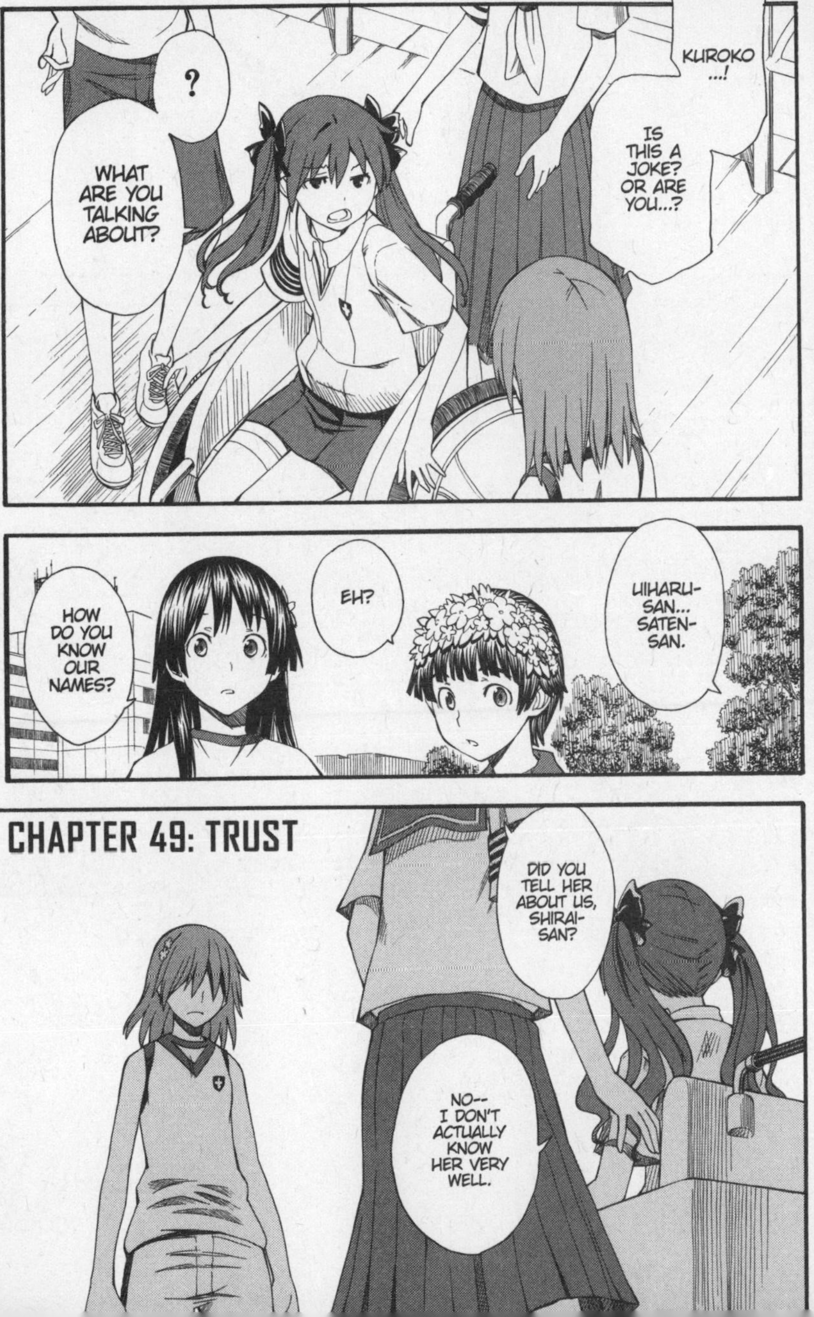
KUROKO ...!
IS THIS A JOKE? OR ARE YOU...?
?
WHAT ARE YOU TALKING ABOUT?
UIHARU-SAN... SATEN-SAN.
EH?
HOW DO YOU KNOW OUR NAMES?
DID YOU TELL HER ABOUT US, SHIRAI-SAN?
NO-- I DON'T ACTUALLY KNOW HER VERY WELL.

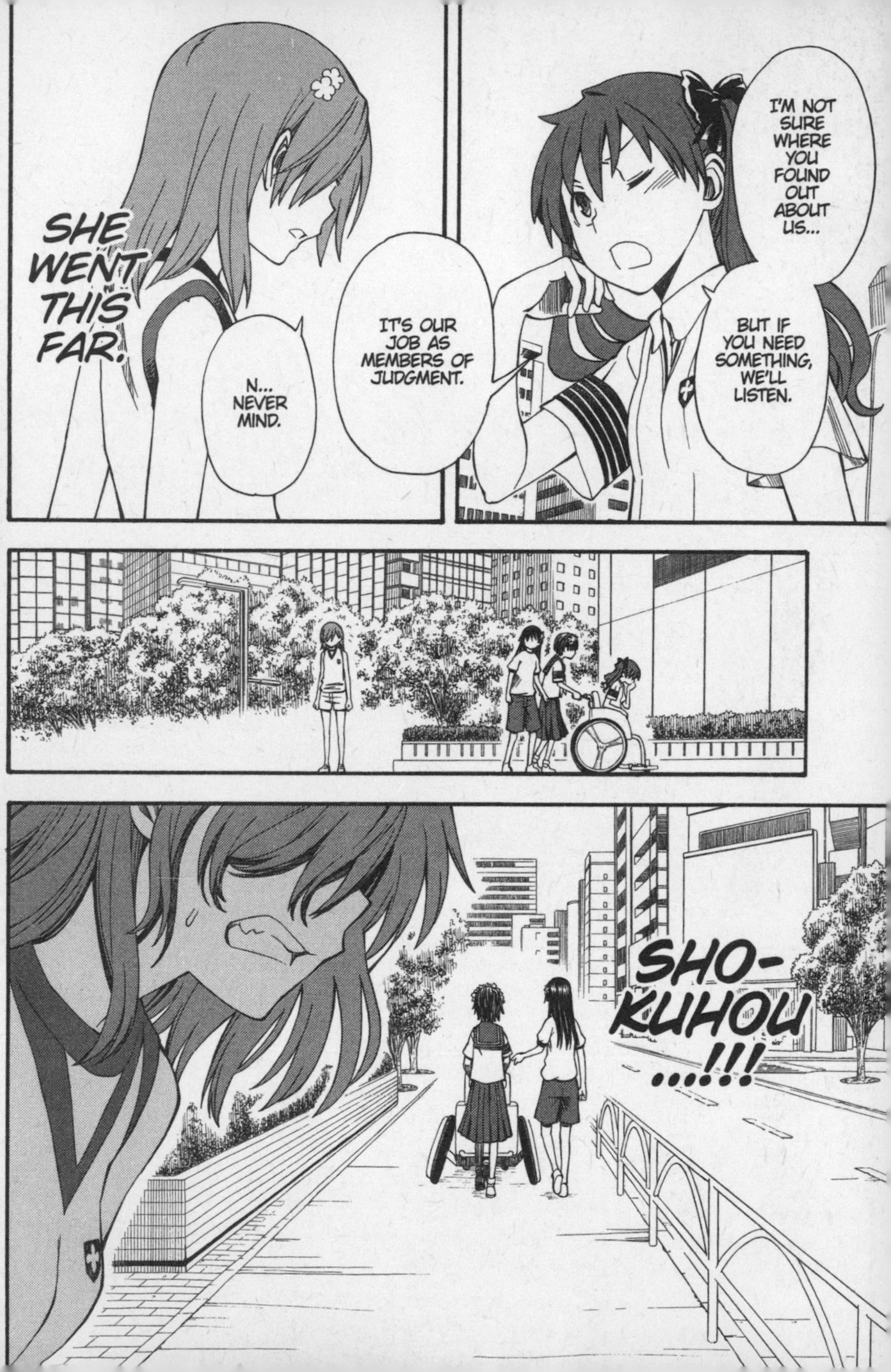
I'M NOT SURE WHERE YOU FOUND OUT ABOUT US...
BUT IF YOU NEED SOMETHING, WE'LL LISTEN.
IT'S OUR JOB AS MEMBERS OF JUDGMENT.
N... NEVER MIND.
SHE WENT THIS FAR.
SHO-KUHOU ...!!!

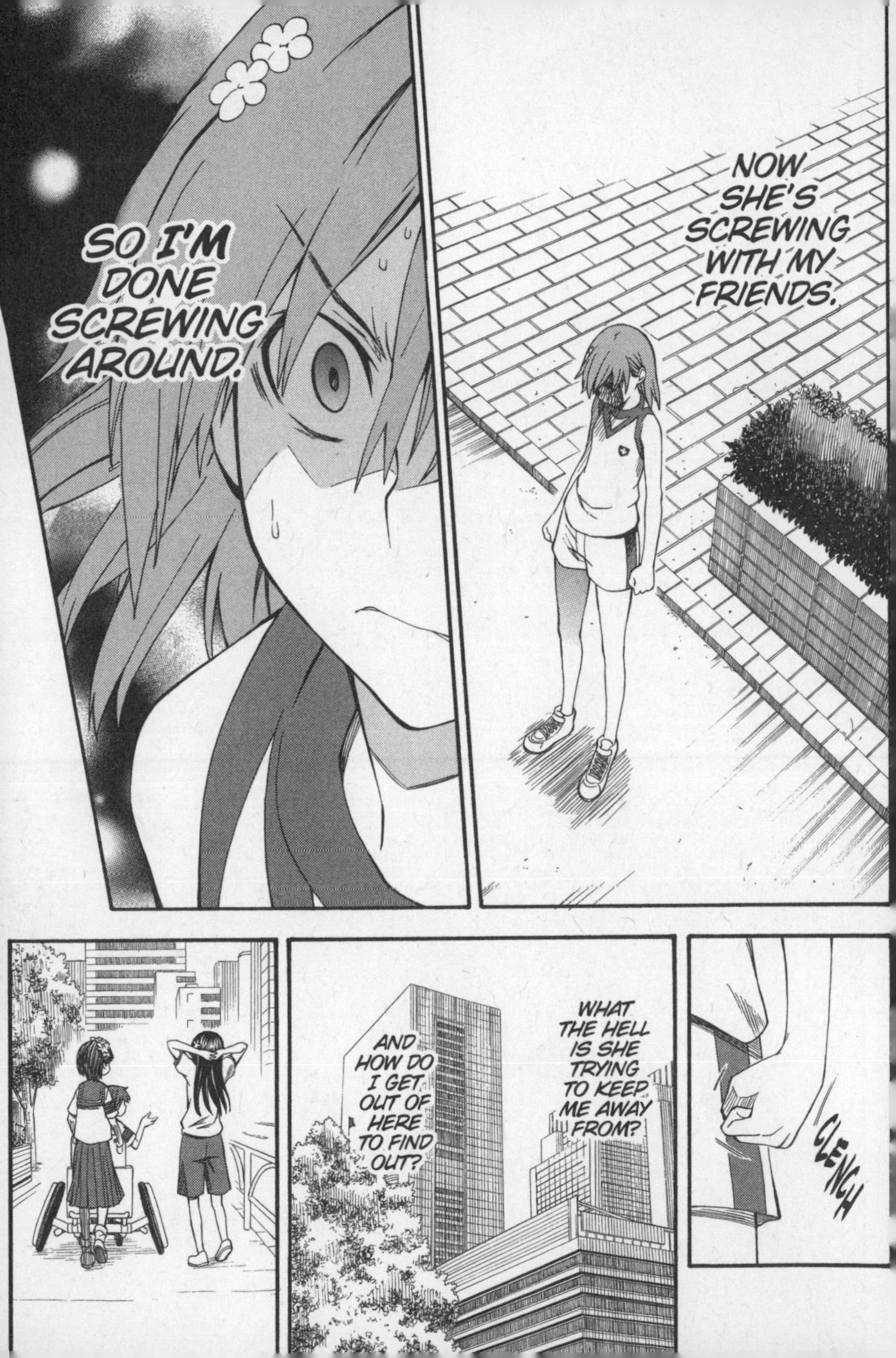
NOW SHE'S SCREWING WITH MY FRIENDS.
SO I'M DONE SCREWING AROUND.
CLENCH
WHAT THE HELL IS SHE TRYING TO KEEP ME AWAY FROM?
AND HOW DO I GET OUT OF HERE TO FIND OUT?

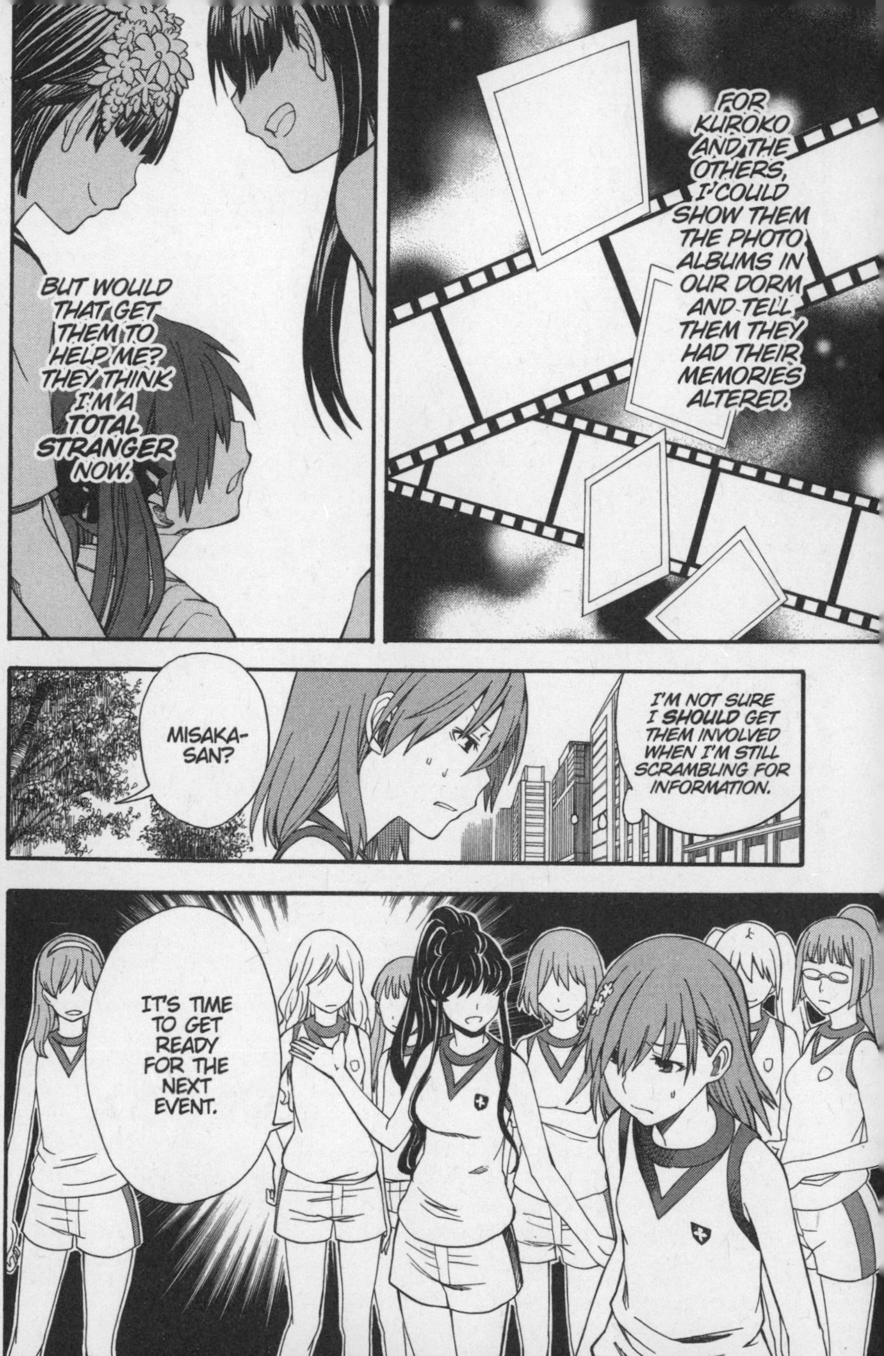
FOR KUROKO AND THE OTHERS, I COULD SHOW THEM THE PHOTO ALBUMS IN OUR DORM AND TELL THEM THEY HAD THEIR MEMORIES ALTERED.
BUT WOULD THAT GET THEM TO HELP ME? THEY THINK I'M A TOTAL STRANGER NOW.
I'M NOT SURE I SHOULD GET THEM INVOLVED WHEN I'M STILL SCRAMBLING FOR INFORMATION.
MISAKA-SAN?
IT'S TIME TO GET READY FOR THE NEXT EVENT.

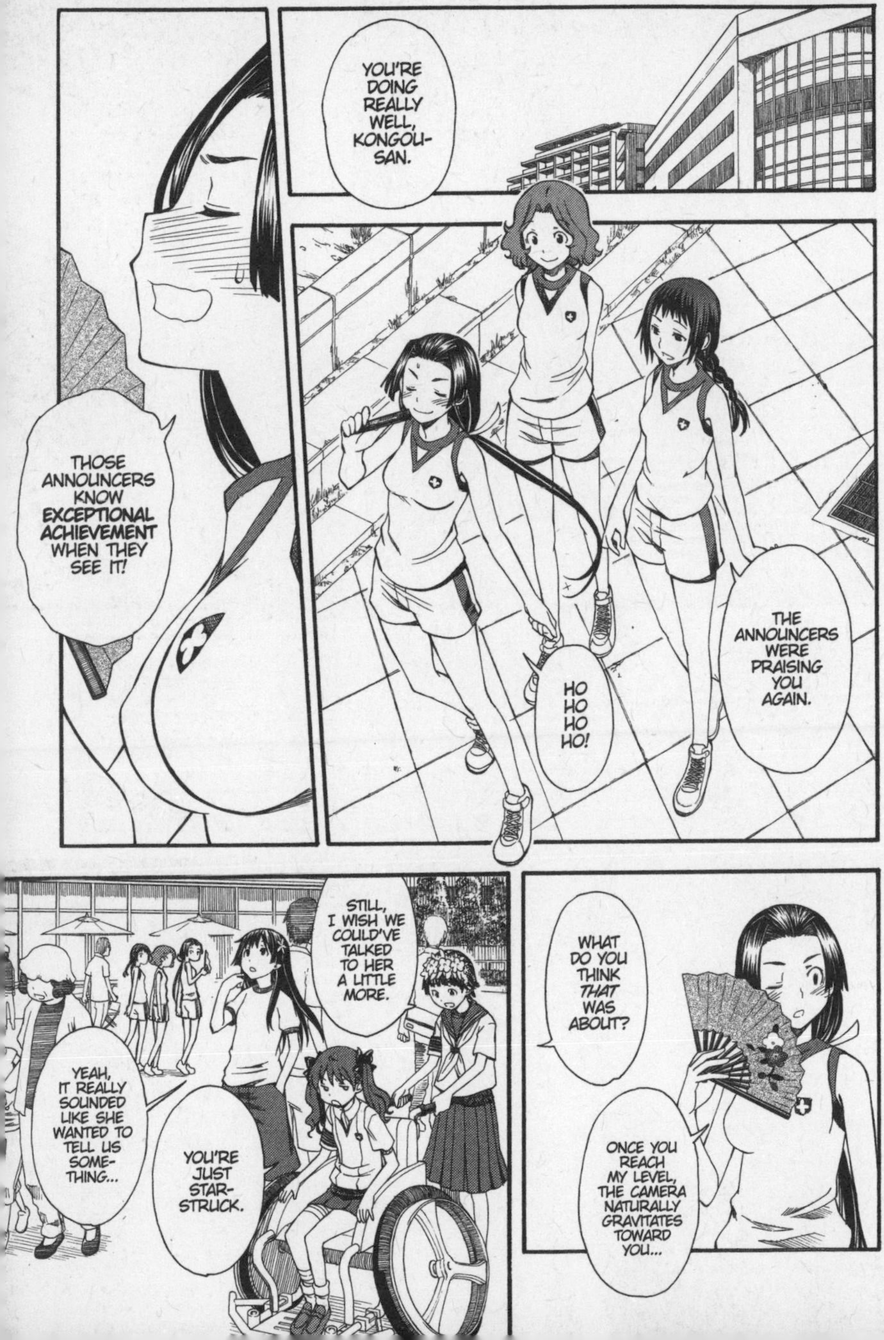
YOU'RE DOING REALLY WELL, KONGOU-SAN.
THE ANNOUNCERS WERE PRAISING YOU AGAIN.
HO HO HO HO!
THOSE ANNOUNCERS KNOW EXCEPTIONAL ACHIEVEMENT WHEN THEY SEE IT!
WHAT DO YOU THINK *THAT* WAS ABOUT?
ONCE YOU REACH MY LEVEL, THE CAMERA NATURALLY GRAVITATES TOWARD YOU...
STILL, I WISH WE COULD'VE TALKED TO HER A LITTLE MORE.
YOU'RE JUST STAR-STRUCK.
YEAH, IT REALLY SOUNDED LIKE SHE WANTED TO TELL US SOME-THING...

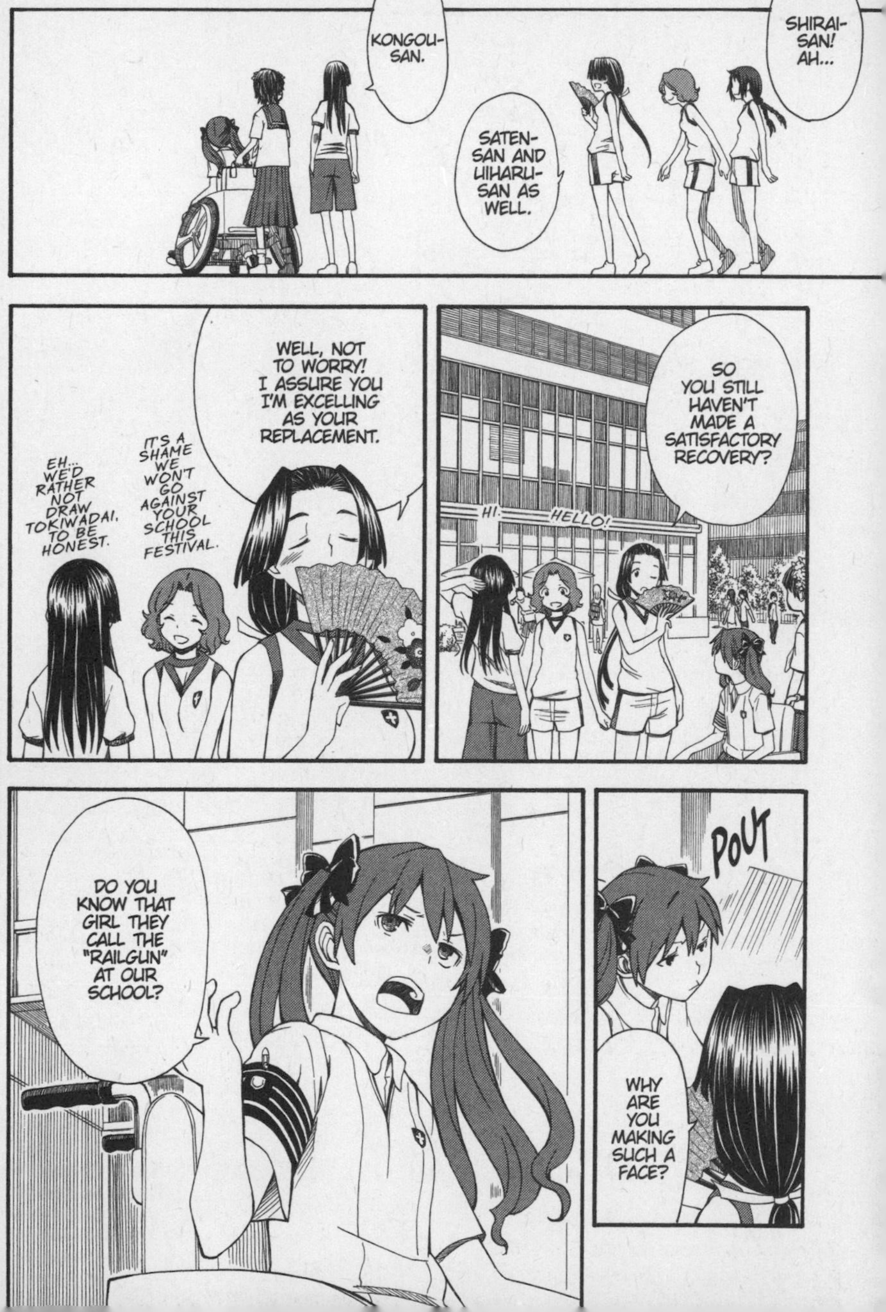
SHIRAI-SAN! AH...
OH.
KONGOU-SAN.
SATEN-SAN AND UIHARU-SAN AS WELL.
SO YOU STILL HAVEN'T MADE A SATISFACTORY RECOVERY?
HI.
HELLO!
WELL, NOT TO WORRY! I ASSURE YOU I'M EXCELLING AS YOUR REPLACEMENT.
IT'S A SHAME WE WON'T GO AGAINST YOUR SCHOOL THIS FESTIVAL.
EH... WE'D RATHER NOT DRAW TOKIWADAI, TO BE HONEST.
POUT
WHY ARE YOU MAKING SUCH A FACE?
DO YOU KNOW THAT GIRL THEY CALL THE "RAILGUN" AT OUR SCHOOL?

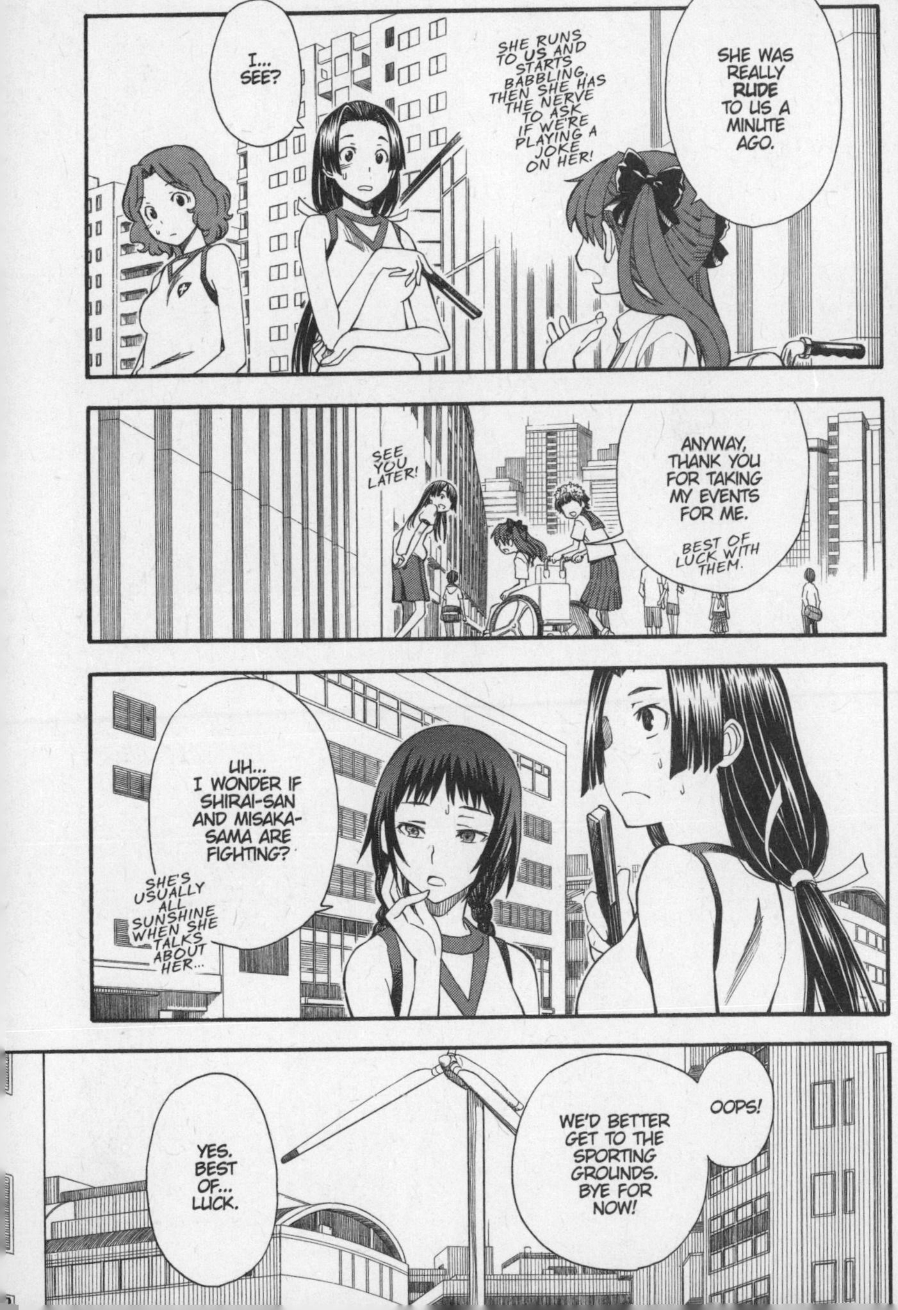
SHE WAS REALLY RUDE TO US A MINUTE AGO.
SHE RUNS TO US AND STARTS BABBLING, THEN SHE HAS THE NERVE TO ASK IF WE'RE PLAYING A JOKE ON HER!
I... SEE?
ANYWAY, THANK YOU FOR TAKING MY EVENTS FOR ME.
BEST OF LUCK WITH THEM.
SEE YOU LATER!
UH... I WONDER IF SHIRAI-SAN AND MISAKA-SAMA ARE FIGHTING?
SHE'S USUALLY ALL SUNSHINE WHEN SHE TALKS ABOUT HER...
OOPS!
WE'D BETTER GET TO THE SPORTING GROUNDS. BYE FOR NOW!
YES. BEST OF... LUCK.

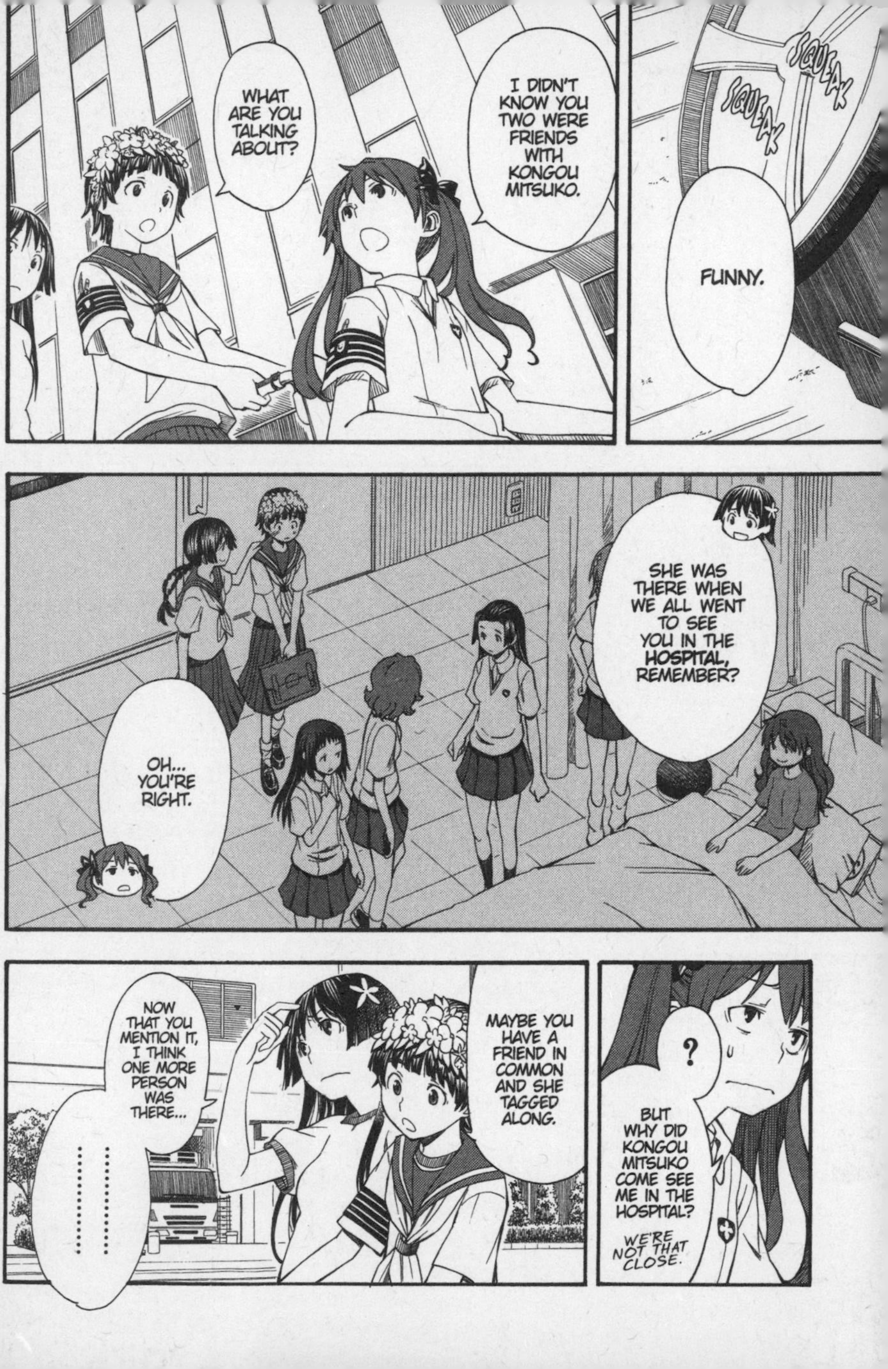
SQUEAK
SQUEAK
FUNNY.
I DIDN'T KNOW YOU TWO WERE FRIENDS WITH KONGOU MITSUKO.
WHAT ARE YOU TALKING ABOUT?
SHE WAS THERE WHEN WE ALL WENT TO SEE YOU IN THE HOSPITAL, REMEMBER?
OH... YOU'RE RIGHT.
?
BUT WHY DID KONGOU MITSUKO COME SEE ME IN THE HOSPITAL?
WE'RE NOT THAT CLOSE.
MAYBE YOU HAVE A FRIEND IN COMMON AND SHE TAGGED ALONG.
NOW THAT YOU MENTION IT, I THINK ONE MORE PERSON WAS THERE...
......

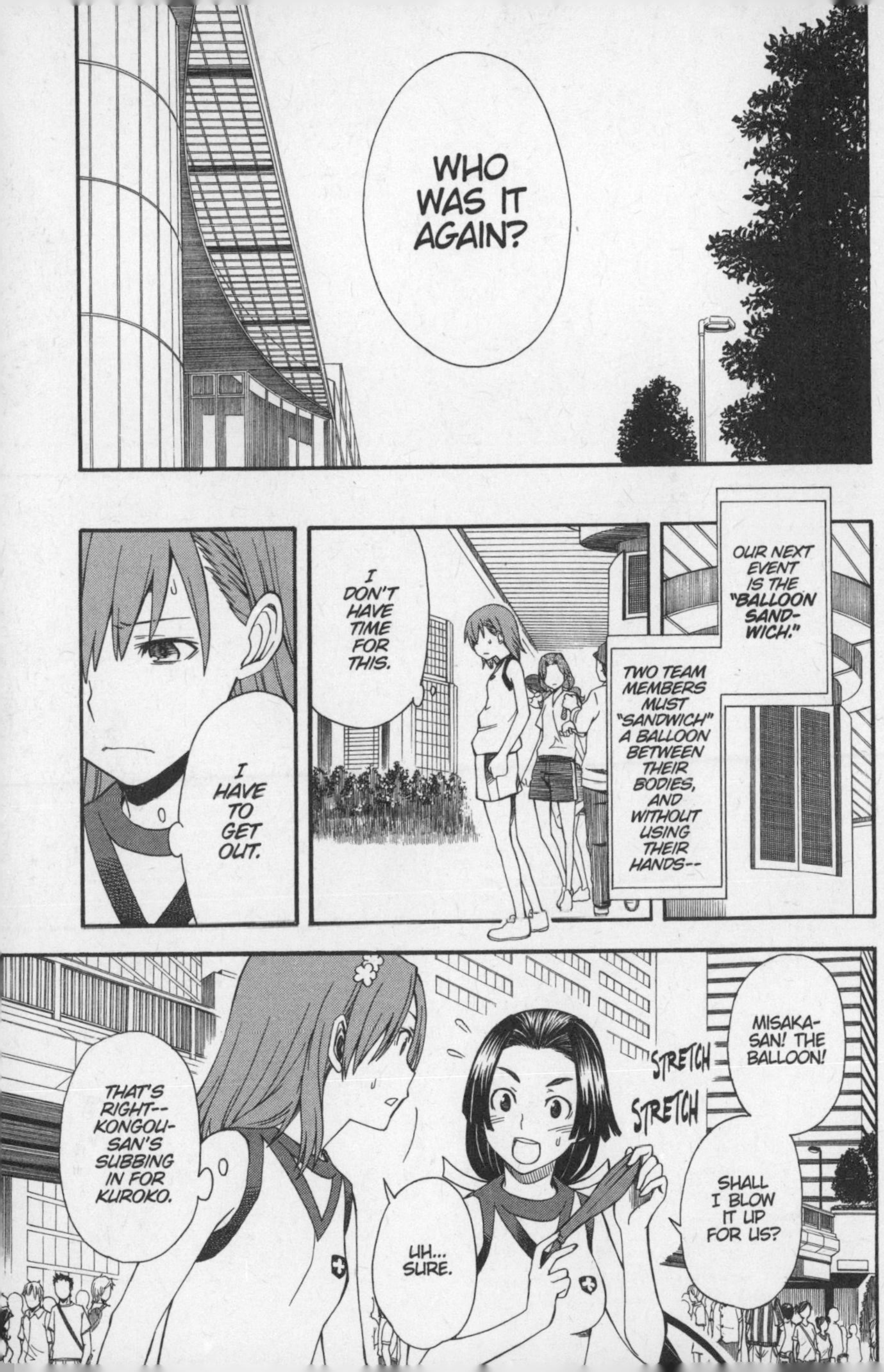
WHO WAS IT AGAIN?
OUR NEXT EVENT IS THE "BALLOON SANDWICH."
TWO TEAM MEMBERS MUST "SANDWICH" A BALLOON BETWEEN THEIR BODIES, AND WITHOUT USING THEIR HANDS--
I DON'T HAVE TIME FOR THIS.
I HAVE TO GET OUT.
MISAKA-SAN! THE BALLOON!
STRETCH
STRETCH
SHALL I BLOW IT UP FOR US?
THAT'S RIGHT-- KONGOU-SAN'S SUBBING IN FOR KUROKO.
UH... SURE.

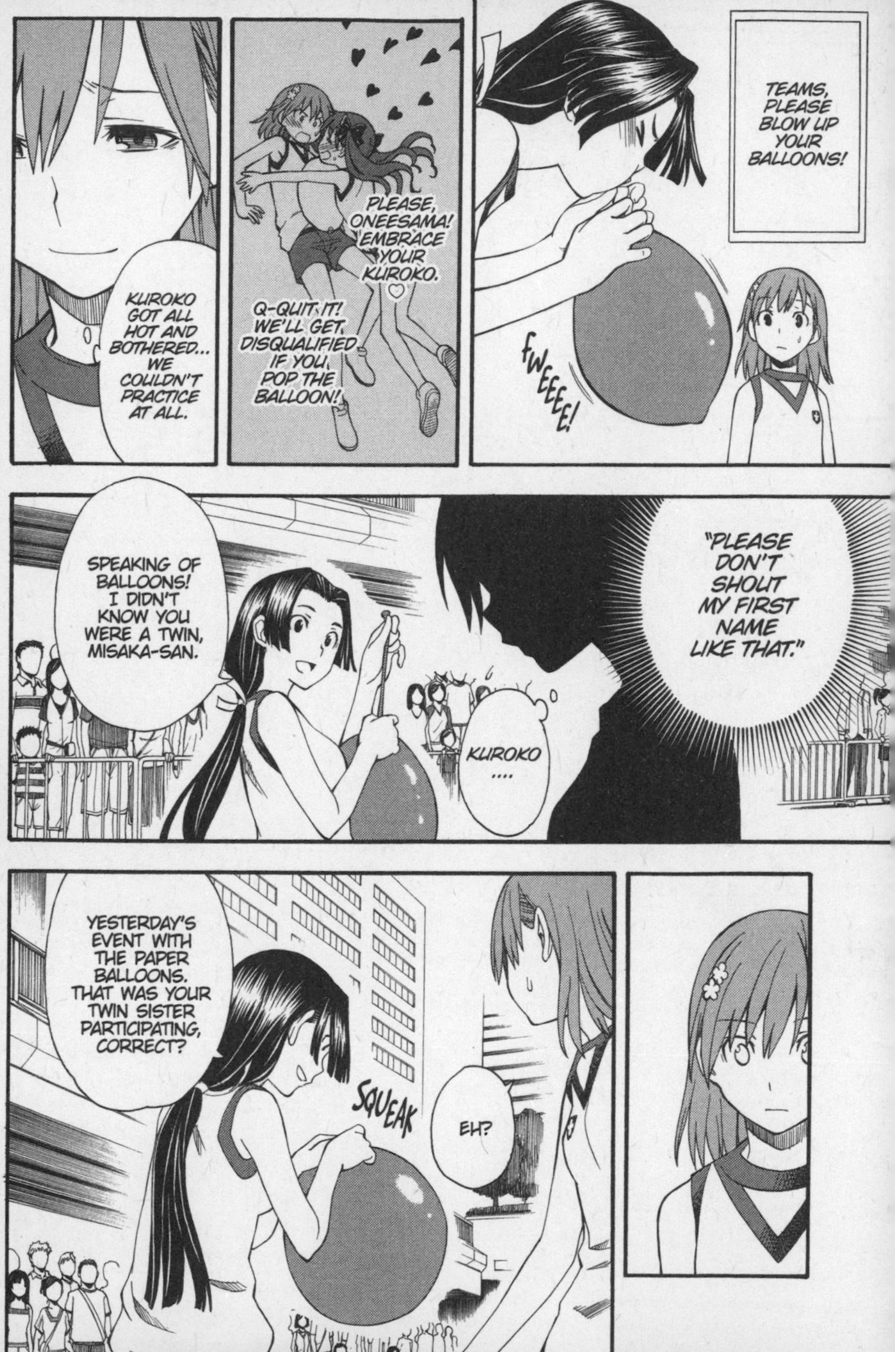

TEAMS, PLEASE BLOW UP YOUR BALLOONS!
FWEEEE!
PLEASE, ONEESAMA! EMBRACE YOUR KUROKO. ♡
Q-QUIT IT! WE'LL GET DISQUALIFIED IF YOU POP THE BALLOON!
KUROKO GOT ALL HOT AND BOTHERED... WE COULDN'T PRACTICE AT ALL.
"PLEASE DON'T SHOUT MY FIRST NAME LIKE THAT."
KUROKO ....
SPEAKING OF BALLOONS! I DIDN'T KNOW YOU WERE A TWIN, MISAKA-SAN.
YESTERDAY'S EVENT WITH THE PAPER BALLOONS. THAT WAS YOUR TWIN SISTER PARTICIPATING, CORRECT?
EH?
SQUEAK

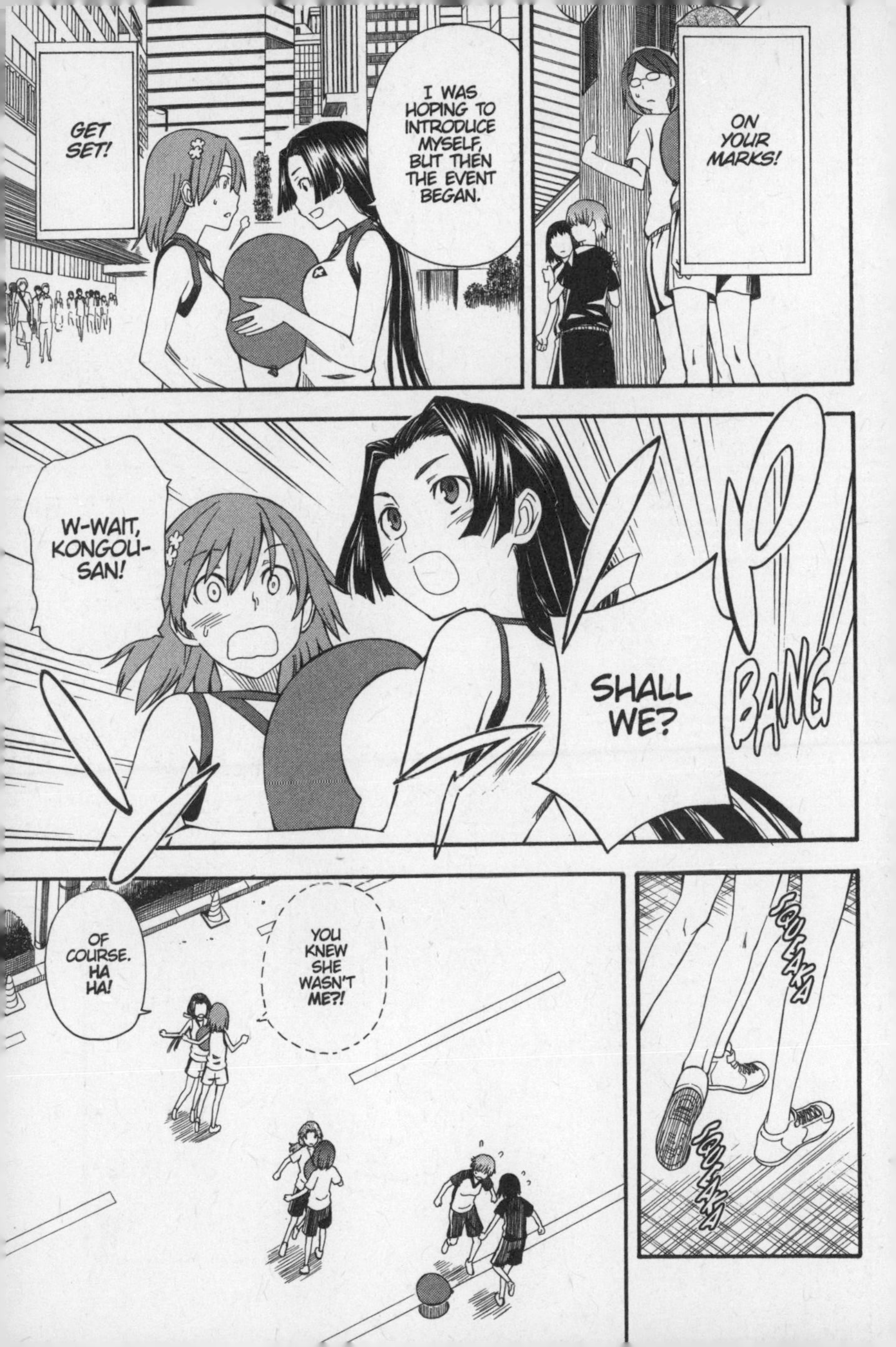
ON YOUR MARKS!
I WAS HOPING TO INTRODUCE MYSELF, BUT THEN THE EVENT BEGAN.
GET SET!
BANG
SHALL WE?
W-WAIT, KONGOU-SAN!
SQUEAKA
SQUEAKA
YOU KNEW SHE WASN'T ME?!
OF COURSE. HA HA!

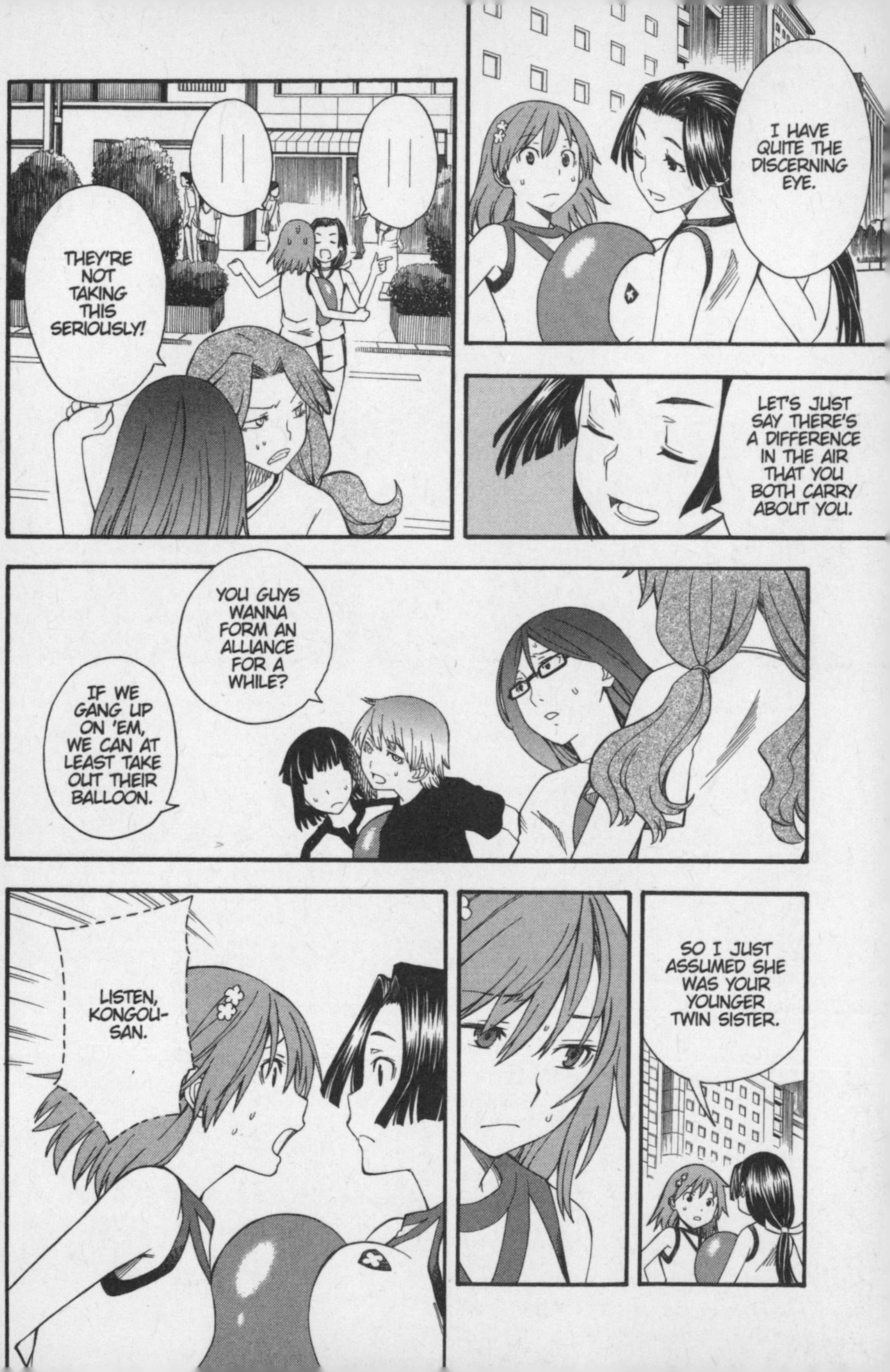
I HAVE QUITE THE DISCERNING EYE.
LET'S JUST SAY THERE'S A DIFFERENCE IN THE AIR THAT YOU BOTH CARRY ABOUT YOU.
THEY'RE NOT TAKING THIS SERIOUSLY!
YOU GUYS WANNA FORM AN ALLIANCE FOR A WHILE?
IF WE GANG UP ON 'EM, WE CAN AT LEAST TAKE OUT THEIR BALLOON.
SO I JUST ASSUMED SHE WAS YOUR YOUNGER TWIN SISTER.
LISTEN, KONGOU-SAN.

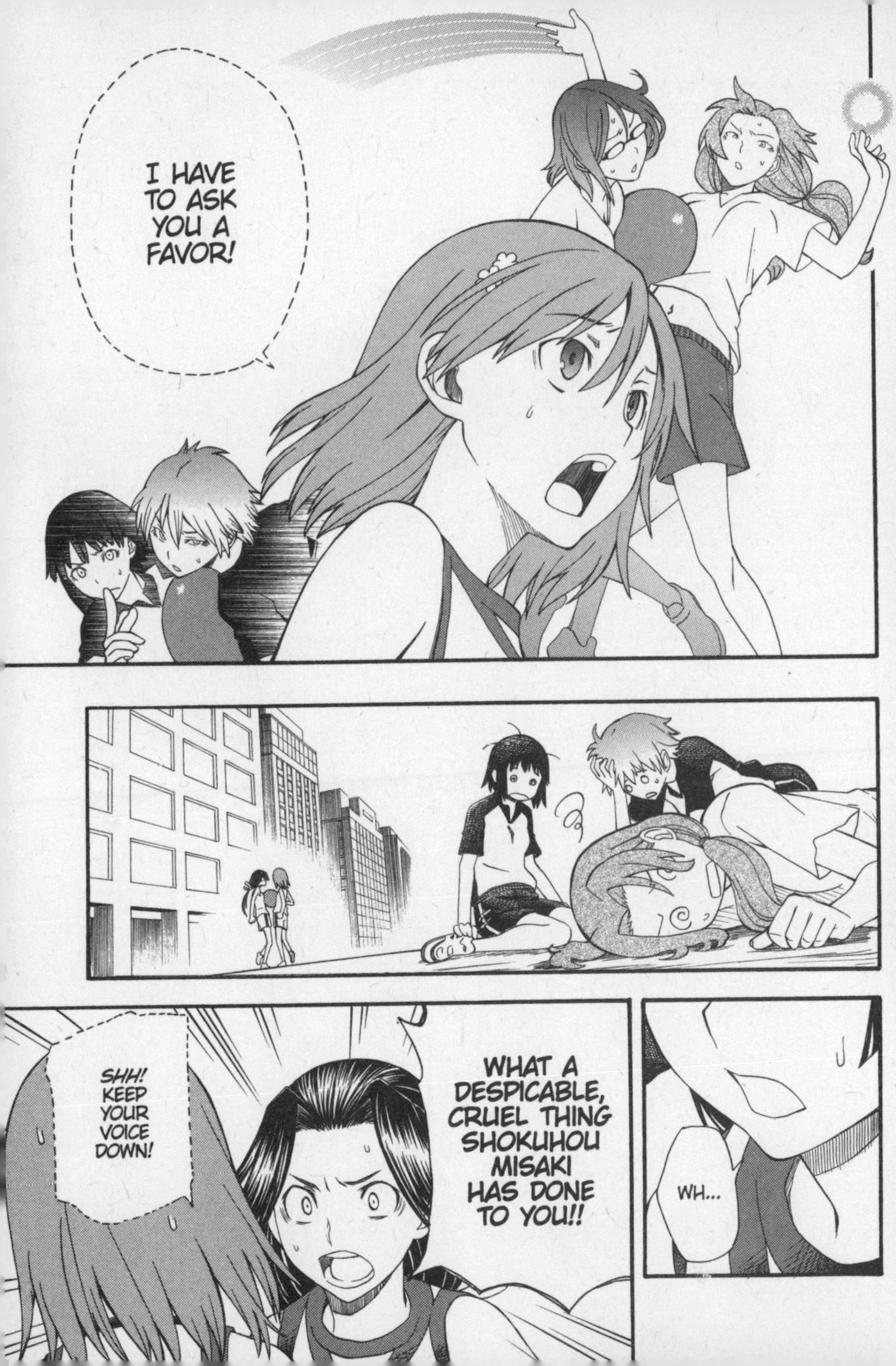
I HAVE TO ASK YOU A FAVOR!
WH...
WHAT A DESPICABLE, CRUEL THING SHOKUHOU MISAKI HAS DONE TO YOU!!
SHH! KEEP YOUR VOICE DOWN!

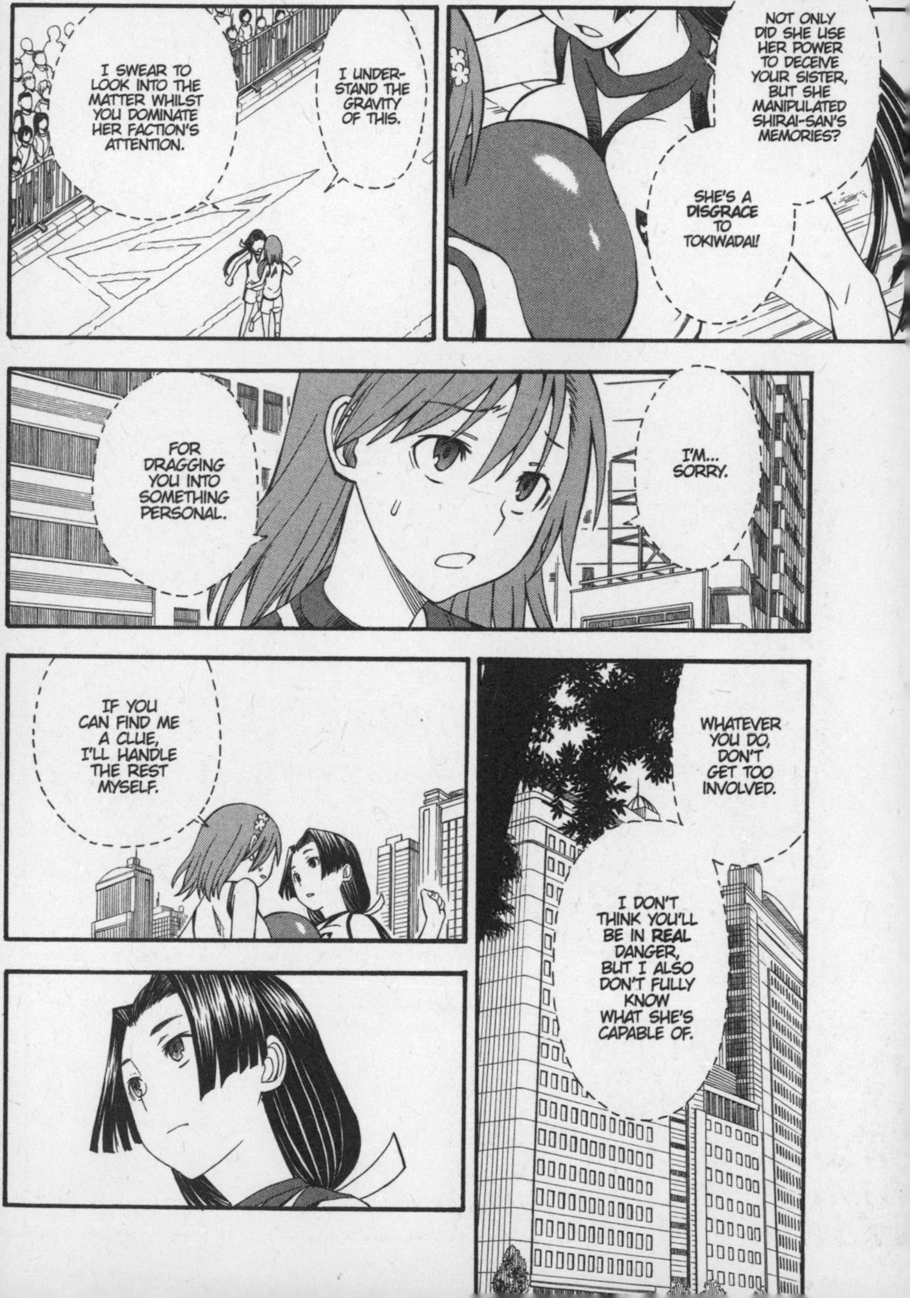
NOT ONLY DID SHE USE HER POWER TO DECEIVE YOUR SISTER, BUT SHE MANIPULATED SHIRAI-SAN'S MEMORIES?
SHE'S A DISGRACE TO TOKIWADAI!
I UNDER-STAND THE GRAVITY OF THIS.
I SWEAR TO LOOK INTO THE MATTER WHILST YOU DOMINATE HER FACTION'S ATTENTION.
I'M... SORRY.
FOR DRAGGING YOU INTO SOMETHING PERSONAL.
WHATEVER YOU DO, DON'T GET TOO INVOLVED.
I DON'T THINK YOU'LL BE IN REAL DANGER, BUT I ALSO DON'T FULLY KNOW WHAT SHE'S CAPABLE OF.
IF YOU CAN FIND ME A CLUE, I'LL HANDLE THE REST MYSELF.

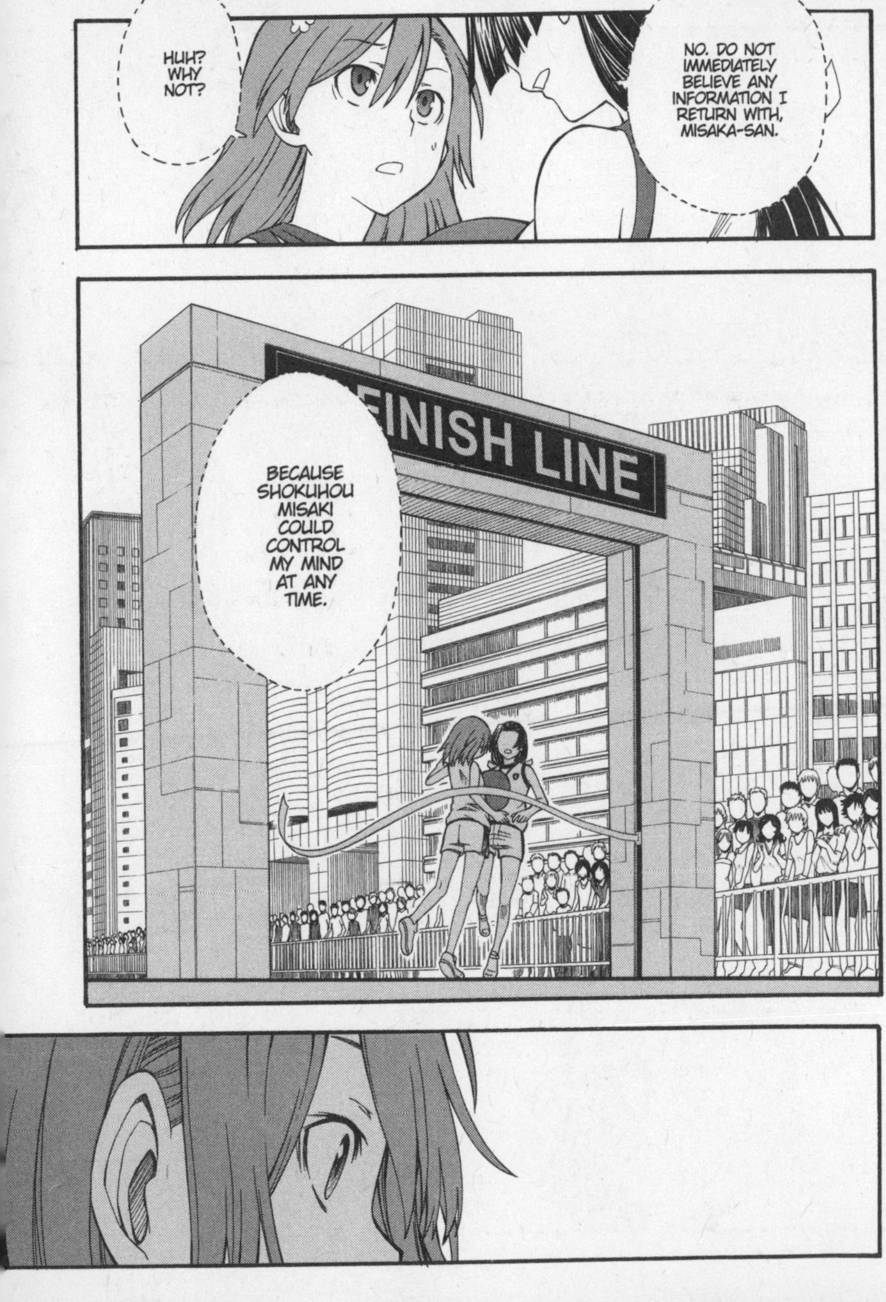
NO. DO NOT IMMEDIATELY BELIEVE ANY INFORMATION I RETURN WITH, MISAKA-SAN.
HUH? WHY NOT?
FINISH LINE
BECAUSE SHOKUHOU MISAKI COULD CONTROL MY MIND AT ANY TIME.

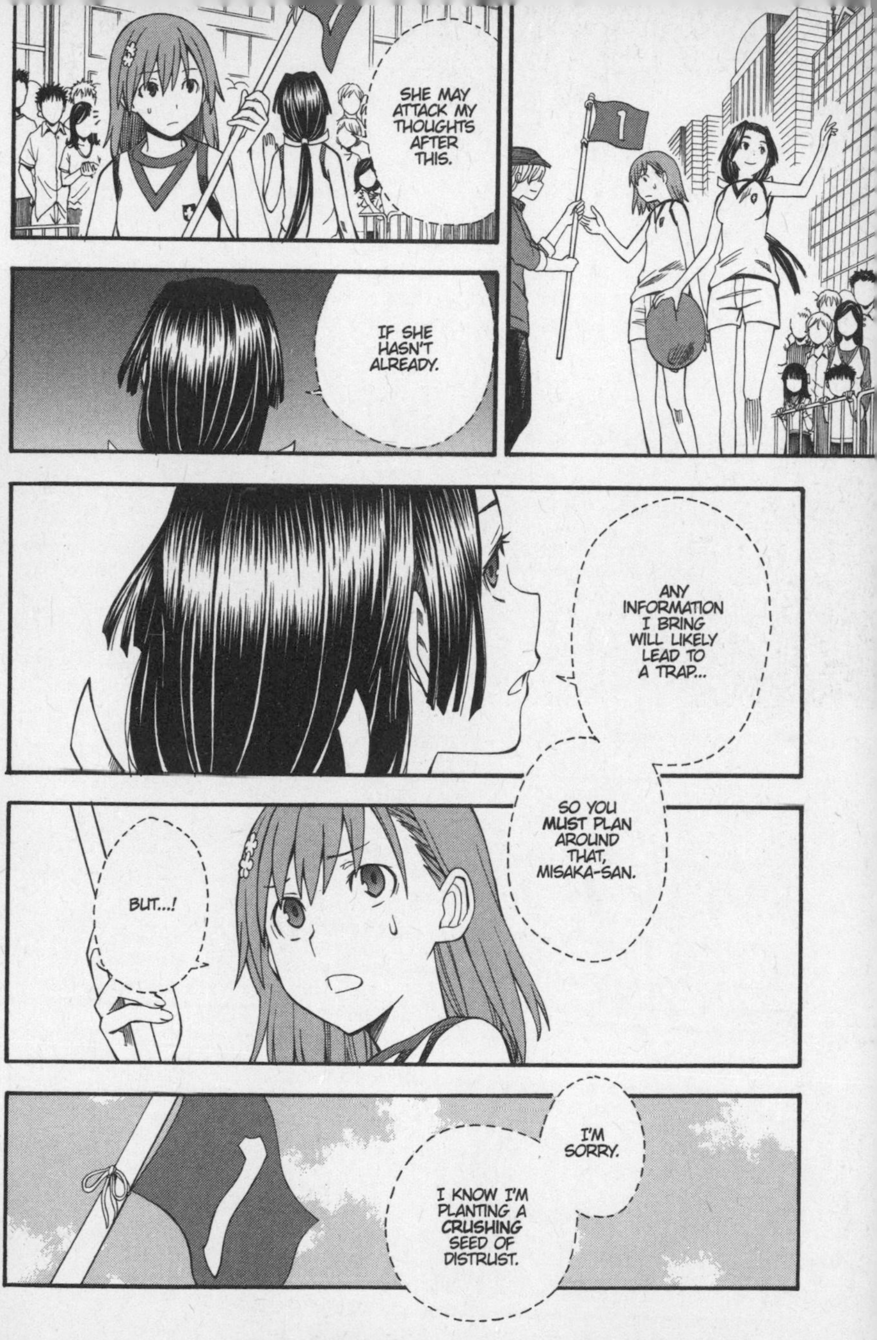
SHE MAY ATTACK MY THOUGHTS AFTER THIS.
IF SHE HASN'T ALREADY.
ANY INFORMATION I BRING WILL LIKELY LEAD TO A TRAP...
SO YOU MUST PLAN AROUND THAT, MISAKA-SAN.
BUT...!
I'M SORRY.
I KNOW I'M PLANTING A CRUSHING SEED OF DISTRUST.

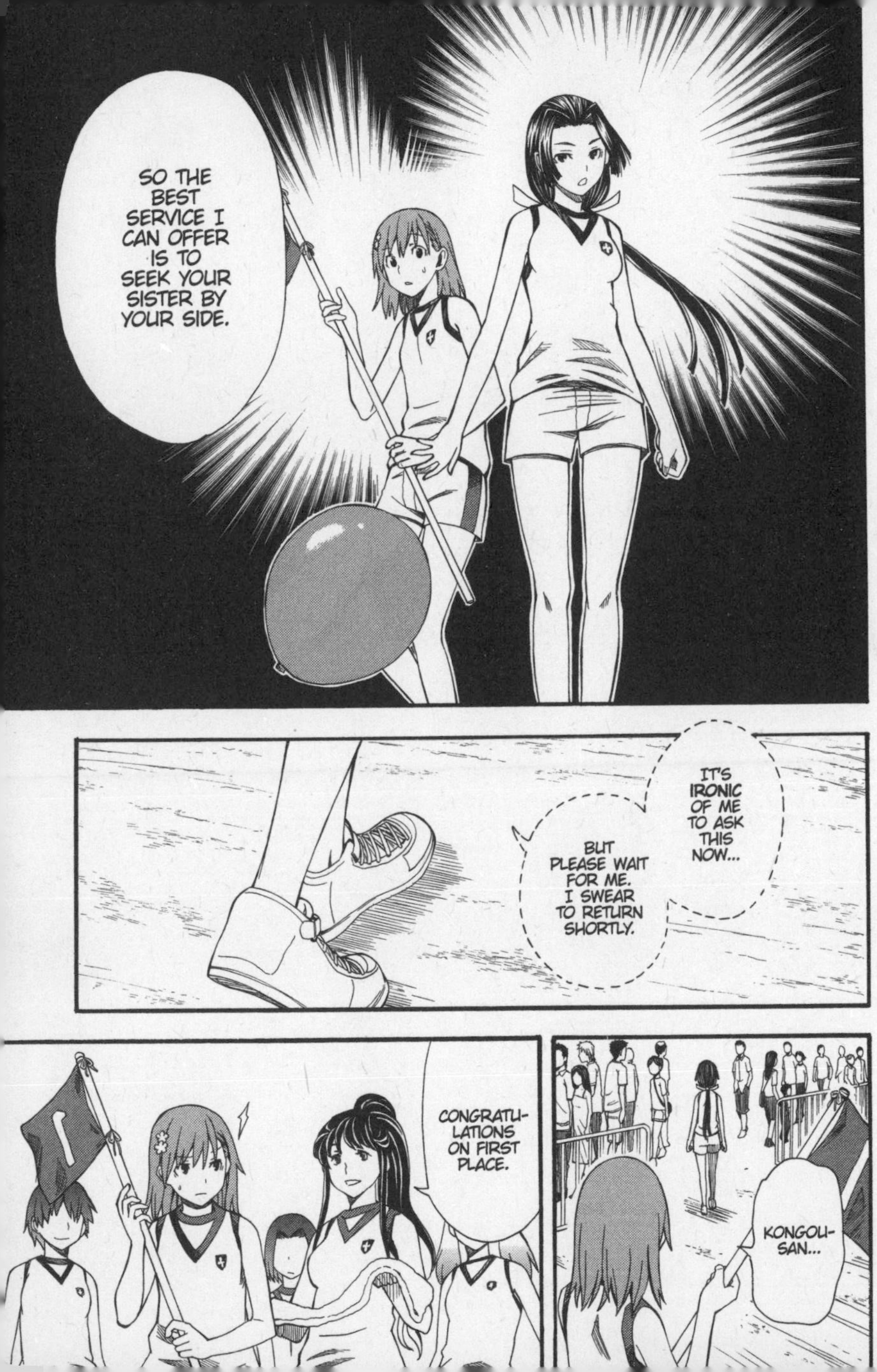
SO THE BEST SERVICE I CAN OFFER IS TO SEEK YOUR SISTER BY YOUR SIDE.
IT'S IRONIC OF ME TO ASK THIS NOW...
BUT PLEASE WAIT FOR ME. I SWEAR TO RETURN SHORTLY.
KONGOU-SAN...
CONGRATULATIONS ON FIRST PLACE.

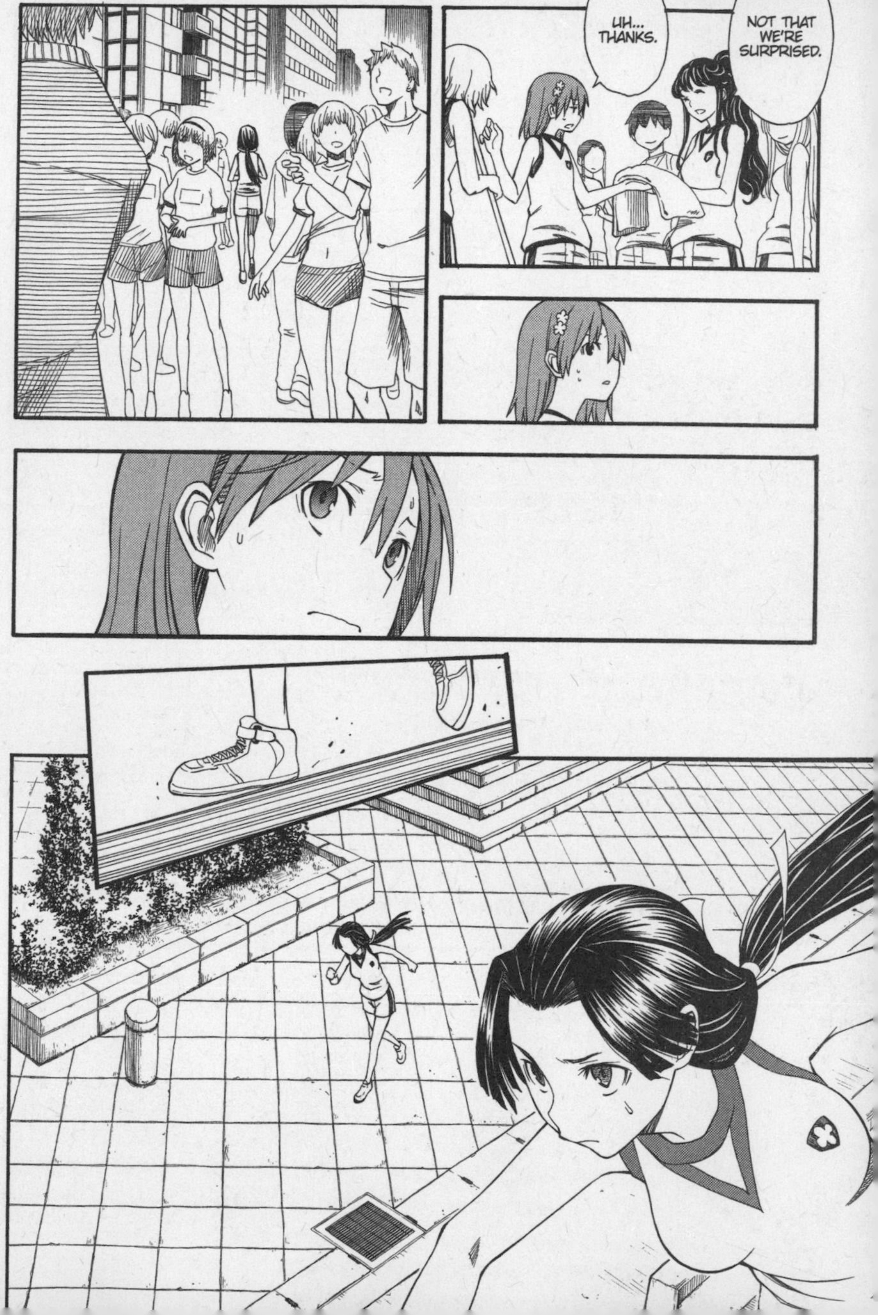
NOT THAT WE'RE SURPRISED.
UH... THANKS.

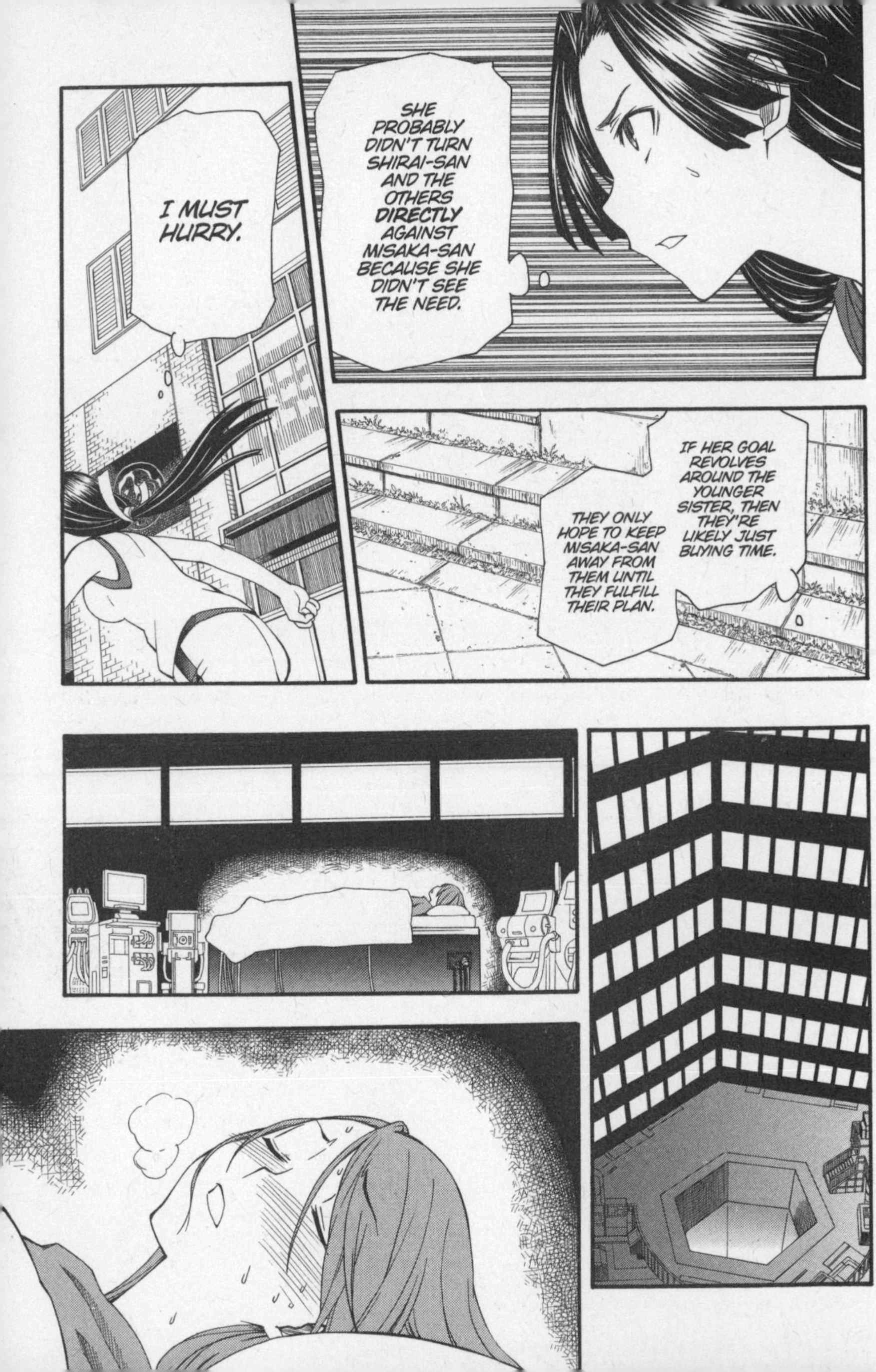
SHE PROBABLY DIDN'T TURN SHIRAI-SAN AND THE OTHERS DIRECTLY AGAINST MISAKA-SAN BECAUSE SHE DIDN'T SEE THE NEED.
IF HER GOAL REVOLVES AROUND THE YOUNGER SISTER, THEN THEY'RE LIKELY JUST BUYING TIME.
THEY ONLY HOPE TO KEEP MISAKA-SAN AWAY FROM THEM UNTIL THEY FULFILL THEIR PLAN.
I MUST HURRY.

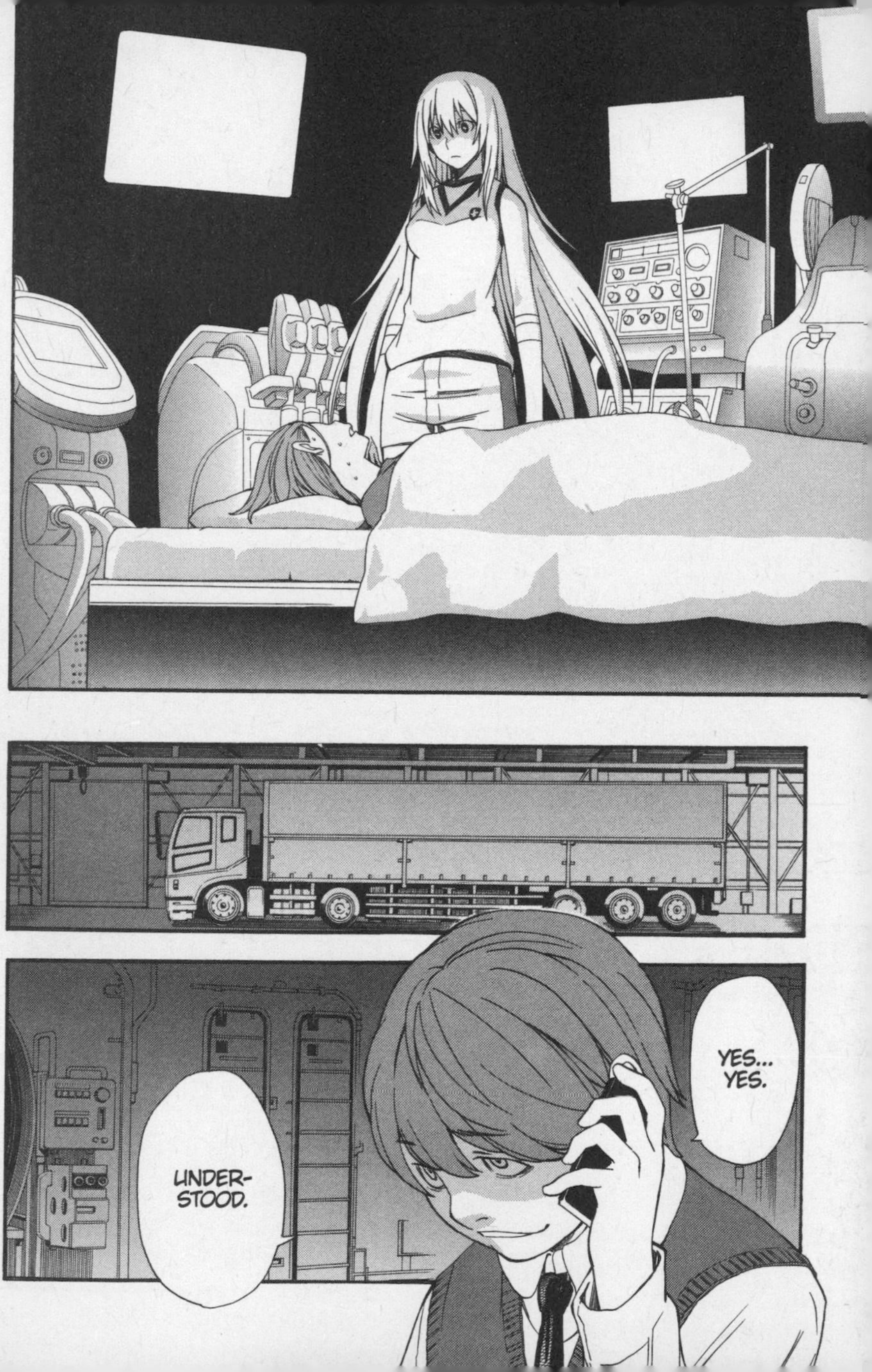
YES... YES.
UNDER-STOOD.

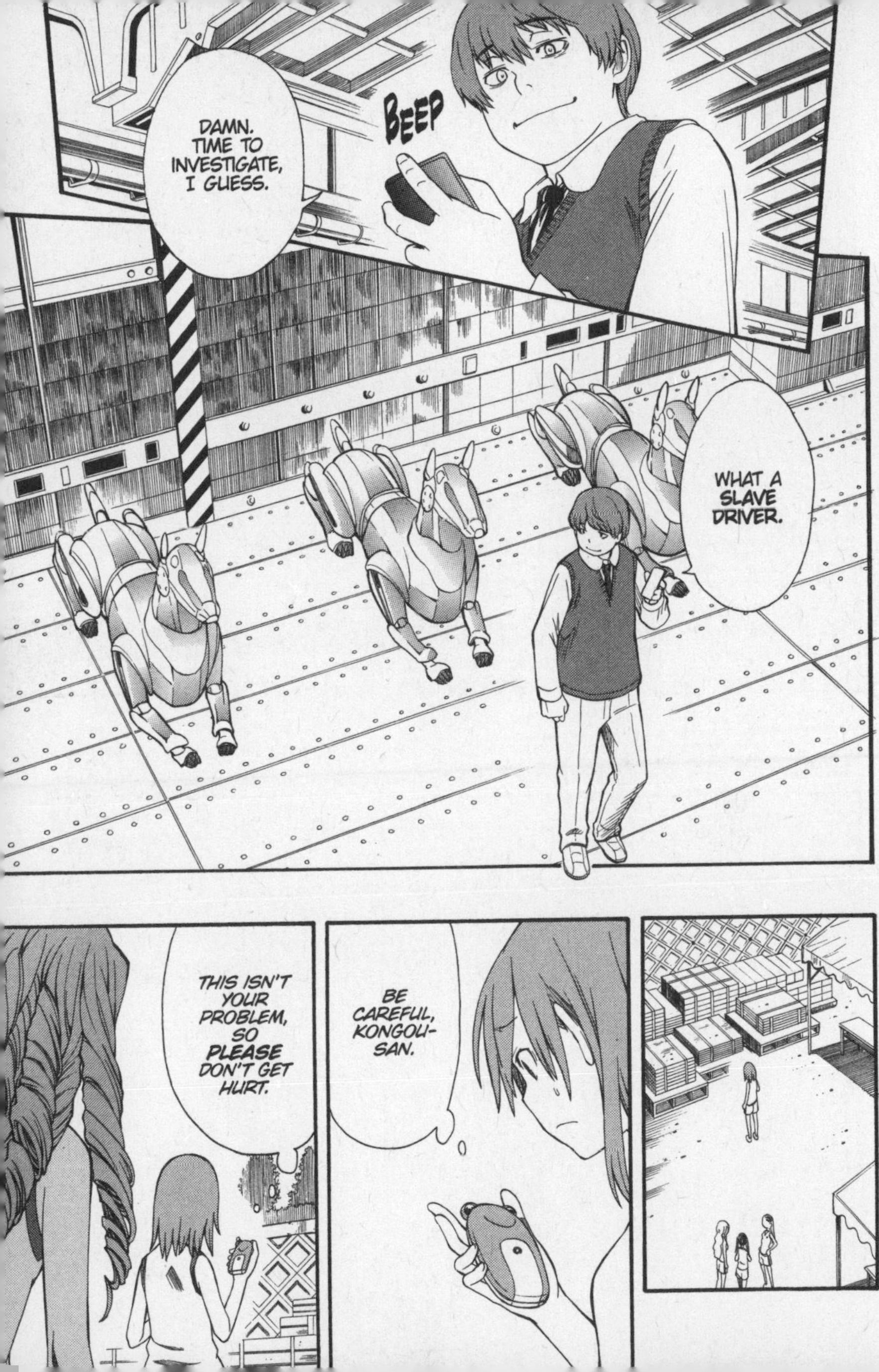
BEEP
DAMN. TIME TO INVESTIGATE, I GUESS.
WHAT A SLAVE DRIVER.
BE CAREFUL, KONGOU-SAN.
THIS ISN'T YOUR PROBLEM, SO PLEASE DON'T GET HURT.

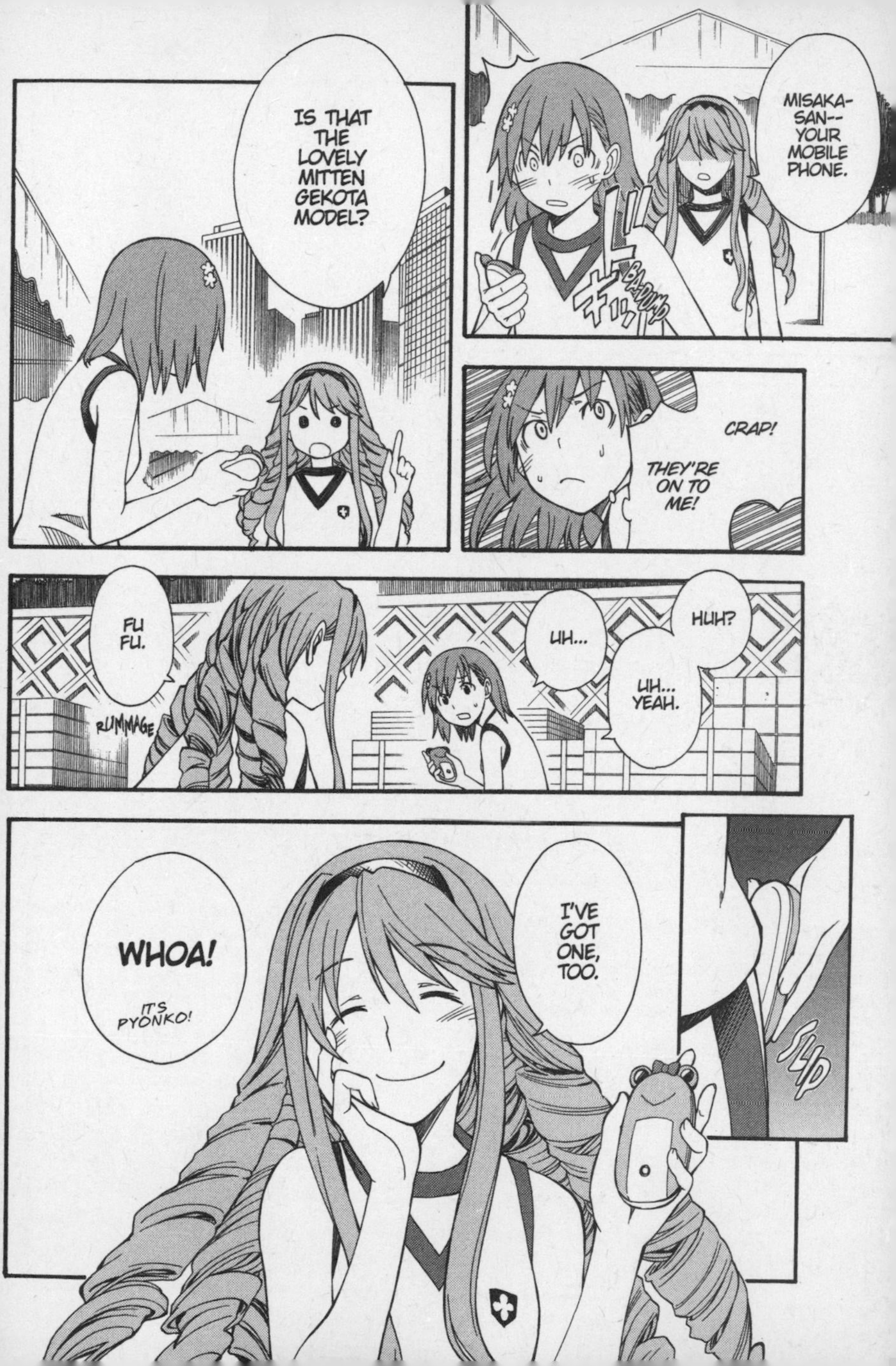
MISAKA-SAN-- YOUR MOBILE PHONE.
BA-DUMP
CRAP!
THEY'RE ON TO ME!
IS THAT THE LOVELY MITTEN GEKOTA MODEL?
HUH?
UH... YEAH.
UH...
FU FU.
RUMMAGE
SLIP
I'VE GOT ONE, TOO.
WHOA!
IT'S PYONKO!

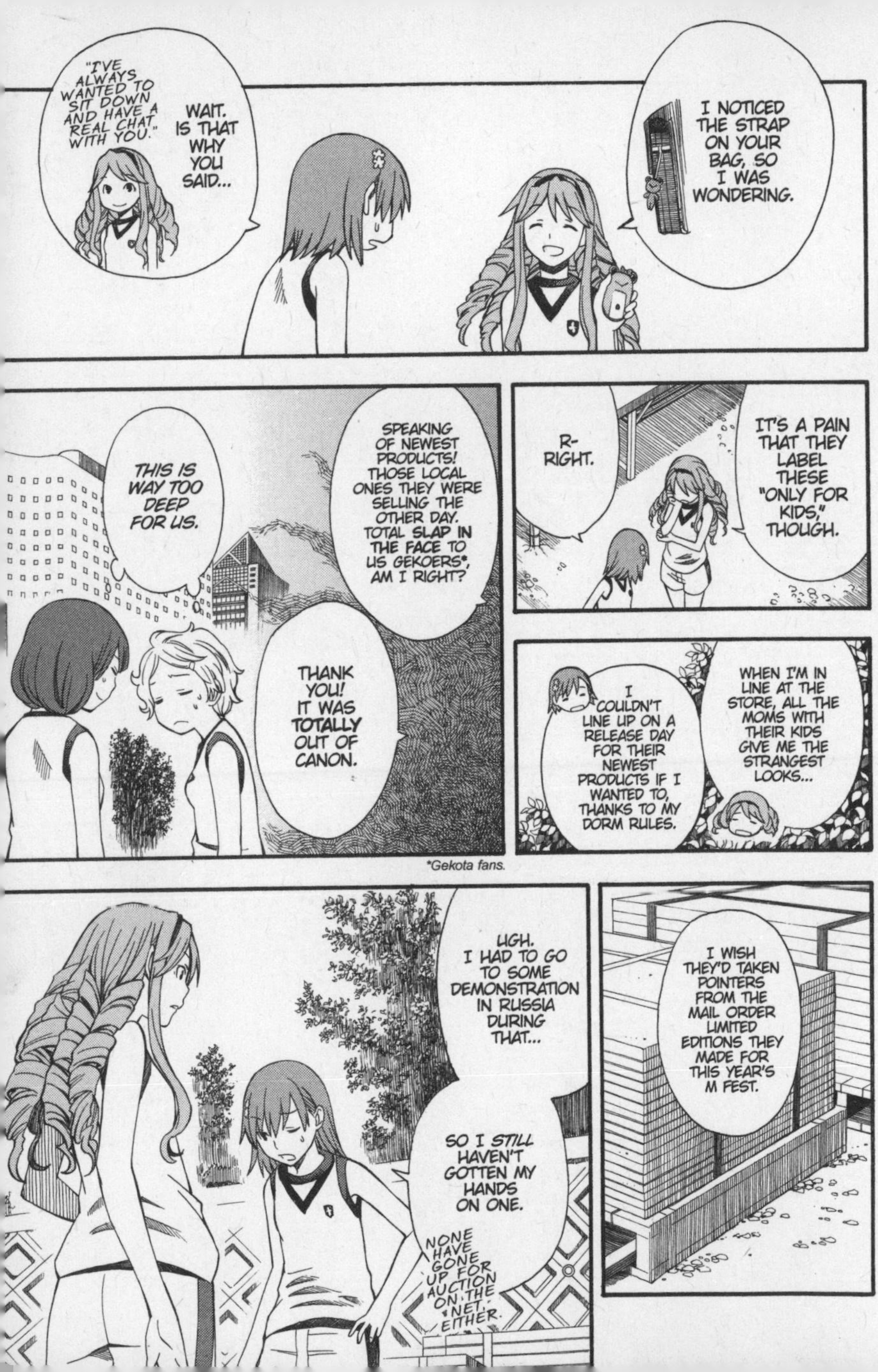
I NOTICED THE STRAP ON YOUR BAG, SO I WAS WONDERING.
WAIT. IS THAT WHY YOU SAID...
"I'VE ALWAYS WANTED TO SIT DOWN AND HAVE A REAL CHAT WITH YOU."
IT'S A PAIN THAT THEY LABEL THESE "ONLY FOR KIDS," THOUGH.
R-RIGHT.
WHEN I'M IN LINE AT THE STORE, ALL THE MOMS WITH THEIR KIDS GIVE ME THE STRANGEST LOOKS...
I COULDN'T LINE UP ON A RELEASE DAY FOR THEIR NEWEST PRODUCTS IF I WANTED TO, THANKS TO MY DORM RULES.
SPEAKING OF NEWEST PRODUCTS! THOSE LOCAL ONES THEY WERE SELLING THE OTHER DAY. TOTAL SLAP IN THE FACE TO US GEKOERS*, AM I RIGHT?
THIS IS WAY TOO DEEP FOR US.
THANK YOU! IT WAS TOTALLY OUT OF CANON.
I WISH THEY'D TAKEN POINTERS FROM THE MAIL ORDER LIMITED EDITIONS THEY MADE FOR THIS YEAR'S M FEST.
UGH. I HAD TO GO TO SOME DEMONSTRATION IN RUSSIA DURING THAT...
SO I STILL HAVEN'T GOTTEN MY HANDS ON ONE.
NONE HAVE GONE UP FOR AUCTION ON THE NET, EITHER.

*Gekota fans.

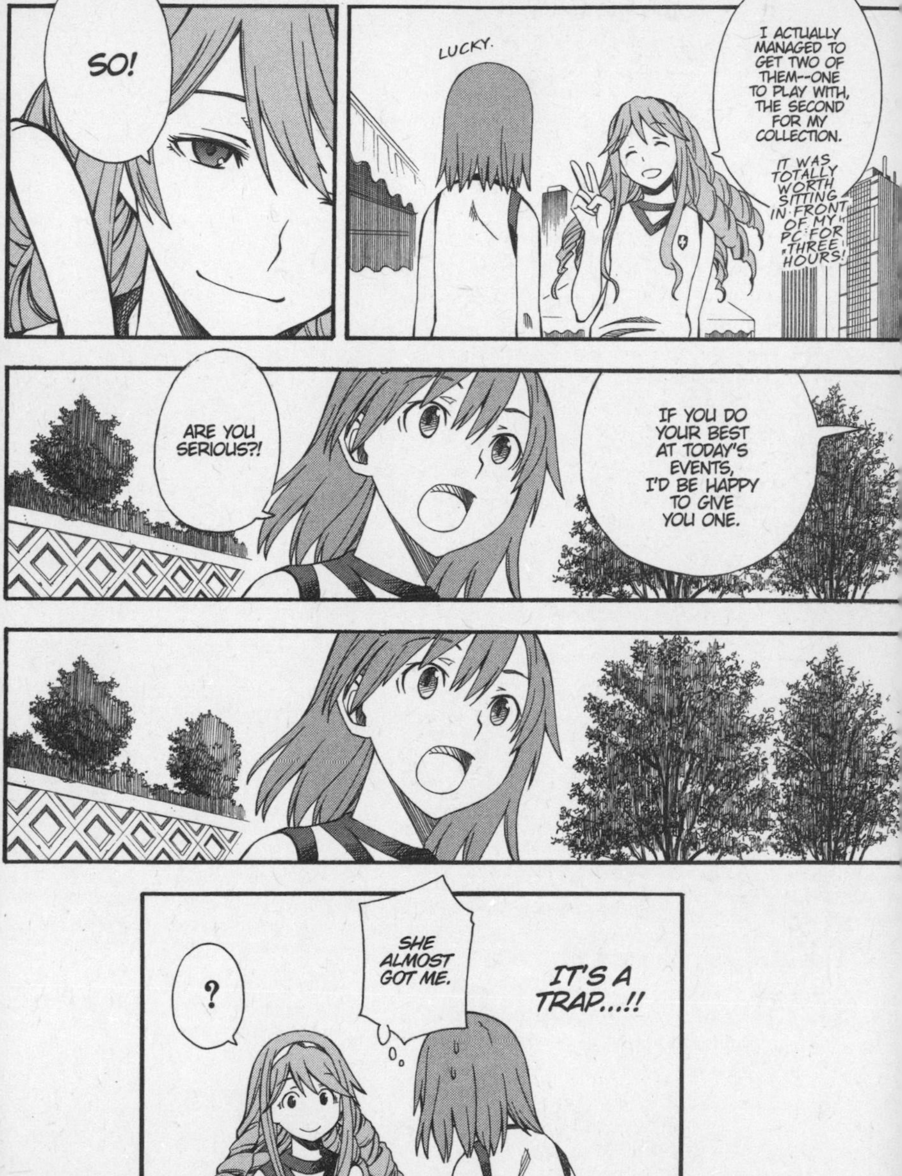
I ACTUALLY MANAGED TO GET TWO OF THEM--ONE TO PLAY WITH, THE SECOND FOR MY COLLECTION.
IT WAS TOTALLY WORTH SITTING IN FRONT OF MY PC FOR THREE HOURS!
LUCKY.
SO!
IF YOU DO YOUR BEST AT TODAY'S EVENTS, I'D BE HAPPY TO GIVE YOU ONE.
ARE YOU SERIOUS?!
IT'S A TRAP...!!
SHE ALMOST GOT ME.
?

A Certain Fan Club for Kindred Spirits

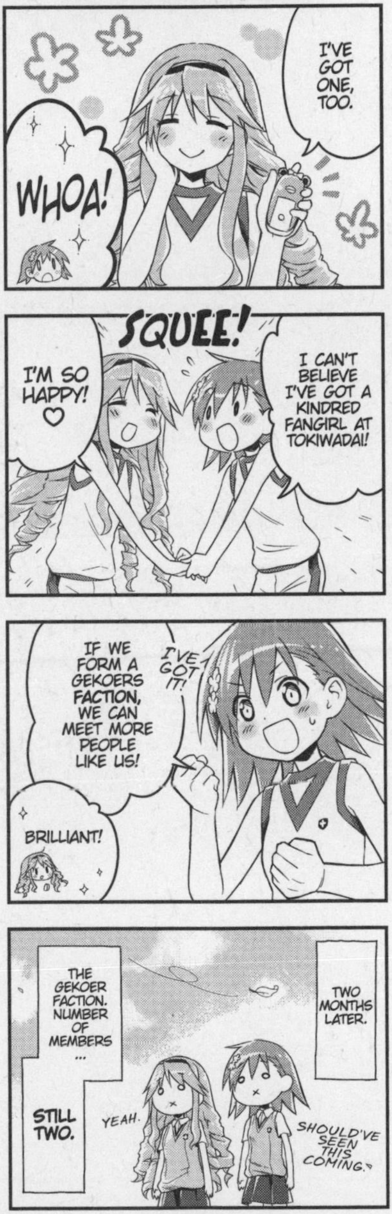
I'VE GOT ONE, TOO.
WHOA!
I CAN'T BELIEVE I'VE GOT A KINDRED FANGIRL AT TOKIWADAI!
SQUEE!
I'M SO HAPPY! ♡
I'VE GOT IT!
IF WE FORM A GEKOERS FACTION, WE CAN MEET MORE PEOPLE LIKE US!
BRILLIANT!
TWO MONTHS LATER.
THE GEKOER FACTION. NUMBER OF MEMBERS ...
SHOULD'VE SEEN THIS COMING.
YEAH.
STILL TWO.

A Certain Event's Sudden Death

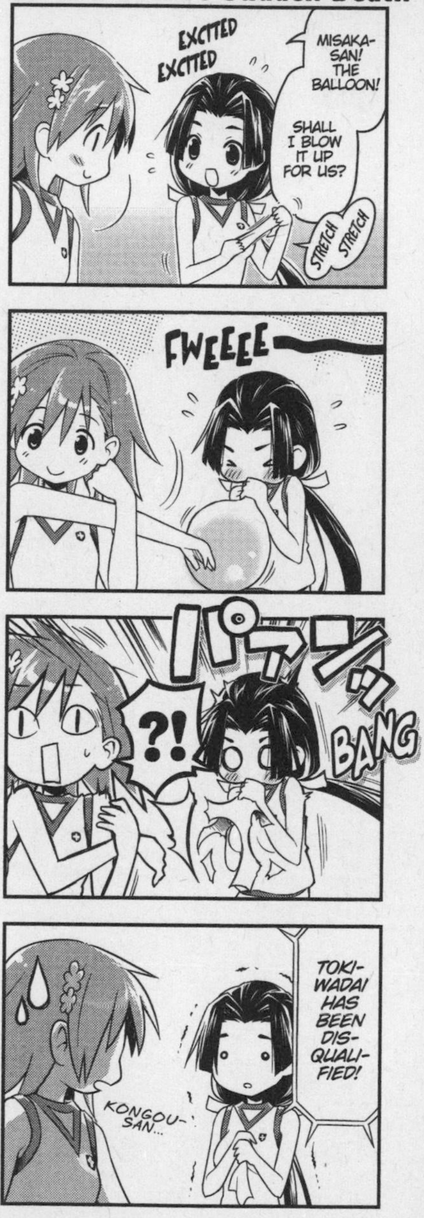
MISAKA-SAN! THE BALLOON!
SHALL I BLOW IT UP FOR US?
EXCITED EXCITED
STRETCH STRETCH
FWEEEE
パン
BANG
?!
TOKI-WADAI HAS BEEN DIS-QUALI-FIED!
KONGOU-SAN...

CHAPTER 50: OUTBREAK

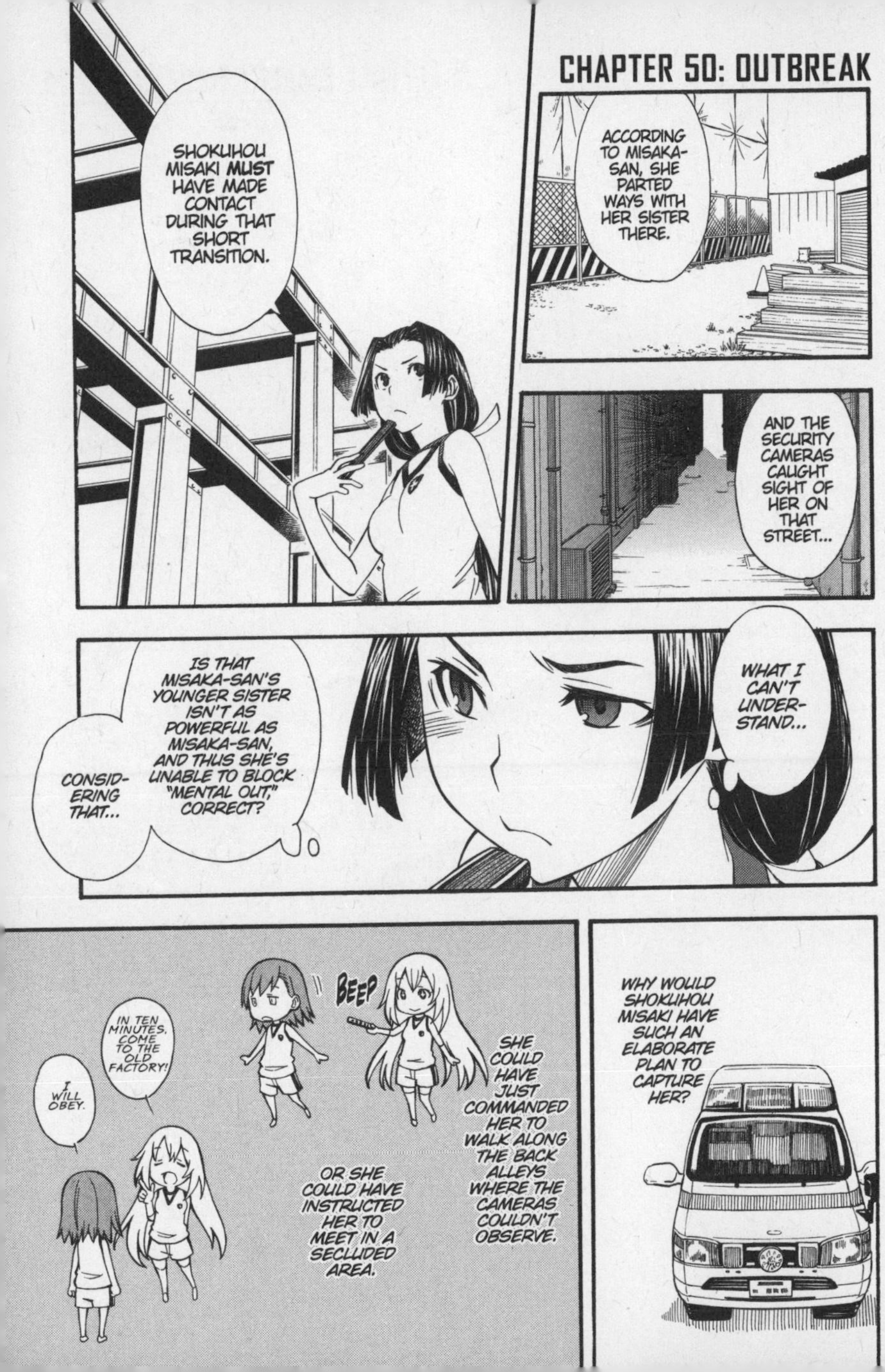
ACCORDING TO MISAKA-SAN, SHE PARTED WAYS WITH HER SISTER THERE.
AND THE SECURITY CAMERAS CAUGHT SIGHT OF HER ON THAT STREET...
SHOKUHOU MISAKI MUST HAVE MADE CONTACT DURING THAT SHORT TRANSITION.
WHAT I CAN'T UNDERSTAND...
IS THAT MISAKA-SAN'S YOUNGER SISTER ISN'T AS POWERFUL AS MISAKA-SAN, AND THUS SHE'S UNABLE TO BLOCK "MENTAL OUT," CORRECT?
CONSIDERING THAT...
WHY WOULD SHOKUHOU MISAKI HAVE SUCH AN ELABORATE PLAN TO CAPTURE HER?
SHE COULD HAVE JUST COMMANDED HER TO WALK ALONG THE BACK ALLEYS WHERE THE CAMERAS COULDN'T OBSERVE.
BEEP
IN TEN MINUTES, COME TO THE OLD FACTORY!
OR SHE COULD HAVE INSTRUCTED HER TO MEET IN A SECLUDED AREA.
I WILL OBEY.

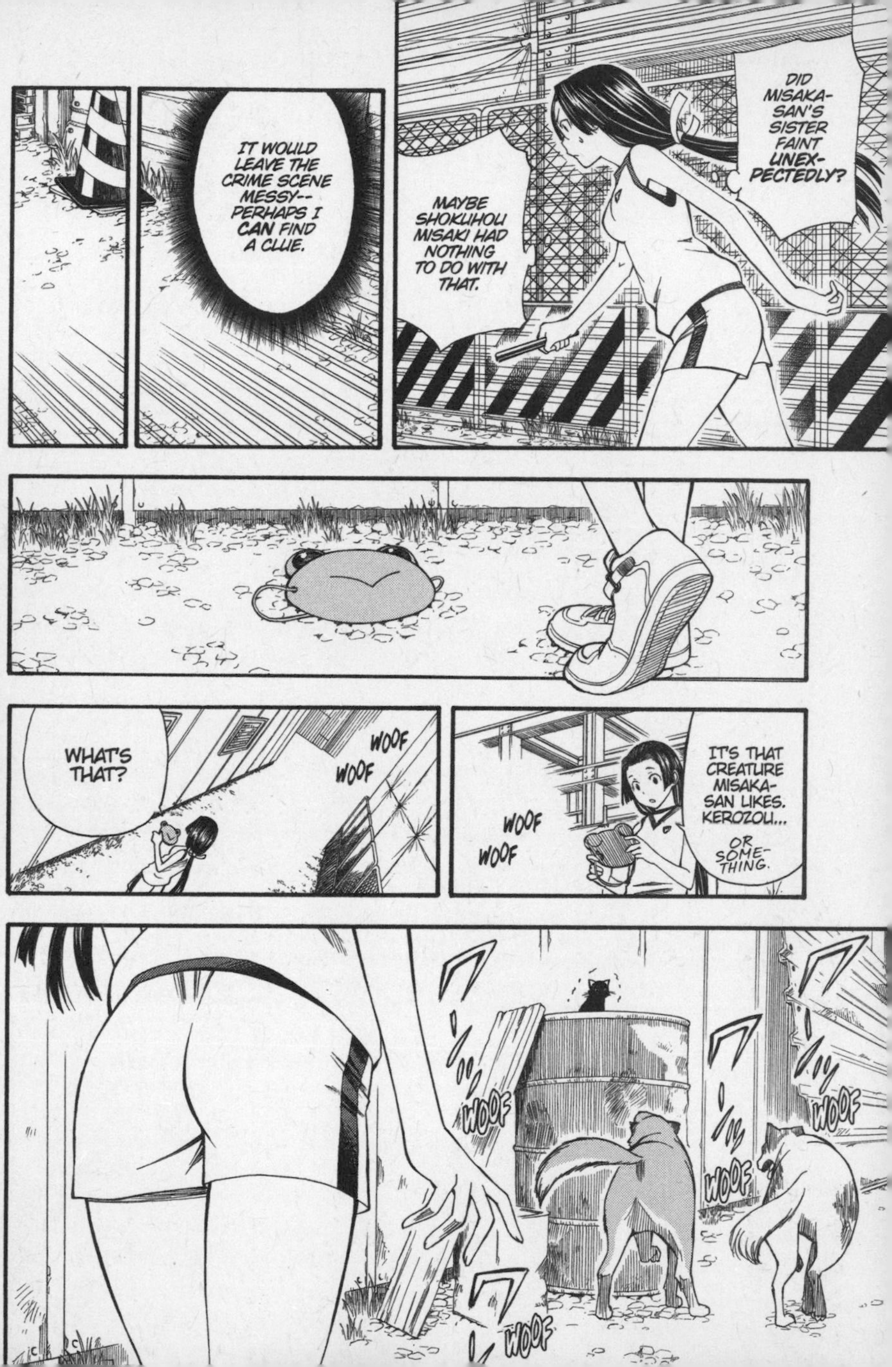
DID MISAKA-SAN'S SISTER FAINT UNEXPECTEDLY?
MAYBE SHOKUHOU MISAKI HAD NOTHING TO DO WITH THAT.
IT WOULD LEAVE THE CRIME SCENE MESSY-- PERHAPS I CAN FIND A CLUE.
IT'S THAT CREATURE MISAKA-SAN LIKES. KEROZOU...
OR SOMETHING.
WOOF
WOOF
WHAT'S THAT?
WOOF
WOOF
WOOF
WOOF
WOOF
WOOF

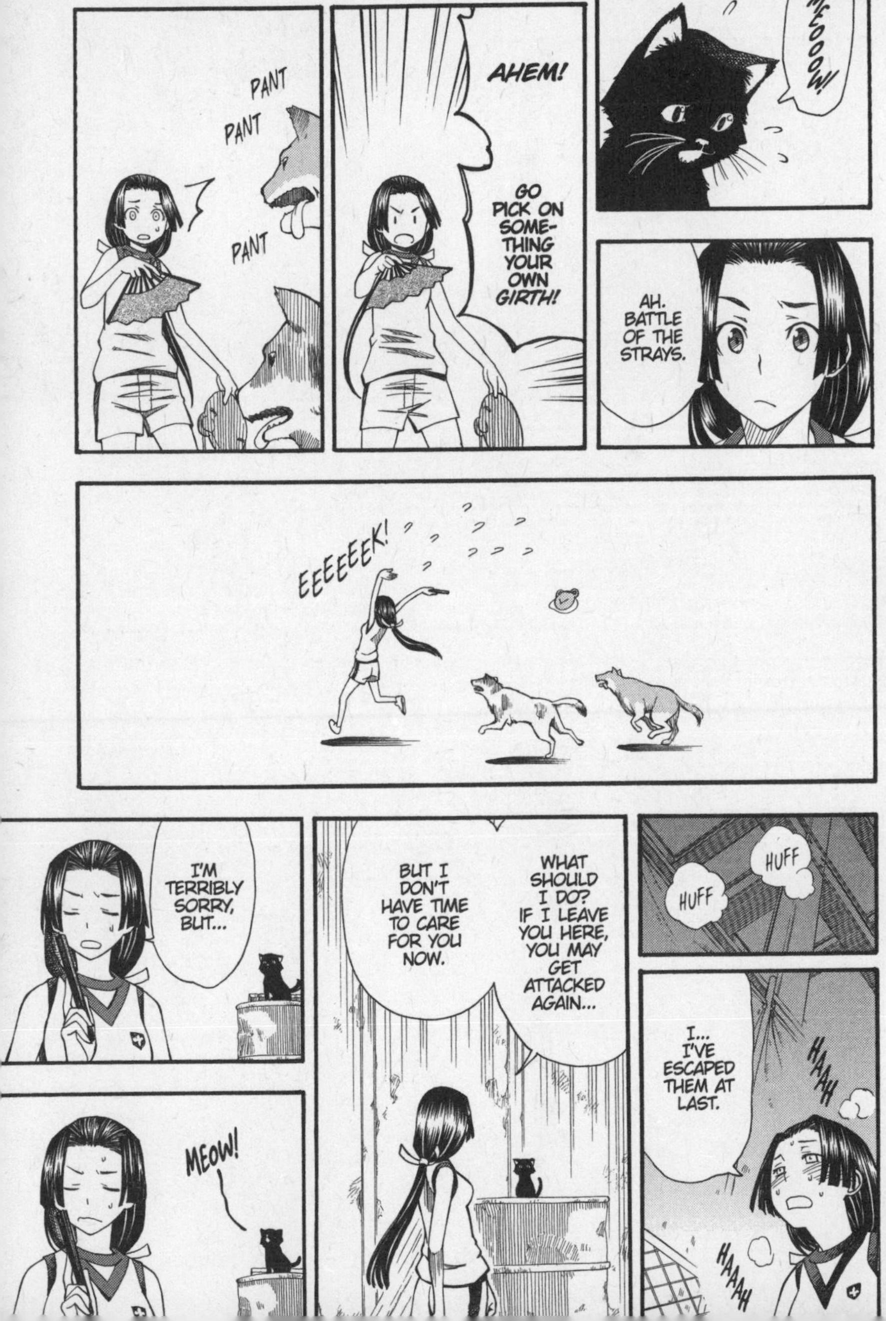
MEOOOW!
AH. BATTLE OF THE STRAYS.
AHEM!
GO PICK ON SOMETHING YOUR OWN GIRTH!
PANT
PANT
PANT
EEEEEEK!
HUFF
HUFF
I... I'VE ESCAPED THEM AT LAST.
HAAAH
HAAAH
WHAT SHOULD I DO? IF I LEAVE YOU HERE, YOU MAY GET ATTACKED AGAIN...
BUT I DON'T HAVE TIME TO CARE FOR YOU NOW.
I'M TERRIBLY SORRY, BUT...
MEOW!

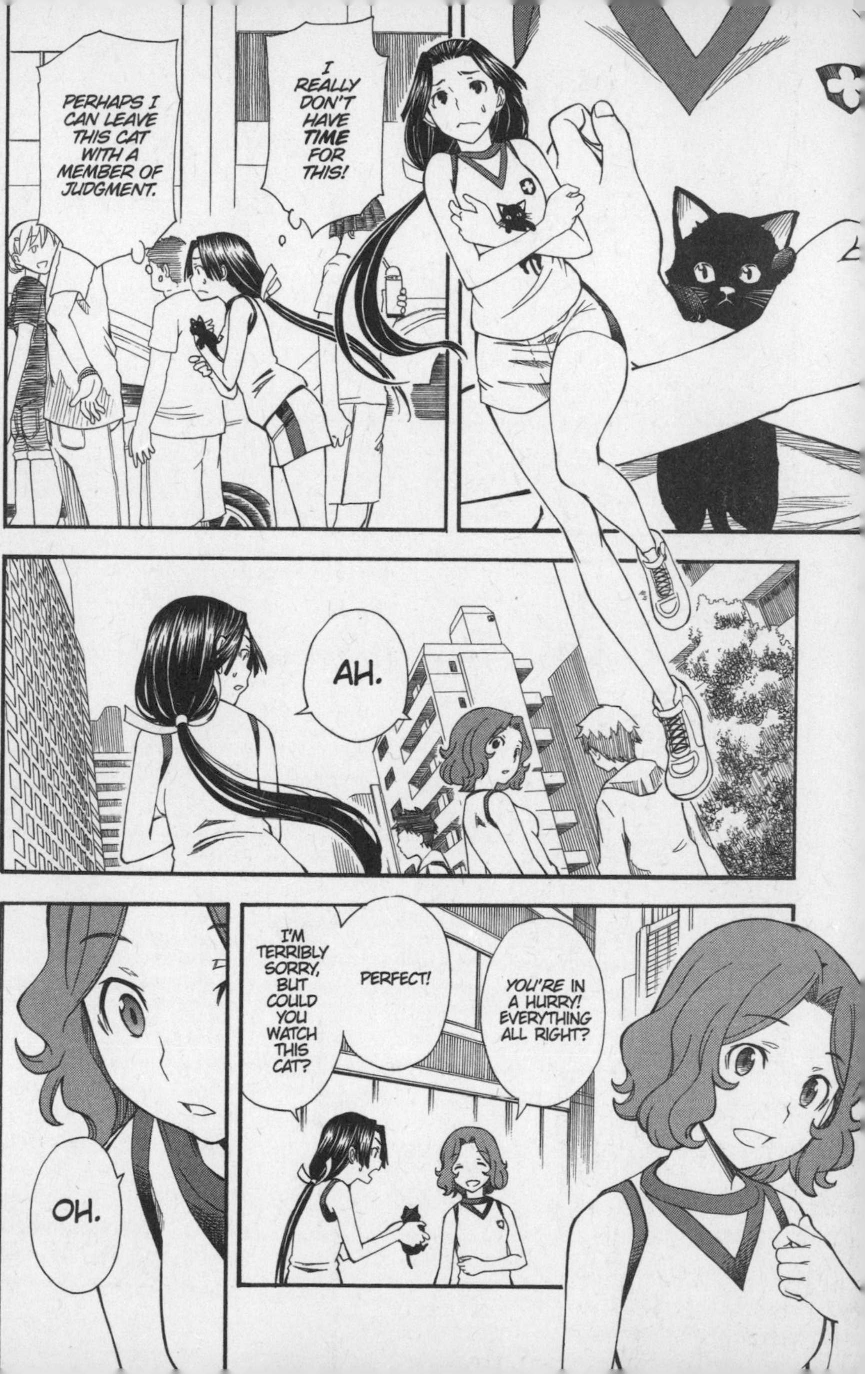

I REALLY DON'T HAVE TIME FOR THIS!
PERHAPS I CAN LEAVE THIS CAT WITH A MEMBER OF JUDGMENT.
AH.
YOU'RE IN A HURRY! EVERYTHING ALL RIGHT?
PERFECT!
I'M TERRIBLY SORRY, BUT COULD YOU WATCH THIS CAT?
OH.

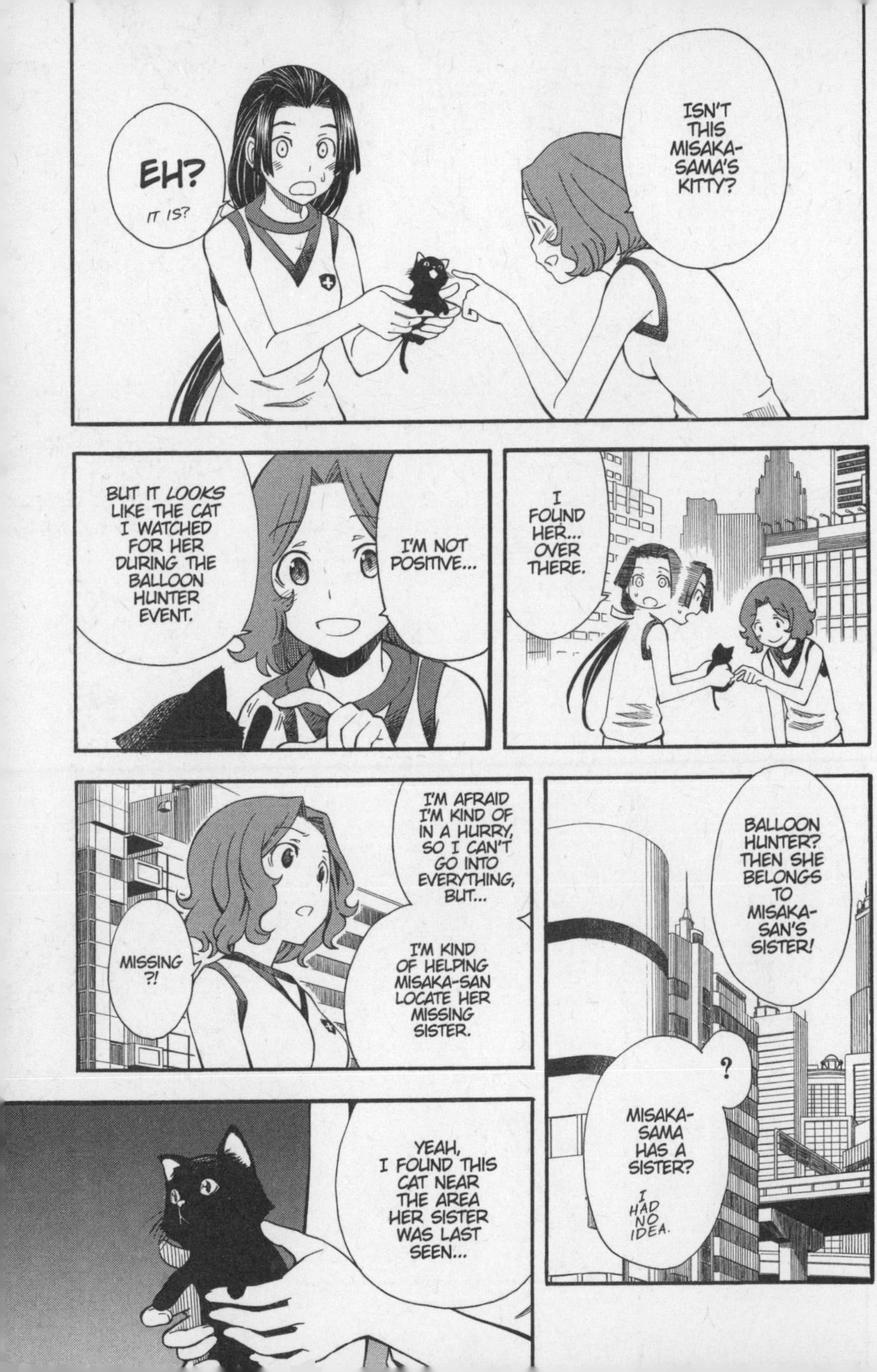

ISN'T THIS MISAKA-SAMA'S KITTY?
EH? IT IS?
I FOUND HER... OVER THERE.
I'M NOT POSITIVE...
BUT IT *LOOKS* LIKE THE CAT I WATCHED FOR HER DURING THE BALLOON HUNTER EVENT.
BALLOON HUNTER? THEN SHE BELONGS TO MISAKA-SAN'S SISTER!
?
MISAKA-SAMA HAS A SISTER?
I HAD NO IDEA.
I'M AFRAID I'M KIND OF IN A HURRY, SO I CAN'T GO INTO EVERYTHING, BUT...
I'M KIND OF HELPING MISAKA-SAN LOCATE HER MISSING SISTER.
MISSING?!
YEAH, I FOUND THIS CAT NEAR THE AREA HER SISTER WAS LAST SEEN...

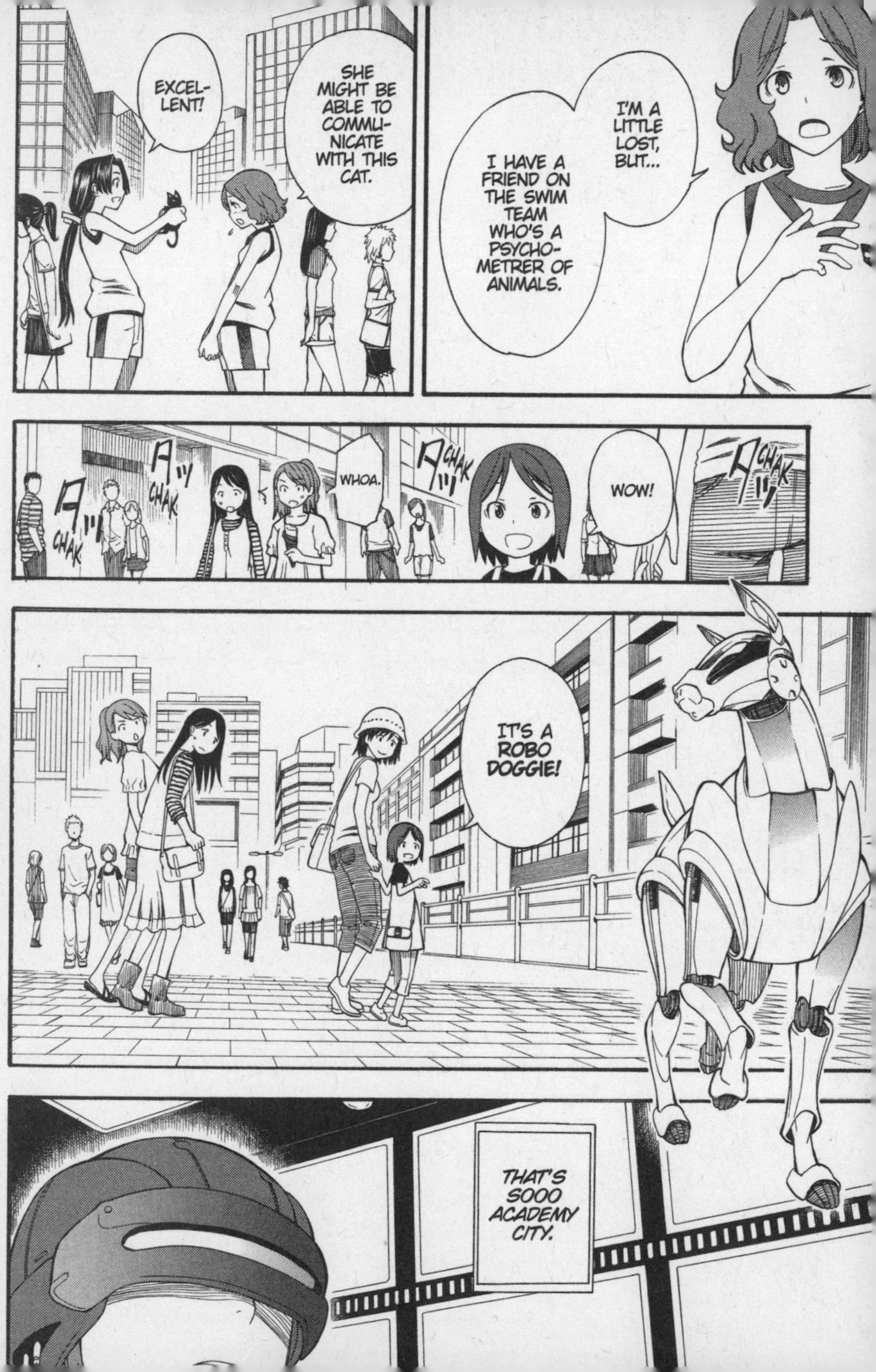
I'M A LITTLE LOST, BUT...
I HAVE A FRIEND ON THE SWIM TEAM WHO'S A PSYCHOMETRER OF ANIMALS.
SHE MIGHT BE ABLE TO COMMUNICATE WITH THIS CAT.
EXCELLENT!
CHAK
WOW!
CHAK
WHOA.
CHAK
CHAK
IT'S A ROBO DOGGIE!
THAT'S SOOO ACADEMY CITY.

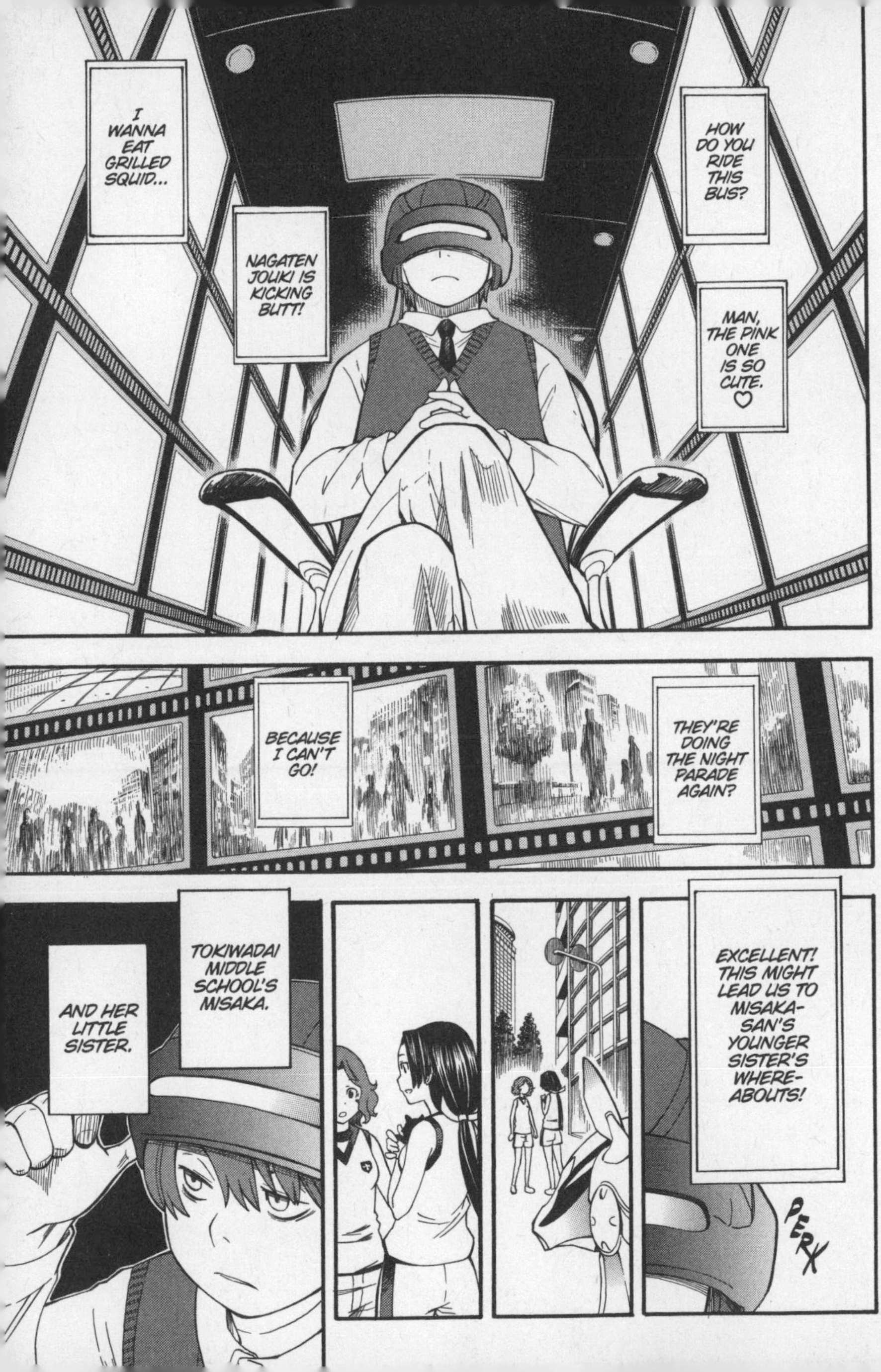
HOW DO YOU RIDE THIS BUS?
MAN, THE PINK ONE IS SO CUTE. ♡
I WANNA EAT GRILLED SQUID...
NAGATEN JOUKI IS KICKING BUTT!
THEY'RE DOING THE NIGHT PARADE AGAIN?
BECAUSE I CAN'T GO!
EXCELLENT! THIS MIGHT LEAD US TO MISAKA-SAN'S YOUNGER SISTER'S WHERE-ABOUTS!
PERK
TOKIWADAI MIDDLE SCHOOL'S MISAKA.
AND HER LITTLE SISTER.

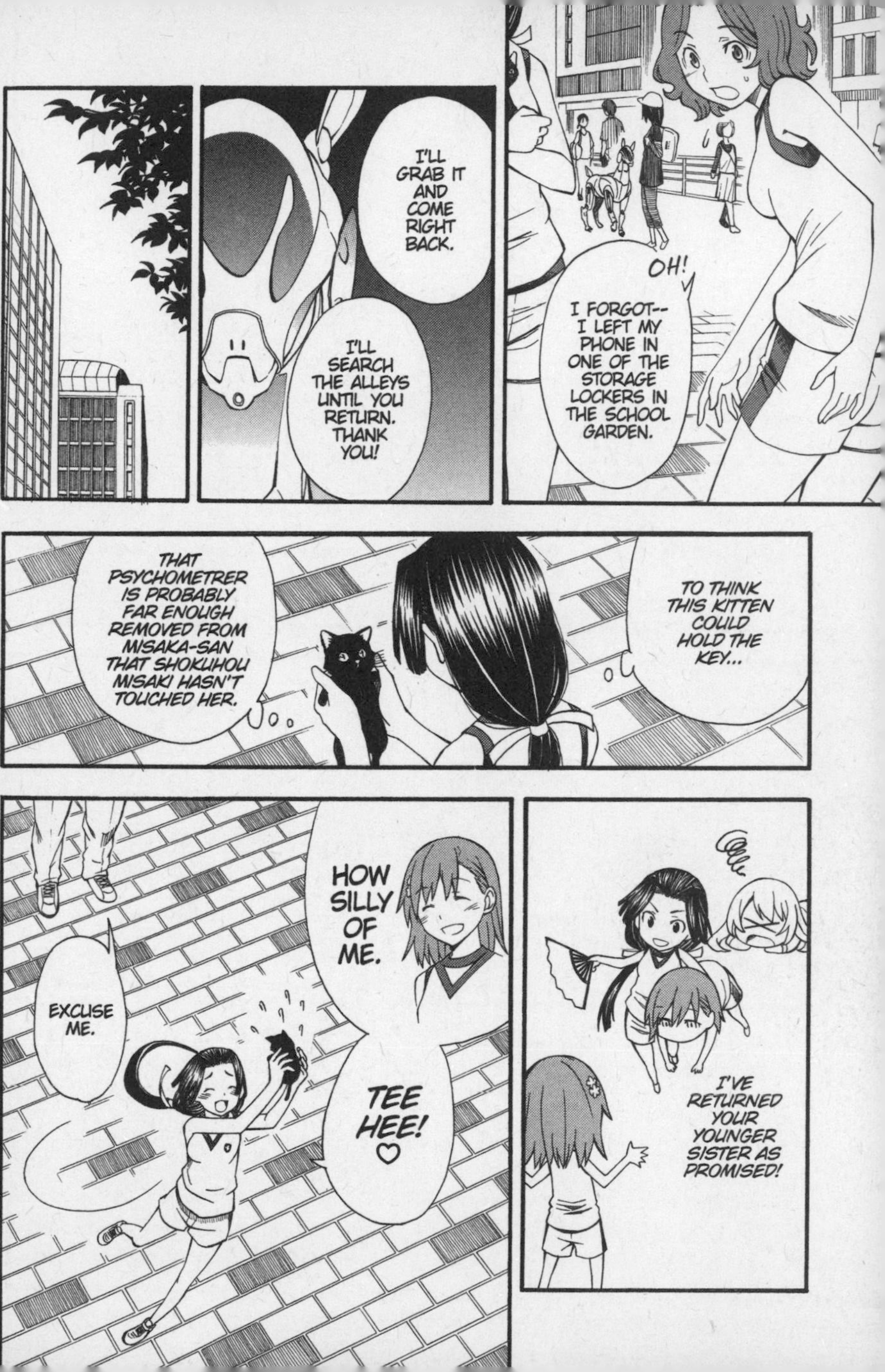
OH!
I FORGOT-- I LEFT MY PHONE IN ONE OF THE STORAGE LOCKERS IN THE SCHOOL GARDEN.
I'LL GRAB IT AND COME RIGHT BACK.
I'LL SEARCH THE ALLEYS UNTIL YOU RETURN. THANK YOU!
TO THINK THIS KITTEN COULD HOLD THE KEY...
THAT PSYCHOMETRER IS PROBABLY FAR ENOUGH REMOVED FROM MISAKA-SAN THAT SHOKUHOU MISAKI HASN'T TOUCHED HER.
I'VE RETURNED YOUR YOUNGER SISTER AS PROMISED!
HOW SILLY OF ME.
TEE HEE! ♡
EXCUSE ME.

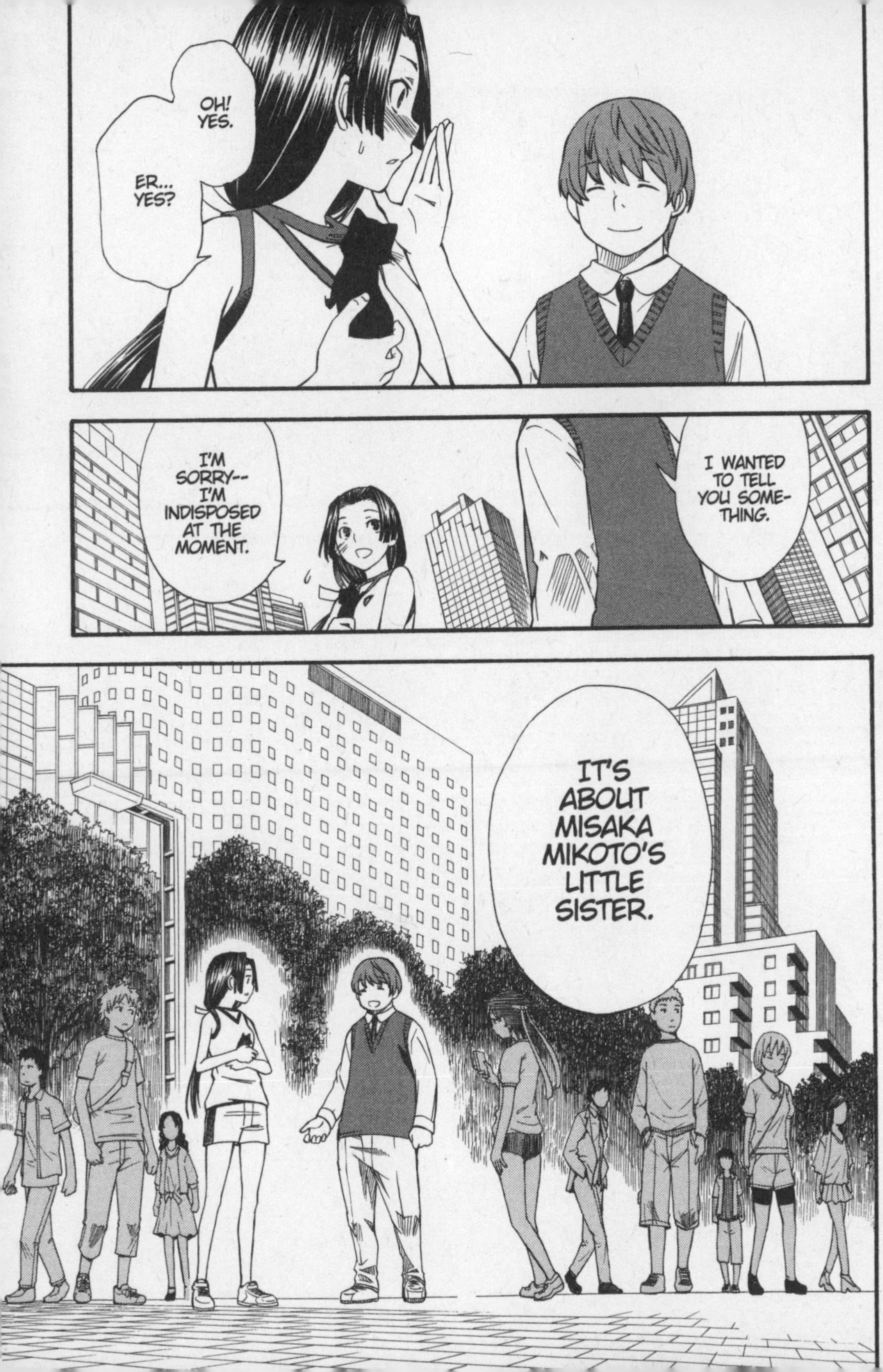
OH! YES.
ER... YES?
I WANTED TO TELL YOU SOME-THING.
I'M SORRY-- I'M INDISPOSED AT THE MOMENT.
IT'S ABOUT MISAKA MIKOTO'S LITTLE SISTER.

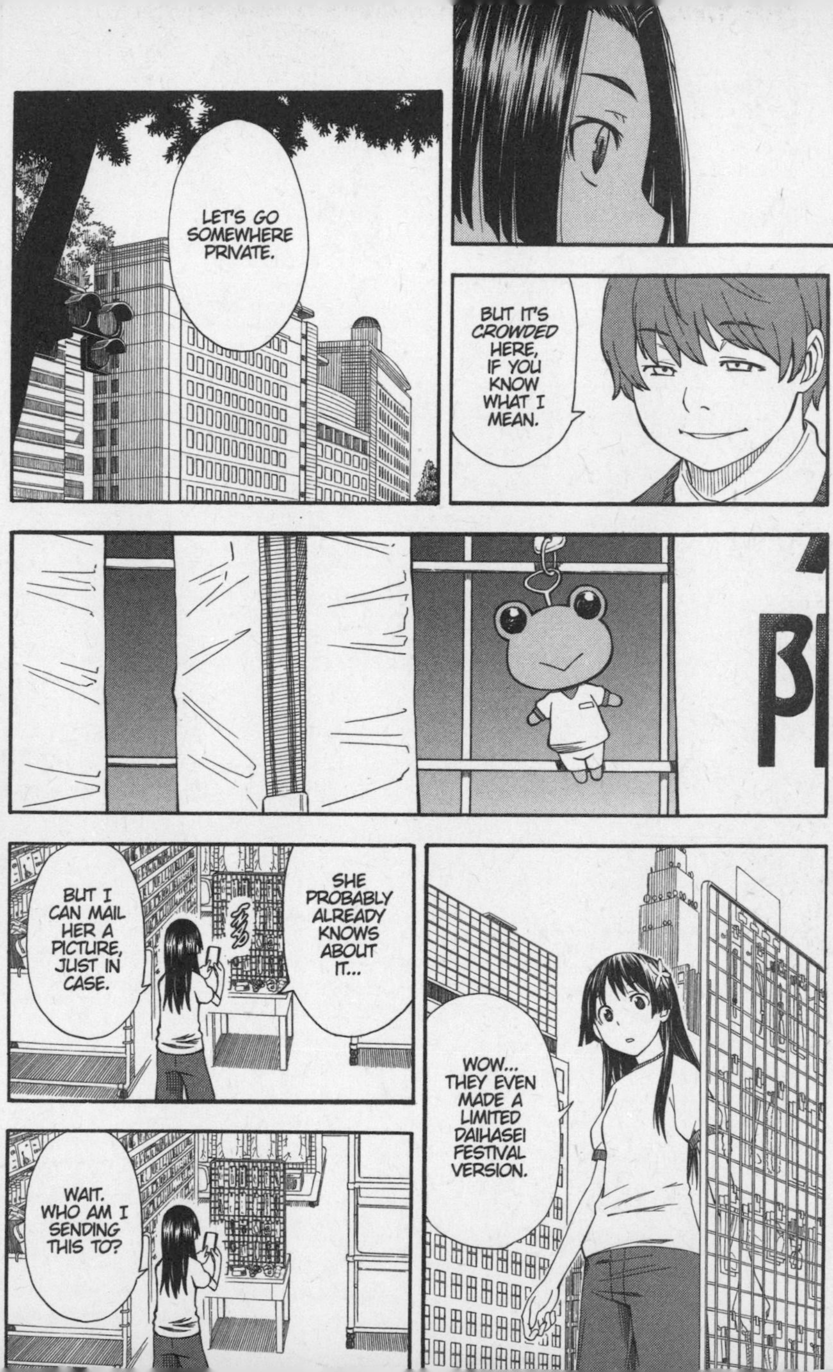
BUT IT'S CROWDED HERE, IF YOU KNOW WHAT I MEAN.
LET'S GO SOMEWHERE PRIVATE.
WOW... THEY EVEN MADE A LIMITED DAIHASEI FESTIVAL VERSION.
SHE PROBABLY ALREADY KNOWS ABOUT IT...
BUT I CAN MAIL HER A PICTURE, JUST IN CASE.
WAIT. WHO AM I SENDING THIS TO?

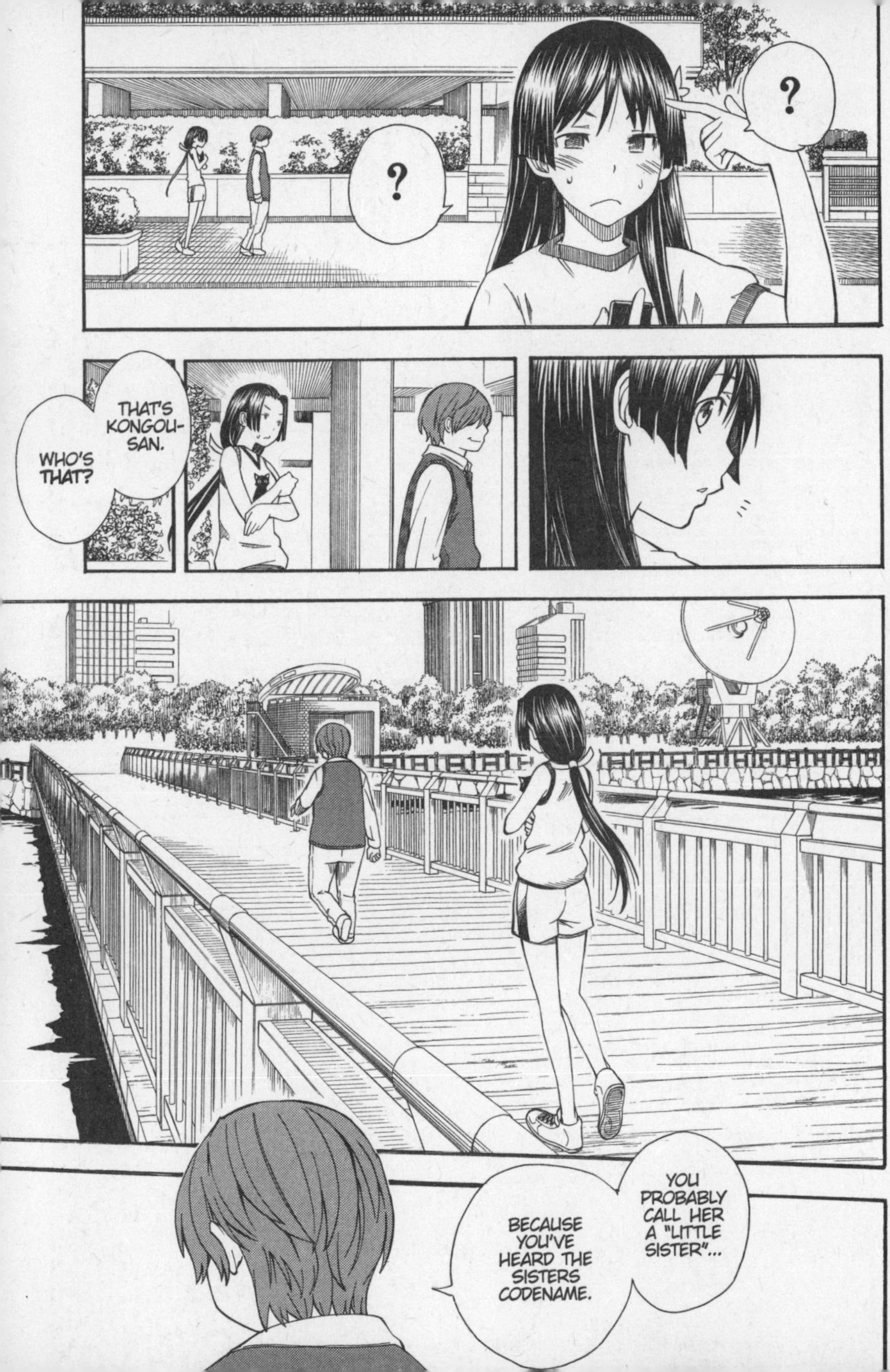
?
?
THAT'S KONGOU-SAN.
WHO'S THAT?
YOU PROBABLY CALL HER A "LITTLE SISTER"...
BECAUSE YOU'VE HEARD THE SISTERS CODENAME.

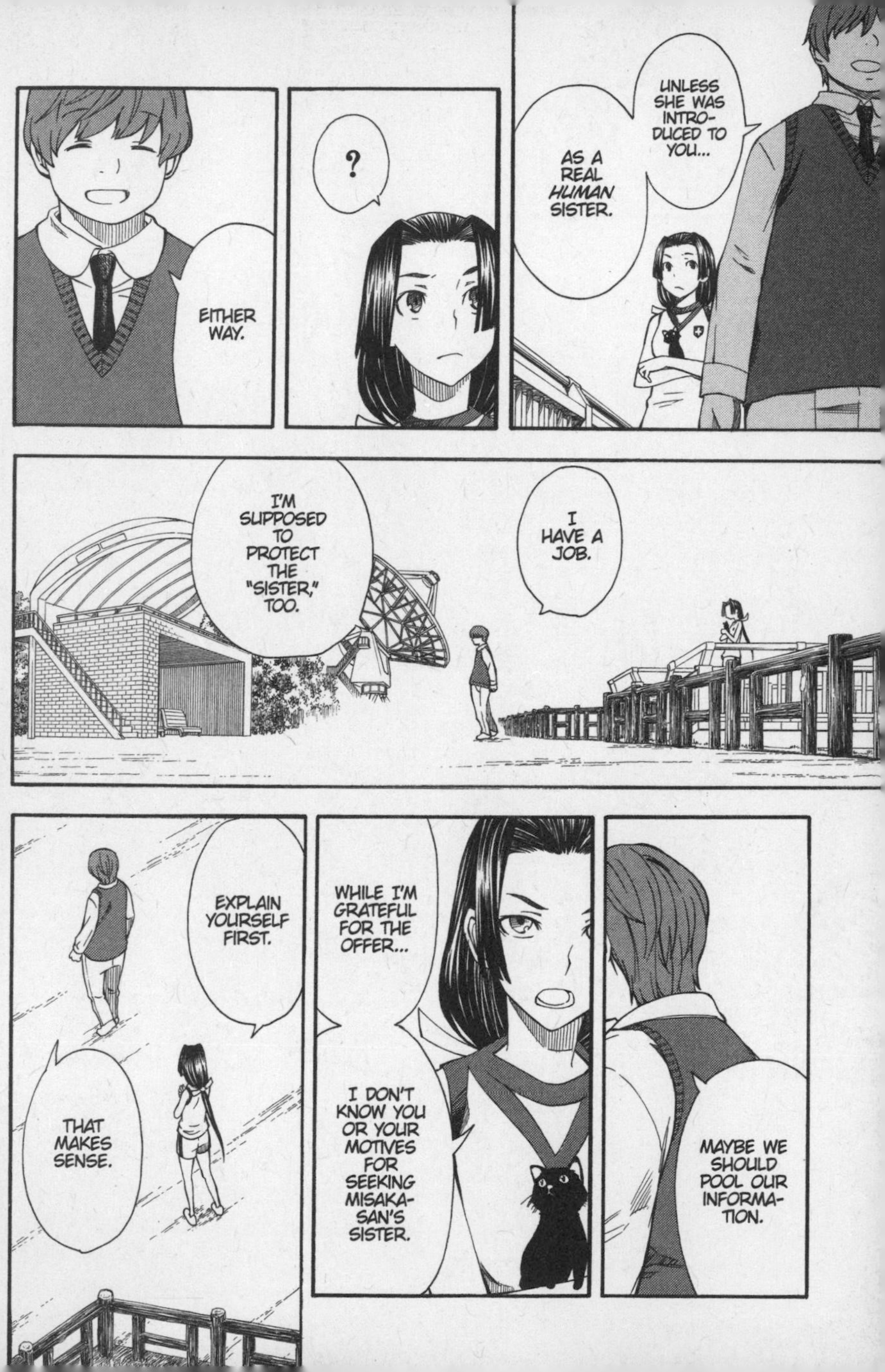
UNLESS SHE WAS INTRO-DUCED TO YOU...
AS A REAL *HUMAN* SISTER.
?
EITHER WAY.
I HAVE A JOB.
I'M SUPPOSED TO PROTECT THE "SISTER," TOO.
MAYBE WE SHOULD POOL OUR INFORMA-TION.
WHILE I'M GRATEFUL FOR THE OFFER...
I DON'T KNOW YOU OR YOUR MOTIVES FOR SEEKING MISAKA-SAN'S SISTER.
EXPLAIN YOURSELF FIRST.
THAT MAKES SENSE.

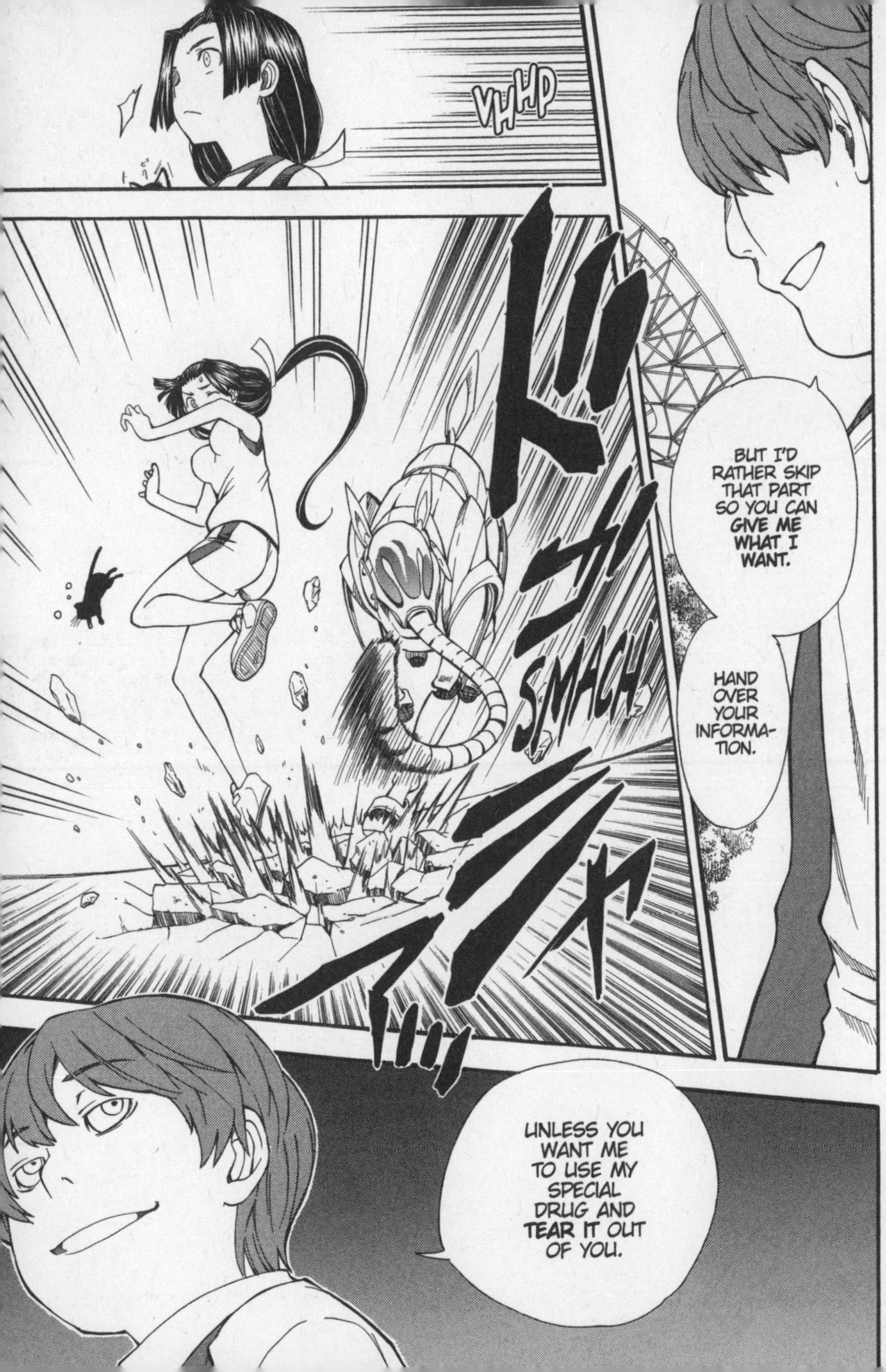
BUT I'D RATHER SKIP THAT PART SO YOU CAN GIVE ME WHAT I WANT.
HAND OVER YOUR INFORMATION.
VHHP
SMACH
UNLESS YOU WANT ME TO USE MY SPECIAL DRUG AND TEAR IT OUT OF YOU.

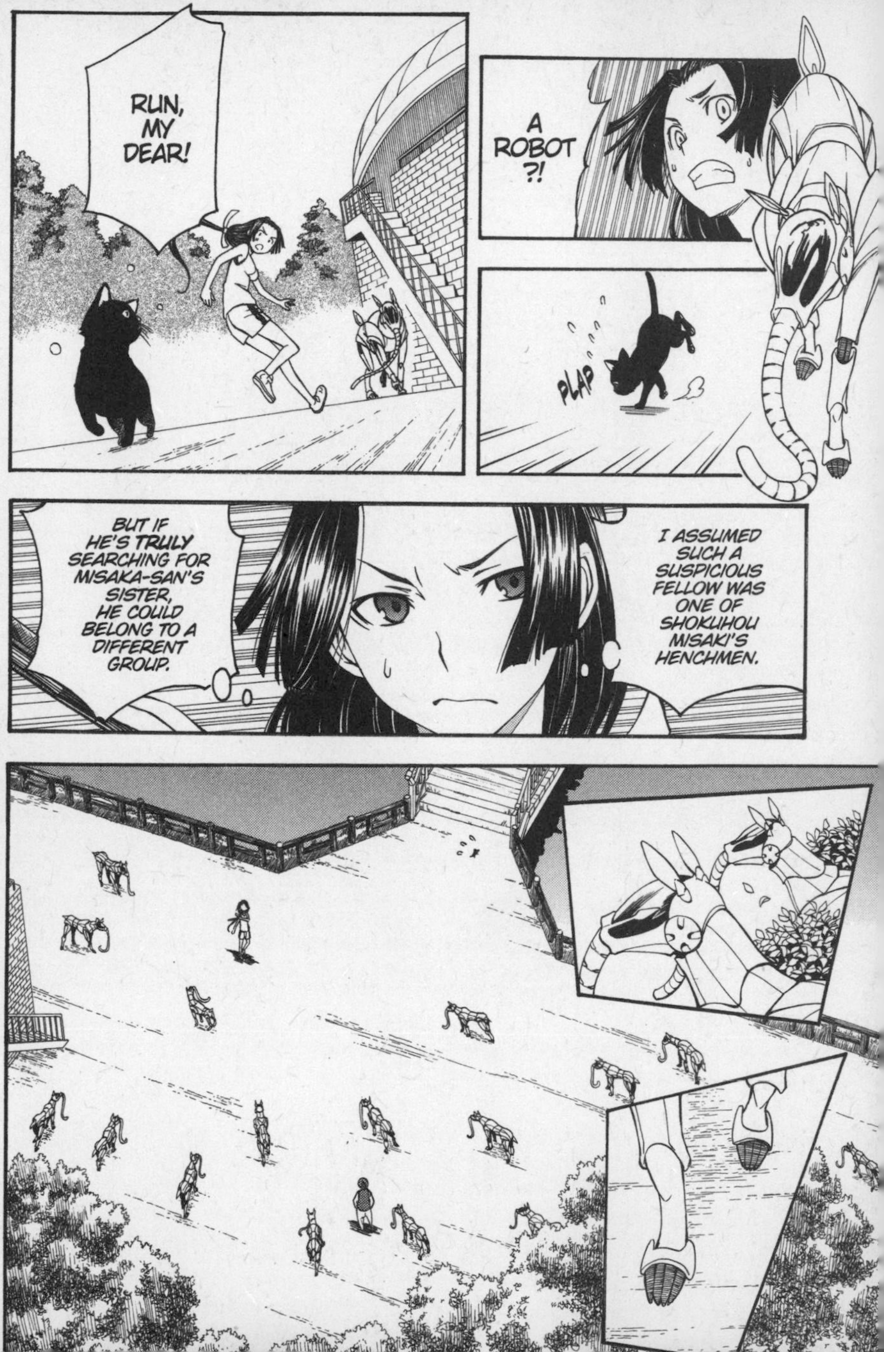
A ROBOT ?!
PLAP
RUN, MY DEAR!
I ASSUMED SUCH A SUSPICIOUS FELLOW WAS ONE OF SHOKUHOU MISAKI'S HENCHMEN.
BUT IF HE'S TRULY SEARCHING FOR MISAKA-SAN'S SISTER, HE COULD BELONG TO A DIFFERENT GROUP.

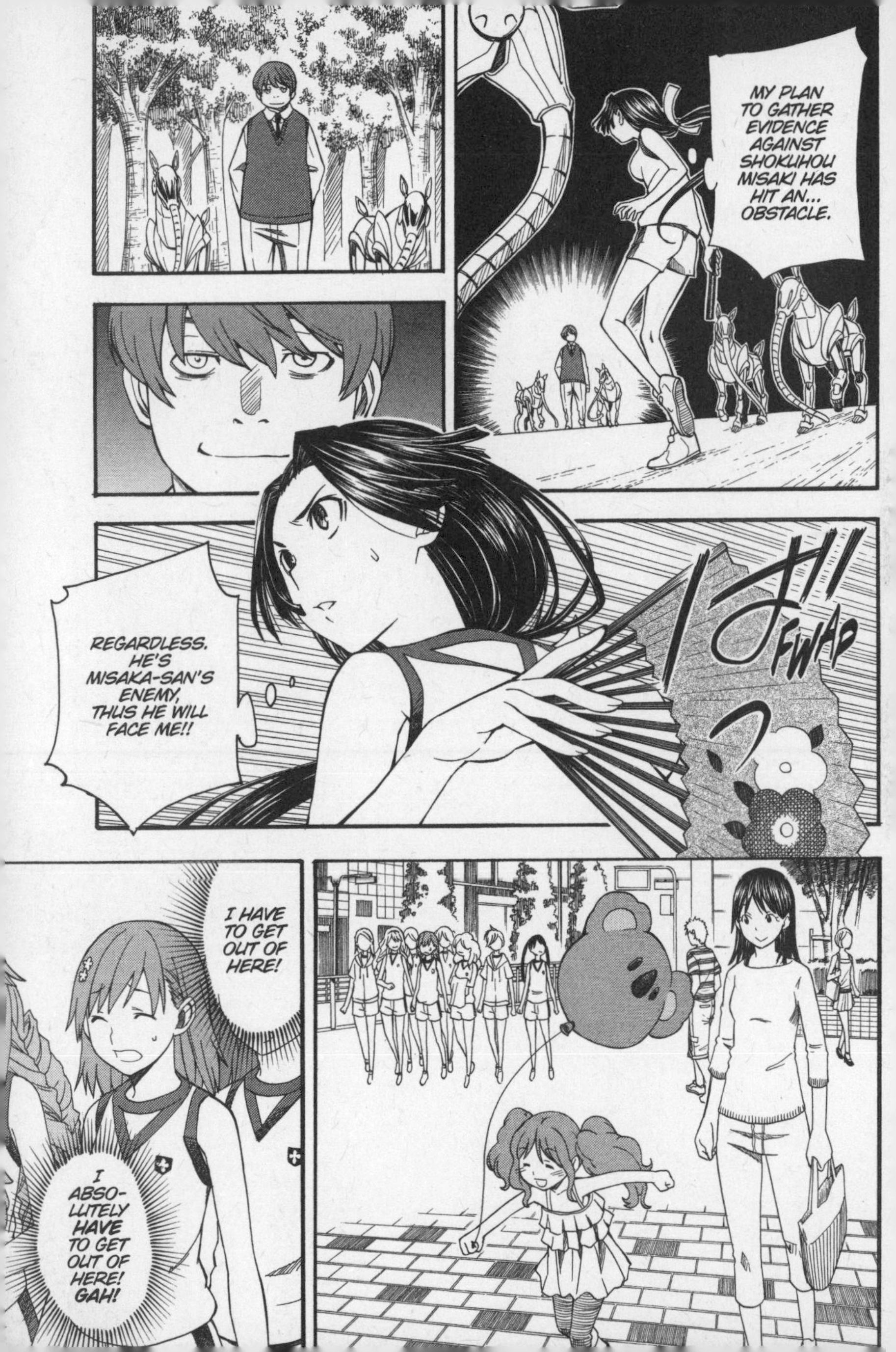
MY PLAN TO GATHER EVIDENCE AGAINST SHOKUHOU MISAKI HAS HIT AN... OBSTACLE.
FWAP
REGARDLESS. HE'S MISAKA-SAN'S ENEMY, THUS HE WILL FACE ME!!
I HAVE TO GET OUT OF HERE!
I ABSOLUTELY HAVE TO GET OUT OF HERE! GAH!

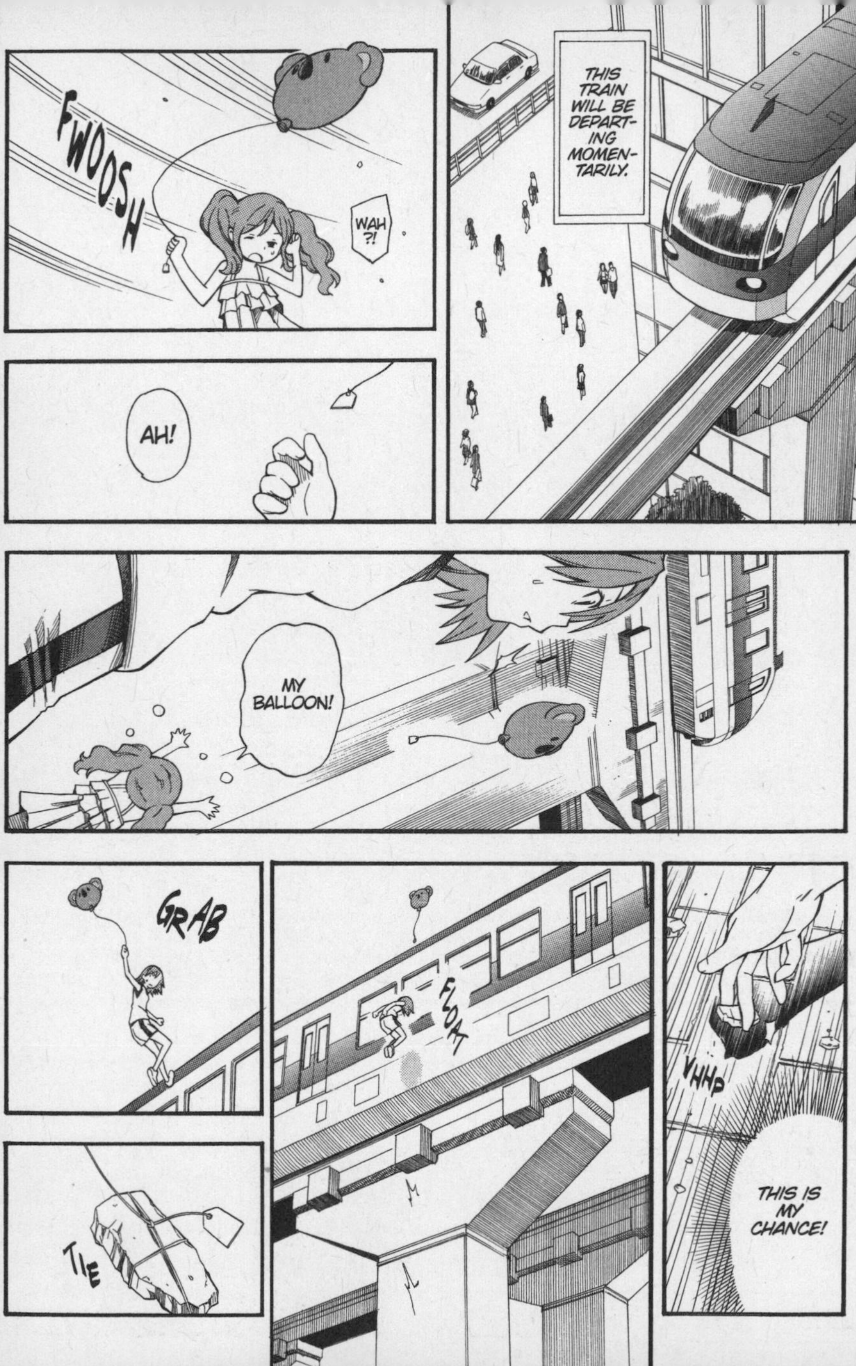
THIS TRAIN WILL BE DEPART-ING MOMEN-TARILY.
FWOOSH
WAH?!
AH!
MY BALLOON!
VHHP
THIS IS MY CHANCE!
FLOAT
GRAB
TIE

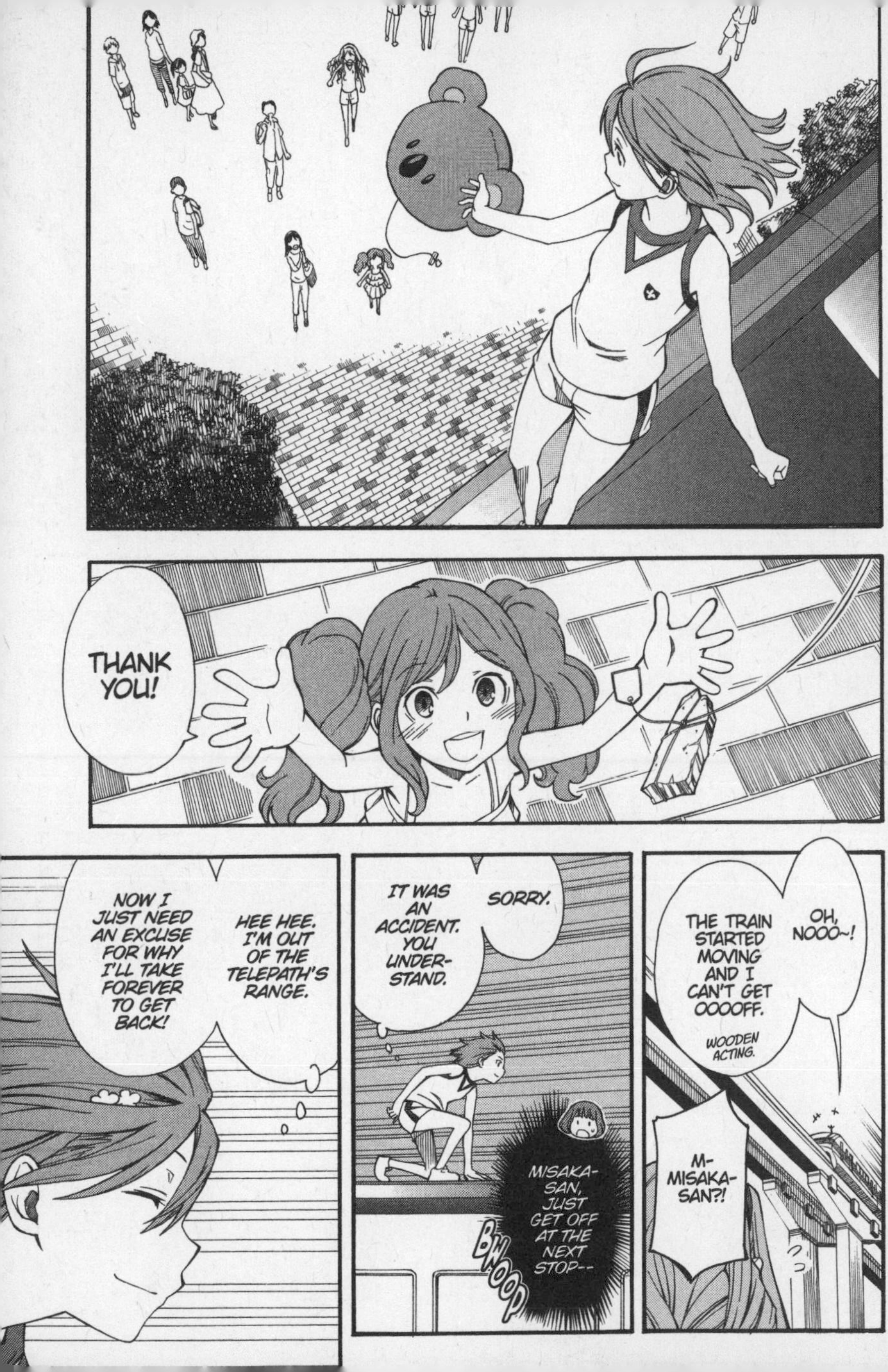
THANK YOU!
OH, NOOO~!
THE TRAIN STARTED MOVING AND I CAN'T GET OOOOFF.
WOODEN ACTING.
M-MISAKA-SAN?!
SORRY.
IT WAS AN ACCIDENT. YOU UNDER-STAND.
MISAKA-SAN, JUST GET OFF AT THE NEXT STOP--
BWOOP
HEE HEE. I'M OUT OF THE TELEPATH'S RANGE.
NOW I JUST NEED AN EXCUSE FOR WHY I'LL TAKE FOREVER TO GET BACK!

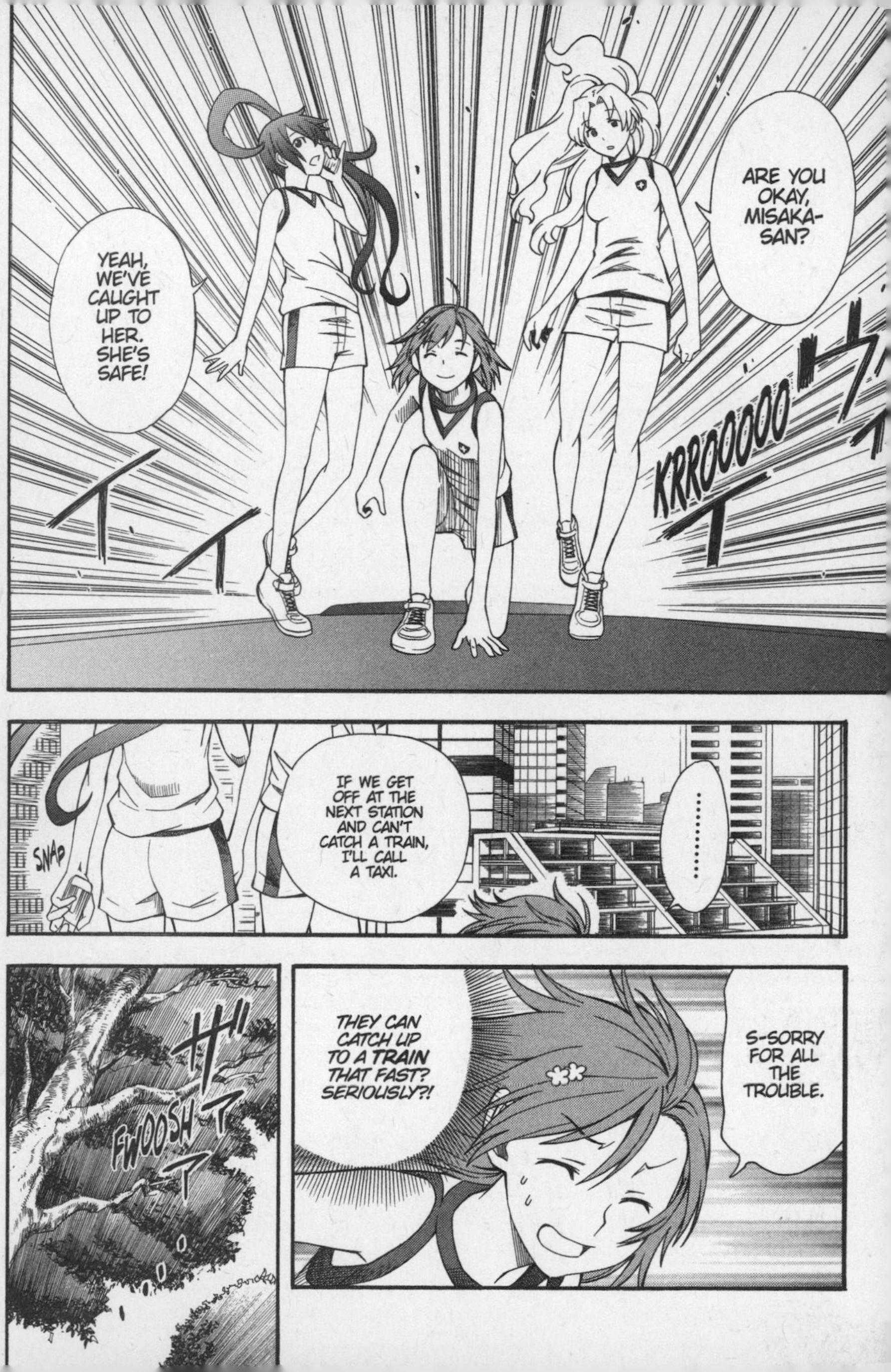
ARE YOU OKAY, MISAKA-SAN?
KRROOOOO
YEAH, WE'VE CAUGHT UP TO HER. SHE'S SAFE!
......
IF WE GET OFF AT THE NEXT STATION AND CAN'T CATCH A TRAIN, I'LL CALL A TAXI.
SNAP
S-SORRY FOR ALL THE TROUBLE.
THEY CAN CATCH UP TO A TRAIN THAT FAST? SERIOUSLY?!
FWOOSH

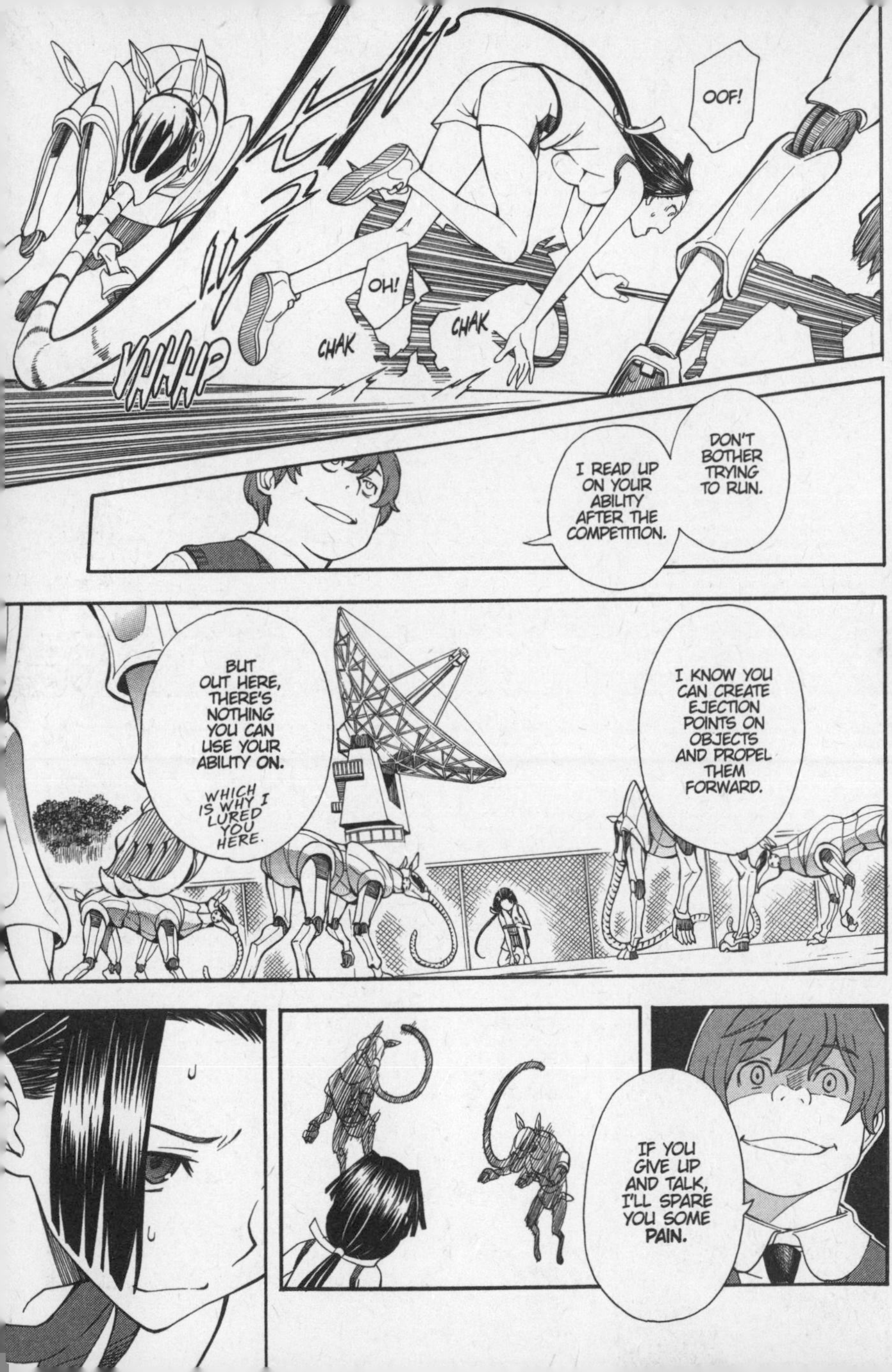
OOF!
OH!
CHAK
CHAK
DON'T BOTHER TRYING TO RUN.
I READ UP ON YOUR ABILITY AFTER THE COMPETITION.
I KNOW YOU CAN CREATE EJECTION POINTS ON OBJECTS AND PROPEL THEM FORWARD.
BUT OUT HERE, THERE'S NOTHING YOU CAN USE YOUR ABILITY ON.
WHICH IS WHY I LURED YOU HERE.
IF YOU GIVE UP AND TALK, I'LL SPARE YOU SOME PAIN.

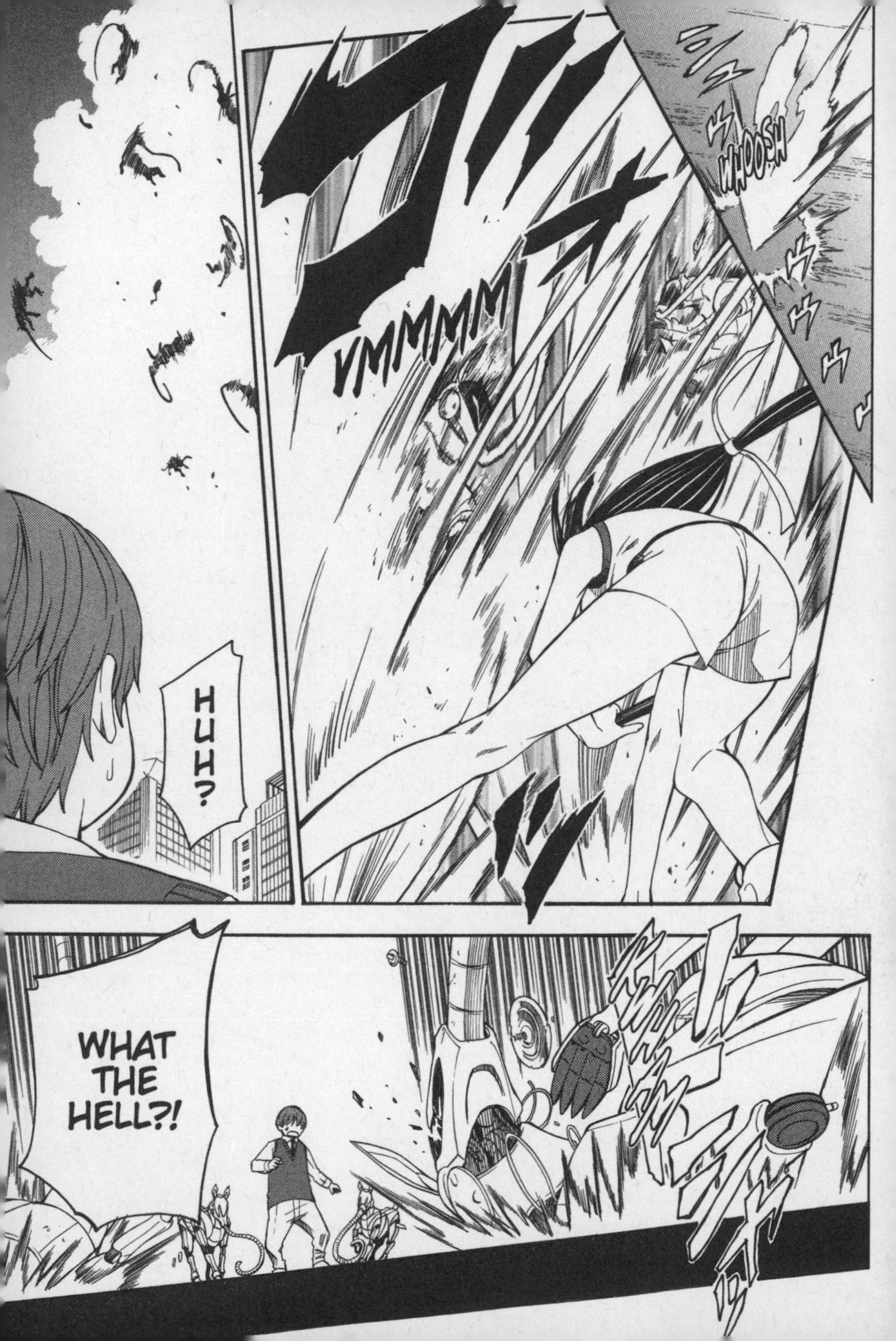
WHOOSH
VMMMMM
HUH?
WHAT THE HELL?!

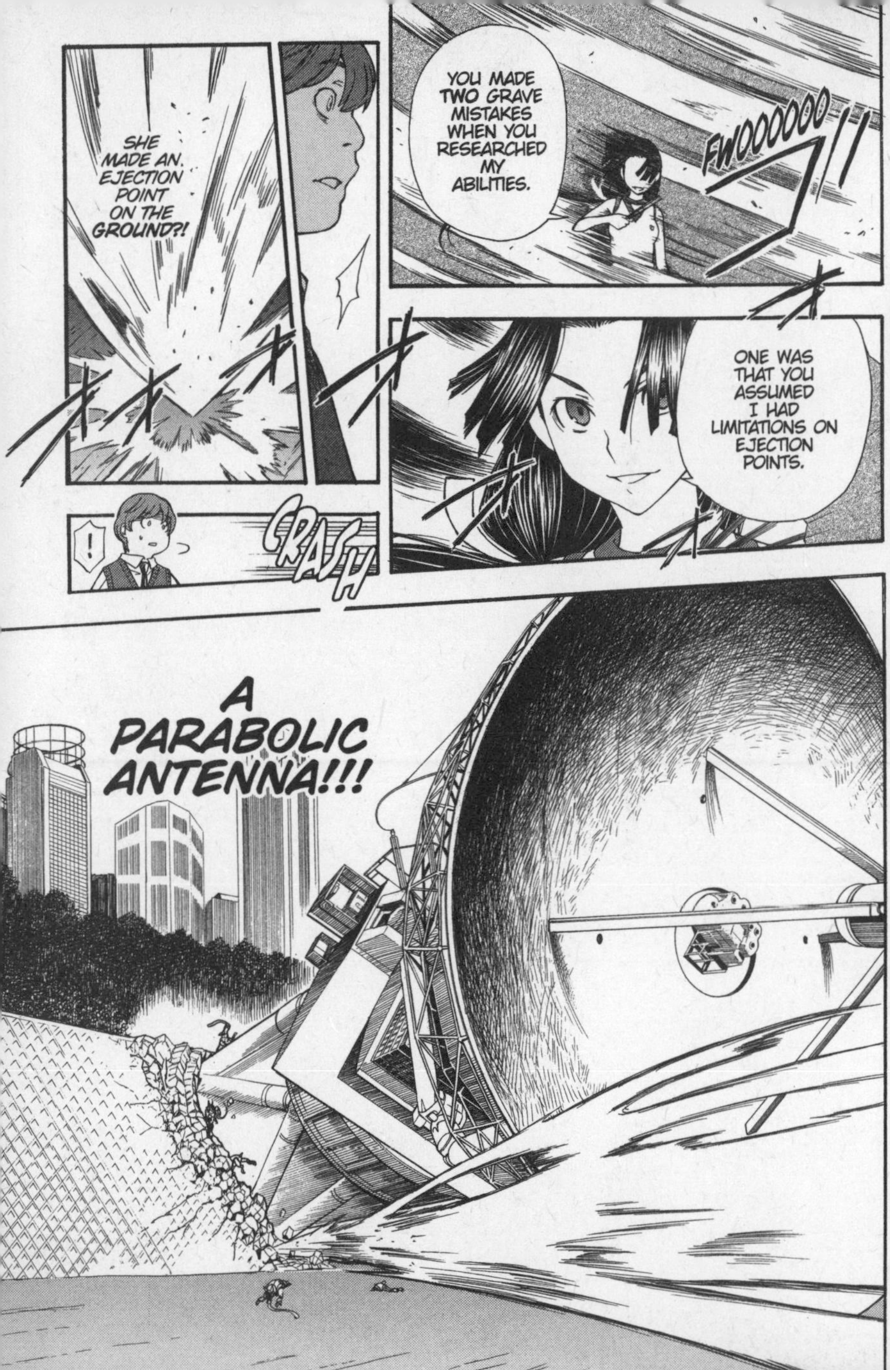
YOU MADE TWO GRAVE MISTAKES WHEN YOU RESEARCHED MY ABILITIES.
FWOOOOOO
ONE WAS THAT YOU ASSUMED I HAD LIMITATIONS ON EJECTION POINTS.
SHE MADE AN EJECTION POINT ON THE GROUND?!
!
CRASH
A PARABOLIC ANTENNA!!!

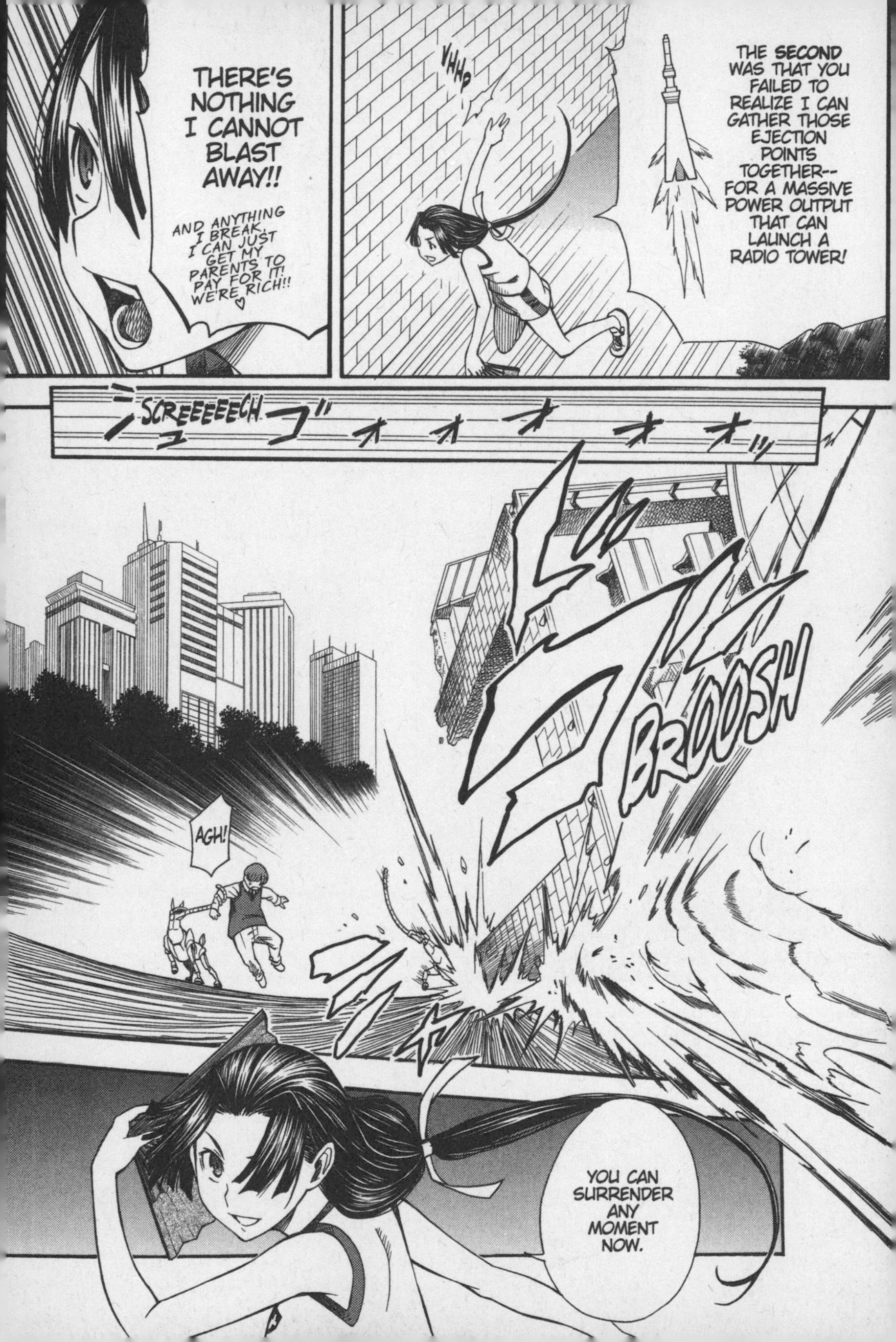
VHHO
THE SECOND WAS THAT YOU FAILED TO REALIZE I CAN GATHER THOSE EJECTION POINTS TOGETHER-- FOR A MASSIVE POWER OUTPUT THAT CAN LAUNCH A RADIO TOWER!
THERE'S NOTHING I CANNOT BLAST AWAY!!
AND ANYTHING I BREAK, I CAN JUST GET MY PARENTS TO PAY FOR IT! WE'RE RICH!! ♡
SCREEEEECH
ゴォォオオオッ
BROOSH
AGH!
YOU CAN SURRENDER ANY MOMENT NOW.

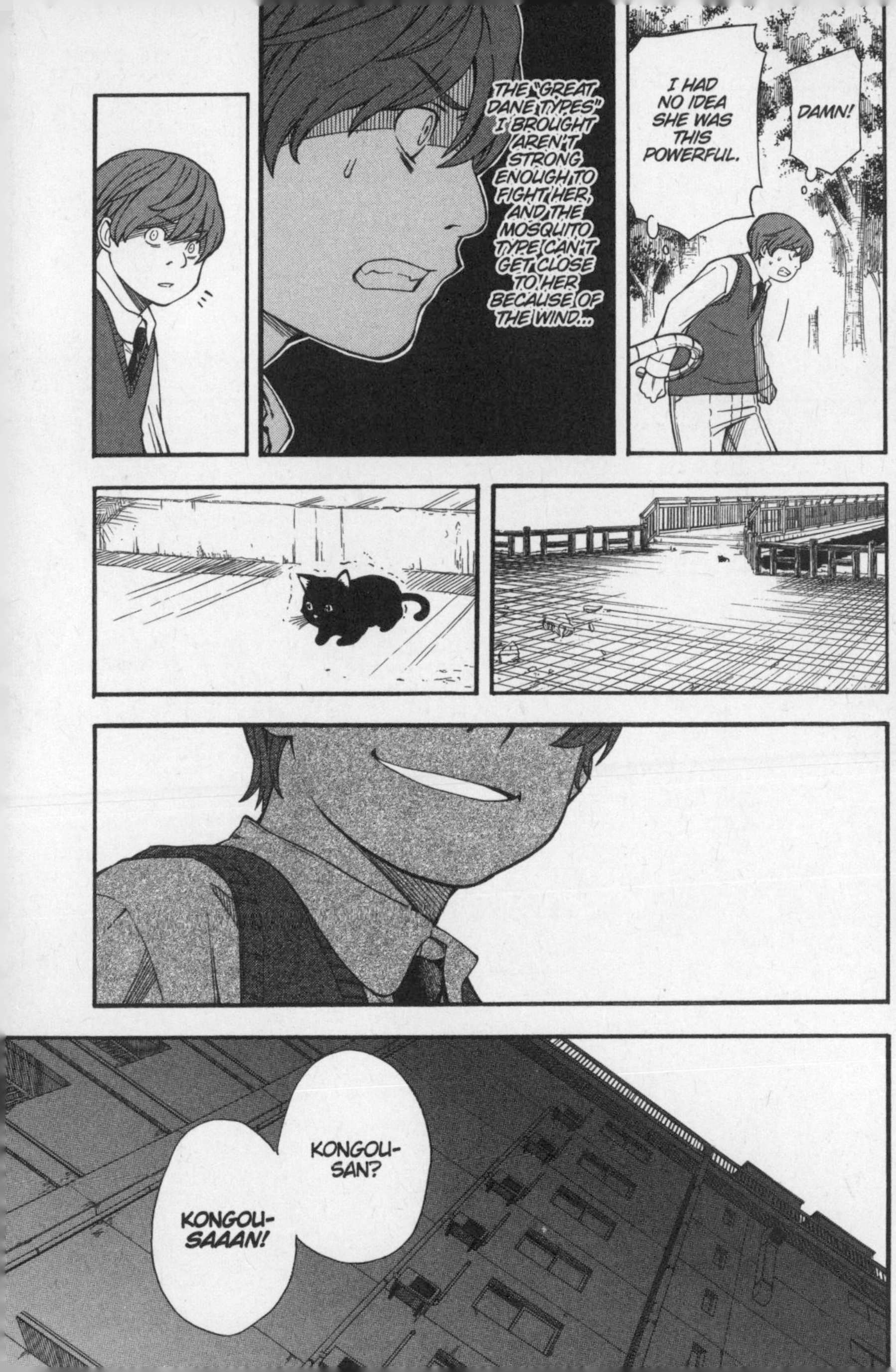
DAMN!
I HAD NO IDEA SHE WAS THIS POWERFUL.
THE "GREAT DANE TYPES" I BROUGHT AREN'T STRONG ENOUGH TO FIGHT HER, AND THE MOSQUITO TYPE CAN'T GET CLOSE TO HER BECAUSE OF THE WIND...
KONGOU-SAN?
KONGOU-SAAAN!

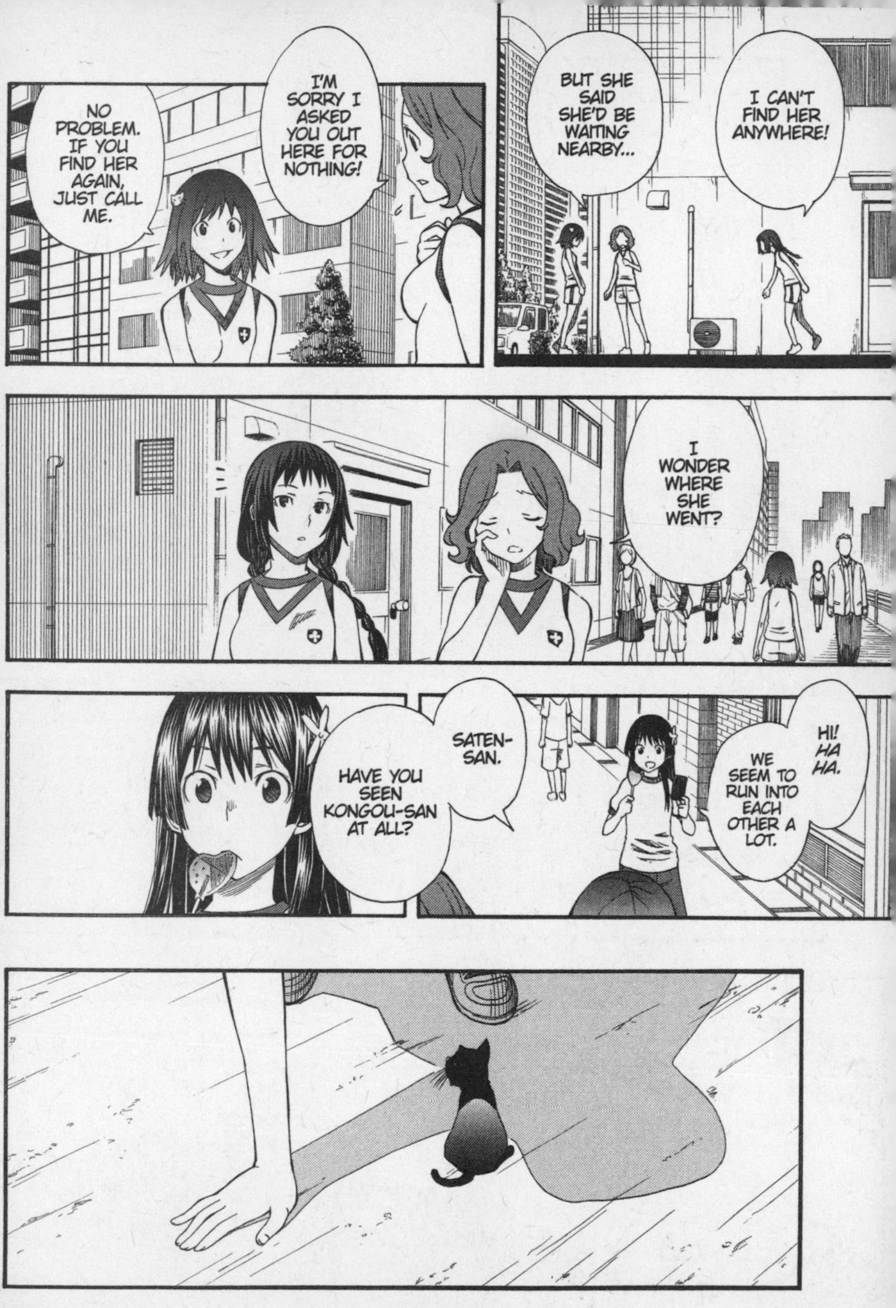
I CAN'T FIND HER ANYWHERE!
BUT SHE SAID SHE'D BE WAITING NEARBY...
I'M SORRY I ASKED YOU OUT HERE FOR NOTHING!
NO PROBLEM. IF YOU FIND HER AGAIN, JUST CALL ME.
I WONDER WHERE SHE WENT?
HI! HA HA.
WE SEEM TO RUN INTO EACH OTHER A LOT.
SATEN-SAN.
HAVE YOU SEEN KONGOU-SAN AT ALL?

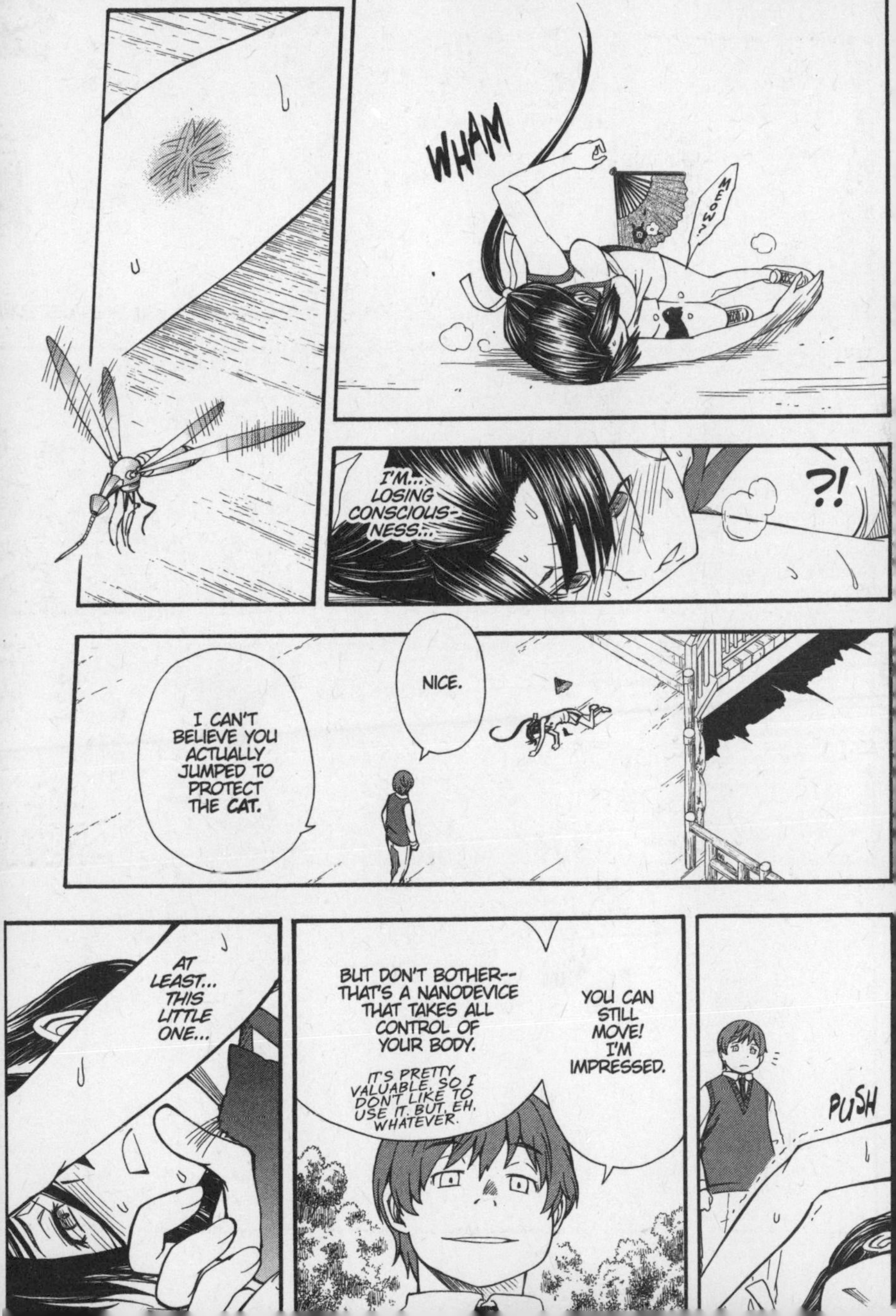
WHAM
MEOW?
I'M... LOSING CONSCIOUS-NESS...
?!
NICE.
I CAN'T BELIEVE YOU ACTUALLY JUMPED TO PROTECT THE CAT.
PUSH
YOU CAN STILL MOVE! I'M IMPRESSED.
BUT DON'T BOTHER-- THAT'S A NANODEVICE THAT TAKES ALL CONTROL OF YOUR BODY.
IT'S PRETTY VALUABLE, SO I DON'T LIKE TO USE IT. BUT, EH, WHATEVER.
AT LEAST... THIS LITTLE ONE...

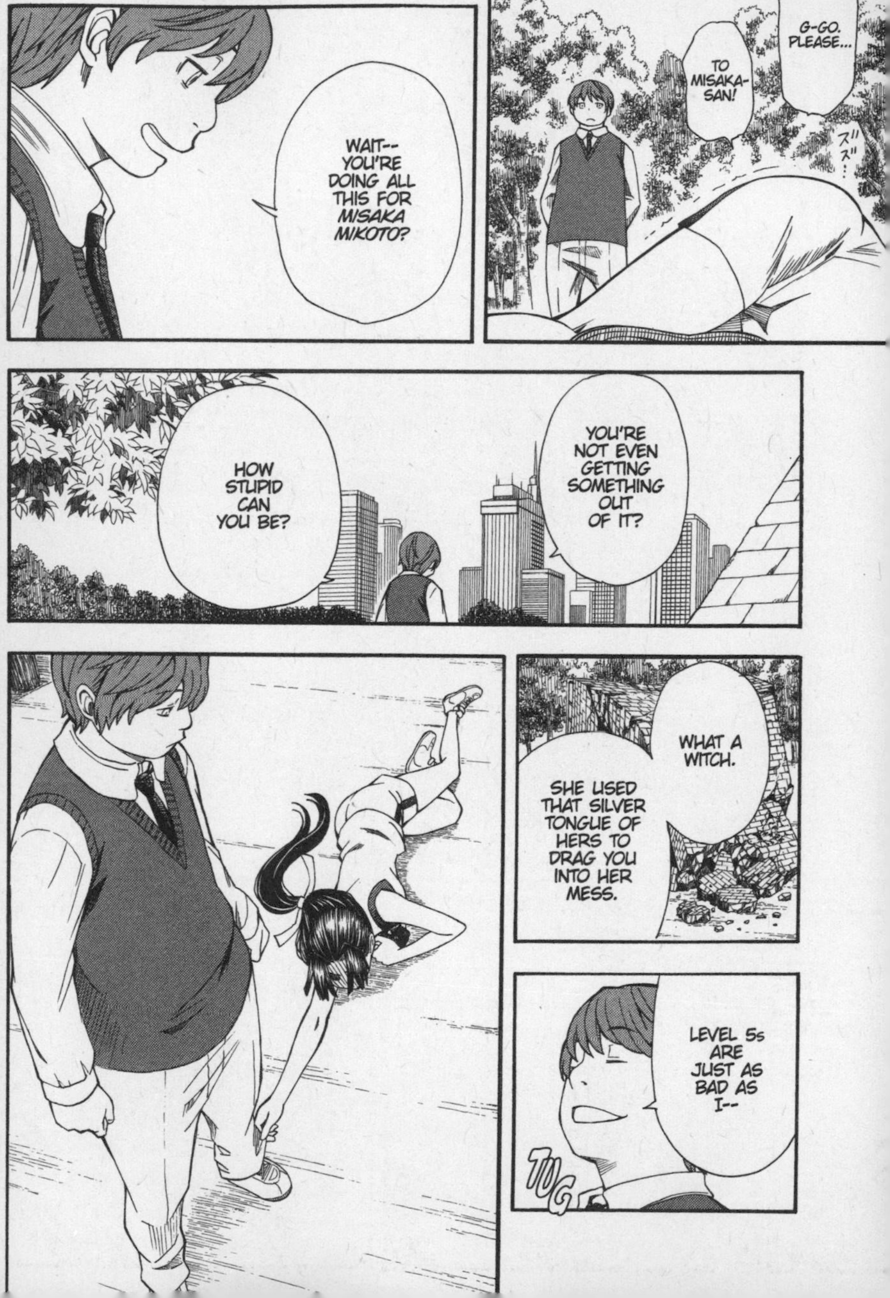
G-GO. PLEASE...
TO MISAKA-SAN!
ズズ...
WAIT-- YOU'RE DOING ALL THIS FOR *MISAKA MIKOTO?*
YOU'RE NOT EVEN GETTING SOMETHING OUT OF IT?
HOW STUPID CAN YOU BE?
WHAT A WITCH.
SHE USED THAT SILVER TONGUE OF HERS TO DRAG YOU INTO HER MESS.
LEVEL 5s ARE JUST AS BAD AS I--
TUG

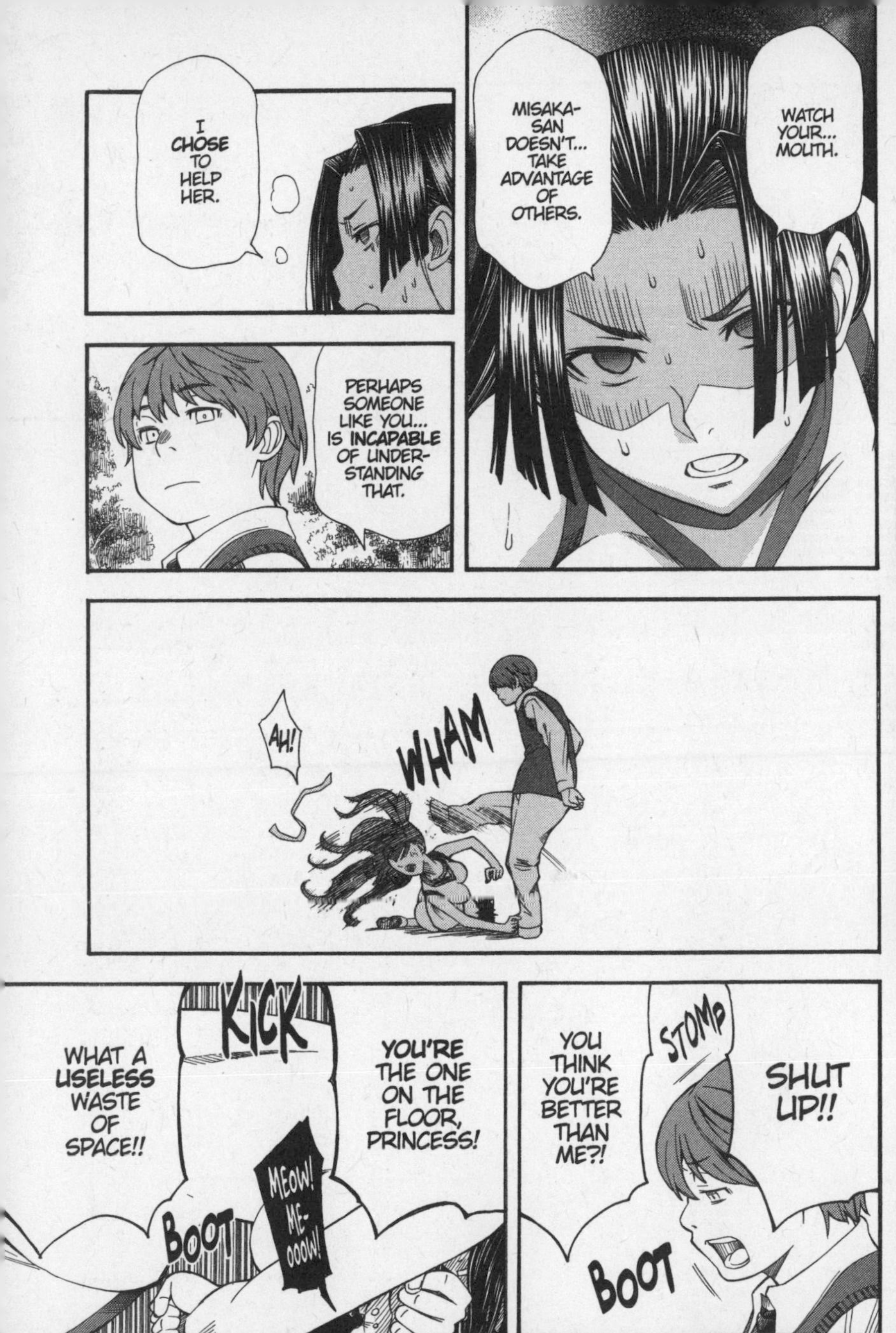
WATCH YOUR... MOUTH.
MISAKA-SAN DOESN'T... TAKE ADVANTAGE OF OTHERS.
I CHOSE TO HELP HER.
PERHAPS SOMEONE LIKE YOU... IS INCAPABLE OF UNDERSTANDING THAT.
WHAM
AH!
STOMP
SHUT UP!!
YOU THINK YOU'RE BETTER THAN ME?!
BOOT
YOU'RE THE ONE ON THE FLOOR, PRINCESS!
KICK
WHAT A USELESS WASTE OF SPACE!!
MEOW! ME-OOOW!
BOOT

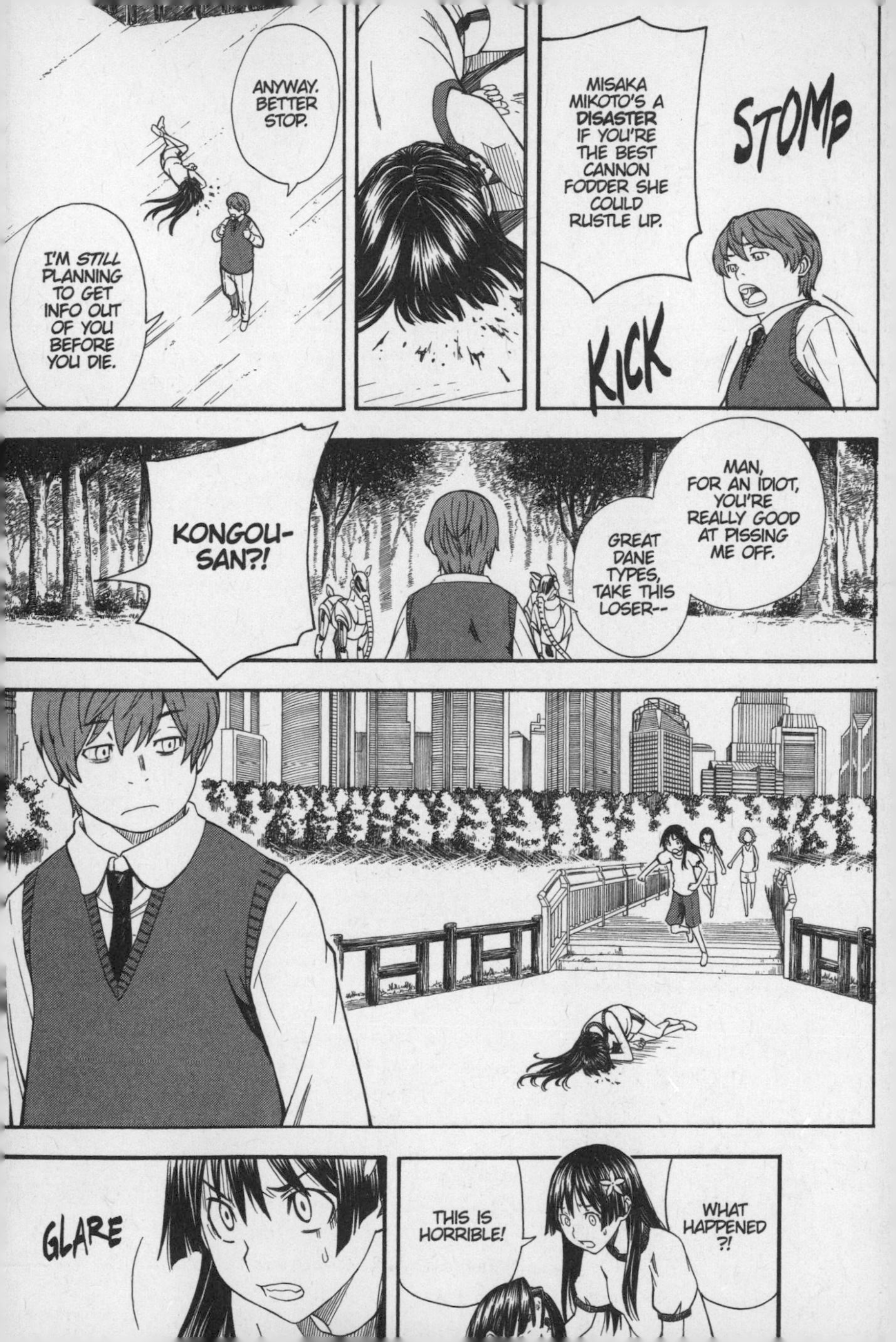
STOMP
MISAKA MIKOTO'S A DISASTER IF YOU'RE THE BEST CANNON FODDER SHE COULD RUSTLE UP.
KICK
ANYWAY. BETTER STOP.
I'M STILL PLANNING TO GET INFO OUT OF YOU BEFORE YOU DIE.
MAN, FOR AN IDIOT, YOU'RE REALLY GOOD AT PISSING ME OFF.
GREAT DANE TYPES, TAKE THIS LOSER--
KONGOU-SAN?!
WHAT HAPPENED?!
THIS IS HORRIBLE!
GLARE

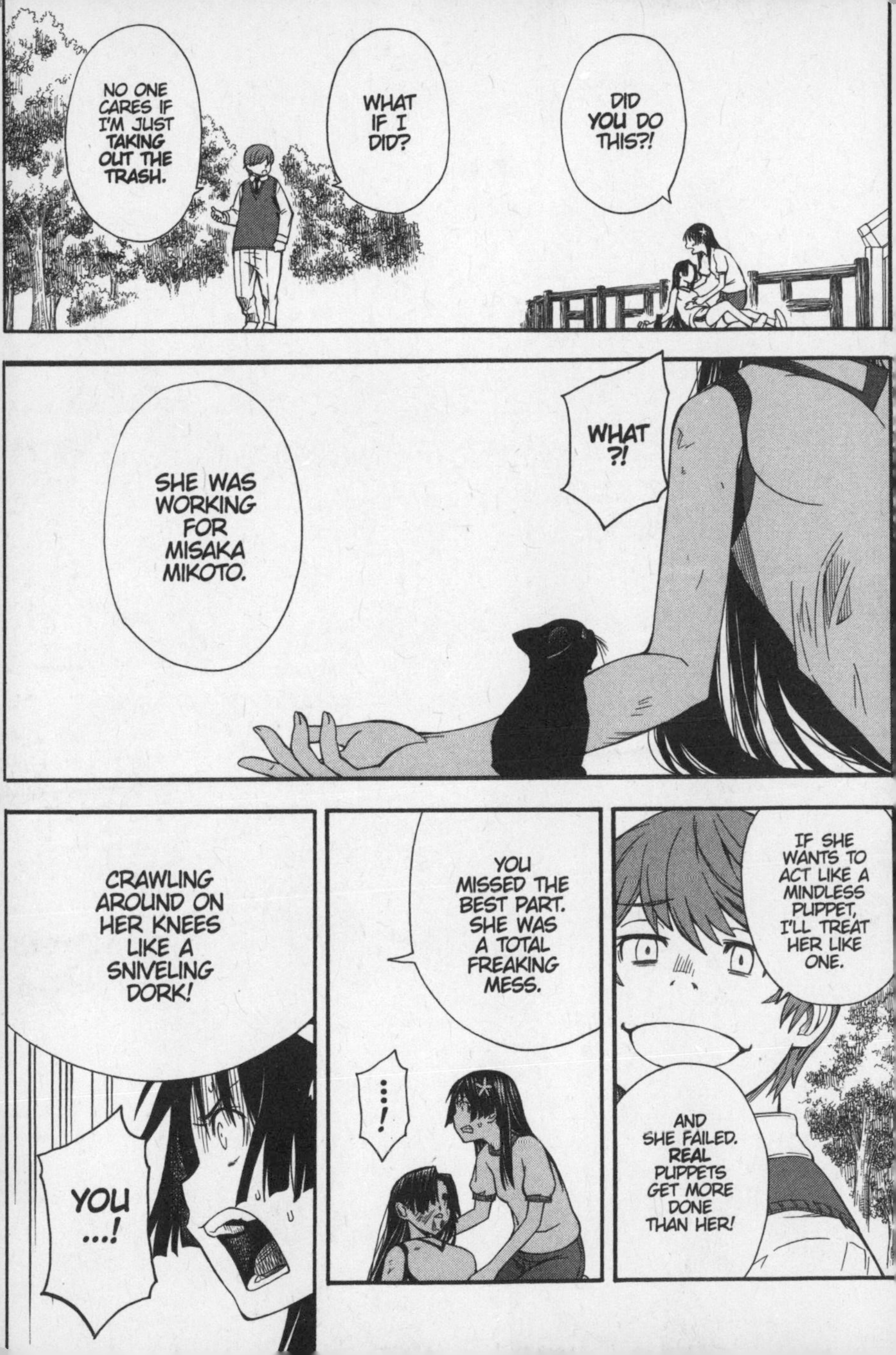
DID YOU DO THIS?!
WHAT IF I DID?
NO ONE CARES IF I'M JUST TAKING OUT THE TRASH.
WHAT ?!
SHE WAS WORKING FOR MISAKA MIKOTO.
IF SHE WANTS TO ACT LIKE A MINDLESS PUPPET, I'LL TREAT HER LIKE ONE.
AND SHE FAILED. REAL PUPPETS GET MORE DONE THAN HER!
YOU MISSED THE BEST PART. SHE WAS A TOTAL FREAKING MESS.
...!
CRAWLING AROUND ON HER KNEES LIKE A SNIVELING DORK!
YOU ...!

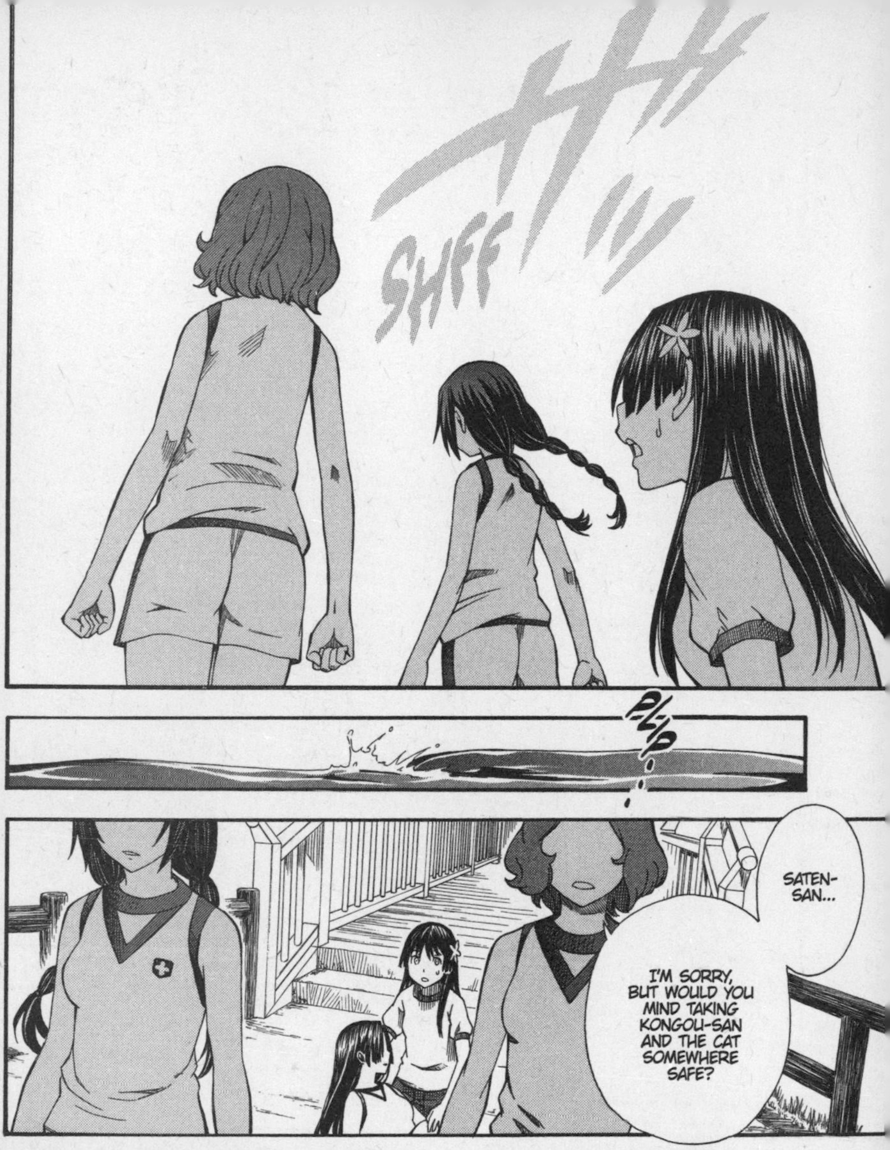
SHFF
PLIP...
SATEN-SAN...
I'M SORRY, BUT WOULD YOU MIND TAKING KONGOU-SAN AND THE CAT SOMEWHERE SAFE?
SPLASH
SPLASH!!
SPLASH

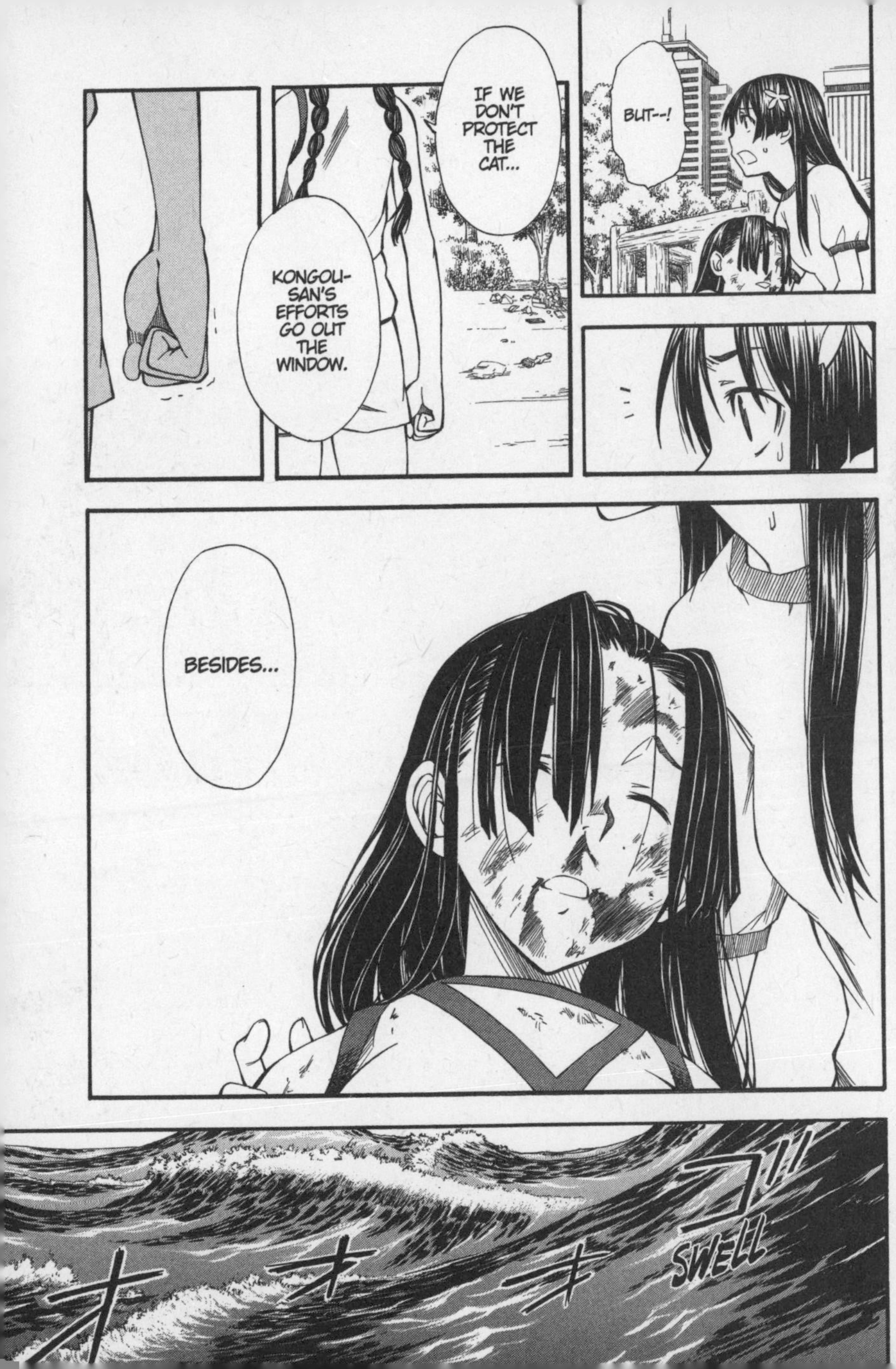
BUT--!
IF WE DON'T PROTECT THE CAT...
KONGOU-SAN'S EFFORTS GO OUT THE WINDOW.
BESIDES...
SWELL

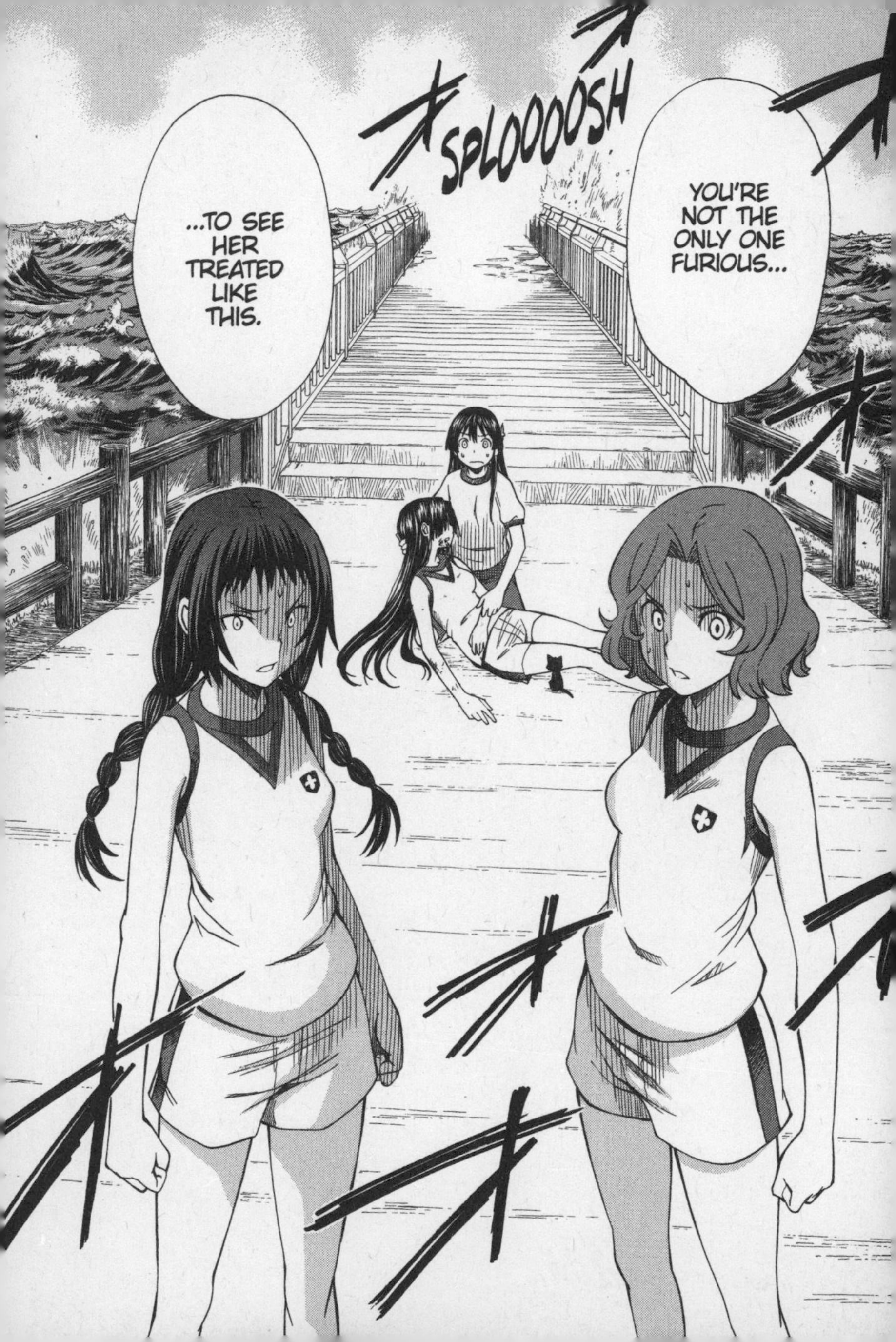
YOU'RE NOT THE ONLY ONE FURIOUS...
SPLOOOOSH
...TO SEE HER TREATED LIKE THIS.

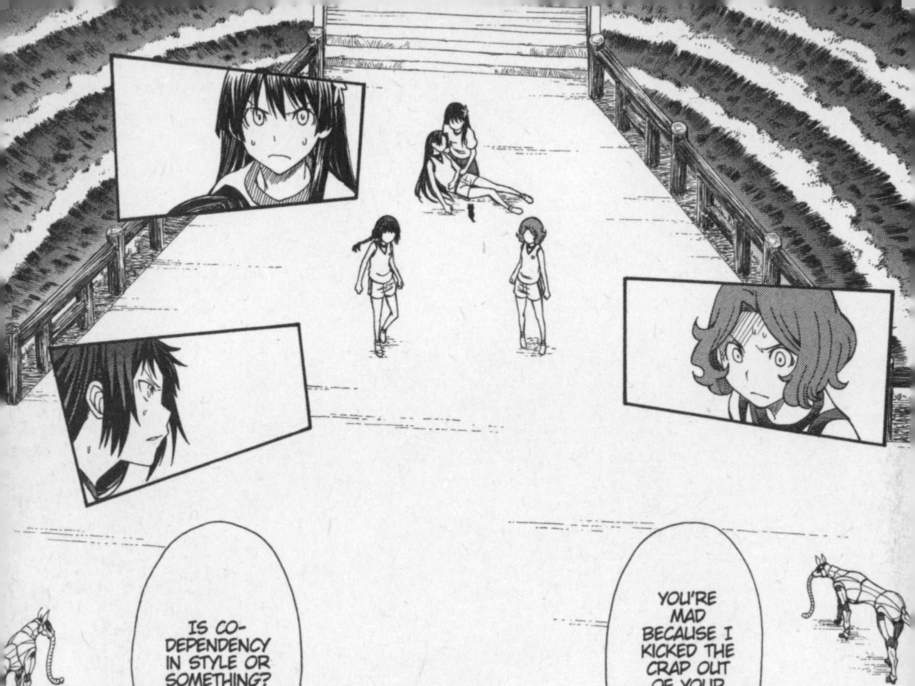
YOU'RE MAD BECAUSE I KICKED THE CRAP OUT OF YOUR *FRIEND*?
IS CO-DEPENDENCY IN STYLE OR SOMETHING?

CHAPTER 51: ANALYSIS

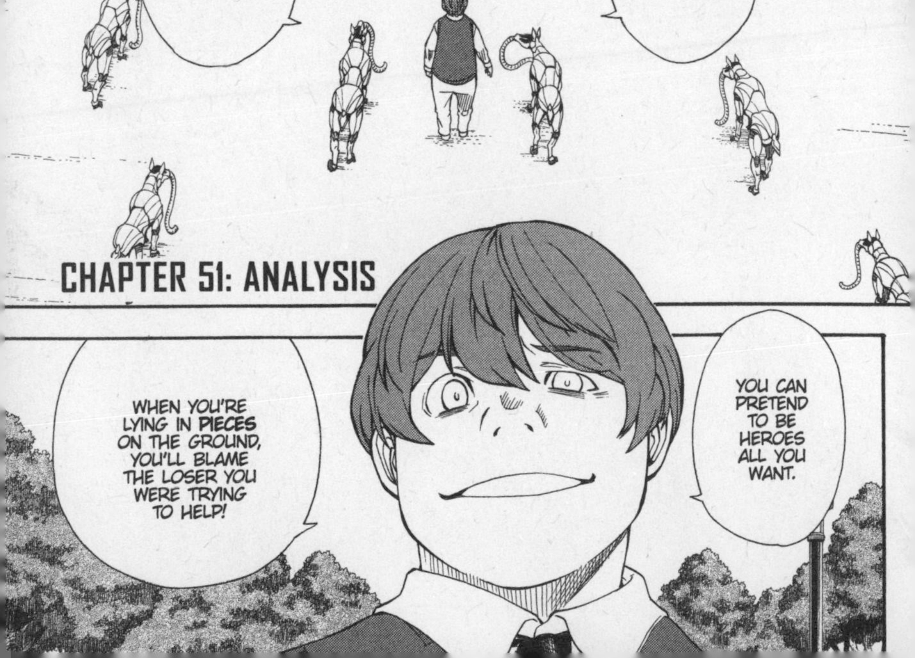
YOU CAN PRETEND TO BE HEROES ALL YOU WANT.
WHEN YOU'RE LYING IN PIECES ON THE GROUND, YOU'LL BLAME THE LOSER YOU WERE TRYING TO HELP!

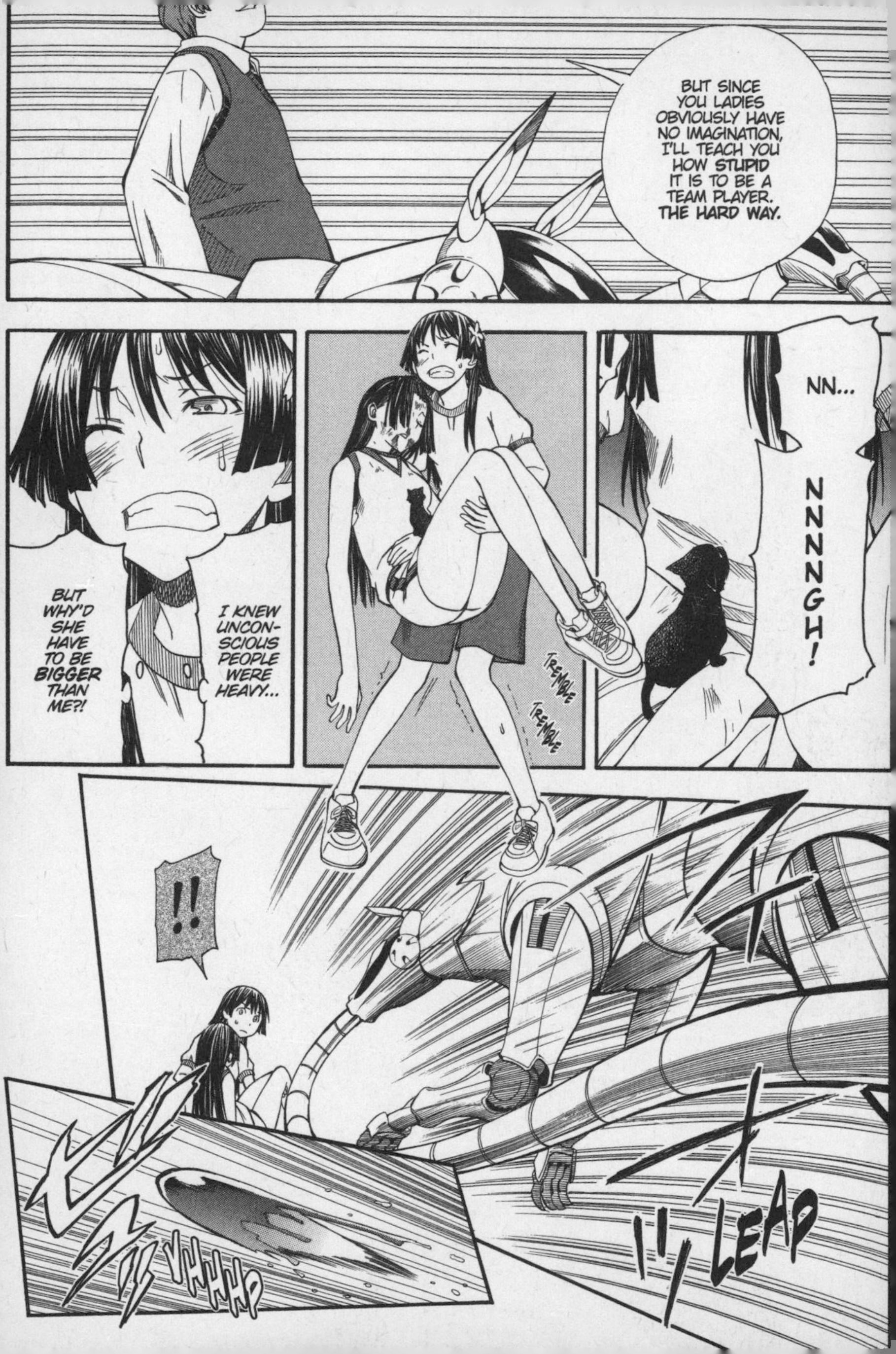

BUT SINCE YOU LADIES OBVIOUSLY HAVE NO IMAGINATION, I'LL TEACH YOU HOW **STUPID** IT IS TO BE A TEAM PLAYER. **THE HARD WAY.**
NN...
NNNNGH!
TREMBLE
TREMBLE
I KNEW UNCON-SCIOUS PEOPLE WERE HEAVY...
BUT WHY'D SHE HAVE TO BE BIGGER THAN ME?!
LEAP
!!

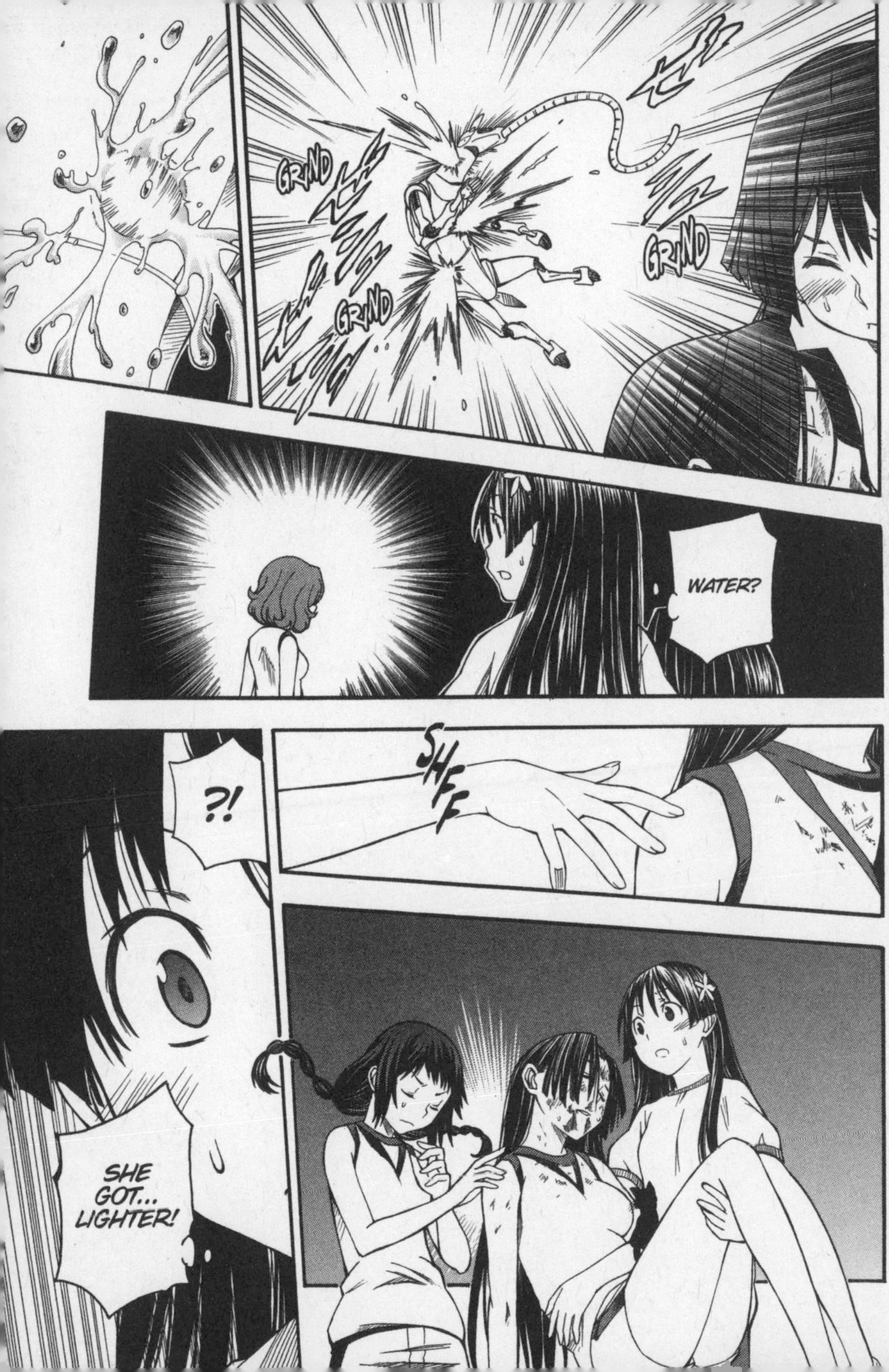
GRIND
GRIND
GRIND
WATER?
SHFF
?!
SHE GOT... LIGHTER!

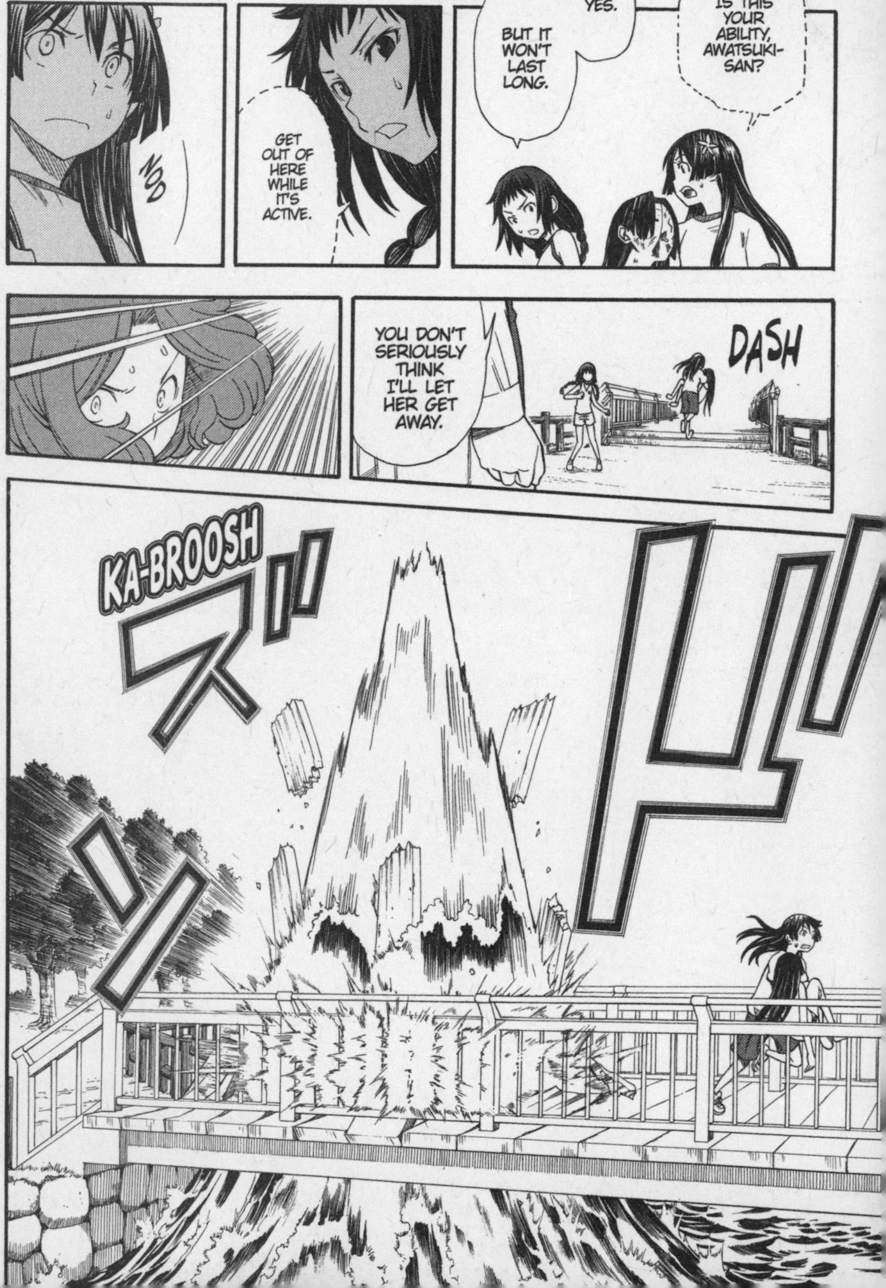
IS THIS YOUR ABILITY, AWATSUKI-SAN?
YES.
BUT IT WON'T LAST LONG.
GET OUT OF HERE WHILE IT'S ACTIVE.
NOD
DASH
YOU DON'T SERIOUSLY THINK I'LL LET HER GET AWAY.
KA-BROOSH

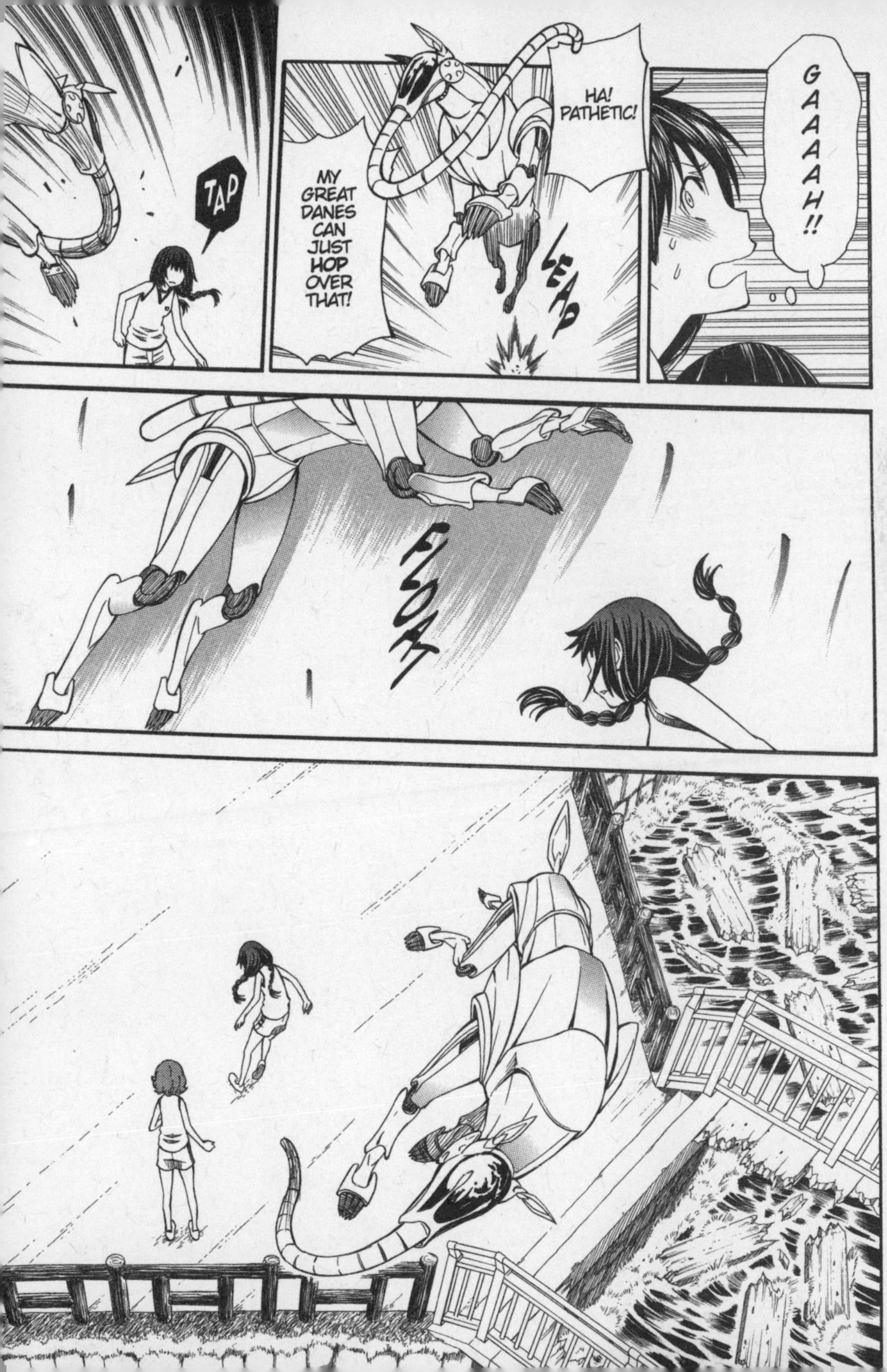
GAAAAAH!!
HA! PATHETIC!
MY GREAT DANES CAN JUST HOP OVER THAT!
LEAP
TAP
FLOAT

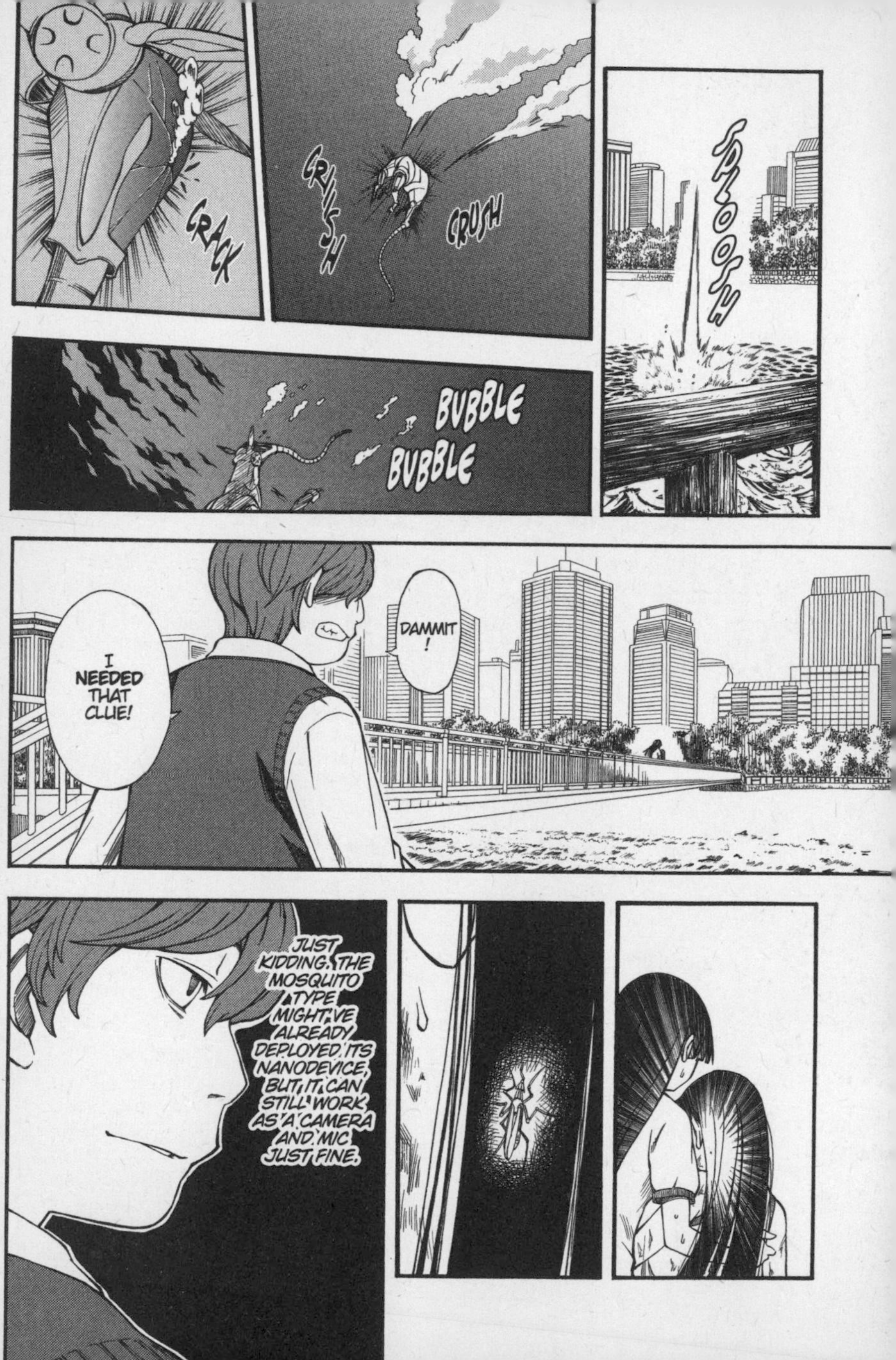
SPLOOSH
CRUSH
CRUSH
CRACK
BUBBLE
BUBBLE
DAMMIT!
I NEEDED THAT CLUE!
JUST KIDDING. THE MOSQUITO TYPE MIGHT'VE ALREADY DEPLOYED ITS NANODEVICE, BUT IT CAN STILL WORK AS A CAMERA AND MIC JUST FINE.

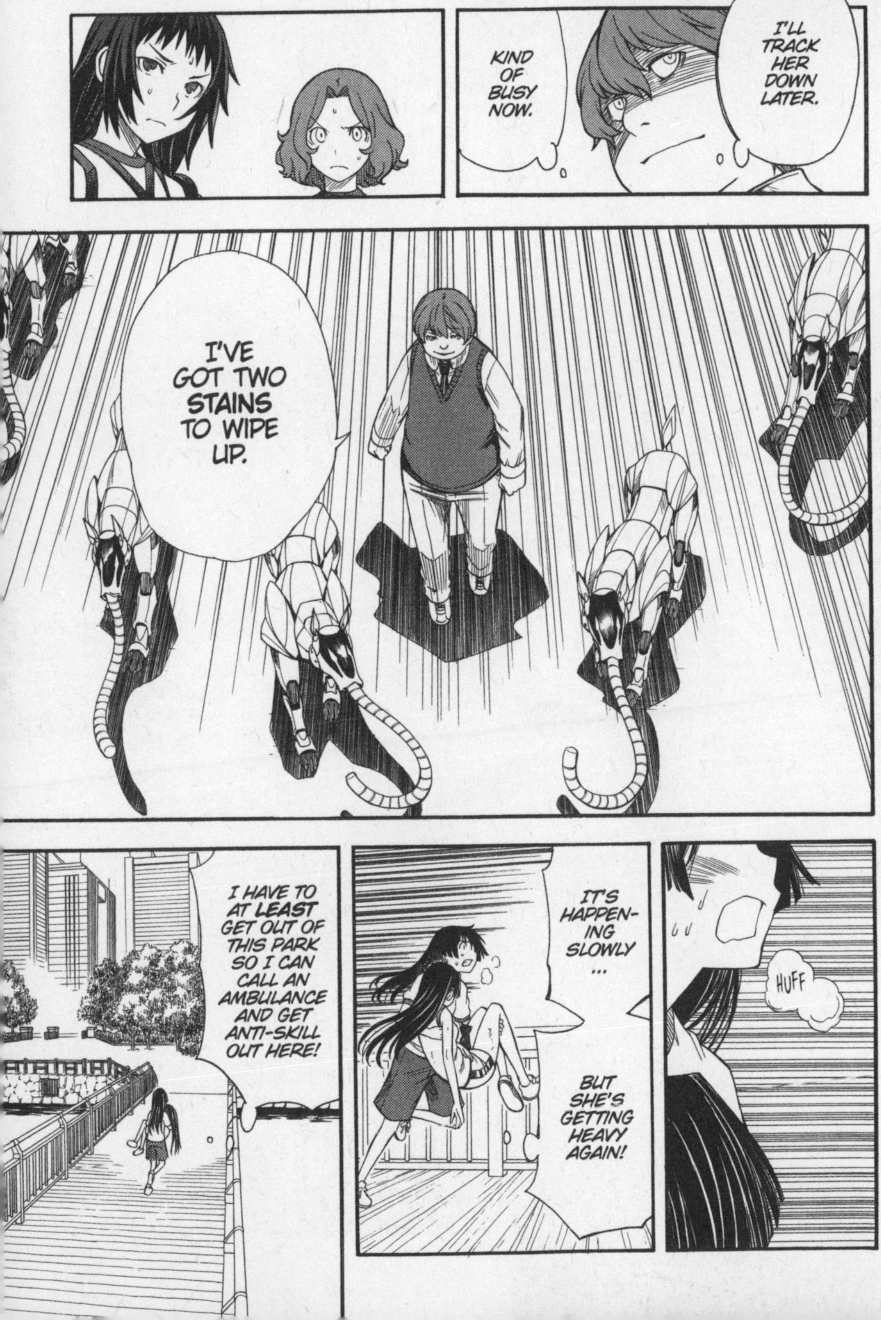
I'LL TRACK HER DOWN LATER.
KIND OF BUSY NOW.
I'VE GOT TWO STAINS TO WIPE UP.
HUFF
IT'S HAPPENING SLOWLY...
BUT SHE'S GETTING HEAVY AGAIN!
I HAVE TO AT LEAST GET OUT OF THIS PARK SO I CAN CALL AN AMBULANCE AND GET ANTI-SKILL OUT HERE!

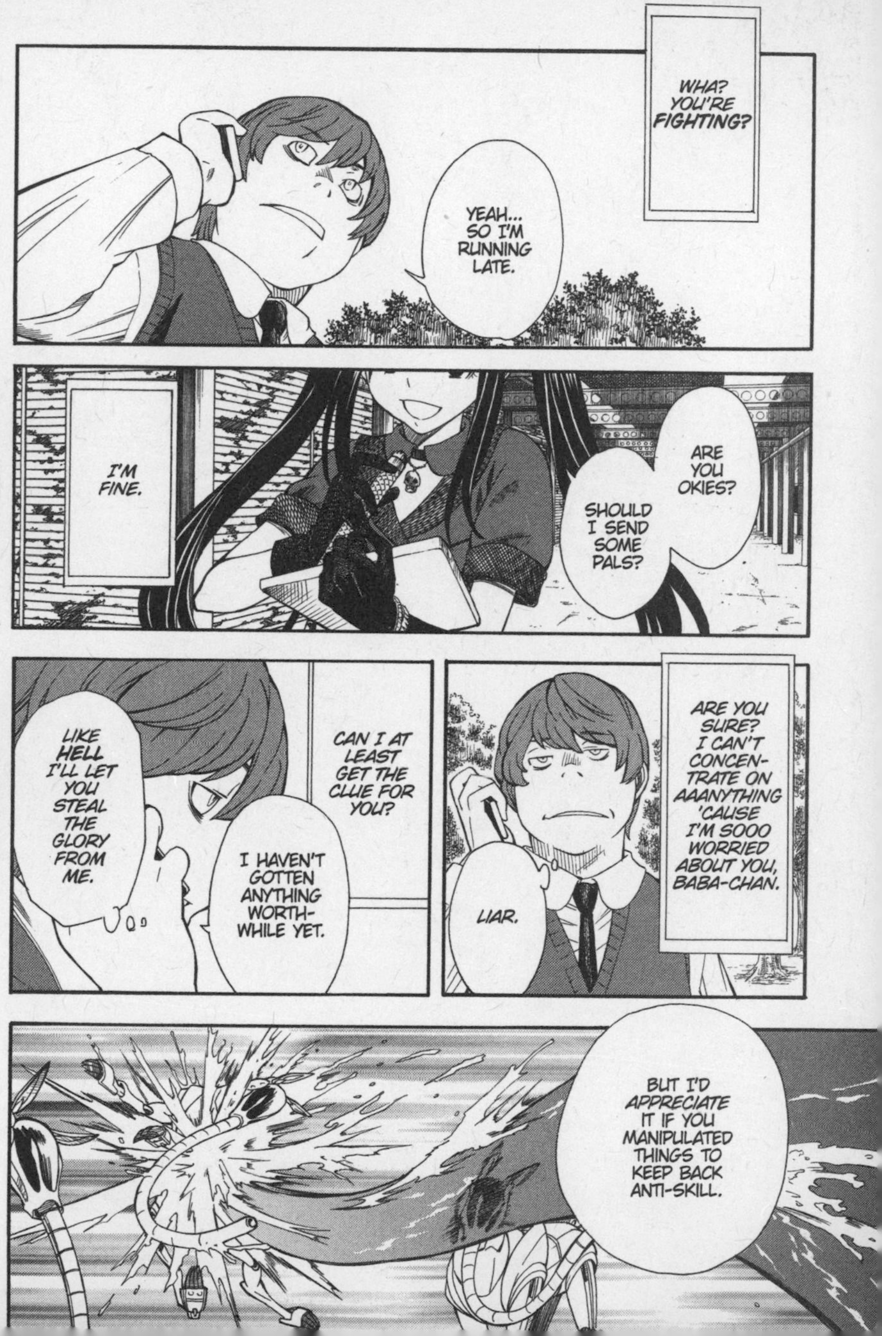
WHA? YOU'RE FIGHTING?
YEAH... SO I'M RUNNING LATE.
ARE YOU OKIES?
SHOULD I SEND SOME PALS?
I'M FINE.
ARE YOU SURE? I CAN'T CONCENTRATE ON AAANYTHING 'CAUSE I'M SOOO WORRIED ABOUT YOU, BABA-CHAN.
LIAR.
CAN I AT LEAST GET THE CLUE FOR YOU?
I HAVEN'T GOTTEN ANYTHING WORTHWHILE YET.
LIKE HELL I'LL LET YOU STEAL THE GLORY FROM ME.
BUT I'D APPRECIATE IT IF YOU MANIPULATED THINGS TO KEEP BACK ANTI-SKILL.

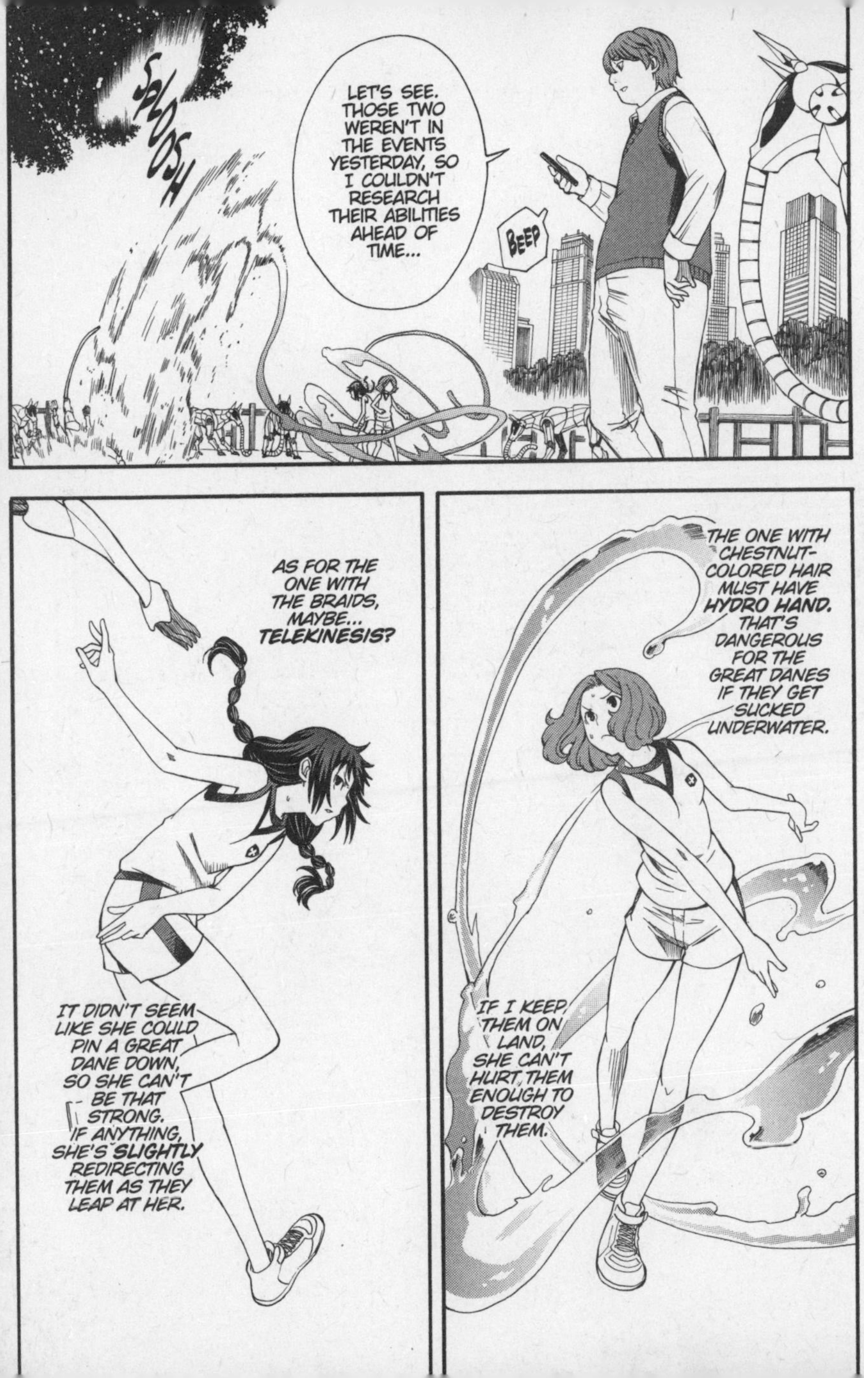
LET'S SEE. THOSE TWO WEREN'T IN THE EVENTS YESTERDAY, SO I COULDN'T RESEARCH THEIR ABILITIES AHEAD OF TIME...
BEEP
SPLOOSH
THE ONE WITH CHESTNUT-COLORED HAIR MUST HAVE HYDRO HAND. THAT'S DANGEROUS FOR THE GREAT DANES IF THEY GET SUCKED UNDERWATER.
IF I KEEP THEM ON LAND, SHE CAN'T HURT THEM ENOUGH TO DESTROY THEM.
AS FOR THE ONE WITH THE BRAIDS, MAYBE... TELEKINESIS?
IT DIDN'T SEEM LIKE SHE COULD PIN A GREAT DANE DOWN, SO SHE CAN'T BE THAT STRONG. IF ANYTHING, SHE'S SLIGHTLY REDIRECTING THEM AS THEY LEAP AT HER.

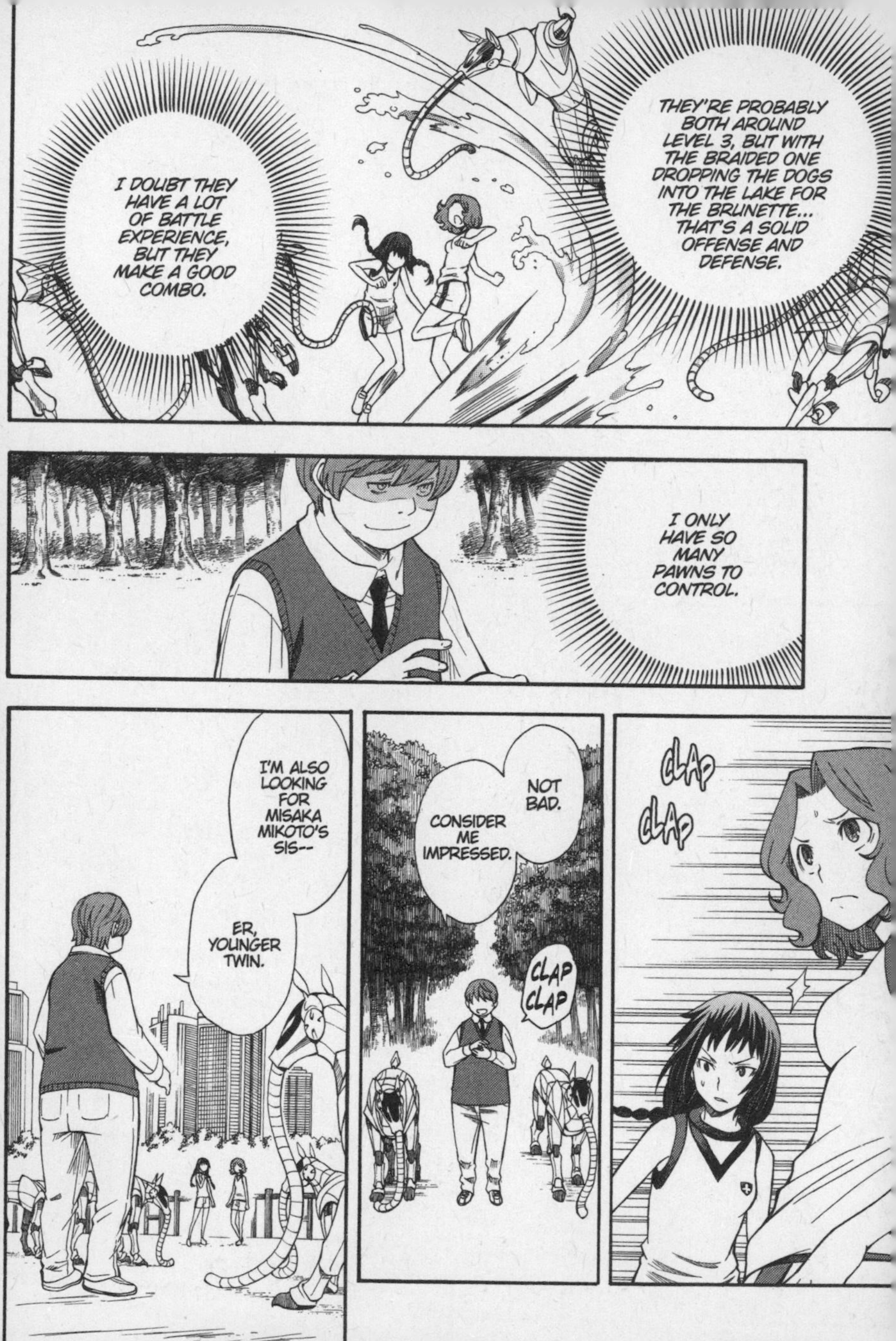
THEY'RE PROBABLY BOTH AROUND LEVEL 3, BUT WITH THE BRAIDED ONE DROPPING THE DOGS INTO THE LAKE FOR THE BRUNETTE... THAT'S A SOLID OFFENSE AND DEFENSE.
I DOUBT THEY HAVE A LOT OF BATTLE EXPERIENCE, BUT THEY MAKE A GOOD COMBO.
I ONLY HAVE SO MANY PAWNS TO CONTROL.
CLAP
CLAP
NOT BAD.
CONSIDER ME IMPRESSED.
CLAP CLAP
I'M ALSO LOOKING FOR MISAKA MIKOTO'S SIS--
ER, YOUNGER TWIN.

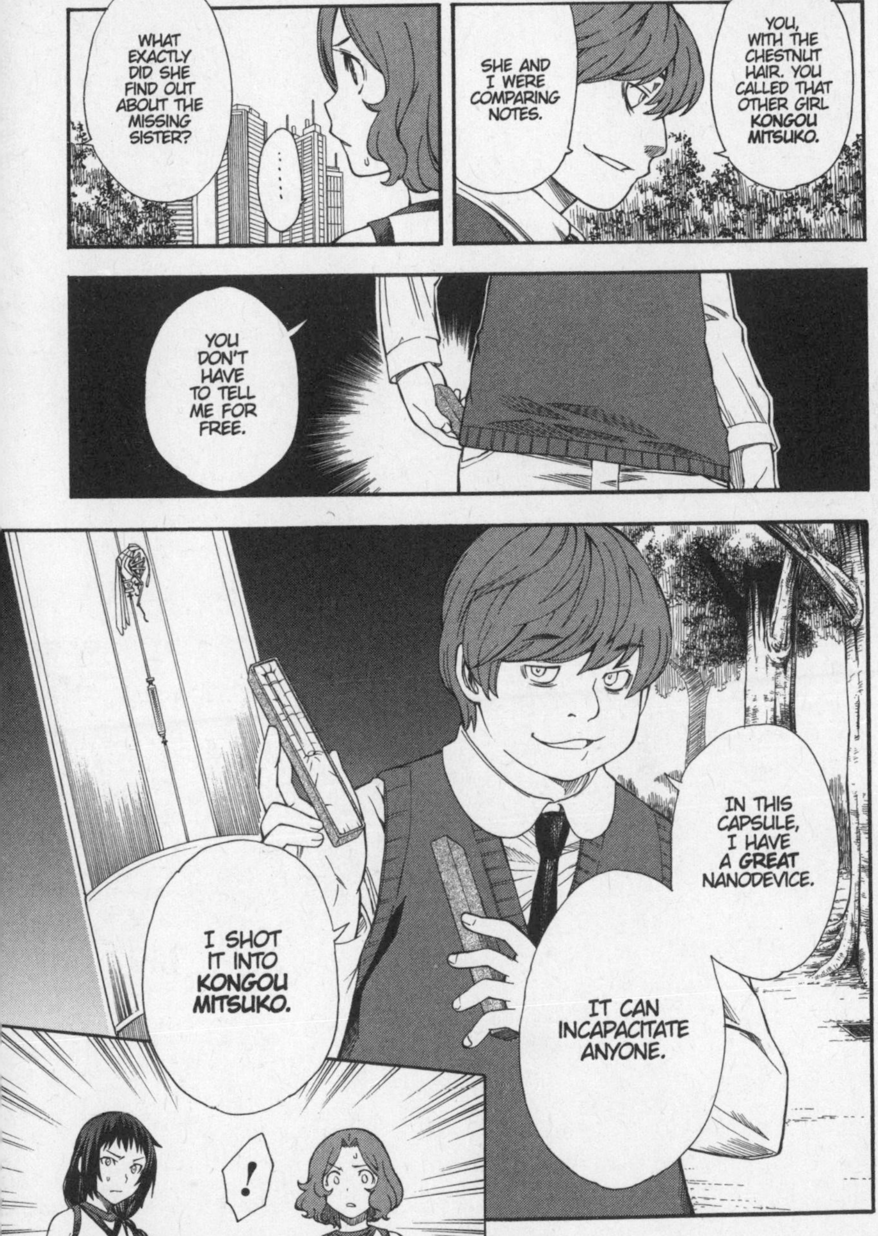
YOU, WITH THE CHESTNUT HAIR. YOU CALLED THAT OTHER GIRL KONGOU MITSUKO.
SHE AND I WERE COMPARING NOTES.
......
WHAT EXACTLY DID SHE FIND OUT ABOUT THE MISSING SISTER?
YOU DON'T HAVE TO TELL ME FOR FREE.
IN THIS CAPSULE, I HAVE A GREAT NANODEVICE.
IT CAN INCAPACITATE ANYONE.
I SHOT IT INTO KONGOU MITSUKO.
!

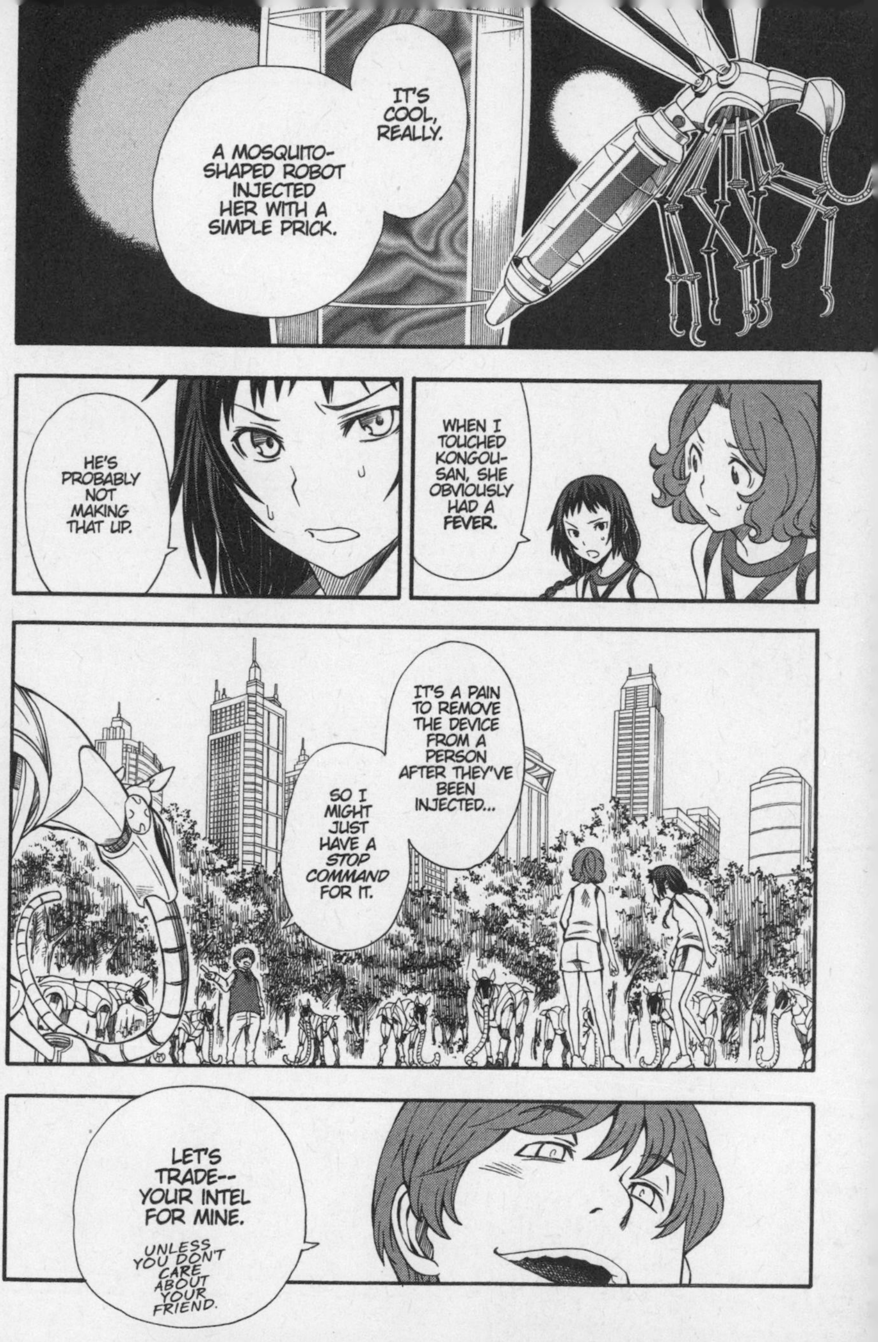
IT'S COOL, REALLY.
A MOSQUITO-SHAPED ROBOT INJECTED HER WITH A SIMPLE PRICK.
WHEN I TOUCHED KONGOU-SAN, SHE OBVIOUSLY HAD A FEVER.
HE'S PROBABLY NOT MAKING THAT UP.
IT'S A PAIN TO REMOVE THE DEVICE FROM A PERSON AFTER THEY'VE BEEN INJECTED...
SO I MIGHT JUST HAVE A *STOP* COMMAND FOR IT.
LET'S TRADE--YOUR INTEL FOR MINE.
UNLESS YOU DON'T CARE ABOUT YOUR FRIEND.

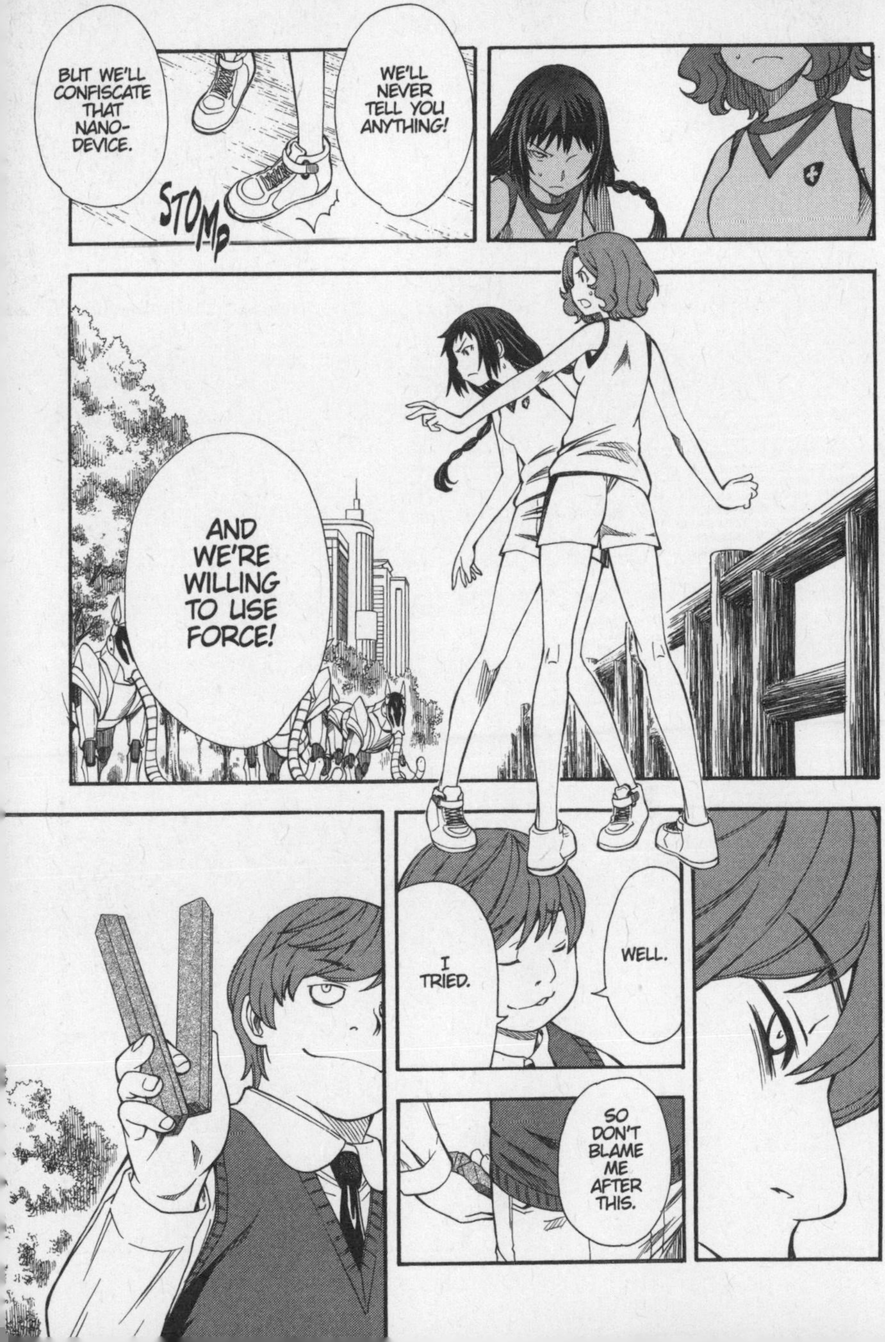
WE'LL NEVER TELL YOU ANYTHING!
BUT WE'LL CONFISCATE THAT NANO-DEVICE.
STOMP
AND WE'RE WILLING TO USE FORCE!
WELL.
I TRIED.
SO DON'T BLAME ME AFTER THIS.

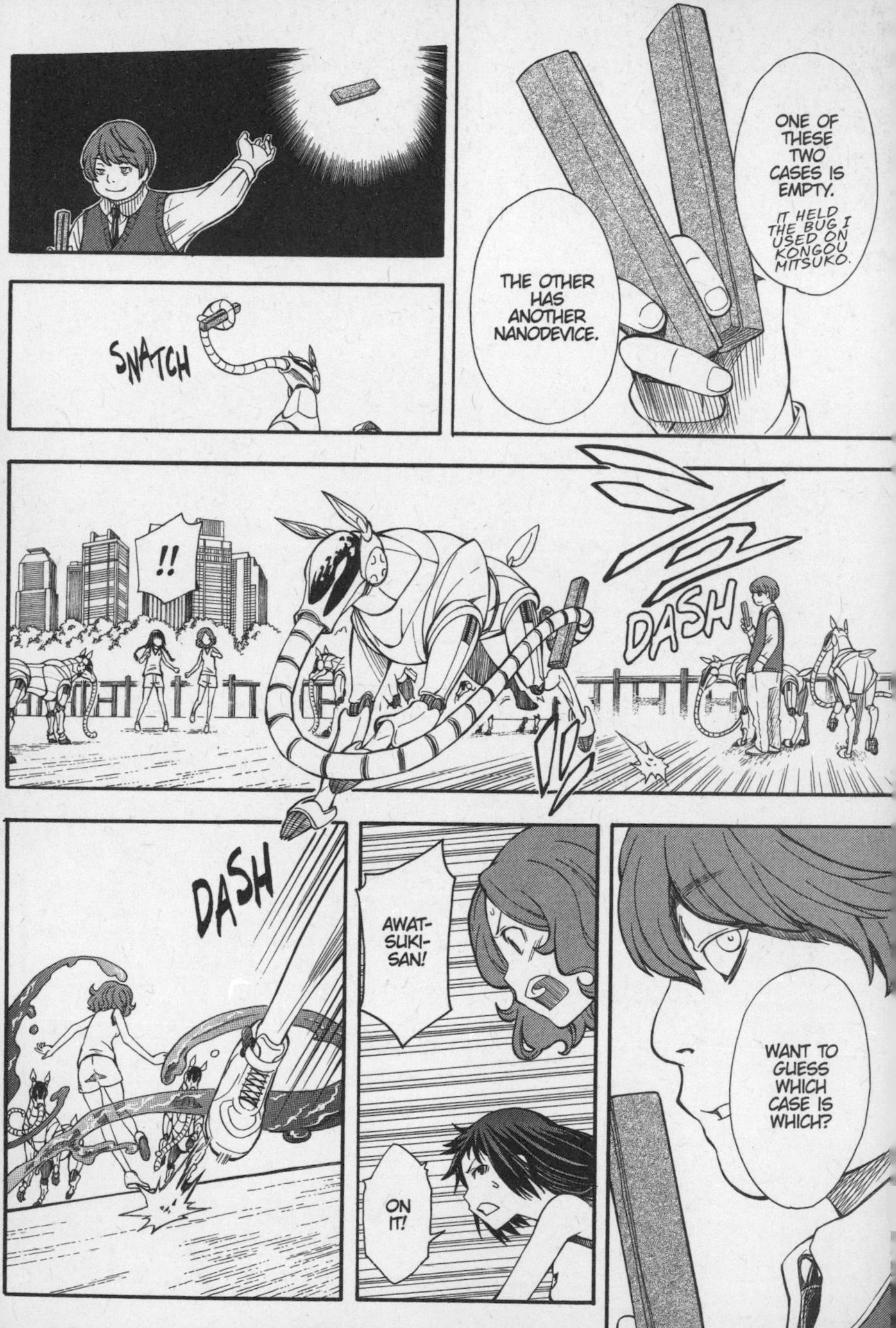
ONE OF THESE TWO CASES IS EMPTY.
IT HELD THE BUG I USED ON KONGOU MITSUKO.
THE OTHER HAS ANOTHER NANODEVICE.
SNATCH
DASH
!!
WANT TO GUESS WHICH CASE IS WHICH?
AWAT-SUKI-SAN!
ON IT!
DASH

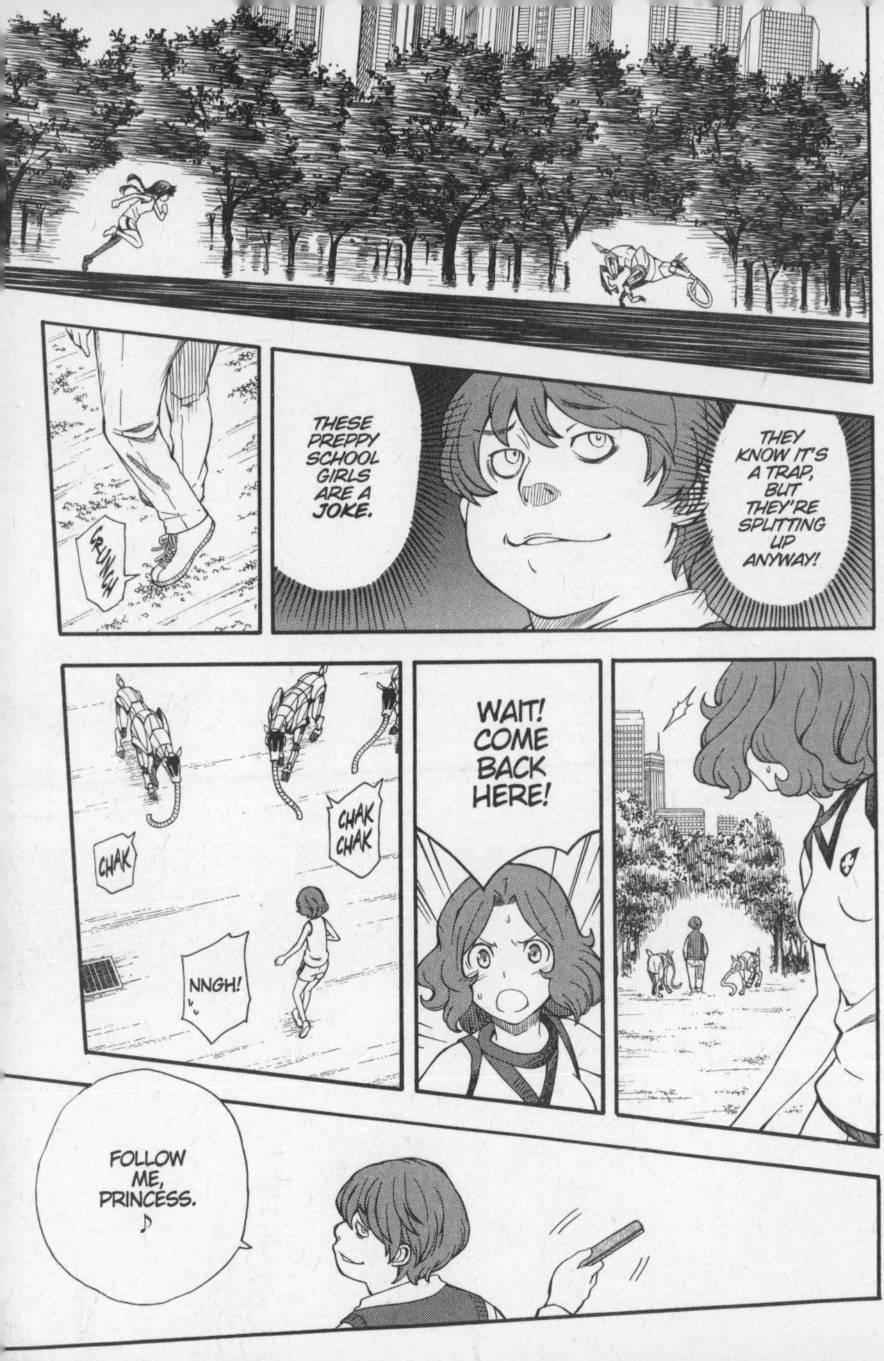
THEY KNOW IT'S A TRAP, BUT THEY'RE SPLITTING UP ANYWAY!
THESE PREPPY SCHOOL GIRLS ARE A JOKE.
CRUNCH
WAIT! COME BACK HERE!
CHAK CHAK
CHAK
NNGH!
FOLLOW ME, PRINCESS. ♪

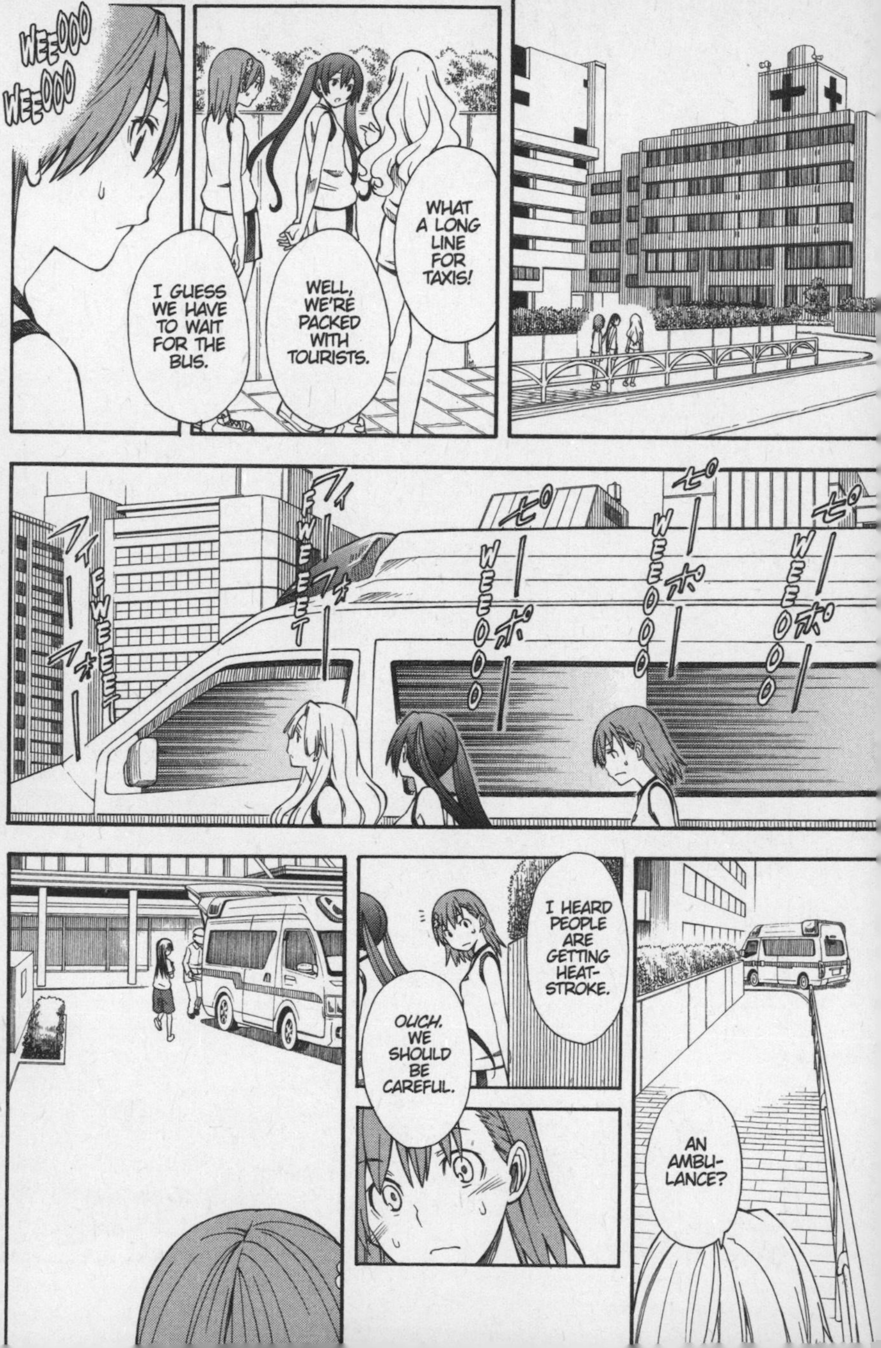
WHAT A LONG LINE FOR TAXIS!
WELL, WE'RE PACKED WITH TOURISTS.
WEE-OOO WEE-OOO
I GUESS WE HAVE TO WAIT FOR THE BUS.
ピーポー WEE-OOO
ピーポー WEE-OOO
ピーポー WEE-OOO
フィーフォー FWEEET
フィーフォー FWEEET
AN AMBULANCE?
I HEARD PEOPLE ARE GETTING HEAT-STROKE.
OUCH. WE SHOULD BE CAREFUL.

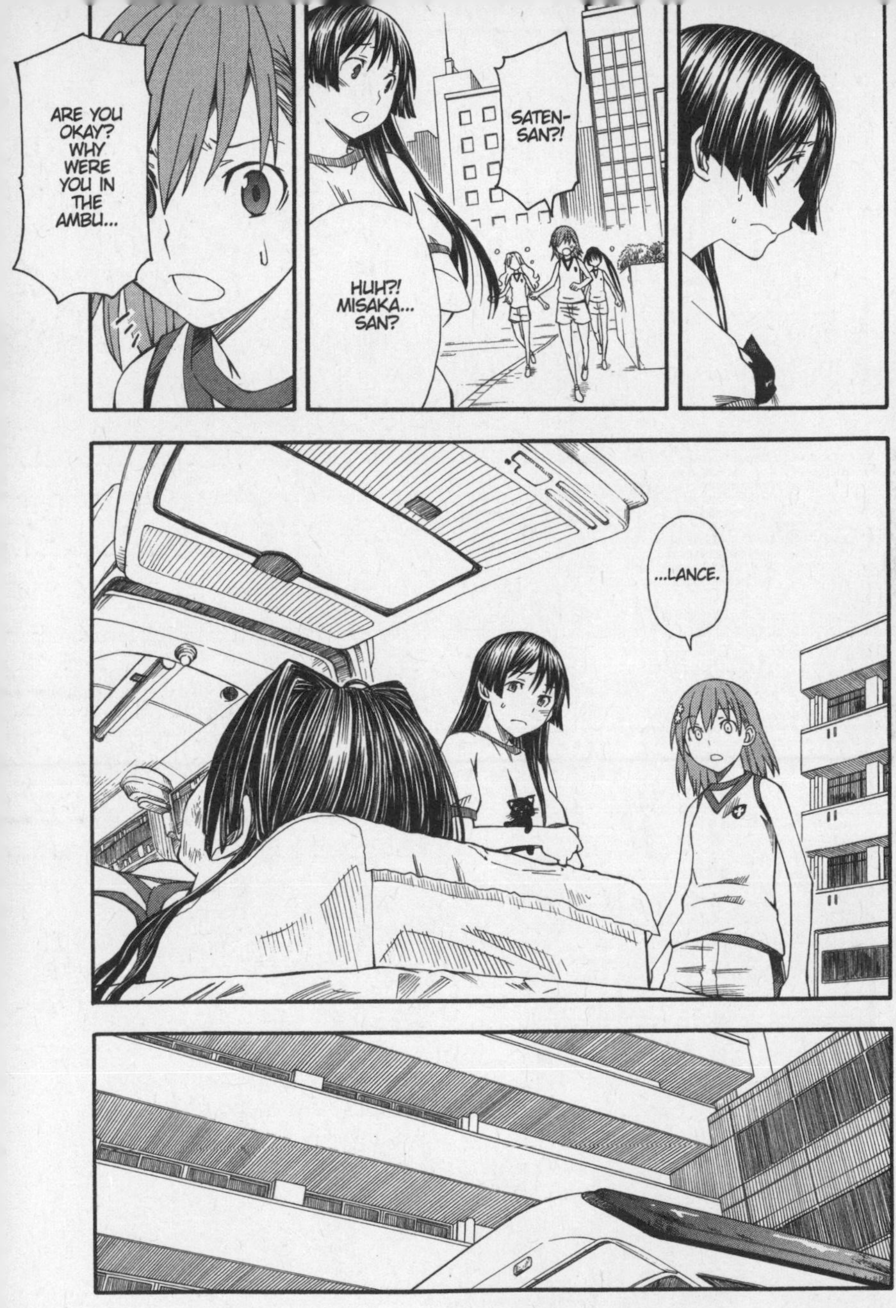
SATEN-SAN?!
HUH?! MISAKA... SAN?
ARE YOU OKAY? WHY WERE YOU IN THE AMBU...
...LANCE.

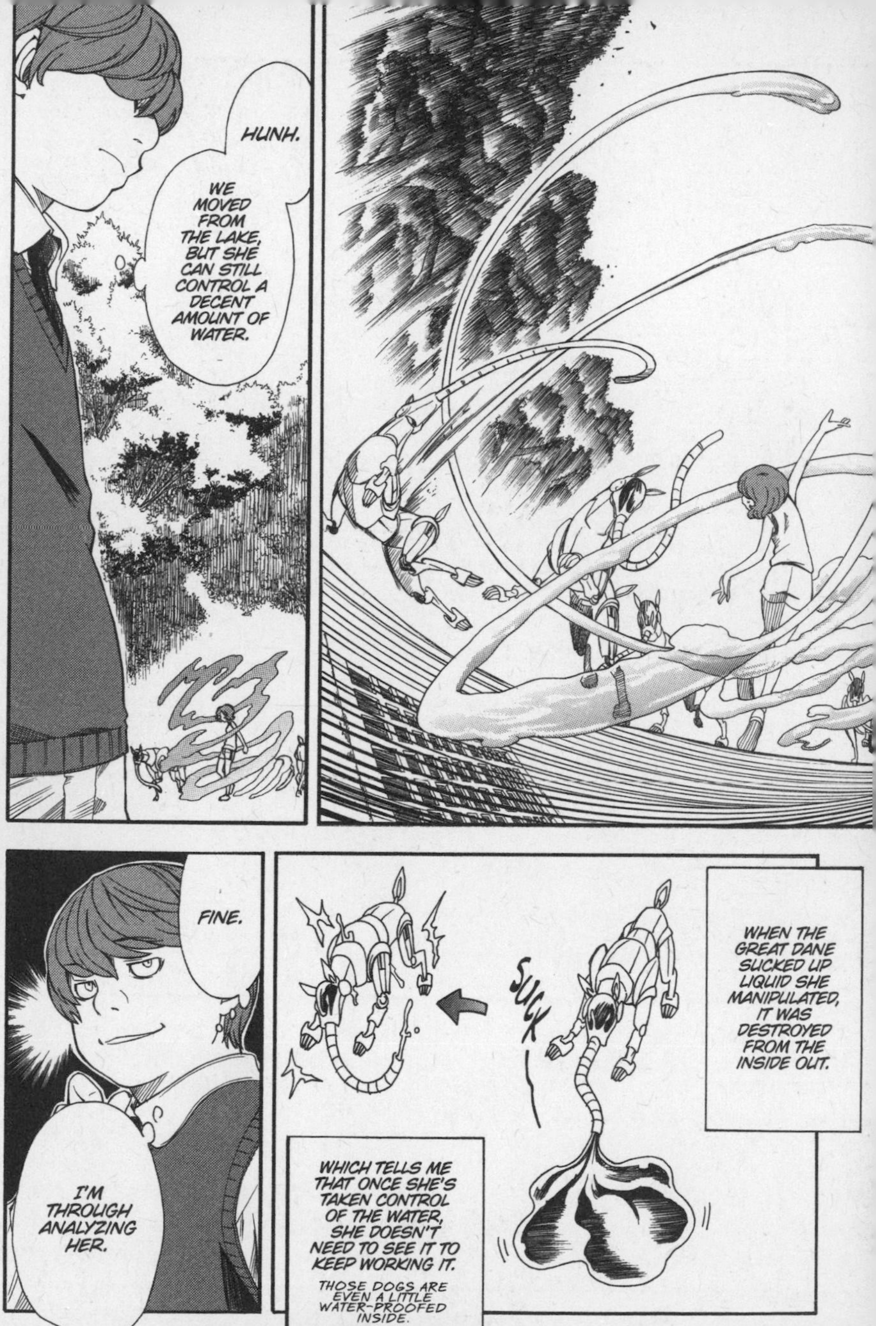
HUNH.
WE MOVED FROM THE LAKE, BUT SHE CAN STILL CONTROL A DECENT AMOUNT OF WATER.
WHEN THE GREAT DANE SUCKED UP LIQUID SHE MANIPULATED, IT WAS DESTROYED FROM THE INSIDE OUT.
SUCK
WHICH TELLS ME THAT ONCE SHE'S TAKEN CONTROL OF THE WATER, SHE DOESN'T NEED TO SEE IT TO KEEP WORKING IT.
THOSE DOGS ARE EVEN A LITTLE WATER-PROOFED INSIDE.
FINE.
I'M THROUGH ANALYZING HER.

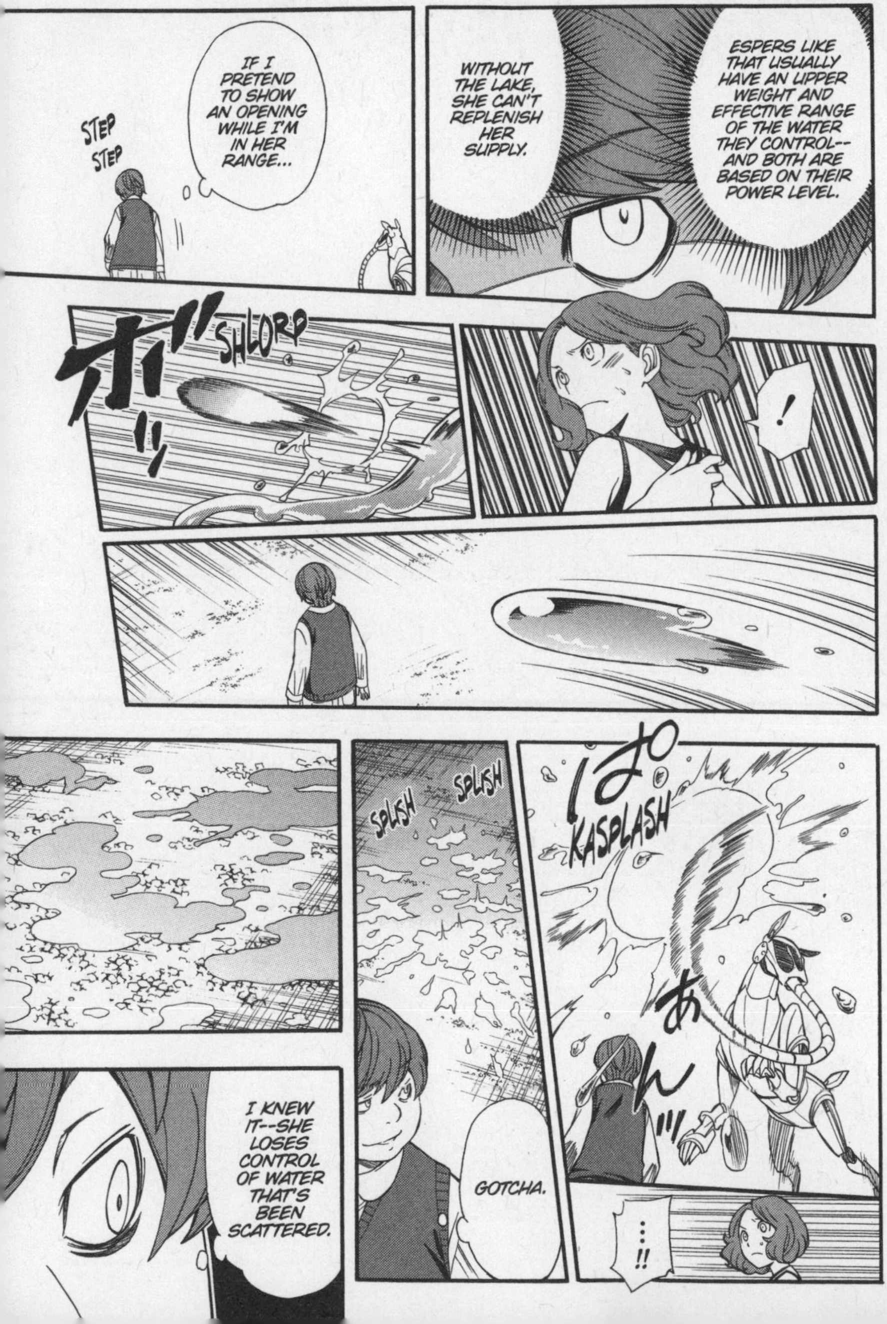
ESPERS LIKE THAT USUALLY HAVE AN UPPER WEIGHT AND EFFECTIVE RANGE OF THE WATER THEY CONTROL--AND BOTH ARE BASED ON THEIR POWER LEVEL.
WITHOUT THE LAKE, SHE CAN'T REPLENISH HER SUPPLY.
IF I PRETEND TO SHOW AN OPENING WHILE I'M IN HER RANGE...
STEP STEP
!
SHLORP
KASPLASH
SPLISH
SPLISH
...!!
GOTCHA.
I KNEW IT--SHE LOSES CONTROL OF WATER THAT'S BEEN SCATTERED.

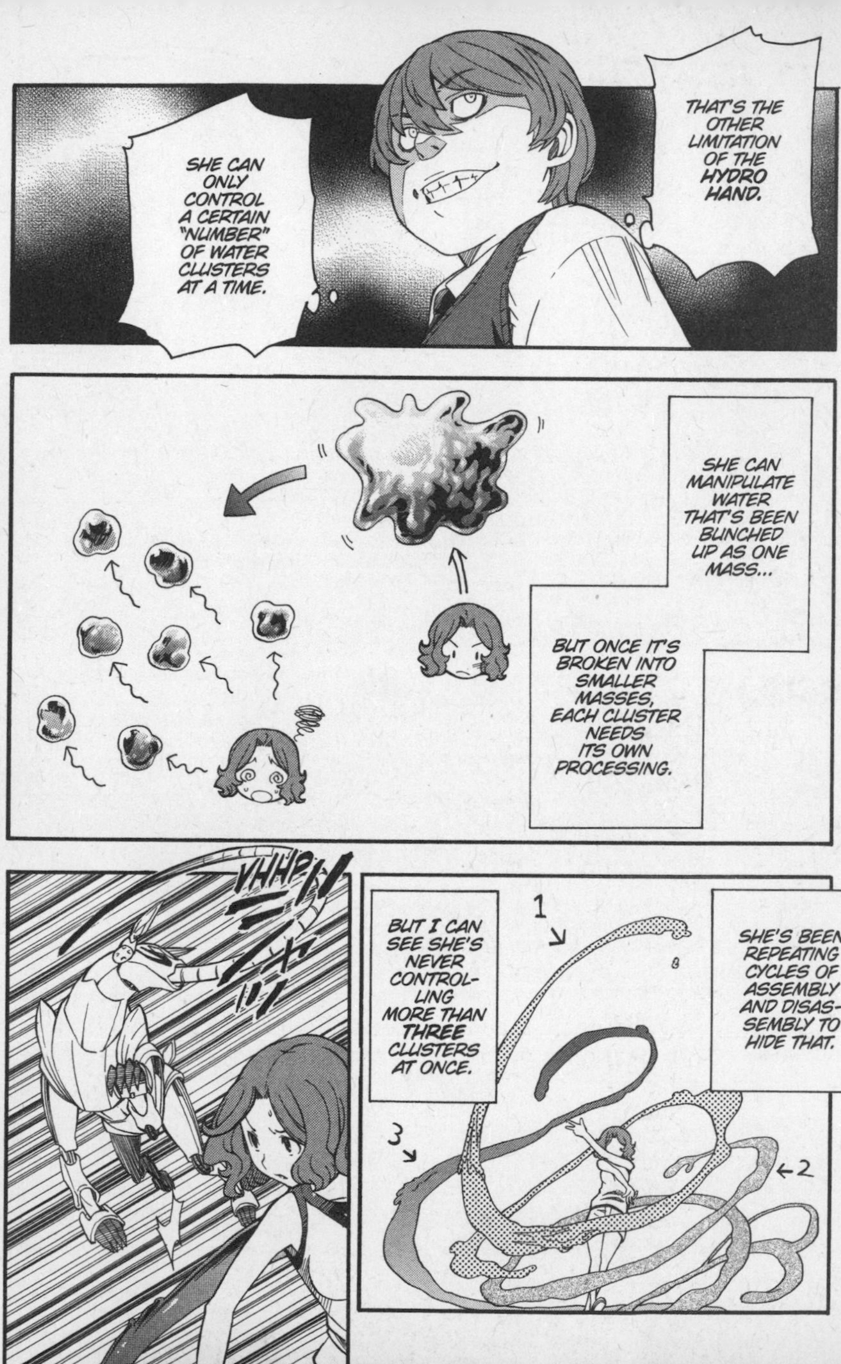
THAT'S THE OTHER LIMITATION OF THE HYDRO HAND.
SHE CAN ONLY CONTROL A CERTAIN "NUMBER" OF WATER CLUSTERS AT A TIME.
SHE CAN MANIPULATE WATER THAT'S BEEN BUNCHED UP AS ONE MASS...
BUT ONCE IT'S BROKEN INTO SMALLER MASSES, EACH CLUSTER NEEDS ITS OWN PROCESSING.
SHE'S BEEN REPEATING CYCLES OF ASSEMBLY AND DISAS-SEMBLY TO HIDE THAT.
1
2
3
BUT I CAN SEE SHE'S NEVER CONTROL-LING MORE THAN THREE CLUSTERS AT ONCE.
VHHP!!

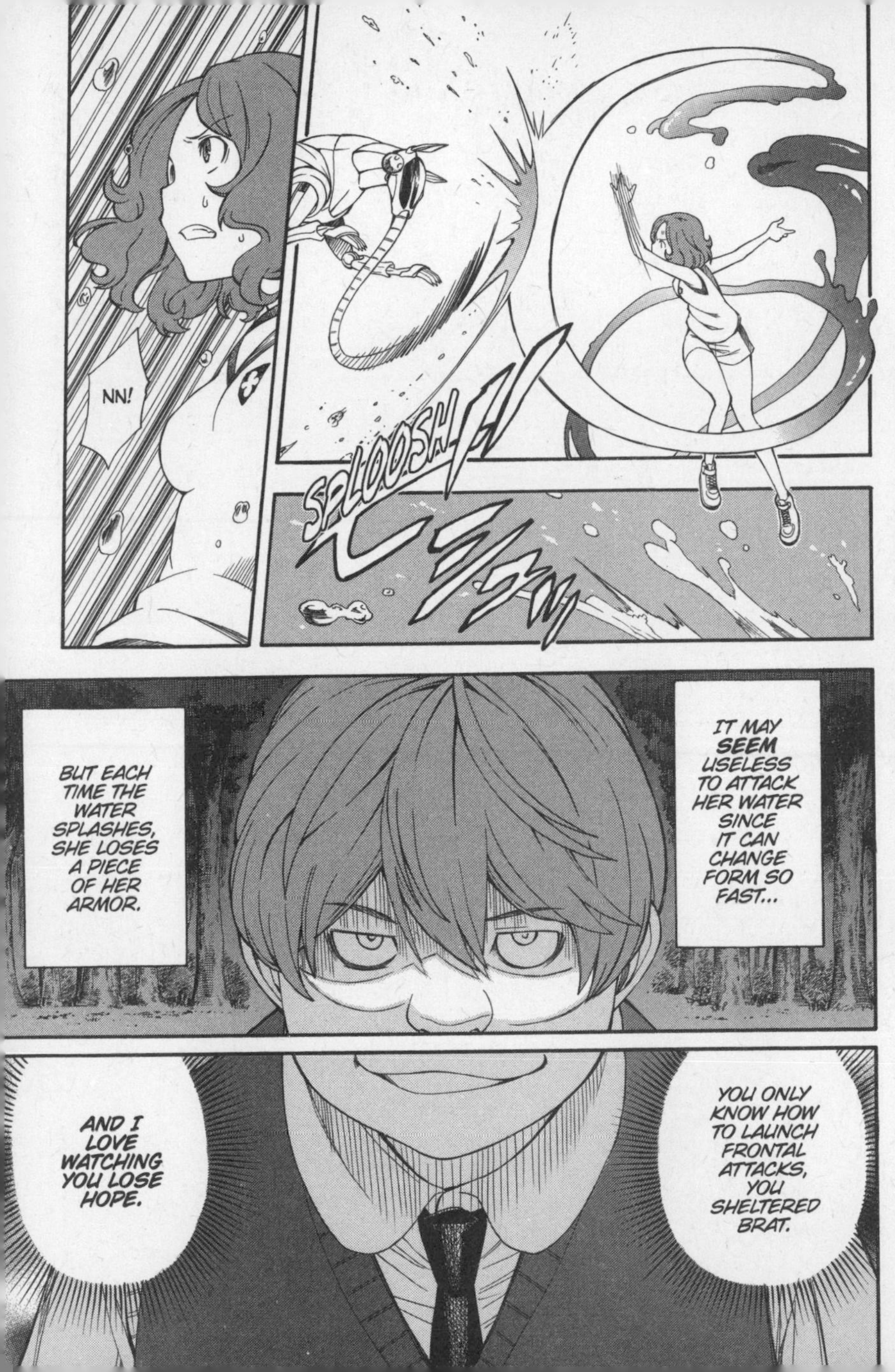
SPLOOSH
NN!
IT MAY SEEM USELESS TO ATTACK HER WATER SINCE IT CAN CHANGE FORM SO FAST...
BUT EACH TIME THE WATER SPLASHES, SHE LOSES A PIECE OF HER ARMOR.
YOU ONLY KNOW HOW TO LAUNCH FRONTAL ATTACKS, YOU SHELTERED BRAT.
AND I LOVE WATCHING YOU LOSE HOPE.

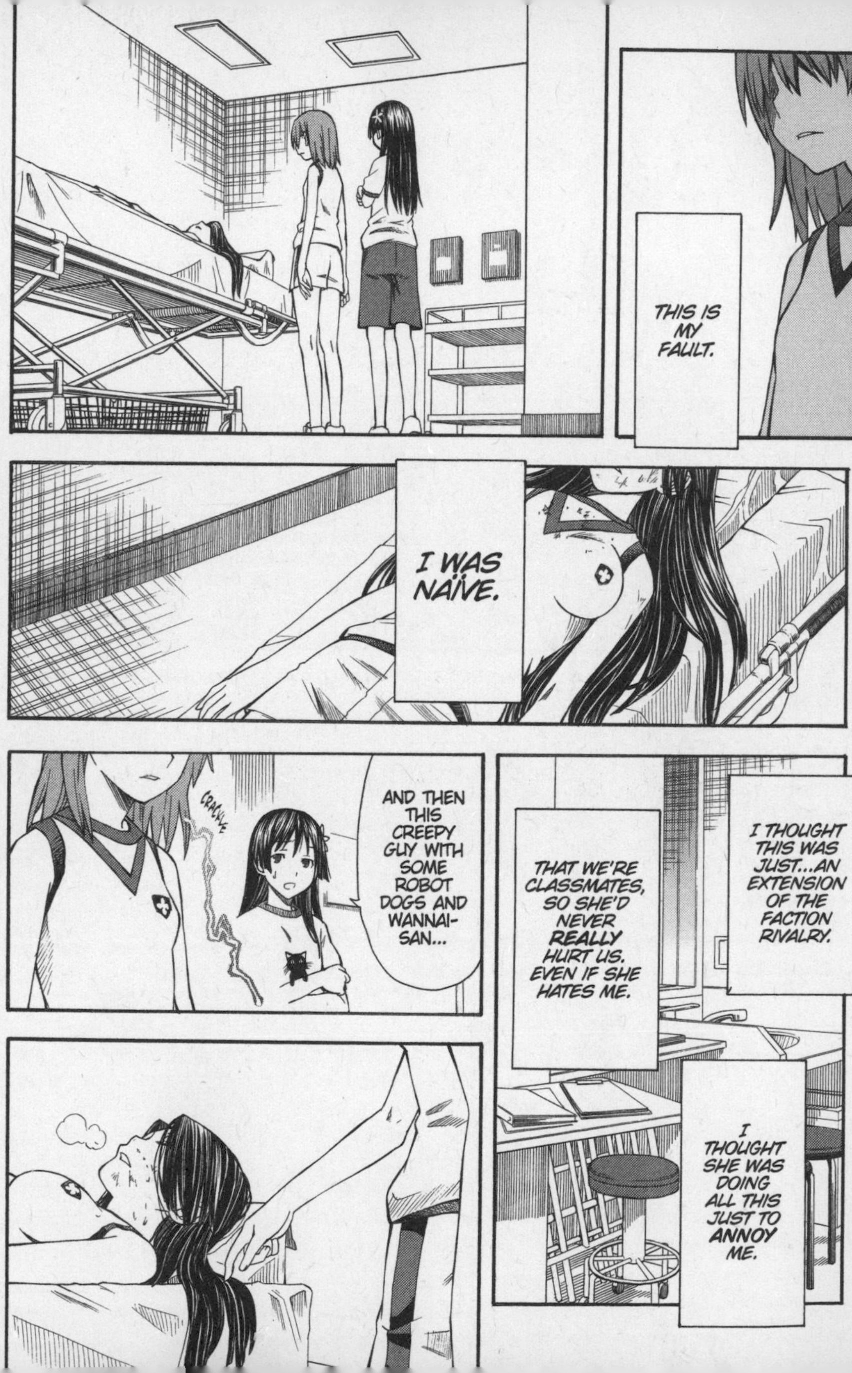
THIS IS MY FAULT.
I WAS NAÏVE.
I THOUGHT THIS WAS JUST...AN EXTENSION OF THE FACTION RIVALRY.
THAT WE'RE CLASSMATES, SO SHE'D NEVER REALLY HURT US. EVEN IF SHE HATES ME.
I THOUGHT SHE WAS DOING ALL THIS JUST TO ANNOY ME.
AND THEN THIS CREEPY GUY WITH SOME ROBOT DOGS AND WANNAI-SAN...
CRACKLE

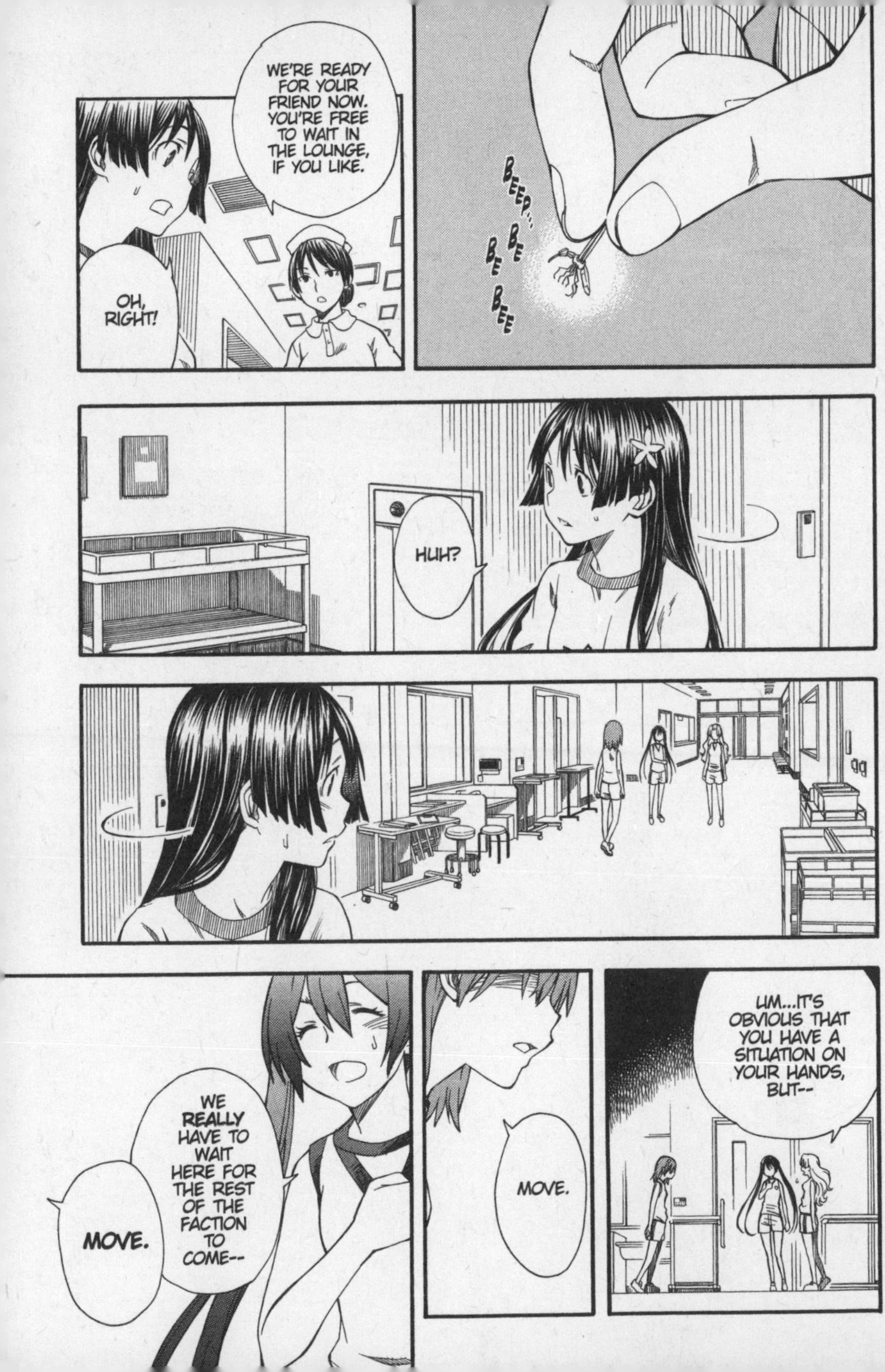
BEEP... BE BE BEE
WE'RE READY FOR YOUR FRIEND NOW. YOU'RE FREE TO WAIT IN THE LOUNGE, IF YOU LIKE.
OH, RIGHT!
HUH?
UM...IT'S OBVIOUS THAT YOU HAVE A SITUATION ON YOUR HANDS, BUT--
MOVE.
WE REALLY HAVE TO WAIT HERE FOR THE REST OF THE FACTION TO COME--
MOVE.

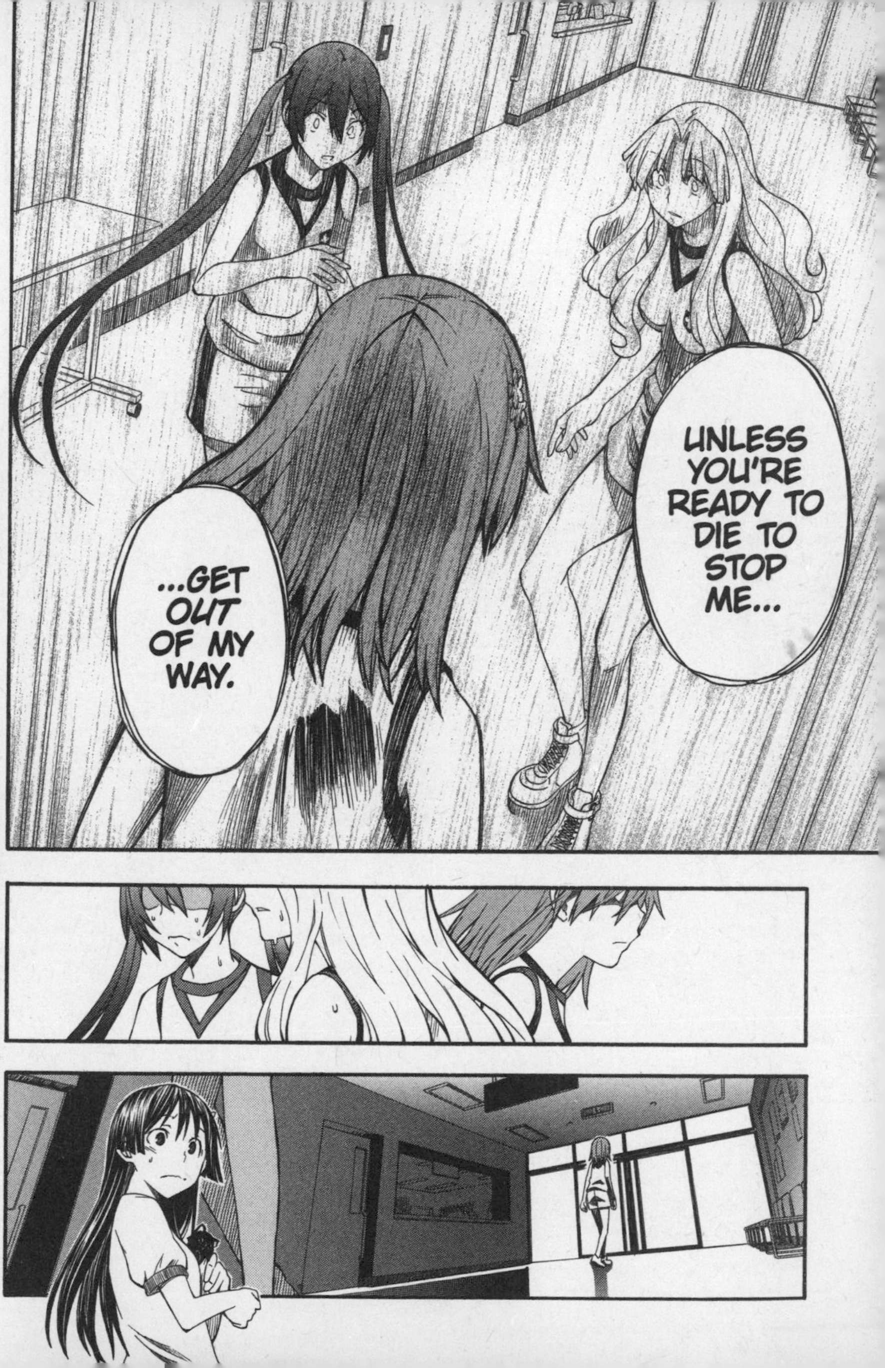
UNLESS YOU'RE READY TO DIE TO STOP ME...
...GET OUT OF MY WAY.

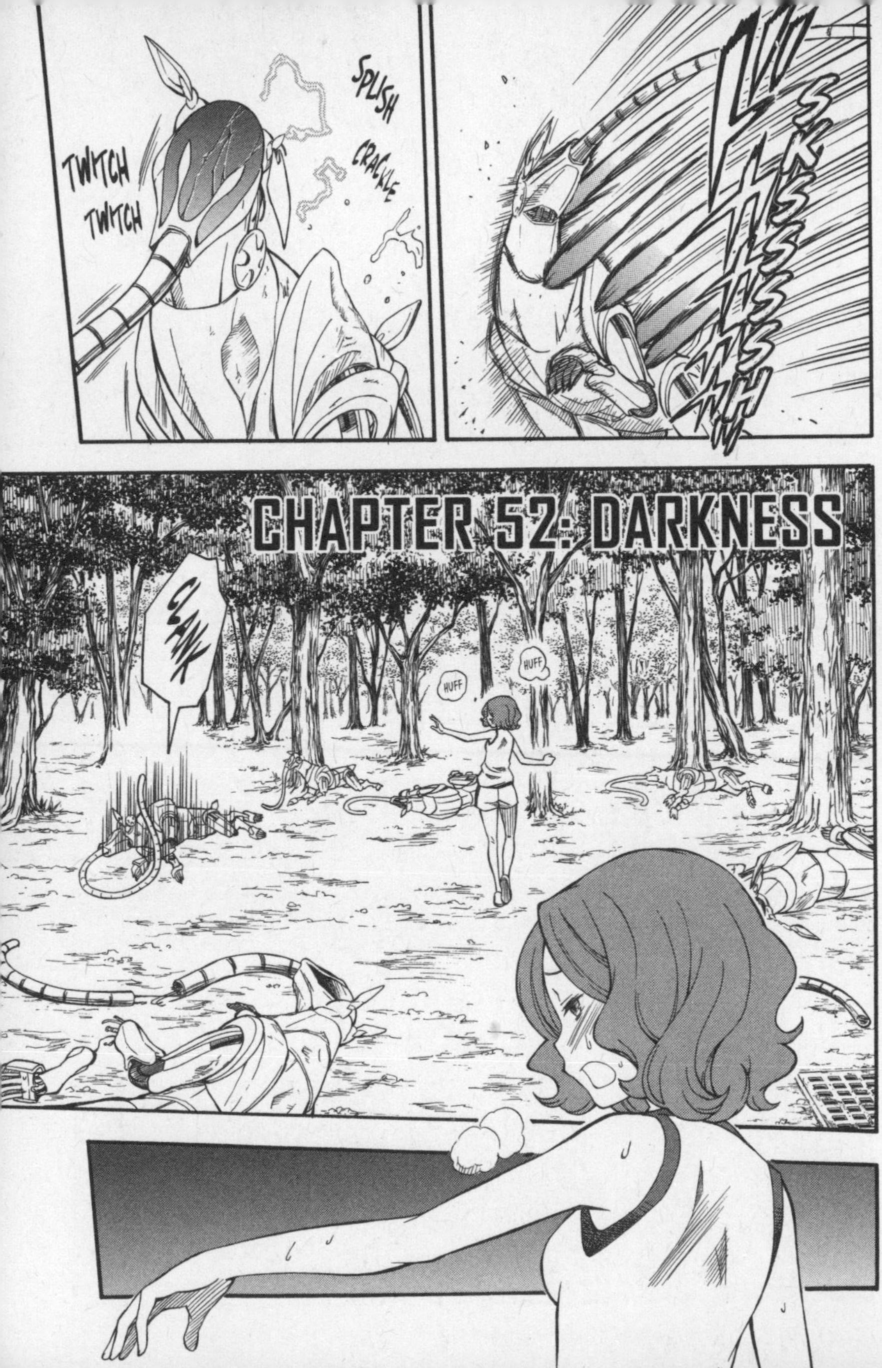
SKSSSSSH
TWITCH TWITCH
SPLISH
CRACKLE
CHAPTER 52: DARKNESS
CLANK
HUFF
HUFF

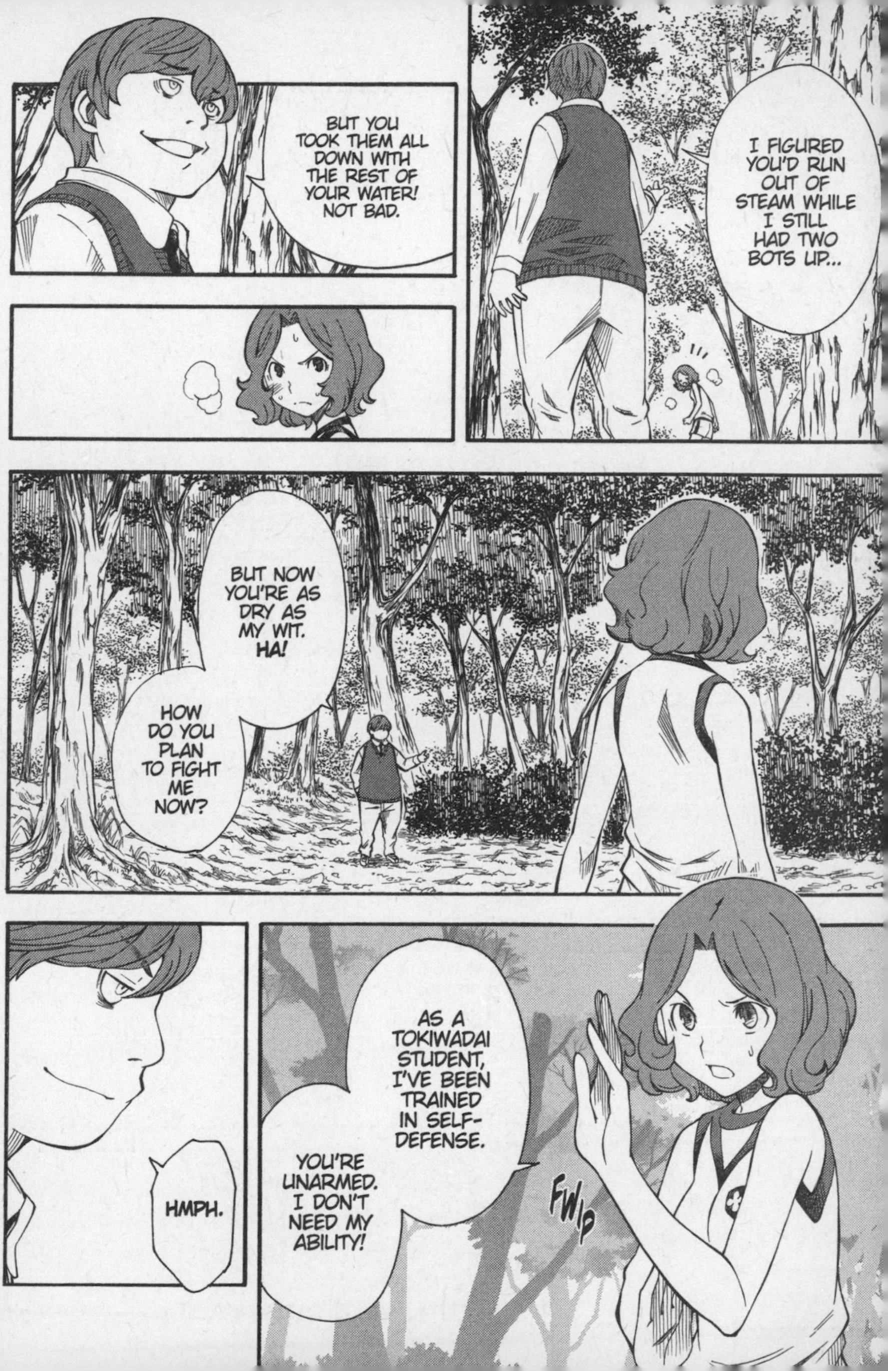
I FIGURED YOU'D RUN OUT OF STEAM WHILE I STILL HAD TWO BOTS UP...
BUT YOU TOOK THEM ALL DOWN WITH THE REST OF YOUR WATER! NOT BAD.
BUT NOW YOU'RE AS DRY AS MY WIT. HA!
HOW DO YOU PLAN TO FIGHT ME NOW?
AS A TOKIWADAI STUDENT, I'VE BEEN TRAINED IN SELF-DEFENSE.
YOU'RE UNARMED. I DON'T NEED MY ABILITY!
FWIP
HMPH.

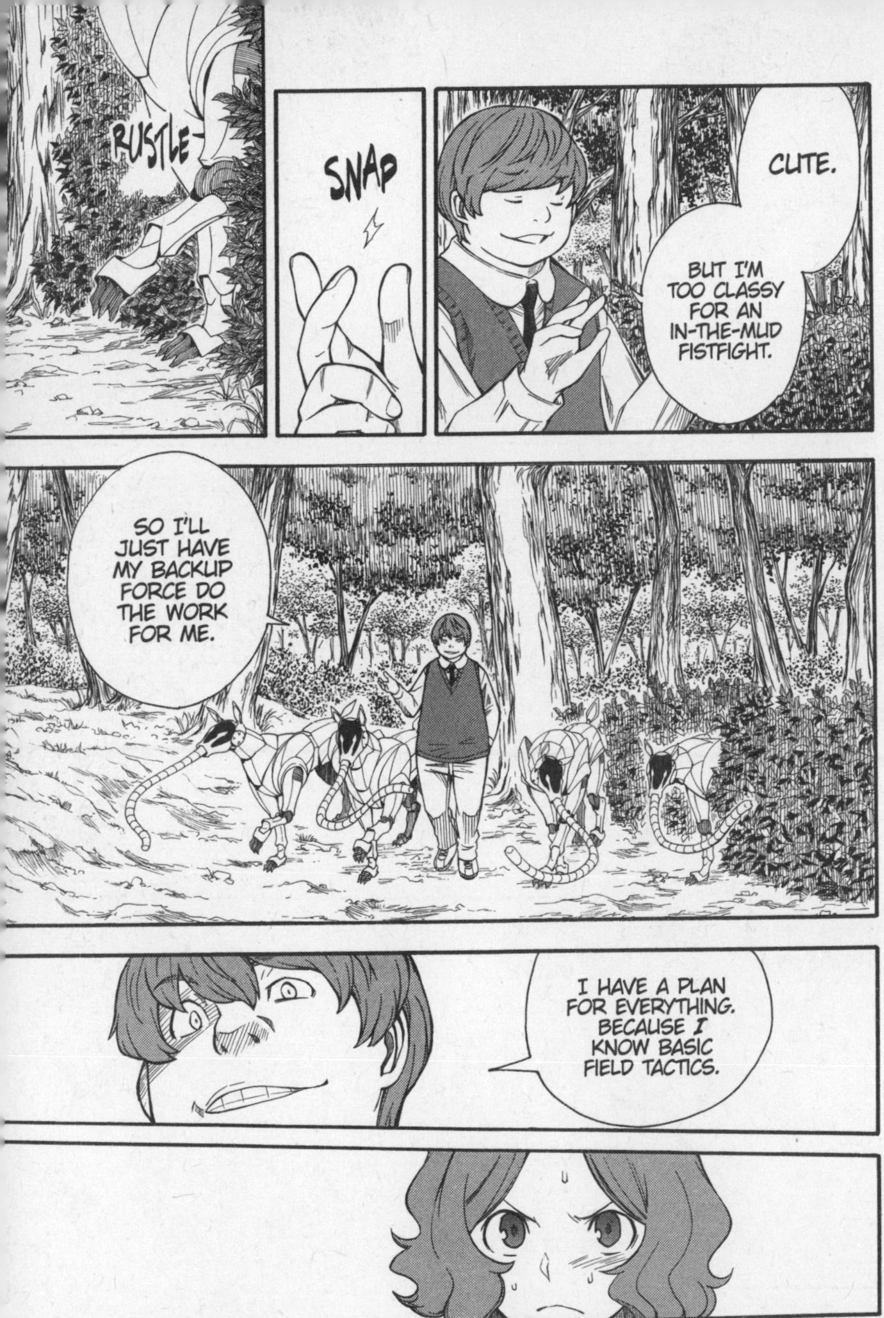
CUTE.
BUT I'M TOO CLASSY FOR AN IN-THE-MUD FISTFIGHT.
SNAP
RUSTLE
SO I'LL JUST HAVE MY BACKUP FORCE DO THE WORK FOR ME.
I HAVE A PLAN FOR EVERYTHING. BECAUSE *I* KNOW BASIC FIELD TACTICS.

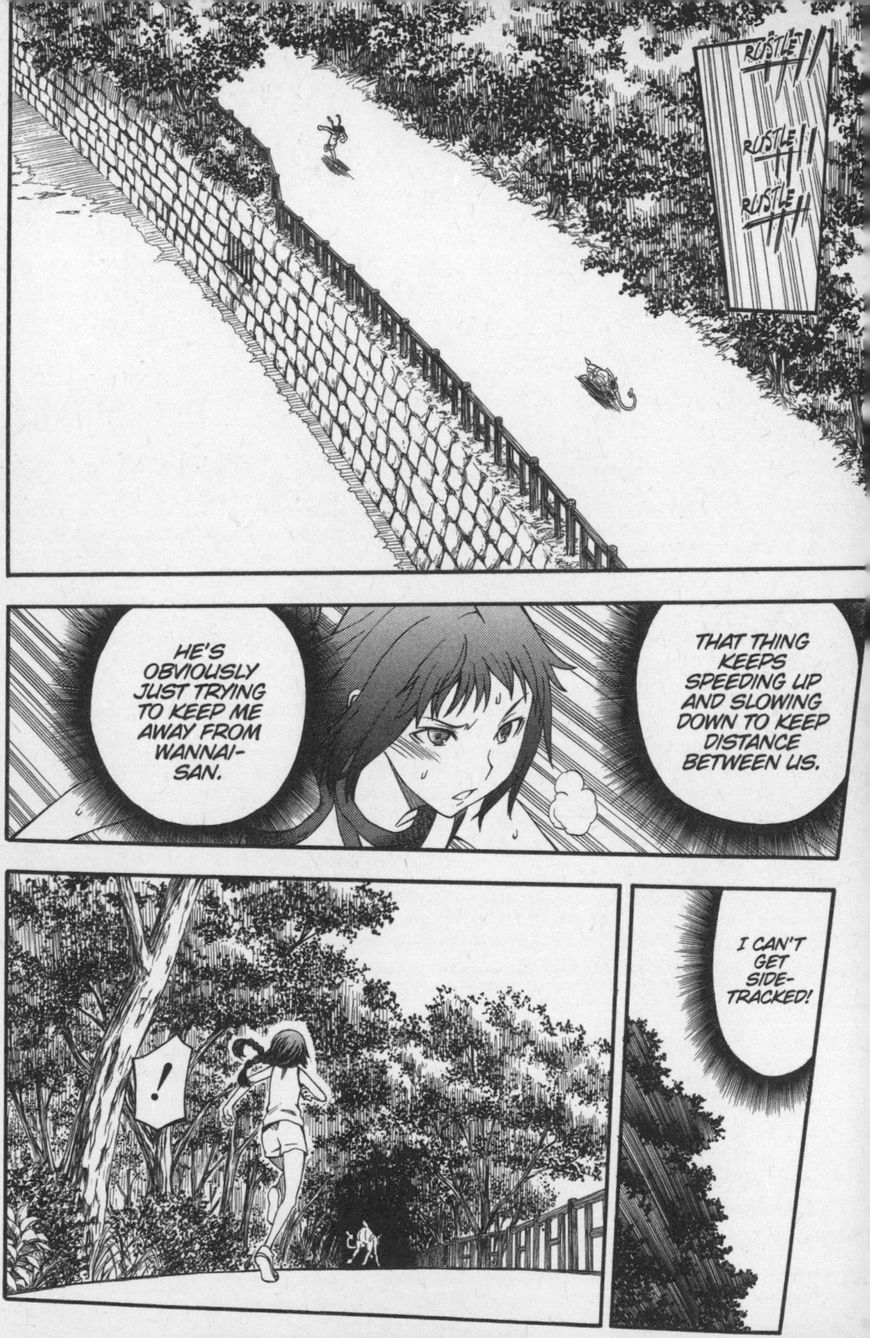
RUSTLE
RUSTLE
RUSTLE
THAT THING KEEPS SPEEDING UP AND SLOWING DOWN TO KEEP DISTANCE BETWEEN US.
HE'S OBVIOUSLY JUST TRYING TO KEEP ME AWAY FROM WANNAI-SAN.
I CAN'T GET SIDE-TRACKED!
!

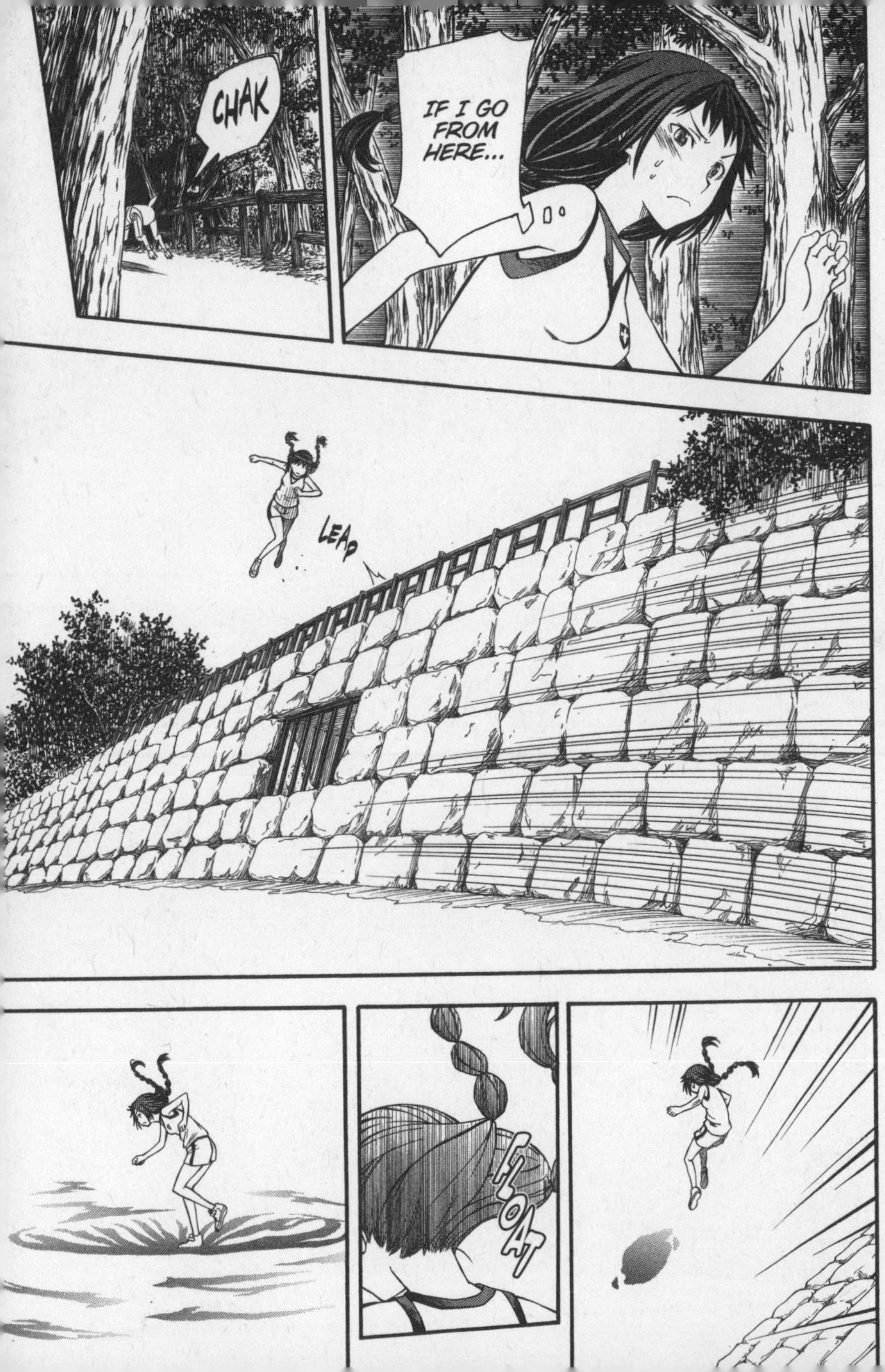
IF I GO FROM HERE...
CHAK
LEAP
FLOAT

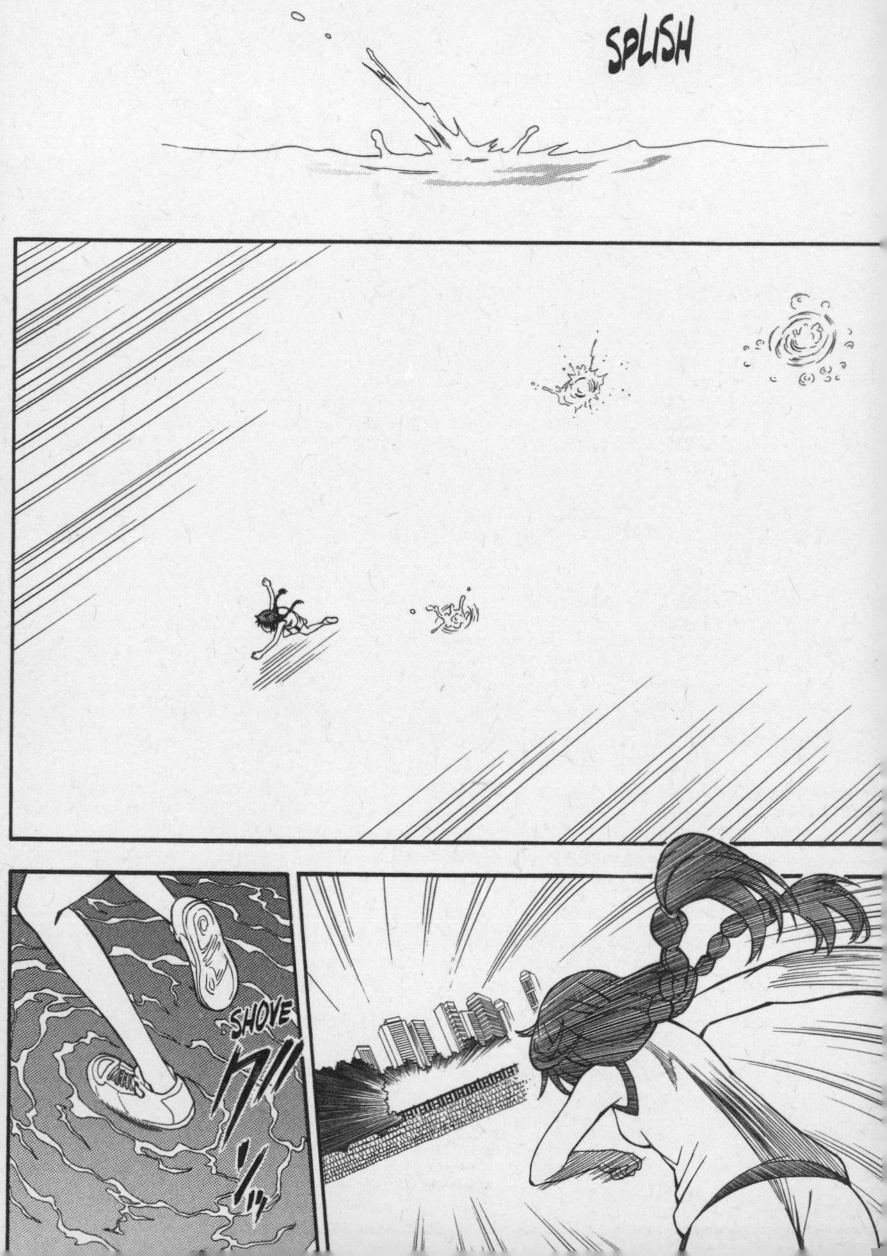
SPLISH
SHOVE

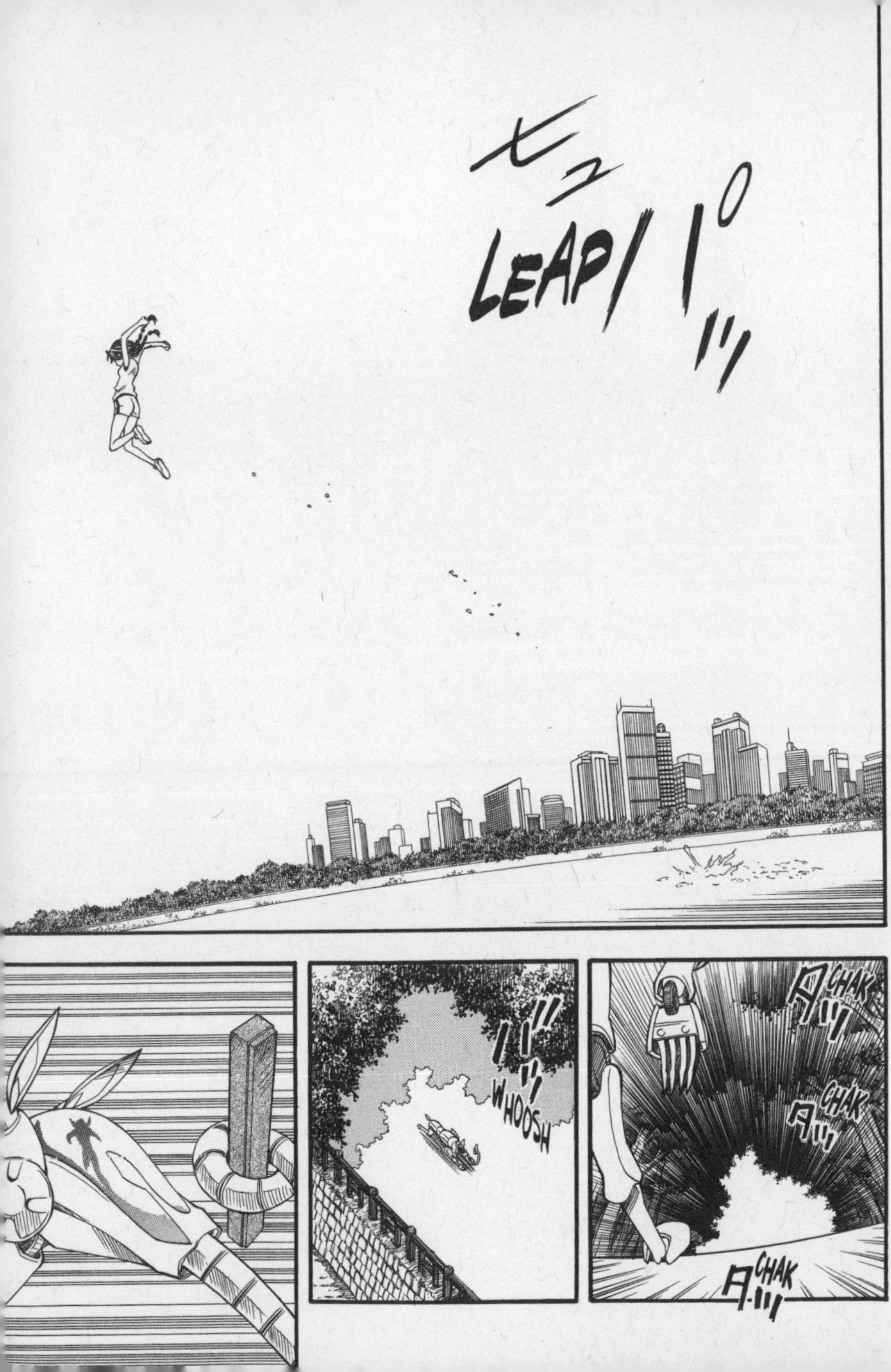
ヒュ
LEAP!
パッ
CHAK
CHAK
CHAK
WHOOSH

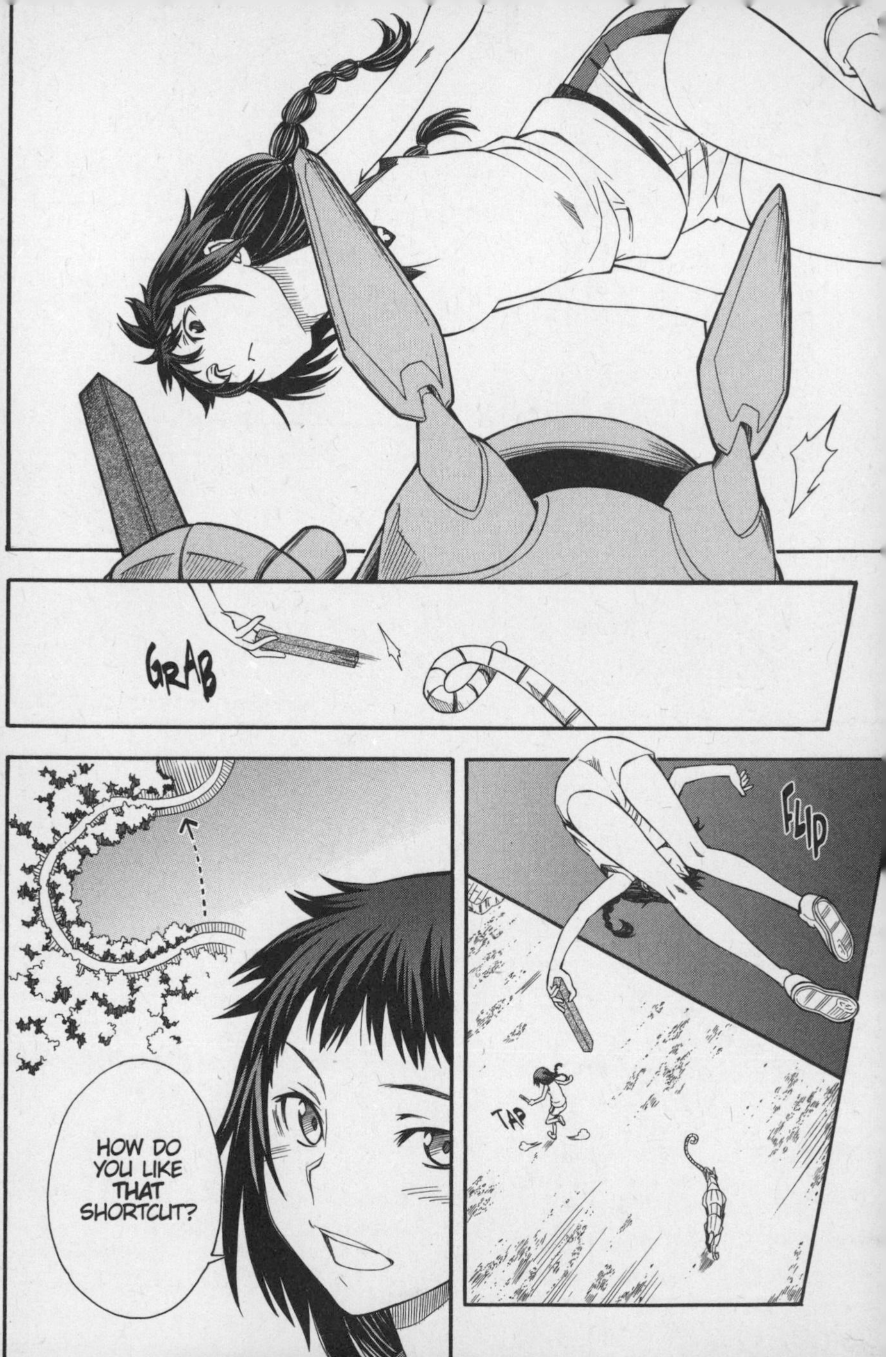
GRAB
FLIP
TAP
HOW DO YOU LIKE THAT SHORTCUT?

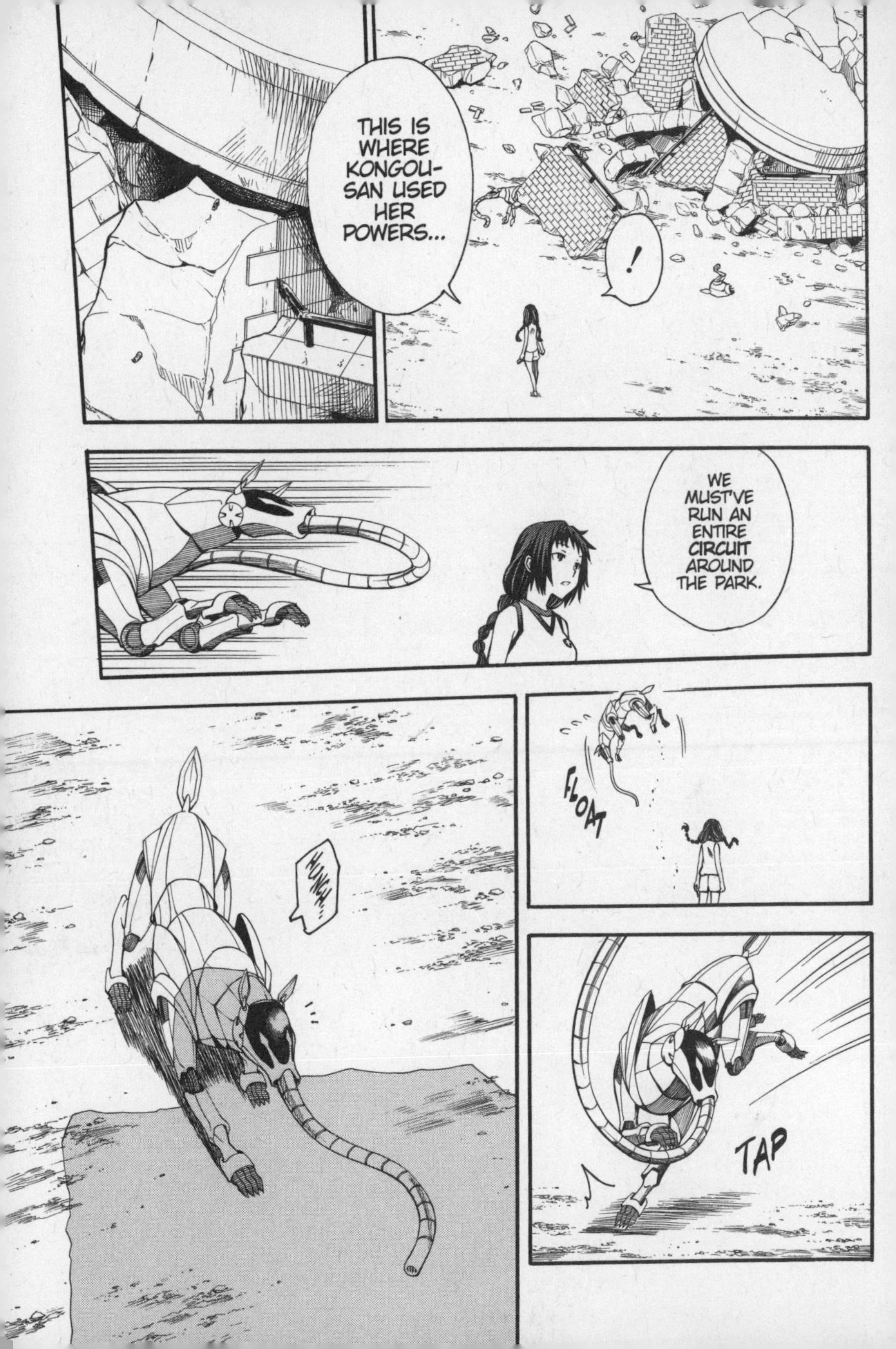
THIS IS WHERE KONGOU-SAN USED HER POWERS...
!
WE MUST'VE RUN AN ENTIRE CIRCUIT AROUND THE PARK.
FLOAT
TAP
HUNGH...
!

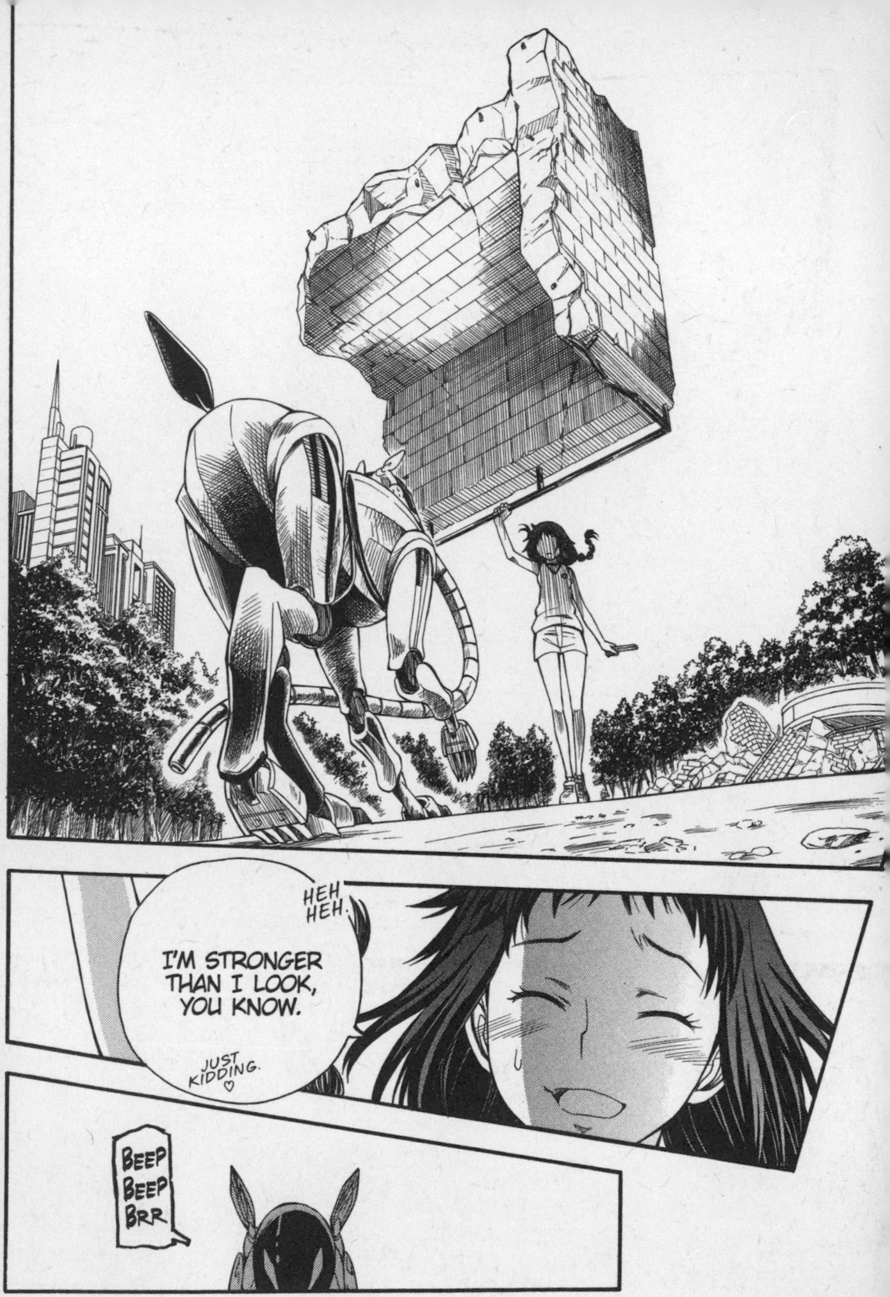
HEH HEH.
I'M STRONGER THAN I LOOK, YOU KNOW.
JUST KIDDING. ♡
BEEP BEEP BRR

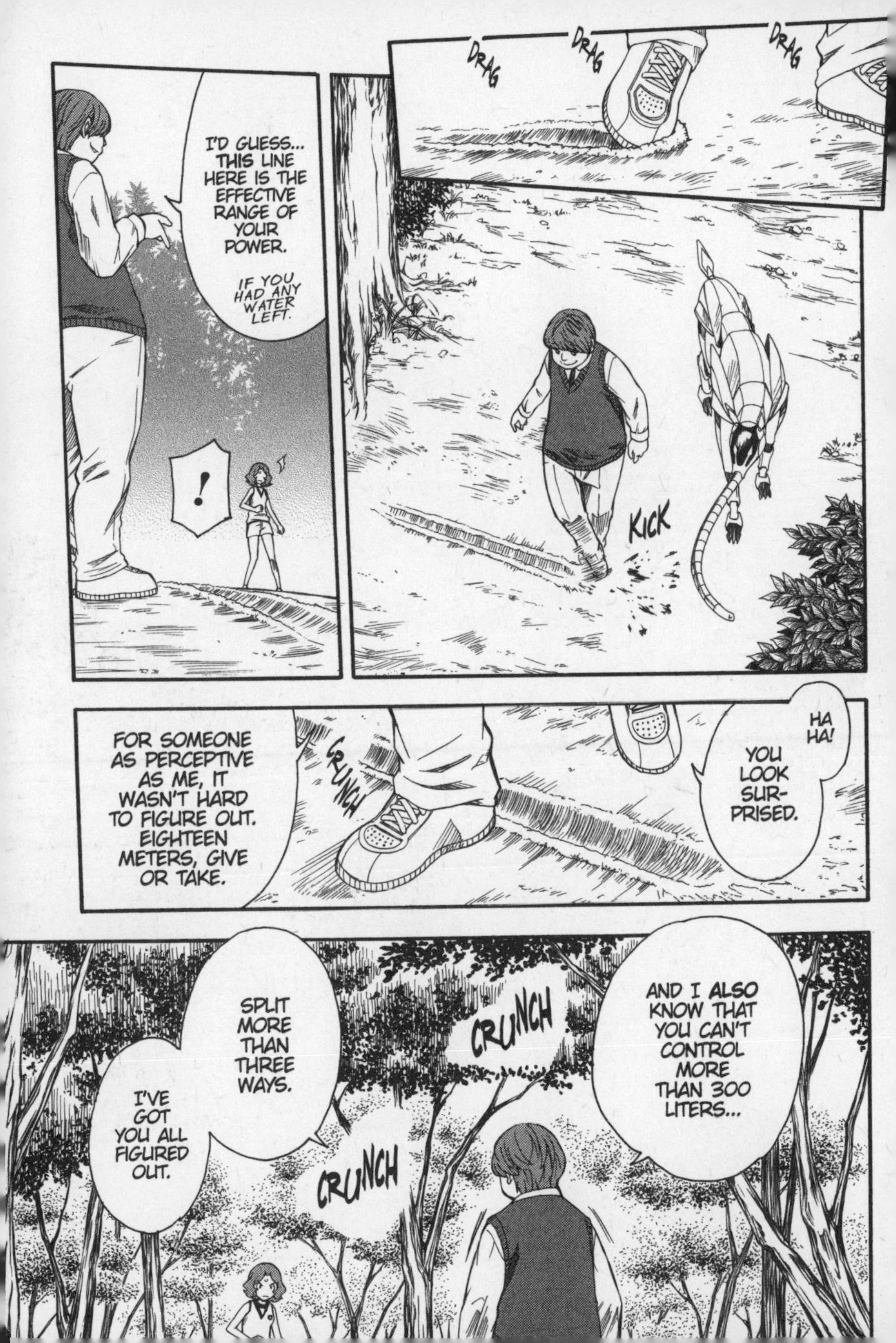
DRAG
DRAG
DRAG
KICK
I'D GUESS... THIS LINE HERE IS THE EFFECTIVE RANGE OF YOUR POWER.
IF YOU HAD ANY WATER LEFT.
!
HA HA!
YOU LOOK SUR-PRISED.
CRUNCH
FOR SOMEONE AS PERCEPTIVE AS ME, IT WASN'T HARD TO FIGURE OUT. EIGHTEEN METERS, GIVE OR TAKE.
AND I ALSO KNOW THAT YOU CAN'T CONTROL MORE THAN 300 LITERS...
CRUNCH
SPLIT MORE THAN THREE WAYS.
CRUNCH
I'VE GOT YOU ALL FIGURED OUT.

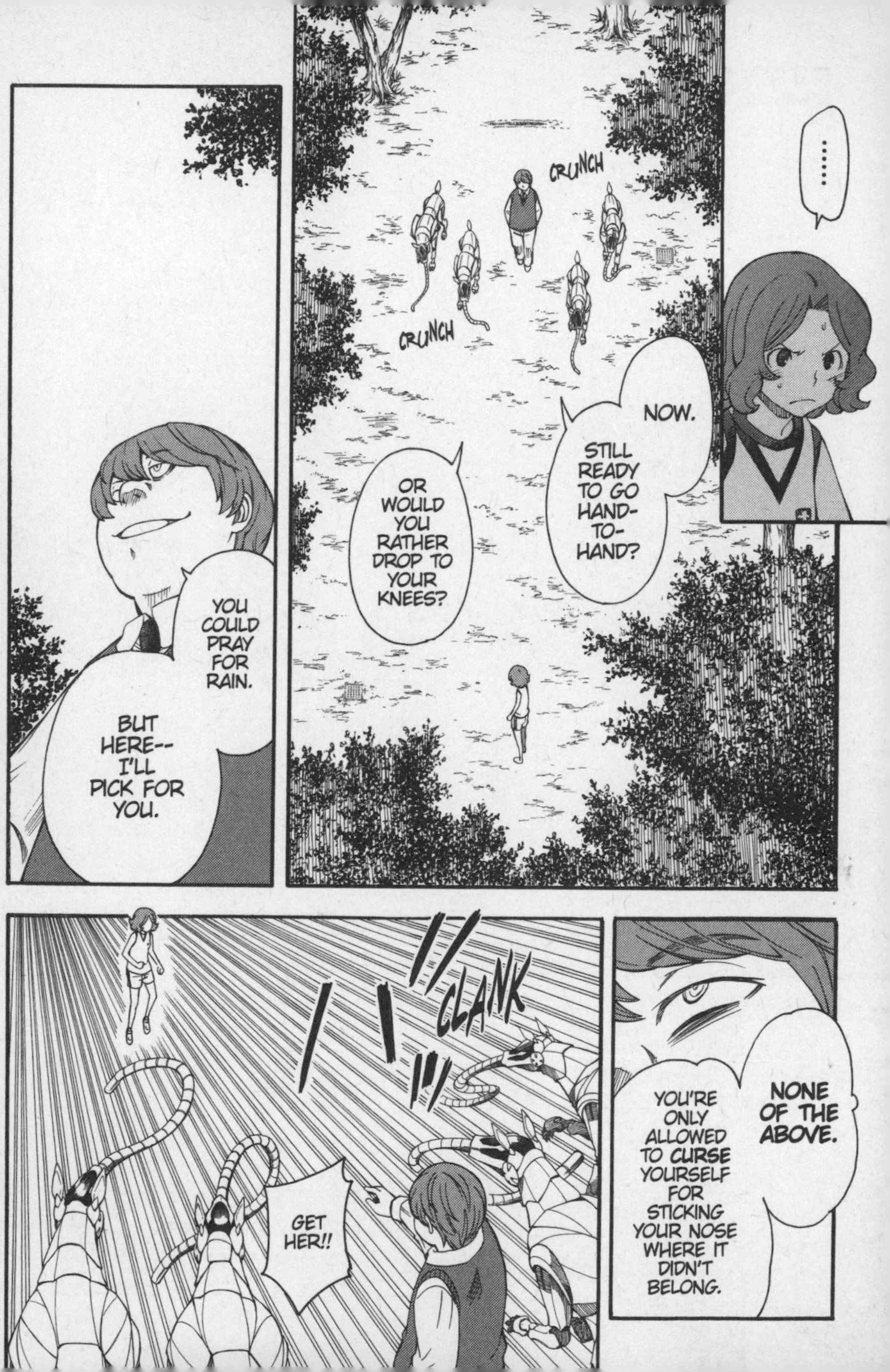
......
CRUNCH
CRUNCH
NOW.
STILL READY TO GO HAND-TO-HAND?
OR WOULD YOU RATHER DROP TO YOUR KNEES?
YOU COULD PRAY FOR RAIN.
BUT HERE-- I'LL PICK FOR YOU.
NONE OF THE ABOVE.
YOU'RE ONLY ALLOWED TO CURSE YOURSELF FOR STICKING YOUR NOSE WHERE IT DIDN'T BELONG.
CLANK
GET HER!!

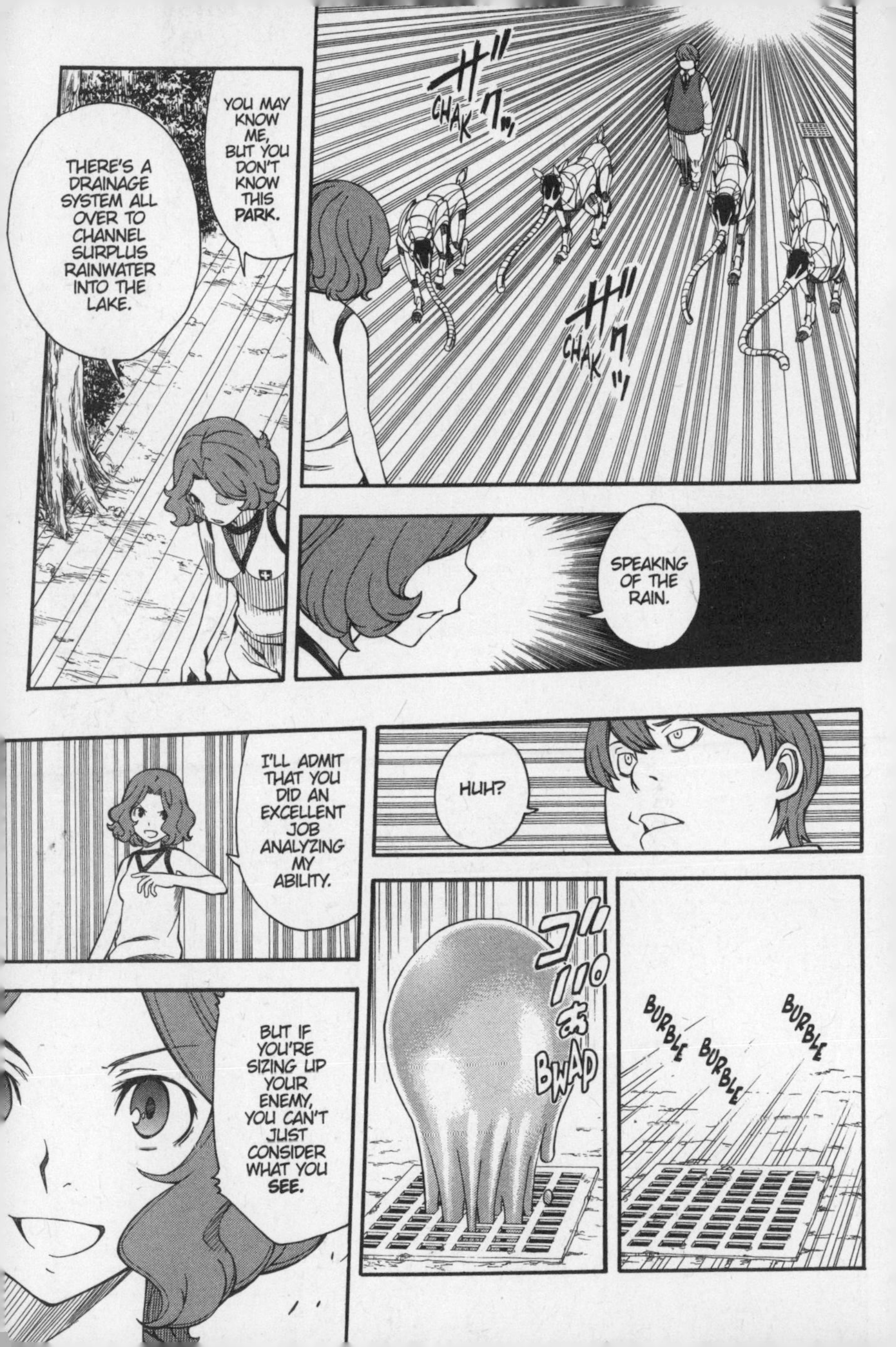
CHAK
CHAK
SPEAKING OF THE RAIN.
YOU MAY KNOW ME, BUT YOU DON'T KNOW THIS PARK.
THERE'S A DRAINAGE SYSTEM ALL OVER TO CHANNEL SURPLUS RAINWATER INTO THE LAKE.
HUH?
I'LL ADMIT THAT YOU DID AN EXCELLENT JOB ANALYZING MY ABILITY.
BURBLE BURBLE BURBLE
BWAP
BUT IF YOU'RE SIZING UP YOUR ENEMY, YOU CAN'T JUST CONSIDER WHAT YOU SEE.

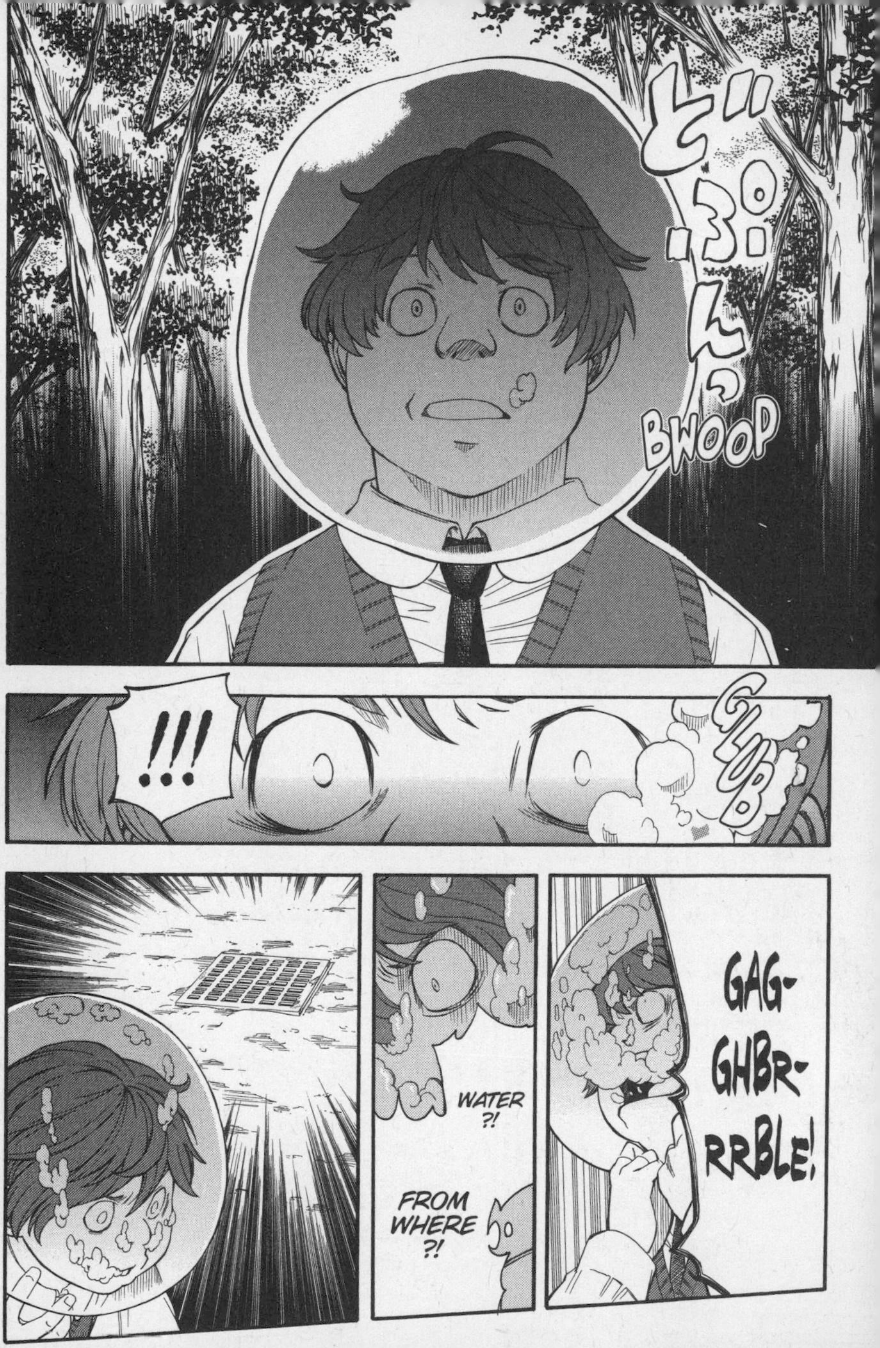
どぷんっ
BWOOP
!!!
GLUB
GAG-
GHBR-
RRBLE!
WATER ?!
FROM WHERE ?!

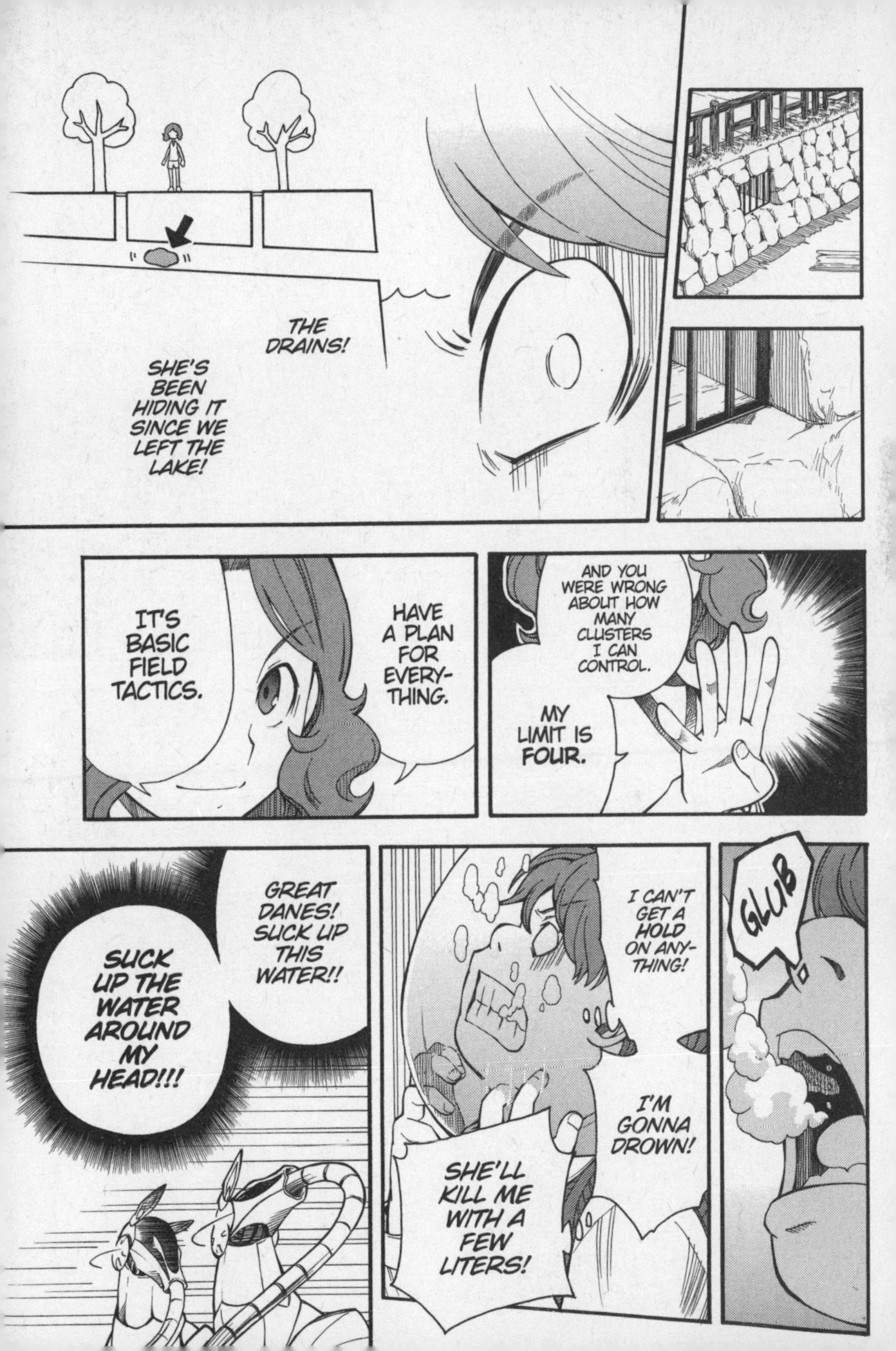
THE DRAINS!
SHE'S BEEN HIDING IT SINCE WE LEFT THE LAKE!
AND YOU WERE WRONG ABOUT HOW MANY CLUSTERS I CAN CONTROL.
MY LIMIT IS FOUR.
HAVE A PLAN FOR EVERYTHING.
IT'S BASIC FIELD TACTICS.
GLUB
I CAN'T GET A HOLD ON ANYTHING!
I'M GONNA DROWN!
SHE'LL KILL ME WITH A FEW LITERS!
GREAT DANES! SUCK UP THIS WATER!!
SUCK UP THE WATER AROUND MY HEAD!!!

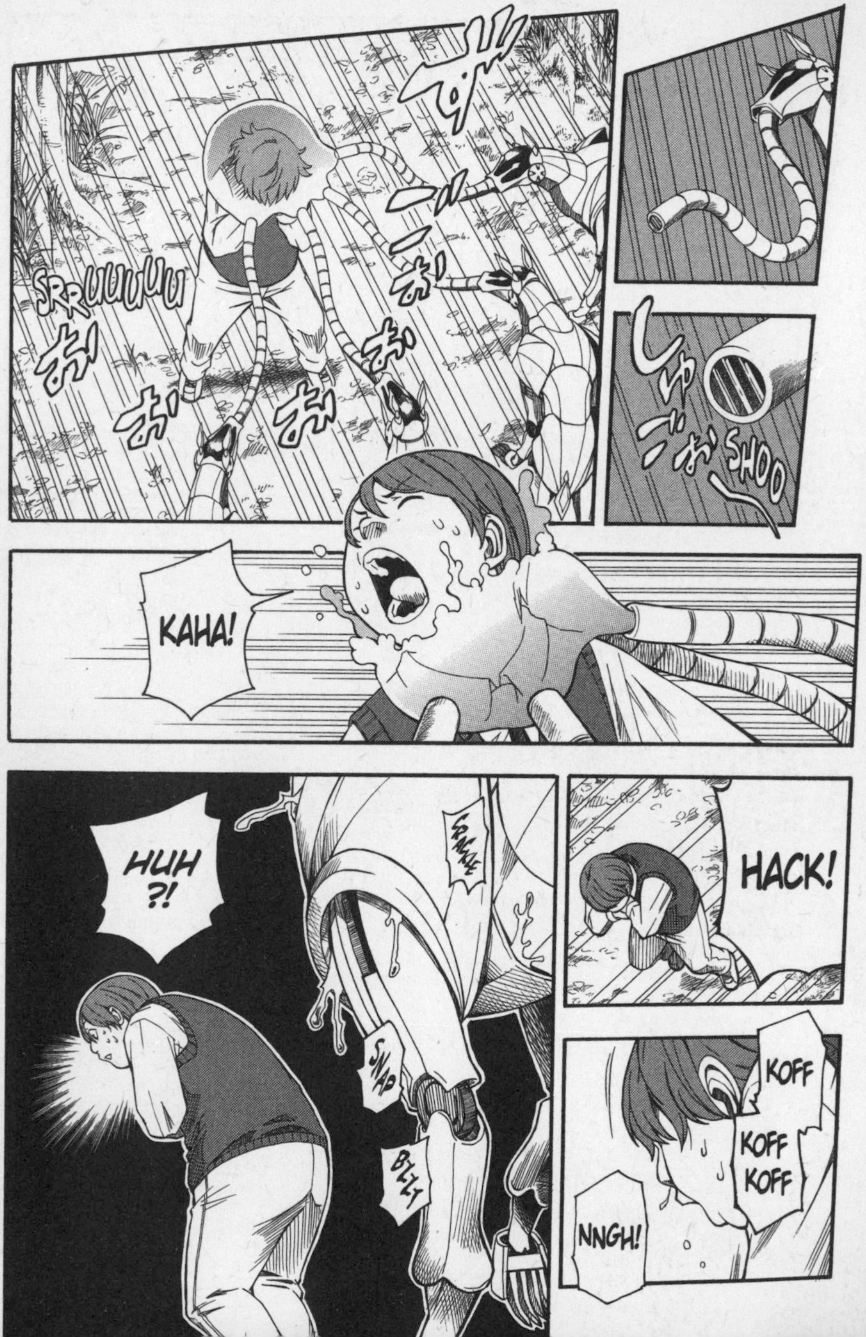
しゅごぉ SHOO
SRRUUUUU
KAHA!
HACK!
KOFF
KOFF KOFF
NNGH!
HUH ?!
SNAP

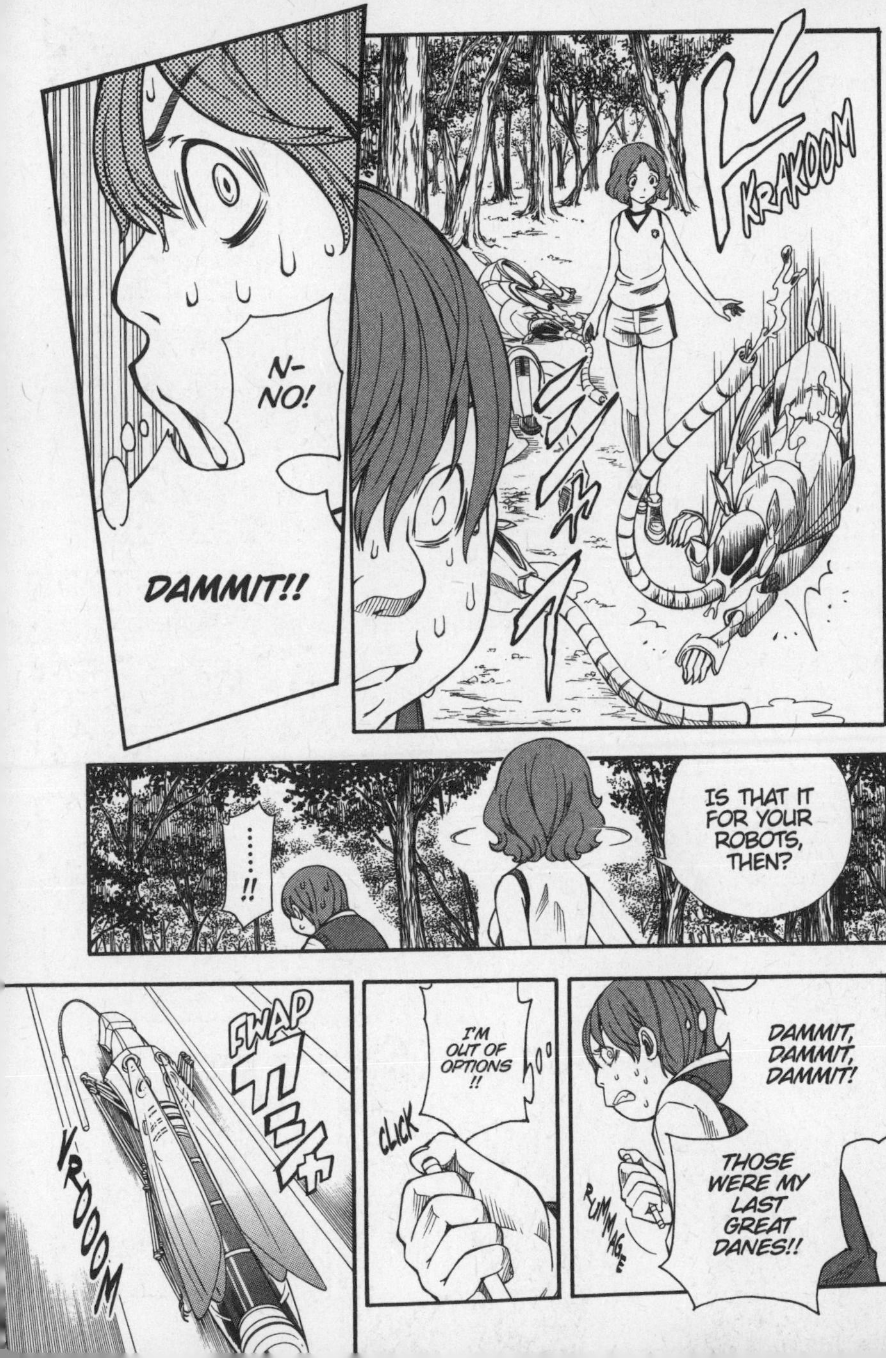
KRAKOOM
N-NO!
DAMMIT!!
IS THAT IT FOR YOUR ROBOTS, THEN?
......!!
DAMMIT, DAMMIT, DAMMIT!
THOSE WERE MY LAST GREAT DANES!!
RUMMAGE
I'M OUT OF OPTIONS !!
CLICK
FWAP
VR-OOOM

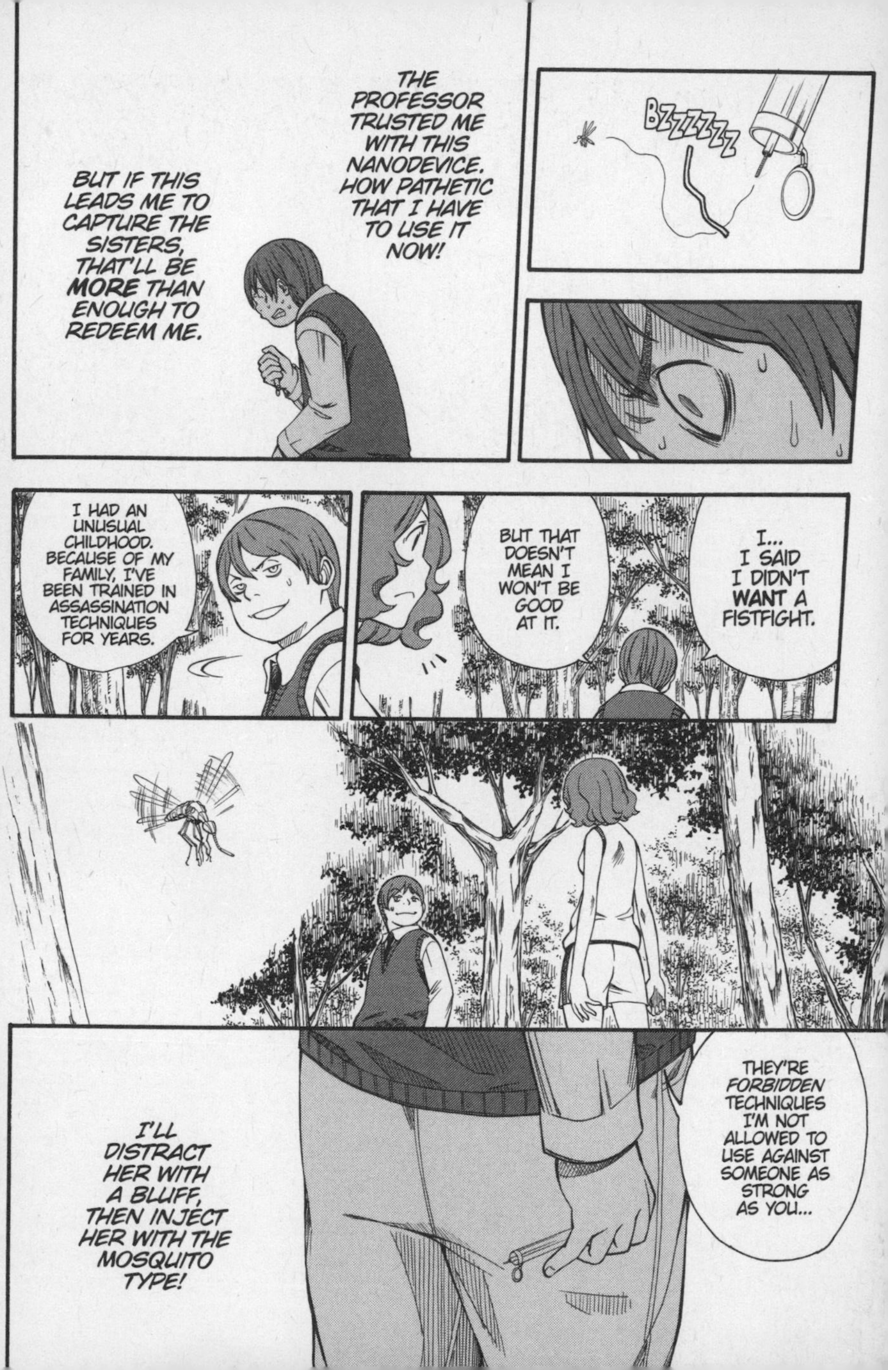
BZZZZZZ
THE PROFESSOR TRUSTED ME WITH THIS NANODEVICE. HOW PATHETIC THAT I HAVE TO USE IT NOW!
BUT IF THIS LEADS ME TO CAPTURE THE SISTERS, THAT'LL BE **MORE** THAN ENOUGH TO REDEEM ME.
I... I SAID I DIDN'T **WANT** A FISTFIGHT.
BUT THAT DOESN'T MEAN I WON'T BE GOOD AT IT.
I HAD AN UNUSUAL CHILDHOOD. BECAUSE OF MY FAMILY, I'VE BEEN TRAINED IN ASSASSINATION TECHNIQUES FOR YEARS.
THEY'RE *FORBIDDEN* TECHNIQUES I'M NOT ALLOWED TO USE AGAINST SOMEONE AS STRONG AS YOU...
I'LL DISTRACT HER WITH A BLUFF, THEN INJECT HER WITH THE MOSQUITO TYPE!

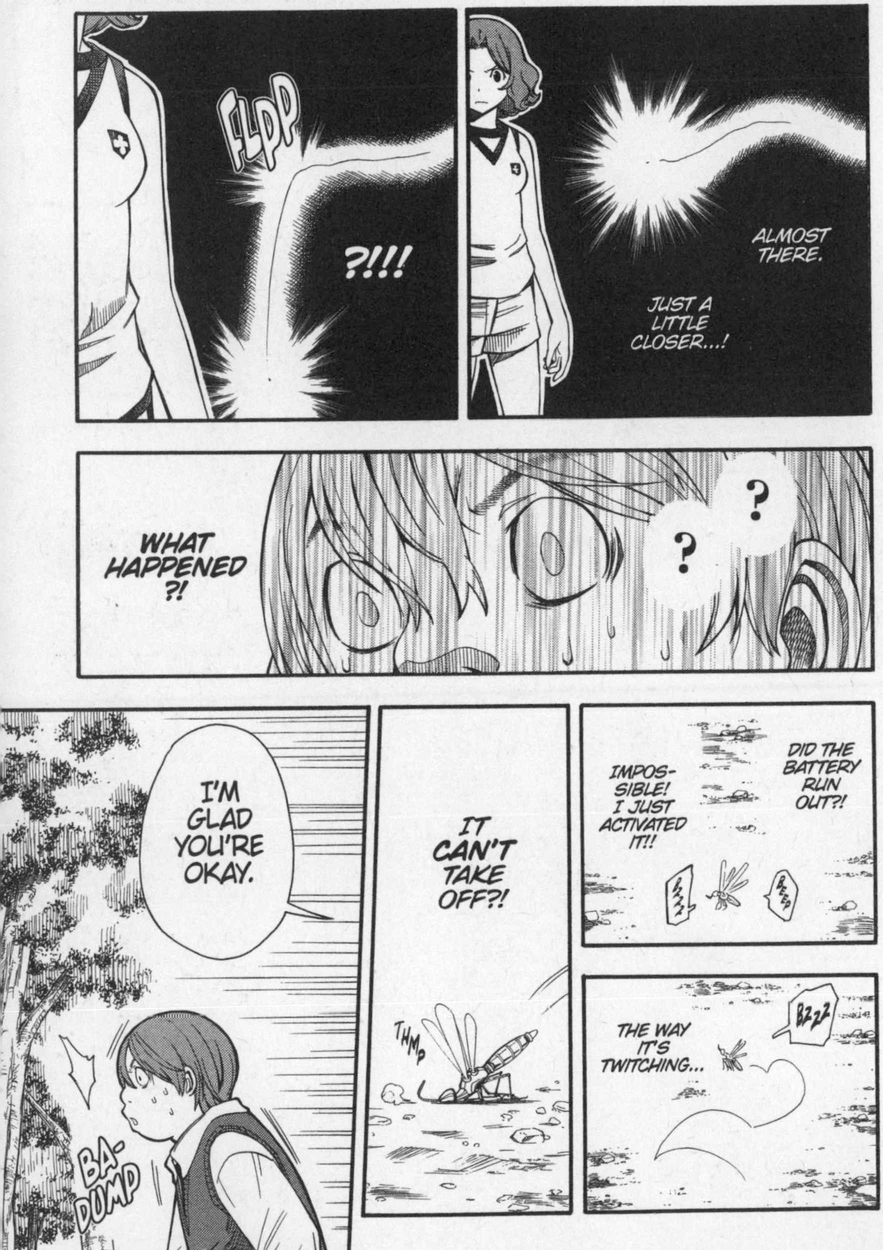
ALMOST THERE.
JUST A LITTLE CLOSER...!
FLPP
?!!!
? ?
WHAT HAPPENED ?!
DID THE BATTERY RUN OUT?!
IMPOSSIBLE! I JUST ACTIVATED IT!!
BEEP
BZZZ
BZZZ
THE WAY IT'S TWITCHING...
IT CAN'T TAKE OFF?!
THMP
I'M GLAD YOU'RE OKAY.
BA-DUMP

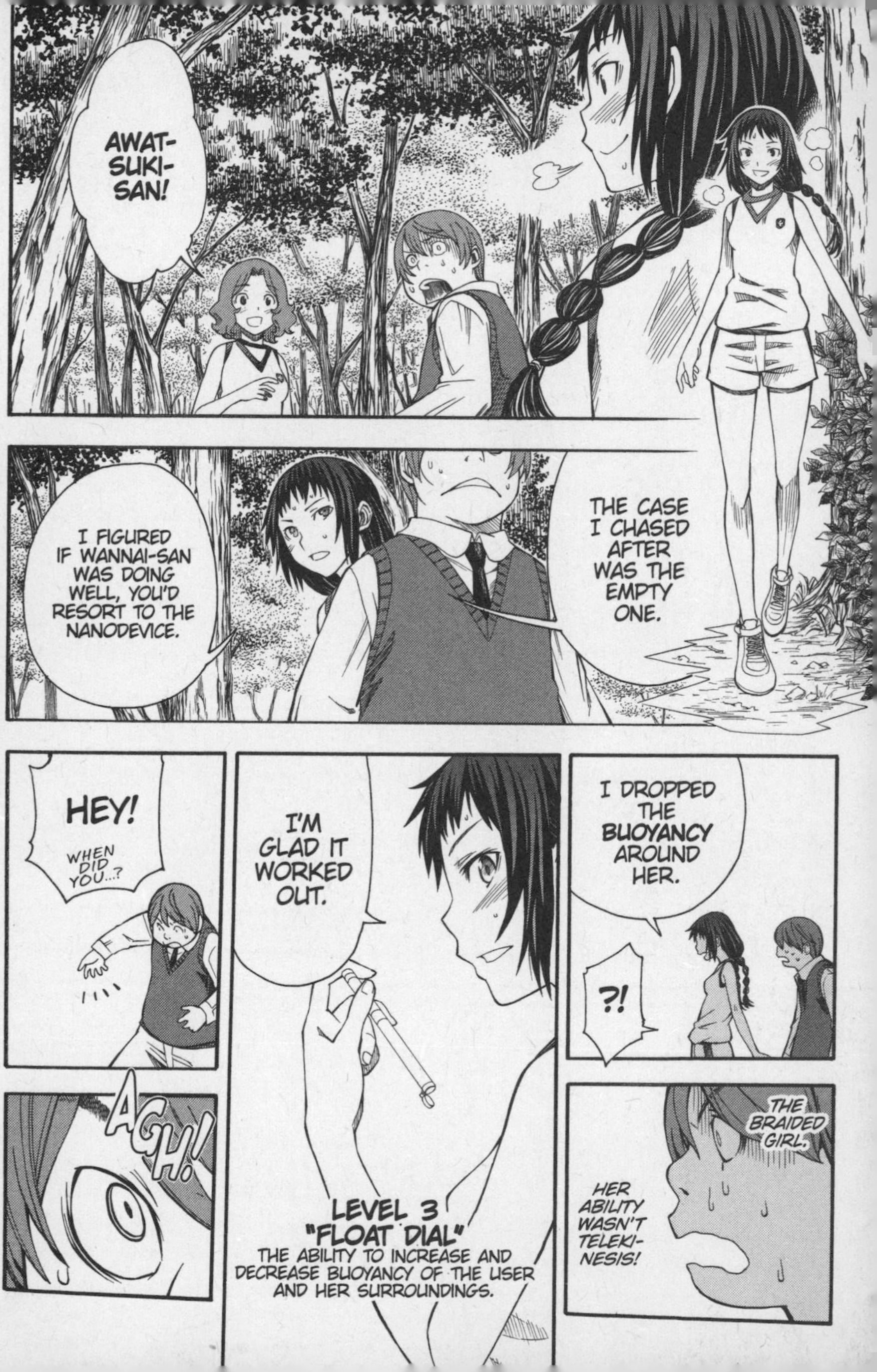
AWAT-SUKI-SAN!
THE CASE I CHASED AFTER WAS THE EMPTY ONE.
I FIGURED IF WANNAI-SAN WAS DOING WELL, YOU'D RESORT TO THE NANODEVICE.
I DROPPED THE BUOYANCY AROUND HER.
?!
THE BRAIDED GIRL.
HER ABILITY WASN'T TELEKI-NESIS!
I'M GLAD IT WORKED OUT.
LEVEL 3 "FLOAT DIAL"
THE ABILITY TO INCREASE AND DECREASE BUOYANCY OF THE USER AND HER SURROUNDINGS.
HEY!
WHEN DID YOU...?
AGH!

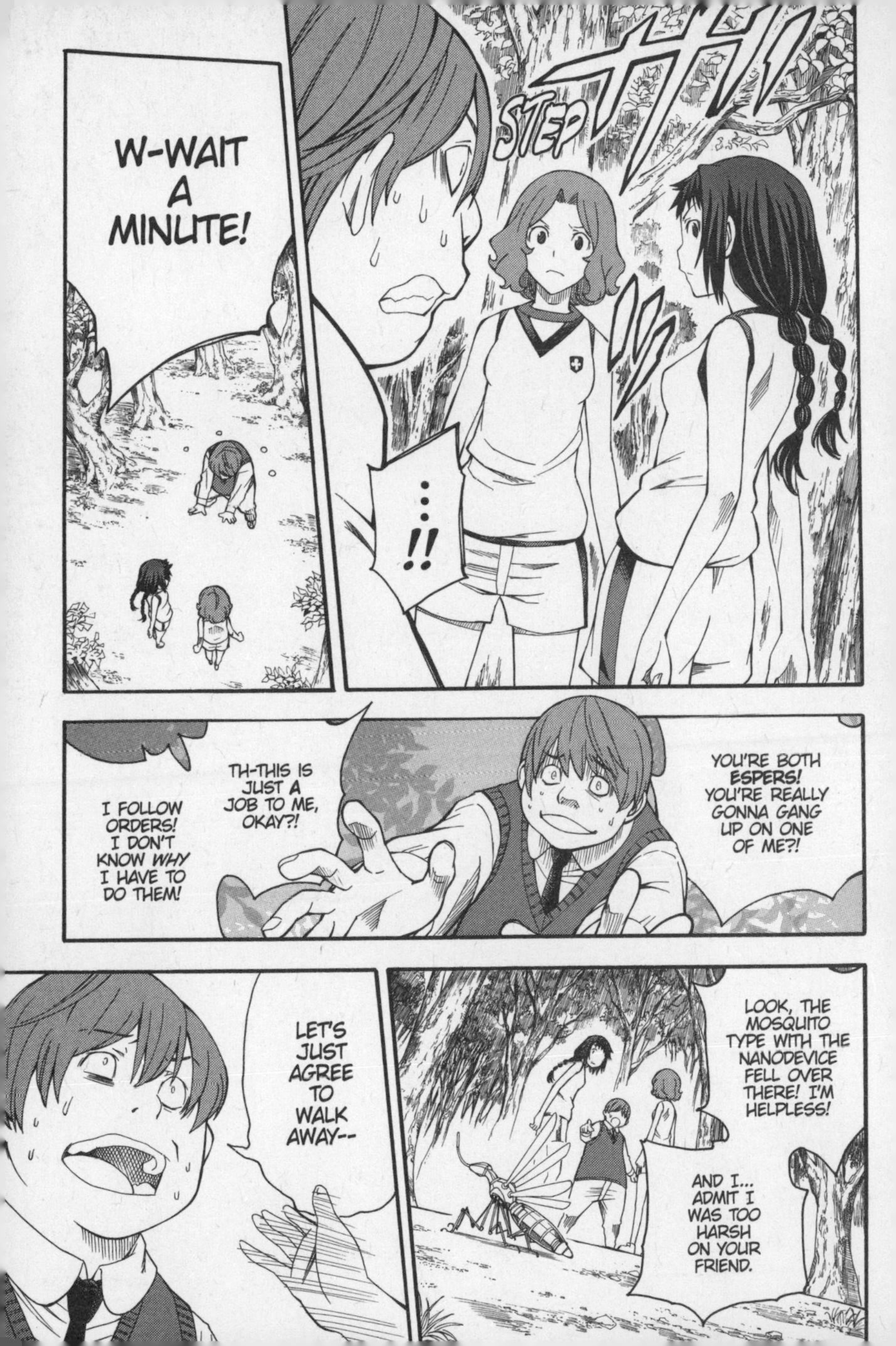

STEP
…!!
W-WAIT A MINUTE!
YOU'RE BOTH ESPERS! YOU'RE REALLY GONNA GANG UP ON ONE OF ME?!
TH-THIS IS JUST A JOB TO ME, OKAY?!
I FOLLOW ORDERS! I DON'T KNOW *WHY* I HAVE TO DO THEM!
LOOK, THE MOSQUITO TYPE WITH THE NANODEVICE FELL OVER THERE! I'M HELPLESS!
AND I... ADMIT I WAS TOO HARSH ON YOUR FRIEND.
LET'S JUST AGREE TO WALK AWAY--

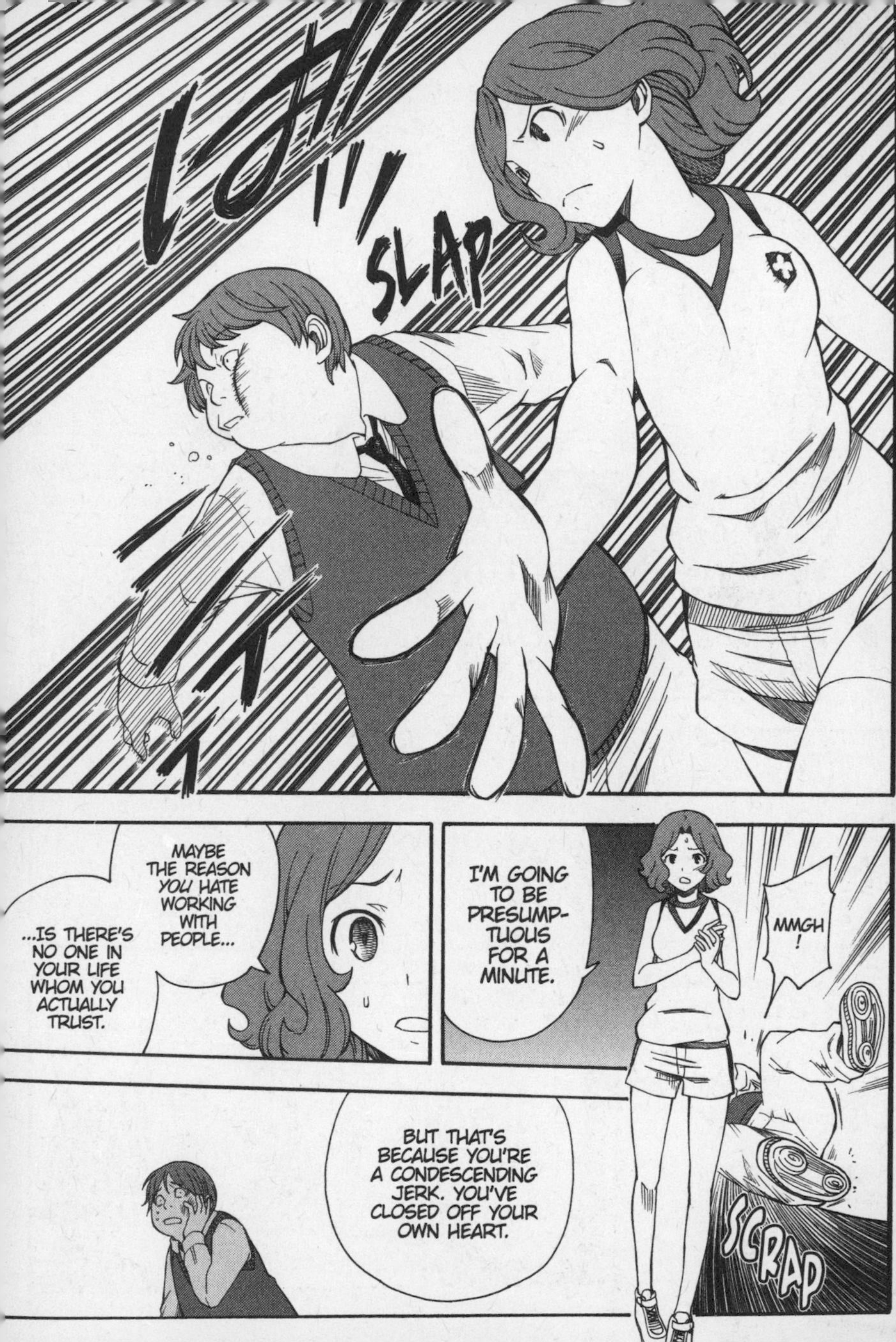
SLAP
MMGH!
I'M GOING TO BE PRESUMPTUOUS FOR A MINUTE.
SCRAP
MAYBE THE REASON YOU HATE WORKING WITH PEOPLE...
...IS THERE'S NO ONE IN YOUR LIFE WHOM YOU ACTUALLY TRUST.
BUT THAT'S BECAUSE YOU'RE A CONDESCENDING JERK. YOU'VE CLOSED OFF YOUR OWN HEART.

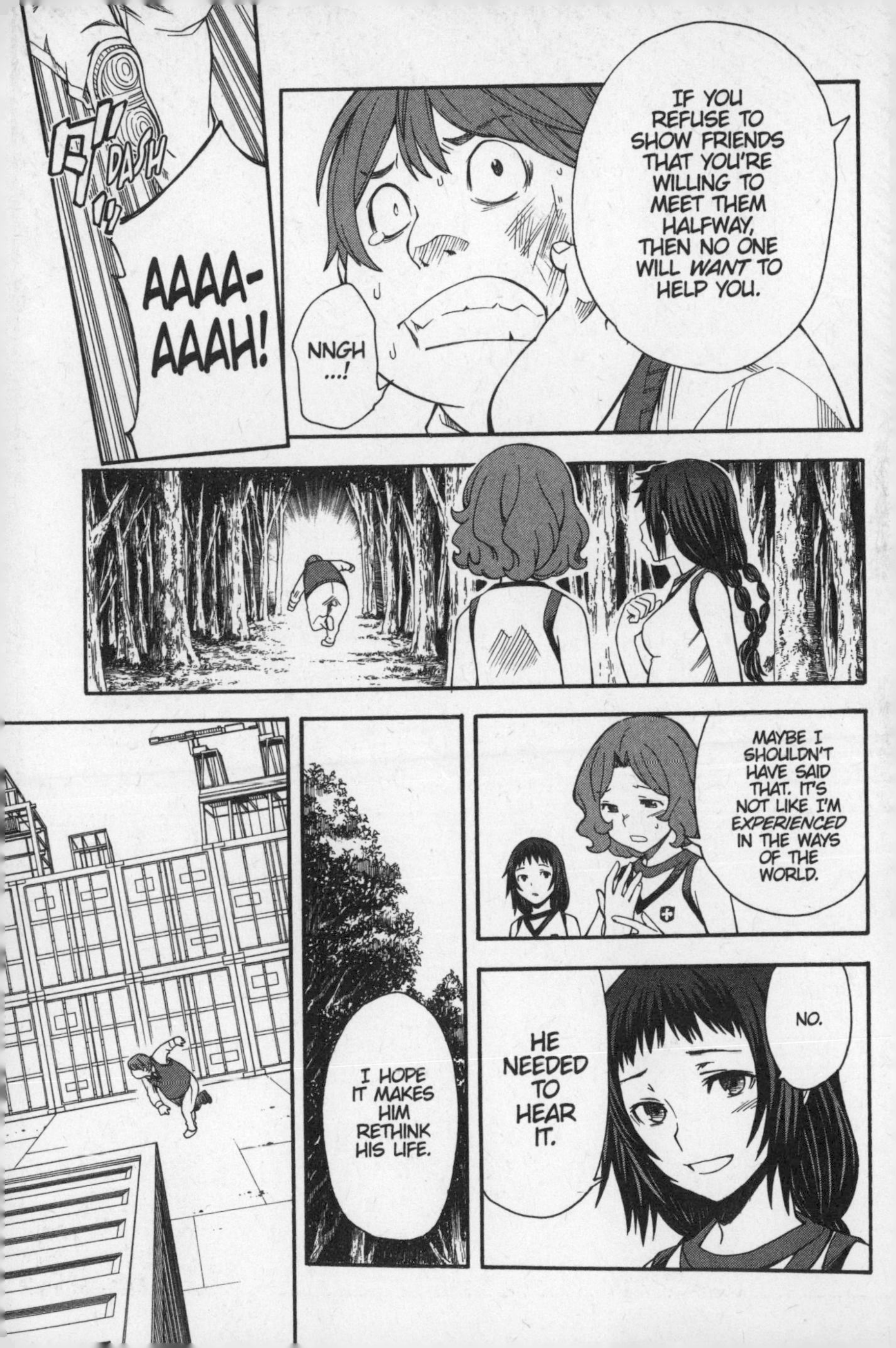
IF YOU REFUSE TO SHOW FRIENDS THAT YOU'RE WILLING TO MEET THEM HALFWAY, THEN NO ONE WILL *WANT* TO HELP YOU.
NNGH ...!
DASH
AAAA-AAAH!
MAYBE I SHOULDN'T HAVE SAID THAT. IT'S NOT LIKE I'M *EXPERIENCED* IN THE WAYS OF THE WORLD.
NO.
HE NEEDED TO HEAR IT.
I HOPE IT MAKES HIM RETHINK HIS LIFE.

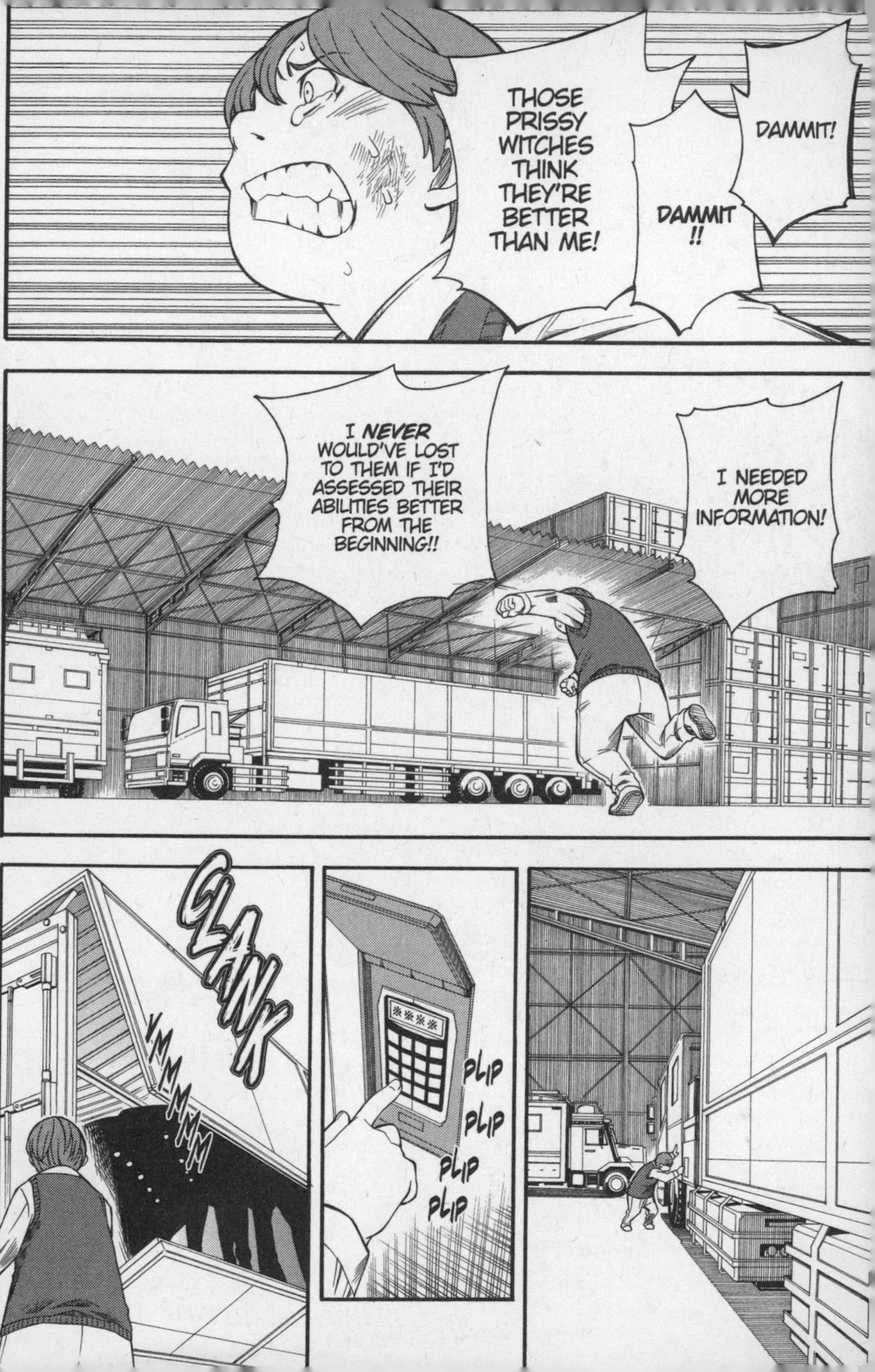
DAMMIT!
DAMMIT !!
THOSE PRISSY WITCHES THINK THEY'RE BETTER THAN ME!
I NEEDED MORE INFORMATION!
I *NEVER* WOULD'VE LOST TO THEM IF I'D ASSESSED THEIR ABILITIES BETTER FROM THE BEGINNING!!
PLIP
PLIP
PLIP
PLIP
CLANK
VMMMMM

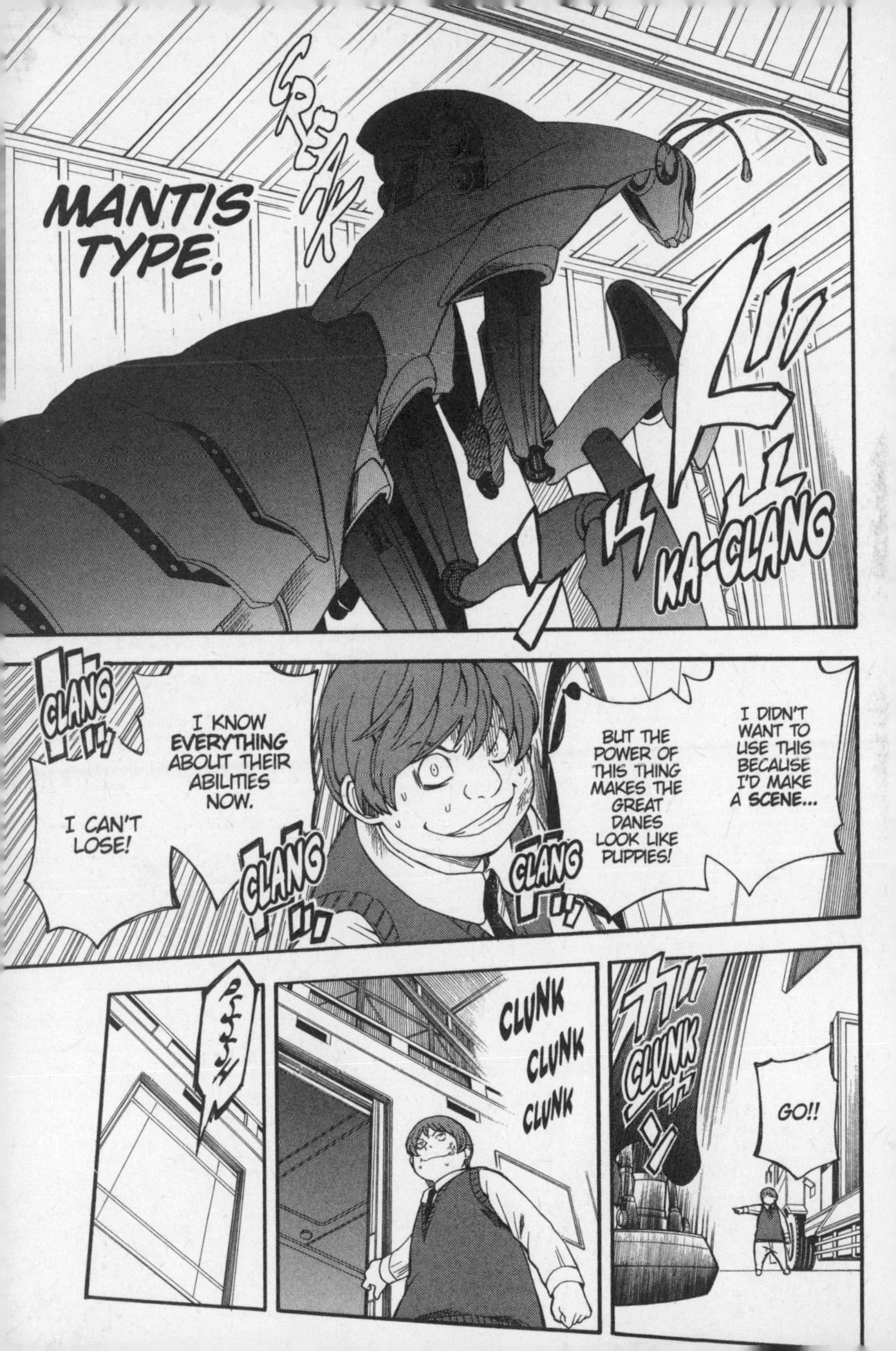
CREAK
MANTIS TYPE.
KA-CLANG
I DIDN'T WANT TO USE THIS BECAUSE I'D MAKE A SCENE...
BUT THE POWER OF THIS THING MAKES THE GREAT DANES LOOK LIKE PUPPIES!
CLANG
I KNOW EVERYTHING ABOUT THEIR ABILITIES NOW.
CLANG
CLANG
I CAN'T LOSE!
CLUNK
GO!!
CLUNK
CLUNK
CLUNK

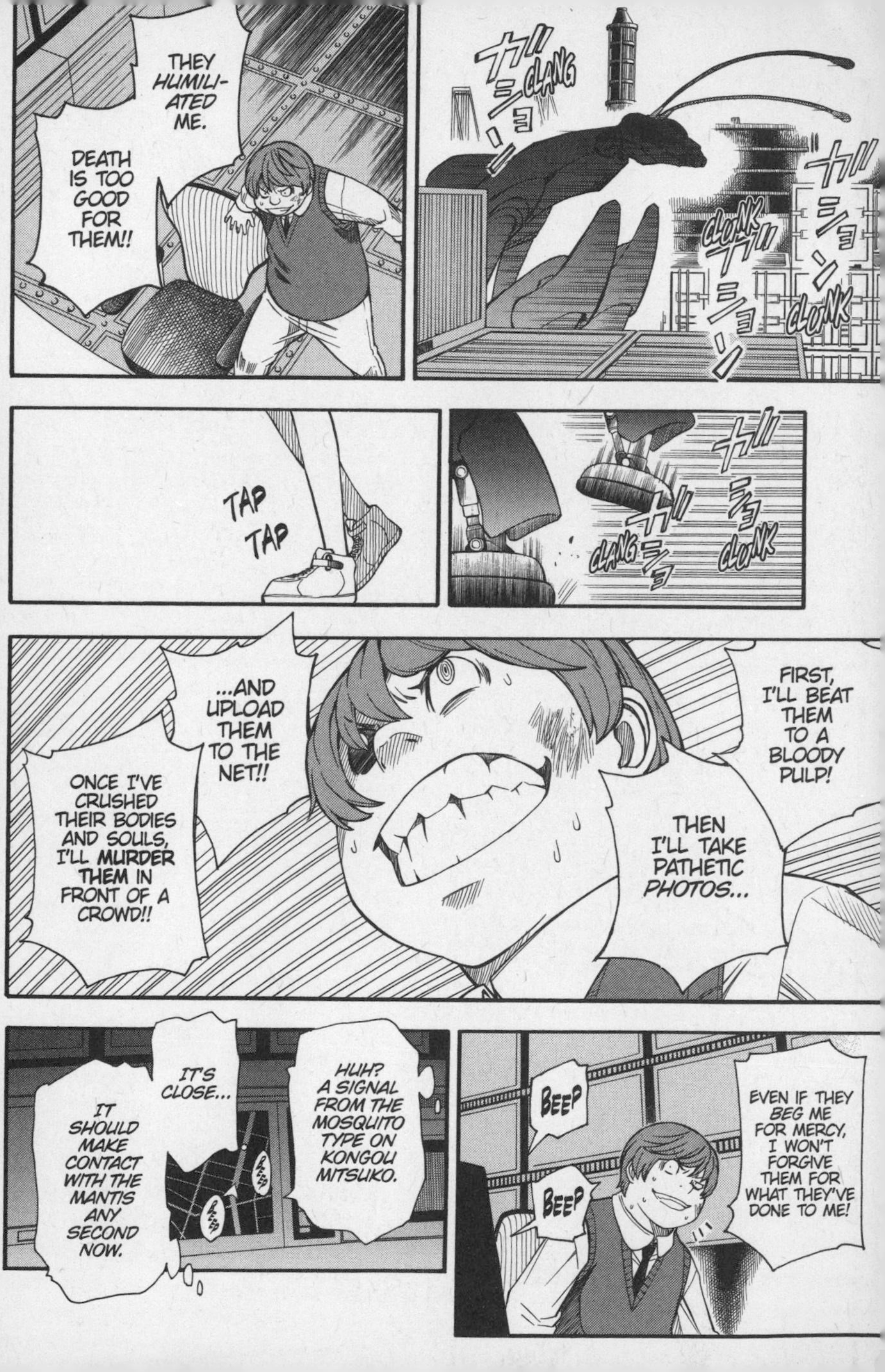
CLANG
CLONK
CLONK
THEY HUMILIATED ME.
DEATH IS TOO GOOD FOR THEM!!
CLONK
CLANG
TAP TAP
FIRST, I'LL BEAT THEM TO A BLOODY PULP!
THEN I'LL TAKE PATHETIC PHOTOS...
...AND UPLOAD THEM TO THE NET!!
ONCE I'VE CRUSHED THEIR BODIES AND SOULS, I'LL MURDER THEM IN FRONT OF A CROWD!!
EVEN IF THEY BEG ME FOR MERCY, I WON'T FORGIVE THEM FOR WHAT THEY'VE DONE TO ME!
BEEP
BEEP
HUH? A SIGNAL FROM THE MOSQUITO TYPE ON KONGOU MITSUKO.
IT'S CLOSE...
IT SHOULD MAKE CONTACT WITH THE MANTIS ANY SECOND NOW.

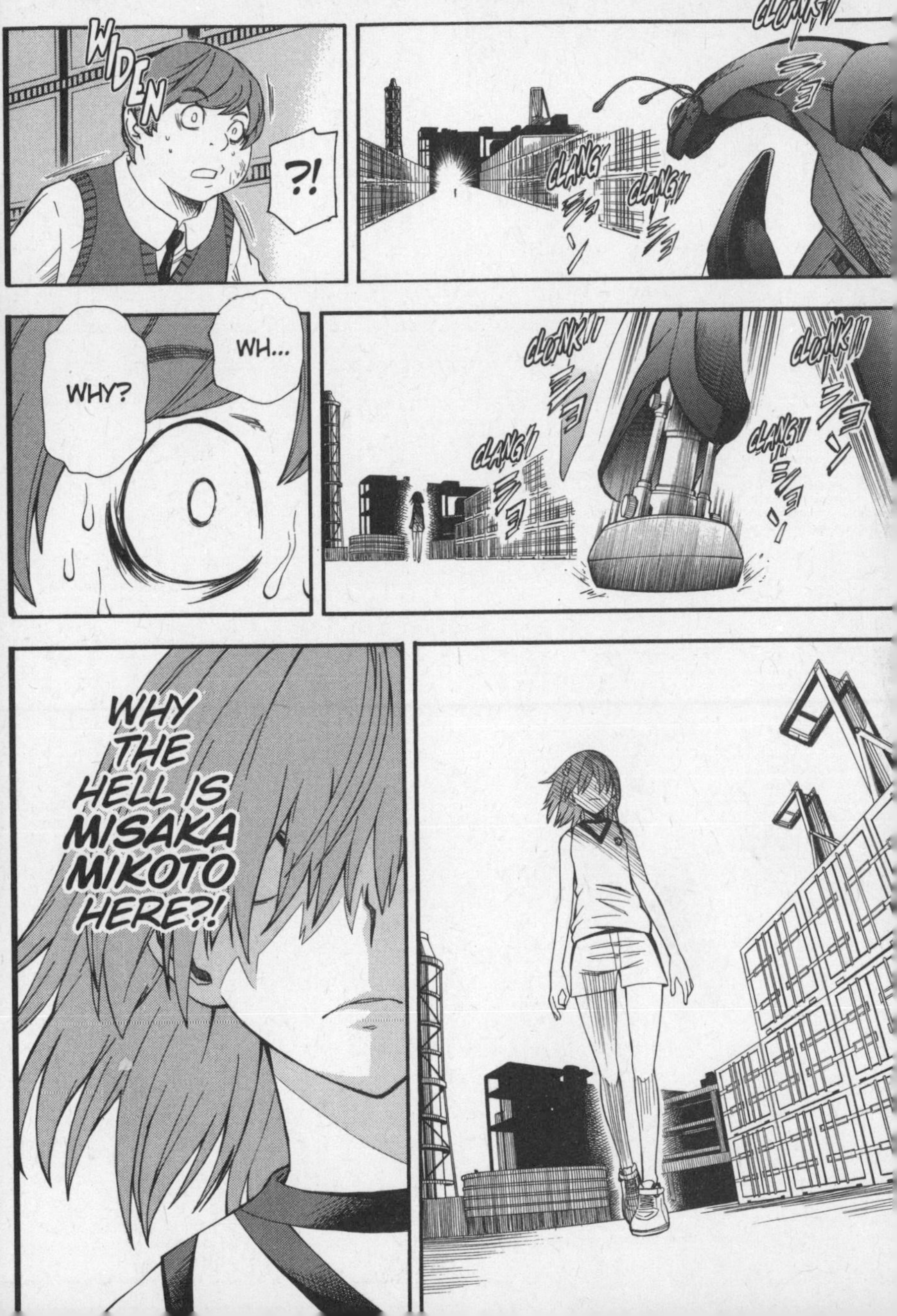
CLONK!!
CLANG!
CLANG!!
WIDEN
?!
CLONK!!
CLONK!!
CLANG!!
CLANG!!
WH...
WHY?
WHY THE HELL IS MISAKA MIKOTO HERE?!

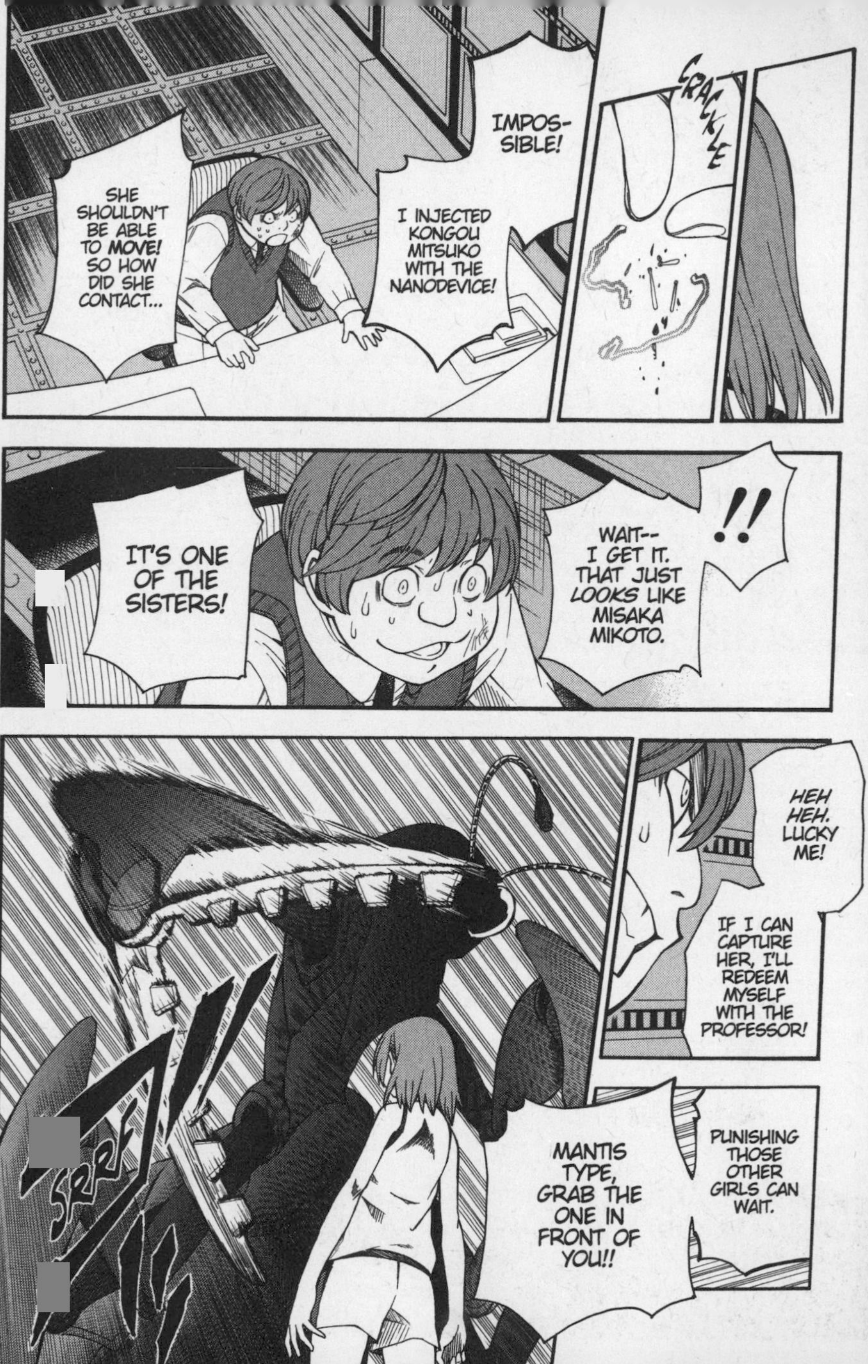
CRACKLE
IMPOSSIBLE!
I INJECTED KONGOU MITSUKO WITH THE NANODEVICE!
SHE SHOULDN'T BE ABLE TO MOVE! SO HOW DID SHE CONTACT...
!!
WAIT-- I GET IT. THAT JUST LOOKS LIKE MISAKA MIKOTO.
IT'S ONE OF THE SISTERS!
HEH HEH. LUCKY ME!
IF I CAN CAPTURE HER, I'LL REDEEM MYSELF WITH THE PROFESSOR!
PUNISHING THOSE OTHER GIRLS CAN WAIT.
MANTIS TYPE, GRAB THE ONE IN FRONT OF YOU!!
SRRF

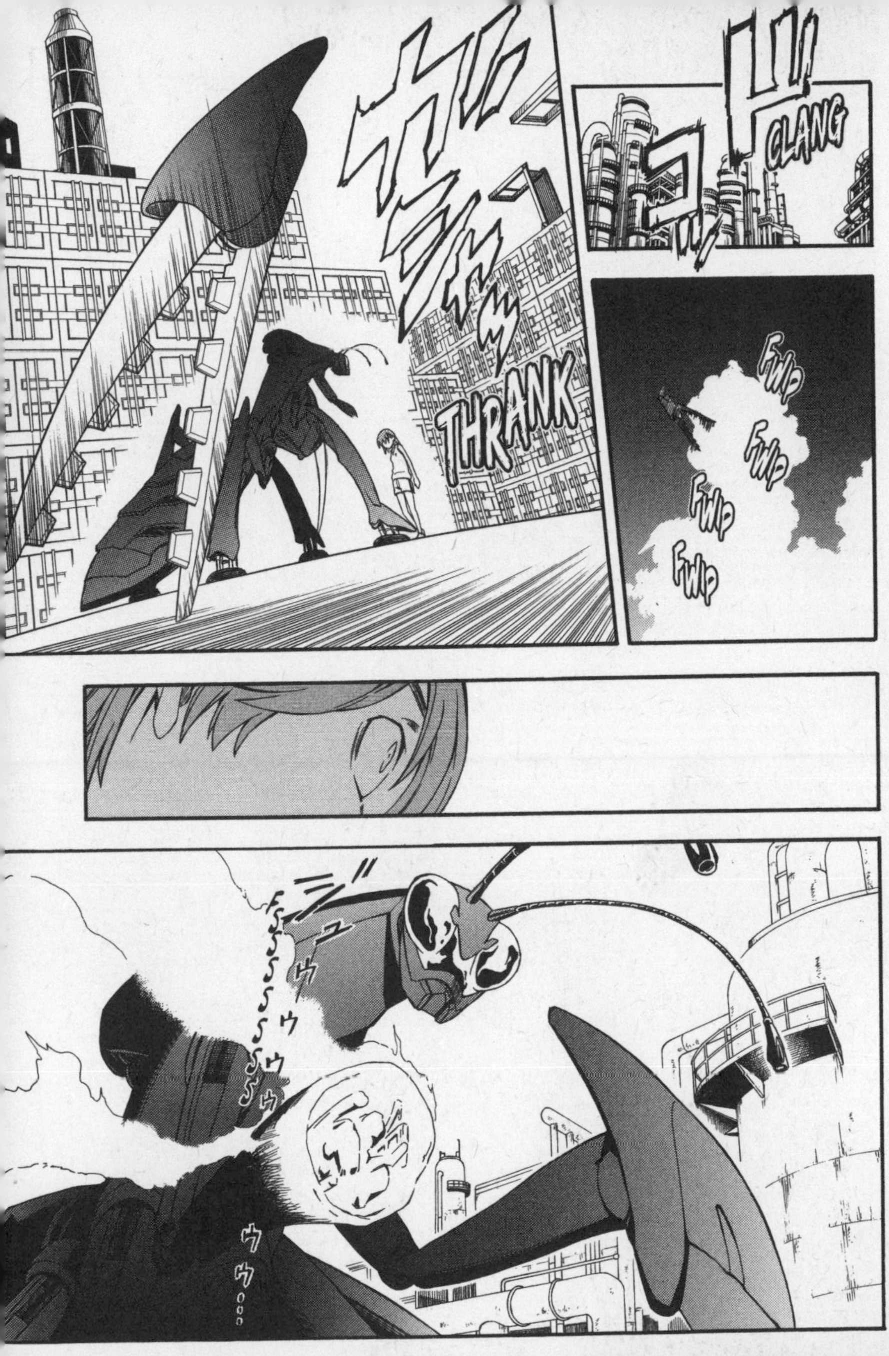
CLANG
FWIP
FWIP
FWIP
FWIP
THRANK
FSSSSSSSS

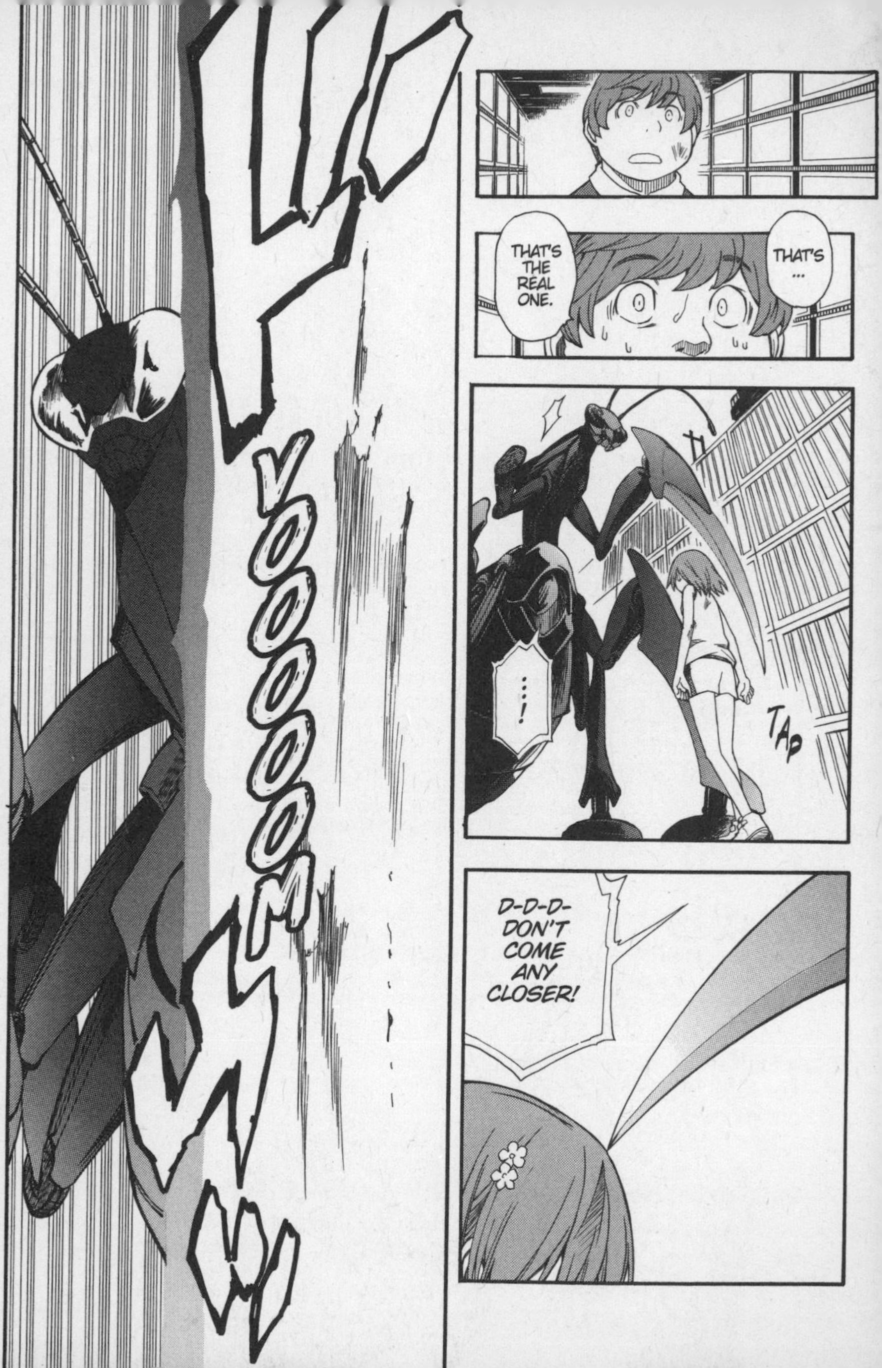
THAT'S ...
THAT'S THE REAL ONE.
...!
TAP
D-D-D-DON'T COME ANY CLOSER!
VOOOOOOM

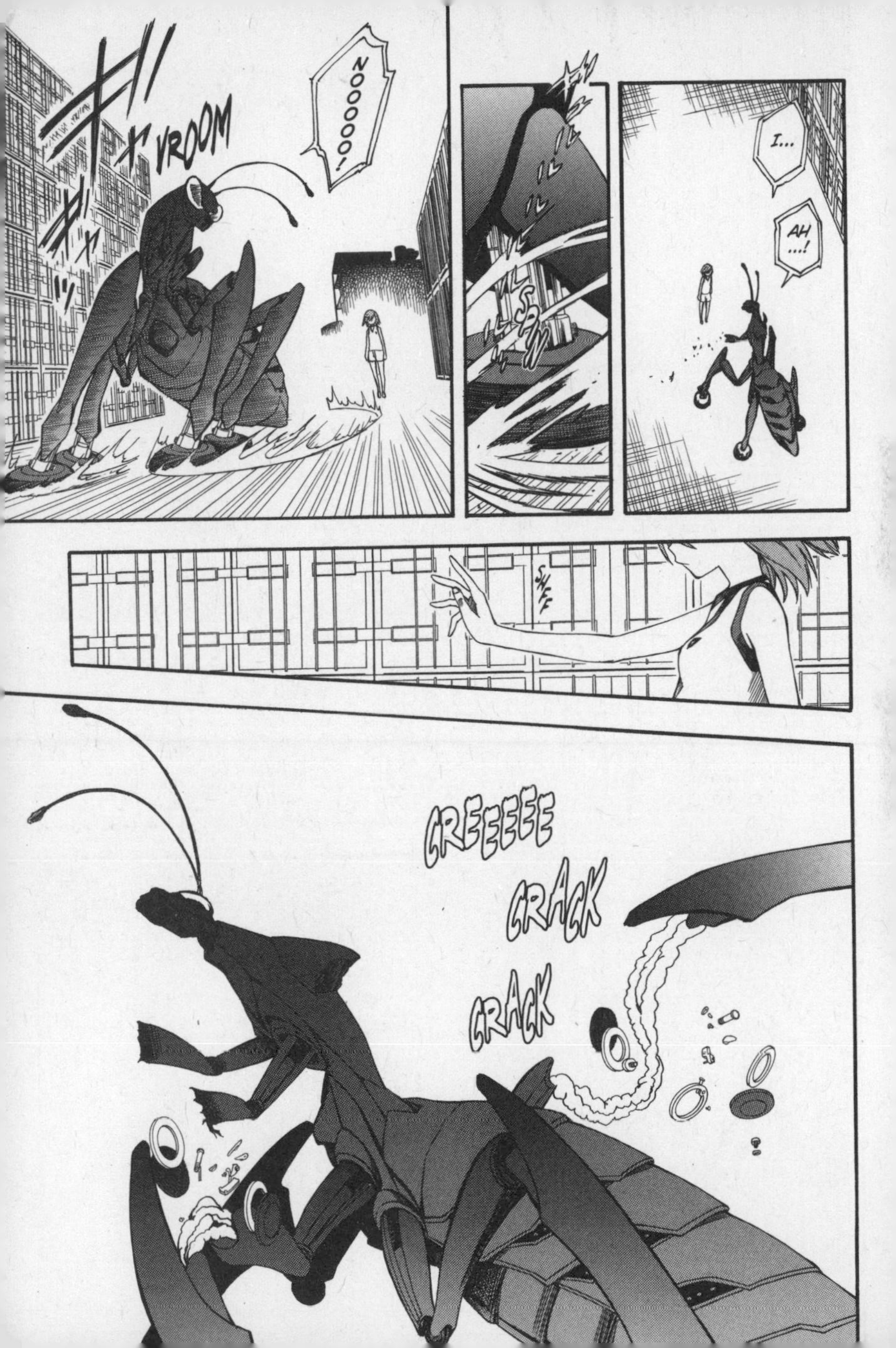
I...
AH ...!
SPIN
NOOOOOO!
VROOM
SHFF
CREEEEE
CRACK
CRACK

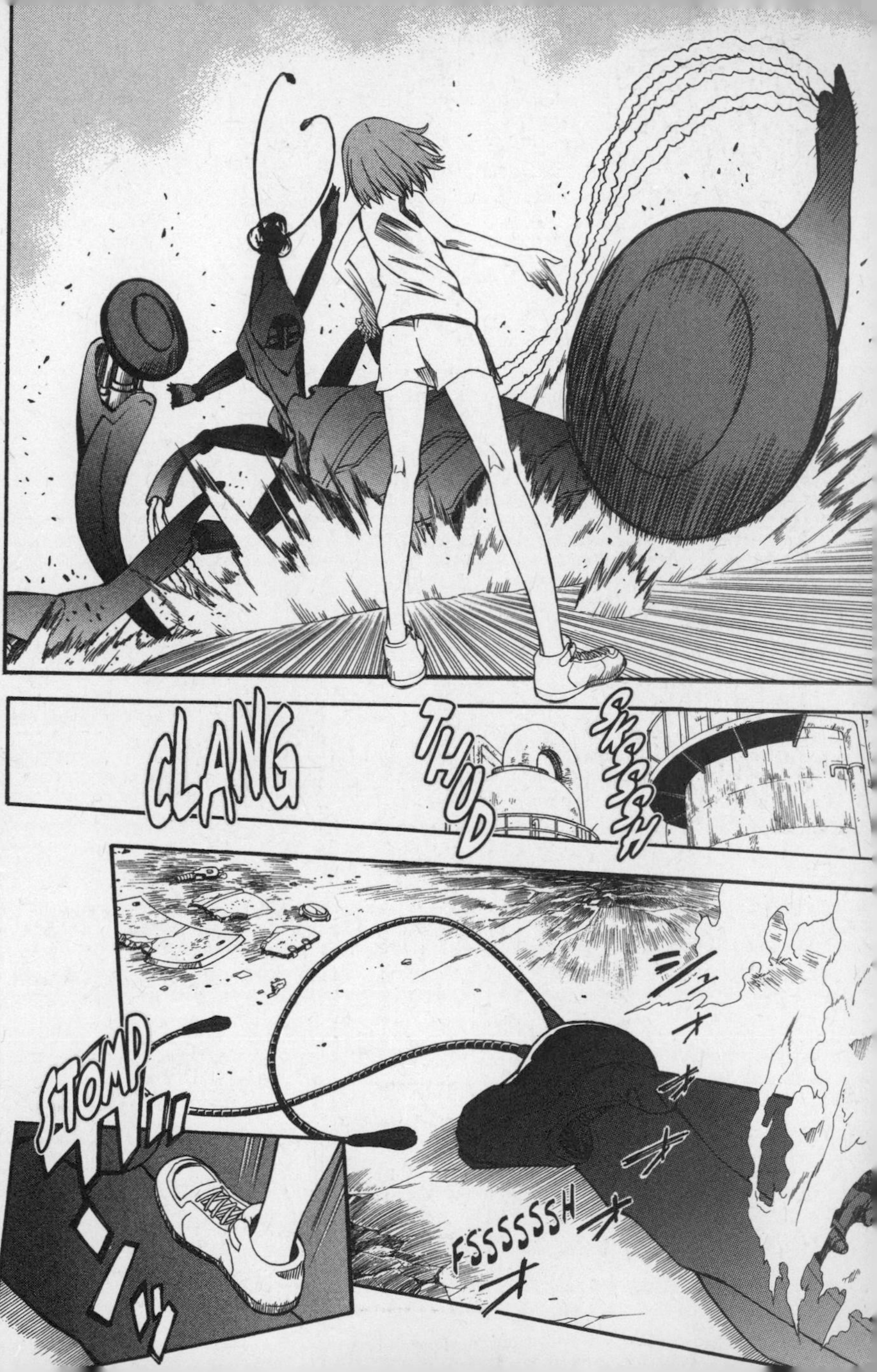
THUD
CLANG
FSSSSSSH
STOMP

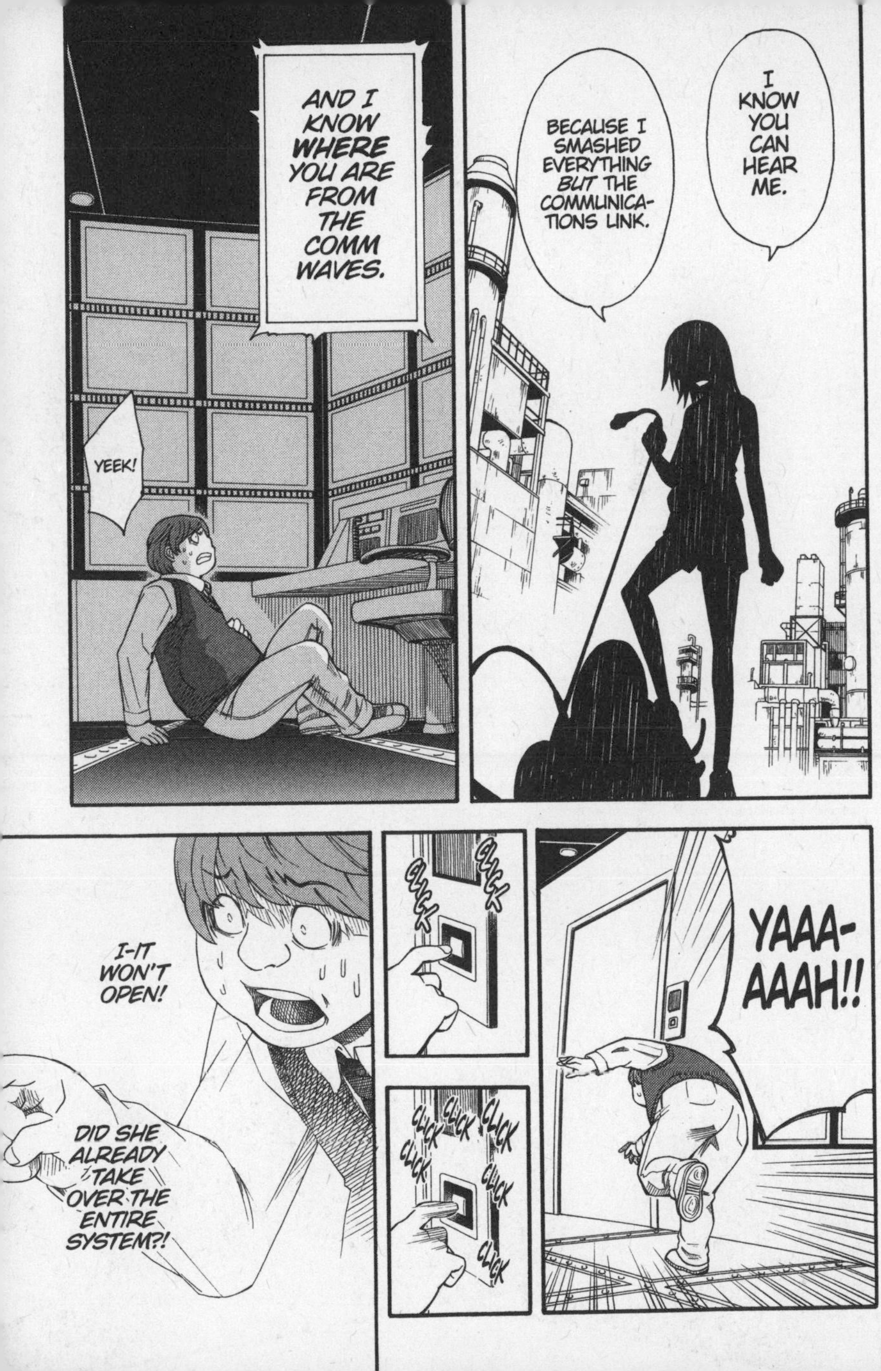
I KNOW YOU CAN HEAR ME.
BECAUSE I SMASHED EVERYTHING *BUT* THE COMMUNICA-TIONS LINK.
AND I KNOW **WHERE** YOU ARE FROM THE COMM WAVES.
YEEK!
YAAA-AAAH!!
CLICK
CLICK
CLICK
CLICK
CLICK
CLICK
CLICK
CLICK
I-IT WON'T OPEN!
DID SHE ALREADY TAKE OVER THE ENTIRE SYSTEM?!

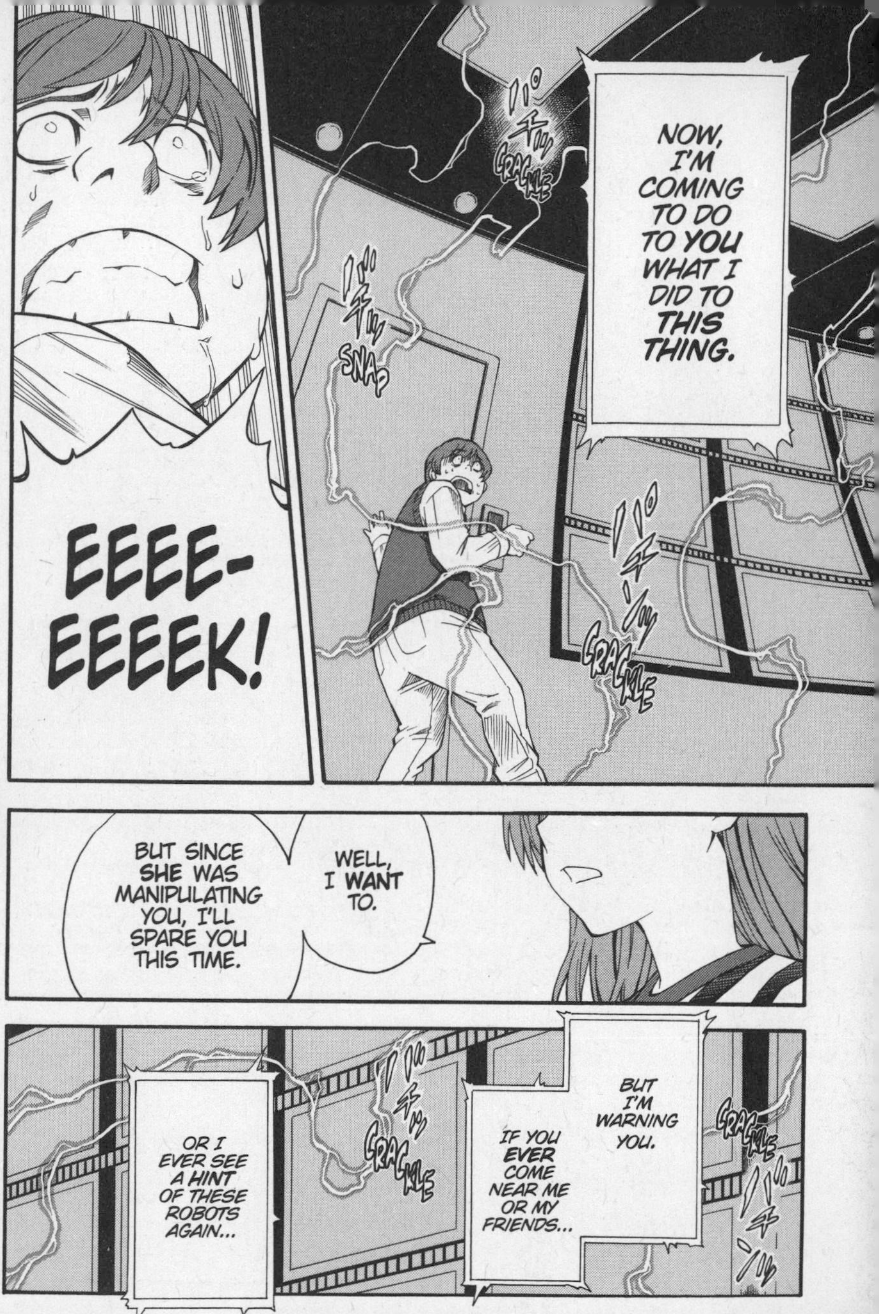
NOW, I'M COMING TO DO TO YOU WHAT I DID TO THIS THING.
CRACKLE
SNAP
CRACKLE
EEEE-EEEEK!
WELL, I WANT TO.
BUT SINCE SHE WAS MANIPULATING YOU, I'LL SPARE YOU THIS TIME.
BUT I'M WARNING YOU.
CRACKLE
IF YOU EVER COME NEAR ME OR MY FRIENDS...
CRACKLE
OR I EVER SEE A HINT OF THESE ROBOTS AGAIN...

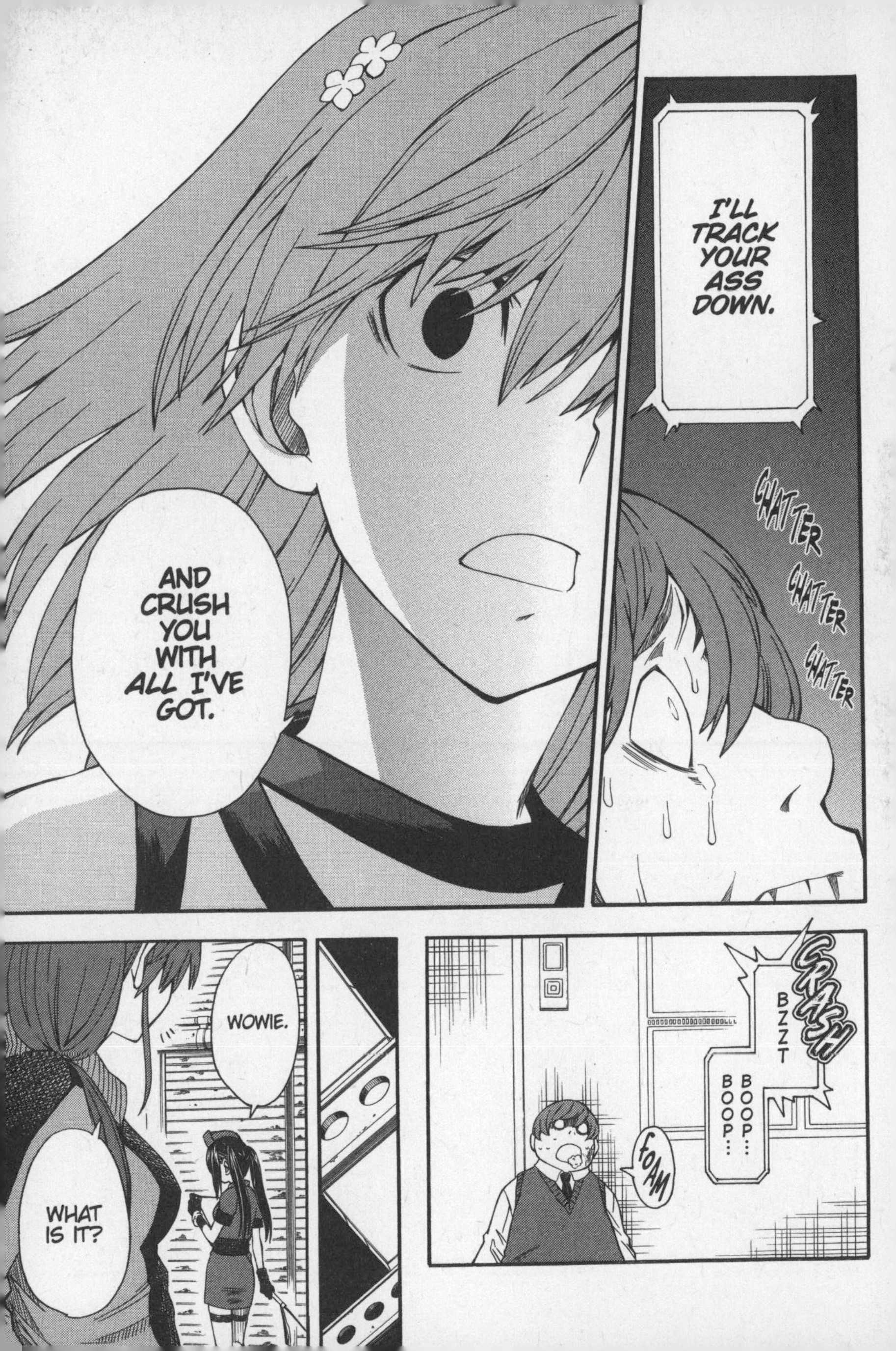
I'LL TRACK YOUR ASS DOWN.
CHATTER
CHATTER
CHATTER
AND CRUSH YOU WITH ALL I'VE GOT.
CRASH
BZZT
BOOP...
BOOP...
FOAM
WOWIE.
WHAT IS IT?

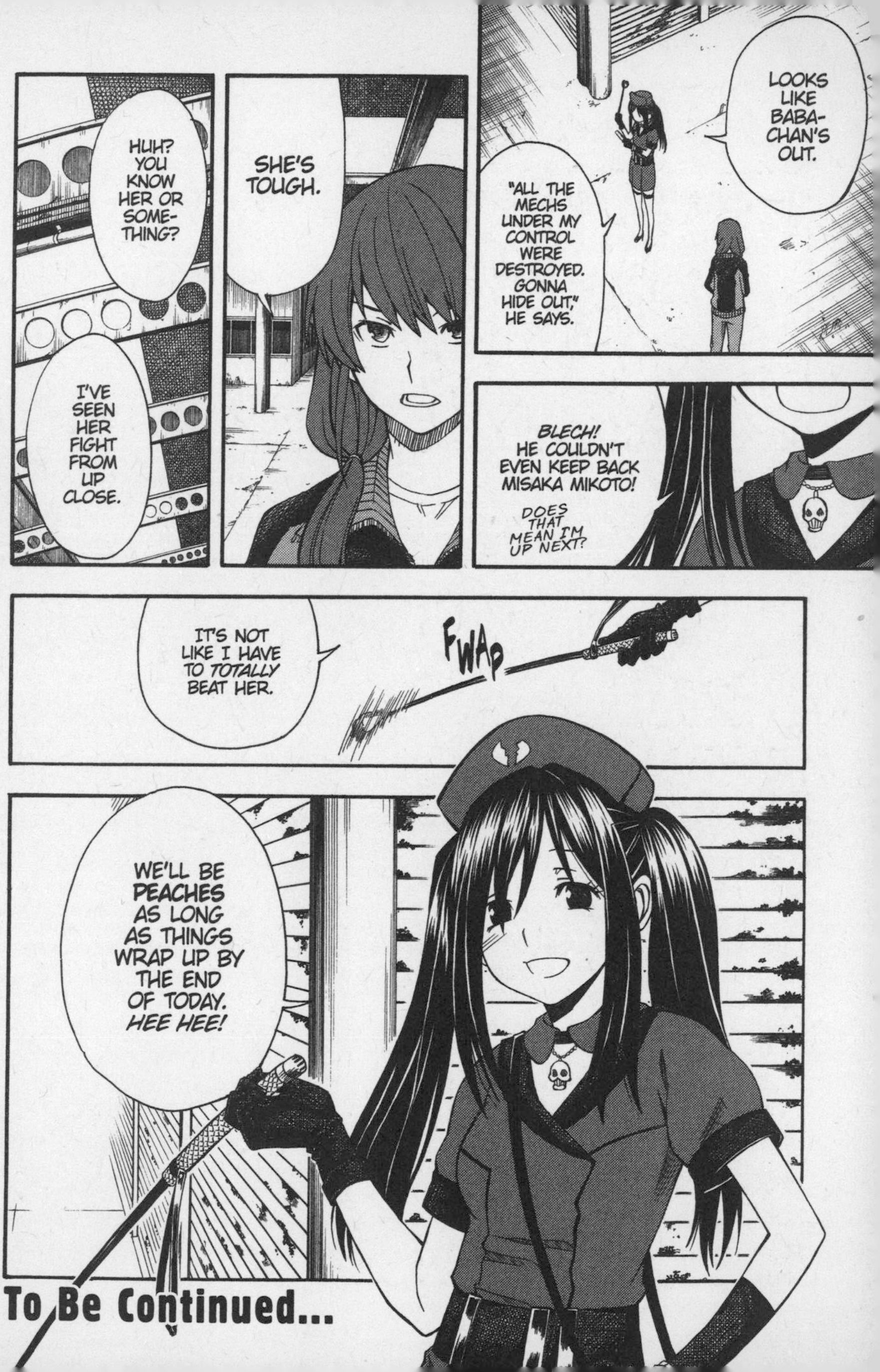
LOOKS LIKE BABA-CHAN'S OUT.
"ALL THE MECHS UNDER MY CONTROL WERE DESTROYED. GONNA HIDE OUT," HE SAYS.
BLECH! HE COULDN'T EVEN KEEP BACK MISAKA MIKOTO!
DOES THAT MEAN I'M UP NEXT?
SHE'S TOUGH.
HUH? YOU KNOW HER OR SOME-THING?
I'VE SEEN HER FIGHT FROM UP CLOSE.
FWAP
IT'S NOT LIKE I HAVE TO *TOTALLY* BEAT HER.
WE'LL BE **PEACHES** AS LONG AS THINGS WRAP UP BY THE END OF TODAY. *HEE HEE!*

To Be Continued...

A Certain Machine's Chivalry

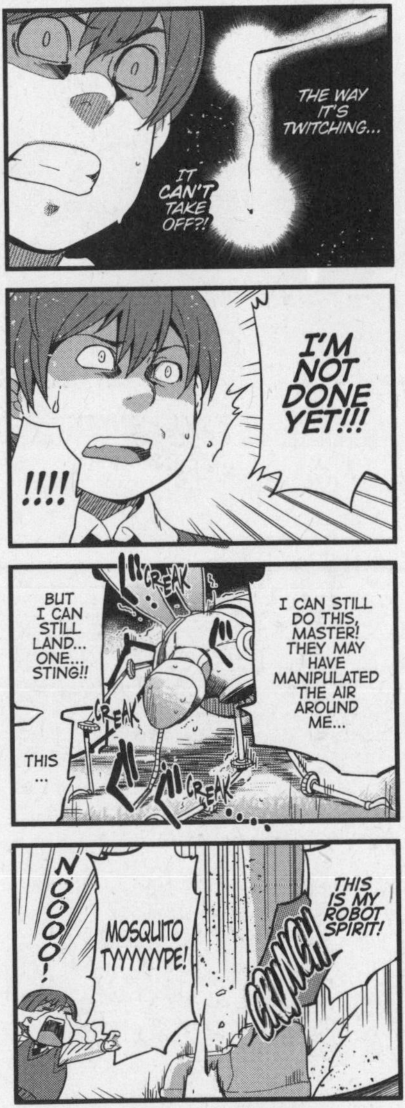
THE WAY IT'S TWITCHING...
IT CAN'T TAKE OFF?!
I'M NOT DONE YET!!!
!!!!
CREAK
I CAN STILL DO THIS, MASTER! THEY MAY HAVE MANIPULATED THE AIR AROUND ME...
BUT I CAN STILL LAND... ONE... STING!!
CREAK
THIS ...
CREAK
THIS IS MY ROBOT SPIRIT!
CRUNCH
MOSQUITO TYYYYYYPE!
NOOOOO!

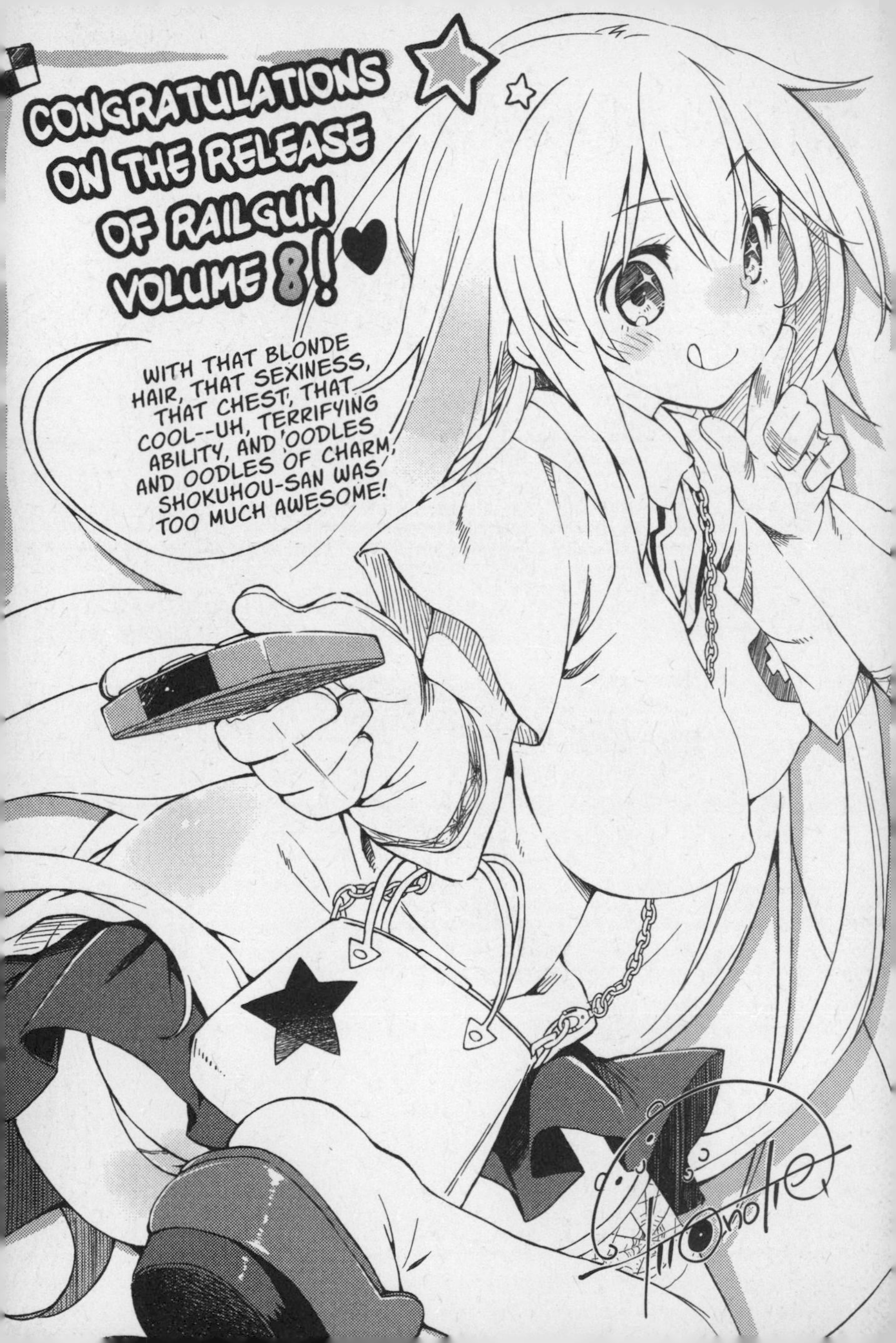
CONGRATULATIONS ON THE RELEASE OF RAILGUN VOLUME 8!
WITH THAT BLONDE HAIR, THAT SEXINESS, THAT CHEST, THAT COOL--UH, TERRIFYING ABILITY, AND OODLES AND OODLES OF CHARM, SHOKUHOU-SAN WAS TOO MUCH AWESOME!

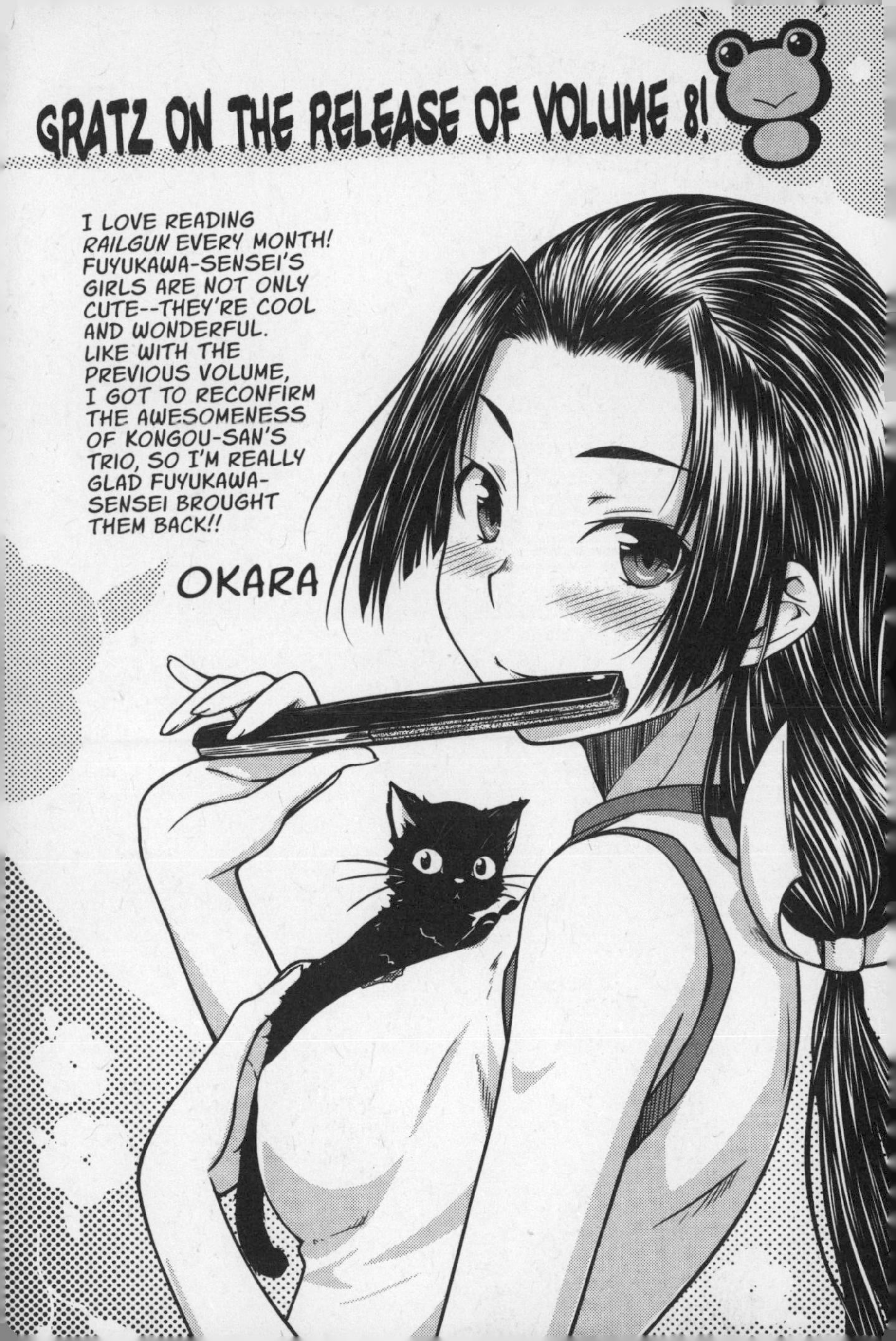
GRATZ ON THE RELEASE OF VOLUME 8!
I LOVE READING RAILGUN EVERY MONTH! FUYUKAWA-SENSEI'S GIRLS ARE NOT ONLY CUTE--THEY'RE COOL AND WONDERFUL. LIKE WITH THE PREVIOUS VOLUME, I GOT TO RECONFIRM THE AWESOMENESS OF KONGOU-SAN'S TRIO, SO I'M REALLY GLAD FUYUKAWA-SENSEI BROUGHT THEM BACK!!
OKARA

Omake!
MOB GIRLS

Tessou Tsuzuri

Essentially, minor characters have been designed with the following things in mind:
(1) This sounds bad, but to ensure that they don't get in the way of the main characters, they can't look too cool--so they have to be a little dull.
(2) They have to be distinguishable from their main character classmates or co-workers.

In Tessou's case, her design was largely based on discerning her from the other female security guard: Yomikawa.

Mako-chin, Muu-chan, and Akemi

In addition to points 1 and 2:
(3) When there are multiple minor characters introduced, each must have a simple trait to differentiate them from one another.

In the case of Saten and Uihara's classmates, you have the tall one, the short one, and the sorta chubby one.

In the anime version, Mako-chin slimmed down.
I bet she dieted once she found out she was going to be on TV. But she didn't lose any of the weight in her chest! Wow.

Wannai Kinuho
Awatsuki Maaya

Wannai was created with a lot
of floating, curved lines,
while Awatsuki was designed
with a lot of sharp lines.

For the anime, Kamachi-sensei
assigned names to each of the
supporting characters,
and I think these two got some
of the most beautiful names.

Konori Mii

Super serious... Really, she's got a
"what else could I be but a class
rep" vibe. That's how she was
planned.

The shield she had the first time
she appeared was borrowed from a
security guard.

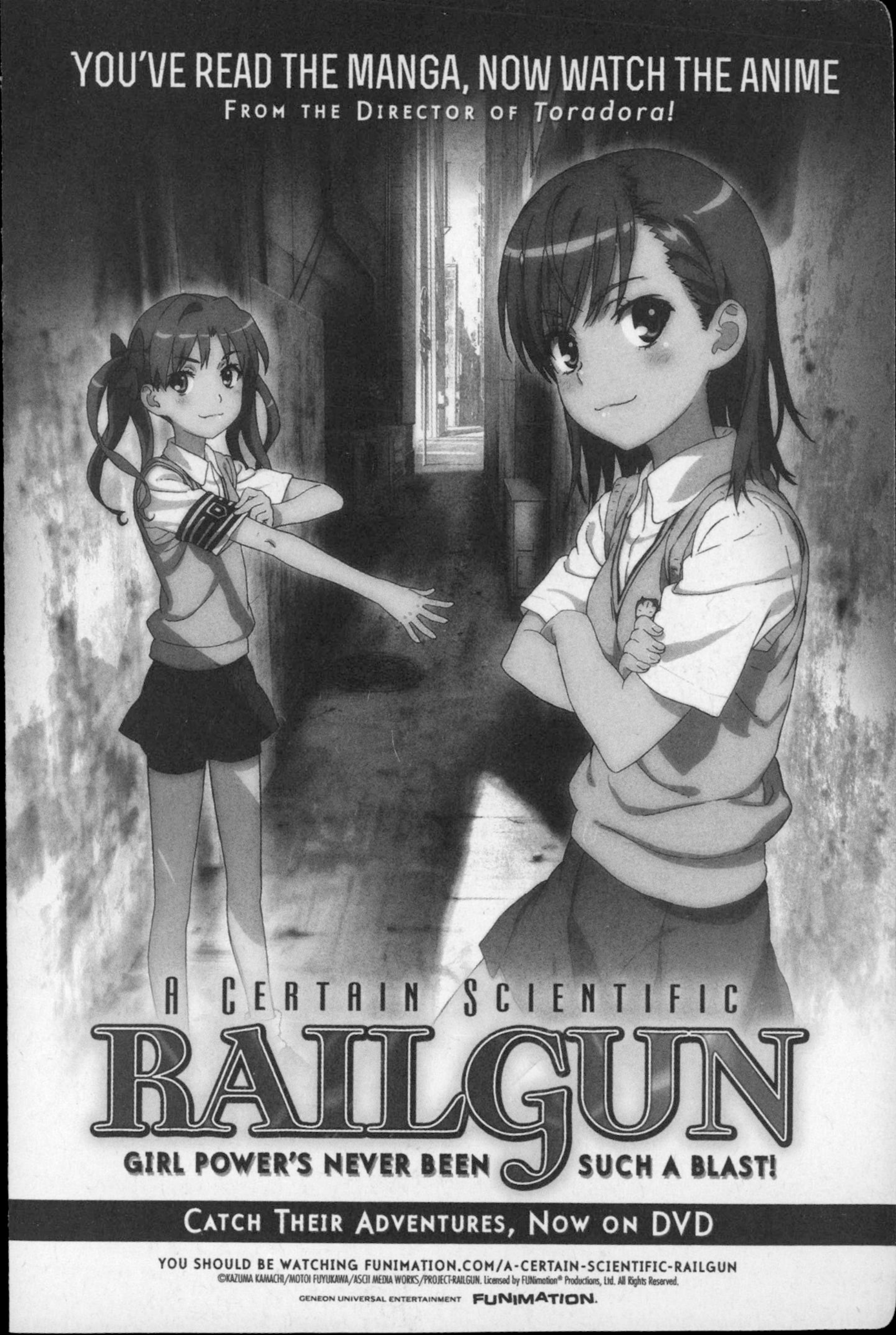
YOU'VE READ THE MANGA, NOW WATCH THE ANIME
FROM THE DIRECTOR OF Toradora!
A CERTAIN SCIENTIFIC
RAILGUN
GIRL POWER'S NEVER BEEN SUCH A BLAST!
CATCH THEIR ADVENTURES, NOW ON DVD
YOU SHOULD BE WATCHING FUNIMATION.COM/A-CERTAIN-SCIENTIFIC-RAILGUN
©KAZUMA KAMACHI/MOTOI FUYUKAWA/ASCII MEDIA WORKS/PROJECT-RAILGUN. Licensed by FUNimation® Productions, Ltd. All Rights Reserved.
GENEON UNIVERSAL ENTERTAINMENT
FUNIMATION.

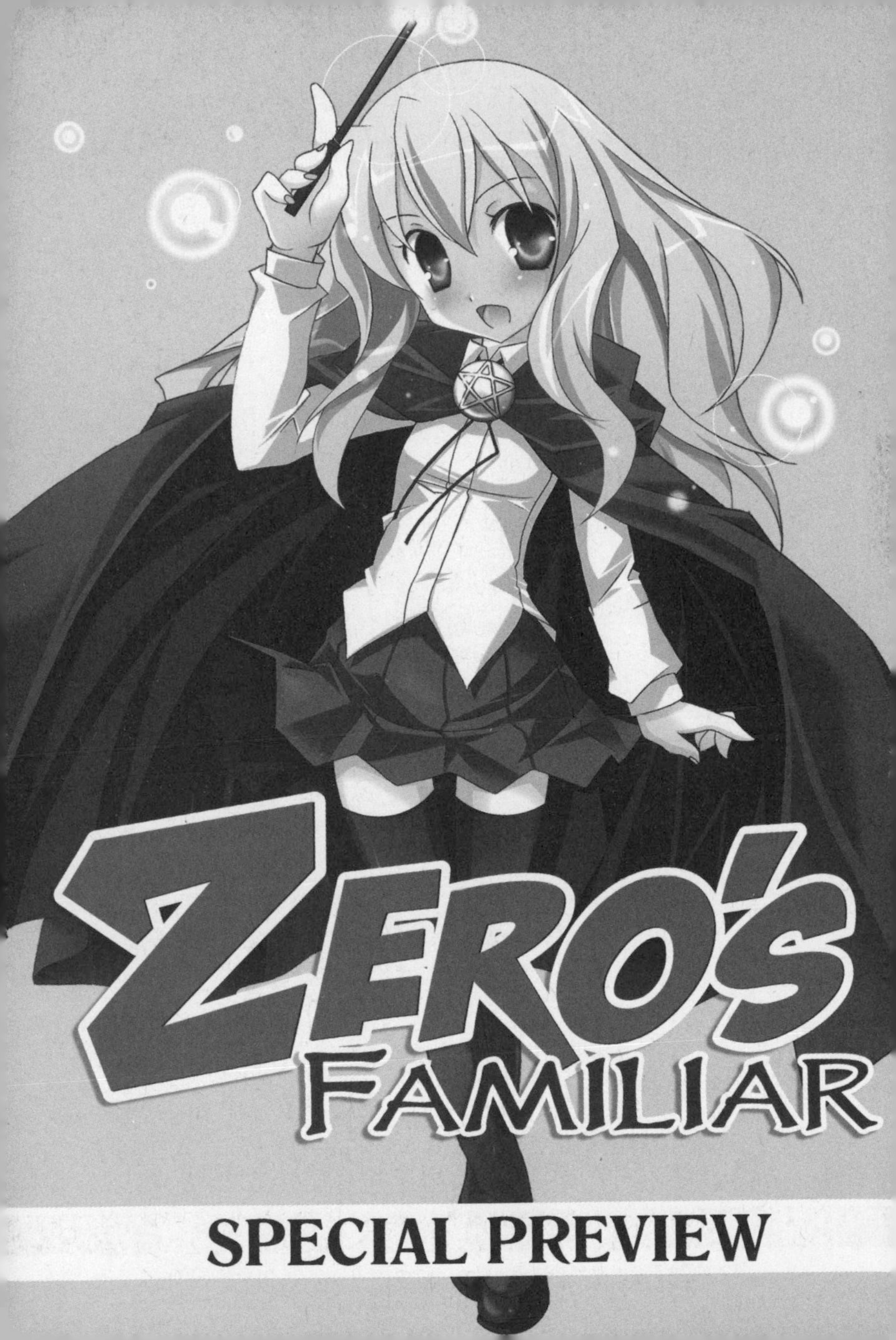
ZERO'S
FAMILIAR
SPECIAL PREVIEW

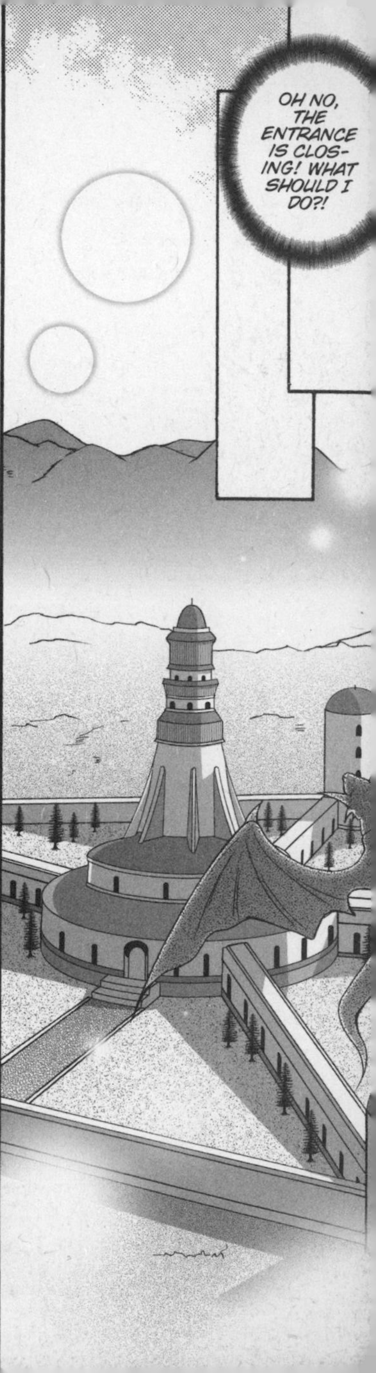
OH NO, THE ENTRANCE IS CLOSING! WHAT SHOULD I DO?!

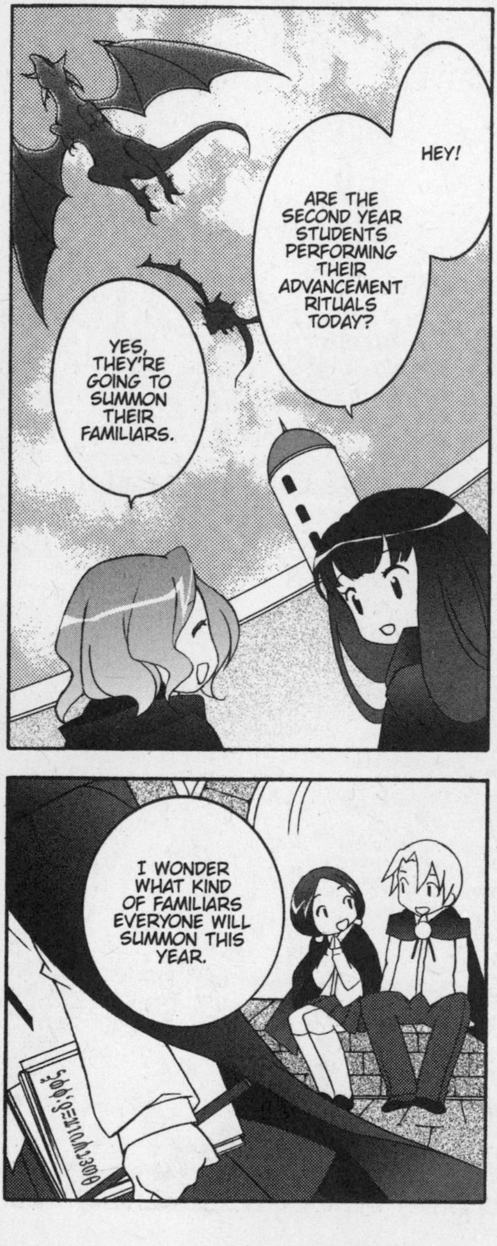
HEY!
ARE THE SECOND YEAR STUDENTS PERFORMING THEIR ADVANCEMENT RITUALS TODAY?
YES, THEY'RE GOING TO SUMMON THEIR FAMILIARS.
I WONDER WHAT KIND OF FAMILIARS EVERYONE WILL SUMMON THIS YEAR.

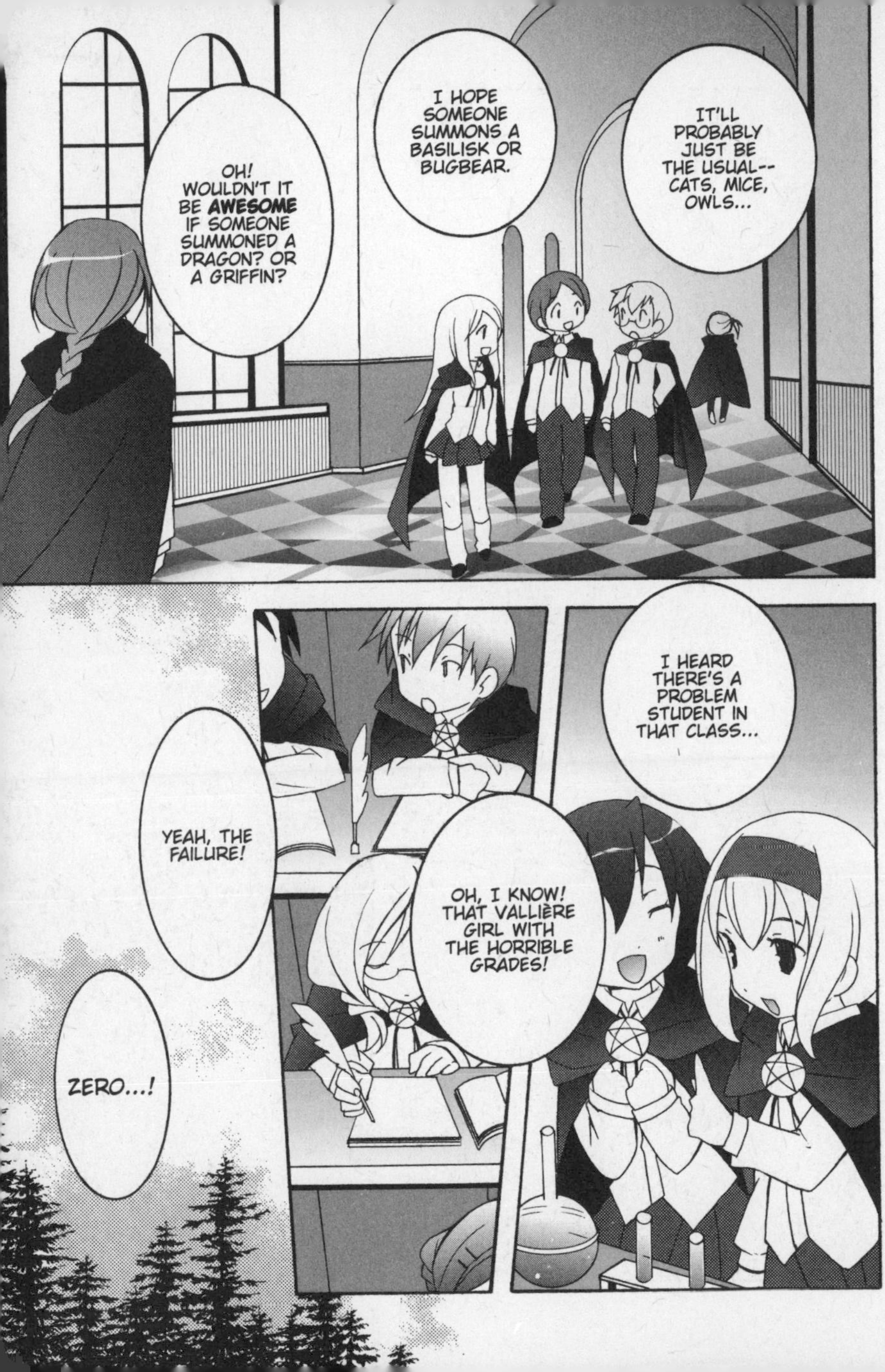
IT'LL PROBABLY JUST BE THE USUAL-- CATS, MICE, OWLS...
I HOPE SOMEONE SUMMONS A BASILISK OR BUGBEAR.
OH! WOULDN'T IT BE **AWESOME** IF SOMEONE SUMMONED A DRAGON? OR A GRIFFIN?
I HEARD THERE'S A PROBLEM STUDENT IN THAT CLASS...
OH, I KNOW! THAT VALLIÈRE GIRL WITH THE HORRIBLE GRADES!
YEAH, THE FAILURE!
ZERO...!

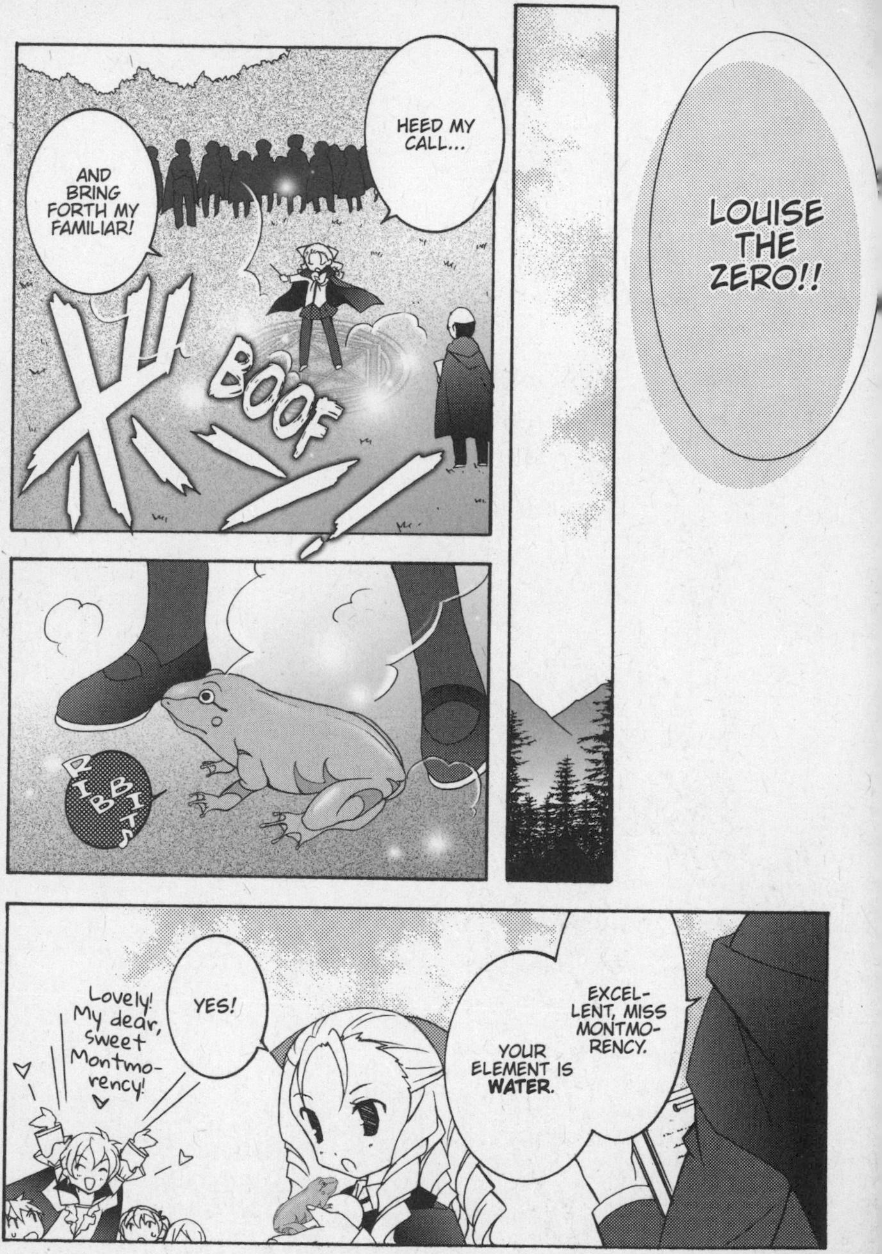
LOUISE THE ZERO!!
HEED MY CALL...
AND BRING FORTH MY FAMILIAR!
BOOF
RIBBITS
EXCELLENT, MISS MONTMORENCY.
YOUR ELEMENT IS **WATER**.
YES!
Lovely! My dear, sweet Montmorency!

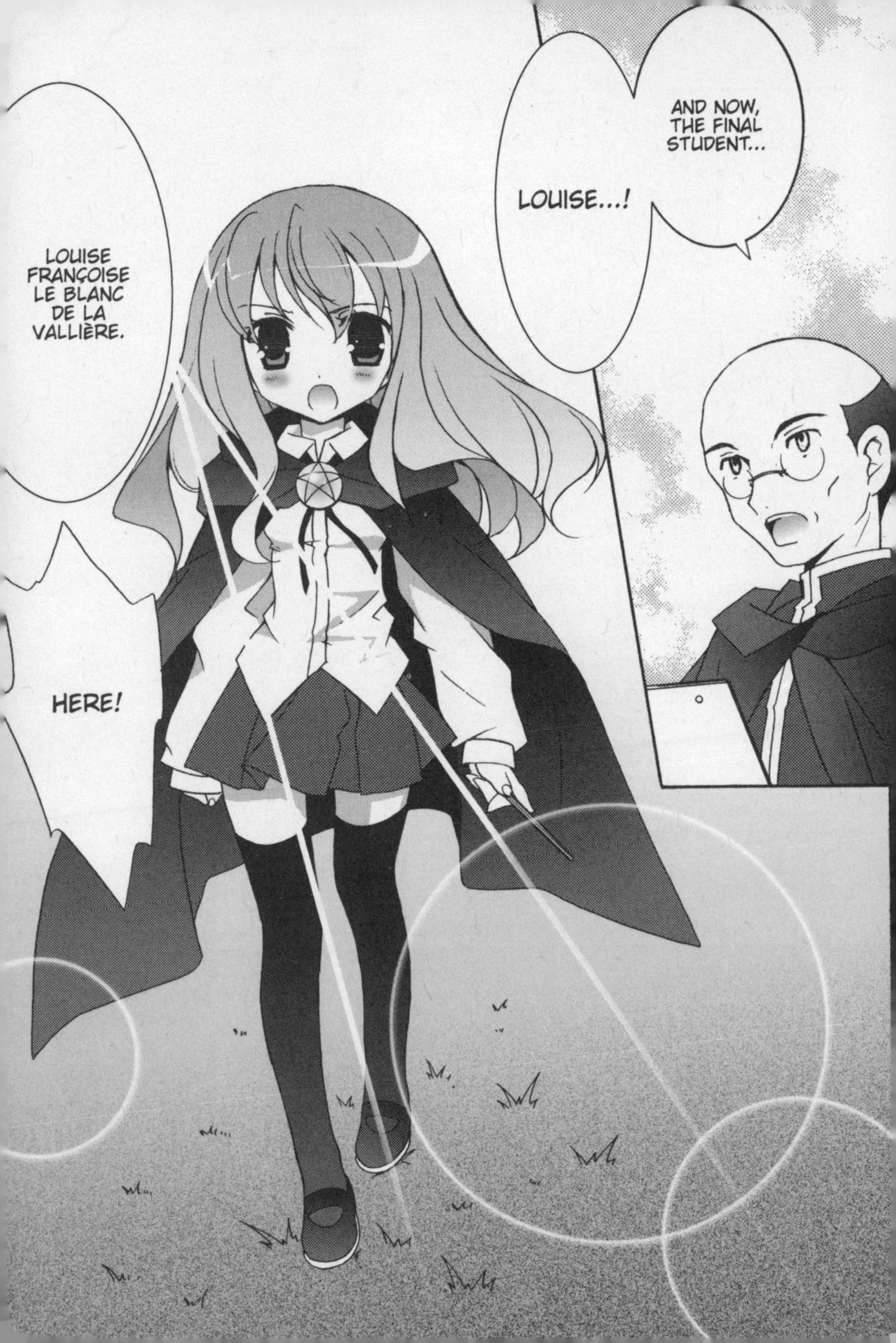
AND NOW, THE FINAL STUDENT...
LOUISE...!
LOUISE FRANÇOISE LE BLANC DE LA VALLIÈRE.
HERE!

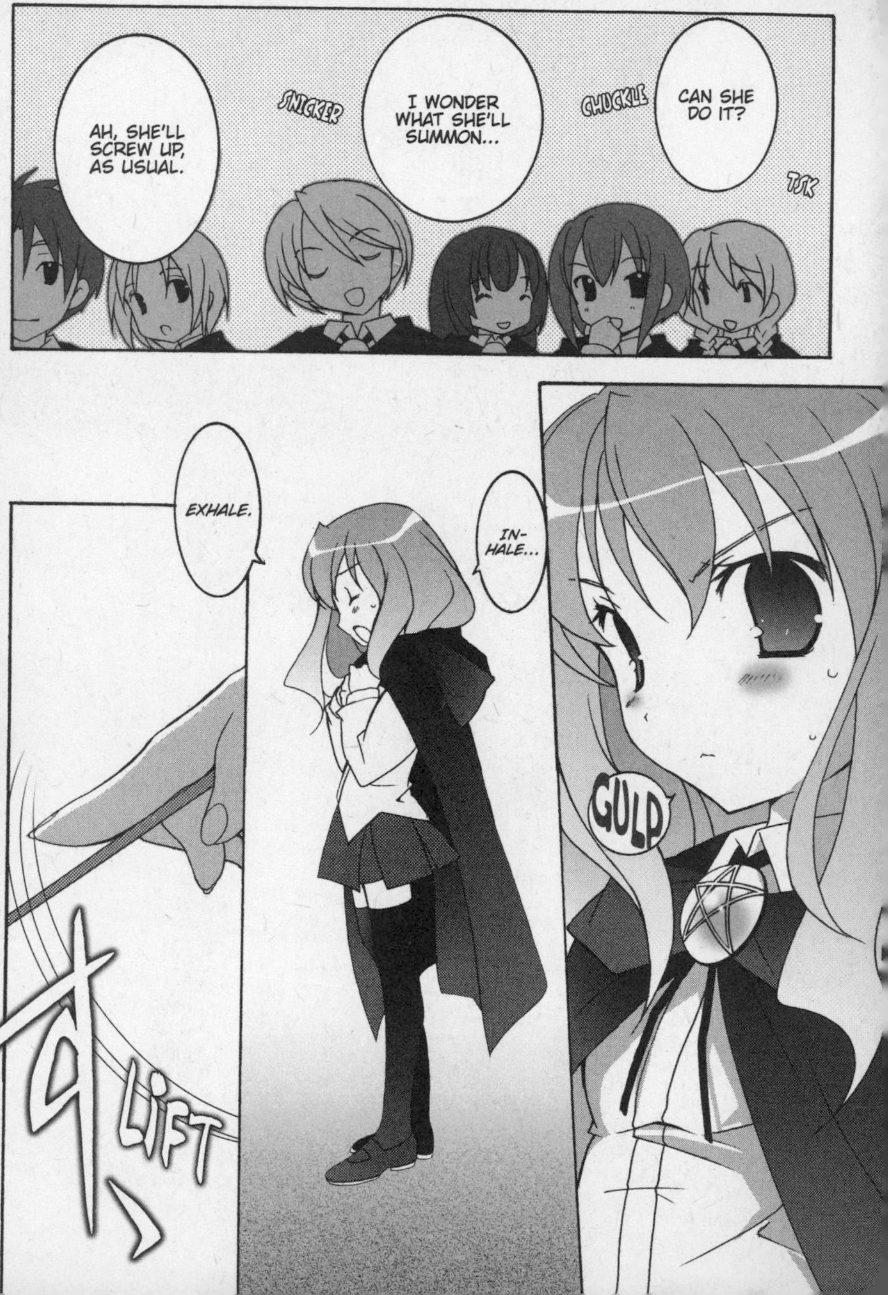
CAN SHE DO IT?
TSK
CHUCKLE
I WONDER WHAT SHE'LL SUMMON...
SNICKER
AH, SHE'LL SCREW UP, AS USUAL.
GULP
IN-HALE...
EXHALE.
LIFT

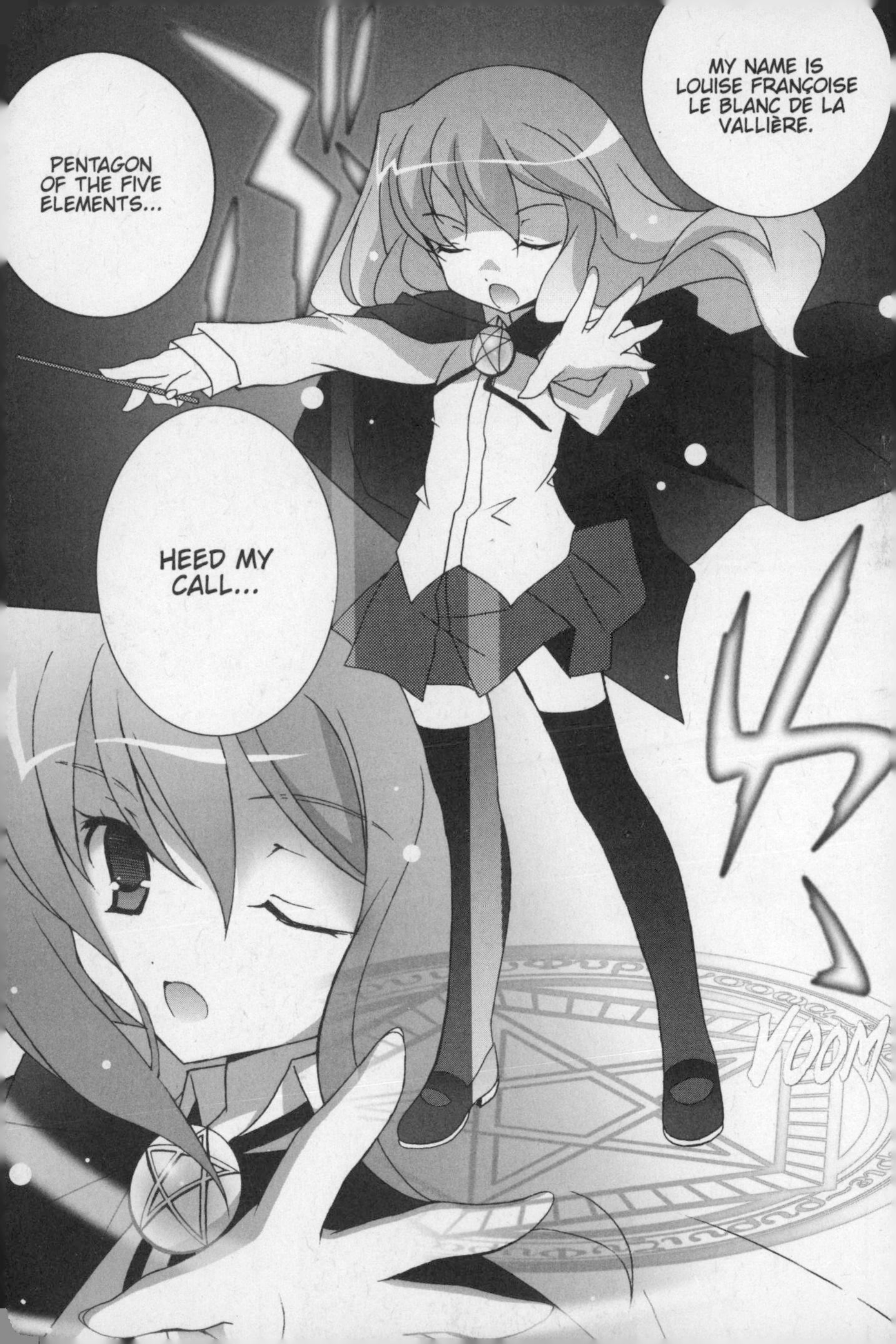
MY NAME IS LOUISE FRANÇOISE LE BLANC DE LA VALLIÈRE.
PENTAGON OF THE FIVE ELEMENTS...
HEED MY CALL...
VOOM

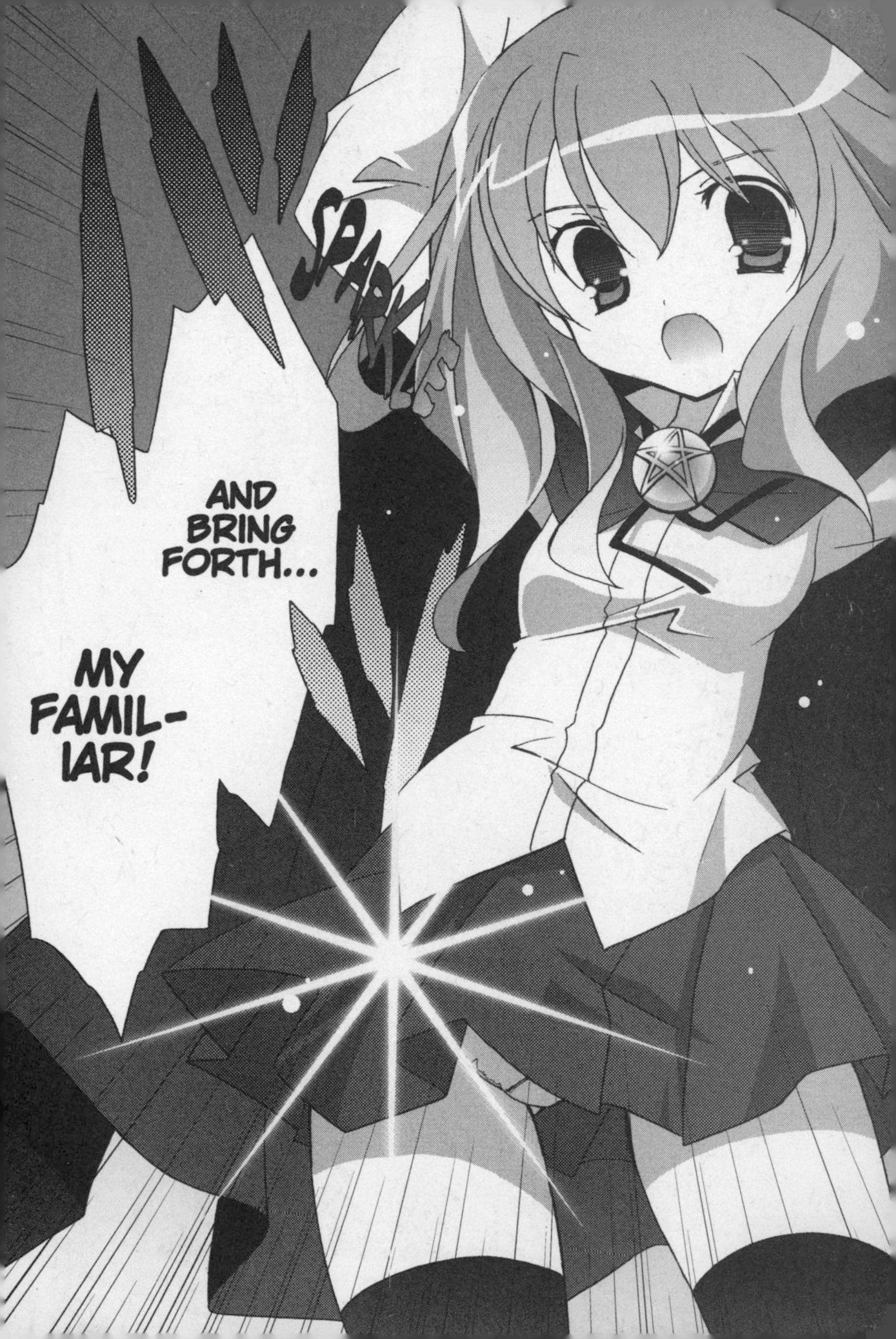
SPARKLE
AND BRING FORTH...
MY FAMIL-IAR!

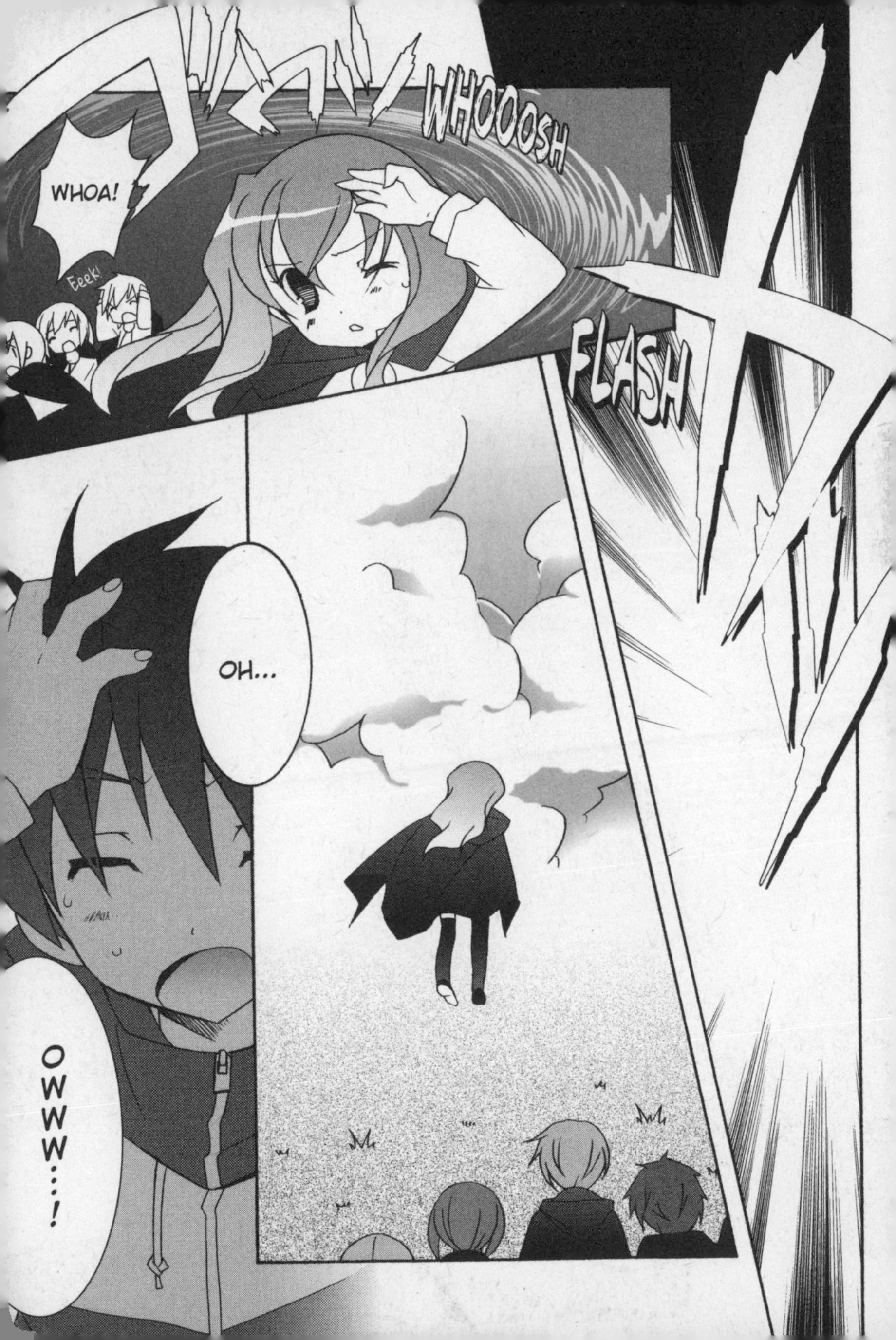
WHOOOSH
WHOA!
Eeek!
FLASH
OH...
OWWW...!

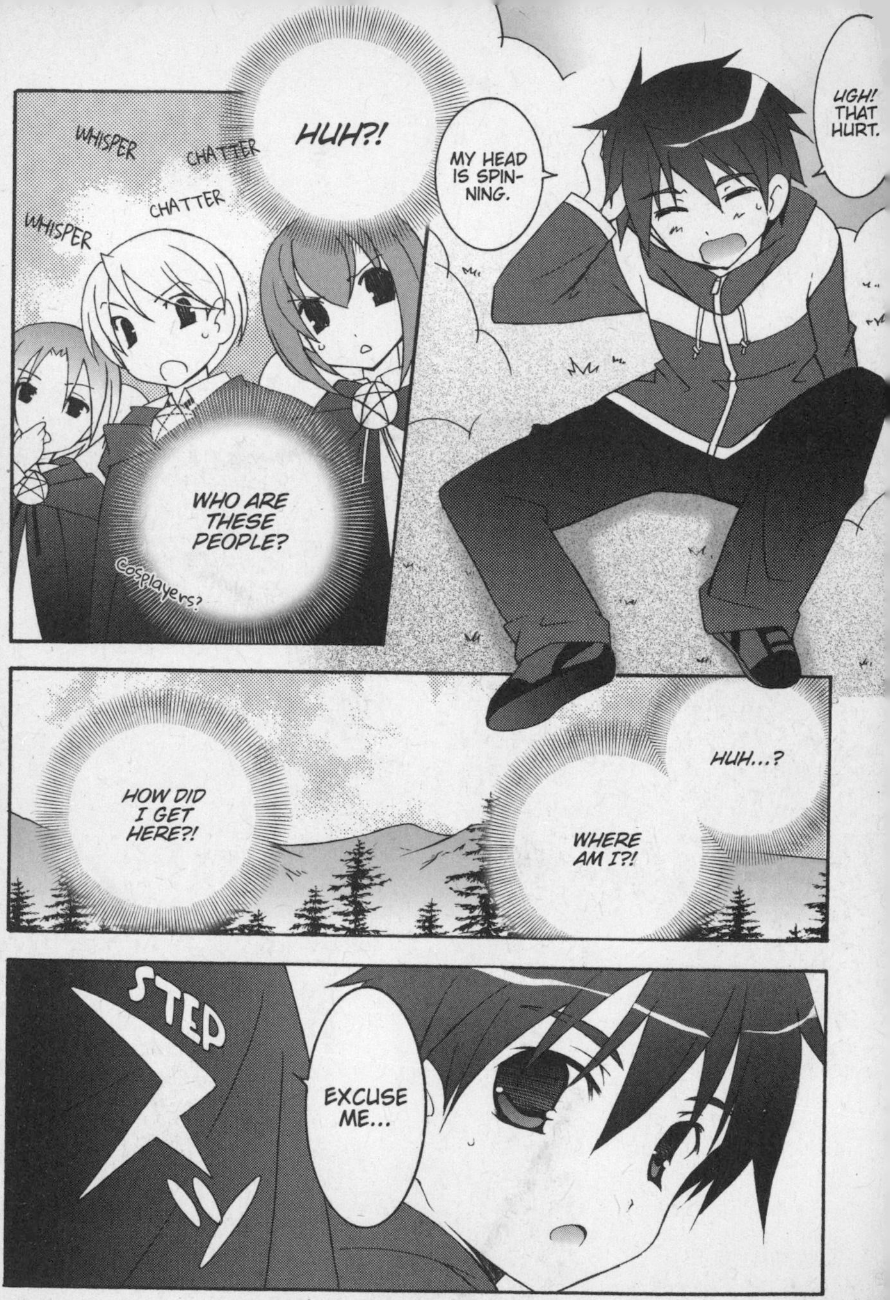
UGH! THAT HURT.
MY HEAD IS SPIN-NING.
HUH?!
CHATTER
WHISPER
CHATTER
WHISPER
WHO ARE THESE PEOPLE?
Cosplayers?
HUH...?
WHERE AM I?!
HOW DID I GET HERE?!
STEP
EXCUSE ME...

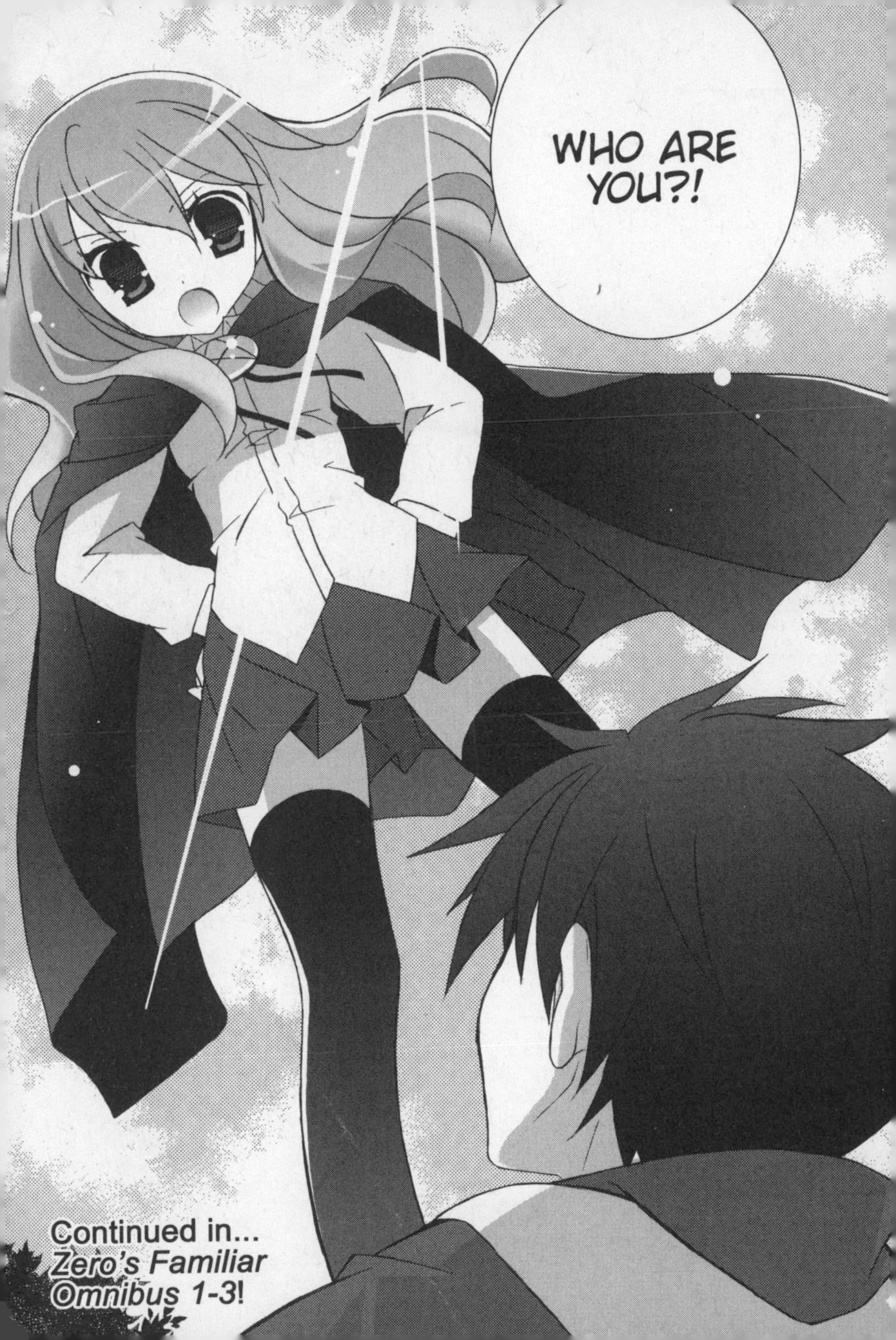
WHO ARE YOU?!
Continued in... Zero's Familiar Omnibus 1-3!